For SEX EDUCATION, *See* Librarian

For SEX EDUCATION,
See Librarian

A GUIDE TO ISSUES AND RESOURCES

Martha Cornog and Timothy Perper

Greenwood Press
Westport, Connecticut • London

Library of Congress Cataloging-in-Publication Data

Cornog, Martha.
    For sex education, see librarian : a guide to issues and resources /
    Martha Cornog and Timothy Perper.
       p. cm.
    Includes bibliographical references and index.
    ISBN 0-313-29022-9 (alk. paper)
      1. Libraries—United States—Special collections—Sex instruction.
    2. Libraries—United States—Special collections—Family life
    education.   3. Public libraries—Collection development—United
    States. 4. Sex instruction—Bibliography. 5. Family life
    education—Bibliography. I. Perper, Timothy. II. Title.
    Z688.S45C67   1996
    026.6139'07—dc20   95-42445

British Library Cataloguing in Publication Data is available.

Library of Congress Catalog Card Number: 95-42445
ISBN: 0-313-29022-9

First published in 1996

Greenwood Press, 88 Post Road West, Westport, CT 06881
An imprint of Greenwood Publishing Group, Inc.

Printed in the United States of America

The paper used in this book complies with the
Permanent Paper Standard issued by the National
Information Standards Organization (Z39.48-1984).

10 9 8 7 6 5 4 3 2 1

For Sandy Berman
. . . long may he wave.

Contents

Acknowledgments

We want especially to thank:

—Martha's Membership Services Section at the American College of Physicians, for putting up with their boss's obsession—Kelly, Michele, and Michael, plus Martha's boss, Eve.

—Our friends and colleagues in the Society for the Scientific Study of Sexuality, Sexuality Information and Education Council of the U.S. (SIECUS), and sexuality libraries and organizations that sent us bibliographies and recommendations. Robert Francoeur, professor of biology at Fairleigh Dickinson University, was especially helpful with his enthusiastic recommendations for new and different titles. And we extend particular thanks to Vern Bullough, distinguished professor of history emeritus at the State University of New York at Buffalo, for reviewing the historical material that comes early in the book.

—Sandy Berman and Chris Dodge, from the Hennepin County Public Library (Minnesota), for sending us hundreds of interesting clippings, newsletters, and miscellanea. Both of them, and Sandy in particular, have consistently stressed the need for library collecting in sexuality among many other areas.

—Francine Fialkoff and Evan St. Lifer at *Library Journal*, for supporting Martha's research on censorship for an article in *LJ*.

—The staff at the W. W. Hagerty Library at Drexel University, especially Ken Garson, for research assistance.

—The former gang at Encore Books, for filling our sometimes bizarre book orders ("You always want the most *interesting* books!") and for their window display on censorship: Tara, Dana, and Ray.

Special thanks go to Harriet Selverstone and Barbara Rader. Harriet, herself a school librarian, urged us to write this book and helped us make contact with our indefatigable editor at Greenwood. Barbara, that editor, has been patient when patience was needed, and urgent when urging was needed.

We also thank the hundreds of publishers and organizations that sent us free materials. Some of the major ones are listed in Chapter 5 and Part II.

Moreover, many individuals contributed solicited and unsolicited advice, documents, and other help: David Azzolina, Joani Blank, Patti Britton, Dorothy Broderick, Bonnie Bullough, Hollis Compton, Sam Gallegos, Cal Gough, Andrew Greeley, Evan Harris, Margaret Harter and staff, Robert Hauptman, Ed Hermance and staff, Amy M. Kautzman, Gary Klein, Jennifer Lee, Will Manley, Donna Minkowitz, Candace Morgan, Raleigh Clayton Muns, Robert Nugent, Anne Penway, James Petersen, Robert Rimmer, Ina Rimpau, Gloria Roberts, Roger Rosen, Howard J. Ruppel, Jr., Edmund Santa Vicca, James L. Sauer, Kara Schaefer, Mark Schoen, Jefferson Selth, Jim Shortridge, Anne Steinfeldt, Samuel Streit, Cecilia Tan, Polly Thistlethwaite, and John Ward. Our many thanks to you all.

Introduction

The author's opinions on the matters with which this book is concerned might be stated . . . : "If by sex, you mean that engine that moves the terrible wheels of lust, that carnal burr under the saddle that hurls men of the gospel down from their pulpits, that tickle that causes kings to abandon their thrones for a sniff of some sweet thing, that demon that turns the heads of captains and generals, so that they whisper breathless nonsense and military secrets into the ear of some doe-eyed double agent, that frenzy that leads men of common sense to thrust aside their loyal wives, weeping children, and vested pension funds to run off with secretaries with half their years and education, that terrible strength that enables an underweight young man to couple with twenty different partners between Friday and Monday in a poorly lit Turkish bath, that dizzying blindness that allows those who brush twice a day and floss every night to risk heartbreak, herpes, AIDS, syphilis, gonorrhea, chlamydia, and lymphogranuloma venereum for the sake of a pelvic spasm, that force that causes altar boys to flog themselves silly in a soapy bathtub, torn between guilt and excitement, if that is what you mean by sex, then I am irrevocably opposed to it.

"However, if by sex you mean that delectable gift of heaven that showers its blessings upon the committed souls so that their hearts beat as one, that force that inspires the long-married to walk holding hands in the cool of the evening, that urge to enjoy the fruit of such unions and provide the twenty-two years of endurance, orthodontia, and tuition hikes that such offspring engender, that force that quickens the pulse when the loved one's footsteps are heard on the porch, that ever-flowing font of shared memories, of binding pleasures, or that drive that causes a pair of geese to mate for life ever-faithful to their troth, generous, companionate, and true, then I am four-square in favor of sex. Clearly, the Prince of Ambivalence has not been dethroned."[1]

Why another book about sex and libraries?

In 1991, we collaborated on *Libraries, Erotica, & Pornography*.[2] With 17 chapters focusing upon different aspects of sexuality and librarianship, the book went on to win the 1992 Eli M. Oboler Award for intellectual freedom from the American Library Association. So why are we back on the same soapbox?

Our focus in that first book was to convince librarians that they could not avoid making decisions about sexuality materials and to point out via a number of voices that "sexuality materials in the library" need not be an oxymoron. But we did not really tell librarians much about what to do next.

In this book, we take a positive approach. Whereas the old—and real—catalog heading "For SEX: See Librarian"[3] meant that sex books were tightly restricted, in the title For *SEX EDUCATION*, See *Librarian* we put forth a proactive mandate for the library. We want to show what the library's role might be vis-à-vis sexuality materials and how to carry out that role. Whereas *Libraries, Erotica, & Pornography* represented a toe in unfamiliar waters, we wrote For *SEX EDUCATION*, See *Librarian* to provide a set of oars for navigation.

In its focus, For *SEX EDUCATION*, See *Librarian* concentrates upon books and services for the public of all ages, pre-kindergarten through adult, rather than professionals and scholarly researchers. Thus our book speaks primarily to public and school librarians. Academic librarians can also use it when considering the extracurricular reading needs of students and faculty.[4]

ORGANIZATION AND STRUCTURE OF THE BOOK

Chapters 1–3 are theoretical, summarizing our hope for the library's role in sexuality education and talking about the history of sexuality education and of sexuality materials in libraries. Chapters 4–7 are practical, providing guidelines for access, collection development, cataloging, retention, reference, and programming, including a chapter on the vertical file, sexuality periodicals, literature, and audiovisuals. Chapter 8 addresses censorship and related issues, from the perspective of different libraries and collections.

Chapters 9–13 comprise annotated bibliographies and recommendations for purchase: 597 books covering 48 topics of sexuality, from "abortion" to "youth and age." Each topical section has a brief introduction that compares titles in that section, covers how to identify additional titles, and mentions other interesting works not annotated. Then follow the annotations, in alphabetical order by author for each section. Annotated works have been given alphanumeric designations, which are used whenever those works are mentioned anywhere in the book. An asterisk (*) before a title or designation number marks books we particularly liked and respected for doing very well what they were trying to do, according to criteria we discuss below. For many books in Chapter 11 and for a few books in other chapters, we have provided grade levels: birth (B), kindergarten (K), grades 1–12 (G1–12), college (C), and adult (A). Books not labeled should be assumed to be suitable for adults and many college students.

HOW WE CHOSE BOOKS FOR INCLUSION

In the beginning, we thought that we *could* in fact choose about 600 "best" sex books, covering a range of topics—particularly if we concentrated on relatively recent titles. Soon our house became awash in sex books of all descriptions, from Christian marriage manuals to guides for home care of AIDS patients, from introductions to S&M to scholarly collections of bawdy cowboy songs. Flyers, newsletters, and bibliographies from every conceivable organization overflowed out of our mailbox: the American Family Association, Homosexuals Anonymous, National Gay and Lesbian Task Force, IntiNet Resource Center, Sexuality Information and Education Council of the United States (SIECUS), the American Educational Gender Information Service, the Kinsey Institute, Non-Circumcision Education Foundation. At times, we found the cacophony confusing and depressing. Yet we were overwhelmed by the collective effort, concern, and pain that had gone into these books. Many were clearly labors of love or of desperation, requiring many years' work and supported by exhaustive references.

So we found that selecting books was not simple. For some topics, the choices *were* relatively easy. Few books were published, so we selected the best, or the only ones. But in many areas the books were legion, with far too many to identify, let alone inspect or review. In addition, topics were legion as well. Let us explain in some detail how we chose both topics and books.

Why We Chose or Eliminated Topics

The 48 sections in Chapters 9–13 represent topics for which we think librarians need the most guidance—by reason of unfamiliarity, controversy, or taboo, or because the subject is highly in demand. We also chose these 48 topics for close relevance to actual sex—that is, copulation—and for that reason most potentially subject to controversy and taboo, plus mis-judgment and censorship.

The following topics are *not* included, or are included only as accessory to one of the 48 topics: appearance/body image, attraction, bioethics, birth (except in books for young people), birth technologies, breast feeding and lactation, cohabitation, emotions (except love), fertility and infertility, male/female relationships (outside sexual involvement), marriage (outside sexual involvement), masculinity/femininity, menopause, menstruation (ex-cept in books for young people), nudism/naturism, parenting (except for sex education of children), population studies, pregnancy, premenstrual syndrome (PMS), and sex/gender roles (general). We feel that these topics, while important, are less controversial, less "hot to handle," and librarians need less encouragement to stock them. (Many are included in the SIECUS *Guidelines for Comprehensive Sexuality Education, Kindergarten–12th Grade*, C97—see Chapter 4.) We also omit almost all book-length bibli-ographies, biographies, curricula, and textbooks.

The Dog in the Night-Time . . .

We note other topics not covered in Chapters 9–13, not because we chose to exclude them but because little or nothing seems to be published in those areas. As with Sherlock Holmes' comment about the dog that did not bark in the night-time, it is easy to miss what is not there.[5] Yet two years of wallowing in sexuality publishing eventually gave us enough experience to detect gaps. Librarians: are there requests in these areas? Authors and pub-lishers: here are unexplored territories to stake out. Anyone interested?

We found almost no books about sex vis-à-vis ethnic groups in this coun-try such as African Americans, Hispanics/Latinos, or Asians.[6] Nor could we obtain works about sex and modern Islamic groups, either here or abroad. Nor did we hear of books on sex in ancient Egypt or in Africa, Polynesia, or among American Indians (although two books address Amer-ican Indian homosexuality). Doubtless, scholarly writings exist, but nothing seems available for the public.

We would also like to see published:

- Books for children about "where babies come from," written by or with older children or adolescents.

- Books to help parents and children deal with dirty words and sexual language.

- More "sexual issue" books for young people from religious perspectives: homo-sexuality, rape, incest, child sexual abuse, abortion.

- Books about all aspects of sex for adult beginning and reluctant readers, including from religious perspectives.

- A nicely done anthology of sexual humor, from Mark Twain to *Playboy*'s Little Annie Fannie.

- Works of sexual literature and folklore from other languages and cultures, modern and historical. (There is probably a fair amount of material buried in anthropology doctoral dissertations that could be anthologized.)

Very little is published about kissing, masturbation, oral sex, or anal sex. Interestingly, the CELIBACY list in *Subject Guide to Books in Print*, although short, has almost doubled in length over the last several years. Also few in number but slowly increasing are books on sex and aging, and sex and disability.

How We Identified the Books: Franklin, Josiah, and DragNet

Having narrowed the potential topics, how did we actually identify 597 sex books? First, we canvassed our large personal library. Next, off to university libraries, where we became acquainted with Franklin, Josiah, and DragNet: online catalogs.[7] In New York City, we visited the Katharine Dexter McCormick Library at Planned Parenthood headquarters and the Mary Calderone Library at SIECUS. The much smaller library at Planned Parenthood of Southeastern Pennsylvania was also helpful, as was an interesting hour with the librarian at Playboy Enterprises in Chicago. We regret that we could not visit the library at the Kinsey Institute or at the Institute for the Advanced Study of Human Sexuality.

At the Hagerty Library of Drexel University, we scanned review periodicals: *Library Journal*, *School Library Journal*, *Booklist*, and many others. We took out a subscription to *Publishers Weekly* as indispensable. We studied the entries under SEX and related headings in *Subject Guide to Books in Print*. We signed up for the Homeschooling Book Club and the Theological Book Service. We requested catalogs from Christian Book Distributors and dozens of publishers.

We compiled a list of about 100 organizations from the *Encyclopedia of Associations*, and we wrote them for bibliographies and catalogs. We ordered bibliographies from SIECUS and Focus on the Family. We scanned bibliographies in the backs of the books we annotated. We identified many items from the innumerable flyers, newsletters, and brochures that cross our desks from our many years' interest in sexuality and membership in various organizations.

We made regular trips to read the shelves at bookstores: Encore and Borders (mass market), Giovanni's Room (gay/lesbian and feminist), Grace Bookstore (Christian), and the Book Trader (secondhand). One of us (MC) went to the 1993 and 1994 American Library Association (ALA) meetings and lived in the exhibit hall, picking up catalogs, buying books, and talking to publishers' representatives. We asked colleagues for recommendations, and we corresponded with numerous authors, librarians, and other experts.

And we personally read or scanned every book we annotated, acquiring 99% of them ourselves through purchase or as complimentary review copies.

As a result, we feel reasonably well acquainted with U.S. sexuality publishing, both regarding what is being published and who is publishing it: mass-market best-sellers, scholarly works, self-published labors of love from individuals and small groups, and most things in between.

Selection Criteria

In selecting books to annotate, our primary criteria were that the books had to be:

- well-written
- cogent and logically presented ("making sense")
- "representative" or "typical" for that topic and viewpoint

Beyond these, we looked for books that:

- take a thoughtful rather than a superficial approach
- are information-rich
- have been cited widely and appear in bibliographies
- have received awards and good reviews
- are up-to-date or classic
- have endured through several editions
- contain referrals to other sources of information
- have author(s)/editor(s) with appropriate qualifications
- are suitable for lay readers rather than highly technical
- are in print and recently published (we did include some older titles)

Few books met all of these secondary criteria, of course! Almost all books have U.S. authors; a few represent Canadian, British, or other non-U.S. perspectives. We were looking for books that would be useful to all ages of the American public in making sense out of sex. We include works on the lighter side, but in general stress solid information over leisure reading. In some ways, our selection process was quite similar to that used by librarians to select books—and we experienced firsthand the bewilderment of a librarian looking at a catalog and asking, "Is this book any good for my library?" Certainly, we had the same three constraints: time, space, and money.

We did not select for "truth," for truth in sex we cannot swear to. Nor did we select for quality in illustrations, since that would have resulted in a tiny bibliography indeed! There are entirely too few books with even passable drawings of male and female sexual anatomy.

We did not discriminate among viewpoints, although we attempted to provide representation more than balance—if "balance" is even possible. We *do* know that there is something here to offend everyone. Overall, we have tried to give librarians a wide sampling of what is available as well as guidelines for choosing. For if there is something to offend, there is also something to *please* everyone. Ignorance of available possibilities can no longer be an excuse to avoid buying sex books on the grounds that they are *all* unsuitable. In fact, our major point is that many more books and viewpoints about sexuality are suitable for libraries than have been so thought in the past, and that librarians should be proactive in collecting *all* of them—or at least a representative selection.

We have our own viewpoints, tending towards liberal/permissive and scientific/medical (see Chapter 4). We could have selected only "the best" according to these viewpoints. But instead we selected books on the basis of representativeness and balance. In sexuality topics where many fine books have been written, we chose a few to represent the range of viewpoint and subject matter. Some of the books included we do not "like," if by *like* one means books that we agreed with, that spoke to us personally, or that appealed to us through style or quirks of opinion. Indeed, we have included books with which we disagree quite heartily. Nor were our own sexual, emotional, erotic, religious, or sociopolitical preferences criteria for deciding to include a title. *Personal tastes and viewpoints are not the important selection criteria for books in a library. Instead, representativeness, range, and balance are the criteria: the debate is the message.*

We cannot stress this enough. When we list a title, do not misunderstand us to think that title is necessarily the most accurate according to our opinion, or the most pleasing, or the most generally acceptable according to "professional" consensus. That is not how we chose it. We chose it because we believe readers should have access to many visions and viewpoints, and because that title represents a particular vision or viewpoint reasonably, with well-written, cogent presentation. In a world of limited time, space, and money—for libraries and ourselves—choices among many books must be made: given quality of writing and cogency, our other major criteria were representativeness, range, and balance—and the point will appear again and again throughout the book.

In the end, these books are our choices, and we take full responsibility for including this one or excluding that one. Some are personal favorites. Some we virulently disagree with—but nonetheless believe that they encapsulate a particular point of view, thoroughly presented and supported. Some we both like *and* disagree with. But notwithstanding these personal affinities and nonaffinities, we chose as objectively and professionally as we could to represent all major views and to include something on every aspect of our topics.

Yet we have probably missed areas. If so, please let us know! We also invite readers to write us with recommendations in areas in which they are expert. Someday perhaps we will update this book and can include them.

We know that there will be those who disagree with us and who would have included different books and emphasized different aspects. To them we say, write your own books and articles—please! This is a virgin field, and there are very few books on collection development and library services relating to sexuality.[8] Librarians need all the help they can get in selecting sex books because sexuality is an immensely complex topic today. In particular, there is need for annotated bibliographies of conservative and Christian sex books.

THE PUBLISHING ENVIRONMENT

We feel lucky to have written this book at a time when sexuality publishing in all areas is flowering. In the 1960s, sexual enhancement books began to appear. Throughout the 1970s, feminist views emerged as well as works on pornography and early popular materials about gays and lesbians. Throughout the 1980s, gay publishing exploded, and books about AIDS and sexual exploitation proliferated and also became highly visible. In the late 1980s and 1990s, books about sex from Christians and conservatives have appeared in greater numbers, although not prominently reviewed or displayed in most bookstores. In the past several years, a number of major sexuality dictionaries and encyclopedias have been published. We have also seen books published recently for librarians and information searchers. Although these new arrivals are few in number, virtually none existed previously.

As professionals, we have been intimately familiar with this explosion of sexuality information, research, and publication. Over a number of years, both of us have written in the professional sexological literature, have served as referees, consulting editors, and associate editors of a major sexological journal, and have written several books on related topics. One of us (MC) reviewed sexuality books for *Library Journal*, and the other (TP) was Book Review Editor for the *Journal of Sex Research*. We contributed to a recent encyclopedia of sexuality, and are co-editors of *The Complete Dictionary of Sexology*, with chief editor Robert T. Francoeur. We have had a fair amount of media experience with print, radio, and television— an experience that forces one to confront not merely TV cameras but the profoundly engrossed curiosity of the American public about sexuality and all its ramifications. We say people are interested in these topics because we know it firsthand. Together, we have some four decades of experience with sexuality information.

And with our experience comes what may be a disadvantage: we bring certain opinions to the book that not everyone else holds. For example, we say that there are "many" works on sexuality out there: how are we to counter someone convinced that these "many" works are all smut, pornography, or just plain worthless junk? Much of this book is directed to that issue.

There are many such amateur experts who think they "know all about it"—and yet they do not, no matter how heartfelt their convictions. We are discussing here approximately three decades of publication in sexuality, with a stronger focus on the past ten years, that have drastically redefined all prior categories of sexuality materials. These new genres or visions of sexuality writing run the gamut from scientific/medical through religious through arcanely specialized works—and none of them junk or porn. If you doubt us, glance at the titles we have annotated in Chapters 9–13.

In these decades, and especially in the last ten years, sexuality writing and books have become a major force in publishing. These works come from mainstream publishing houses as well as little presses. Unfortunately, library practice in acquiring these works and making them available to library-goers has not kept pace. We argue that it must: librarians must take these works seriously, collect them, protect them, and make them accessible. In a very real way, it is a new world in sexuality information.

As we finish this book, the breaking news concerns the Internet: first, allegations of widely available pornography accessible to children and adults via modem and home computer, and, second, the Communications Decency Act, that prohibits very broad classes of sexually explicit material from distribution on the Internet. Today, there are computer bulletin boards, chatlines, collections of graphics, and interactive games that all deal explicitly with sex. Even if only some of these matters directly concern libraries, legal opinion and court decisions are needed to settle if, for example, an interlibrary computer-linked catalog network is exempt from provisions illegalizing transmission of "lewd" and "lascivious" material. Or, more pointedly, should libraries providing on-line access for patrons serve up netsex along with business and sports? We are not experts in the area—and it seems as yet no one is. The library press will increasingly deal with these issues.

However, one aspect of the Communications Decency Act is familiar: the issue of censorship of sexual materials. Censorship questions raised by print material have a millennium of precedent, but on-line "publishing" has no precedents. Is it legally more akin to print publishing, to the telephone, or to radio and television? Each has a quite different legal history concerning censorship. Controversies will certainly grow more intense legally, emotionally, and socially, and it would take credentialled seers and prophets to anticipate how these intricate matters will finally resolve. The questions are so new, so large, and so fast-changing that speculation would be out-of-date before this book sees print. Accordingly, our focus will remain on print materials about sexuality.

One of our purposes is to describe this plethora of materials, and another is to suggest how to collect it. Fundamentally, our recommendation is for library collections to embody an evenhanded and balanced representation of this array of views and visions. And an underlying theme is how to prevent would-be censors from hacking it all to pieces. We do not expect you to agree with all of our views, but we do hope you will think about our suggestions and the points we raise, and attempt to apply and modify them for yourselves and your libraries.

There is *so much* that is worthy and valuable in sexuality writing today that decisions must be made about what to collect and what to omit. With this, too, arises the ugliness of censorship, because omissions can be biased. Thousands of interesting books are in print, and dozens more are being published as we write. We are sorry that we could not examine and include more of them. The best we can say is that we tried very hard not to bias our suggestions and our annotations. We hope, recommend, and urge that you as librarians in your own communities contribute your own expertise and skills in building collections that reflect the variety of voices and visions in sexuality information.

NOTES

1. *The Story the Soldiers Wouldn't Tell* (D73, Lowry): 6–7. Note: the designation D73 refers to a book annotated in Part II, where full citation information may be found.

2. *Libraries, Erotica, & Pornography* (D115, Cornog).

3. L. B. Woods, "For SEX: *See* Librarian," *Library Journal* (September 1, 1978): 1561–1566.

4. An excellent bibliography of more scholarly work pertaining to sexuality is *Studies in Human Sexuality* (D116, Frayser & Whitby). See also *A Research Guide to Human Sexuality* (D120, Lichtenberg).

5. From Arthur Conan Doyle, "Silver Blaze," in *The Complete Sherlock Holmes* (Garden City, NY: Doubleday, n.d.): 347. The fact that the dog did not bark during the night when Silver Blaze was stolen indicated to the perceptive Holmes that the horse thief was known to the dog and therefore an insider to the household.

6. "Understanding the complex role that sexuality plays in the lives of African-Americans requires much more information than is now available about the sexual attitudes and behavior of a broad spectrum of African-Americans." Herbert Samuels, "Sexology, Sexosophy, and African-American Sexuality: Implications for Sex Therapy and Sexuality Education," *SIECUS Report* 23.3 (February/March 1995): 8–10.

7. Franklin (as in Benjamin, we assume) is the online catalog of the University of Pennsylvania library system, Josiah that of Brown University (after the completely legendary psychoceramics professor Josiah S. Carberry), and DragNet that of Drexel University (the Drexel mascot is the dragon).

8. See the Librarians and Sex section in Chapter 12.

I LIBRARIANS, EDUCATION, AND SEXUALITY

1 The Role of Libraries in Sexuality Education

> Although parents and schools should be the basic providers of sound
> sex education, they seldom are. This leaves the library as the only
> source of sex education for young people, unless we want to abandon
> the job to sexploitation movies, rock lyrics, graffiti, and the dubious
> counsel of peers.[1]

Libraries have three choices about sexuality materials. They can attempt to
maintain a traditional posture of silence; they can tread cautiously, buying
only a few books that reflect majority views (their own or their community's); or to one extent or another they can try to present "all points of
view on current and historical issues" as guided by the Library Bill of
Rights.[2] In this book, we assume that silence is no longer an option.

Now, we do not expect that librarians, upon reading our words, will
suddenly see a Mystic Light and instantly devote large percentages of their
budgets to sexuality topics. More realistically, many libraries will tiptoe
cautiously and experimentally between the second and third options above.
Yet we *do* hope to convince you that sexuality education is a valid and
necessary function of librarianship, at whatever reasonable commitment of
staff and funding any particular library accepts.[3]

But why is sex education a function of librarianship, as opposed, say, to
the role of parents, teachers, physicians, and pastoral counselors? The rea-

son is that "opposed" is the wrong word: we—*all citizens*—must cooperate in providing sexuality education for ourselves and for our children.

Parents, all too often embarrassed or ignorant, may mumble about the birds and the bees or provide misinformation, sometimes in good faith, but sometimes to stop a child's probing questions. Indeed, adults have a vested interest in lying, for example, about situations of sexual abuse. Ideally, parents should provide sexuality information and ethical-moral guidance. But who educates *them*? Where do *they* find out what they do not know?

Most states require or recommend sex education programs in public schools, and all states require or recommend HIV/AIDS education. But who educates the teachers? True, many excellent teacher-training programs provide information to many educators. Yet none of these can be fully comprehensive or unbiased. More important, sex education in the schools is itself bound up with bureaucratic concerns and agendas, as we will discuss in later chapters, and curricula may be mandated that do not tell a full story about sex. Parents, children, and teachers need access to sexuality information *not* supplied via school programs.

Only rarely do physicians ask about a patient's sexual health or welcome volunteered comments about it. Many physicians are themselves poorly educated in sexual matters and to hide their own embarrassment may avoid questions or respond only with medical jargon. Ultimately, for health problems, the physician is the *only* person to consult for diagnosis and treatment. So when our health is at stake, it is wise to prepare ourselves with at least a layperson's knowledge of what ails us. Then we can more intelligently search out medical experts who *will* discuss our sexual symptoms and gladly take our sexual histories. Common sense? Of course. But where can *we* find that layperson's information?

Pastors and denominational leaders are likewise often poorly educated in sexuality other than in the traditional moral teachings of religion. Those teachings are indeed necessary guides. But they are not enough if two religious leaders on a television talk show differ strongly about the moral meanings of types of sexuality that were hidden in Victorian times but are now scrawled over every inner-city bus and subway car in America. One example will suffice, and it is a terrible story.

Towards the end of 1994, serial killer Jeffrey Dahmer was beaten to death in a Wisconsin prison where he was serving 15 consecutive life sentences for killing 17 boys and young men, then having sex with and dismembering some of their corpses. Earlier that year, in May, he had "made a public profession of faith and was baptized. After praying that God would forgive his sins, Dahmer became remarkably calm about his fate."[4] For many Americans, Dahmer represented the demonic brought to fleshly life. *Theologically*, will God forgive him, assuming his repentance was sincere? Yet there is another way of posing the question. *Sexologically*, what was Dahmer's demon? Thus we encounter a deeper question: Was Dahmer's life one of pure, unchangeable demonism beyond God's forgiveness, or one of perhaps treatable psychopathology, capable of repentance before God and therefore of obtaining God's forgiveness? Was it the Devil or Disease? Or both? Where shall we go to find out more—not solely about criminological sexology, which has a history of some depth—but also about sexual sin, no longer the garden variety "lust in my heart" stuff, but deeper and far more troubling?

If you have answered, "Why, the library, of course," then you have given the only right answer there is. Yes, *of course* we ask parents, teachers, physicians, and pastors. But we need to know more—often much more—about sexuality and the myriad viewpoints that swirl around it and that are so well represented among current and historical issues of importance. Library sexuality collections are needed to support the entire community's efforts in sex education: to support efforts of parents, schools, physicians, and churches; to work with community and national groups with many viewpoints; to help individual patrons to self-educate themselves; and to assist in supplementing, correcting, and counteracting inaccurate information disseminated by the media, among other sources. Sex education materials thus have a home in the library because so many library patrons have needs for sexuality information and because providing this information fits with larger library goals of community support.

And because many people are frightened, panicked, and hysterical about sexuality and the associated dangers they foresee. As we put the finishing touches on this chapter, a preprinted letter arrived from Gary L. Bauer, president of the conservative, pro-family Family Research Council (FRC). He describes how the Wellesley (Massachusetts) Public Library refused requests to limit children's access to *Playboy*, citing the American Library Association's position against limiting access to materials on the basis of patron age.

Bauer goes on to suggest that the United Nations Convention on the Rights of the Child could be used to

force the ALA's policy on every community in the nation—by international law. . . . I cannot say it more emphatically. These travesties must be stopped! License is not liberty. Exposing children to *Playboy* has as much to do with intellectual freedom as giving poisoned lollipops to them has to do with the free market. I have not spent the majority of my adult life fighting bureaucrats in Washington only to see decisions affecting my family and yours turned over to a bunch of UN bureaucrats.[5]

He urges readers to request a copy of FRC's UN information packet and to write their senators and congressmen, and also describes FRC's efforts to monitor the UN.

We in the library community have much to offer people like Bauer and

FRC members. They are genuinely frightened, and they see us as enemies. So we must seize this opportunity to defuse their paranoia and explain what libraries can do for them and for everyone. We must tell them the truth about what the Library Bill of Rights really says—including that parents have the sole right to control their children's reading.

Libraries are one of the only institutions in America that can encompass the needs of FRC members as well as the needs of liberals, hedonists, religious people, atheists—even the apathetic. But the public must be shown that the library *itself* is neither liberal nor conservative but above both. Libraries can be storehouses of information on all sides, subscribing to FRC and Focus on the Family periodicals as well as *Playboy*.

If we cannot forthrightly explain to all people about the library's role in education—about sex as with all other topics—we risk more centuries of book-burning. We must tell everyone that libraries correct their collections not by removing books and magazines but by adding them. Modern sexuality upsets and fascinates people; *therefore* libraries must commit themselves to providing a full range of information about it.

MANY TOPICS, MANY VIEWS

> Collection development and the selection of materials are surely functions for which Christians ought to seek divine guidance. In the first place, we can acquire materials that portray a Biblical perspective on a variety of topics and thus maintain a balance of world views in the marketplace of ideas and ideologies. . . . Secondly, we can genuinely support intellectual freedom and select broadly across the spectrum of topics and perspectives, choosing the best examples of unpopular or minority points of view. This is possible because Christian collection developers believe that ultimate truth, not defined by a temporary fashion, will be victorious when given the opportunity for fair comparison.[6]

> In the United States, the sex educators have been cast as liberals, the noneducators as conservatives. . . . Mind you, it is only when proponents of all political persuasions break the sex taboo [of silence] that we will have the chance for a truly informed debate about sexual matters.[7]

Sexuality topics have become regular media fodder over the past 30 years. Even *Reader's Digest* and *Prevention* magazines now run articles about sex. We suspect that anyone who can read—or hear—would be inclined to agree with us: no debate about it. Sex is news.

Where the debate *does* lie is in viewpoints about the topics. And it has been this debate that librarians have found so distressing and confusing. If the United States—or even one community!—had a cultural consensus on sex, there would be no problem. But we do not have consensus, micro or macro. Who's right? Which messages should the library support?

Why, all of them, of course! *The debate is the message.* As we will elaborate in other chapters, all political persuasions, including sexual conservatives, *have* broken the taboo of silence about sexual matters. We personally think that this is wonderful—the more the merrier. But the reality of limited budgets makes it impossible to purchase everything, and choices indeed must be made.

The worst is the default option, so to speak, of doing as little as possible and responding only after protests from individuals and groups. Then libraries can become arenas of loud and angry battles between factions representing nastily opposing sides of political debate. Neither really cares about librarianship, but they do care about Winning This Round—which, in the language of sexual realpolitik, seems to mean PUTTING OUR BOOKS into the library and KEEPING THEIRS OUT. So the default option leaves libraries extraordinarily vulnerable to sudden cyclones of political furor, and the only Land of Oz at the end of the cyclone is a mass of bad feelings.

We believe that the answer is that libraries must be proactive about balancing their collections. And such balance should be sought before community annoyance rises so high that *everyone* is telling the library that its collection is just plain inadequate—because, in a sort of perverted reversal of the Library Bill of Rights, all views on everything have been simply omitted. That sort of ostrich-headedness cannot be allowed. Taking into account budgets and community needs, libraries must seek to stock their shelves with a representative variety of views and topics about sexuality.

BUT THERE AREN'T ANY BOOKS

Not long ago, we were invited to talk at a multistate library conference about sexuality books in the library. After our presentations, a woman asked one of us (TP) how come, in my list of suggested books libraries might purchase, I had left out works of—not about, *of*—child pornography. Feeling truly bewildered, I slowly explained that such works are probably illegal to purchase, possess, or distribute, but the questioner interrupted sarcastically, "You have included everything else, so why not kiddie porn?"

Our impression is that some librarians—like this woman—think that there are only a few books about sexuality, and that they come in two types: medical/academic/professorial, and filth ranging from popular smutty sorts of stuff to material that is utterly illegal. Part of the attractiveness of the default option—not doing much—arises because librarians, like parents, educators, physicians, and pastors, are often not professionally trained about sexuality studies and collections. For them, as for this woman, works about sexuality automatically belong with technical books or in the categories of smut, filth, dirt, and pornography unless otherwise proven. But it is not so.

In Chapters 9–13 of this book, we annotate some 597 titles about sexuality and describe hundreds more without annotation. Most have been written within the past decade or so, were published by mainstream publishing houses, and are written solidly and informatively. In parallel, there also exists a fascinating world of marginalia, titles published in small numbers by individuals or small presses, some discoursing on exotic behavior but others addressing quite common topics from a fresh perspective. And if not all are suitable for library purchase, many of them are. Many thousands of other sexuality titles, mainstream and marginal, are in print: there is no dearth of material. And in today's publishing world, the default is neither medical treatise nor pornographic novel and is certainly not kiddie porn, but nonfiction trade books carried by major bookstore chains.

The only question is whether or not librarians know that such titles exist. The woman at the conference with her sarcastic question did not. When someone believes that all sexuality books in today's world are equivalent to kiddie porn, you know you have problems. And when that person is a librarian, the need for educating the educators has reached crisis proportions.

As a cultural phenomenon, this upwelling of writing and publication about sexuality, especially prolific since about 1970, deserves its own thoughtful analysis. We suspect it comes from two sources. One is the First Amendment, which allows anyone to print anything at all, provided only that someone pays for printing and a court does not rule it obscene. Moreover, a long-standing tradition of U.S. culture says that anyone's opinion is as good as anyone else's. Accordingly, a great diversity of opinion and belief lies at the base of our culture, and given the freedom of the press, people feel free—and *are* free—to publish and publish and publish. But a second factor also intervenes: the waning of Victorian and post-Victorian silence about sexuality. After World War II, many literary figures, followed by scholars, then scientists, and now laypeople, have put into print their sexual opinions. And we *mean* "opinion": beliefs, philosophies, observations, interpretations, stories, and ideas about every possible form of a topic that was once a darkly hidden secret.

Simultaneously came a release into the light of printed reality a world of sexually arousing material, variously called erotica or pornography. It ranges from the vanilla and "girlie show" sexuality of *Sports Illustrated* swimsuit issues through specialized sexual material that only a very few people find even remotely interesting. Some of this material is collected by archival libraries, but—surprise!—some of it is relevant even to public libraries. Yet such materials are not our major concern in this book. Instead, we focus primarily on mainstream publishing, where the emphasis is not on arousing you, the reader, but on what sexual arousal is and means.

We were genuinely surprised by the range and variety of what has been published about sexuality in recent years. There are serious and thoughtful books on virtually every topic one can imagine, and some—often published in oversize format—are elegant, very beautiful, and expensive. The art books alone cover the world, and books on history and sexuality range from the delightfully and sometimes wickedly chatty through ponderous tomes that nonetheless deal with issues of profound modern debate, for example, about Christianity and homosexuality.

Some sex-related topics have produced a genuine explosion of publications. One is the psychological–sexological–self-help genre, with titles covering sexual development, gender differences in sexuality, sexual language and communication, and psychosexual functioning. Now, we do not mean textbooks of academic psychology, although many of these titles are written by practicing psychotherapists. We are discussing mass-marketed trade books—hundreds of them.

More general than merely sexological are books written by and for women about women's sociosexual lives and realities. The vast majority are written by feminists, but feminism is no monolithic entity. These works cover everything from attacks on the patriarchy to discussions of why the Goddess wants you to enjoy sex whenever you want it, with whomever you want, and wherever. Here we plead the great plea of authors on topics as wide as ours: for reasons of space, we could not annotate most of these titles.

A large how-to subgroup also includes nearly everything: how to pick up girls (the title of a real book for men); how to flirt (a title aimed at women); how to find the perfect mate; how to fix him (usually) when he breaks down and won't talk; how to have a better sex life; how to try new and wonderful variations of what you already like; how to—well, how to virtually anything you wanted to know how to, including how to have sex via computer.

On one topic essentially nothing has been published: books advocating or illustrating how adults may have sex with children. These may be illegal to purchase, possess, or distribute, and we made no effort whatever to search out titles in any area that could be deemed illegal obscenity. Yet we found works *about* pedophilia—the technical term for sexual attraction of an adult for a child—and *about* child sexual abuse and incest, including treatment and prevention. These we annotate and urge libraries to purchase.

Another topic of prolific publication comprises rape and related crimes of sexual violence: discussions of prevention, avoidance, survival, and treatment plus social and psychological theories about why men rape. A fair number of books cover sexual harassment from legal, social, personal, and prevention viewpoints. Many are written by victims of sexual misconduct, a general term that covers a variety of evils from rape through obscene phone calls. These books are moving, frightening, and above all needed on library shelves as thrilling stories of triumph over abuse.

Still other books deal with abortion: personal tirades for or against it, religious treatises and legal histories, and serious discussions of the abortion debate itself.

Pornography as well has produced a publishing explosion. We do not refer here to authors seeking to arouse readers but to writers debating what pornography is, whether we should or should not censor it, and why it does—or does not—empower women.

Yet another group comprises books about homosexuality. Pro and con, histories, personal stories, psychology, sociology, religion: they are all there in the publishers' catalogs and can be obtained by any library—and ought to be.

Then come religious books on sexuality, an immense variety, many recent, and taking as many viewpoints as one can imagine. Some are conservative, others liberal. Some argue that only procreative sex within marriage is God's way; others argue that God has blessed us with many forms of eros. And they pose some special problems because many titles of great potential interest to library-goers are hidden, like the light under the proverbial bushel, deep within Christian book catalogs. We have made something of an effort to ferret out these titles, but our research cannot be considered complete.

Again and again, topic after topic, viewpoint after viewpoint, we found books, books, and more books. Whatever conspiracy of silence once surrounded sexuality has been drastically broken. All that remains is for libraries to select and shelve some of these titles.

WILL ANYONE READ THEM?

Over the years, both of us have been interviewed on radio and television about various topics in sexual communication. Invariably, the phone rings afterwards: "Where can I get your book?" One man had a fascinating story to tell us: he had wanted a sex-related book one of us had written and had gone to his local library in Virginia. The librarian consulted the catalog and told him they didn't have it. "Huh," he grumbled. "I happen to know your library has interlibrary loan." So the librarian tried the county interlibrary loan (ILL) system. "Nothing here, sir." "Huh," he grumbled again. "I happen to know where there is a copy." "I see," the librarian said, perhaps a bit nettled that he had not said so at the start. "Where is that?" "The Library of Congress!" he announced. "I'll go there and read it!" (However, he tried the radio station next and from them obtained our phone number.)

Or another call, from a woman. "I'm out of work, you see, so I can't buy it. Can I get it from my library?" We told her about ILL. She was excited. "Is that what they call it! Oh, thank you very much!"

Not all patrons are so determined to lay their hands on a book, and not all patrons know about the Library of Congress and its function as the great repository library of the United States. But these anecdotes make their point. When readers are motivated by a topic, they will go out of their way to find material on it. Why make it hard for them?

All kinds of people need information about sexuality: young people trying to supplement inadequate information or to correct misinformation; parents, educators, physicians, and clergy with needs pertaining to their roles as sex educators; people with sexual dysfunctions, stigmatized obsessions, or other sexual troubles in the family; students working on classroom assignments about "current events"; advocacy groups gathering information to advance their cause; random folk with questions about health, family planning, an issue raised on a TV show, and so on.

And because sexuality is emerging from a Victorian and post-Victorian conspiracy of silence, more and more readers are making an information transition from the popular media, like radio, television, and newspapers, to wanting more detailed knowledge. They know that a three-minute television sound bite or a half-column in a newspaper tells only the tiniest part of a story that interests them very much, and on topics covering the full range of sexual problems and fascinations. They *do* want more, and if you do not believe us, a visit to your local chain bookstore will convince you otherwise, for you will find quite a sample of titles on sexuality. Consider this: if the big chain bookstores carry these titles, then people are buying them.

So, in a very minor way, writing this book was an act of self-defense. Over years of telephone calls asking, "Where can I get your book?" came the ever-repeated explanation, "I tried the library, but they didn't have it." Why did our callers explain that their library did not have the book? They expected us to reply, "Well, try your library," and they were forestalling us. They had *already* tried the library. And they wanted us to know that they really were serious about their search, sufficiently so to dig out telephone numbers sometimes half-way across the country and through various intermediaries. Yet in this is a truly American ethos. Of course the library is the place to go. *Of course.*

So let's make it true.

HOW TO CHOOSE?

There is a fundamental group of books on sexuality that libraries should have because they are the classics of human thought and feeling about sex: Plato's *Symposium*, Ovid's *Art of Love*, the Kinsey reports, Masters and Johnson, Margaret Mead, Bertrand Russell, and Sigmund Freud, among others. (See Chapter 5.) No library is complete without titles like these—although each library must choose individual works to suit needs of the collection.

In principle, these kinds of basic books ought to inspire little debate or difficulty in most libraries. But in reality, difficulties do exist for books both in this group and outside it: censorship, doubts about quality, scarcity of reviews, unfamiliarity with what is available, perceived lack of need, vandalism and theft, concerns about children's access to sexuality titles, and—very important they are, too!—traditions in librarianship itself that have greatly limited library holdings in sexuality. Accordingly, a basic question arises that we address throughout the entire book: How should libraries approach the problem of selecting books on sexuality?

Throughout the history of U.S. librarianship, two great principles have affected what books libraries purchase. One we have called "the guardianship of society" ethos.[8] It is the older of the two, and if in fact it is not simple, it surely sounds simple enough: purchase only the best and most uplifting of works, those that elevate the reader towards the great Ideals of life, culture, and religion. And sex has, historically, *not* been among them. The other is the "Freedom to Read" ethos, emerging later in U.S. library history, which urges a doctrine of equal time on the shelves. No topic or viewpoint is intrinsically unworthy, though individual works might remain unbought. Because sex is something about which people have a right to know, onto the shelves it goes. Librarians seem deeply torn between these two images of the Ideal Library—and, for our topic, that means a constant tension between two poles. On one end lies distrust of the topic of sexuality itself plus a desire to stock only "classic" and "time-tested" books about it; on the other end, a desire to round out the collection with material that is new and culturally significant, such as books on abortion, homosexuality, contraception, and so on.

We cannot decide for you as an individual or for your library where you will put the balance point between these visions. But we ourselves feel strongly that libraries can no longer treat sexuality as an intrinsically unworthy topic, nor disguise individual or institutional disgust and suspicion with pieties about "not knowing if a book is really of high quality." The books we urge you to consider in Chapters 9–13 are works that you yourself might buy at your local bookstore, or give to your spouse or an adolescent you know, or read to your children. Quality—which we define as well-written, thoughtful, and cogent—will be no issue for any work we discuss.

But once beyond the classics and once beyond never-ending budget crunches, what might a library want to acquire? Themes that will recur throughout this book include making acquisition decisions based on local clientele and its interests; asking for participation from various community groups ranging from church-based to sexual minority–oriented; keeping up with the offerings of publishers and bookstores; and above all, stocking a range of titles that represent the diversity of America.

SPECIAL TOPICS, SPECIAL HEALINGS

We hope to pursuade you as librarians to experience firsthand as we did the quality, variety, and—yes—passion of some of these books about sexuality. Writing about sex is not easy for most people: one must involve oneself deeply in a variety of personal issues. Indeed, the best works are those by people whose personal lives are part of the work itself: the personal stories of sexual harassment, child abuse, or rape are among the most powerful of all.

Writing a book is a form of triumph over these past horrors, and despite the nasty ugliness of some of the stories, a sense of victory pervades these books. Indeed, we doubt if a person still victimized *could* write a book: reliving the horrors via word processor might well be too traumatic, and the book would not be finished until the writer can triumph over them. But think what reading such a book might do for a victim still feeling destroyed, damaged, hurt: here in this book *itself* is proof that others have come back from horror, not unchanged, but with a clarity and purpose that is beyond value.

We found especially impressive those sexual enhancement manuals that were written from deeply devout Christian perspectives, stressing that within marriage not only is sex God's gift, but that it is intended for pleasure. To readers familiar only with the Sex-And-Damnation traditions of American preaching, these books will be startling indeed. Yet other readers will feel themselves in the presence of the divine eros:

The church is challenged in this day to unmask these fears [of sexuality] and liberate women as well as men to experience the wholeness of their sexuality. In exquisite theological poetry the Song of Solomon proclaims that the fiery flashes of love are as a raging flame—in some translations, a most vehement flame of God. Energized by the divine eros, human beings were created by God with the fiery flame of God's own passion, to love each other as God has loved us.[9]

The quote is from a 1991 Presbyterian Church document, which we compare with an excerpt from a Christian sexual enhancement manual:

[T]he husband-wife sexual relationship is used throughout Scripture to symbolize the God-man relationship. This imagery begins in Genesis. . . . [In addition, t]he Old Testament frequently refers to Israel as God's Bride . . . [and t]he sexual symbolism in the New Testament describes the church (the body of believers) as Christ's bride. . . . We *do* believe that it is in this mystical union of two bodies that body and spirit come closest to merger. Most of the time we let our minds control us. But in the moment of orgasm we are released from that control; climax is something that we experience as a totality. Everything about us enters into it. Perhaps this is how the sexual experience represents our relationship to God. In this total, intense fusion of body, emotion and spirit we are connecting with what it can be like to be totally one with God.[10]

The point is not so much whether you agree or not but whether or not you think that these are the equivalent of kiddie porn, as the sarcastic woman at the conference seemed to think we were discussing. And if *that* suggestion is deeply offensive—it is to us—then we are beginning to make our point. Do libraries have the right to disregard such writing because it is about sex, or is there a positive responsibility of libraries nationwide to make available such works to all?

That is a book selection issue far transcending choices about purchasing a specific title. When, through default, ignorance, or sarcastic malice, a library fails to stock such materials, it denies a place on the shelves not to pornography, but to a deeply felt American effort to understand God. Of course, not everyone agrees with this vision of God, and the library has the equal duty to shelve other visions, such as the companion report to the same General Assembly of the Presbyterian Church that demurred in many ways from these conclusions about eros.[11]

So "the selection issue" has two faces. One is specific to titles: shall we purchase this one or that? The other is a deeper challenge to ideals of librarianship as well as to citizenship. It requires that we install a *new* default option, of examining works on a broad spectrum of sexuality as a routine part of library acquisition policies and practice, seeking out those works which have general or specific interest to a library's community, and shelving them where citizens, adult and younger, can read them and learn.

VOICES AGAINST: OBJECTIONS FROM WITHIN AND WITHOUT

> As a profession we're officially committed to the "library Bill of Rights." In practice, the traditional "guardianship" reflex kicks in, mixing potently with erotophobia. The practical result is that we basically don't feel good about buying and offering sex materials. We do so with pain and anxiety. And often we don't buy or offer them at all.[12]

And yet objections are raised against what we at least see as common sense and as a reasonable policy. As we discuss at greater length later, ever since the 1880s librarians have avoided most materials about sex, especially any that are controversial or potentially so. For the same reasons relating to controversy, libraries have also avoided some works from religious viewpoints.[13] So books about sex and religion, like those we have quoted, may be doubly avoided because "the patrons will complain," or "the board will object," or—more honestly, at least—"*I* don't like it."

These are sad voices, defeatist, surrendering to pressures they seem able to foresee but powerless to weather. Yet if controversy is seen as a negative outcome of buying sex books, might not positive outcomes be foreseen as well? A teenager avoids rape because she read a book about date rape in the young adult section; or a father is able to welcome home his dying homosexual son because the parents have checked out a Christian book about AIDS ministry; or a group of children does *not* taunt another child for early pubertal development because they have all learned via sex education books that growing up happens at a unique pace with each person.

We sense that most librarians are willing to look less defeatedly at the problems besetting America and the world. Issues that form the penumbra of sexuality include contraception and world population growth; international efforts to prevent and eradicate disease; a group of profound and deep-set changes in family, particularly in the role of women; and a worldwide moral-ethical-religious ferment about what is and is not right and proper sexually. For many, including the defeatist, such variety of problems, books, and ideas is chaos. But we do not agree: the debate is the message and perhaps even the response. In those many voices is a richness of ideas—and potential solutions. Ultimately, truth is itself like the words on a page: because each is different, together they make sense. If libraries are to play a role in slowly—ever so slowly—changing that world, then we may no longer have voices objecting to sexuality books in the library. Instead, we need voices urging libraries to become involved proactively in helping solve these problems within the great tradition of librarianship: the acquisition, distribution, and preservation of books.

In the chapters that follow, we provide detailed guidelines for enhancing the role of libraries and librarians in sexuality education. Silence is no longer an option, but the cacophony is overwhelming; we hope to assist librarians in understanding and organizing the cacophonous voices so that individual voices and rational debate may emerge.

NOTES

1. *Sex Guides* (D111, Campbell): 323.

2. American Library Association, Office of Intellectual Freedom, *Intellectual Freedom Manual*, 4th ed. (Chicago: ALA, 1992): 3.

3. Recent sexology writing often refers to *sexuality education* rather than *sex education*. We have used mostly the older term for its familiarity and brevity.

4. Terry Mattingly, "Dead Reckoning: Dahmer's Death Reveals Paradox of Belief in Damnation," *St. Louis Post-Dispatch* (December 3, 1994): D5.

5. Gary L. Bauer, letter on behalf of the Family Research Council, August 25, 1995, p. 2.

6. Donald G. Davis, Jr., & John Mark Tucker, *The Master We Serve: The Call of the Christian Librarian to the Secular Workplace* (Virginia Beach, VA: Fellow-

ship of Christian Librarians and Information Specialists/Austin, TX: Font & Fire Books, 1993): 10.

7. James D. Weinrich, *Sexual Landscapes* (B55): 386–387.

8. Martha Cornog & Timothy Perper, "For Sex, See Librarian: An Introduction," in *Libraries, Erotica, & Pornography* (D115, Cornog): 1–35.

9. General Assembly Special Committee on Human Sexuality, Presbyterian Church (U.S.A.), *Keeping Body and Soul Together: Sexuality, Spirituality, and Social Justice, A Document Prepared for the 203rd General Assembly (1991) of the Presbyterian Church (U.S.A.)*. Reports to the 203rd General Assembly (1991), Part I (Baltimore: Presbyterian Church U.S.A., 1991): 63.

10. *The Gift of Sex* (A65, Penner & Penner): 38–40.

11. General Assembly Special Committee on Human Sexuality, Presbyterian Church (U.S.A.), *Minority Report of the Special Committee on Human Sexuality, Prepared for the 203rd General Assembly (1991) of the Presbyterian Church (U.S.A.)*. Reports to the 203rd General Assembly (1991), Part II (Baltimore: Presbyterian Church U.S.A., 1991).

12. Sandy Berman, "Hot Stuff: Getting Sex in the Library," *Collection Building* 13.1 (1993): 46.

13. Alice Norris, "Should We Buy Religious Fiction?" *School Library Journal*, January 1993: 42; Eric Bryant, "Librarian-Evangelical Cross-Talk," *Library Journal*, May 1, 1994: 44–45.

2   Sex Education: Past and Present

Some background on the history of sex education will lend perspective to our discussion of the library's role. Consider a story from the early days of public sex education, presumably just about Kinsey's time in the 1940s, when delicately and with trouble, U.S. colleges and universities were grudgingly introducing the rudiments of formal instruction about sexual function.

The male instructor was explaining something of the anatomy of the sexual organs. He had come to the male genitalia and was—with difficulty—trying to conquer his embarrassment. "The human male's testicles," he said, "are approximately the size and shape of plovers' eggs—"

Voice from the audience (female): "Well, now we know how large plovers' eggs are."[1]

This instructor was clearly far behind his audience, perhaps not surprising when considering their age group. But today, sex educators risk being far behind *their* audiences if they do not begin when children are quite small.

Why should this be?

In the last 50 years, it has become increasingly acceptable to talk about sex in print, on radio, on television, in film, the theatre, restaurants, magazines, sidewalks, offices. Children receive messages about sex from the first time they see a TV screen or page through *Ladies Home Journal*. In a 1992 "Calvin and Hobbes" cartoon, Calvin sidles up to his mother: "Mom, I have a question." "Sure, honey." "Why would it be worth four dollars a minute to talk on the telephone to goofy ladies who wear their underwear on TV commercials?" Mother exclaims, "When were you watching THAT?!" "Um . . . it was on—uh—during my morning cartoons." He trudges off, obviously unenlightened: "Somehow whenever I ask a question, I end up with a lot of them to answer."[2]

The fictional Calvin is a precocious kid who tries to inveigle librarians into telling him about dirty words. "County library? Reference desk, please. Hello? Yes, I need a word definition. Well, that's the problem. I don't know how to spell it and I'm not allowed to say it. Could you just rattle off all the swear words you know and I'll stop you when . . . Hello??" Later, he turns to trickery: "Allo? Eez thees der pooblic lahbrorry? Yah? I em beeg eeemportant rezearcher oond I require Eenglish voolgar zynonyms for dis-gustink body vunktions, yah? Allo? Allo?"[3] We laugh at Calvin's antics; but they reveal classic parental avoidance of sexual issues, and *that* is no joke.

What did parents tell their kids when Michael Jackson was accused of child sexual abuse? When Pee Wee Herman was arrested for exhibitionism? When Magic Johnson was diagnosed with AIDS? When Loreena Bobbitt was all over the news for cutting off her husband's penis? When Anita Hill complained about Clarence Thomas' unwanted sexual remarks? Over the past five years, these events have dominated the media and popular con-sciousness.[4]

Countless soap opera characters have passionate extramarital sex, but few get pregnant or get sexually transmitted diseases.[5] These media mes-sages can give children—and adults!—inaccurate and lopsided ideas about sex. Stanton and Brenna Jones reported watching with their nine-year-old son a TV couple kissing passionately. The child stated confidently that "married couples don't kiss like that."[6]

Other reasons speak for sex education beginning as soon as children can talk. As a society, we have gradually become aware of how widespread child sexual abuse is—and also how difficult it is for children to verbalize even to *themselves* how they feel victimized. Teaching correct sexual terms and familiarizing children with matter-of-fact discussion of sexual devel-opment, etiquette, and values lay the groundwork for reporting exploitative behavior.

A stream of books and articles show how uninformed many people have been about sex from their earliest years and how unfortunate the outcomes. Some women have no words for their genitals. *Voice of Youth Advocates* editor Dorothy Broderick once mentioned a 1970 letter to a newspaper from a woman complaining that her daughter was being taught words in class that she, the mother, did not know—her example was *vagina*.[7] With-out such a class, her daughter may have been in danger of having her first menstrual period come as a complete shock, a terrifying event that has befallen all too many girls. Unenlightened boys can be equally distressed by their first nocturnal emission.[8]

Even the most conservative Americans are joining liberals in espousing some sort of sex education for everyone and starting the earlier the better. For one thing, it spares us the embarrassment of talking about plovers' eggs—and only through knowledge can we understand sexual processes, learn comfort with our own bodies and sexuality, and make choices about appropriate and healthy sexual expression. In doing so, we integrate our ethical, emotional, and sexual lives into personally appropriate systems of values and morality. And when we become ill, we can even tell the doctor where it hurts.

SEX EDUCATION: A BRIEF HISTORY

Despite its critics, sex education is not a recent innovation of liberalism. The Kahun Papyrus from 1900 B.C.E. in ancient Egypt gives contraceptive formulations based on such interesting ingredients as crocodile dung, to be inserted into the vagina. Impotence and STDs were also addressed in ancient papyri.[9] Chinese sex manuals are reported as the world's earliest, most comprehensive, and most detailed, dating back at least to several centuries B.C.E. Some had illustrations, and some attributed sexual expertise to women in the same way that Plato identifies Diotima of Mantinea as Socrates' instructress in love.[10] The well-known Indian *Kama Sutra* (c. 0–600 C.E.) and the Arabic classic *The Perfumed Garden* (c. 1400 C.E.) originated in later eras, but they precede Masters and Johnson—or high school sex education—by many centuries.

Ever since The Beginning, people have spoken and taught about sex. "How-to-pick-up-girls" books were not invented by the modern American author Eric Weber but date back at least to Ovid's *Art of Love* from the first century C.E. Ovid recommended the theatre and the race track as hot spots for finding "one to love, or possibly only to have fun with." He gave women explicit instructions for comportment during sex, advising them to fake orgasm, if necessary, to captivate their partner: "And if nature, alas! denies you the final sensation, cry out as if you had come, do your best to pretend."[11] While few modern advisors would counsel women to fake orgasm, it was probably sage advice in ancient Rome, where society was run entirely by men and only the very wealthiest women had resources and opportunities for independent living.

Although Catullus, Martial, or Horace may be little read today, except as exercises in now vanishing Latin courses, they were intensely popular then. Catullus in particular was widely read for his truly extraordinary skill with the sexual insult. And Ovid was perhaps the best known and most beloved poet of Europe from late medieval to Shakespearean times and, up to 1453 and Gutenberg, all in hand-copied versions.

From ancient times to the 1800s, the West has more records of erotica than sex education writings, although doubtless many people used the former for the latter purpose. The period sometimes called the "Little Renaissance" (the 1100s and 1200s in Provence and elsewhere) saw the emergence of troubadour love poetry and traditions of "courtly love"—and some sexual jokes.[12]

In Europe, the first known explicitly "dirty" book was the so-called *Aretino's Postures*, actually a series of 20 engravings of "the various ways, attitudes, and positions in which licentious men have intercourse with women; and, what is worse, for each plate Messer [Master] Pietro Aretino wrote a most indecent sonnet."[13] The poems themselves were entitled *Sonetti lussuriosi*, but it was the combination of word and drawing, published in 1524, that became notorious. Obviously, the "postures" could be used as inspiration and instruction for sporting couples.

Over a century later, a work appeared in Restoration London that became a major source of sex education for two centuries and over two continents. The misleadingly titled *The Works of Aristotle the Famous Philosopher in Four Parts*, best known as *Aristotle's Masterpiece*, is a household manual about sexual anatomy, function, and reproduction. It was surprisingly accurate for its day—the 1680s, approximately, although parts of the work are much older—and by the 1800s had been reprinted throughout America. It frankly celebrated sexual joy and achieved broad distribution even into the twentieth century.[14]

Certainly folk and medical remedies for sexual matters circulated in the 1800s, especially among women: to promote abortion, contraception, and—for both men and women—increased sexual desire and stamina (aphrodisiacs). The 1844 *United States Practical Recipe Book* gave detailed directions for making condoms out of sheep intestine: "Used to prevent infection or pregnancy."[15]

Effects of Science and Medicine on Sex Education

Meanwhile, advances in medicine set certain changes in motion. Their history is a wonderful convolution of knowledge attained in classical years of ancient Egypt, Greece, and Rome, codified by the Hippocratic physicians and later by Galen, translated and preserved by Arab and Islamic scholars, and early in the 1200s, brought to Europe via North Africa and Spain to Salerno, where schools of physicians studied ancient wisdom and wrote to the great doctors of the church in Paris for moral enlightenment about these new discoveries. Later in the 1200s, St. Thomas Aquinas further codified Aristotelian knowledge, some of it quite erroneous, into doctrine that has permeated many Western beliefs about sexuality, for example, the idea that a male fetus takes on human life—"quickens"—after 40 days in the uterus, whereas a female fetus quickens at 80 days.[16]

As the Renaissance dawned, it again became possible to study, dissect, and draw the nude human body, which the church had previously forbidden. Beginning with the first modern textbook on anatomy by Vesalius in 1543, physicians began to develop "scientific" theories about sexual maladies and processes that formerly had been linked by the church and in the popular mind to magic, witchcraft, demons, and sin. One tradition, not medical in the modern sense but nonetheless not demonology, is associated with the publication in the early 1700s of *Onania*, whose title refers to Onan in the Bible and therefore to the "wastage of a man's seed." It linked many physical and social harms, including venereal disease, to masturbation and excess of sexual activity, even within marriage. It led to later "balance theories" of sexual health, where loss and expenditure of sexual fluids and energies had to be balanced by their preservation lest excessive losses lead to degeneration, debilitation, and death. Still later versions of this notion, for example, in the 18th and 19th centuries and associated most with the 18th century Swiss physician Simon Tissot, elaborated the concept of loss of male (or female) semen into very general theories of social, physical, and moral health. Known broadly as "degeneracy theory," this concept supported various efforts to purify society of moral and venereal disorders, particularly in the 19th century, by eradicating "sexual excess" of all sorts.

These efforts, misdirected according to modern views, nonetheless provided a secular alternative to the equally frightening but disembodied notion that God punishes sin with disease. In brief, these years saw the emergence if not of sexual education in any modern way, then of medicalizing theories that could be explained to the public. For example, they were incorporated into sporadic efforts towards public sex education in France and Germany, both before and after the French Revolution in 1789.[17]

In the United States and England, the sex-phobic trend begun with *Onania* and elaborated by Tissot blended with Victorianism and strongly influenced 19th century U.S. social reformers Sylvester Graham and John Harvey Kellogg, better known now for their links with graham crackers and breakfast cereal, respectively. Both wrote anti-masturbation manuals: Graham's 1834 *A Lecture to Young Men*, and Kellogg's 1888 *Plain Facts for Old and Young*.[18]

These degeneracy theories emerged prior to "the germ theory of disease," which originated in the second half of the 19th century and developed into modern medical epidemiology and pharmacology only in the 20th. To be fair to history, partnered sex has always been dangerous—ironically for the *Onania* school, masturbation is completely safe. In the past, venereal diseases were incurable, contraception unreliable, and abortion deadly; childbirth was a social and economic hazard for unmarried women and a medical menace for all women. Today, the medical hazards of abortion and childbirth are small, and contraception usually works. But unmarried childbirth is still a social and economic liability, and STDs—including HIV/AIDS—can still cripple or kill. In AIDS, we moderns can sense some of the terror and superstition of times when *no* STD was treatable.

Not all Victorian medical thought focused on the "degenerative" effects of sex. Russell Thatcher Trall wrote about contraception extensively in his *Sexual Physiology* (1866), and Charles Knowlton's *Fruits of Philosophy* (1832) counseled readers that sexual desire (within reason) was another normal body appetite. Yet a scandal rocked the 1899 annual meeting of the American Medical Association when senior gynecologist Denslow Lewis read a paper describing quite accurately sexual response and advocating sex education, especially for women. "The Gynecologic Consideration of the Sexual Act" was refused publication in *Journal of the American Medical Association*, and he came under much criticism from other physicians who did not believe in speaking about sexual matters publicly or in sex instruction beyond "botany and the elements of zoology."[19]

This "medicalization" of sex, sex-positive or sex-negative, was able to reach a wider audience of average citizens in an increasingly education-hungry society than previous, mostly theological, visions of sexual sin. Although medically inaccurate, degeneracy theory brought sexual behavior into public discourse as a vital area for investigation, discussion, cure, and public education. By defining these "sins" as secular events, public attention was focused in a way not hitherto possible.

We can draw a broader conclusion. The effect of medicalized discourse was not completely salutary from the anti-sex viewpoint. In theory, people ought to have recoiled in horror from sex once they knew it "caused" degeneracy. Yet we have here a paradox of moralizing sexuality education: not everyone was horrified. The French poets Baudelaire and Verlaine adopted images of sexual sin as icons of liberation and descent, for example, in Baudelaire's *Les Fleurs du Mal*. Marcel Proust's *Sodome et Gomorrhe*, part of his masterpiece *A la Recherche du Temps Perdu* (*Remembrance of Things Past*), was unmistakably about homosexuality.[20] Although English and American literature were slower to follow, medicalization led not only—and not even primarily—to prophylaxis and chastity but to broadening of the borders of acceptable discourse. Divorced by medicalization from his fatherhood of sexual sin, the Devil dwindled, while simultaneously Baudelaire established himself as the granduncle of modern sexual counterculture.

The purist may object that such is not "real" sex education. In the narrow sense, the purist is right: sex education is taught through formal, organized classroom curricula and concerns sexual anatomy, physiology, and (maybe) behavior. Thus Baudelaire, Madonna, and MTV can be easily dismissed as "not really education at all" and even *anti*-educational. While we respect this definition and its historical locus in education reform, we nonetheless propose a wider concept that we use throughout this book: sex education is a *totality* of experiences and learning. Some sex education occurs in the classroom under teacher supervision, but many forms of sexual learning occur in settings external to schools—including supplemental self-education via libraries!

So we view "sex education" in far broader contexts of history, literature, art, religion, and philosophy. Accordingly, to the extent that Baudelaire wrote about lesbianism as a sexualized icon of freedom, he was a sex educator. The researcher then asks *how* Baudelaire educated people about sex, for once one lifts one's eyes beyond the classroom, educator he assuredly was.

The advantage of our broader definition is that it permits us to state the greatest paradox of all that developed around the older concept of sex education, which, like medicalization, has directed itself to social purity, abstinence, and heterosexual monogamy. The more strictly such education insists on limiting itself to moral education, the more it invites and invokes the opposite. The mother of one of us (TP) had a favorite saying that illustrates the paradox: "Don't tell children not to put beans up their noses." The image is vivid because we visualize the poor child instantly becoming intrigued by the idea. *Alfie's Home* has been hailed by conservatives as a story modeling how a young person can overcome homosexuality and become "normal." The book nonetheless describes a lad having sex with his uncle and then deciding that he will grow up and have sex with women. We grownups recognize the message, driven home by quotes on the back cover. But will a young reader conclude that *maybe one can do both?* Sex education—in all possible senses—brings to the fore matters that we are biologically and culturally prepared to find interesting. So does—and did—medicalization, even if intended as moral prevention.

Effects of Socioeconomic Change

To describe more fully other factors inspiring both sex-negative and sex-positive 19th century social reformers and physicians, we must go back to the industrial revolution, roughly 1750–1850. For generations previous, the economy of the United States, Britain, and Europe had been based primarily on farms and small businesses run by extended families, which in turn fell under the social and moral leadership of both church and state acting together. But as people left home to work in factories, these connections were severed. Families lost much of their control over children's education and morality, and religious authority over all aspects of life, including reproduction, was weakened. In the United States in particular, waves of immigrants brought different family and sexual customs, which themselves waned as families acculturated. Throughout these changes, older information, kinship, and religious networks and systems became weaker and less influential. Simultaneously, fledgling science and medicine began to cast doubt on the inerrancy of church authority in sexual as in other matters, further weakening older controls on behavior. Cities grew, populated by growing numbers of single young people sundered from the influence of kin and church.

Because farming families were giving way to factory worker parents and because by the 1890s and early 1900s child labor laws restricted children's economic contributions, larger families gradually became more of a financial liability than an asset. More so than previously, children were nonproductive drags on family time and resources: they had to be schooled and looked after, rather than being integrated usefully into the family farm or home business. The result was greater interest in and need for contraception.

With the factory system and proletarianization came rebellion, reform, and radicalism.[21] These—the three R's of the day—incorporated increasing awareness of sexual misfortune and inequality, particularly among working class women and their more educated middle class sisters. Nineteenth century socialists, reformers, and radicals alike wrote about "The Woman Question," meaning issues of gender inequality in work, family, and home. Building on first-wave feminism, such as Mary Wollstonecraft and her 1792–93 *A Vindication of the Rights of Woman*, 19th century women writers and activists championed a set of issues very recognizable today: education, reproductive rights, job equality, and political equity for women. Sex education—though not necessarily so called—was a central component to this vision of a changed future. Later, through vocal involvement of women reformers of society at large, it focused more and more clearly on education about pregnancy, disease, and contraception.

Simultaneously, industrialization created a growing middle class of merchants and small business folk, with greater prosperity and leisure. They sought and increasingly had time for education and reading, and money for buying books. Publishers sprang up to print the books these people bought: the consumer movement, the media, and the information explosion all arose together.

The romance novel, begun in England with Samuel Richardson's *Pamela* in 1740, blossomed as a genre both here and throughout England and Europe. It attracted great and hack writers serving a voracious reading public. In England, Jane Austen, Mary Wollstonecraft Shelley, Frances Burney, Charles Dickens; in America, Nathaniel Hawthorne, James Fenimore Cooper, and Herman Melville—all became the recorders and shapers of an increasingly cultured and socially aware lifestyle not merely for a few men, but for women and their children. Today, Austen's *Pride and Prejudice* seems to have nothing to do with sex education, but it was a profound novel of gender and implicitly of the sexual duties and travails that for

women underlay the romance of Elizabeth and Darcy. Given a time when
Aristotle's Masterpiece could provide the nitty-gritty how-to's, the novel
provided meaning, sense, and value in a world that had lost its prior connections to church and kin as storehouses of sexual meaning.

If women of middle class wealth and comfort read novels, men of comfort read the erotica increasingly available in Europe, England, and the
United States. Greater literacy and education also gave rise to greater curiosity, and the growing concentration of people in cities provided populations to study. The pioneer endeavor of modern social science research
into sexuality is considered to be Jean Baptiste Parent-Duchâtelet's investigation into the lives of Parisian prostitutes, published in 1836.[22]

Indeed, loosening family and church influences, increased leisure and in-
come among young city folk, the growing consumer ethic beginning to
replace the earlier mandates of hard work and sacrifice—all led to an increase in, and a growing consciousness of, an array of sociosexual "evils."
If sexual activity outside of marriage, homosexuality, birth control, abortion, "venereal" disease, and prostitution had always existed, by the 1800s
they had become concentrated and noticeable, by 1900 had become more
concentrated and noticeable, and—hmm, things don't change, do they—
by the year 2000, will have become *very* concentrated and noticeable. Indeed, they have spawned such an immense industry of writing and publishing that we are writing this book just to make a few suggestions about
what libraries might acquire.

Social Reform Education

By the 19th century, the time was ripe for social reformers like Graham
and Kellogg, and they came aplenty and in surprising diversity. And with
them, they ultimately brought systematic sex education—for, ironically,
you cannot warn against something without talking about it! The very
efforts to reform sexual "evils," beginning with *Onania* in 1724, led to
increased tolerance for public discussion of sex, if only to speak against it.

This trend had opponents, foremost among them Anthony Comstock,
who organized the Society for the Suppression of Vice in 1873. Known for
attacks on erotica, he had reformer Margaret Sanger indicted for her writings on contraception. But Comstock, while highly influential for awhile,
was doomed to failure as other reformers with different views and agendas
fought to influence public sexual thinking—and the battleground then as
now was public discourse.

For Sanger, the greatest evil was unwanted pregnancy. The birth control
movement, which she helped found, had from the start a strong education
component despite censorship of its early literature by opponents such as
Comstock. Other reformers took on other evils. Medicine was beginning
to lose its preoccupation with sexual excess and masturbation. As early as

1912, some marriage manuals declared that nothing but "happy and joyous sex relations can keep the world moving and progressing."[23] Havelock Ellis, a pioneer sexologist and physician in the early 20th century, wrote in favor of sexual tolerance, particularly for homosexuality. He also supported contraception, marriage reform, and rights for women.

Arrayed against Sanger and the few permissive physicians and scholars were those who took up the burden of *Onania* in the "social purity" and "social hygiene" movements.[24] Social purity generally referred to reforming immorality; social hygiene, to eliminating venereal disease and prostitution. These movements were made up of a dozen or so groups, and all held one way or another that sexual pleasure and indulgence, outside and even within marriage and especially solo, led to great social and personal harm. Whereas their late Victorian morality seems repressive by today's standards, their discourse impossibly euphemistic and romantic, and their knowledge certainly based on medical inaccuracies, the social purity and social hygiene groups did believe in public education and discussion of sexual topics. In this, they were quite un-Victorian and represented a change from Comstock.

As early as the 1880s, the White Cross, a general social purity group, urged parents to instruct their offspring in proper sexual standards. But by 1900, many purity-type reformers despaired of parental success and began to favor the schools as the most effective channel for applying preventive and corrective measures to potentially wayward youth.[25] Although many reformers continued to favor exclusive home instruction, the advocates of sex education in the schools triumphed. Taking the lead was the American Society of Sanitary and Moral Prophylaxis, founded in 1905 and allied in 1910 with the newly formed American Federation for Sex Hygiene (AFSH). In 1913, the AFSH was renamed the American Social Hygiene Association upon merger with the anti-prostitution American Vigilance Association. While venereal disease and prostitution had been the targets of these groups, all agreed that a broader agenda was desirable.

The public school establishment had already become receptive to the idea; the National Education Association first discussed sexuality education in 1892, passing a resolution in favor of "moral education in the schools." By the 1920s, between 20% and 40% of U.S. school systems had some sort of provision for social hygiene and sexuality instruction.[26] By the 1930s, the U.S. Office of Education began to print materials and train teachers.

Early school sex instruction taught sexual morality centering on the restriction of sex to marital procreation, the dangers of venereal disease, especially from "illicit" (i.e., nonmarital) encounters, and the notion that promiscuous intercourse was likely to contribute to "race degeneracy." Meanwhile, the birth control movement and the advocates for (nonprocreative) sexual pleasure continued their efforts independently through private organizations and publications. These elements were not introduced into public school sex education for many years, and are still controversial. Early sex education programs focused on "disaster prevention" and to a considerable extent still do.

Even though founded upon "social purity" and moral standards wholly compatible with the most conservative Victorian ideas of sex, the early public school sex education movement was highly controversial. Opposing it were, in part, some of the physicians who were sexual liberals before their time and, in part, those who defended the earlier conspiracy of silence to preserve youthful morals. Still others favored home or church as the desirable milieu. Many were concerned that public discussion would promote licentiousness and hedonism.

Modern Bases of Sex Education

To the agendas of radicals, reformers, and conservatives pressing for moral and ethical content in sex education courses, the 20th century has added a new ingredient: the knowledge explosion, particularly in biomedicine but, increasingly in the last three decades, in social and behavioral scientific knowledge as well.

Modern biological interest in sexuality dates back to Vesalius but grew immensely after the 17th and 18th centuries, when Antonie van Leeuwenhoek built the first microscopes and saw sperm, William Harvey proposed his doctrine that all life arises from eggs, and Reinier de Graaf described the internal structure of the mammalian ovary. By the mid-1800s, fertilization was first observed under the microscope (many people imagine it was seen much earlier, but not so), and by 1900 the cellular events of egg and sperm formation, as well as of fertilization, were beginning to be understood. The role of the high power microscope from the 1890s cannot be underestimated for elucidating the events of embryonic development: for the first time in history, it was possible to *see* embryonic development unfolding. By 1915, the science of genetics had established that inheritance occurs by transmission of genes carried on chromosomes contained in egg and sperm. By 1940, genetics and embryology were among the most advanced of the biological sciences.

Medical, surgical, and anesthesiological advances in understanding pregnancy and fertility likewise followed. In addition, microbiologists had come to understand the origin of the true venereal killer: syphilis. By 1905, the first genuinely effective treatment for syphilis was announced: Salvarsan. And with Salvarsan, gone was half a millennium of syphilitic horror. With penicillin—first used medically during World War II—gonorrhea and syphilis were both, in theory at least, mere shadows of their former selves. But progress was not unilateral. At all points, conservatives opposed medical research and, when that proved impossible, opposed its therapeutic consequences in hospital and medical practice and, when *that* proved impossible, opposed educating the public about what medicine and biology had found.

Yet the crux for sexuality was the discovery, during the 1930s and 1940s, of the hormones associated with mammalian ovulation and reproduction: estrogen, progesterone, follicle stimulating hormone, and luteinizing hormone (LH). These were not pure academic findings, curiosa of distant physiological interest to specialists. Because the mutually and cross-interacting roles of hormones in ovulation were understood, it was clear that estradiol-progesterone formulations could block LH release and thereby impede follicular release of the ovum.

And if you are unfamiliar with those terms, you have not learned what all people need to know about basic sexual physiology. We have described nothing less than how the contraceptive pill works—The Pill itself. Be not too quick to say you do not need to understand the esoterica of physiology to understand what it does, for assessment of technology requires technical knowledge—and sometimes the most profound matters are hidden when we are ignorant of basic biomedicine.

If "Xq28" means nothing to you, know this: that if its properties are confirmed, it will obliterate 2,000 years of moralizing. It refers to the hypothesized so-called gay gene, and if further research validates the preliminary findings, there will be no question that at least some forms of male homosexuality are due in part to built-in genetic predispositions and are not merely sinful habits acquired because some men have chosen the morally disordered life of sodomy. Can we afford to be ignorant?[27]

The answer is no—an absolute *No*. And accordingly, the work of sex education has been made far more complex than mere moral and value-decision judgments, as vital as those are to people. It has become essential to know a good deal about sexuality if we are to carry forward rational discussion of these moral and ethical issues. Some beginnings have been made, and more will come.

Growth and Expansion of Sex Education

Over decades and despite controversy, sex education spread to a majority of school districts. Gradually, curricula have changed, becoming broader and more detailed, incorporating elements such as birth control and sexual pleasure from other camps of reformers. Further impetus was provided by pressure from health professionals and the public for AIDS education in the mid-1980s. Today, 47 states require or recommend sex education programs in the public schools, and all 50 states require or recommend HIV/AIDS education.[28] Courses in human sexuality for college students began in the 1940s and 1950s.

The two organizations most responsible for continuing expansion and improvement of sex education in schools and colleges were the Sexuality Information and Education Council of the United States (SIECUS), begun in 1964, and the American Association of Sex Educators, Counselors, and Therapists (AASECT), begun in 1967. SIECUS was founded partly to challenge the hegemony of the American Social Hygiene Association, which then dominated sex education curriculum development. ASHA fought back but finally disbanded, and today other organizations continue to oppose SIECUS-style education (see below). AASECT has been a major education and credentialling body for elementary, secondary, and college level educators. In 1968, New York University received a grant from the U.S. Office of Education to develop graduate programs for training sex education teachers; degrees were first offered in 1970.[29] In 1990, SIECUS established the National Coalition to Support Sexuality Education, which by 1994 had 80 nonprofit organizations as members, including the American Library Association, the American Medical Association, the YWCA of the USA, and the U.S. Conference of Mayors.[30]

Sex Education Today

Sex education in the schools has remained controversial, despite polls over the decades showing that large majorities of parents support it.[31] In the late 1960s, groups such as the Christian Crusade and the John Birch Society attacked SIECUS and sex education in general for promoting immorality and promiscuity; by the late 1970s, sex educators were accused of promoting "humanism" as a religion. By the 1980s and 1990s, however, many religious and conservative groups had shifted their emphasis to the content of sex education in the schools, rather than whether it should be taught at all.[32] Schools are urged to teach sexual abstinence only, through use of curricula such as Teen-Aid and Sex Respect. Some schools have adopted these curricula, although one state judge barred a school system from using them, saying they unconstitutionally promote religion.[33] Meanwhile, SIECUS and other more liberal sex educators refer to these programs disparagingly as "just say no" and "fear-based." SIECUS-approved curricula stress abstinence as a smart choice but also provide information about birth control, abortion, safer sex, and nonexploitive adolescent sexual expression. SIECUS calls its approach "reality-based" and often uses the terminology "delaying (or postponing) intercourse" rather than "abstinence."

The schools have not been the only vehicle for U.S. sexuality education, although they have been a major locus for controversy. The antiprostitution and anti–venereal disease campaigns conducted by the armed services during World Wars I and II were not officially connected to sex education in the reformers' mode, but once again represented discussion— if that term can be used for the army—of matters that could not be left to silence or to mere abstinence harangues directed at the troops.[34] These campaigns too were forms of social or cultural "education" about sex, and no matter how much they left to be desired from modern viewpoints, they brought sexuality into consciousness in ways unprecedented.

Over the years, many public and private organizations have conducted programs, sometimes with government funding, such as the "Education for Parenthood" programs in the Boy Scouts and 4-H, funded by federal agencies in the 1970s. In recent years, churches have developed their own programs and curricula, particularly centering on the teen years and preparation for marriage. Other church educational efforts address adult sexuality and AIDS. Today, a wide variety of sex education courses and programs are offered by government, medical centers, universities, nonprofits, and for-profit organizations: for example, the Masters and Johnson Institute, Planned Parenthood, the Menninger Clinic, and the Athletes for Sexual Responsibility program from the University of Maine.

Sex Education in Print

We have noted above a number of different groups, viewpoints, and agendas. While some have become more accepted by the public, administrative, and/or scientific communities than others, *all* show their faces in books, pamphlets, newsletters, and fact sheets. What began in the United States with *Aristotle's Masterpiece* has become a tumult of cacophonous voices. The sexual purity reformers published heavily in the 1800s, with pamphlets, circulars, and works like *Plain Points on Personal Purity, or Startling Sins of the Sterner Sex*, by George F. Hall (1892). Marriage manuals began as a genre in the 1800s, some touting "purity," others being more permissive. In the 1890s was born the "teen sex manual," two early series being "Self and Sex" and "Teaching Truth."[35]

A 1906 book urged parents to talk to their children about sex: *The Renewal of Life: How and When to Tell the Story to the Young*, by Margaret Morley. Soon thereafter followed Margaret Sanger's pamphlets and books on birth control. The explosion of sex information was sufficiently unprecedented to lead the magazine *Current Opinion* to remark in 1913 that it was "sex o'clock in America."[36]

Teen manuals, marriage manuals, and medical works about sex have continued to develop, gradually becoming more comprehensive, detailed, and accurate as taboos on sex in print have been relaxed. In 1948 and 1953 came Kinsey's milestones, which inspired unprecedented publicity, discussion, and debate on topics previously unmentionable. The Kinsey reports set the tone for open investigation and instruction about a full range of sexual expression. In 1966, Masters and Johnson contributed the first scientific, physiological descriptions of sexual response. For the first time, people could read about what was common statistically and normal physiologically. Kinsey and Masters and Johnson paved the way for continued investigation into, and publication about, sexual matters, with the aim of providing ever more useful and accurate information to a public very curious and sorely in need.

The public is still sorely in need. Will sex education reduce or end AIDS, adolescent pregnancy, prostitution, sexual exploitation? Frankly, we do not know. But silence on sexual matters does not appear to be an option either ideologically or practically. Ideologically, ignorance is no advantage when others have knowledge, especially knowledge misused, and people who know nothing of sex can take risks unknowingly and be taken advantage of. From its earliest foundations, the American educational system stressed equal access to knowledge for everyone, and so it must be for sexuality information also. Practically, sexual messages in the media and elsewhere are not going to go away. The United States is run on a free-market capitalist economy, and so long as sex sells, it will. We had better face up to teaching people to make sense out of sex rather than telling them simply to ignore it.

Thus there is no longer any "whether" to sex education or even "when"—only "what" and "who." The playing field is crowded and the voices legion. More populist than the schools, the books and publications

available today represent *all* these voices, from amateur rants of sadomasochism (S&M) aficionados, to scholarly gynecological treatises, to exhortations from clergy about homosexual immorality, to pleas for gay liberation. There has been a particular and largely unrecognized explosion of religious/conservative books about sex, dealing with morality, teenage dating and deferring sex until marriage, marital sexual enhancement, AIDS, and sexual exploitation, as well as homosexuality and the church.[37]

And where books are, there should librarians be also. But library dealings with sexuality have been ambivalent to say the least, as we will summarize in the next chapter.

NOTES

1. A *true* story: one of us (MC) received a rudimentary form of sex education in junior high school. The young (and married) female gym teacher had just finished describing the male genitalia. A hand went up. "I have a question—" my classmate fidgeted with embarrassment. "Uh, how do they [men] *sit down?*" The teacher promised to explain it to her after class. The girl did find out, but not (only) from the teacher. Somewhat later, she became pregnant and dropped out of school for half a term. Sex education in those days did not cover the rudiments of either contraception or communication and how to say no.

2. Bill Watterson, *The Days Are Just Packed: A Calvin and Hobbes Collection* (Kansas City: Andrews and McMeel, 1993): 104.

3. Watterson: 49, 95.

4. Anyone missing TV and radio news would have to be living in a cave to

miss the jokes circulating as a result of these incidents: Why did Michael Jackson hurry over to K-Mart? Because he could get boys' pants half off.

5. In the 1987–1988 season, a typical adolescent viewed nearly 14,000 instances of sexual material on TV. Of these, only 165 referred to topics such as sexuality education, STDs, or birth control. H. Louis et al., "Sexual Material on American Network T.V. During the 1987–1988 Season" (New York: Planned Parenthood Federation of America, 1988), cited in James Shortridge, comp., "Did You Know?" *SIECUS Report* (February/March 1994): 5.

6. *How & When to Tell Your Kids About Sex* (C98, Jones & Jones): 20. In a telephone poll of teenagers, 15% of those aged 13–15 and 18% of 16- and 17-year-olds reported learning the most about sex from "entertainment." Nancy Gibbs, "How Should We Teach Our Children About Sex?" *Time* (May 14, 1993): 61.

7. Dorothy Broderick, "Hill, Thomas, the 'P' Word and SEX, SEX, SEX, Education," *Voice of Youth Advocates* (April 1992): 6–7. Since the Bobbitt case, there is little danger of the word *penis* being unknown.

8. See, for example, "What the Young Want to Know About Sex," in *Show Me Yours!* (C86, Goldman & Goldman): 102–117.

9. *Sex in History* (D79, Tannahill): 64–65, 71–72.

10. *Sex in China* (D78, Ruan): 1–2, 29–32; *The Yin-Yang Butterfly* (D62, Chu): 81–92; Plato, *Symposium of Plato*, trans. by Tom Griffith (Berkeley, CA: University of California Press, 1989): 210a–212a.

11. *The Art of Love* (D40, Ovid): 108, 177.

12. Punning and bawdy jokes can be found in John W. Baldwin, *The Language of Sex: Five Voices from Northern France Around 1200* (Chicago: University of Chicago Press, 1994): 108–115. A 12th century fabliau tells how a peasant and his wife obtained a great blessing from St. Martin. The husband was given many penises, and she many vaginas—for which she became really quite famous. You see, she was "bien coneüe." *Connaître*, modern French past participle feminine *connue*, means "to know" in both common and Biblical senses, but there is a second pun as well, explained if you need it in *Merde!* (D94, Geneviève): 20–21.

13. *The Secret Museum* (D11, Kendrick): 58. *Aretino's Postures* was by no means the first Western sexually explicit work. Earlier Greek and Roman works such as the play *Lysistrata* are extraordinarily bawdy even by today's standards. But sex in classical literary contexts was usually linked to humor or satire. Aretino's work is reputed to be the first recorded book clearly having the sole intent to arouse so-called prurient interest.

14. The work was *not* written by Aristotle, although his very savvy observations of plants and animals formed the basis of Western biology and medicine. It has been reprinted as *The Works of Aristotle, the Famous Philosopher, in Four Parts Containing I. His Complete Masterpiece; II. His Experienced Midwife; III. His Book of Problems; IV. His Last Legacy*, 1813 ed., repr. (New York: Arno Press, 1974). See *The Destroying Angel* (D74, Money): 77–79; Vern L. Bullough, "An Early American Sex Manual, Or, Aristotle Who?" in *Sex, Society, and History* (New York: Science History Publications, 1976): 93–103. The Kinsey Institute library catalog shows several editions published 1700–1817.

15. *Woman's Body, Woman's Right* (A120, Gordon): 44, 492. Don't try this at home—only latex works against the HIV virus.

16. Material on the Salerno physicians and their relationship to the church is in

Baldwin: 10–16. On quickening, see physician Richard Lewinsohn's *A History of Sexual Customs* (Greenwich, CT: Fawcett, 1958): 178. Scholarly histories of early European sexual knowledge include James A. Brundage, *Law, Sex, and Christian Society in Medieval Europe* (Chicago: University of Chicago Press, 1987). See also the History and Culture section in Chapter 12.

17. Money: 49–55; William R. Stayton, "Onanism," in *Human Sexuality: An Encyclopedia* (A3, Bullough & Bullough): 424–426. Erwin J. Haeberle, *The Sex Atlas*, rev. ed. (New York: Continuum, 1983): 503–505, discusses French and German sexuality education at the time of the French Revolution. We thank Vern L. Bullough for additional observations, personal communication, February 13, 1995. The notion that "spending" semen depletes males has been found in many cultures; see, for example, Weston LaBarre's *Muelos: A Stone Age Superstition About Sexuality* (New York: Columbia University Press, 1984). It was parodied in Jack D. Ripper's concern for his "vital bodily essences" in the movie *Dr. Strangelove* and survives today when athletic coaches warn teams to avoid sex before a game.

18. Money: 50–87.

19. Sex-positive physicians: Sidney Ditzion, "Moral Evolution in America," in *Encyclopedia of Sexual Behavior, Vol. I: Modern Sex Practices*, ed. Albert Ellis & Albert Abarbanel (New York: Ace, 1967): 17–18. See also *The Story the Soldiers Wouldn't Tell* (D73, Lowry): 16–18, 93–98. American Medical Association scandal: Money: 116.

20. J.E. Rivers, *Proust & the Art of Love: The Aesthetics of Sexuality in the Life, Times, & Art of Marcel Proust* (New York: Columbia University Press, 1980).

21. This and the following discussion draw on a number of sources, especially Bonnie K. Trudell, "The First Organized Campaign for School Sex Education: A Source of Critical Questions About Current Efforts," *Journal of Sex Education and Therapy* 11.1 (Spring/Summer 1985): 10–15; and Bonnie Epstein, "Family, Sexual Morality, and Popular Movements in Turn-of-the-Century America," in *Powers of Desire* (A36, Snitow): 117–130. Other sources: Lynn R. Penland, "Sex Education in 1900, 1940 and 1980: An Historical Sketch," *Journal of School Health* (April 1981): 305–309; Bryan Strong, "Ideas of the Early Sex Education Movement in America, 1890–1920," *History of Education Quarterly* (Summer 1972): 129–161; *Science in the Bedroom* (D60, Bullough); Michael Imber, "Toward a Theory of Curriculum Reform: An Analysis of the First Campaign for Sex Education," *Curriculum Inquiry* 12.4 (Winter 1982): 339–362; Lester Kirkendall, in "Sex Education in the United States: A Historical Perspective," in *Sex Education in the Eighties: The Challenge of Healthy Sexual Education*, ed. Lorna Brown (New York: Plenum, 1981): 1–17; William L. Yarber, "Past, Present and Future Perspectives on Sexuality Education," in *The Sexuality Education Challenge* (C93, Drolet & Clark): 3–28.

22. *Science in the Bedroom* (D60, Bullough): 31–32. Duchâtelet's work was followed in England by Henry Mayhew's *London Labour and the London Poor*, first published 1849–1850. Its fourth volume devotes some 250 pages to prostitution in a tone remarkably enlightened for then—and for now. (Mayhew's masterwork has been reprinted in 4 volumes by Dover, 1968.)

23. Strong, p. 133.

24. For the complex history of these organizations, see *Science in the Bedroom* (D60, Bullough): Chapter 4.

25. Then, as now, parents were not the major providers of sex education to young people. Several studies in 1914–1915 indicated that around 20% of college age youth received sex instruction at home (Strong: 153). More recently, in a survey conducted by *Time* and CNN, 22% to 30% of teenagers said that they had learned most about sex from parents (Gibbs: 61). *Plus ça change.*

26. The 20% figure comes from Richard K. Means, *A History of Health Education in the United States* (Philadelphia: Lea & Febiger, 1962), cited by Clint E. Bruess & Jerrold S. Greenberg, *Sexuality Education: Theory and Practice*, 2nd ed. (New York: Macmillan, 1988): 54. The 40% figure is from Newell Edson, "Status of Sex Education in High Schools," Bureau of Education, Department of Interior, *Bulletin* 14 (1922): 3, 5, cited by Strong: 152.

27. Dean Hamer & Peter Copeland, *The Science of Desire: The Search for the Gay Gene and the Biology of Behavior* (New York: Simon & Schuster, 1993).

28. Sex education: Alan E. Gambrell & Debra Haffner, "Unfinished Business: The Executive Summary from the SIECUS Assessment of State Sexuality Education Programs by the United States," *SIECUS Report* (December 1993/January 1994): 27. HIV/AIDS education: Patti O. Britton, Diane de Mauro, & Alan E. Gambrell, "HIV/AIDS Education: SIECUS Study of HIV/AIDS Education for Schools Finds States Make Progress, but Work Remains," *SIECUS Report* (October/November 1992): 1–8.

29. Deryck Calderwood, "Educating the Educators," Brown: 191–201.

30. "The National Coalition to Support Sexuality Education," *SIECUS Report* 22.4 (April/May 1994): 13–14.

31. For example, 85% of adults support teaching sex education in the schools, according to the 22nd Annual Gallup Poll of Public Attitudes Toward Public Schools, published in a 1990 *Phi Delta Kappa Magazine* and cited in James Short-ridge, comp., "Did You Know?" *SIECUS Report* (February/March 1994): 5.

32. Leslie M. Kantor, "Attacks on Public School Sexuality Education Programs: 1993–94 School Year," *SIECUS Report* (August/September 1994): 11–16.

33. Abstinence curricula: Gibbs: 65. Court ruling: "Judge Blocks Pro-Abstinence Course," *Chicago Tribune* (March 21, 1993): Section 1, 15.

34. *No Magic Bullet* (E70, Brandt).

35. *Sex Guides* (D111, Campbell): 13–14, 29–34.

36. *Current Opinion* (August 1913): 113, quoted in Brandt: 49.

37. Apparently, many religious conservatives learn much more about sex from books than from parents, schools, or other sources. Conservative Christian counselors Tim and Beverly LaHaye wrote that 53% of wives and 47% of husbands attending their Family Life Seminars reported "reading" as their main source of sex education before marriage (*The Act of Marriage*, A61: 199). These people obviously represent potential library clientele.

3 History of Libraries and Sexuality Materials

> The libraries' censorship, except at the provincial lending level . . . has paradoxically had the opposite effect: that of preserving, in many cases, the very books that would otherwise have been destroyed. . . . For essentially, the libraries' effort is to protect the books for and sometimes *against* the readers, and not to protect the readers from the books.[1]

The role of the library as a repository for sexuality materials dates back at least to the early 1800s with the "Enfer" (hell) collection of the Bibliothèque Nationale in Paris.[2] The French were among the first to attempt a formal program of sex education; they also seem to have been in the avant garde in sexuality collections. The Bibliothèque Nationale is also the only great library that always frankly listed its erotic holdings in the printed catalog.[3]

In the English speaking world, the earliest erotica preservatory is the Private Case in the British Museum Library, dated tentatively to the 1866 receipt of a collection on "phallicism." The catalog to the Private Case was as tightly sequestered as the books, only a few researchers being allowed to examine the handwritten "P.C." catalog kept in the office of the Principal Keeper of Printed Books.[4] Nonetheless, this—and other sequestered collections first held by private individuals, then by libraries—preserved many early erotic writings from destruction by church, state, and readers like Samuel Pepys, who described burning an erotic novel after masturbating.[5] While not "sex education" in the modern sense, early erotic writings sometimes challenge received wisdom and have considerable educational value for modern historians, therapists, and policy makers.[6] But in those days burning, censorship, and sequestration all served the Victorian notion that silence was the best way to speak about sexuality.

FREE LIBRARIES AND UNCLEAN BOOKS

> There are people in San Francisco who are not pure. Among them, in my opinion, are those who try to supply themselves with dirty reading from the library.[7]

But when we turn to the "provincial lending level," the record is somewhat different. Librarians accustomed to poking around in the history of their profession will recognize Cannons' *Bibliography of Library Economy* (ALA, 1927) as the oldest index to library literature, covering 1876–1920. Two of its subject headings illuminate the issue: DOUBTFUL BOOKS: LITERARY CENSORSHIP and SEX HYGIENE, for these two headings crystallize the ambivalent, indeed Janus-like approach towards sex taken by U.S. public libraries for over a century.

The earliest entry under the first heading is F.B. Perkins' 1885 article, "Free Libraries and Unclean Books."[8] Subsequent articles ring a thesaurus of changes on undesirable acquisitions: *improper fiction, bad books, poisonous literature, "weeds" in library work,* materials termed *pernicious, nasty, doubtful, immoral, questionable,* and—with more rhetorical flourish—*"exotic," "erotic," and "tommy-rotic" literature.*[9] These proscribed readings seem to have been mostly fiction, a genre already suspect for its ability to stimulate fantasy, imagination, and yearnings for experiences beyond everyday life, erotic or not.

Under the heading SEX HYGIENE, the entries start somewhat later with a 1912 "Bibliography on Sex Education." It lists seven works directed to various age groups: two published by the Society of Sanitary and Moral Prophylaxis, three by the Spokane Society of Social and Moral Hygiene, one by Appleton publishers, and one by the American Medical Association.[10] The following year, the "Question Box" column from *Wisconsin Library Bulletin* was asked, "What books should the small library purchase on sex hygiene?" Columnist "Miss Helen Turvill" responded with four books, three described in the *A.L.A. Catalog* 1904–1911 and one in *A.L.A. Booklist* of January 1913.[11] One "may be safely put into the hands of the girls themselves"; another "[m]eets a definite need, but should not be placed on the open shelves." In prescribing their painfully ordained lists of delicately sanitized nonfiction, this second group of librarian authors were valiantly trying to swing with the time of "sex o'clock in America."

In the 1920s, a survey by Louis Feipel about "questionable books" in public libraries specifically addressed "books honestly or otherwise offering physiological information" as well as " 'suggestive' fiction" and such classics as Boccaccio and the "Arabian Nights." Most respondents did buy "physiological information," but usually restricted these books. Yet responses varied widely:

In the matter of sex hygiene books . . . , these books are held for restricted circulation, to such persons only as exhibit satisfactory evidence of normal tendencies and good faith.

In the case of sex-books, an endeavor is made to have available enough of the best of these written for laymen or young people, discussing sex questions in a clear, serious, but non-technical way, such as . . . the approved list of the American Hygiene Association.

Of the sex-books we buy those which are well reviewed and seem of some value, and circulate them freely. Certain titles are reserved for the use of students and physicians; but the majority of the books are circulated without question.

The sex series we do not buy at all, because we think that this is not a subject that any public library is competent to handle.

[A] popular series on sex hygiene is issued to adults only.

[S]ex-books are given, with discrimination, to minors.[12]

One respondent wrote the best summary possible for this study of "questionable books": "Our state of mind in regard to it is so chaotic, and subject to change, that there would be no use in trying to record it."[13]

In Perkins' era, the split had been clear: fiction books with sexual content were bad, nonfiction permissible if suitably credentialled and restricted. By Feipel's era, the picture had become muddy. In the 1920s, these librarians were just on the edge of an ongoing conflict that persists to this day: opposition between the older, classic library goal of holding only the highest and best Fruits of Civilization and a newer "freedom to read" ideology, ultimately culminating in—but not resolved by—the 1939 adoption of the Library Bill of Rights. This landmark document stated that "all sides of questions on which differences of opinion exist should be represented fairly and adequately."[14]

Librarianship was making a transition from the Victorian and ivory tower moral elitism of 19th century scholarship, wherein lay some of its origins, towards a more populist, democratic vision better suited to an American society where all citizens received public education, and many were college graduates. Furthermore, the librarians' consensus was breaking down as to precisely what comprised the Fruits of Civilization. At the height of Victorianism, even the Bible could be considered too freely written. Indeed, the collective level of the era's sexual frankness was exemplified by the *expurgated* Bible, upon which surgery had been performed by Thomas and Harriet Bowdler, dictionarian Noah Webster, and many others.[15] By Perkins' time (1885), this chasteness had dissolved somewhat, so that even he could hold the uncensored Bible as a standard for comparison with "suspect" works: "Whenever it shall be generally agreed that the merits of any given book are as much superior to its defects as the Bible, I will concede that it should be allowed to circulate freely."[16] This is the essence of the so-called Roth and Miller tests for pornography, where "importance" or "value" redeems sexual frankness. So as Bowdlerism waned, later librarians may have felt that some sexual content in otherwise classic or excellent works may not be so harmful as previously supposed.

Moreover, "Victorianism" was not monolithic, but an ill-at-ease congress of yearnings for moral uplift, desire for education (of the right kind), genteelism of a new bourgeois class, radical criticisms of sexual evil from moral reformers, ditto from suffragists, and campaigns against excesses of all sorts from drunkenness to licentious bordello-crawling, gambling, cursing, prostitution, the plight of the working girl, spiced up with Socialism, Trade Unionism, Oneida Community Bible Communism, bomb throwing anarchists, and writers about sex—in brief a true hodgepodge that centered on not much at all except our Monday morning hindsight that calls the entire stew "Victorianism." It was no homogeneous moral tapioca pudding. Then came World War I—and the movies.

External to the library world, both morals and reading habits were changing. Freud's work was already sufficiently known to be mentioned by Feipel's respondents. World War I had shown thousands of American homeboys that Europe had different sexual customs, and the 1920s flappers reeked of risqué demeanor. Bertrand Russell and Margaret Mead followed soon after; these two scholars made sexuality even more accessible to a reading public than did Freud.

Russell, Mead, and Freud were the intellectual children of Victorian ferment. They codified a vision of sexual prudery perhaps more an intellectual invention than a real description of life a half century before. For them, Victorianism was a mantle of censoring repression cast over sex. For others, in retrospect it had become a cleansed golden age of pure, innocent hominess. But a memory it was, nostalgia or a bad example. Today was the Great Depression, and World War II was looming: the Grapes of Wrath flowered at Hiroshima.

The end of World War II brought more changes, then in 1948 the "K-bomb": *Sexual Behavior in the Human Male* (A48, Kinsey et al.). Time for another survey, and Roger Bristol asked, what do librarians do "when faced with books that are too hot to handle[?] . . . Do they [buy them] or don't they? How do they justify their decisions? And if they do buy them, how do they solve their 'handling problems?' " Eleven libraries responded about the Kinsey male volume and Mailer's then controversial *The Naked and the Dead*. Bristol concluded: "So far as the library is concerned, the basic conflict seems to be between two conceptions of the librarian's job: (1) maintaining taboos of society, and (2) providing wide variety of community fare, even including material personally repugnant to the librarian."[17]

We could not imagine a clearer statement of the tension and outright conflict between the older classic library ideal of protecting the clientele from "poisonous literature" and the newer notion of the freedom to read and *serving* the clientele, even if they had repugnant needs. In the years following, this conflict sharpened, fueled by the literary/intellectual movements of the 1950s and the cultural phenomena now simply called "The Sixties."

It was a good time for still another survey about "problem materials." Eric Moon and Dorothy Broderick asked librarians whether they had purchased any of 44 books selected as "controversial"—21 so designated because of sexual content. And again, responses varied widely. A few librarians bought all 44 books, but many bought few or none. "[M]uch more common than judgments on literary merit or quality were judgments on content, assessments of moral values or taste, with a protective attitude toward a public described with alarming frequency and condescension as 'unsophisticated.' " Sometimes librarians chose not to purchase certain titles *because* they were controversial—whether the topic was sex, race, or politics. Other librarians "balanced their collections without second thoughts about 'demand' "—or controversy.[18]

A 1970s survey by Michael Pope, aptly published as *Sex and the Undecided Librarian*, also showed diversity. University librarians were shown to be more liberal in buying sex materials than public librarians, who in turn were more liberal than school librarians. Yet somewhere between the 1940s and the 1970s, a shift had occurred in the profession. Questions about sexuality books became posed more in the framework of expediency than morals: "unclean" and "questionable" books had become "problem" and "controversial" works. Guardianship of society has been recast as censorship, and librarians were now expected to guard the freedom to read instead. Thus the 1960s respondents' protective attitude was seen as "alarming," and the 1970s "undecided librarians" were characterized disparagingly: "Research indicates that librarians gave strong support to the concepts of intellectual freedom and open access to information, but do not necessarily implement these concepts in their libraries."[19]

It is perhaps not surprising that librarians lacked consensus about handling sexuality materials. Ever since the Victorian world ideal crumbled, U.S. society has lacked consensus about sex. For pornography alone, we have seen both the anti-pornographic Meese Commission *and* quite an explosion of recent sex writing, from explicit materials on how to avoid AIDS to women-written erotica to dozens of underground "zines" of sexual subcultures. Librarians even have their own uninhibited zine: *Fugitive Pope*.

On the one hand, we have had the Parents Music Resource Center, Jesse Helms, and the (now defunct) "Gag Rule"; on the other hand, Robert Mapplethorpe, Madonna, X-rated videos, dial-a-porn, a naked woman in *Publishers Weekly*, and a penis in *Library Journal*.[20]

Everyone has an opinion about these phenomena. Throughout the 1960s, sexual pleasure and birth control were debated. In the 1970s, abortion and gay rights came to the fore. By the 1980s, we all became newly conscious of sexual harassment, child sexual abuse, and pornography. All of these issues are still controversial, with vocal factions of American society contending in different voices What Should Be Done. Abortion is morally and legally acceptable . . . it is an individual moral, not a legal matter . . . it should be regulated "without undue burden" by the states . . . it should be outlawed by constitutional amendment. Homosexual acts and relationships are "just one more kind of love"[21] . . . gays should live married, monogamous lives, like responsible heterosexuals . . . homosexual behavior is a moral outrage against God and man. Looking at sexy pictures is great fun and makes your sex life better . . . erotica is sensuous and inspiring, pornography is degrading and promotes violence . . . sexually explicit images and nudity have no place outside medical settings. And so on.

Yet in one thing, there is consensus. We argue that ever since the 1980s, talk and writing about sex have represented *the* dominant cultural event. Upholders of all viewpoints, librarians or otherwise, agree on this: the way to convince people is to talk to, at, and around them, drown them if need be, but above all, get the words out there. *The debate is the message.*

We will use two major issues to illustrate how debate has expressed itself in recent library literature: the rise of gay and lesbian librarianship and the explosion of censorship regarding sexuality materials.

MAKING THINGS PERFECTLY QUEER

The Gay, Lesbian, and Bisexual Task Force of the American Library Association was founded in 1970, the first gay interest group in any professional association.[22] Now with an awards program, regular and popular presentations at conferences, and publications such as "How to Get Gay Materials into Libraries," the task force has matured into an active and influential presence in librarianship. Gay and gay-friendly librarians have added to the literature such contributions as *Gay, Lesbian and Bisexual Library Service* (D118, Gough & Greenblatt), plus many articles.[23]

Librarians have prepared exhibits for Gay and Lesbian History Month, staffed booths at gay and lesbian pride fairs, and marched in gay pride parades. The new San Francisco main library, to open in 1995, is planned to house a Gay and Lesbian Center, which will include "one of the most ambitious archives ever assembled of materials on lesbian and gay history, literature, and culture."[24]

However, not all librarians approve. When the July/August 1992 cover of *American Libraries* featured the Gay, Lesbian and Bisexual Task Force marching in the San Francisco Gay Pride Parade, reader responses ranged from applause to nausea.[25] In *School Library Journal*, a review of a book about homosexuality in young people's reading brought several critical letters and then a barrage of more letters responding to the first set.[26] An *RQ* article on "Problems of Access to Lesbian Literature" brought a response, "The best service for homosexuals is a recognition that repentance, not bibliography, will satisfy their needs."[27]

IS SEX SAFE IN YOUR LIBRARY?

Of the three great historical arenas for censorship—sex, religion, and politics—only sex has maintained widespread power to evoke the censor as we enter the 21st century. We still have laws against certain forms of sexual writing, art, and performance but not against religious or political expression. In library censorship, sex-related concerns take the number one place even more than a century after F.B. Perkins. A recent change has been increased efforts to censor homosexuality-related materials, with challenges to pro–gay/lesbian books now making up about a third of sex-related library challenges. The most frequently challenged book in both 1993 and 1994 was *Daddy's Roommate* (C26, Willhoite).[28]

All library censorship attempts, including those about sex, have radically increased since 1966, when library researchers began to collect systematic data. Between 1966 and 1975, a fourfold increase in incidents and a thirteenfold increase in number of different titles have been reported. The curve was relatively flat until the 1980s, when it began to rise again. More recent data show increases ranging from double to fivefold between 1990 and 1993. Challenges to school materials alone are reported to have increased fivefold from 1982 to 1992. The percentage of libraries reporting challenges has more than doubled, from 20% before 1980 to 40–50% more recently. Some of these increases may be due to increased reporting, but the ALA's Office of Intellectual Freedom estimates that only 15% of censorship attempts ever reach tabulation.[29]

Library press reports suggest increased censorship from religious groups, especially the "Christian right," and from feminist and civil rights groups. Yet individuals, especially parents, probably account for the bulk of challenges. Part of this phenomenon is undoubtedly fallout from greater cultural support for activism in general, together with encouragement from schools and libraries for community participation. Said one PTA president about a series of Florida school library incidents, "We say, 'Please, please be involved in your children's education.' To turn around and say, 'Your opinion isn't valid,' isn't fair."[30]

Four particularly press-worthy censorship cases in the last decade reveal hand-to-hand combat over sexuality materials from the highest to the more humble levels of librarianship.

- Librarian of Congress Daniel Boorstin's withdrawal in 1985 of *Playboy* from magazines brailled by the National Library Service for the Blind and Physically Handicapped (NLS). The removal was precipitated by an appropriations bill amendment from Congressman Chalmers P. Wylie (R-OH), cutting the Library of Congress budget by exactly the cost of brailling *Playboy*. Wylie indicated clearly in discussions on the House floor his intent to cause the NLS to drop the magazine. A coalition composed of Playboy Enterprises, several blind individuals and advocacy organizations, and the ALA subsequently sued successfully for its restoration.[31]

- H.W. Wilson president Leo Weins' termination of Will Manley from his 12-year stint as *Wilson Library Bulletin (WLB)* columnist because of a lighthearted "Librarians and Sex" questionnaire in the June 1992 issue. *WLB* editor Mary Jo Godwin quit in protest and received the 1992 Robert B. Downs Intellectual Freedom Award from Greenwood Publishing Group and the University of Illinois Graduate School of Library and Information Science. The library press and letters to the editor in *WLB* and elsewhere solidly supported Manley and excoriated Weins, and sympathizers at the 1992 ALA conference handed out "Free Will" buttons. Manley, somewhat shaken, was later hired by *American Libraries*, and Mary Jo Godwin by Oryx Press.[32]

- The Fairfax County Public Library Board of Trustees' struggle with the Fairfax County Board of Supervisors over distributing the gay newspaper, the *Washington Blade*, available at no cost in branch lobbies. County supervisors pressured the library to remove the *Blade* or restrict access, responding to complaints from patrons and conservative Christian activists after papers were first put out with other free publications in December 1992. However, the library board voted on two separate occasions to retain the newspaper, which had in the interim moved its sexually explicit personals ads to a separate section not included with library copies. County supervisors then threatened to abolish the library board, but lacked the authority to do so. More recently, one supervisor proposed prohibiting county employees from any activity encouraging violation of the state's anti-sodomy law, which would include holding or displaying pro-gay publications. Other efforts focused on promoting selection of anti-gay library board members. Meanwhile, the Fairfax library system purchased 11 titles suggested by a Christian activist, to add balance to its collection of over 100 gay books. These titles offer the conservative Christian perspective that homosexuality can be "cured" or "reformed" through counseling and changes in lifestyle. Among many other escalating complexities, the Fairfax Lesbian and Gay Citizens Association later donated 78 titles to counter the anti-gay books.[33]

- The split level conflict in the library community inspired by Madonna's explicit picture book, *Sex*. On one level, some libraries buying the book faced massive demonstrations, letter and phone campaigns, and civic leader intervention. Nearly all retained the book against protests. On the other level was the war in the library press as to whether libraries should buy the book or not, and for what reasons.

The anti-*Sex* contingent cited lack of enduring value, poor binding, high price, and self-promotional ballyhoo; the pro-*Sex*-ers cried *Censorship!* and cited best-seller list, public interest, author popularity, and desire to spare patrons from purchasing this expensive item out of curiosity.[34]

Two issues are at the heart of library debates about homosexuality and censorship. One is the personal perception of "harm" likely to result from sexual behavior and sexuality materials. It is possible that such perceptions are to some degree outcomes of socioeconomic class and educational background, as Kristen Luker wrote about pro-choice and pro-life activists.[35] In this, the people on one side have a world view utterly different from people on the other side: one group sees sex as by nature sacred and dangerous, the other as situationally hazardous but basically no big deal. The second issue is the function of the library. Should libraries, if no longer concerned with public morals, reassume a primarily educational function?

In this time of lowered educational standards and achievements, the public [library] must reassert its traditional role as an educational provider. . . . [A]way with the stuffed animals; away with the CDs, records and cassettes. . . . Fiction acquisitions of the [Danielle] Steel and [Judith] Krantz genre should be cut back. Tasteless books such as *Sex* should not be purchased.

The goal of libraries would be "promotion of wisdom in the individual and the community" instead of "mak[ing] intellectual freedom their philosophy. . . . Intellectual freedom is not an excuse to purchase unalloyed trash."[36]

And so the words fly and the conflicts rage in all quarters. While intellectual freedom and tolerance of sexual expression have perhaps a majority of supporters, other viewpoints have not withered away, nor have they been silenced. One side preaches repentance, but against repentance comes the slogan, "We're Here, We're Queer, Get Used To It." To every action, a reaction: neither side seems willing to let the other have all the spotlight, particularly if the spotlight confers legitimation to one's viewpoint. So libraries that may have had a dozen—no more—requests for books on gay topics now become centers of book donations, denunciations, and more donations. Libraries are perceived as arenas in which *we* win if *our* books get in.

In the melee, librarian reactions to sex are still "chaotic" and "undecided." Yet whereas in the short term there is a good deal of angry and frightening clashing of viewpoints, in the long term the library and all its readers are the winners if *both* sides get their books in.

AND NOW . . .

Indeed, the only real casualty has been silence itself. Significantly, a major survey of the 1990s on libraries and sexuality materials was published not in *Library Journal* but in *The Christian Librarian* from the Association of Christian Librarians. Respondents from nearly 100 Christian and Bible college libraries answered questions about patron objections to library materials: those relating to sex made up nearly half the objectionable titles.[37]

And yet, if Perkins or Feipel would have seen continuity between their own writings and this latest survey—and its underlying ethos of conservatism—still, change has been greater than preservation of older ways. One could imagine that Perkins and *The Christian Librarian* would see eye-to-eye on at least some doctrinal issues of religion and on the librarian as cultural custodian. Still, in Perkins' day would a library journal have needed to add the qualifier "Christian" to its title? For him, the Bible was the standard, and it needed no special association of librarians to promote it. But today "Bible Christianity" is no longer a culture-wide norm whose premises are accepted without challenge, doubt, or question.

Since Perkins, we have undergone a transformation from a perception of Victorian and Christian unanimity to the reality of modern diversity in which one size no longer fits all. It perhaps never did, but we never really knew that then—or today. With television, the immense distribution of newspapers, and news magazines with their surveys unparalleled—and unthinkable—in Perkins' day, our awareness of diversity has become a central fact of American self-perception. Perhaps there were just as many alternative views then as now, but no *USA Today* reported it on the front page.

A second change is just as significant, perhaps even more so. The official position about sexual matters of the Victorian and Christian majority had been silence. As other views about sex rose up in speech and writing, the conservative religious community nonetheless still retained silence about sexuality well into the 20th century. Today, it has been making its voice heard—not just in censorship attempts but more positively through library surveys and publication of Christian sex books, of which is discussed in more detail later. And that is the change: not even Christian traditionalists are silent about sex any longer. Yet theirs is but one voice among many.

But what of librarians, caught in the whirlwind? Remember: *The debate is the message.* In the next chapter, we explore the topics and viewpoints that fall within a mandate for library-based sexuality education.[38]

NOTES

1. G. Legman, "The Lure of the Forbidden," in *Libraries, Erotica, & Pornography* (D115, Cornog): 41.

2. Some of the discussion in this chapter is based on Martha Cornog & Timothy Perper, "For Sex, See Librarian: An Introduction," in *Libraries, Erotica, & Pornography* (D115, Cornog): 1–35; Martha Cornog & Timothy Perper, "Librarians and Sexologists: Not So Strange Bedfellows," *Collection Building* 13.4 (1994): 33–39.

3. *The Horn Book* (D52, Legman): 11.

4. Legman, "Lure": 44–45.

5. *The Secret Museum* (D11, Kendrick): 64.

6. Vern L. Bullough, "Research and Archival Value of Erotica/Pornography," in *Libraries, Erotica, & Pornography* (D115, Cornog): 99–105.

7. F.B. Perkins, "Free Libraries and Unclean Books," *Library Journal* (December 1885): 397.

8. Perkins: 396–399.

9. "What Shall Libraries Do About Bad Books; Contributions from Various Librarians," *Library Journal* (September 1908): 352.

10. "Bibliography on Sex Education," *Public Libraries* 17.9 (November 1912): 366.

11. Helen Turvill, "What Books Should the Small Library Purchase on Sex Hygiene?" *Wisconsin Library Bulletin* 9 (April 1913): 56–57.

12. Louis N. Feipel, "Questionable Books in Public Libraries—I," *Library Journal* (October 15, 1922): 858, 860–861; Louis N. Feipel, "Questionable Books in Public Libraries—II," *Library Journal* (November 1, 1922): 909 (last two quotations).

13. Feipel, "Questionable I": 857.

14. Office of Intellectual Freedom, American Library Association, *Intellectual Freedom Manual*, 4th ed. (Chicago: ALA, 1992): 5. This was the original wording. The current wording is "Libraries should provide materials and information presenting all points of view on current and historical issues" (see p. 3).

15. See Noel Perrin, *Dr. Bowdler's Legacy: A History of Expurgated Books in England and America* (Boston: David R. Godine, 1992).

16. Perkins: 399.

17. Roger P. Bristol, "It Takes Courage to Stock 'Taboos,' " *Library Journal* (February 15, 1949): 261–263.

18. Eric Moon, " 'Problem' Fiction," *Library Journal* (February 1, 1962): 490; Dorothy Broderick, " 'Problem' Nonfiction," *Library Journal* (October 1, 1962): 3378.

19. Michael Pope, *Sex and the Undecided Librarian: A Study of Librarians' Opinions on Sexually Oriented Literature* (Metuchen, NJ: Scarecrow, 1974): 184.

20. *Fugitive Pope* is edited and published by Raleigh Clayton Muns, 1178 Margaret Lane, Olivette, MO 63132-2319. Naked woman: An ad for the German publisher Benedikt Taschen appearing in *Publishers Weekly* (November 22, 1993): centerfold, depicted the male publisher fully clothed, with the female editor-in-chief nude, seated on the arm of his chair. Angry letters from readers appeared in a subsequent issue of *Publishers Weekly* (December 13, 1993): 6. See also "Nude in *Publishers Weekly* Ad Sparks ALA, ALISE Actions," *Library Hotline* (February 28, 1994): 7. Penis in *Library Journal*: "Ed. Note," *Library Journal* (December 1991): 14.

21. *Daddy's Roommate* (C26, Willhoite): 26.

22. Barbara Gittings, "Gays in Library Land; The Gay and Lesbian Task Force of the American Library Association: The First Sixteen Years," *WLW Journal* 14.3 (Spring 1991): 7–13. The task force was originally named the Task Force on Gay Liberation and recently renamed the Gay, Lesbian, and Bisexual Task Force (GLBTF).

23. For example, Janet A.E. Creelman & Roma M. Harris, "Coming Out: The Informational Needs of Lesbians," *Collection Building* 10.3-4 (1990): 31–41; Cal Gough & Ellen Greenblatt, "Services to Gay and Lesbian Patrons: Examining the Myths," *Library Journal* (January 1992): 59–63; Douglas Eric Anderson, "Gay Information out of the Closet," *School Library Journal* (June 1992): 62; Eric Brant, "Making Things Perfectly Queer," *Library Journal* (April 15, 1993): 106–109; Leonard Kniffel, "You Gotta Have Gerber-Hart: A Gay and Lesbian Library for the Midwest," *American Librarians* (November 1993): 958–960.

24. "San Francisco Library to Be Center for Gay Scholarship," *Equal Time* (October 14–21, 1993): 2.

25. Tom Gaughan, "Ed. Notes: The Last Socially Acceptable Prejudice," *American Libraries* (September 1992): 625. See also "Reader Forum" in *American Libraries* (September 1992): 625; (October 1992): 738–740; (November 1992): 840–843. One letter-writer (November 1992: 843) stated, "I propose that all God-fearing librarians start up an alternative library organization . . . [to the ALA, which is] not a professional organization but a left-wing political group." That letter-writer is unlikely to be reading this book, but for the record, there are two older and one new such organizations: the Association of Christian Librarians, an independent organization of librarians at mostly Christian and Bible colleges (P.O. Box 4, Cedarville, OH 45314), Fellowship of Christian Librarians and Information Specialists, a group that meets yearly at the ALA national meeting (Joe Dalstrom, Secretary, Library Director, Victoria College, University of Houston at Victoria, 2602 North Ben Jordan, Victoria, TX 77901), and Family Friendly Libraries, founded by Karen Jo Gounaud, a patron of the Fairfax County (Virginia) Public Library (see stories in the October and November 1995 *American Libraries*).

26. A positive review from Harriet Selverstone of the book *Out of the Closet and into the Classroom* appeared in *School Library Journal* (January 1993): 37. Donna Baird wrote a letter of outrage printed in the March issue; subsequent letters appeared in the May, June, and July issues.

27. James L. Sauer, letter, *RQ* (Spring 1992): 455.

28. "Challenges to Intellectual Freedom Rise Seven Percent," *Library Journal* (March 1, 1994): 13; "*Daddy's Roommate* Most Challenged Book of 1994," *Newsletter on Intellectual Freedom* (March 1995): 36.

29. Based primarily upon the following sources: L.B. Woods, *A Decade of Censorship in America: The Threat to Classrooms and Libraries 1966–1975* (Metuchen, NJ: Scarecrow, 1979); National Commission on Libraries and Information Science, *Censorship Activities in Public and Public School Libraries 1975–1985* (Washington, DC: NCLIS, 1986); Intellectual Freedom Round Table, American Library Association, *Report from the States 1991–1992* (Chicago: IFRT/ALA, 1992); People for the American Way, *Attacks on the Freedom to Learn: 1991–1992 Report* (Washington, DC: PFAW, 1992). In addition, censorship data for 1982–1992 were provided to us from PFAW and for September 1990–May 1993 from Office of Intellectual Freedom/ALA.

30. Reported in the *Newsletter on Intellectual Freedom* (July 1992): 106.

31. Martha Cornog, "A Case Study of Censorship? The Library of Congress and the Brailling of *Playboy*," in *Libraries, Erotica, & Pornography* (D115): 130–143.

32. See letters to the *Wilson Library Bulletin* (September & October 1992); plus John N. Berry & Francine Fialkoff, "Censorship at H.W. Wilson," *Library Journal*

(July 1992): 6; "Wilson Editor Mary Jo Godwin Resigns over Will Manley Column," *American Libraries* (July/August 1992): 543. For Manley's reactions, see his "Sex," in *The Manley Art of Librarianship* (Jefferson, NC: McFarland, 1993): 207–232. For Godwin's reactions, see her "A Difficult Choice: Censorship or Credibility," *The Public Image* 4.3 (Fall 1992): 1–2 (published by the Neuse Regional Library, 510 North Queen Street, Kingston, NC 28501).

33. See stories reported in the *Newsletter of Intellectual Freedom*: "Libraries: Fairfax, Virginia" (July 1993): 101–102; "Fairfax Board Retreats on Gay Paper" (January 1994): 7–8; "Battle Continues over Gay Paper" (July 1994): 105–106; "Fairfax Library Board Stalemate" (September 1994): 142; "Libraries: Fairfax, Virginia" (November 1994): 194; "Fairfax Library Rejects Minors' Restrictions" (January 1995): 3; plus Public Information Office, Fairfax County Public Library, "Statement on Homosexuality Titles Added to the Collection," rev. (February 7, 1994).

34. See "Has the American Public Library Lost Its Purpose?" *Public Libraries* (July/August 1993): 191–196. When the Madonna *Sex* wars were at their height, we wondered idly if Madonna had ever done or been invited to do a "celebrity read" poster. A phone call to the American Library Association enlightened us: Madonna had been invited to do a poster in the past, we were told, but she had refused.

35. *Abortion and the Politics of Motherhood* (A110, Luker).

36. Daniel F. Ring, "Defending the Intended Mission," *Public Libraries* (July/August 1994): 191–193; quote above is from p. 192.

37. Creighton Hippenhammer, "Patron Objections to Library Materials: A Survey of Christian College Libraries, Part I," *The Christian Librarian* (November 1993): 12–17; Creighton Hippenhammer, "Patron Objections to Library Materials: A Survey of Christian College Libraries, Part 2," *The Christian Librarian* (February 1994): 40–47.

38. We address sex education of *librarians* in Chapter 11.

4 Topics, Viewpoints, and Genres for Sex Education Collection Development

If you thumb through the annotations or browse through the titles in the index to this book, you will be impressed by the sheer mass of available material on sexuality. When one recalls that these selections are culled from many more titles, that we have omitted most pre-1985 works, and that the publication lag of this book itself guarantees that more titles have been published since we finished our annotating, the amount of material available appears even greater. Can these materials be organized so librarians can make sense out of sex books, or are they merely a random hodgepodge of the kind found in yard sales?

GOOD OLD DEWEY?

Actually, there are several different questions here. At the narrowest are issues of cataloging these titles. Later, we consider that problem in more detail, but for now we note that most modern books come equipped with cataloging-in-publication (CIP) data, either from the Library of Congress or the British Library. To be sure, cataloging poses practical problems of training personnel and making tricky distinctions among various possibilities, but no unique philosophical problem inheres in assigning call numbers to sex books.

However, it would not do much good for you, the reader, if we merely reprinted call numbers from various cataloging protocols. By itself, cataloging does not provide a synoptic guide to available works on sexuality. In a sense, it is too fine-grained, assigning each book its own unique niche in an extremely complex taxonomy. Moreover, cataloging alone does not set forth the *relationships* of books within the now very large area of sexuality publishing. We must try to make sense of the diversity and range of these works quite independently of good old Dewey and his modern followers and modifiers.

In biology—a field in which one of us was trained long ago—it is an aphorism that taxonomists come in two types: lumpers and splitters. Likewise with books: if we had to create piles and heaps of these works according to their similarities and differences, how would we do it? With this question, we encounter personal judgment: this book is more like that book than another book. Some people will make many smaller piles (the splitters), and others will make a few larger heaps (the lumpers). Such similarities and dissimilarities ought to be recognized quite independently of CIP data.

But identifying non-CIP taxonomic groups is not total whimsy or personal idiosyncrasy. If it were, then librarians would sort books by their jacket color or by whether they have photographs of the author. Any cataloging system—that is, any microscopically fine-grained taxonomy—and any effort to create larger groups of books that already have CIP data will encounter an empirical fact: books about sex fall into identifiable viewpoints and genres that only sometimes match up with call numbers in the Library of Congress Classification (LCC) or Dewey Decimal Classification (DDC) schedules and protocols.

One reason—and it is consistent with the history of how libraries have dealt with sexuality titles—is that by and large sexuality publishing has developed both recently and independently of librarianly efforts to catalog such works. Although great strides have been made in subject headings, especially by the Hennepin County Library System, both LCC and DDC were created (dare we say fossilized?) at a time when books on sexuality were anathema. LCC and DDC call numbers can be adapted to accommodate present-day sexuality publications, but it can be like squeezing too many books into a cardboard box: it begins to bulge at the edges and some books don't fit. Certain traditional catalog niches can quickly be overburdened: DDC's 306.76(6) for homosexuality, for example. Even if a computer based catalog can be expanded endlessly, lumping the hundreds of books on gay/lesbian issues into one or a few call numbers cannot reflect their intellectual content and diversity.

We intend no profound critique of either DDC or LCC, but wish merely to note that sexuality authors do not feel compelled to remain within boundaries set down explicitly or implicitly in either schedule. When we also remember that many works published today would have, a century ago, been seized and destroyed by Comstock or other censors, we see that today's sexuality publications deal with matters that in the old days they did not think fit to catalog at all.

So, regardless of whether a library uses LCC, DDC, or another system, it confronts in sexuality titles an essentially new phenomenon: heaps and piles of books representing new genres, new subgenres, and even newer sub-subgenres. Making sense of the diversity requires a good look at what is actually in the heaps and piles, but it also means rethinking old taxonomies.

REFLECTING THE NEW TRENDS

Professional librarians will be professionally competent to place any given book within its DDC or LCC niche even if that takes bending and stretching. However, the mere act of cataloging a book does not tell us how to create a collection of sexuality works in a library. By that, we do not mean acquisition policies, but a more basic issue. If one does not know what the genres, subgenres, and sub-subgenres are, how can one develop an acquisition policy at all?

To reiterate, the older "acquisitions" policy of not acquiring anything at all on sexuality is no longer realistic or even possible. We sympathize with traditional librarians who today are trying to maintain a "We-don't-have-sex-books-here" policy when suddenly confronted with angry patrons donating boxes of books for, against, about, and related to some incendiary sexual issue, such as homosexuality. "I never heard of these titles," says the librarian plaintively. Well, you have now—or, more accurately, we hope that you can learn about them in the calmer ambience of reading a book like this one rather than suddenly confronting angry conservative Christians, angrier friends of the gay/lesbian community, and even angrier proponents of Christian acceptance of gay/lesbian sexuality into God's love, all represented by boxes and boxes and *boxes* of books.

SEXUALITY VIEWPOINTS AND BOOK GENRES

Over their lifetimes, people create from their sexual experiences, knowledge, beliefs, and moralities a more or less coherent vision of what sexuality is and means: the experiential component of sex education mentioned below. Because our personal sexuality is private—and widely cherished as private—probably few people think of themselves as belonging to schools of thought about sex or as deliberately modeling their sexual habits and beliefs on what teachers, philosophers, or "society" might mandate or condemn. Nonetheless, human beings are social creatures, and despite our prized autonomy and privacy, we are strongly influenced by what others believe and do. So, in a sense all of us do belong to, or have allegiances towards, various broad *visions* of sexuality.

These emerge over time, history, and culture, even when we think we have discovered our own sexual principles all by ourselves. Although individuals certainly differ, nonetheless overarching viewpoints and visions of sexuality can be identified independent of DDC or LCC categories. No one holds monolithically to any one of them, and allegiances to different ideals change with life experience. Instead, individual diversity exists within broadly similar sociosexual patterns of interest and emotion, often presented in uniquely individual ways but still identifiably akin to ideas held by other individuals.

We believe that library holdings should have some representation of all these visions and viewpoints. How completely a given library covers them will vary by availability of materials, and according to the librarian's judgment about community need. Yet we do believe that adult collections, at minimum, will best serve community needs if librarians recognize the existence in sexuality works of diversity within similarity—and of similarity within diversity.

As we collected and read for this book, we soon developed rough and ready categories for visions of sexuality that exist in modern U.S. society. Some of these categories might be called *viewpoints*, others more appropriately *genres*, but they are not topics. They represent styles of cooking, if you will, rather than types of foods. Our descriptions below are fuzzy sets with porous boundaries, and rigid classification is next to impossible. Moreover, they are not mutually exclusive but overlay and cross-cut each other in unpredictable and interesting ways. But as we refined the descriptions, we realized that they are not peculiarities of publishers' catalogs or mere inventions of marketeers trying to sell books. These are the ways, it seems to us, in which diversity of sexual viewpoints builds itself into larger communities of shared vision.

1. Scientific/Medical. Topics and treatments range from extremely technical to popular and semi-popular works reporting discoveries in basic biomedicine, discussing prevention and treatment of sexually transmitted diseases (AIDS looms large), and describing sexual behavior, anatomy, and physiology. Some titles discuss reproductive technologies from contraception through artificial insemination, in-vitro fertilization, and even more futuristic possibilities. Still others report on scientific surveys of sexual behavior and attitudes. The basic assumptions of the entire genre are that sex can and should be investigated objectively and that the results of such investigations can be fruitful for humanity. Writing informed by this viewpoint often draws on a variety of scholarly disciplines, ranging from medicine and biology through psychology, sociology, and anthropology. Often, but not always, the social scientific approach accepts "cultural relativism," the notion that other cultural practices are legitimate in their own frameworks, even when they repel Westerners—for example, adult/child sexuality or female circumcision. By and large, most readers will feel that

this is the "real stuff": data-based, quantitative, well-reasoned, and factual. But others will be upset by the lack of overt moral judgment against behavior they themselves condemn.

2. Historical and Social Critical. This genre includes works drawing primarily on scholarly disciplines, like history, law, and literary criticism, but whose authors do not see themselves as either natural or social "scientists." Indeed, they are often suspicious of the sciences or believe that science is only one of many ways to look at sexuality. Books with this vision range from compendious tomes suitable only for large academic collections through chattily written popular works. The basic view is that sexuality has been around for a long time, that it disturbs and fascinates people, and that it is appropriately studied in social and historical context. Some writers may express opinions critical of the status quo and propose radical alternatives, while other writers in this genre are equally critical of these radical alternatives. But all insist that sexuality is at least in part a human creation, as opposed to being solely biologically determined or theologically set down for us as an eternal given of God's will. Although topics vary considerably, the approach is quite similar: humanistic with special stress on human history, and society, and their vicissitudes. Before the modern days of biomedical and scientific sexology, this was one of the major genres of sexuality writing.

3. Art Books. By virtue of their size, cost, and copious illustrations, art books are unique. In their approach to sex, they share much with the humanistic and historical visions. They include books of painting, drawing, photography, sculpture, and crafts. Some range across the world and history, while others focus on eras or locales. The overall tone is of supreme confidence—arising in part from the sheer antiquity of the subject matter, for among the most ancient human artworks are nude sculptures of the female body such as the Venus of Willendorf—allied to an aesthetic vision of sexuality as intrinsically beautiful and/or visually interesting. Today, under the rubric of modernism and its post-modernist, hyper-post-modernist, and still more recent offspring, images of sexuality include a far broader range of aesthetics, seen not as exercises in offending people (which they nonetheless invariably do) but as reactions against social prettification of sex by advertising, the media, and bourgeois culture. Madonna's *Sex*, infamous in the library world, belongs in this category, although reviewers did not make the connection between its photos and the larger history of art to which its images belong. These will be the books that elicit the loudest protests and that will need the greatest physical protection against vandals. Some exemplars recall specifically American art forms, including paintings of naked ladies on the fuselages of World War II bombers.

4. Psychological/Psychotherapeutic. This vision produces work ranging from dense psychoanalytic material inaccessible to most lay readers, through modern "reformist" psychotherapies such as family therapy, cou-

ples therapy, and sex therapy itself, to books written for general audiences by practicing psychotherapists about an astoundingly wide range of sexuality topics, to pop-psych, self-help books. The basic idea is that sexuality is a central part of life, that sexual urges are healthy and normal though sometimes underdeveloped or inappropriately directed, that love and sex are deeply linked, that sexual exploration and experimentation can sometimes be psychologically valuable, and that open talk about sexual activities and feelings should be a personal and social norm. Many stress that *You can make sex better for yourself and your loved ones*, and suggest how: what we have called "enhancement" in Part II.

5. "Sex Crime." A closely related genre contains works written about specific sexual problems like rape, child sexual abuse, sexual harassment, incest, adultery, sexual addiction, and other troubling or dangerous sexual issues. However, nearly any sex-related behavior can be treated from this perspective. Books range from specialized works in psychiatry or the law to a large group of trade books recounting personal experiences and healing. Many are written with anger and deep feeling, often by women survivors. Some deal with pornography and are connected directly to the feminist viewpoints below, but an important if small subset has been written by men who sympathize with feminism. Other titles are primarily how-to's and recommend social and personal methods for prevention. Overall, this is a prolific genre of modern sexuality writing.

6. Liberal/Permissive. This viewpoint, well represented in sexology, holds that sexuality is yours to explore and feel good about, no matter what other people may say. Virtually all of these books emphasize consensuality in social/sexual contexts of mutual respect and permission-giving. The classic phrase is, "It's OK if it doesn't hurt you or your partner." These books often stress that "love" and "commitment," however defined, are not obligatory prerequisites for sexual activity or sexual health but add an immensely important dimension when present. Many have a tone of gleeful exploration and seem genuinely to want the reader to share the author's enthusiasms for sexuality.

7. Spiritual/New Age. Most readers probably associate this genre with the 1960s, either as leftovers from a bygone era or as harbingers of further social change and spiritual development. It is actually much more complex than that. To the extent that one can make overarching comments about the genre at all, books here share the view that sexuality is embodied but, infinitely more important, connects to spiritual domains that are only vaguely, if at all, associated with traditional Western religious beliefs. Often these works take Tibetan Tantric sexuality as a starting point—or at least what they interpret to be Tantric sexuality—and seek wholeness, health, and goodness in sexuality as one of life's avenues to realms beyond our day-to-day experiences. Included here are a number of works on "sexual astrology" that we did not annotate: the author presents sometimes arcane

connections between the stars and planets and sexuality. (Historically, sexual astrology goes back to Babylonia.) Much of the writing is deeply emotional, often poetic, and never exactly what you expect.

8. Occultist. We may offend people by our word choice, but we know of no other. This genre is the Dark Side of the Force, that is, it inverts the preceding and connects "sexual magic" to spiritual rebellion, often with cults and their practices and often with heavy-handed (to us) invocations of various deities and forces for whom Christians reserve the phrase "demons and devils." Perhaps its most famous adherent was Aleister Crowley, but his Ordo Templi Orientis has produced a number of imitators and descendants.[1] Much of this genre is tongue-in-cheek, satiric, and represents a sexual theatre-of-the-absurd. Nonetheless, it will deeply offend some readers, while greatly amusing others. It blends into the next category.

9a. Radical/Anarchist. Herein we find books proclaiming that all sexuality is acceptable so long as it does not involve coercion of clearly unwilling partners. Such works may urge and highly recommend promiscuous coupling, multiple relationships, open exploration of all consensual forms of sexuality, among a number of other possibilities. These books connect on one side to the liberal/permissive group, and on another to the occultist, but differ from each in their socio-sexo-political views. These writers see sexuality as systematically oppressed by Capitalism, by The Establishment, by The System, or by a Horde of Other Evils, against whom rebellion is always advisable and surely welcome. This is the "Let's do it in the streets to annoy people" view, and has a serious edge to it that distinguishes it from the theatre-of-the-absurd. Sex is seen as a way to strike back while having a good deal of fun at the same time.

9b. Radical/Anarchist, Youth Brigade. This genre is so diverse as to beggar categorization and includes zines through comix through underground newspapers. It is virtually always scurrilous, offensive, or scatological, all weapons for thumbing one's nose individually and collectively at The Grown-Ups and Their System. The purpose is not sexual arousal but eliciting strong emotional-political responses. There is also a good deal of humor, some inadvertent. Collecting this genre takes special knowledge and sources.

10a. Conservative Christian. A far broader and diverse group than one might think. As a generalization, books with this viewpoint accept sexuality as natural and God-given but welcome it only in monogamous heterosexual marriage. Abortion is seen as a grievous wrong, homosexuality as an abomination, and nearly all premarital sexuality as dangerous, coital or not. Characteristically it is suspicious of all forms of school-based sex education except for the so-called abstinence-only programs, a topic about which conservative Christians have had much to say—and write. This vision of sexuality is rooted both in American social conservatism ("family values") and in religious conservatism (the Word of Christ is always right for everyone). It connects to political conservatism, but the political and religious conservative movements have different goals and objectives. Lay readers often call this approach "fundamentalism," but the term is inexact because Christian fundamentalism refers to a movement desiring to return to Bible fundamentals in all ways, not merely about sexuality.[2] Conservative Christian writing about sexuality is primarily a phenomenon of the past two decades, and has much less of a public profile than some of the preceding viewpoints. It might be characterized as sincerely upset that sexuality in the modern world does not follow Biblical or Christian principles.

10b. Roman Catholic. With its 2,000 year history, Roman Catholicism has produced some of the most significant writing about sexuality in the history of Christianity, including St. Augustine and St. Thomas Aquinas. *Humanae Vitae* and *Evangelium Vitae* cannot be ignored by any library. Nonfiction books on sexuality by modern Roman Catholic writers fall into two groups, according to their positions on a variety of more or less controversial modern statements by the magisterium and the Pope about marriage, family, contraception, homosexuality, divorce, and premarital sexuality. Writers adhering to positions adopted by the magisterium develop their ideas with great care and scholarship rooted in the church's 2,000 year history. Writers critical of papal views do so equally carefully, but repeatedly refer to how modern realities are changing around the church. Both sides write with passion and deep conviction.

10c. Protestant. By virtue of its history, Protestantism is far more diverse than official Roman Catholicism, and many Protestant writers of great authority have held—and still hold—quite different views on sexuality. Some accept abortion, while others do not, and some accept premarital sexuality, while others demur. Points of agreement include acceptance of contraception and of divorce; indeed, the idea of family planning is itself deeply resonant with Protestantism. The notion of sexual sin is extremely varied. Some hold that sex in itself is sinful if done with wrong intentions or with wrong partners. Others hold that sex cannot be sinful because it is "God's good gift," although human beings can individually assuredly misuse that gift to hurt others.

An additional point needs to be made. All Christian denominations, including Roman Catholicism, accept the ideal of ministering to the ill, including those ill with sexually transmitted diseases. Yet there have been considerable heartache and agony in Christian writing about AIDS because its association with homosexuality creates real tension between a desire to minister and a desire to condemn, if not on Christian grounds, then on grounds of old-fashioned American homophobia. Books about AIDS and the church form a small group of their own and include some of the most heartfelt writing in all the works we have examined.

10d. Liberal Christian. Books here cross denominational boundaries to share a common vision of sexuality as more than merely a way to procreate, or as a basis for marriage, or as a social reality. Instead, they delve more deeply into Christian spiritual connections through and with eros, considered as a human aperception of the Divine attributes of passion and love. They differ from New Age spiritualism in their specifically Christian view, and seek to transcend what are felt to be human—and necessarily therefore tinged with sin—institutions of gender inequality, sexual exploitation, marital pain, and worldwide population crisis. Among Catholics, the vision is sometimes called "seamless web" theology, wherein all life forms a unity under God's great love.

10e. Jewish and Muslim. We found very few books on sexuality written either from Jewish or Islamic perspectives, certainly far too few to speak of a genre or viewpoint, let alone attempt to characterize it. It therefore appears that among the major religions in America, changes in modern sexual mores have most greatly affected Christianity.

11a. Homosexuality. Books herein have a sole or primary focus on, or are informed by, gay or lesbian sexuality, usually written by members of those communities. For reasons of space, we have had to omit a great many works of general interest about gay and lesbian topics, so that our lists focus largely on sexuality itself. Within this genre, there is considerable variation, particularly among lesbian writers (see 12b, below). Within this group, books fall into other major categories listed—scientific, scholarly, historical, theological, and so on.

11b. Anti-homosexuality. A relatively small genre, often written by conservative Christians or the so-called radical right. It ranges from virulently homophobic through discussions of ministering to homosexuals with the purpose of curing or preventing homosexuality, or enabling celibacy as an alternative to sin. Some attention to details is required in collecting such works, for they can suddenly veer into conspiracy theorizing about "homosexual plots" and the like.

12. Feminist. Feminists can take virtually any of the viewpoints above, but throughout stress women's experiences, lives, and realities. The "Youth Brigade" feminist writers can be extremely funny and sometimes very nasty about the evils of the Patriarchy.[3] Even so, two general categories seem to exist:

12a. Middle-Ground ("Liberal") Feminist. Books herein are similar to the Liberal/Permissive group, but stress how women's growth depends on gender and sexual equality with men. There is less emphasis on sex as a good in itself and more insistence that women's desires lead to relationship and affiliation.

12b. Radical ("Separatist") Feminist. Writers in this genre demand a complete break with masculine sexuality, stressing female relationships. Heterosexuality is perceived as intrinsically unequal and necessarily oppressive of women. The concept of a global and history-encompassing Patriarchy is the central organizing theme in much of this writing, which emphasizes that women must free themselves in order to be truly human. Much of this work is extremely critical of heterosexually explicit materials but divided about lesbian erotica. By and large, this movement has made considerable effort to expand the meaning of words like "politics" from voting and partisanship to sexuality and gender.

13. Specialists. Herein are books written by aficionados of particular sexual activities. Almost never political and rarely spiritual or religious, these are works of specialized enthusiasm for one or another sexual lifestyle or activity. Many can be called happily cheerful, as opposed to grim, pornographic, or psychotic. Often these works are treasure troves of curious and interesting information, much unavailable anywhere else.

GETTING MORE SPECIFIC

These viewpoints and genres, complex and multifaceted, represent focal areas of sexuality writing and publishing. We can argue about the precise limits of each genre, but the centers of each—the heaps we mentioned before—are most heavily populated. Moreover, they are not merely our arbitrary taxonomic inventions. They represent foci of great significance to writers and readers. Some of the titles are moral, some analytical, some chatty, even gossipy. But these issues of style and flavor are not primary in distinguishing one sort of book from another. The real issue is that they have a common viewpoint or vision. And, for the librarian, they form focal areas in which collections must grow.

These genres are also salient because library-goers know what bookstores carry, and readers often identify with specific visions. The genres are not ivory tower exercises in abstract taxonomy but are practical guides to a book's content, point of view, and audience. At a minimum, they represent where America's reading habits are for sexuality.

BUT WHAT ABOUT SEX EDUCATION?

But do these genres have anything to do with sex education? That depends on what we mean by the term. It can mean what you learned in school, or it can be far broader. We have drawn from several sources to develop our own definition:

• Sex education is instruction about the biological, psychological, cultural, social, ethical, and spiritual aspects of human sexuality and reproduction, and addresses knowledge, attitudes, feelings, and behavior. Formal sex education may be conducted in schools or churches, or by other organizations. Informal sex education is provided by parents, other family members, peers, and the media, including books.[4]

• Experiential sex education is the sum of one's own sexuality, throughout one's

life, as experienced with others and alone, for example, in fantasy and masturbation.

• Formal sex education and a good deal of informal sex education are designed to
impart information, influence attitudes, instill values, strengthen relationships and
interpersonal skills, and promote responsibility.[5]

If these definitions sound idealized, to an extent they are: they represent
goals, not universal current practice in schools or anywhere else. Yet they
suggest practical ways we might improve sex education.

One way is to consider sex education *not* as the sole possession of school
systems. These systems operate under sometimes extremely stringent rules
and procedures, often mandated by statute and differing from state to state.
Furthermore, school sex education programs are the purview of professionals trained in education and educational psychology on one hand, and
of state educational administrators on the other. And, like all publicly
funded education, sex education exists in the highly politicized arenas of
state budgets, legislatures, and bureaucracies. But citizens have no excuse
if they say *Let the government do it*, and then do not like the outcome.

So in this book, we are not evaluating curricula or generating reading
lists for students taking school sex education courses. Nor are we proposing
bibliographic support for college and university training of sex educators.
We propose our lists of books not for bureaucrats or even solely for educators, but for working librarians who wish to collect in areas of sexuality
for their patrons. Our view is that sex education should involve all of us,
not merely a few. And specifically, we consider the definition of *sex education* to include supplemental self-education via libraries. The basic reason
is that formal sex education curricula are compromises worked out between
opposing political parties and bureaucratic factions, where even the presence of a word like "contraception" can stir up angry debate. So our definition of sex education is far broader than the idea of a "curriculum"
designed by a committee and imposed by state law on everyone who goes
to school.

Libraries can play a large and increasing role in making information
about sexuality available to the general populace, particularly materials
that for reasons of politics or bureaucratic decision were omitted or un-
derstressed in state-mandated or "official" curricula. It also means that
imbalances of viewpoint in formal sex education can be remedied, at least
to some extent, by cooperative efforts of libraries and citizens' groups. This
approach allows sex education to be tailored to meet community needs for
people of all ages, preferences, and levels of sophistication, however one
might judge such things.

What else does our non-bureaucratic definition mean for library collections? It means more for how one thinks about sexuality books than it
means for the details of technical lumping or splitting or even deciding

whether to purchase this book or that. Above all, it opens up sexuality education to broader involvement by more people, librarians and readers both, than the school-based definition. Now, we are not criticizing school systems for narrowness or for being undemocratic. We are merely pointing out that schools and libraries have different missions, histories, audiences, and accountabilities. Accordingly, libraries are freer to encompass a far wider range of materials than can a time-limited school sex education course, whether they are public libraries or school libraries. And above all, libraries are not only free to collect and offer, but are *responsible* for collecting and offering to the public a wide variety of highly controversial materials that would rarely be included in a school sex education curriculum.

Furthermore, public libraries serve all ages, including grown-ups. It would be insufferable condescension to limit a library collection to titles confined to an age-graded curriculum. If one's high school sex education course did not even breathe a word about group sex (also known as orgies), then it would be making children of grown-ups if a library for adult readers followed suit in misplaced exclusion of such ungenteel topics. Yes, politicians and school leaders might *not* want to discuss Arno Karlen's *Threesomes: Studies in Sex, Power, and Intimacy* (A94) or Burgo Partridge's *A History of Orgies* (Bonanza/Crown, 1960) in front of supposedly innocent 16- and 17-year-olds, but observe: both Crown and *Threesomes'* Morrow are distinctly mainstream publishing houses. Adopting a version of school education as the guideline for selecting books —in especially the nonschool library—infantilizes the library patron, denies the existence of vast publishing realms, and dismisses reader interest.

School library collections are necessarily narrower in scope than public library collections, as they serve a narrower age group. Yet we argue that even school libraries should offer a broader menu of topics and viewpoints than those directly reflected in the curriculum, for sex as well as for other subjects.

How can one convert the diversity of books, classification schemes, and viewpoints/genres into tools that librarians can use for developing collection philosophies, plans, and procedures? The need is real. Library policies are still highly varied, and indeed sometimes still seem chaotic. School and curriculum development approaches are strongly influenced by the public school mandate, and although highly organized, cannot be used directly in the context of general librarianship. A generalized notion of sex education implies developing a comprehensive and wide-ranging series of topics that transcend the usual subjects discussed in school sex education curricula.

Nonetheless, we cannot disregard educators' efforts to categorize sexuality education materials, if only because considerable experience has gone into those efforts. Even though curriculum development is not collection building—different criteria enter the two processes—the issue is to build library policies and viewpoints based on the best of both worlds. We therefore examine one of the most significant curriculum/material guidelines.[6] Careful study of these guidelines will repay librarians who wish to familiarize themselves with the issues and controversies that surround sexuality materials and will also help them select and evaluate materials.

SEXUALITY TOPICS AND CATEGORIES

In 1991, SIECUS published *Guidelines for Comprehensive Sexuality Education* (C97), developed by a task force of leading education, health, and sexuality professionals. The *Guidelines* is a conceptual framework of categories recommended for planning new sex education curricula and assessing existing ones. The framework can also be used as a collection evaluation and book selection aid for librarians.

Central to the *Guidelines* are six "key concepts," each with associated topics. Together, concepts and topics form an outline for a comprehensive school-based sexuality education program (see Table 4.1).

We recommend that librarians interested in improving their sex collections start with the SIECUS "key concepts and topics" as a checklist, although we have a caveat. The *Guidelines* were designed for grades K–12, and some topics are not developed in the range and depth needed for adult sexuality education. For example: for adults, topic "Sexuality and society" (Key Concept 6) ought to include sexual folklore, history, anthropology, and language. Sexual language could also fit under "Communication" (Key Concept 3). Moreover, sexuality and disability should be added to Key Concept 4, Sexual Behavior, and sexual harassment added to "Sexual abuse" under Key Concept 5, Sexual Health.

The SIECUS key concepts and topics are particularly helpful for alerting us to subjects that are not necessarily concerned with sex exclusively but which have immense ultimate impact on sexual decisions and behavior. These include all topics within Key Concept 3: Personal Skills, and Key Concept 2: Relationships. Other topics—such as "Body image" (Key Concept 1) as well as "Gender roles" and "Diversity" (Key Concept 6)—also have effects on sexuality rather than being about sexuality directly. We may call all of these *indirect sex education* topics as opposed to *direct sex education* topics. Educators and librarians can easily overlook these areas when sex education initiatives are planned.

We admit that this book concentrates primarily on the direct topics and addresses the indirect topics only when they affect sexuality. This we have done because we believe that the direct topics need remedial acquisition and collecting, whereas the indirect topics require lesser such efforts. Thus, books and materials treating the indirect topics are widely reviewed, easy to locate, noncontroversial, and seldom censored. However, materials treating the direct topics are less widely reviewed, less easy to locate and pur-

Table 4.1
Key Concepts and Topics in a Comprehensive Sexuality Education Program

Key Concept 1: Human Development
  Reproductive anatomy and physiology
  Reproduction
  Puberty
  Body image
  Sexual identity and orientation

Key Concept 2: Relationships
  Families
  Friendship
  Love
  Dating
  Marriage and lifetime commitments
  Parenting

Key Concept 3: Personal Skills
  Values
  Decision-making
  Communication
  Assertiveness
  Negotiation
  Finding help

Key Concept 4: Sexual Behavior
  Sexuality throughout life
  Masturbation
  Shared sexual behavior
  Abstinence
  Human sexual response
  Fantasy
  Sexual dysfunction

Key Concept 5: Sexual Health
  Contraception
  Abortion
  Sexually transmitted diseases and HIV infection
  Sexual abuse
  Reproductive health

Key Concept 6: Society and Culture
  Sexuality and society
  Gender roles
  Sexuality and the law
  Sexuality and religion
  Diversity
  Sexuality and the arts
  Sexuality and the media

Source: Guidelines (C97): 9. Copyright © Sexuality Information and Education Council of the U.S., Inc., New York, N.Y. The *Guidelines* may be purchased quite inexpensively from SIECUS.

chase, often highly controversial, and more often subject to censorship attempts. The direct topics need emphasis that the others do not. Nonetheless, titles on indirect topics should form a major part of a library's *overall* collection on sex education and must not be overlooked even if we cannot emphasize them in the space we have.

COLLECTION BUILDING IS NOT CURRICULUM DEVELOPMENT, AND VICE VERSA

The full-length SIECUS document, *Guidelines for Comprehensive Sexuality Education* (C97), specifies "life behaviors" for each key concept and desirable "developmental messages" for each topic according to target age group. This didactic style is very much in keeping with the traditional "goals and outcomes" approach of professional educators but has some potential disadvantages for use with libraries that have significant adult clienteles.

First, not all adults like being told what their "life behaviors" should be. Many readers dip into books for reasons not fitting any classroom pattern of planned outcomes or behaviors: they browse the shelves and find something that "looks interesting." They read for curiosity's sake or to fulfill interests not satisfied in school. Some readers may not even know in advance that they *will* become interested in a topic: they just pick up the book and start—and then find themselves strongly drawn to what they are reading. To the very extent that the SIECUS approach is appropriate for planning formal educational programs, it may be inappropriate for library-goers who browse, pick and choose, and who, thinking themselves free of exactly such formalities, read whatever they want.

The second potential disadvantage of using only the SIECUS system for library book acquisitions—or using it literally and without thought—is that not everyone agrees with its recommended messages and life behaviors.[7] Thus, an important aspect of the SIECUS approach is learning responsible contraceptive behavior. Many, *but not all*, Americans would agree that learning how to use contraception is a significant, even vital, part of growing up into a sexually mature person. But there is an alternative. It does not urge irresponsible contraception: it states that interfering with the natural purposes of sexuality is sinful in the eyes of God. And that "natural purpose" is procreation, so that abortion and artificial contraception are equally sinful. This, of course, is the position of the Roman Catholic magisterium, most recently reiterated in the 1995 papal encyclical letter *Evangelium Vitae*.

Accordingly, if one uses only the SIECUS approach, with its recommended messages and behaviors, one can inadvertently pose oneself in opposition to Roman Catholic official teaching. That posture is legitimate in a pluralistic society, but we urge librarians to be aware that one *does* select a moral, ethical, and religious position whenever one adopts categories of sexuality that include pro-contraceptive messages. Furthermore, the identical conclusion holds if categories for sexuality titles take an *anti-contraception* position. For example, one might place works about natural family planning—which is legitimate for Roman Catholics—under a topic "Family Planning" but put books about condoms, the diaphragm, and the pill under a potential topic, "Abuses of Sexuality." We can imagine still other ways of categorizing books that might omit all mention of contraception on the theory that including such books "promotes promiscuity."

The issue takes on real significance for librarians who, familiar with the large, venerable, and impersonal Dewey Decimal System and Library of Congress Classification System, may feel that all approaches to categorizing books are likewise value-neutral—or are supposed to be. But one should not underestimate the potential for importing moral judgments into categories, classifications, and indexes, even into the highly respected LC system.[8]

HOW DO WE CATEGORIZE BOOKS?

If we had been writing a literary critical essay or formulating ivory tower hypotheses, we might have contented ourselves by categorizing books in the genres we listed at the beginning of the chapter. But our goal was more practical, and the genre list has some major disadvantages for collection building. To use the genres as categories for acquisition requires that the librarian be quite familiar with a wide variety of books and approaches. The "genre classification" of any given book is not necessarily obvious, so that whereas the genre list describes the landscape, it is not a practical selection tool. So in organizing titles and annotations for this book, we tried other approaches. At first we tried arranging books according to topics in the SIECUS *Guidelines*, but the books we were encountering did not always naturally clump into SIECUS categories. Moreover, as we have already observed, these categories were insufficiently detailed to cover everything we wanted to include, especially for adults.

Accordingly, we developed our own outline of 48 topics from the books themselves. We then created broader classes to lump the 48 topics into five groups of roughly comparable size, convenient for "chapterizing" Part II. These topics seemed to make sense for comparing and contrasting a very great variety of titles (see Table 4.2).

Above all, we recognize that whereas value judgments are central to sexuality itself, we also feel that value judgments must not be built into the superstructure of how books are grouped. Value judgments should be the *subjects* of categorization schemes, classifications, and indexes, not built into the systems themselves. Instead, we had to develop a more objective system.

Table 4.2
Outline of Sexuality Topics Included in Part II of This Book

1. **Sexuality and Behavior**
    General and reference works
    Female sexuality
    Male sexuality
    Sexual enhancement
    Variations
    Sexual sadomasochism (S&M, S/M, S-M, or SM)
    Sex for one—or none: masturbation and celibacy
    Nonmonogamy: adultery, infidelity and sexual addiction, "swinging,"
        group marriage, open marriage, group sex
    Reproductive control: Abortion
    Reproductive control: Birth control
    Natural history/evolution

2. **Homosexuality and Gender Issues**
    Homosexuality—General works
    Homosexuality—Coming out
    Homosexuality—Couples and mateships
    Homosexuality—Families and children
    Homosexuality—History and cultural studies
    Gay reform/critique
    Homosexuality—Religion
    Homosexuality—Scientific and scholarly research
    Homosexuality—Sexual behavior and enhancement
    Homosexuality—Social issues and problems
    Homosexuality—Youth and age
    Bisexuality
    Transgenderism (transvestism, transsexualism, drag, female impersona-
        tion, butch)

3. **Life Cycle Issues**
    Books for young people (wide age range)
    Books for children
    Books for pre-adolescents
    Books for adolescents
    Sexuality in youth and age
    Sex education

4. **Sex and Society**
    The arts and the media
    Courtship and love
    Ethics and philosophy
    The folklore of sex
    History and culture
    Humor and/or cartoons
    Language and sex
    Law and sex

Table 4.2 (continued)

   Libraries and sex: books for and about librarians
   Sex and religion
5. **Sexual Problems**
   Disabilities and dysfunctions
   Sexual exploitation (general works)
   Incest and child sexual abuse
   Rape
   Sexual harassment
   Sexually transmitted diseases (STDs) and safer sex
   HIV/AIDS
   Prostitution and other sex work

Broadly, our approach to categorization is behavioral and age-graded, and our topics are such as might appear in a list of college courses: herein we find books on history; herein books for and against abortion; herein books on sexual variations. Indeed, in retrospect, it startled us how much our outline of topics *did* resemble a college course catalog.

Does that mean that we recommend to public and other nonacademic libraries that they adopt the acquisition policies and subject range of university libraries? By no means. The vast majority of titles that we suggest are trade books, not scholarly or academic. Indeed, we made some effort to find nonacademic works. To be sure, the outline of topics we developed reflects our own education—college and university, with advanced degrees—which we share with many library professionals. However, the content of the books and the purpose for acquiring them are not intended to create a heavy-handed approximation to a university. The great bulk of the works we include are written for, and can be read by, anyone with a high school background and very often not even that. Our approach to selecting was populist, and our selection of topics exemplifies not educational goals, but the realities of publishing—and therefore the marketplace for—works on sexuality written for the general public.

Our outline therefore reflects the recent and current state of sexuality publishing and how writers and publishers have de facto addressed various aspects of sexuality. But since librarians can choose only among books that *are* published, we thought that just such an outline might be an advantage.

Our topics overlap those of SIECUS by about 80%. The SIECUS approach gives more coverage to relationships and personal skills, and ours more coverage to variations in sexual behavior and aspects of sex and society. The *Guidelines* understandably emphasize priorities of high schoolers and other relatively young people whose main interests are in what sex means, how it fits in with love, and how to find a partner, all in the context of a growing awareness of oneself as sexual. By contrast, our topics were drawn from books that cover the entire life cycle and include many written by adults for adults about adult questions and problems. Yet adults also need information about "personal skills," "body image," and "gender roles," all of which the SIECUS approach emphasizes.

Although our topic outline represents beliefs, ideas, and opinions that range far wider than a particular set of educational goals, there is no question that librarians should acquire the full SIECUS *Guidelines* to better understand the scope and intention of its topics. Indeed, we believe that a good sex education collection in public and school libraries should encompass the full range of topics specified both in the SIECUS *Guidelines* and in our own outline. Accordingly, we urge librarians to use both schemes for evaluating their collections. But we also recommend that librarians should include a broader range of viewpoints than those endorsed in SIECUS messages.

In particular, adult collections should encompass fully both approaches. Children and young adult collections in school and public libraries will in all likelihood give more weight to the *Guidelines* topics, supplemented by materials in our Books for Children, Books for Pre-Adolescents, and Books for Adolescents sections (Chapter 11). If, with time, other groups propose book-based educational programs, these too should be consulted and used for acquiring sexuality titles, whether those groups be Christian conservative, radical, feminist, or oriented towards sexual minorities.

BUT DON'T WE HAVE TO MAKE MORAL CHOICES?

In our personal lives and in the voting booth, yes. But our personal moralities are no sure guides for creating selection/acquisition policies for libraries. One reason is that each of us tends to function sexually and morally within one or several of the major viewpoints we have outlined, and therefore can begin to think that the rest are uninteresting, statistically insignificant, immoral, or downright foolish. When we whereupon earnestly select "the best *and* most moral" books, we tend to pick titles from one category—our own. This problem can become acute if simultaneously we are unaware of books that represent other viewpoints. We become inadvertent censors—and the solution is once again to recognize that diversity is the reigning principle in sexuality, as it is in so much else. Historically, librarians could have once claimed ignorance as an excuse for not including diverse materials about sexuality. With the varied materials discussed in Part II of this book, ignorance can be claimed no longer.

Yet there is a second reason to hesitate in choosing sexuality titles on moral grounds. Sometimes moral choices are made not as innocent expressions of our own experience, but to proselytize for *our side* and oppose *their side*. In this, we are not being moral so much as moralizing: we are trying to gain converts, win votes, fight the good fight—in brief, we are competing with other people and their viewpoints. Now, this may be a natural human propensity, but if so, remember this: when *you* try to win converts, then by the same token so will your competition. You are now not engaged in collection building or sexuality education in broad or narrow senses, but in battles external to such matters, where books are merely tokens of who is winning. It becomes a war of all against all—not, in our view, a way to build a solid, lastingly significant collection.

WHAT LIBRARIES CAN DO FOR SEX EDUCATION

But the third approach is most important of all, for it reverses the poles, so to speak, and says Yes, let us choose books on moral bases—*all of them.* Let us review a few points to support this proposition. First, the Library Bill of Rights says that libraries should carry "all points of view on current and historical issues." This mandates inclusion in the library of both conservative Christian and radical anarchist views—and all points in between. Moreover, it is only fair for libraries to serve different segments of the community. Some parents of young people would prefer the guidance of *A Parent's Guide to Teenage Sexuality* (C95, Gale), while others might prefer *Raising Them Chaste* (C94, Durfield & Durfield) or *How to Help Your Child Say "No" to Sexual Pressure* (C100, McDowell).

A more practical consideration: representing many viewpoints will probably not stop censorship efforts, but it may diminish them as libraries gain credibility for being responsive to the community and truly impartial, rather than being seen as either a bastion of librarian be-bunned sexual propriety or as a vehicle exclusively for the "advancement of sexual relativism and the toleration of homosexuality."[9] Certainly, proponents of any one view should be able to find in the library *the other viewpoints,* so that they may learn about the opposition, clarify their own views, and understand the issues more generally. "Why not invite everybody to 'read with the enemy'?"[10] In many cases, the library will be the only place in which people *can* be exposed to views different from what they grew up with, what their friends and families believe, or what they see in the media. Conviction by default is no conviction at all.

Libraries also have an obligation to researchers (from term paper to Nobel levels) and policy makers who are studying an issue objectively and need to be able to find in libraries materials from all viewpoints—whether or not mainstream thinking considers some of these positions inaccurate, invalid, or even "lies." And about "lies," Jefferson Selth makes a final point: "[E]ven if they [certain viewpoints and publications] turn out to be lies, they are still less harmful than their suppression would be. . . . For one thing, as history has shown us many times, they may be proven in the end *not* to be lies, no matter how many experts now testify to the contrary. And even if they are lies: if we allow *them* to be suppressed, what credibility do we have when we defend *The Satanic Verses* or *Catcher in the Rye?*"[11]

We stress again and again that the best collection of sexuality materials is one that in balanced fashion represents a *full* range of visions, ideals, and preferences people feel about sexuality. For today, essentially by definition, that range expresses today's issues and, for tomorrow, will provide invaluable insight into what motivated us as a society at a time of great upheaval and change. A good current collection also becomes a reliable, valuable historical record.

What we propose for viewpoints and genres also holds for topics. A library collection about sex should reflect the SIECUS topics, our topics, and the viewpoints and genres listed above while still being fine-tuned to reflect the needs of the community. Such a collection is diverse enough, yet focused enough, to help patrons now and for many decades to come.

There is a philosophical calm in the idea of filling the shelves with a range of titles. It speaks more to the ages than to the transitory tumult and hubbub of media-style debate. In some perhaps romanticized—or ideal— sense, it is more librarianly than constantly trying to align the collection with whatever faction seems at the moment to be winning. And in the long run, it is much more interesting!

NOTES

1. See J. Gordon Melton, "The Magic Family," in *Encyclopedia of American Religion*, 4th ed. (Detroit: Gale, 1993): 173–183. Crowley's works are among the most banned in the history of modern sexual censorship. Now some are available in new editions (a few available from AK Distribution, P.O.B. 40682, San Francisco, CA 94140). His *Snowdrops from a Curate's Garden* (Chicago: Teitan Press, 1986, originally published privately in 1904) is perhaps the wackiest book of sexual literature we have read, ranging from genuinely very funny to utterly outrageous to deranged. And yet it is dated, too. Written at the turn of the century in reaction against Victorianism, it now reads more mildly than some material we have seen in comix and zines and is certainly more literate.

Not all occultists were—or are—as sexually wild-eyed as Crowley, yet 19th century occultism in both the United States and Great Britain had its share of sex radicals. For an inter alia summary, see Peter Washington, *Madame Blavatsky's Baboon: A History of the Mystics, Mediums, and Misfits Who Brought Spiritualism to America* (New York: Schocken, 1995), which embodies a book seeming to have nothing to do with sex, yet with sexual content.

2. An invaluable resource on all "fundamentalist" religious groups is the projected five-volume work, "The Fundamentalisms Project," edited by Martin E. Marty & R. Scott Appleby (University of Chicago Press). Volumes 1–4 are currently in print: *Fundamentalisms Observed* (1991); *Fundamentalisms and Society: Reclaiming the Sciences, the Family, and Education* (1993); *Fundamentalisms and the State: Remaking Polities, Economies, and Militance* (1993); *Accounting for Fundamentalisms: The Dynamic Character of Movement* (1994).

3. For example, see Diane DiMassa, *Hothead Paisan: Homicidal Lesbian Terrorist* (Cleis Press, 1993), not annotated, a cartoon collection described in the pub-

lisher's catalog as "an irresistible fusion of violence, television, caffeine, sex and spiritual enlightenment." Hothead "is an equal opportunity avenger" and "practices preventative homicide."

4. By *formal*, we mean a structured, predesigned program taught by trained individuals. It is conceivable—and often recommended—that parents provide formal sex education to their children, but in actual practice they rarely do so.

5. For this definition, we drew from *The Complete Dictionary of Sexology* (D93, Francoeur et al.): 583; *The Language of Sex from A to Z* (D95, Goldenson & Anderson): 249; and *Guidelines for Comprehensive Sexuality Education, Kindergarten–12th Grade* (C97): 3.

6. We uncovered a number of other ways to subcategorize sexuality, including classification systems in the SIECUS, Planned Parenthood, and Kinsey libraries; and in the book *Studies in Human Sexuality* (D116, Frayser & Whitby).

7. Debates about sex education curricula have yielded a large and highly polemic literature. A recent example criticizing the SIECUS and similar programs for schools is Barbara Dafoe Whitehead's "The Failure of Sex Education," *Atlantic Monthly* 274.4 (October 1994): 55–80. Debra Haffner, SIECUS executive director, and other sex educators replied in *Atlantic Monthly*, 275.1 (January 1995): 6–12. Additional material about Whitehead's article appeared as Leslie M. Kantor & Debra W. Haffner, "Responding to 'The Failure of Sex Education,' " *SIECUS Report* 23.3 (February/March 1995): 17–18; and as a letter sent to the *Atlantic Monthly* but not published: "Douglas Kirby Responds to the *Atlantic*," *SIECUS Report* 23.3 (February/March 1995): 19.

8. Cataloging, classification, and indexing systems have come under major attack for inadequate treatment of sex topics. See, e.g., Martha Cornog, "Providing Access to Materials on Sexuality," *Libraries, Erotica, & Pornography* (D115, Cornog): 166–187; Sanford Berman, "The 'Fucking' Truth About Library Catalogs," *Alternative Library Literature 1992–1993*, ed. Sanford Berman & James P. Danky (Jefferson, NC: McFarland, 1994): 336–341; Gary M. Klein, "Sex Education and Sexuality Before Stonewall: A Historical Look at Subject Headings Used in the *Education Index*, 1929–1969," *Reference Services Review* (Winter 1994): 29–50.

9. James L. Sauer, "Community Service" (letter), *Library Journal* (October 15, 1993): 8.

10. James LaRue, "Reading with the Enemy," *Wilson Library Bulletin* (January 1994): 45.

11. Jetterson P. Selth, *Ambition, Discrimination, and Censorship in Libraries* (Jefferson, NC: McFarland, 1993): 126–127.

5 Selection and Evaluation

Lists of topics, genres, and viewpoints like those in Chapter 4 are only a map of sexuality publishing—and although we can lay out this map, we cannot tell libraries where they should go. Instead, the first step in collection building is for you, working librarians, to develop a philosophy from which will flow plans and policies for selecting sex books. In this, the selection philosophy specifies the destination—"where to go"—and the plans, policies, and procedures comprise the navigation instructions.[1]

Without plans and policies underlain by such a philosophy, you will not know where you are going, and you will wind up someplace else. That "someplace else" may readily be a collection policy or agenda forced on the library by outsiders—or even by the library board or school board or Board of Education—whose motivations may be primarily political and who may represent only a few community pressure groups speaking from expediency rather than after deliberation and serious discussion of available choices. Historically, these have been the usual origins for a pattern of sexuality collecting we see as problematic: ignoring sexuality or selecting so narrowly as to be unrepresentative of modern sexuality publishing and readers' needs. Without a collection philosophy developed by librarians themselves, a collection develops as a hodgepodge without form or function, without coherent purposes, and without organized rationale.

Accordingly, philosophy, plan, and policy function like an architectural blueprint and permit one to build a collection as a coherent whole, capable of many functions, including growth and responsiveness to future needs. Moreover, a coherent philosophy lets you explain to the citizenry exactly why the library has this book but not that one, no small matter when library holdings in sexuality become politicized and controversial.

Because every library is different, each must develop its own philosophy, plans, policies, and procedures. After all, if every library in America had identical holdings and philosophies, what dull places libraries would be! But worse, such uniformity would bespeak bureaucratization of librarianship to a terrible degree and would violate the very principle we uphold on philosophical grounds: that libraries exist to represent reasonable diversity.

Still, we are writing this book to offer concrete suggestions about collecting in sexuality. And we raise questions that only you and your colleagues can resolve rather than offer cut-and-dried solutions. The problems may display uniformity, but their solutions need not.

If collecting sexuality books were emotionally and socially neutral, like building a collection of local historical memorabilia, then the effort needed to develop the "Four P's"—philosophy, plan, policy, and procedure—might well be unnecessary. But because library collections have so often avoided sexuality topics and because library history has so steadfastly denied their importance, there is a great deal for modern librarians to do—a task, challenge, and opportunity all at once.

PHILOSOPHY, PLAN, POLICY, PROCEDURE

The library's philosophy states the purpose and goals of the sex collection; its plan covers how goals will be accomplished; policies cover day-to-day contingencies; and procedures are the nitty-gritty of everyday library life. We could fill pages with detail about each, but we assume instead that our readers already know how to run a library. What is needed is to connect existing library philosophies/procedures to a proactive decision for widening and modernizing a library's holdings in sexuality.

Deciding to Do It

It is a commonplace in industrial quality control that upper management must totally support any corporate scheme to enhance product quality. An indifferent or hostile upper management will undercut changes initiated by middle management or factory employees. Although libraries and corporations are quite different, nonetheless a similar principle holds: a decision to enhance the sexuality collection must have the active support of the library director, staff, and governing board. If the library or school board, for example, rejects such a concept, individuals lower on the totem pole may find their hopes thwarted by indirection, indifference, and above all by arguments that "it costs too much" or "the board won't support it" or "the parents will be up in arms."

However, hierarchies of power and status in libraries differ very greatly from those of the corporate world. These differences are not in type of service offered—after all, many for-profit corporations offer services to the public and thereby resemble libraries. Instead, the greatest difference is that at all levels librarianship is infused by a larger ethic: the view that collecting, protecting, and disseminating books and other works is a good in itself.

In a real sense, libraries can afford to view idealistically their role in the community and society. Their bottom line is measured not in widgets per week or in dollars per quarter or in shareholder profits. Instead, the library's bottom line is how well its holdings represent the world of books and writing, and how well it makes those holdings available to its public. This commitment to idealism alters the power structure of a library compared to that of a corporation.

Thus, the chief executive officer of Amalgamated Widget Corporation decrees, "We're cutting back on semi-involuter production." And, like people in a medieval fiefdom, the lackeys—if they want their jobs—scurry to cut back accordingly. By contrast, a library director says, "We're not going to waste money buying sex books," and the other librarians eye the director suspiciously. "Why?" they ask. "We think it's a good idea to develop that collection."

Of course, library directors can wield power over subordinates. Yet the existence of a shared ethical groundwork in librarianship undercuts efforts by a few individuals, even highly placed ones, to oppose library purposes. Instead, library ethics, particularly the ideal of collecting, protecting, and disseminating books, permit any trained librarian to contribute substantially and significantly to how a library achieves its goals.

So, by contrast to corporate life, where a plan for improving services must come from on high or die, *all* librarians can significantly affect how their library works. If a few individual librarians wish to develop the sexuality collection, they can make an excellent case for doing so based on ethical and professional considerations. Their view will then likely shape the decisions of the library as a whole, even in the face of internal or external opposition. Such a library is then much closer to deciding to enhance the sexuality collection because it is arguably the right thing to do, as opposed to the most profitable, the most comfortable, or the most convenient.

So let us assume that this decision has been made by someone—we hope, by several someones. What comes next?

What Is a Philosophy?

The philosophy of a sexuality collection defines its purposes: finding focal areas of collecting, deciding what clientele will or might be served, preparing criteria for acquiring and retaining books, and searching for ways to balance existing collections. The philosophy ought to address, for example:

- Who are the patrons? The collection might serve all ages, only young people, or only adults. What are their interests? How many will be interested, and how can one attract more people?

- What are the purposes of the collection? For example, leisure vs. research vs. general information vs. coursework/classroom support. To what extent, for example, might a school library support recreational reading? While potentially everything is valuable for *some* purpose, specialization is always needed for practical reasons of limited money and shelf space.

- What are the needs of parents and community groups? Although we argue that these groups cannot *force* a determination of the library's collection policies, nonetheless libraries exist to serve a public that includes such groups, even if it is not limited to them. Parents have many questions about child sexuality, particularly the inflammatory and frightening issues of abuse; they also need straightforward information about what is and is not normal. Likewise, community groups, whether of adults or children (such as religious youth groups) have needs that must be understood and reflected in collections.

- Will the collection deal archivally or in depth with specialized topics? Will it be based on a donated special collection? Should the library seek such collections, and if so, how?

- To what extent will a public library serve students from local high schools or colleges? Academic and school libraries must fulfill coursework requirements, but all libraries can offer auxiliary materials to students.

We stress again that we cannot tell you what your choices should be. Instead, individual libraries and staff must make individual decisions. Nonetheless, some general principles seem to exist. A sex collection philosophy should be idealistic and should address the roles of all interested parties. Moreover, the ideals expressed should be relatively free of factional agendas and incorporate both currently competing overall library philosophies: that of providing the "best fruits of civilization" and that of providing a wide variety of materials on all points of view. These overall philosophies are not necessarily compatible, as we all know! We also know that one can almost never have simultaneously low price, high quality, and speed of delivery. But as we consistently aim for thrift, quality, and speed in most of our affairs, we should also aim for quality *and* representativeness in sex collections.

In addition, the philosophy should deal with the sorts of objections so often raised about sexuality collections, including:

- How to handle the patron complaint, "This work does not belong in the library." Here we are not talking about convening the selection committee and wading through forms and petitions, but making it clear to oneself that library functions transcend local politics. It is a question of library philosophy for a librarian to respond, "We shall consider your objection seriously, but please understand that libraries collect books and do not make judgments only *you* can make," rather than saying, "Well, personally I agree that this is a terrible book, but what can you do? *They* bought it and put it on the shelves."
- How to deal with frightening or dangerous patrons. One must be aware from the philosophical outset that sexuality collections *can* attract strange people. Not many, perhaps, but sometimes one is too many! Under this heading comes a commitment to security and protection. Some librarians may think that these issues are purely practical, but addressing them in the philosophy can help avoid panicky prognostications that Undesirable Visitors will arrive the moment the library stocks, for example, *The New Joy of Gay Sex* (B62).
- How to develop access and anti-vandalism policies. Again the question is not solely practical. It is no philosophy at all if one decides to purchase expensive books and then allows them to be stolen or destroyed.

But, above all, the philosophy we are urging librarians to consider is not cast in negatives. Instead, we urge that sexuality collecting be an extension of traditional library ethics rather than a novelty, and that all librarians can contribute significantly and substantially to building the philosophy needed to create a good sex collection.

Plans, Policies, and Procedures

If the philosophy is idealistic, plans and policies should be realistic. Building a library sexuality collection means first identifying a wide range of likely titles for purchase and then choosing some. As no one can "buy it all," serious practical consideration must be given to developing a larger wish list and then making hard choices among the possibilities.

Ideally, all library staff could contribute to the initial wish list, but after that, a series of management questions arise that must be considered in detail. As managers know, without policies and plans, life in The Organization is chaos. Among other issues that need to be dealt with at planning stages are the following:

- Who selects and approves sexuality materials for purchase? Selection at all stages is potentially the most contentious process of all because it so clearly lends itself to covert bias. Selection, approval, and disapproval at the early stages of modernizing and extending the sexuality collection are focal points for avoiding censorship—or for subtly implementing it. A homophobe can work serious damage to representativeness; indeed, *any* agenda-laden individual will immediately focus on the selection function. All plans and policies must incorporate appropriate monitoring but in ways that do not offend individuals' deeply held moral views. One imagines that the library director's tact will be much exercised.

- From whom else will suggested titles be accepted for consideration? What published or other sources of titles will be sought by librarians or accepted from others? ("Can you buy this book? I heard about it on Phil Donahue.") Once the news spreads that a library *is* collecting sexuality works, many people will express opinions. Some such opinions may be quite unique, but we must recall that libraries serve patrons, unique and otherwise. Amalgamated Widgets can ignore screwball ideas about their semi-involuters, but a library must and should respond to its public.

- What sorts of public relations are desirable about the sex collection? Traditional librarians might say "None!" but that is the problem, isn't it? We suggest informative and evenhanded announcements that do not stridently advertise but inform the public about the library's intentions and ideals, and therefore its materials and services. "We provide information" is the basic—and very true—slogan.

- What broad criteria will be used for purchasing? Good reviews? Expert opinion? Anticipated high use? Mention in the media? Patron petition? Update of, or fit with, area within current collection? Filling gaps in the current collection? Representative of new and popular (or unpopular) views? Excellent writing, organization, and grasp of subject? All or some of the above?[2] And who decides *these* questions?

- Will criteria for selecting sexuality works differ from those applied to other potential purchases? In this perhaps more than anywhere else, we encounter the need for a philosophical underpinning to collecting in sexuality, for no plan will function if the philosophy does not first address the issue of "special criteria" for sexuality titles. Once again: there is considerable opportunity for covert and overt censorship and agenda-mongering when it comes to selecting books. It is all too easy to impede collecting in sexuality by supporting book selection criteria that seem reasonable—but in fact permit nothing to pass through the sieve. Characteristically, such efforts are presented as the best of librarianly and moral reasoning; yet they can deeply sabotage the ideal. A well-thought-out philosophy will go a long way in enabling plans and policies for evenhanded collecting—as opposed to requiring, for example, that any sexuality title considered for purchase must have only excellent reviews or additional qualifications not applied to other books. At a minimum, a "special criteria" policy requires extremely careful justification.

- How do philosophy, plans, and policies for sexuality materials compare with those for other controversial materials? Perhaps the first might serve as a broader model for the latter. Certainly there will be similarities, especially in relation to any library board or school board or Board of Education policies for dealing with controversial materials in general.

Plans and policies can also specify particular genres and topics on which the library wishes to focus as well as procedures for collecting in these areas—and also for specifying any excluded categories such as, say, textbooks. If the library decides to exclude any particular sort of sexually explicit materials, this is the place to state that policy and justify it. As a point of philosophy, we do not recommend such exclusions—but if a library wants to impose such exclusionary policies, the least it can do is to be open and honest about it.[3]

An excellent book selection strategy is including representatives of many interests via a selection committee or committees. Particular individuals or groups can be responsible for particular subject areas. Committees should be headed by library staff and may include other staff, library administration, members of library boards and "friends" groups, representatives of community organizations, plus library patrons of all ages including parents and children. As well as recommending new titles, committee members can also review books for which inadequate reviews or none are available. This strategy is a good way to involve the entire community, while at the same time ensuring that the collection represents a diversity of needs and views.

Committees studying these issues must themselves be balanced and represent a variety of viewpoints just as surely as the library's holdings must do so. An overly negative report from the "Sex Book Committee" is a danger sign that the committee is unbalanced and perhaps under sabotage from some of its members who lack the courage to oppose it openly. Help here can be obtained by discussing the issue with the director and with other librarians, both in and out of the library, in an effort to reassert egalitarian collegiality in the committee.

A necessary complement to a book selection philosophy, plan, and policy is the policy for reconsideration—that is, coping with challenges to library materials. This is discussed together with censorship in Chapter 8.

THE CORE COLLECTION

Just as philosophy, plan, and procedures for a sex collection are unique to each library, so too every library can create a core collection of sexuality titles unique to its own needs. When the subject is uncontroversial, so is the list of titles in the core collection. But considerable debate can break out concerning which sexuality books are "basic, fundamental, and necessary" because so many historical and moral issues surround the area. But even so, the notion of the core collection is still an extremely valuable part of the library's philosophy/plan/policy for its sex collection.

A core collection contains books collectively covering with quality and representativeness a great deal of key information. Accordingly, and consistent with our philosophical ideal that libraries serve all viewpoints and needs, the core collection must represent a diverse range of genres, experiences, and visions. Some books in the core collection deliver information in highly concentrated fashion: encyclopedias, dictionaries, handbooks. Others present past and present statistical survey data, whereas still others represent books widely deemed fundamental for their roles in the past and present. From Chapters 9–13, we mention for illustration the types of books we mean:

Human Sexuality: An Encyclopedia (A3, Bullough & Bullough)

Sex in America (A11, Michael et al.)

Sexual Behavior in the Human Female (A33, Kinsey et al.)

Sexual Behavior in the Human Male (A48, Kinsey et al.)

The Hite Report (A30, Hite)

The Hite Report on Male Sexuality (A46, Hite)

The Complete Dictionary of Sexology (D93, Francoeur et al.)

Another example: Alfred Kinsey's colleague Wardell Pomeroy contributed a list of the "10 Most Important Books About Sex" to *The Book of Lists*. Indeed, the authors and titles are among the classics:

Havelock Ellis, *Studies in the Psychology of Sex* (Random House, 1936)

Sigmund Freud, *Three Essays on the Theory of Sexuality* (Basic Books, 1962)

Th. H. van de Velde, *Ideal Marriage* (Random House, 1930)

Alfred C. Kinsey et al., *Sexual Behavior in the Human Male* and *Sexual Behavior in the Human Female* (A48, A33)

C.S. Ford and F.A. Beach, *Patterns of Sexual Behavior* (Harper & Row, 1972)

William Masters and Virginia Johnson, *Human Sexual Response* and *Human Sexual Inadequacy* (A9, E7)

Alex Comfort, *The Joy of Sex* (*The New Joy of Sex*: A59)

Helen Singer Kaplan, *The New Sex Therapy* (Times Books, 1974)[4]

It is, in fact, a fine list, and we could discuss it extensively.[5] These titles date only through the 1970s, and nowadays different individuals would add a variety of recent titles, for example, about homosexuality, rape, abortion, contraception, and religious perspectives—including *Evangelium Vitae*. One could add older titles too, like Plato's *Symposium*. Certainly public and school library core collections will include books for various ages, with selections for young people such as those listed in Chapter 11. But that is not the point. Pomeroy's list succeeds in illustrating one approach to a basic core collection.

Accordingly, our purpose is *not* to urge all libraries immediately to purchase the titles on either Pomeroy's list or ours. Instead, the lists provide exemplars of what to think about. By analyzing topics and approaches used in lists like these, librarians can build a custom core collection of their own.

A few caveats about core collections. Foremost is that collecting can stop there and become hopelessly outdated. So a library's commitment to collecting in sexuality cannot stop with a core collection. The philosophy must incorporate the idea of continued development and enhancement around the basic books already stocked. Otherwise, why bother? Another problem is labeling: heated arguments can break out if such-and-such a book is or is not needed for the "core collection." Such arguments may be efforts to censor further collecting. Indeed, under some circumstances, it may be unwise to even talk about a core collection. Some staff may see the core as a seed for further growth; others will say, "You've got the core, that's enough." In our opinion, it is not.

BEYOND THE CORE COLLECTION

Any core collection, including choices made from the 597 books in Part II, eventually becomes static and dated. Pomeroy's list, assembled for a 1977 book, is now dated, no matter how important these works. A striking feature of modern sexuality publishing is its flux and constant expansion. Thus too a library's collection, no matter how good it *once* was, must be kept up. New genres of writing appear—for example, much modern work deals simultaneously with sexuality and gender roles. The absence of feminist writers is striking in Pomeroy's list.

It is a lesson librarians know well from other areas of book acquisition: in a fast moving field, collections become out of date rather too quickly for comfort. So libraries must systematically incorporate into philosophy, plan, and policy the notion of keeping the core collection up to date and supplementing it with coverage of many topics and views in more depth, always tailored to that library. Here we can offer tips for identifying possible new titles and evaluating them for inclusion. From our suggestions, each library can discover what works for its particular community and for its sex book collection.

TURNING TO THE PRACTICAL

In the rest of this book, we deal increasingly with practical issues of establishing, modernizing, and extending a sexuality collection. No longer are historical and philosophical issues at the center, but instead we reach the nitty-gritties of librarianly life. We move on to sources for identification of new (and older) sexuality books: book reviews, bibliographies and lists, mail order catalogs, publishers, bookstores, other libraries, organizations, experts—including teachers, patrons, and library staff. We concentrate upon selection of nonfiction books for adults and young people; selection of other types of materials will be discussed in the following chapter. Considerations particular to specific topics are covered with that topic in Part II.

BOOK IDENTIFICATION

Initially, we feared that identifying sex books would be difficult. Many are not reviewed or mentioned in common sources. But we were soon awash in publishers' catalogs, flyers, journals, bibliographies, letters from colleagues, and articles clipped from the library press, all describing sexuality titles of striking relevance. So we modified our assessment. People and organizations *want* you to know about sex books, and they will be delighted to tell you about them if you ask. The catch: the information is not all in one place.

Book Reviews

Librarians are familiar with the major review periodicals written for them: *Library Journal, School Library Journal, Horn Book Magazine, Booklist, Kirkus Reviews, Choice*, and *Publishers Weekly*, plus general review periodicals such as the *New York Times Book Review*.[6] These pick up perhaps a third to half of the interesting sex books. Most thorough coverage seems to be given to abortion, AIDS, homosexuality, and sexual exploitation of various types.

Some coverage is accorded to female sexuality and sexual issues, sex education, particularly of children and young adults, books *for* children and young adults, sexual enhancement, and erotica from mainstream presses. Much less coverage is accorded to celibacy, masturbation, variations in sexual behavior and lifestyle other than homosexuality, transgendered concerns, and religious or conservative perspectives.[7]

Many professional sexuality journals and newsletters offer reviews. That most helpful for public and school libraries is *SIECUS Report*. For more scholarly collections, *Journal of the History of Sexuality* carries a large number of reviews and would be especially helpful. Other scholarly journals of sexuality, most carrying reviews, are listed in Chapter 6.

But since reviews do not begin to cover some of the most interesting and wide-ranging sexuality materials, libraries should depend upon many other avenues for selection, as we will describe.

Bibliographies and Lists

Bibliographies, especially annotated ones, are the major source of information about unreviewed sex books. Four sources are especially noteworthy:

Sexuality Information and Education Council of the U.S. (SIECUS)
Publications Department
130 West 42nd Street, Suite 350
New York, NY 10036
   Publishes 14 annotated bibliographies, updated regularly, of materials largely
suitable for public and school libraries: books for the general public, religious perspectives (2 bibliographies, including some conservative materials), child sexual
abuse, sex education (curricula and textbooks), talking with children about sexuality, books for children and adolescents, gay/lesbian issues, gender dysphoria
(transvestism and transsexualism), global sexuality, disability, sexuality in middle
and later life, sexuality periodicals for professionals, and AIDS/HIV.

Focus on the Family
Correspondence Department
Colorado Springs, CO 80995
   This is one of the few sources of bibliographies covering conservative and religious sex education materials. Annotated resource lists are available on sex education, sexuality, sexuality-special situations (homosexuality, masturbation, pornography, unmarried pregnancy, sexual addiction, and STDs), premarital materials,
and pro-life materials (2 bibliographies). A few sexuality books also are included
on: teen materials, singles, women-related issues, materials for men, parenting: age
9 to pre-adolescent, special parenting situations, and health. However, the Focus
on the Family (FOTF) lists are neither complete nor definitive. We estimate that at
least several hundred conservative/religious books about sexual issues are in print;
unfortunately, the only way to identify most of them is to use *all* the tips recommended in this chapter and in Part II, especially publishers' catalogs and
bibliographies in other books. Librarians should pressure FOTF to expand their
bibliographies and keep them up to date.

The Kinsey Institute for Research on Sex, Gender, and Reproduction
Information Service
416 Morrison Hall
Indiana University
Bloomington, IN 47405
   Nearly 500 specialized topic bibliographies relating to sexuality, most older ma-
terials. Covers books and scholarly journals; some popular periodical articles. Re-
quest the complete list of bibliographies. No annotations. Useful for older materials.

Subject Guide to Books in Print
   Sometimes the only way to locate items about a topic—such as celibacy—is to
look up the topic in *Subject Guide to Books in Print*. One can then contact the
publishers of likely books to obtain catalogs, reprints of reviews, or examination
copies.

   Bibliographies in book form or those contained within books are another
source, particularly for older and classic materials. *Studies in Human Sexuality* (D116, Frayser & Whitby) is indispensable for academic and large

public libraries. See also books recommended in Chapter 12's Libraries and Sex section. Many topic bibliographies have been published, and some can be located by checking *Subject Guide to Books in Print* under the topic, subhead BIBLIOGRAPHIES. Others appear in *A Research Guide to Human Sexuality* (D120, Lichtenberg).

Mail Order Catalogs

Many catalogs include sex books; most are discussed under the appropriate topic in Part II. Some more general catalogs:

The Sexuality Library
938 Howard Street, Suite 101
San Francisco, CA 94103
   Annotated catalog of several hundred books: nonfiction and erotica, heterosexual/homosexual. Geared towards enhancement: no sexual exploitation, no STDs. Books are selected with help of an expert review panel.

Ivan Stormgart
P.O. Box 470883
San Francisco, CA 94147-0883
   "Antiquarian bookseller specializing in books relating to all aspects of sexual behavior," including out-of-print and rare works, and materials in 12 languages. Twenty-five topic lists/catalogs available. Brief annotations.

Michael Neal
6 rue des Bas-Jardins
Feugères
91650 Saint-Yon
France
   "Erotica-curiosa-sexualia-pornographica" catalog of several hundred items, no annotations. Much out-of-print and rare. Fiction and nonfiction.

Loompanics
P.O. Box 1197
Port Townsend, WA 98368
   A major access point to small press, underground, and literature of "the strange, the useful, the arcane, the oddball, the unusual, the unique, and the diabolical. Controversial and unusual books on a wide variety of subjects. Most of these books cannot be found in even the largest libraries"—but some of them should be. The 1994 catalog listed 31 books on sex, 5 of which we included in Part II. Not a primary source of sex books, but unique in its coverage of libertarian and semi-anarchist titles. Annotations.

Big Books from Small Presses
Upper Access Books
P.O. Box 457
Hinesburg, VT 05461

A smaller and tamer Loompanics, with a selection of high quality small press titles. One-page section on sexuality, with other sex-related works scattered throughout. Annotations. Loompanics and Upper Access both list books on the nudist/naturist movement.

Publishers

Sometimes the only description one can find of a book is in the publisher's catalog. These publishers have more than a few nonfiction sexuality titles: Cassell, Garland, Greenhaven, Greenwood, Harper and its subsidiaries (especially Harper San Francisco), Haworth, McFarland, Oryx, Plenum, Prometheus, and Sage.

The major conservative Christian publishing houses with sex titles are Bethany House, InterVarsity, Multnomah, NavPress, Paulist Press, and Word. Word and Multnomah both refused to send us catalogs, saying that they provided catalogs only to bookstores having accounts with them. A contact at a local bookstore arranged to get us catalogs. When Word exhibited at the 1994 ALA meeting, one of us (MC) complained to the representative, who seemed surprised at the stonewalling and interested in courting the library market. Librarians dealing through major jobbers may have less trouble, but who knows? If you have problems, call the publisher's marketing department and complain loudly.

For all publishers, make sure you get backlist as well as current catalogs.

Bookstores

Yes, bookstores. Take a field trip to your local chain bookstore (Borders, B. Dalton, Encore, Walden) and read the shelves for interesting sex books. You will see titles you would not have found any other way, and some you will want for your library. Check sections labeled sexuality, psychology, self-help, health, erotica, gay/lesbian, how-to. Gay bookstores can be good sources for materials about AIDS, male sexuality, female sexuality, S&M, transgendered and other sexual variations, as well as about homosexuality. Feminist, radical/anarchist, and "alternative" bookstores can also be useful.

If there is a Christian bookstore near you, you are lucky. Browsing will uncover some of those hard-to-find conservative and religious viewpoints—look for sections labeled "social issues" or "the church in the world." Moreover, bookstore staff can help you get catalogs and order materials when publishers will not deal with a library or jobber directly. (See the Sex and Religion section in Chapter 12.)

And don't forget secondhand bookstores, which can turn up classics like the Kinsey reports at bargain prices.

Other Libraries

Other libraries, especially those with special sexuality collections, can suggest titles for purchase, provide acquisitions lists, send copies of cataloging records for inspection, and (sometimes) lend books through interlibrary loan. The major sexuality libraries are those of the Kinsey Institute, SIECUS, Planned Parenthood (New York and local affiliates), the Institute for Advanced Study of Human Sexuality in San Francisco, and the Vern and Bonnie Bullough collection at California State University, Northridge.

There are many other places with interesting special collections. The index to the 1995 edition of the *Directory of Special Libraries and Information Centers* (Gale Research) lists 32 libraries under topics beginning with "sex," 39 under homosexuality and lesbianism, 44 under birth control, 31 under abortion, and 29 under acquired immune deficiency syndrome.[8]

Other lists of sex-related collections may be found in the following:

Alternative Lifestyles: A Guide to Research Collections on Intentional Communities, Nudism, and Sexual Freedom, by Jefferson P. Selth (Greenwood Press, 1985). Describes 6 collections on nudism and 18 on "sexual freedom."

"Special Collections of Gay and Lesbian Materials: A Directory" (in *Gay and Lesbian Library Service*, D118, Gough & Greenblatt). Over 80 collections in the U.S., Canada, and Mexico, academic and nonacademic.

Libraries, Erotica, & Pornography (D115, Cornog). See chapters "Erotica Research Collections," by Gwendolyn Pershing, and "Homosexuality Research Collections," by Daniel C. Tsang.

Some nonacademic lesbian/gay collections are listed as a group and by city in *Gayellow Pages* (B7).

Organizations

Organizations can be sources for monographs, flyers for the vertical file, and more bibliographies. As part of research for this book, we sent a form letter requesting information and bibliographies to at least a hundred organizations listed in the *Encyclopedia of Associations*. Any library can do the same, as we describe in relation to vertical file enhancement (Chapter 6).

Local organizations can also be queried for interesting materials—check the Blue Pages and the Yellow Pages of the telephone directory.

Experts, Including Teachers

"Never do yourself," muttered Quinn, "what you can con an expert into doing for you."[9]

Experts can suggest books, evaluate materials that have not been reviewed or have been challenged by would-be censors, provide bibliographies and syllabi used in college courses, and contribute to library programming.

Experts in sexuality can be found by contacting the Society for the Scientific Study of Sex (SSSS, P.O. Box 208, Mt. Vernon, IA 52314) and the American Association of Sex Educators, Counselors, and Therapists (AASECT, P.O. Box 238, Mount Vernon, IA 52314). Both provide referrals to local experts. Another source of experts is any of the 24 university degree programs in human sexuality; a list may be obtained from SSSS. Organizations can also suggest experts. *A Research Guide to Human Sexuality* (D120, Lichtenberg) lists organizations and indicates which groups will recommend experts.

Teachers/faculty as a subclass of experts must not be neglected: in schools, teachers of health, lifestyle, and "social studies"; in academia, faculty in sociology, psychology, anthropology, and religion—for starters.

Patrons

Patrons can be a source for book requests and donations. Both should prove helpful for sex collections. We noted above that patrons should be included in book selection committees.

We assume that most libraries accept book requests from patrons other than through library committees with patrons on them. Although these requests are processed through standard procedures and do not necessarily result in purchases, they are still valuable because they alert library staff to patron interests.

The major problem is letting patrons know that requests will be taken seriously, if not always actually filled, and that requests for sex books are welcome. Stereotypes of anti-sexual librarians die hard. Perhaps a list could be posted of recently requested items that the library has bought, including a few sex books—no names of requesters, of course. This might prime the pump.

Censorship efforts are the flip side of book requests. They offer a different challenge but can be just as valuable. While processing the request for reconsideration, ask the censor to suggest books more in line with his or her needs. If someone wants to remove *Changing Bodies, Changing Lives* (C53, Bell), ask them what books for teens they—or the organization they represent—would recommend. Then buy some of them. Hopefully, this will nudge conservative organizations to develop their own annotated bibliographies of sex books, lists that at present are a rare commodity.[10]

Pruning is a natural function in a library. However, it really should be done by staff according to established policies and procedures rather than by responding ad hoc to angry patron demands. Nonetheless, patron protests alert libraries about areas of controversy—and, paradoxically, the need to retain "objectionable" titles in the name of freedom of information and debate. Indeed, censorship efforts spotlight a need to acquire materials on both sides of the debate. Ideally, censorship efforts should result in *more* books, not fewer.

Donations are a good way to sidestep those who claim that taxpayers' money should not be used to buy "trash"—when *trash* is used to mean sex books the speaker disagrees with. However, an organized citizens' group playing "War of the Books" with their opponents can overwhelm a library with boxes of stuff no one will probably ever read. So philosophies, plans, and policies must incorporate the possibility of unwanted donations made not to enhance a collection but to score political points. We personally think all donations should be accepted—*we* never turn down free books!—but we understand that libraries may have limitations on shelving that make such idealism impractical.

Some libraries discovered the donation ploy during the Great Madonna *Sex* Wars (see Chapter 3). Local lesbian/gay organizations may be encouraged to donate gay newspapers and a few books about homosexuality. For other controversial books, cash contributions from patrons could be solicited or sympathetic donors sought.

Library Staff

Library staff should serve on selection committees, as we noted. In addition, librarians who have developed expertise on sexual topics by reading and attending classes may obtain free sex books by reviewing them for library periodicals or local newspapers.[11]

Summary of Selection Sources

Most school and small public libraries can select sexuality materials via standard library review media, SIECUS and Focus on the Family bibliographies, and the Sexuality Library catalog, plus occasional bookstore visits. Larger public libraries, academic libraries, and libraries with special interests and/or collections will need to try some of the other approaches suggested above. All selection techniques should be customized to each library and incorporated into the plan and policy for the sex book collection.

Difficulties in Selection and Acquisition

Some additional issues deserve brief comment.

• Many excellent and valuable works are published by very small presses, virtually mom and pop operations, or even self-published. These are impossible to obtain through standard jobbers and must be ordered individually—even paid for in advance—from the source. Moreover, such folks cannot afford to give library discounts, but they *will* probably be thrilled that a librarian is interested in their work!

• Some works are small and/or slender, requiring special support binding both for protection during use and against too-easy theft.

EVALUATING SEX BOOKS

We feel that sex books, like other books, should be evaluated for purchase in two major ways: how well they do what they attempt to do and how well they fit with the needs of the collection and patrons. Book evaluation criteria should be customized to each library and incorporated into plans and policies.

Easy to say, harder to do. If selection criteria are prone to debate, evaluation can be even worse. Assuming a large wish list of possible purchases, one can—in principle—be strict or be flexible in applying evaluation criteria. Again, it is clear that the opportunity for censorship is very great, again on reasonable sounding grounds of demanding quality and excellence. It just turns out that the evaluator's notions of quality and excellence eliminate anything he or she disagrees with morally, politically, or personally. This person feels, say, that "quality" means only books in the scientific-medical genre and excludes as ephemeral trivia anything mentioning religion. A colleague holds the directly opposite view, and feels that science and medicine dehumanize human sexuality. And so it goes, until the list of criteria chosen to compromise between all possible views is unworkable in practice. The result is predictable: books on sex are once again evaluated according to personal taste and preference.

An alternative is a "paint-by-numbers" rule book that mechanically applies evaluation criteria in strict adherence to written specifications, as if books were evaluated the way the U.S. Army evaluates widgets. Yet here too problems lurk: who sets the specifications? Eventually, the mere rumor of another meeting on the issue is enough to send cold shudders through everyone involved.

Well, we have a recommendation. In real life, all evaluation criteria for anything—books included—are interpreted via custom and habit by people who have become familiar with the area. And so it is here as well: clearly, the importance of collecting in sexuality warrants appointing appropriate staff to make it their business professionally and ethically to make the right choices. Appoint a good committee, let them do their work, and listen to what they say. And therefore it is for such people—whom we take to be well-meaning, serious, and reasonably well informed—that we include some suggestions about evaluation.

The Book Itself

We were able to identify in the library literature only a few sets of guidelines for evaluating sex (education) books. The most comprehensive was originally published in 1982 and subsequently adapted by another library writer. In this tradition, we present our own adaptation in Figure 5.1.[12]

These criteria were designed for evaluating comprehensive sex education books for young people, and naturally not every sex book fulfills them—or should. It depends upon what the author is trying to do, what the library wants, and who the patrons are.

Another, very simple set of criteria for evaluating books in general has been proposed: representativeness, cogency of argument, and quality of writing.[13] We found this quite useful for selecting items for Part II, especially works from the more extreme viewpoints.

Between these two poles of sample evaluation criteria—one elaborate and one quite simple—each library will need to develop its own standards for evaluating new materials on sexuality. The more stringent criteria list was developed for judging nonfiction. However, the representativeness-cogency-quality of writing criteria apply quite well to fiction and periodicals. Is the item representative of issues, topics, and points of view that resonate with patrons? Does the plot or content make sense? Is it well written in an appropriate style? And for magazines, are the graphics and layout well done? Do they complement the prose and add meaning?

On the other hand, a set of "instant disqualifiers" has been proposed for sex books: "excessive description of sexual pathology, gross factual errors, (such as claiming that abortion is illegal or that homosexuals are child molesters), warnings of hellfire or other scare tactics, outdated 'teen slang,' or a heavily condescending tone."[14] We don't fully agree with this list, and following it strictly might eliminate a number of conservative/religious sex books and even more of the permissive titles. So applying the criteria is an art as much as a science, and should be handled with ethical generosity. "Factual errors," sometimes termed *lies* in the library literature, is a very tricky concept when used as an exclusionary criterion for books, as discussed by a number of library writers on intellectual freedom.[15] After all, lying—or at least optimistic hyperbole—is standard fare in several types of books routinely bought by libraries: diet books ("Take off five pounds in five days!") and financial success books. We are not suggesting that accuracy as a selection criterion be completely disregarded but that it is a less firm concept than it might seem.

The Book in Context of the Collection

One may also evaluate sex books by considering balance and redundancy within the collection. "Everyone talks about balancing the collection, some

Figure 5.1
A Checklist for Evaluating Sex Education Books

Anatomy, Physiology, and Sexual Behavior
Does the book cover the following:
  Sexual development
  Sex organs and their function
  Puberty in both sexes, including menstruation in females and nocturnal emission
    in males
  Masturbation
  Intercourse
  Noncoital partner sexuality (petting, oral sex, etc.)
  Homosexuality
  Contraception
  Pregnancy
  Abortion
  Childbirth

Sociological Aspects of Intimate Relationships
Does the book reflect awareness of recent social changes in sexual attitudes and
  behavior?
Does the book stress emotional as well as physical aspects of sexual relationships?
Does the book deal equitably with the roles of males and females in sex?

Ethical/Moral Aspects of Intimate Relationships
Does the book discuss sex before marriage?
Is support offered to those who wish to abstain from sexual activity?
For the sexually active, does the book stress:
  —mutual consent?
  —caring and consideration for partner?
  —responsible contraception (via various methods, including abstinence and natural family planning) and STD prevention?

Problems in Sex
Does the book discuss
  —negative feelings about sex?
  —sexual exploitation (rape, harassment, incest, child sexual abuse)?
  —sexually transmitted diseases?

Amount and Kind of Information
Is the amount of basic sex information sufficient to make key concepts clear?
Does the book suggest further references and resources?

Reliability of Information
Is the basic sex information accurate?
Does the book show awareness of recent relevant changes in law and scientific
  knowledge?
Does the author have appropriate credentials?

Format and Readability
Do layout and design promote readability?
Is text clearly written?
Does the book use appropriate illustrations?
Is there a glossary?
Is there an index?

Style
Does the writing style establish audience rapport?
When possible, does the author use nonclinical terminology?
If humor or colloquialisms are used, is the inclusion effective?

people do something about it, but no one seems to have written about it."[16] A very good set of guidelines has been suggested for balancing a collection, which we quote in its entirety:

- As far as size will permit, there should be at least one informative work on every subject in which any patron has expressed interest, or in which interest would probably be generated by the presence of such a book in the library.

- For a public or academic library of *any* size, there should be at least one book on each side of a controversial issue. Budget constraints cannot justify a violation of this principle. For libraries with larger capacities, an attempt should be made to balance the sides.

- If only one book, or a limited number, can be afforded on a topic or position, the works acquired should be those which by the most reliable accounts are the best available, judged by representativeness, cogency of argument and quality of writing.

- The balance spoken of two paragraphs above need not mean arithmetic equality (six books on one side if six on the other), but may be qualified by such factors as usage, quality of writing or the academic curriculum.

- There is no basic difference in these principles as they apply to public or academic institutions, except for the curriculum in an academic, or demand in a public, library. In each case there must be at least a minimum of opportunity to explore any topic and each side of any controversy.[17]

We think that library collections should include many of the topics, viewpoints, and genres given in Chapter 4. As for redundancy, libraries obviously will want to consider overlap among books as a significant factor in evaluation. But sometimes books with a good deal of content overlap differ greatly in tone, style, and accessibility to different readers. Once again, one cannot apply strict criteria in knee-jerk fashion. We can imagine that the selection committee will try to pick the "best" of the lot when budgets are tight and reader interest lower.

Another type of balance is by format and mode of presentation. For any given sexuality topic, librarians may consider the following format variations: anthologies, collections of first person or reported stories/case reports, pro/con treatments, question/answer, and nonfiction presented through fiction (common in books for young people). When multiple books are bought on a topic, variety may be sought in presentations as well as in points of view.

CONCLUSIONS

Overall, we recommend some idealistic and some realistic approaches to building a library's sex collection. The philosophy of collecting should be idealistic and should try to represent a balance of the best. Practically, the major issues are avoiding censorship, overt and covert, and dealing with subtle bias by clarifying selection and evaluation criteria as explicitly as can be done. Library administrators need to support these efforts actively, and to appoint enthusiastic individuals to committees that can perform the selection and evaluation functions in ethical and professional ways. Moreover, the public needs to be informed what the library is doing and, above all, why. With good faith, the effort will be greatly repaid.

NOTES

1. What we call *philosophy*, *plan*, and *policy* are incorporated within the concept sometimes called a *materials selection program*. See the basic resource: Office of Intellectual Freedom, American Library Association, "Development of a Materials Selection Program," *Intellectual Freedom Manual*, 4th ed. (Chicago: ALA, 1992): 207–214. Another good resource is Phyllis J. Van Orden, *The Collection Program in Schools: Concepts, Practices, and Information Sources* (Englewood, CO: Libraries Unlimited, 1988), especially Chapter 6, "Policies and Procedures," and Chapter 7, "Developing Policy Statements."

2. Rightly or wrongly, some librarians seek as much "supporting evidence" as possible when contemplating purchase of controversial books, such as positive reviews *and* user demand. See Ann Curry, "*American Psycho*: A Collection Management Survey in Canadian Public Libraries," *Library & Information Science Research* 16.3 (Summer 1994): 201–217.

3. See Will Manley, "Pornography in the Library? No!" *Libraries, Erotica, & Pornography* (D115, Cornog): 92–98.

4. David Wallechinsky, Irving Wallace, & Amy Wallace, *The Book of Lists* (New York: Bantam, 1977): 340–341.

5. Other suggestions for core collections: Timothy Perper, "For Sex, See Librarian: Reprise," in *Libraries, Erotica, & Pornography* (D115, Cornog): 273–284.

6. We are aware that many more periodicals for librarians carry useful reviews and bibliographies, but we cannot list them all here.

7. To be fair, we have to admit that AIDS, homosexuality, and sexual exploitation are producing proportionately more books than the other categories.

8. We took counts for these categories from the 1991 edition also. Between 1991 and 1995, the number of libraries having special collections in every category increased, from a minimum of 3 additional libraries (for homosexuality and lesbi-

anism) to a maximum of 12 (for AIDS). The total of new libraries for all categories is 39—increasing from an overall total of 136 to 175. This shows an encouraging library response to the need for collecting on sexual issues.

9. Lois McMaster Bujold, *Ethan of Athos* (New York: Baen Books, 1986): 162.

10. One of us has corresponded with a Christian conservative librarian who favors materials on chastity in the library. I urged that person to join with other Christian conservatives in preparing annotated bibliographies to assist librarians in balancing collections. In a subsequent letter, my correspondent admitted having more time for letters to the editor and less for bibliography: "Would that I had more time for both." Exactly. Personally, we feel that solid, carefully prepared annotated bibliographies published and made widely available to librarians and educators have more potential for real social change than the flashy but short-lived scattershot of vituperative letters.

11. One of us (MC) got started in the study of sexuality in the 1970s by reviewing books about sexuality for *Library Journal*. I would like to thank Anneliese Schwarzer, Kyle Ahrold, and Francine Fialkoff, successive editors for *LJ*'s "The Book Review" section, for furthering my development as a writer about sex and librarianship.

12. The original checklist was compiled by William S. Palmer from a survey of "most recommended" sex education books and published as "Evolving Criteria for Evaluating Sex Education Books," *Voice of Youth Advocates* (April 1982): 23–24. It was modified and condensed slightly in *Sex Guides* (D111, Campbell): 326–327. Our Figure 5.1 further edits and modifies this list. Another, shorter, list of criteria is included in Dorothy Broderick, "Sex and Sexuality in Children's Books," in *Library Work with Children* (New York: H.W. Wilson, 1977): 47–61.

13. Jefferson Selth, *Ambition, Discrimination, and Censorship in Libraries* (Jefferson, NJ: McFarland, 1993): 106. Dorothy Broderick proposes waiving the requirement for quality of writing in cases of children's books presenting attitudes not presently represented in the collection, because such books are so rare. See her "Building a Library Collection," in *Library Work with Children*: 8.

14. *Sex Guides* (D111, Campbell): 325.

15. See John Swan & Noel Peattie, *The Freedom to Lie* (Jefferson, NJ: McFarland, 1989); Jefferson P. Selth, "Waiting in the Wings," in *Ambition, Discrimination, and Censorship in Libraries* (Jefferson, NJ: McFarland, 1993): 113–128; Will Manley, "Does Intellectual Freedom Give Libraries the Right to Lie?" *American Libraries* (October 1994): 880; John N. Berry, "Some Books Demand Rejection," *Library Journal* (February 1, 1995): 6.

16. Selth, "The Librarian as Censor," in *Ambition, Discrimination, and Censorship in Libraries* (Jefferson, NJ: McFarland, 1993): 105. Actually, some quite interesting recent literature discusses collection balance. A good theoretical discussion is Phyllis J. Van Orden's "Issues About Collections," in *The Collection Program in Schools*: 34–62. Two studies attempting to measure balance are Judith Serebnick & Frank Quinn, "Managing Diversity of Opinion in Public Library Collections," *Library Quarterly* 65.1 (January 1995): 1–38; and Dave Harmeyer, "Potential Collection Bias: Some Evidence on a Controversial Topic in California," *College & Research Libraries* (March 1995): 101–111, and following "commentaries": 113–118.

17. Selth, "The Librarian as Censor": 105–106.

6 Other Sexuality Materials: Vertical File Holdings, Periodicals, Literature, and Audiovisuals

So far, we have focused mainly on nonfiction books. Yet vertical file materials, periodicals, literature, and audiovisuals about sexuality are also important. Here we offer suggestions for developing these aspects of collections, and we regret the lack of space and time to cover them more fully.

VERTICAL FILE MATERIALS

An excellent way for librarians to improve their sexuality collections is to start with the vertical file. Acquiring materials is simpler and certainly less expensive. Items are probably less subject to censorship—although theft may be a problem. Because of small size and low cost, a goodly number and variety may be added, representing many points of view. Moreover, their brevity and conciseness may make them preferable to books for some readers.

Vertical file has been defined as "a collection of materials such as pamphlets, clippings, and pictures, which, because of their shape and often their ephemeral nature, are filed in drawers for easy reference."[1] For very useful basic reference about vertical file management, we encourage librarians to consult *The Vertical File and Its Alternatives: A Handbook*, by Clara L. Sitter (Englewood, CO: Libraries Unlimited, 1992), plus *Readings on the*

Vertical File, edited by Michael D.G. Spencer (Englewood, CO: Libraries Unlimited, 1993).

The vertical file represents a fine way for librarians to research and experiment with new topics not represented in the book collection, to complement books already in the collection, and to supplement an already good collection with timely materials. Compiling a vertical file collection about sex topics can be a good educational experience for librarians, who will then have learned enough about the issues to go on to improve their book collections in these areas. Here are a few suggestions for how to proceed.

One may first develop a list of key topics, including abortion, child sexual abuse/incest, contraception, erotica/pornography (the controversy), gay/lesbian, HIV/AIDS, rape, sexual harassment, STDs, and teen sexuality/abstinence. Topics drawn from patron requests, circulation patterns, local controversies, newspaper headlines, and deficiencies in the collection should then be added.

The next step is to identify local and national sources for brochures, fact sheets, and other vertical file items on sexuality topics of interest—a good project for an alert and curious library intern, volunteer, or student from a nearby library school or social science college program.

1. For local sources, consult the Blue Pages in the telephone directory. Look under Sex Related Concerns, and also under Abuse-Assault (for rape), Health—Diseases and Disorders (for HIV/AIDS), Health—Family Planning, Health—Pregnancy and Pregnancy-Related Problems (for pro-choice and pro-life), and Self-Help Groups (may include gay/lesbian, sexual addiction, incest survivors, etc.).

2. For national sources, go through the *Encyclopedia of Associations* (*EoA*). Literally hundreds of groups have some sexual focus. Note, however, that many organizations with positions and materials on sexual issues do not have sex-related names. One must read the descriptive blurbs, particularly for what the *EoA* calls "conservative traditionalist" organizations like the Christian Coalition. (See also "families" and "conservative" categories.)

3. From both local and national sources, choose a group of organizations and build up a mailing list on computer or reproducible labels. As the Blue Pages does not have addresses for local organizations, you will need to get them from the telephone directory White Pages and the Zip Code directory. The list should reflect diverse viewpoints.

4. Create a letter stating that the library is collecting materials representing many viewpoints on topics X, Y, and Z. Then ask for general information and a catalog of items available, with samples, if possible. Send the letter to those on your list and wait. If the subject matter is especially important, a more personalized letter may establish an especially productive relationship.

This method will yield a true embarrassment of riches over two to six weeks. Not all materials will be worth keeping, of course, and a few organizations may not respond. When you find particularly valuable items, you can order multiple copies. To keep material current, you should probably resend a request to those on your (continuously updated) list every year or so. We gathered much information for this book using this technique, and, in our experience, nearly all associations are quite willing to provide information and materials.

A shortcut may be taken by first referring to two other works that list organizations and publishers of sex-related vertical file–type materials:

Free or Inexpensive Sources for Sex, Health & Family Education (D113, Charlton): Sources of materials ideal for vertical files, listed by topic, *abortion* to *teens—life planning*. Many items are free; most are under $10.

A Research Guide to Human Sexuality (D120, Lichtenberg): Chapter 30, over 100 pages, lists organizational sources of sexuality information, arranged by topic. Entries indicate whether an organization provides bibliographies, directories, publications, or statistics.

However, neither lists much in the way of conservative or religious sources. Note that many of the organizations, catalog suppliers, and publishers listed in Chapter 5 and Part II of this book have materials quite suitable for the vertical file: brochures, pamphlets, fact sheets, statistics, posters, reports.

A kind of hybrid between book and vertical file item is the "instant reference book," created by compiling key vertical file items on a topic and binding them in-house. The subsequent "book" may be shelved in the reference section or in the stacks, or placed on reserve.[2] Materials thus treated are easier to use, being all together, and more difficult to steal. We suggest that more than one copy be made of such "books," allowing both reference and circulation use.

PERIODICALS

With periodicals, we reach increasingly controversial areas of library collecting. To begin, there are serious professional periodicals about sexuality that correspond more or less to the scientific-medical genre for books (see Chapter 4). Other genres of sexuality writing also have flowerings in periodicals. These range from *Playboy*'s vanilla images of heterosexual nudity through highly specialized, small circulation magazines like *The American Matriarch* and *Hermaphrodites with Attitudes*. This diversity is as recent a phenomenon as the diversification of book titles.[3] No longer is it a matter of *Reader's Digest* and *National Geographic* versus, say, *Spicy Detective Stories*. Those were the divisions of the bygone 1950s and offer no clues about the diversity of the 1990s—and beyond. Yet old categories die hard.

> Sex sells magazines of any nature, including *Sports Illustrated*, but the inclusion of topics other than sex ultimately must be the criterion used to judge the real value of a magazine for library use.[4]

You may by now guess that we do not fully agree with this quotation. If inclusion of "topics other than sex" is a criterion for magazines, then it is also a criterion for books, and the librarian we just quoted would de facto deny a place in the library to the Kinsey reports, Dr. Ruth, or indeed any of the works cited in Part II of this book. And perhaps he *would* exclude such works. But we cannot agree that sex has no "real" value.

Perhaps the author meant not "sex" exactly, but pictures of naked women in magazines like *Playboy* and *Penthouse*—the "skin magazines." But here we encounter a genuinely modern paradox about the "value" and "quality" of sexual depictions. By today, widely applied standards exist for defining excellence of quality for pictures of naked women—and men—and even for images of people sexually involved. For example, the photography in *Playboy* is of the highest quality in composition, coloring, balance, and related criteria of professional photography. The erotic cinematography of Laird Sutton's oeuvre is of the highest technical, sexological, and emotional quality—and value, as *A Ripple of Time* and *Going Down to Bimini* display.[5]

Are such considerations what this commentator meant by "real" value? Obviously not: he meant that the mere *presence* of sex, if unaccompanied by other features, is by itself a reason to reject a magazine. To which we ask: why?

Part of the answer is ignorance of modern styles of sexual depiction: if one has not seen *A Ripple of Time*, one could unknowingly imagine a 1950s style nudie flick. Yet, below the trivial answer "I never heard of it" is something deeper. Indeed, only two answers are traditionally offered to justify this critic's view. One is to say that sexual depictions are bad, period, no further discussion. Of course this is not an argument but an imitation of a parent talking to a child. So we can eliminate that answer as no argument at all.

The other answer bedecks sexuality and its images with an enormous array of ancillary, auxiliary, and additional evils, wrongs, and sinfulnesses. But what happens when people refuse to so burden sexuality and simply do not agree? In the past two decades, an immense number of writers and publishers in fact have *not* agreed that sex is wrong. Whether or not one laments this change, it is the basic approach to sexuality publishing in modern America. And—this is the crux—*therefore* selection of library magazines cannot be made solely on whether or not sexual or erotic graphics are included, just as the quality of art and photography books obviously would not be judged solely on whether or not they contain nudes or depictions of sex (see The Arts and the Media section in Chapter 12).

In today's magazine world, sex is not merely *Sports Illustrated* swimsuits. Instead, as sexuality becomes integrated more and more openly into American life, so too the mass-market magazines have come to deal with it differently: not as pinup window-dressing for heterosexual young men but as a matter of interest to all readers, men and women. No longer do we have the 1950s division between sex magazines and the clean stuff. So, genuinely sexual material beyond pinup photo-pix is in most libraries already—in *Time, Glamour, Rolling Stone*, and many others. The range is far greater today.

Even so, two major types of primarily sex-related periodicals do exist: popular/recreational and scholarly. We deal with each in turn.

Popular/Recreational Periodicals

One of us (MC) collected survey data on *Playboy* in the library, finding that not many libraries subscribed to *Playboy* and that subscribing libraries varied in how much they welcomed the magazine.[6] These doubts are understandable given anti-sexual library philosophies and given public doubts about erotica/pornography. While we respect such doubts, nonetheless strong reasons exist why libraries ought to subscribe to wide readership magazines like *Playboy*.

One is the sheer popularity of periodicals that, like *Playboy*, mix politics, fashion, and sexuality into a distinctly post-Comstockian recipe—*Playboy*'s coverage of sex-related legal and censorship issues is unparalleled in any mass magazine. *Playboy* and possibly *Penthouse*[7] are currently the highest quality mass-market general interest heterosexual sex magazines with informative nonfiction—mixed in with those naked women. *Playgirl* is much less substantial, although worthy of consideration.

But the playing field contains more than just the glossy, high circulation periodicals. A number of newer, smaller, and mostly recreational sex magazines offer a more or less broad variety of sex-related nonfiction, plus stories, poems, and graphics. For example:

Eidos—"Sexual freedom tabloid of erotic entertainment . . . for all sexual orientations and lifestyles"; many reviews of publications and products, plus swingers' ads.

Frighten the Horses—For all persuasions; "a document of the sexual revolution." A British woman is supposed to have said that she didn't object to sex so long as people didn't do it in the streets and frighten the horses.

Future Sex—Hard-edged, mostly heterosexual techno-sex, with intrusive explicit ads.

Journal of Erotica—Fiction and photographs, beautifully produced; British. (Recently ceased publication, but back issues worth acquiring.)

Libido—All persuasions; "the journal of sex and sensibility."

Taste of Latex—Gender-bending, post-punk magazine, "erotica with a rock and roll attitude."

Yellow Silk—"Journal of the erotic arts, all persuasions, no brutality."

Many are edited largely by women—Lisa Palac of *Future Sex*, Lily Burana of *Taste of Latex*, Lily Pond of *Yellow Silk*, and Mariana Beck of *Libido*—and are published for audiences far broader than merely heterosexual males. Probably the best for libraries are *Journal of Erotica*, *Libido*, and *Yellow Silk*: they have the best writing and high production values as well as being tastefully intellectual and aesthetic. The others, while fascinating, make *Playboy* look pretty tame in topics, viewpoints, advertisements, and graphics. *Eros* from the 1960s was an excellent, beautifully produced magazine and rather restrained by today's standards, but is now a collector's item.

Unfortunately, there is no lively and substantial (hetero)sexual equivalent of *Atlantic Monthly*, *American Health*, or *Reader's Digest*. Someone really ought to publish a nonfiction sexuality magazine at about the level and style of *Time* or *Prevention*. Articles could cover legal developments, sex research, and reports from experts, plus a question/answer column and graphics of the quality of Time-Life books. But, alas, there is no such thing. (We have heard that Penthouse's *Forum* will take an approach of this sort, starting in December 1995.)

Popular/Recreational Periodicals—Gay and Lesbian Division

The situation with gay and lesbian periodicals is completely different: the gay and lesbian communities have some good, informative general interest magazines, with mostly nonfiction:

The Advocate—"The national gay and lesbian news magazine" comparable to *Time* or *Newsweek*; started in 1967 and one of the most widely read.

BLK—Magazine for the African American lesbian and gay community.

Curve (formerly Deneuve)—"The lesbian magazine," general interest.

Out—General interest: arts, books, entertainment, people, travel.

10 Percent—General interest; similar to *Out*.

Lesbian sexuality, including fiction and graphics, is emphasized in:

Black Lace—Magazine of erotica by and for African American lesbians.

On Our Backs—Magazine of "entertainment for the adventurous lesbian." The title refers not only to the sexual position but more pointedly is a jab at the feminist periodical *Off Our Backs*.

These are only some of the most prominent gay periodicals. There are many others, with literary, commentary, erotic, and other emphases. Gay newspapers are a separate category, and all public libraries should carry the local gay newspaper if one exists. Larger public libraries should add the *Washington Blade*.

There are also hundreds of magazines and newsletters, zine-like and not, from and about special interest groups, some heavy on nonfiction, some on erotica. Those of wider interest include:

Anything that Moves—"The magazine for the discriminating bisexual," from the Bay Area Bisexual Network.

Diseased Pariah News—By and for people with HIV/AIDS; black humor, no holds barred.

It's Okay!—On "sexuality, sex, self-esteem, and disability."

POZ—Well-produced magazine "about life with HIV for people whose lives have been affected by AIDS." "POZ" is shortening of *positive*, as in HIV-positive. One of *Library Journal*'s "best magazines of 1994."

The Sandmutopia Guardian—"The Farmer's Almanac of S&M."

Sex over Forty—Newsletter about enhancement, dysfunctions, and other sexological news. Medical/scientific, but for laypeople.

The transgendered community has numerous periodicals, some mentioned in the Transgenderism section, Part II, and most listed in the *1994 Who's Who & Resource Guide to the International Transgendered Community* (B87, Roberts). Range is from general interest such as *TV/TS Tapestry Journal* to specialized, such as *Grace and Lace Letter*, a newsletter for "Christian crossdressers, transgenderists, and transsexuals."

Then there are zines. *Factsheet 5*, the *Ulrich's* of zines, defines *zine* as "a small handmade amateur publication done purely out of passion, rarely making a profit or breaking even." However, *Frighten the Horses*, *Taste of Latex*, and other nicely produced publications named above are often included in lists of sex zines. So we are not sure at what point a periodical stops being a zine. Librarians interested in sex zines should check out the Queer, Grrlz, and Sex sections of *Factsheet 5* for several issues back, as listings are not cumulative. We have seen one conservative sex zine: *VIP: Virgin Pride*, "uniting the virgin community" (P.O. Box 433, Norwalk CT 06851-0433).

Scholarly Periodicals

Scholarly sex periodicals will be mostly the domain of academic libraries. They include:

AIDS Education and Prevention

Annals of Sex Research

Archives of Sexual Behavior

Family Life Educator

Family Planning Perspectives

GLQ: A Journal of Gay and Lesbian Studies

Journal of Gay and Lesbian Psychotherapy

Journal of Homosexuality

Journal of Psychology and Human Sexuality

Journal of Sex and Marital Therapy

Journal of Sex Education and Therapy

Journal of Sex Research

Journal of Social Work and Human Sexuality

Journal of the History of Sexuality

Maledicta (language)

Paidika: The Journal of Paedophilia

Sex Roles

Sexual Addiction and Compulsivity

Sexual and Marital Therapy

Sexuality and Disability

SIECCAN Journal—from the Sex Information and Education Council of Canada

SIECUS Report

All carry research articles and reviews; some report on news and events.

Other specialized periodicals deal with sexuality in ways that do not quite fit the definition of either popular or scholarly. For example, *The Human Life Quarterly* is a serious, somewhat literary periodical on pro-life issues. Furthermore, every conceivable type of sex-related organization has a newsletter.

Periodical Selection

It is not easy to compile lists of general or heterosexual sexuality periodicals, whether popular or scholarly. The *Ulrich's*-type directories are virtually useless because the entries are scattered among non-sex headings such as LITERATURE, MEN'S INTERESTS, and PSYCHOLOGY; moreover, the indexing is inadequate for sexuality topics. Some popular/recreational items are included in *Factsheet 5*, others in the catalog of Desert Moon Periodicals/Xines, Inc. (1226 A Calle de Comercio, Santa Fe, NM 87505). *Utne Reader* occasionally publishes lists (see July/August 1993: 72). SIE-

CUS issues an annotated bibliography, Sexuality Periodicals for Professionals.

The periodical directories give better treatment to gay/lesbian periodicals, often via separate sections. Other sources of titles include *Gay and Lesbian Library Service* (D118, Gough & Greenblatt) and *Gayellow Pages* (B7). One can also browse in gay bookstores.

Most of the scholarly sex journals are covered by Sociological Abstracts, PsycINFO, and the like. But as Sanford Berman noted in 1981, there is no "sex index,"[8] and almost no popular titles except *Playboy* are indexed anywhere. This has also been the case for gay and lesbian periodicals until recently. Since at least 1990, gay and lesbian librarians have urged H.W. Wilson to include the *Advocate* and other popular gay magazines in *The Reader's Guide to Periodical Literature*, but without success.[9] However, other indexing companies have begun to cover the gay and lesbian press, including the Alternative Press Center, Gale Research, Information Access Company, and University Microfilms.

Still, while *Alternative Press Index* includes *Off Our Backs*, no one indexes *On Our Backs* or *Libido*—let alone such unlibrarianly documents of current culture as *Hustler* and *Screw*. The result can be self-fulfilling, de facto censorship: because it's not indexed, we never heard of it and we won't carry it.

Yet a startlingly wide range of materials does exist, despite inadequate coverage by indexing and reference tools. Having examined issues of all the popular periodicals listed above, we can authoritatively tell you that these are nicely composed and printed, and competently written, proofread, and edited. While some zines may be stapled-together, flaked-out ephemera run off on a borrowed mimeograph, this is not true for the sexuality periodicals described here. They are serious and significant products of a new view of sexuality in America.

LITERATURE

Though the climate for sexual experimentation has chilled since the advent of AIDS, . . . there is a growing readership for . . . boudoir *laissez-faire*. At one of New York's largest erotic emporiums, Come Again Bookstore, owner Helen Wolff reports no letup in the public's appetite for sexual material. "Erotic literature has gone through the roof since AIDS," she says.[10]

Few of us will ever murder someone, travel to Mars, punch cows on the open range, or satisfy a dozen strangers at an orgy; but we can live these experiences vicariously. Obviously one of the attractions of fiction is that it enables us to experience vicariously a thousand lives we wouldn't have the courage, time, or inclination for in reality; erotic fiction dramatically increases the number of vicarious experiences available to us.[11]

The AIDS catastrophe and vicarious living are only two facets of a remarkable and complex upwelling of erotic and sexualized fiction.[12] Characteristically, the mainstream media present these changes only in a single context of "pornography" versus "erotica." But other factors are more significant, if harder to reduce to sound bites.

For librarianship, these issues center on hitherto unthought-of complications in what once were simple matters. As social mores have changed increasingly rapidly since the 1950s, erotic fiction has emerged from pulp towards the mainstream, attracting mass-market publishers, durable binding, shelf space in chain bookstores, and even reviews. At least four types of sexual literature now may be distinguished, each with a potential place in the library:

- Works that have given rise to major obscenity trials and censorship efforts, such as Henry Miller's *Tropic of Cancer*.
- Older and classic works, such as Balzac's *Droll Stories*, Aristophanes' *Lysistrata*, or the writings of Pierre Louÿs.
- Modern fiction of various persuasions, some of it mainstream, including genre fiction, such as works of Jean Genet, William Burroughs, Marco Vassi, and many others.
- Materials from cultures other than the Eurocentric West, such as "The Arabian Nights" and *Chin P'ing Mei*.

But there is also a fifth category: pulp sex fiction. We have a hunch that many librarians think this is the *only* category of sexual literature, and might have been surprised by the preceding four. Indeed, many people associate sexual fiction solely with the likes of *Sex Slaves of the Astro-mutants* or *Hot Nurses in Chains*. However, we will not stress this category of pulp pornography, not from sudden anti-sexual prudery, but for reasons embedded in library actualities. We will explain briefly.

For the moment, set aside the perhaps shocking titles in category five and imagine them as simply a form of genre fiction. Should a library acquire these pulp titles? Some libraries must—the archival and special collections in sexual culture. But with budgets and shelf space being finite, most libraries can probably omit the pulp sex genre.

Now, libraries do buy genre fiction—westerns, romances, gothics, and science fiction—but they usually buy the highest quality and best reviewed of the lot. The first four categories of sexual literature assuredly meet those criteria, but most pulp sex fiction is of poor quality, never reviewed, and ephemeral; as with other genre fiction, much sex fiction is read once and never again. So, utterly regardless of "moral" issues, pulp sex fiction books

pose the identical questions of genre fiction in general: many are poor quality, high-turnover, low-endurance materials with an audience as voracious
in its appetite for them as the fans of westerns, romances, gothics, and
science fiction are for the absolutely newest book by their favorite hack
writer. A case can be made for keeping all such titles to a minimum on
purely practical, collection management bases. Accordingly, it makes reasonable sense to put this fifth category into abeyance for most libraries and
to focus on the first four. When a given pulp title achieves some modest
recognition for originality, characterization, or writing, then it can be considered to move up into the "modern sexual fiction" category.

The Erotica/Pornography Controversy

Even for the four categories of sexual literature, many librarians and
citizens will raise questions and doubts about erotica-pornography-decency
controversies. These pose a subtle challenge to the library, not so much
about collecting sexual fiction, but about definitions.

If by consensus or otherwise, everyone agrees that the library should not
collect "pornography" because it is sexist, offensive, or for other reasons,
opponents of general sexuality materials will be quick to assign *all* titles
they do not like to the proscribed category. Thus the opponents of *The Joy
of Sex* will assert that it "really is pornography," hoping to prevent its
purchase. It makes no difference whatever what the proscribed category is:
if books with purple covers were proscribed, then opponents of sexuality
collecting would say that sex books "really" have purple covers, no matter
what the color seems to be.

Although this definitional maneuver may represent heartfelt anxiety and
moral opposition to a detested genre, it nonetheless so weakens labels like
"pornography" or "sexist" that they become empty phrases. They end up
meaning nothing more specific than "bad and ugly," thereby reducing the
debate to personal taste that makes vacuous whatever "pornography" or
"sexism" once meant. By widening the net to include Henry Miller, Pierre
Louÿs, or Jean Genet, the risk is diluting differences between them and the
hack authors of pulp.

We might seem to be castigating unfairly people who deeply believe that
the works of Miller, Louÿs, Genet, and others are genuinely pornographic
or sexist. Not so: instead, we suggest that these accusations have today
become so general and vague as to be meaningless, and therefore of little
use in selecting or rejecting a title. When the accusation of "Pornography!"
is made, it is best recorded merely as opposition in *general*, rather than as
representing a *specific* objection to titles thus labeled.

A related issue arises next. Characteristically, individuals who use labels
like "pornographic" or "sexist" as generic terms of condemnation will simultaneously assert that "most people" see it the same way. A psycholog-

ical mechanism must be understood here: all people with strong moral views and anxieties want very much to believe that they are not alone in thinking that the world is awash in sexually terrible material.

Such a person might gently be asked what titles *are* acceptable, but the answer may be too easily cast in negatives to be useful in practice. Thus, he or she replies that "decent works" are acceptable, but cannot name any, or can point only to a few works of sexual morality published under denominational auspices. Excellent! Those are titles to consider purchasing— but their purchase cannot be used as an excuse to reject other works.

The moralist who uses generic labels might retort with a version of the Good Books Ethos, asserting that *only* the best should be shelved, and meaning that the moralist alone is capable of selecting best and proper titles. Against such exclusionary approaches, the inclusionary philosophy we have been stressing comes to the fore: purchase *representative titles of all views, all genres, and all visions*, not merely those acceptable to moralists of whatever kind. The ethical answer to exclusionists is "Yes, we will stock titles you recommend, but we will stock those you oppose as well." In this, no individual—and no single generic vision—has the final say about what is and is not acquired.

Some Practical Observations About the First Four Categories

For many, especially larger libraries, a well-chosen collection of sexual literature may be appreciated by some patrons, although not by all—nor by librarians either! So, be forewarned that these works may elicit challenges. And for those tempted to challenge, does one need lengthy apologia for including sexual literature of the first four categories? Well, no. Most public libraries already have some sexual literature. Moreover, sexual literature may be evaluated with the same standards as other literature and nonfiction: quality of writing and making sense. In addition, sexual/erotic literature is among the oldest genres of writing, including as authors Catullus, Chaucer, Boccaccio, Mark Twain, Benjamin Franklin, Aphra Behn, ancient Chinese scholars, and traditional Indian erotologists. The genre has attained notoriety because it has so often been censored and condemned while nonetheless remaining extraordinarily popular.

We recommend a collection philosophy that does not from the start rule out sexual fiction. Yet some specific issues need to be addressed when deciding what to include. In particular, much sexual fiction does pose a problem for lack of reviews. Michael Perkins comments wryly:

Erotic literature possesses a raw, innocent power which general literature has lost for many readers. . . . There is an audience for this kind of writing, perhaps larger than that for science fiction and mystery stories, but unfortunately few critics . . . are willing to guide readers to a deeper understanding of it. There have been some critical studies devoted to those erotic classics which have survived the centuries, but modern erotic literature, by which I mean a large number of books written from a sexual perspective and published in Europe and America in this century, has been met with silence by critics and reviewers.

An important result of this neglect of erotic literature has been that the constructive processes of public appraisal and literary criticism have not been available to it. Erotic writing is therefore peculiarly virginal, for in the absence of these reactions there are no standards by which its real achievements can be measured."[13]

Only the passage of time will remedy the problem of evaluating more recent sexual fiction. But the issues are somewhat clearer for the other categories, as we shall see as we examine each in more detail.

Subjects of Major Obscenity Trials and Censorship Efforts

We think that all public libraries should have these books because they occupy a prominent place in the history of censorship, of books, of reading, and of libraries themselves. Lack of reviews is not a problem as these works are all well known and have inspired pro and con treatments many times their own length. A core list could include:

The Decameron, by Giovanni Boccaccio

Jurgen, by James Branch Cabell

Justine, or the Misfortunes of Virtue, by the Marquis de Sade (his name gave us the term *sadism*)

Lady Chatterley's Lover, by D.H. Lawrence

Madame Bovary, by Gustave Flaubert

The Memoirs of a Woman of Pleasure ("Fanny Hill"), by John Cleland

My Secret Life[14]

Tropic of Cancer, by Henry Miller

Ulysses, by James Joyce (strictly speaking not sexual fiction, but impetus to one of the great censorship trials)

To expand this list, sources on the history of censorship may be consulted, such as *The Encyclopedia of Censorship*[15] or *The Secret Museum* (D11, Kendrick).

Other Older and Classic Works

The second category includes a rich variety of fascinating material from the 1st century C.E. to the 19th century, often humorous and often overlooked by modern readers. These works too—or at least their authors—are well known and have stood the test of time. Suggestions for purchase:

The Canterbury Tales, by Geoffrey Chaucer

The Complete Poems of John Wilmot, Earl of Rochester (Yale University Press, 1968)

Droll Stories, by Honoré de Balzac

Fart Proudly: Writings of Benjamin Franklin You Never Read in School, edited by Carl Japiksi (Enthea Press, 1990)

Lysistrata, by Aristophanes

"Mammoth Cod," "1601," and "The Stomach Club: Some Remarks on the Science of Onanism," by Mark Twain

The Memoirs of Jacques Casanova de Seingalt

The Poems of Catullus

Venus in Furs, by Leopold von Sacher-Masoch (his name gave us the term *masochism*)

A good reference for expanding this list is *Erotic Literature: A Connoisseur's Guide* (D15, McCormick).

Modern Sexual Literature

Modern sexual literature dates from roughly 1930 and has been expanding ever since. We suspect that several processes have been at work in its emergence.

The genre has been condemned by "decent" and "proper" society for many centuries, forcing it to become an underground enterprise tainted with "lower-class" corruption—which of course has been part of its appeal.[16] With the advent of mass publication from the late 19th century, huge quantities of cheaply produced and poorly written materials were generated on virtually anything that would sell, from vampire novels to sexual fiction. Partly because of official suppression, authors, publishers, and printers worked quickly, surreptitiously, and with what time and talent was available. So the world was flooded with junk erotica. Some of sexual literature's shoddy image has been well deserved.

Yet there has always been a market for sexual literature, and readers have been willing to buy whatever was available—even of dubious quality and outside mainstream channels. It is a testimony to how much sexual literature must have been produced in the past that some works have survived with enduring quality and appeal for hundreds of years. However, as production standards changed in the past two decades or so, the faces of sexual fiction have also changed. Writing quality—always the first criterion in reviewing—has moved sharply upwards, as have printing and binding.

One example will do for all: the writing of Piers Anthony, an immensely popular modern fantasy/science fiction author. Among his best known works are the Xanth novels, set in a magical kingdom of sorcerers, spells, centaurs, and man-eating trees located on a peninsula remarkably similar to Florida and immediately south of the bourgeois and boring country of Mundania. Often his heroes and heroines are children, but Xanth is no innocent Land of Oz. One novel describes a marriage of centaurs that is recognized officially only when the loving couple consummates the union, much to the guests' enthusiastic good cheer. The Xanth novels constantly play with sexual themes and episodes without ever becoming explicit. Anthony also wrote short stories dealing explicitly with sexuality, collected under the title *Pornocopia*. In no way can his work be assimilated to the older, pulp-porn tradition. It's a new world, folks.

Time has not yet had the chance to serve as de facto reviewer for these books. Yet distinctions can be made, and we found useful Michael Perkins' categorization scheme for modern sexual literature as a pyramid with three horizontal slices. The broad base is the mass of unimaginative and minimally skilled formula fiction—the stuff one associates with the bottom tier of bus station book racks and the pulp porn of category five. The middle group of novels, "although written to formula, are examples of writers working to the limit of their abilities."[17] The point of the pyramid belongs to work demonstrating not only superior ability of the novelist but the fertility of the genre when so handled.

Top Level Modern Sexual Fiction. Modern works of sexual literature that have received national prominence and might be considered at or near the pyramid's top include:

Candy, by Terry Southern and Mason Hoffenberg

Fear of Flying, by Erica Jong

Little Birds and *Delta of Venus*, by Anaïs Nin

Lolita, by Vladimir Nabokov

Oh, Calcutta! by Kenneth Tynan

Our Lady of the Flowers and other works, by Jean Genet

Portnoy's Complaint, by Philip Roth

Story of O, by "Pauline Réage" (Dominique Aury)

Tropic of Capricorn and other works, by Henry Miller

Vox, by Nicholson Baker

Middle Level Modern Sexual Fiction. We add a short list of other writers of popular sexual fiction, these more in the middle of the pyramid—and our thanks to Hollis Compton, writer and critic, for helping us with this list. Many of the following are described in the catalogs of Masquerade Books or Blue Moon Books and some in *The Secret Record* (D20, Perkins).

Olympia Press Authors (1950s)

Van Cardui—*Coral Lips Smiling at You* features a Vietnam vet put to work satisfying the women patients of a mad scientist.

"Akbar del Piombo" (Norman Rubinston)—Aristocratic rogues, erotic satire.

Alexander Trocchi—Best known works include *White Thighs* and *Helen and Desire*; passion, sex, melodrama, and madness.

Grove Press Authors (1960s–70s)

"Emmanuel Ansan" (Maryat Rollet-Andriane)—Best known title is *Emmanuelle*, made into an X-rated film of the same name; lush and philosophical sensuality.

Jean de Berg—Best known work is *The Image*, well-crafted story of dominance and submission in the tradition of *Story of O*; made into an X-rated film, *The Punishment of Anne*.

Marcus Van Heller—Historical novels of sexual decadence and corruption.

Blue Moon Books (1980s–90s)

John Barcelett—Best known work is *The Captive*: dominance, submission, and a white slavery ring.

Maria Madison (a.k.a. Rachel Longford)—Modern-day dominance and spanking.

David Redshaw—Victorian "maiden punishment" themes, set in modern times.

Don Winslow—The *Ironwood* novels; sexuality and innocence, power and submission.

Masquerade Books (1980s–90s)

Jocelyn Joyce—Flamboyant, orgiastic romps with strong female leads.

Paul Little—Historical S&M and dominance and submission.

Marco Vassi—Known for his pansexual "metasex" and considered by publisher Maurice Girodias a successor to Henry Miller.[18]

Subgenres of Modern Sexual Literature. Several modern subgenres have expanded in recent years: women-written heterosexual, women-written lesbian, and gay male (interestingly, some also written by women). These have always existed, but not in the quantity now available. Prominent authors/anthologists include:

Susie Bright—the "Herotica" and "Best American Erotica" anthologies

Pat Califia—lesbian, some S&M

John Preston—gay male, some S&M, including the "Flesh and the Word" anthologies

Anne Rice—"A.N. Roquelaure," vampire stories, some S&M

Michele Slung—women-written erotica.

Gay and lesbian fiction of all types has greatly proliferated: gay and lesbian science fiction, mysteries, westerns, gothics, and so on. Not all of these could be called sexual literature. Interestingly, the gay/lesbian mystery is beginning to cross over to straight readers. Said one bookseller, "One of my older women customers told me recently that she enjoys reading lesbian and gay mysteries because they teach her about a way of life she didn't know much about."[19]

A subgenre unto themselves are Robert Rimmer's utopian sexuality novels. A classic, *The Harrad Experiment* belongs in all public libraries, especially since it includes an annotated bibliography on sexuality, relationships, and values (25th anniversary edition, Prometheus, 1990). Other titles include *The Rebellion of Yale Marratt, Proposition 31*, and *Thursday, My Love*.

Another growing subgenre is science fiction/fantasy with sexual themes. Anthologies include *Alien Sex*, edited by Ellen Datlow and others (NAL/Dutton, 1992), *Pornocopia*, by Piers Anthony (Tafford Publishing, 1989), *Technosex* and *Worlds of Women*, edited by Cecilia Tan (Circlet Press, both 1993), *Worlds Apart: An Anthology of Lesbian and Gay Science Fiction and Fantasy*, edited by Camille Decarnin and others (Alyson, 1986), *Love in Vein*, edited by Poppy Z. Brite (Harper, 1994), and *Daughters of Darkness: Lesbian Vampire Stories*, edited by Pam Keesey (Cleis, 1993).

We must not neglect romance novels, many of which have strong erotic content. *The Romance Revolution* (D29, Thurston) is a good beginner's guide. *Library Journal* has started reviewing romance novels—see columns in the May 15, August, and November 15 issues. Manderley (P.O. Box 880, Boonville, CA 95415) is a romance fiction catalog giving plot summaries, but it does not indicate erotic content except by broad category in the table of contents.

Cross-Cultural Materials

Cross-cultural materials are the hardest to identify because most are not in print and not translated. An old standby is *The Book of the Thousand Nights and One Night*—the "Arabian Nights."[20] Only some of the tales have sexual content; all have surprising plot twists, treacherous folk of all sorts, and a distinct sense of the exotic "other."

The most celebrated and perhaps longest Chinese sex novel—*Chin P'ing Mei*—was reportedly being retranslated into English.[21] Several previous translations have been done of this fascinating and panoramic work of passion and vengeance, but all seem to be out of print. Currently available and suggested are *The Carnal Prayer Mat*, written in the 1600s by Li Yu (Blue Moon Books, 1994), and *The Fragrant Flower: Classic Chinese Erotica in Art and Poetry*, by Hua Ying Jin Zhen (Prometheus, 1990). Recently written and published is *Pleasure in the Word: Erotic Writing by Latin American Women*, edited by Lizabeth Paravisini Gebert and Margarite Fernández-Olmos (White Pine Press, 1993).

Several years ago, one of us came across a charming and unlikely collection, *Sex Songs of the Ancient Letts*, translated by Bud Berzing (University Books, 1969). Clearly some sexual literature from other cultures *is* in print, but one seems to find it only accidentally.

How to Begin: Anthologies and Onwards

Librarians wanting to venture cautiously into collecting sexual literature may start with anthologies. Indeed, anthologies are popping up in profusion from large and small publishers. Some suggestions:

An Anthology of Classic Anonymous Erotic Writing, edited by Michael Perkins (Rhinoceros/Masquerade, 1993)

Banned: Classical Erotica, edited by Victor Gulotta & Brandon Toropov (Bob Adams, 1991)

Best American Erotica 1993 and *Best American Erotica 1994*, edited by Susie Bright (Collier, 1993; Touchstone/Simon & Schuster, 1994)

The Best of the Badboys, edited by Michael Lowenthal (Richard Kasak/Masquerade, 1995)

The Erotic Edge: Erotica for Couples, edited by Lonnie Barbach (NAL/Dutton, 1994)

Erotic Literature: Twenty-Four Centuries of Sensual Writing, edited by Jane Mills (Harper Collins, 1993)

Erotique Noire/Black Erotica, edited by Miriam Decosta-Willis, Reginald Martin, & Roseann Bell (Doubleday, 1992)

The Faber Book of Blue Verse, edited by John Whitworth (Faber & Faber, 1990)

Flesh and the Word 1 and *Flesh and the Word 2*, edited by John Preston (Plume, 1992, 1993)

Games of Venus: An Anthology of Greek and Roman Erotic Verse from Sappho to Ovid, edited by Peter Bing and Rip Cohen (Routledge, 1991)

The Gates of Paradise: Erotic Short Fiction, edited by Alberto Manguel (Clarkson Potter, 1992)

Herotica, *Herotica 2*, and *Herotica 3*, edited by Susie Bright (Down There Press, 1988; Plume/NAL-Dutton, 1992 [with Joani Blank]; Plume/NAL-Dutton, 1994)

The Literary Companion to Sex: An Anthology of Prose and Poetry, edited by Fiona Pitt-Kethley (Random, 1993)

The Olympia Reader and *The New Olympia Reader*, edited by Maurice Girodias (Blue Moon Books, 1993 repr.)

An anthology of quite a different stripe is *Bad Sex*, edited by John Hoyland (Serpent's Tail, 1993): "tales . . . of misunderstandings and misadventures; tales of people being used, or denied passion; tales of collisions between fantasy and reality. . . . [T]hese are stories to be enjoyed—partly because many are funny, partly because many are brave, partly because they tell us much about people that a book about good sex, for example, might well miss" (p. 2).

Where to Obtain Sexual Literature. Major publishers of sexual literature include Blue Moon Books, Carroll & Graf, Grove Press, and Masquerade Books. New arrival Circlet Press specializes in erotic science fiction/fantasy. Many other publishers offer titles; a scan of our local bookstore's "erotica" shelf yielded Ballantine, Clarkson Potter, Dutton, Harper, Plume, Random House, and Routledge.

Reviews and annotations of these materials *are* available. Some of the newer anthologies are covered by *Publishers Weekly* and *Library Journal.* The Sexuality Library catalog is a particularly good source of women-written work, both lesbian and heterosexual (see Chapter 5). New and classic gay and lesbian sexual literature is highlighted in the free *Lambda Rising News*, plus the other gay/lesbian sources noted in Chapter 10. Paradoxically, it is most difficult to locate lists and reviews of male-oriented heterosexual fiction—the standby of the genre for centuries. Blurbs in publishers' catalogs are often the only guides to current titles, although *The Secret Record* (D20, Perkins) covers some of the 1920s–1980s literature retrospectively.

An interesting but unannotated bibliography of anthologies and individual works of "sex in science fiction" is available from Cecilia Tan, c/o Circlet Press (P.O. Box 15143, Boston, MA 02215).

Librarians should preview carefully all purchases of sexual literature, or request assistance from a colleague experienced in this area, to confirm representativeness and quality of the materials and to ensure suitability for the collection and the community.

See also Chapter 12: the Folklore section, particularly for cross-cultural material; the Humor and/or Cartoons section for sex-themed stories in the form of comics; and the Arts and the Media section for works *about* sexual literature and for books of and about erotic art.

AUDIOVISUAL MATERIALS

Audiovisuals (AVs) about sexuality include videos/films, slide sets, audiotapes, personal computer CD-ROMs and software, and television programs. Videos are by far the most numerous and probably of most interest for libraries.

We admit that, first, we are not experts in AVs and, second, we have not the space to treat these media as fully as print—even more so since videos about sexuality have proliferated just as have books about sexuality. In fact, nearly every other catalog that crossed our desks in the course of writing this book seemed to have a couple of sexuality videos, on AIDS at least. This scattering of resources across suppliers makes it difficult to give advice about AV collection building.

Our first advice is to read chapters 26–28 of *A Research Guide to Human Sexuality* (D120, Lichtenberg), covering basic techniques for identifying educational and entertainment videos/films and TV shows. In addition, Chapter 30 lists hundreds of sex-related organizations by topic and indicates which ones distribute AVs. Beyond this, we can only summarize some of the most prominent sources of titles.

Audiovisuals about sexuality comprise educational materials about sexual matters or issues like puberty, abstinence, homosexuality, sexual abuse, and AIDS; sexual enhancement educational materials for adults; and adult "erotic" materials—designed for arousal and recreation rather than education.

The first group is an expanding genre, especially for young people. There are literally hundreds of videos for all ages on various topics. Most are not explicit. Major liberal/middle of the road catalog distributors, largely for young people, include At Risk Resources (645 New York Avenue, Huntington, NY 11743), ETR Associates (P.O. Box 1830, Santa Cruz, CA 95061-1830), Health Edco (P.O. Box 21207, Waco, TX 76702-1207), and Sunburst (39 Washington Avenue, P.O. Box 40, Pleasantville, NY 10570-0040). Videos are the standard stock-in-trade, although At Risk Resources offers three software packages for grade 6 through adult: on sexuality decision making, STDs, and AIDS.

Mostly for adults, the liberal Multi-Focus, Inc. (1525 Franklin Street, San Francisco, CA 94109) has interesting videos and slide sets on many topics and is particularly strong on sexuality and disability. Filmmakers Library (124 East 40th Street, Suite 901, New York, NY 10016) also has a few interesting items, as does Focus International (1160 East Jericho Turnpike, Huntington, NY 11743). For a conservative/religious view, see the Focus on the Family bibliographies noted in Chapter 5 and the Josh McDowell Ministry catalog (Box 130, Wheaton, IL 60189), which list audio and videotapes for youth and adults.

AIDS videos are particularly numerous. Interested librarians should consult *AIDS Crisis in America* (E89, Hombs), pages 229–234; *AIDS: Library in a Book* (E85, Flanders & Flanders), pages 183–196; and *How to Find Information About AIDS* (E91, Huber), pages 227–224. Whether by accident or design, these three sources complement rather than duplicate each other.

There is some overlap in concept and effect among the second and third groups—sexual enhancement educational materials are often erotic and erotic videos often educational. However, selection tools for the two groups are quite different. The major sources for enhancement videos—how to do it better—are Focus International and Multi-Focus, mentioned above; also, the Sexuality Library offers two "erotic educational series." Some enhancement videos involve "talking-head therapist" sequences, while others lyrically depict sexual encounters in romantic environments. Most have some explicit content.

For erotic videos, one selection source stands out: *The X-Rated Videotape Guide* (D22), multivolume and continuously updated. Some of the best of these videos are described in *Libraries, Erotica, & Pornography* (D115).[22] For a more concise selection, chosen as "outstanding exceptions to the mediocrity, erotophobia and sexual illiteracy that plague the American erotic scene," consult the sizable video section of the Sexuality Library catalog—which also has a half-page of audio erotica. For erotic CD-ROMs and software, consult *The Joy of CyberSex* (D23, Robinson & Tamosaitis) and—again—the Sexuality Library catalog.

Should libraries acquire audiovisuals about sex? If a library collects AVs at all, we think there would be little problem with adding some issue-based materials for all ages and with various views. Sexual enhancement videos, if chosen carefully for quality and taste, might also be readily integrated into the collection and appreciated by singles of both sexes and couples. Larger libraries with major AV holdings, especially in feature and recreational films, might want to go still further and add some of the best of the erotic videos, selected to appeal to women and men.[23]

We note that librarians should preview all sex-related AVs before purchase.

SOME SUMMARY THOUGHTS

To be sure, nonfiction books remain a significant focus for library collecting in all areas. But nonetheless we urge consideration of other materials on sexuality, particularly for the vertical file. Many pamphlets and flyers representing a range of viewpoints can be obtained at little cost, and some can be given out freely. Vertical file collections can be easily customized to the community and kept up to date with, for example, newspaper clippings.

Nor should periodicals be neglected. Magazine publishing has greatly expanded in recent years, and entries into sexuality publishing are appearing from many sources. These require examination and selection.

Other important formats are not print-based, but audiovisual. Here, there has also been a positive trend, with an increasing number of high quality videos available from many sources, covering as many topics as the books themselves. The catalogs we have seen contain much material for young people on sexual issues and problems. Other catalogs center on sexual enhancement videos. Even "erotic film" quality has been upgraded and diversified.

Things really *have* changed in recent decades. Sexual fiction and magazines—where once "smut" defined the bad stuff—have crossed over to the mainstream in dramatic and unprecedented ways and quantities. Quality has gone up as competition for increasingly educated readers requires new marketing strategies and new content approaches. Women are increasingly producers and consumers of sexual fiction, magazines, and videos. Even Christian writers, once the most reluctant to talk about sex, are emerging as new voices. And we think that librarians should be proactive in collecting all of it.

NOTES

1. From the ALA *Glossary of Library and Information Science*, quoted by Clara L. Sitter in *The Vertical File and Its Alternatives: A Handbook* (Englewood, CO: Libraries Unlimited, 1992): 1.

2. Andrew Garoogian, "Making Book at the Reference Desk," *Readings on the Vertical File*, ed. Michael D.G. Spencer (Englewood, CO: Libraries Unlimited, 1993): 66–68.

3. *The American Matriarch* explores adult "domestic discipline" as a "powerful, romantic and practical method of enhancing and strengthening the bonds of loving relationships." (From TNV, P.O. Box 3292, Annapolis, MD 21403-3292.) *Hermaphrodites with Attitudes* is a forum for the Intersex Society of North America (P.O. Box 31791, San Francisco, CA 94131), written by, about, and for people born with components of both male and female genitalia. Our thanks to Robert Francoeur for sending us a sample. You will probably not find these in *Ulrich's*—or in X-rated bookstores either.

Widespread de facto censorship of (quite legal) modern sex periodicals probably ensures that many librarians have never seen—and might not guess at!—their extraordinary diversity of opinion and focus. Some are reviewed in *Factsheet 5* and range from "riot grrrlz" through punkzine sex through Gothic through body piercing, S&M, queerzines, and so on. By comparison, *Playboy* is not only tame but positively reeks with nostalgia for the Good Old Days of pretty girls—and boys who liked pretty girls, nice clothes, good manners, cars, and sports. Space limitations prohibit more detailed analyses of these striking changes.

4. Richard M. Moritz, "A Brief Guide to Provocative Publications," *Serials Review* (Winter 1983): 10.

5. *A Ripple of Time*, filmmaker Laird Sutton, prod. National Sex Forum, 1974 (24 min.); *Going Down to Bimini*, filmmaker Laird Sutton, prod. National Sex Forum, 1978 (22 min.). Both are distributed by Multi-Focus.

6. Martha Cornog, "What Happens When Libraries Subscribe to *Playboy*?" in *Libraries, Erotica, & Pornography* (D115, Cornog): 144–165.

7. For a good pro-con discussion of *Playboy*, *Penthouse*, and *Oui* in the library, see Bruce A. Shuman & Karen Dalziel, "Sex Magazines: Problems of Acquisition, Retention, Display, and Defense in Public and Academic Libraries," *Sex Magazines in the Library Collection* (D117, Gellatly): 27–46.

8. Sanford Berman, "If There Were a *Sex Index* . . . " in *Sex Magazines in the Library Collection* (D117, Gellatly): 99–135.

9. "Gay/Lesbian Task Force Seeks Index Access," *Library Journal* (September 15, 1990): 16–17; "GLTF Petitions H. W. Wilson to Include Gay/Lesbian Press," *American Libraries* (April 1991): 365; Polly Thistlethwaite, "No Queers Here,"

Lesbian Herstory Archives Newsletter 12 (June 1991): 9; Polly Thistlethwaite, "GLTF Indexing Project Update," *GLTF Newsletter* (ALA) 4.3 (Fall 1992): 7–8; Gary Klein, personal communication, February 24, 1995.

10. Nicholas Nicastro, "Double Reissue of Literary Erotica: A Sudden Influx of the Works of Marco Vassi," *Publishers Weekly* (May 31, 1993): 22.

11. Perkins: 17.

12. In this chapter, we do an end run around the erotica/pornography debate and use the term *sexual literature* for adult fiction, plays, and poetry dealing explicitly and mostly with sexuality, whether or not written for purposes of sexual arousal. See Maurice Charney's *Sexual Fiction* (London: Methuen, 1981): 1–14. Similarly, Michael Perkins defines *erotic literature* as "any imaginative writing that is mainly about sexuality": *The Secret Record* (D20, Perkins): 19. We focus on fiction, but note that erotic poetry, and plays about sexuality topics (notably AIDS), have also proliferated, albeit more modestly.

13. Perkins: 14–15.

14. The anonymous *My Secret Life* is considered a treasure trove of information about Victorian social and sexual mores, not documented in standard historical sources. See Vern L. Bullough, "Research and Archival Value of Erotica/Pornography," in *Libraries, Erotica, & Pornography* (D115, Cornog): 99–105. The full work runs to 11 volumes but has also been condensed into one 700-page paperback (Blue Moon Books, 1988).

15. Jonathan Green, *The Encyclopedia of Censorship* (New York: Facts On File, 1990).

16. See John C. Burnham, *Bad Habits: Drinking, Smoking, Taking Drugs, Gambling, Sexual Misbehavior, and Swearing in American History* (New York: New York University Press, 1993): 193–203. Burnham, taking a conservative and rather moralistic view, sets the origin of much of today's sexual mores in the Victorian "lower class" underground. See also Timothy Perper & Martha Cornog, "Sexual Fantasy," review of *Bad Habits*, by John C. Burnham, *Journal of Sex Research* 30.3 (August 1993): 295–296.

17. Perkins: 59.

18. Nicastro: 22.

19. Carolyn Anthony, "Many Ways to Mayhem," *Publishers Weekly* (October 17, 1994): 52. See also M. Kenon Breazeale, "The Postmodern Politics of the Lesbian Mystery," *Lesbian Review of Books* 1.1 (Autumn 1994): 14–15.

20. We own a four-volume edition of the "Arabian Nights," "rendered into English from the literal and complete French translation of Dr. J.C. Mardrus by Powys Mathers" (New York: St. Martin's, 1972). This is probably the same edition currently available from Routledge, 1986.

21. Anthony C. Yu, "The One About the Scholar and the Hermit's Daughter," review of *The Carnal Prayer Mat*, by Li Yu, *New York Times Book Review* (July 15, 1990): 3.

22. Robert H. Rimmer, "A Connoisseur's Selection of X-Rated Videotapes for the Library," in *Libraries, Erotica, & Pornography* (D115, Cornog): 240–249.

23. See Judith A. Geer (Erie Community College/South, Orchard Park, NY 14127), "The Use and Selection of Nonprint Erotica in Public Libraries in New York State," presentation given at the New York Library Association Conference, October 30, 1992, Lake Placid, NY.

7   From Access to Vandalism

How should sexuality books be cataloged and shelved? What is "user-friendly" reference service about sex? Will the staff, patrons, and community support the library's new role as sex educator? How about theft and mutilation? We discuss these questions from A to V: access restrictions, cataloging and classification, finding aids, programming, recruiting support, reference tips, and vandalism and theft.[1]

ACCESS RESTRICTIONS

> A majority of nearly 2/3 restricted *Playboy* behind the reserve or circulation desk; a patron would need to request it from a librarian and would sometimes be required to show or leave identification (62.2% or 69/111). Sometimes only the current issue or year was restricted. A small number of these libraries also specifically mentioned permitting access to *Playboy* only to those over 18 years old or with an adult library card; no other type of patron was specifically denied or permitted access (5 out of 69).[2]

In the ideal library functioning in the ideal community, all books are on the open shelves and circulate freely to all patrons.[3] Yet real-life libraries do restrict access to books, via shorter circulation periods, noncirculation, closed stacks, and reserve rooms. Smaller libraries sometimes use the "behind-the-desk" approach instead of a reserve room. In addition, books may be kept out of sight or out of reach in a variety of informal ways such as kept perpetually "in storage" or retained in a director's or librarian's office. One librarian told us how her director de facto limited access to *The Joy of Sex* by placing it on the very top of one of the tallest shelves. This can often be functionally equivalent to *no access*—in which certain books are completely off limits to patrons or—more usually—particular classes of patrons such as children.

Whether these methods or others are used, all tend to serve three broad functions. The first is to assure availability to the greatest number of readers for popular items or materials held in limited quantities. Everyone has an equal chance at using them because no individual can monopolize them. Such policies guarantee sharing of materials across all users, thereby ensuring access to all. The second has the goal of protecting rare or valuable items against too-enthusiastic use or deliberate vandalism. Thus both these functional categories, while limiting access through perhaps temporary inconvenience in the short run, actually increase or ensure access in the long run.

However, the third category of access limitation erects barriers *denying* access to certain works or for certain users on the basis of principles, often moral, unrelated to how many patrons use—or might use—a given work. Sometimes individuals in power impose these limitations ad hoc. No matter how well intended, there is always the odor of censorship or high moral tone when it is decided to limit access for the patron's "own good." When children are involved, American family traditions unquestionably grant that right to parents, but it is not clear that libraries should act in the parent's place without obtaining an explicit mandate from individual parents, or even at all. By contrast, when *adult* library patrons are involved, no mandate seems possible: who is able, in America, to prohibit adults from reading what they want? Nonetheless, sexuality materials are often restricted in ways that prevent adults from obtaining them. Now we encounter the full force of censorship by access limitation: Yes, the library has the book, but no one can get it—or get at it easily.

We have urged librarians to develop philosophies about sexuality materials. Assuredly, one philosophy is to declare forthrightly that certain views or types of sexuality will not be included in the collection or will be included only with access restrictions. Should a library take this approach, the decision should be publicly acknowledged. Too often such decisions have been made ad hoc and single-handedly, and kept secret except in their effects. But such actions have similarities to old-fashioned cowardice. The least the library can do is openly acknowledge the position and be prepared to deal with the consequences. For example, we sense that Christian librarian James Sauer's defense of "Judeo-Christian-based" censorship fits this model of honestly stating the pro-censorship position and attempting to justify it.[4] We ourselves do not agree, but we acknowledge the self-consistency of that philosophy. Yet we also feel that few libraries will openly adopt his view or that it will attract a major following in the ALA or among librarians in general.

Accordingly, libraries must develop ways of dealing with access to highly used, valuable, and/or controversial items. Here are some suggestions for minimizing access restrictions to sexuality materials.

1. When high use or damage is the problem, consider obtaining two copies of the item, with one circulating and one restricted.

2. When the issue is "protecting" young people from certain books or collections, consider access by default, with parental signature to restrict, instead of the reverse.

3. Consider approaches where people sign to enter an area, but can access and choose books directly without needing to request specific titles.

4. Consider milder forms of restriction before more drastic restrictions—placing items in reference rather than behind the desk with request required.

5. Consider alternatives to restriction whenever possible, such as purchasing multiple copies, photocopying key excerpts and binding them as pamphlets in multiple copies, and buying microfilm.

6. Whatever access restrictions are used, they should be implemented evenhandedly according to policies laid out in advance and communicated to patrons, not applied ad hoc and kept secret.

Problems of access will not be solved easily or quickly. Yet we suspect that ingenious solutions are evolving across the nation's libraries as more and more librarians encounter the combination of increasing publication of sexuality materials *and* increased patron tolerance and demand for them.

CATALOGING AND CLASSIFICATION

> The centerpiece of the show's first hour . . . featured [humorists Garrison] Keillor and [Dave] Barry as children going to the NYPL looking for books about sex—preferably French ones. "We have a rather large collection of sex books," the librarian tells them. "I'd estimate about 3,327. You'll find them indexed over there under SEX, FRENCH, or else under COLLECTIONS, FRENCH, SEX. You can also check SEXUALITY, CARNALITY, CONCUPISCENCE, FORNICATION, and MARITAL SCIENCE."[5]

What is unexpected and therefore funny is that this imaginary library *has* lots of sex books *and* that the librarian admits it! But we also laugh because we see here some of the same problems in real-life cataloging and classification of sex books: inappropriate, outdated, overlapping, and un-specific headings.

Classification

Many patrons and not a few librarians browse the stacks when hunting books. Therefore, shelf order as determined by the classification scheme can help or hinder access.

Most libraries use either the Dewey Decimal Classification (DDC), typically school and public libraries, or the Library of Congress Classification (LCC), typically academic and research libraries. Both systems have call numbers assigned at the Library of Congress, although by different staff for each system, and both tend to split most sex works among psychology (155.3 or BF692), sociology (306.7 or HQ), and medicine (600 or R, numerous subclasses). But assignments are inconsistent both within DDC or LCC *and* between them. *Sexual Loving* by Joseph and Lois Bird is classed in DDC as psychology and in LCC as sociology. *The New Joy of Gay Sex* (B62, Silverstein & Picano) and *Heterosexuality* (A10, Masters et al.) are classed in medicine by DDC but in sociology by LCC.

DDC differs from LCC in its shorter length and less detail about all subjects. DDC also has an additional and problematic feature, that many sex topics—for example, extramarital/premarital sex and homosexuality—may be classed within sociology as either "institutions pertaining to relations of the sexes" (306.7) or as "controversies related to public morals and customs" (363.4). It may be that the 363.4 numbers are rarely used; our recent books on homosexuality are all classed in 306. "Pornography" has a 363.4 number; however, collections of erotica plus history and criticism are supposed to be classed in the 800s, with literature.

In LCC, sexual literature is split three ways: erotica (HQ450–460), pornography (HQ471), and literary collections/history and criticism in the Ps.

The upshot is that if the librarian accepts the assigned DDC or LCC classifications, similar books can be dispersed to different places throughout the collection. It can be made worse if the original class notation is really *wrong*—as does happen. Sanford Berman, head cataloger at the Hennepin County Public Library (HCL) in Minnetonka, Minnesota, cites a book called *Tales from Times Square*, which was classified by LCC as 974.71, a "New York" notation appropriate for history and civilization books. It sounds reasonable—after all, Times Square is in New York, it does have history, and maybe even some civilization. But that was not what the book was about: it was about hookers and peep show parlors—yet not a peep about sex in the classification numbers.[6]

Now, the catalog is supposed to solve these problems by providing multiple access points through subject headings—and we discuss such remedies below. But proliferation of subject headings is no panacea for bad-faith or incompetent classification, and there are other things librarians should do.

First, class numbers for new sex books should be checked for simple accuracy and modified as appropriate. Second, each class number should be compared with those of similar books. Should it be reclassed with more similar works according to practices specific to this library? Third, *see also* references to related class numbers could be inserted *in the stacks* in the form of dummy "books." Wrap a wood or styrofoam block with contact paper, and label the spine with "Homosexuality—Additional information" and the 306.75 call number, for example. Then on the front of the "book," paste an abbreviated pathfinder, listing other call numbers where books on homosexuality may be found.

Librarians can also explore other classification options. The ALA Gay, Lesbian, and Bisexual Task Force (GLBTF) makes available a list of classification schemes for lesbian/gay materials. Libraries specializing in sexuality or homosexuality may be contacted for advice and copies of their own classification schemes.[7]

Subject Headings

Even when appropriate classification codes are assigned, sexuality materials will still be dispersed throughout the collection. Thus librarians and patrons must rely heavily upon subject headings.

Most libraries use either *Sears List of Subject Headings* (Sears)—typically school and smaller public libraries—or the *Library of Congress Subject Headings* (LCSH)—typically medium-sized to larger public libraries and academic libraries. In both, subject headings, like classification codes, are assigned at the Library of Congress.

LCSH is extremely detailed; the "sex-to-sexuality" headings alone run to 17 columns of small print. The "erotic" headings are also ample. By contrast, in Sears, "sex-to-sexuality" headings occupy less than five columns.

What can go wrong with subject headings assigned to sex books? A good deal:

- No headings may be assigned, as for adult fiction. Fiction about AIDS, rape, or telephone sex—such as *Vox* by Nicholson Baker—are often not retrievable by topic. Fortunately, fiction books for young people *are* assigned subject headings.

- Not enough headings may be assigned. Valerie Kelly's *How to Write Erotica*, assigned LCSH's EROTICA—AUTHORSHIP, should also be assigned PORNOGRAPHY—AUTHORSHIP and SEX ORIENTED BUSINESSES.

- Incorrect, misleading, or inadequate headings may be assigned: *Tales from Times Square*, mentioned above, had been assigned only LCSH headings beginning with TIMES SQUARE— and NEW YORK—. The book clearly needed headings such as SEX INDUSTRY and PROSTITUTION.

- The headings available may be insulting, outdated—or nonexistent. Sanford Berman is well known in the library literature for his efforts to induce LC to update its headings. He cites such examples as no heading in LCSH for HETEROSEX-UALITY; outdated headings such as LITERATURE, IMMORAL; SEX IN-STRUCTION instead of SEX EDUCATION and NOCTURNAL EMISSIONS instead of WET DREAMS; and lack of such common concepts as SEXUAL REV-OLUTION, SEX MANUALS, and ANTIPORNOGRAPHY MOVEMENT.[8] To LC's credit, the latest LCSH edition *does* include HETEROSEXUALITY and does *not* include LITERATURE, IMMORAL. Sears has also improved coverage of sexual concepts in the last few years, adding SEXUAL DISORDERS and SEX THERAPY. Yet the shortness of the Sears "sex" list inevitably means that some concepts will not be represented as narrowly as might be desired. Older books in particular may completely lack all cataloging-in-publication information and be included in hopelessly outdated categories.

• Cross-referencing in the library's catalog may be inadequate. When separate head-ings exist for EROTICA and PORNOGRAPHY, for example, *see also* references are needed. Sanford Berman suggests SAFE SEX: *see also* CONDOMS, EROT-ICA, MASTURBATION, and so on.[9]

Librarians must review seriously all headings assigned to new sex books, with a view towards adding new headings and substituting better ones. We suggest as a source for new headings the *Hennepin County Library Cata-loging Bulletin*, published bimonthly since 1973 and available from the library in Minnetonka, Minnesota. While certainly not all libraries will want to adopt HCL's approach, HCL's topical forms nonetheless serve as a fruitful source for ideas for headings and represent detailed attention to current distinctions among topics.

A comment about the bibliographic record. Greater use of bibliographic notes on the record, such as phrases from tables of contents, goes a long way towards enriching the catalog. Is Maurice Charney's *Sexual Fiction* a compilation of short stories, a critique of novelistic sex, or a discussion of erotica/pornography? The table of contents quickly reveals that it is the last. Such enrichment can greatly help in triaging many records under one heading. Moreover, content-type notes facilitate keyword searching in on-line catalogs.

Cataloging, Classification—and Labeling

Librarians should correct call numbers and subject headings about sex for an additional reason: patrons may want to avoid these materials. Imag-ine someone looking for a travel book about New York City and encoun-tering *Tales from Times Square* next to a tourist's history of the Statue of Liberty. Our traveler could well feel misled or deceived in some way—not necessarily because the library has this book about sex, but because the book *is not in its proper category* and so the patron could not recognize its nature.

This raises the question of how to handle books that clearly belong in non-sex sections but that have incidental sexual content. An example is

Terence Conran's *The Bed and Bath Book* (Crown, 1978), described by a *Booklist* reviewer as "a gold mine of information and ideas for anyone remodeling or planning these rooms from scratch." But *The Bed and Bath Book* bothered at least one patron because of nude photos and discussion of orgasms. "This book is totally out of line for the 747.77 section," the patron wrote on the reconsideration form. "This book should be rated or [have] a warning label on it!!"[10]

Should warning labels be placed on books when sexual content is not obvious in either classification or title? (*Sensuous Spaces: Designing Your Erotic Interiors*, by Sivon Reznikoff, Whitney Library of Design/Watson-Guptill, 1983, might not engender problems.) The ALA has come out strongly against labeling of books, defined as "affixing a prejudicial label and/or segregating them by a prejudicial system . . . [as] means for predisposing people's attitudes toward library materials." Of course, ALA does not rule out "adoption of organizational schemes designed as directional aids or to facilitate access to materials."[11] What prejudice means in the case of sex can be a bit tricky, as some people *want* to access titles with sexual content, in whatever context they may be found, and might appreciate such labeling. It is a truism of censorship that "banned in Boston" designations lead to sales, and record album labeling proposed by the Parents Resource Music Center may have led to more rather than fewer albums being sold.

A relatively benign form of labeling sexuality materials would be to consider erotic fiction as genre fiction, parallel to romances, gothics, science fiction, and westerns, and use spine labels (such as the biological symbols for male and female) to distinguish such books. Beyond that, we do not recommend any labeling system, especially for nonfiction! But the problem may arise in some public libraries, and librarians need to consider how to respond.

FINDING AIDS

> Librarians censor by refusing to authorize or obstructing attempts to promote the use of materials through displays, bibliographies, bookmarks, and the like.[12]

When the topic is sensitive and the catalog mysterious, how do patrons find books? By browsing the stacks—perhaps the patron has learned that some sex books are located "on the second shelf down, over by the stairwell." But since books on sexuality will always be dispersed throughout the entire collection, the patron's favorite group of books will probably not include all relevant titles.

A way out of this dilemma is through what we call "finding aids," which can give patrons a convenient and private way of locating books:[13]

- Bookmarks. Cheap, colorful, and easy for patrons to pick up, bookmarks can list key books and periodicals with call numbers and even short annotations. They can be used by any library to improve access for popular topics. In essence, they are mini-pathfinders.

- Book lists. You can pack more into a book list than onto a bookmark. Here, annotations are a definite plus—they can be cribbed from book jackets and tables of contents. Book titles should be arranged by subtopic, again with call numbers. Other approaches can also be used, such as "Ten Myths About Sex (or AIDS or Rape . . .) and Where to Find Answers."

- Study guides. Also known as pathfinders, these describe how to research a particular topic. A study guide lists key indexes and other reference works and gives relevant call numbers and subject headings rather than book titles. An excellent sample pathfinder on gay/lesbian history and culture is Appendix XII of *Gay and Lesbian Library Service* (D118, Gough & Greenblatt).

- Union lists. These list materials available in the city, community, or state. There may be a gay archives in the next town or a collection on sex education at a neighborhood community college library.

- Organization and referral lists. The starting point for these is the telephone directory Blue Pages.

Many sexuality topics may be used as the focus for such aids. Obvious candidates are abortion, birth control, rape, sexual harassment, child sexual abuse, talking with children about sex, and teen sexuality. "Gay/lesbian" alone can lead to a number of topics, for example, the categories in Chapter 10.

We make a number of general suggestions about such aids:

- Colored paper and clip-art graphics can be used to enhance attractiveness and eye-catching appeal.

- Whereas sexuality topics can be given their own aids, sexuality materials can also be incorporated into topics such as "new acquisitions," "multiculturalism," "summer leisure reading," "women's history," "families," and so on. A World War II book list for Veterans Day could include *Virtue Under Fire: How World War II Changed Our Social and Sexual Attitudes* (D63, Costello).

- Different points of view should be represented, with clear and diplomatic labels. An excellent example is a brochure/book list from the Fort Vancouver Regional Library in Vancouver, Washington, *Sexuality and Sex Education for Parents and Their Children*. This brochure is divided into three sections: selections recommended by Planned Parenthood, by SIECUS, and by Phyllis Schlafly's Eagle Forum. We hope that many libraries adopt this extremely clear format: it saves time for readers and it alerts them to what they may *not* want to see. All finding aids can include a caveat, such as, "These materials represent different points of view. Should a particular book not seem appropriate to your needs, we invite you to consult other books."

- All finding aids should be made available at more than one location. Don't just stack them at the reference or circulation desk. Try a rack in the stacks or near the catalog or photocopy machine. Post samples on bulletin boards.

- Use finding aids for community outreach. Send samples with the library newsletter and to community organizations appropriate to the topic. Copies to newspapers may bring writers in to use the collection—or to write a story about the library and sex education.

- Use finding aids to respond quickly to news or community events: protests against an X-rated video store, arrest of a prominent person for child sexual abuse, and of course any major censorship attempts.

PROGRAMMING

> In no other area does information depend so on the availability of services as in sexuality. . . . Do you know what *is* and *is not* available for kids in your community? Are you sponsoring programs to call attention to these unmet needs? Are you giving community leaders information on how to fill the needs? Or are you waiting, like most libraries, for everybody to come to you?[14]

"Programming" is a general concept indeed, if we are any judges: programming is anything other than the standard and expected provision of access, reference, and circulation services. Standard library services, while vital and necessary, are passive—they await demand to take effect. Programming is active and invites participation. Library programming can be as creative as the librarians running the programs. We have already recommended creative approaches to access, reference, and circulation of sexuality information—and we also recommend creative approaches to library programming.

How is library programming about sexuality different from other programming? First, programming draws people's attention to the library. Since libraries have been traditionally anti-sex, programs are a great way to get the word out that *sex is so important that you can read all about it at the library*. For "sex," you really can "see librarian" and a great many books besides.

Certainly library programs about sex run no risk of being buried on page 29 of the local paper. Prominent publicity is likely much more forthcoming when sex is the subject. Simply putting *sex* and *library* into the same sentence is a novel experience for some media folk, partly the reason why the stories about Madonna's *Sex* in the library got such wide play.

So, a menu for library programs about sex: pick one from Column A and one from Column B.

Column A. Topics for Public Libraries

1. About the library and books, examples include:

- Books to help you teach your child about sex
- What kinds of books about sex belong in the library?
- Pro/con views on *Daddy's Roommate* (any current censorship challenge)
- Banned books (for Banned Books Week)

2. About a community controversy
   - Pro/con views on the proposed or actual opening of a new condom emporium or X-rated video store
   - Forum on condom distribution in the high school[15]

3. About a national controversy
   - Adolescent pregnancy: Tragedy or transition?
   - Should homosexuals serve in the military?

4. About a broad issue, topic, or area of education
   - Abortion
   - AIDS
   - Birth control
   - Child sexual abuse
   - Religion and sexuality

Column A. Topics for School Libraries
   - New baby in the family (elementary and middle school)
   - Learning about the opposite sex (grades 5 through 12)
   - Puberty (grades 5 through 12)
   - Understanding censorship (grades 5 through 12)
   - Fiction about social and sexual issues (middle school/junior high and high school)
   - Sexual values, including religious viewpoints (middle school/junior high and high school)
   - Planning your future, including materials about marriage and parenting (middle school/junior high and high school)
   - "The birds and the bees" (all ages)
   - AIDS (all ages)
   - Books about sex to read with your child (for parents)

Some of the topics suggested for public library programs can be adapted for school libraries.

We also suggest that sexuality materials be integrated into other programming. Book displays about prominent women? Include works about Margaret Sanger, Mae West, Mary Calderone, Madonna, Sappho. Sports? Include transsexual Renée Richards and lesbian Martina Navratilova. Civil War? Include *The Story the Soldiers Wouldn't Tell* (D73, Lowry). Health? Include books on HIV/AIDS, STDs, and breast and testicular exams. A good deal of sex information can fit quite neatly within health topics—for which demand has increased in recent years because of the consumer health advocacy movement and health care reform.

Column B. Formats

1. Display (case, tabletop, or bulletin board)
2. Film
3. Lecture
4. Panel discussion
5. Workshop
6. Course
7. Poetry or other book reading
8. Information fair (special event with booths or tables displaying books, handouts, and information)

Another class of programming could be called "out-of-house" as opposed to in-house programming. These ideas are less commonly used by libraries, and they certainly are *not* "waiting for everybody to come to you."

1. Letter writing. Send regular letters to the local paper(s) suggesting books for the public to read as background to help understand recent news stories or trends. For high schools and colleges, this would be the student or campus newspaper. With luck, it could turn into a regular column. Recent sex-related events crying out for such background reading suggestions include the suit against Michael Jackson for child sexual abuse, child sexual abuse by clergy and Boy Scout leaders, and the abortion-inducing drug RU486.

2. Representation at a community event: school fair, county fair, Gay Pride Day, open air market, restaurant festival ("food for thought"), whatever special events bring people out in groups. Include sexuality materials with a variety of others.

3. The "Column B" programs can be held outside the library, co-sponsored by other organizations. Imagine a workshop for parents about "Books to Help You Teach Your Child Sexual Values," customized for various religious groups and held in church buildings.

4. Meeting with community groups to discuss what books they might buy about sexuality and other topics. This service could be quite valuable for groups too small to have their own full-scale libraries: prisons, summer camps, day care centers, physicians' waiting rooms, retirement communities, churches.

5. Conferring and cooperating with other area libraries. Holdings can complement each other if different area libraries agree to specialize in different topics. Thus library A acquires an in-depth collection on homosexuality; library B, on sex and religion; library C, on sexual dysfunctions and disabilities. Naturally, all of

these libraries would have basic popular materials on these topics, but could refer readers looking for more information to the appropriate library.

Whatever the programs, publicize them: in the library and in the community through press releases, bulletin boards, calendars, newsletters, media spots. Be sure to gather feedback and reactions, such as via evaluation sheets, a response log, surveys, and evaluation by speakers. Save letters and log telephone calls. The responses can be used to evaluate the program, fine-tune a rerun, and design new programs. Quotes from attendees can be used to promote future programs. A good collection of data about a controversial program can be turned into an article, flyer, or handout—with suggested bibliography.

And always include staff: in program planning, design, publicity, and implementation. Share the feedback. Should staff be divided into conservative and liberal factions about a topic, build the different views into the program.

We urge that programs as well as collections represent multiple views. Not only is intellectual freedom served, but such diversity can build community support for the library and defuse censorship. The Downers Grove (Illinois) Public Library recently exhibited a pro-life display in response to a local organization's request. But the library at the same time exhibited an "options for women" (including pro-choice) display as well. The result? "We received a number of thank-you letters for one or the other display, as well as comments from residents who simply expressed support for the way the whole issue was handled. And the few patrons who came in to complain about one of the displays were satisfied when they were shown the alternative display right next to it."[16]

RECRUITING SUPPORT

> A group of us librarians from southwest Florida sat around a meeting room about a year ago, voting on the topic we most needed in a continuing education workshop. We chose teen sexuality and AIDS. . . . [When the workshop was held,] Dr. Marilyn Volker, sexologist and sexuality educator from Miami, began speaking. . . . [After the workshop, an] old friend of mine said, "She's wonderful. But I hope she doesn't want us to all go back and do what she's doing, or we would all be fired. Especially after the censorship problem we just had at our library with an AIDS book."[17]

Librarians taking steps to improve sex collections and programs may well be apprehensive about staff, patron, and community reactions—and often with good reason. But let us remember some common sense: no library can please everyone all the time, but libraries *can* please almost everyone to some degree and therefore can earn respect as responsive and evenhanded institutions.

We next suggest ways for librarians to build relationships in providing sexuality information and building a reputation for responsiveness and service. The bottom line is that staff, patrons, and the community all can get involved in the overall effort in providing sexuality information.

Communication *within* the library is an absolute must if a successful program is to be achieved. It does no good to talk about multiple viewpoints to the public if diversity among librarians is not heard—and it can range far more widely than obvious matters such as one librarian is gay while another is a conservative heterosexual Christian. For example, one of the men might be knowledgeable about military sexual medicine because he served as a medic. Perhaps one of the women worked in a church-based prostitution outreach project. If you underestimate your own diversity, you will certainly underestimate diversities external to the library.

The second key element is concern for patrons' opinions. The library must keep up a running dialogue with patrons about sex information, via, say:

- Bookmark inserted at the checkout desk in all books, requesting reactions to the book on one side and suggestions for new books to be purchased on the other side. These can be deposited anonymously in a "suggestion box."
- Response logs, forms, and surveys used in connection with library programs.
- Contests: my favorite/more helpful/most unforgettable book about topic X. Here, topics must be chosen carefully to avoid patron embarrassment. But some sex-related topics are possible: love and marriage, or becoming a man/woman.
- Return form for comments and suggestions in library flyers or newsletters.

When patrons' opinions are solicited, the library must respond, for example, as follows:

- Having the policy that any book requested by a certain number of patrons or under a set price will be bought automatically. (Of course, other criteria may be added.)
- Prominent announcements made when a patron-requested title has been purchased (no names of suggestors, please!).
- Excerpts from patrons' comments about specific books quoted (anonymously) in newsletters, flyers, posters, bibliographies.
- Responses to patron concerns and comments about policy, procedures, issues publicized via newsletter, bulletin boards.
- Development of programs based on patron input.
- Feedback given to patrons about general library use patterns: what events were held and how many people attended, or what topics have seen the most circula-

tion recently. A list could be made of sample titles checked out in the past month, together with patron comments from those bookmarks. A model might be "Middletown Public Library patrons have wide-ranging interests! Here are some of the interesting books that have circulated recently." (No patron names, of course.) Since everyone is nosy, the list will doubtless become an institution and attract wide readership. This may also alert patrons to books and subjects in the collection that they might not have expected, for example, sex.

A third element is cooperation and dialogue with community organizations on all side of issues. Otherwise, the library may be seen as unilaterally imposing itself on an issue, and it will be ignored. By soliciting suggestions for book and vertical file purchases from community organizations, librarians can ensure that organizations know that input is valuable, appreciated, and *acted on*. We suspect that few organizations demand sole monopoly on providing information: they want recognition of their existence and their concerns. Accordingly, they will very possibly be delighted to have the library interested in *them*.

A semi–form letter asking for book recommendations could be sent out once a year or so to such organizations: for example, Planned Parenthood local affiliates, rape crisis centers, AIDS service organizations, pastors/churches, pro-life groups, local units of Focus on the Family and the American Family Association, gay groups such as Parents and Friends of Lesbians and Gays (PFLAG), self-help groups of sexual exploitation survivors, feminist groups such as the National Organization for Women (NOW), the YMCA/YWCA, and so on. The Blue Pages of the telephone directory can help. Organizations can also be asked how the library can help them and their members.

Good relationships with community groups can lead to mutually beneficial cooperation in library programming and even staff training. The 1994 Gale Research–*Library Journal* Library of the Year Award was given to the Brown County Library of Green Bay, Wisconsin, partly because of their support for and partnership with nearly 100 local organizations, from the Boy Scouts to the local HIV/AIDS clinic, in creating innovative and effective programs.

When a community has one or several organizations that threaten to become a thorn in the library's side, it may greatly smooth matters if librarians join these organizations and attend meetings. The idea is not to argue and rebut, but for people to get to know people and find common ground.[18]

Community organizations include other libraries. It might be valuable to start a Middletown Librarians' Network, inviting public, school, academic, and even special librarians to meet and discuss mutual interests such as literacy, public relations, funding, response to civic issues, and topics of wide concern such as providing AIDS information.

It also may be possible to set up mutually beneficial relationships with bookstores. Common areas of interest might include literacy, censorship, coping with the latest book fads, and dealing with jobbers/publishers.

A type of organizational support that libraries should increasingly investigate is outside funding. Grants and contracts are available from public and private sources for programming on AIDS prevention, adolescent sexuality education, and other topics. Libraries could develop the credentials to qualify, perhaps applying jointly with other organizations. In fact, community understanding and goodwill garnered via patron and organizational relationships are quite likely to result in greater success with all fund-raising efforts, from grant-getting to building fund donations to "endow a book" campaigns.

Let us return to library staff. Librarians wishing to improve sex collections must be as solicitous of staff as of public opinions. When staff members have different value systems about sexuality, the library must draw upon this diversity to create better collections and services. This does not mean that staff can censor the collections or veto programs, but any staff objecting to library materials should be invited to suggest acquisitions reflecting their values and to have their points of view included in staff training.

We suggest staff training on sexuality issues as an integral part of library-based sex education. A series of lunchtime speakers could be set up, drawn from organizations with which the library has developed cooperative relationships. Anonymous questions could be collected in advance and submitted to speakers as a starting point for the presentation.

Above all, the library must model within its sexuality collections and programs an evenhanded responsiveness to staff, patrons, and community. The concept of *library* has been associated with sexual silence or conservatism, and the concept of *sex* education associated with sexual liberalism or permissiveness—an irony, given that sex education began with efforts to teach conservative values. No longer need we be weighted down by such stereotypes, as we try to show in this book. When this modern approach is understood by the library's constituencies, the library will grow and thrive in its new role as sex educator, not without conflict, but with much greater support and goodwill.

REFERENCE TIPS

> You should check with the librarian about ways to locate materials. ... Don't be shy. The librarian won't call the police or run away screaming if you ask for information about gender dysphoria. Ask. If you're embarrassed, you can always say you have a friend who is a crossdresser or transsexual person or that you're doing a paper for a class you are taking.[19]

A young man whom I had known vaguely as a neighborhood kid approached the reference desk where I was working in August, 1974. He said, "Do you have a book on pregnancy? I'm getting married Saturday, and I want to make sure that she takes care of herself."[20]

Oddest requests from [bookstore] customers: "Do you have a book about body changes that doesn't discuss sex?"[21]

Welcome to the sex-friendly reference desk! When it comes to sex education in libraries, the reference librarian has two major problems: first, getting the patrons to ask about sex at all, and second, finding out the *real* question. (The third is locating material that answers the question, but that problem is common to all reference questions.) Some tips for professional and competent service:

1. Handle every request for sex-related information in a professional manner: nonjudgmentally, pleasantly, efficiently, helpfully, and thoroughly. Professionalism and politeness also mean appearing comfortable and unfazed, whatever the topic. Keep your voice low and clear, without whispering. No one wants to hear, "WHAT'S THAT?? YOU'VE GOT A QUESTION ABOUT GONORRHEA??" A chair by the reference desk can provide the feel of a more private discussion.[22]

2. Assume patrons will *not* usually ask. To prime the pump and show that librarians welcome sex questions, you can also try posting on a bulletin board or including in the library newsletter "interesting reference questions and how we answered them," including some sex questions. By knowing that other patrons have similar concerns, a questioner feels less lonely.

3. Do not assume that patrons who do ask are telling you their real questions. You will probably need to probe diplomatically. In his lectures about information searching, Rutgers professor Tefko Saracevic used to tell about a young man who approached the reference desk wanting "something about medicine." Ten minutes and much circuitous dialogue later, the bemused librarian managed to learn that what he really wanted was the telephone number of the nearby nurses' dormitory. Imagine how tongue-tied people feel when the topic is, well, *sexier*. The young man who was getting married Saturday probably did not want a book on pregnancy but on birth control. But pregnancy was no longer taboo in 1974, whereas birth control surely was—and he asked circumlocuitously. Be prepared for phrases like "a friend of mine" or "term paper." Act as if you believe it.

4. But never assume that any patron does or does not have any particular sexual interests. That slight young man with long hair and an earring may be a real stud with women and concerned about preventing pregnancy. That feminine woman looking for books for her child may be coparenting with a lesbian lover.

5. Recommend alternative viewpoints where relevant. Anyone asking about abortion should be pointed towards both pro-life and pro-choice works. Patrons asking about religion and sex can be referred to a range of views.

6. Consider reference staff training or exchange-of-information sessions about sexuality topics. "How do we handle questions about X" is a good starting point, which will evoke war stories and discussions of how to do it better. Some role playing exercises can be helpful, both for talking about sex and for empathizing with patrons. Sample situations to role play: a married woman asking about tubal ligation; a teenage girl asking about birth control; a distressed parent of a pregnant teen, looking for materials on abortion; a pre-teen boy concerned about his "different"—i.e., uncircumcised—penis but unable to ask directly; a man in his 50s concerned about prostate disorders.

Two additional issues must be raised from the shadows. One is about professional training in sexuality librarianship, and the other is about come-ons and put-offs.

Much about sexuality is emotionally threatening. Certain topics—like the paraphilias and various medical problems—are not only hard to ask about but, for the layperson, can be difficult to listen to. The listener's signs of embarrassment are mostly nonverbal: the listener averts his eyes; she picks up a pad, starts writing, and comments, "Yes, go on, I'm listening," when obviously she is not; he asks that the question be repeated and then fusses with folders in a drawer. The message is "Go away. You embarrass me." Under these circumstances, do not be surprised if the patron *does* go away.

Unfortunately, few of us are aware of our own nonverbal behavior. In jobs that absolutely require self-control, such as training of psychotherapists, video records might be made of a trainee's behavior and corrective measures taken. However, such techniques are complex, expensive, and sometimes unpleasant, and by no means can be considered routine for libraries. The only alternative is self-honesty and the ability to listen to colleagues' comments.

A second problem also looms. Many sexual questions seem to the listener as having elements of a come-on. We recall the *Playboy* cartoon showing a young man grinning at an attractive female librarian: "It says in the catalog, *For Sex, See Librarian*." We took this book's title from that cartoon because we insist that there is a better way to interpret it. Yet we also know that librarians may be concerned that *any* question about sex comes with a not-so-hidden agenda. The only answer is professionalism: a clear expression that one will answer reference questions, nothing else. If a questioner persists with increasingly personal overtones, call the security guard or a supervisor. Such contingencies need to be worked out in advance at staff meetings. It is another reason why a library as a community in itself must discuss and evolve a philosophy about sexuality information that transcends the older ethos of silence.

VANDALISM AND THEFT

> They even mutilated the [*Playboy*] microfilm. Selected parts were ex-
> cised from the film. Why? They weren't even in color! (#88)[23]

Everyone *knows* that sex books are stolen and mutilated. Aren't they?
Well, sometimes. An informal survey in the 1990s, pieced together despite "imperfect statistics and the reticence of some to talk about the subject," classed *The Joy of Sex* together with other sex books as one of the
top ten most-stolen types.[24] When in 1987 I (MC) surveyed libraries subscribing to *Playboy*, nearly two-thirds of responding libraries reported vandalism of the magazine. More recently, we were hunting a reference for
Chapter 2 of this book in a journal sedately titled *Today's Education*. Unfortunately, the 1976 article—"Sex Education: Yesterday, Today and Tomorrow"—had been neatly razored out.
  What can be done about defacement and theft of sex books? Some libraries respond by restricting sex titles, some by not replacing them—in
effect, giving up. However, we conjecture that at least sometimes vandalism
of sex books is not materially different from vandalism of other materials,
but librarians *act as if it were*. Several responders in the *Playboy* survey
commented, unprompted:

> It would certainly be hard to distinguish between censorship and fear of mutilation
> or theft in our not placing [sexually] explicit material on the open shelves. For
> example, we already face heavy theft and mutilation in our sections on Marilyn
> Monroe . . . and Nazism [presumably on open shelves]. (#102)

> We recently decided to drop [*Playboy*] because of difficulties managing it. . . . [But]
> we put up with theft of all kinds of materials and never consider not purchasing
> anymore [sic]—in fact, if patrons steal Fortune or People, we simply add another
> copy. (#38)

So librarians need to consider whether sex is bearing an unfair burden. If
Fortune and *People* are replaced, *Playboy* should be also. If car repair
manuals are bought in multiple copies and replaced when stolen, the same
policy should apply to sex manuals.
  Neither simple restriction nor nonreplacement is an ideal resolution to
the problem. Nonreplacement in particular seems questionable from a policy viewpoint. What other remedies might help?
  We favor a policy of combining greater protection of sexuality materials
with more convenient use. These approaches need not be as oxymoronic
as they seem.
  Protection: sizable, scholarly, beautiful, and expensive sex books *may*
need restriction via procedures used for other such materials, such as being
placed on reserve or in special collections and requiring patrons to sign for

them. Microform provides some deterrence. This approach should be combined with a collection-wide approach, incorporating techniques such as electronic book tagging, mirrors and/or cameras, "staff-only" areas, good lighting, off-hours intruder detection systems—and staff training. Libraries should publicize widely that all books are protected and that theft and mutilation bring penalties.

Cases of vandalism should be investigated, prosecuted, and likewise publicized. Apparently librarians have been historically loathe to talk openly about vandalism, for fear of "giving patrons ideas." But reports of cases can promote sympathy for the library when news stories take the slant that vandalism reduces access for other patrons and wastes taxpayers' money. Nor do we think book thieves and page-rippers are likely to inspire imitation if it becomes known that these individuals must face the police, pay fines, and lose borrowing privileges, plus risk expulsion from school and loss of scholarships.

But only some sex books require greater protection. A very large majority of essential works about sexuality are available inexpensively in paperback. Key works should be bought in multiple copies, and any vandalized books replaced in multiple copies (restrict one copy if you wish). How do you pay for this? With creative ways of getting freebies. For gay or AIDS books, ask local gay/AIDS organizations to sponsor a book, with credit given in a bookplate. Other types of organizations can donate other books, including conservative organizations and pressure groups. You can give them all credit in a prominently posted donor list. We would be interested to see if Christian sex manuals would be vandalized as often as *The Joy of Sex* is reputed to be.

A complementary approach is providing free photocopying. Yes, that would be expensive, but more expensive than the books lost or defaced? Perhaps seven local businesses would each support one night a week of free photocopying in return for good public relations—or more than seven, if the volume is high.

Convenience and privacy clearly enter into decisions to steal or slash books. Some people do not want to be seen with *Young, Gay, and Proud* (C52, Alyson), or *Sex Crimes* (D106, Holmes), or *If You Are Raped* (E53, Johnson), or *Addicted to Adultery* (A92, Brzeczek et al.). Certainly, they do not want their name associated with any of them in the circulation file. Tables or carrels in the stacks may help people read without fearing surveillance. Also, multiple copier machines in the stacks are more convenient and private than copiers under the noses of the neighbors' kids doing homework in the reference room: "Eeuww, I just saw old Mr. Maddox, and you know what he had?? It was something about SEX!!" The book may have been the highly regarded *Love, Sex, and Aging* (C82, Brecher), but who knows that? Mr. Maddox could be well on his way to a reputation among the puberty set—and ultimately, their parents—as a Dirty Old Man. (And keep copiers in good repair, with handy change machines.)

A somewhat different problem is the "take-and-hide" phenomenon— books not stolen but hidden elsewhere in the library. While depriving other readers may be a motive in law, business, or medical libraries, when sex books are involved the motive is probably a desire to read the book without checking it out. Here, the library must buy extra copies and should prob- ably treat transgressors more gently if they are caught. Linda Perkins, speaking at the 1994 ALA meeting, described finding books about gays and lesbians hidden in odd corners of the Berkeley Public Library, obvi- ously by people who could not bring themselves to check out the books but who wanted to finish reading them.[25] She said that when the staff finds these books, they try to leave them there. Libraries having real problems with this sort of behavior might want to set up some sort of anonymous patron book reserve system or install small lockers that can be used for this purpose.

Vandalism for political motives is still another problem. Its sign is spec- ificity: books and topics are targeted, not idiosyncratic. Multiple copies will not help, as they too may be stolen. In these cases, librarians need to meet with representatives speaking for those viewpoints and attempt to recruit assistance to prevent property destruction. One should enlist their help in selecting acquisitions that represent their viewpoint, as well as follow the usual procedures for challenged books and for theft. This approach may not identify specific vandals, but can nonetheless send a message to them: we will include many viewpoints in the library collection, including yours, but if you steal books you disapprove of, you are committing a crime.

Ultimately, vandalism represents an opportunity for the library. Here is information so desired that people will break the rules of society to possess it. What a selling point! "We have information that some people want to steal. But you don't have to steal it—it's right here for you and everyone." If the library prominently posts an explanation for why it must resort to anti-vandalism measures, most library goers will sympathize. Using van- dalized books—including sex books—for a display, together with materials about vandalism itself, may serve not only to alert people but also to ed- ucate everyone about the causes and costs of vandalism. This publicity tactic undercuts one important reason vandals have for defacing materials on sexuality: to obliterate sexual images and words. But, instead, the library has *displayed* the image and the word, so that the vandal's action has emphasized, rather than obliterated, precisely the information the vandal wants suppressed.

In the final analysis, libraries operate under the ethic of mutual trust. Yet a library that sends mixed messages about its sexuality materials—either by not protecting them at all or by not considering them worth stocking in quantity or replacing—is surreptitiously winking at the obliteration of sexual words and images and de facto collaborates with destructive activities. It cannot then claim with clean hands and pious innocence that They Are Destroying the Books.

NOTES

1. Some of this discussion is condensed, revised, and updated from material published in Martha Cornog's "Providing Access to Materials on Sexuality," in *Libraries, Erotica, & Pornography* (D115): 166–187. The cataloging and classification sources cited are *Library of Congress Classification*, 4th ed., 1989 (for the Medical schedule, 5th ed., 1989); *Dewey Decimal Classification*, 20th ed., 1989; *Library of Congress Subject Headings*, 17th ed., 1994; and *Sears List of Subject Headings*, 15th ed., 1994.

2. Martha Cornog, "What Happens When Libraries Subscribe to *Playboy?*" in *Libraries, Erotica, & Pornography* (D115): 149.

3. See Office of Intellectual Freedom, American Library Association, comp., "Free Access to Libraries for Minors" and "Restricted Access to Library Materials," *Intellectual Freedom Manual* (Chicago: ALA, 1992): 16–17, 66–67.

4. See James Sauer, "In Defense of Censorship," *The Christian Librarian* 36.2 (February 1993): 48–51.

5. Gordon Flagg, "Garrison Keillor Salutes 'Slaves of Literature' at NYPL," *American Libraries* (January 1992): 13–14.

6. Sanford Berman, "Consumer, BEWARE!" *Technicalities* (April 1985): 11–12.

7. Major sexuality collections are located at the Kinsey Institute at Indiana University, Planned Parenthood and SIECUS in New York, the Institute for Advanced Study of Human Sexuality in San Francisco, and California State University, Northridge (Vern and Bonnie Bullough Collection). For gay and lesbian collections, see *Gay and Lesbian Library Service* (D118, Gough & Greenblatt); Daniel C. Tsang's "Homosexuality Research Collections," in *Libraries, Erotica, & Pornography* (D115, Cornog): 199–210; and *Gayellow Pages* (B7). See also Gwendolyn Pershing, "Erotica Research Collections," in *Libraries, Erotica, & Pornography* (D115, Cornog): 188–198.

8. Sanford Berman, "Out of the Closet and into the Catalog: Access to Gay/Lesbian Library Materials," in *Alternative Library Literature, 1982/1983: A Biennial Anthology*, ed. Sanford Berman & James P. Danky (Phoenix: Oryx, 1984): 230–233; "Finding Sex in the Library: New Petition Seeks to Make It Easier," *WLW Journal* (Summer 1993): 6; Sanford Berman, "Man/Woman/Sex," in *Prejudices and Antipathies* (Jefferson, NC: McFarland, 1993): 145–169; Sanford Berman, "The 'Fucking' Truth About Library Catalogs," in *Alternative Library Literature 1992–1993*, ed. Sanford Berman & James P. Danky (Jefferson, NC: McFarland, 1994): 336–341. See also Ellen Greenblatt, "Homosexuality: The Evolution of a Concept in the Library of Congress Subject Headings," in *Gay and Lesbian Library Service* (D118, Gough & Greenblatt): 75–101.

9. Sanford Berman, letter submitted to *Library Journal*, December 12, 1994. LCSH does have a heading, SAFE SEX IN AIDS PREVENTION, which seems unnecessarily narrow. As the concept is used currently, safe sex is designed to protect against unwanted pregnancy and a variety of STDs.

10. Information provided to us from a midwestern library that wished to remain anonymous, December 1994.

11. Office for Intellectual Freedom, American Library Association, "Statement on Labeling: An Interpretation of the Library Bill of Rights," *Intellectual Freedom Manual*, 4th ed. (Chicago: ALA, 1992): 34.

12. Gough & Greenblatt (D118), "Services to Gay and Lesbian Library Patrons": 61.

13. The following list draws heavily upon ideas from Cal Gough's "Making the Library More User-Friendly for Gay and Lesbian Patrons," in Gough & Greenblatt (D118): 109–124, which describes at greater length some excellent suggestions.

14. Mary K. Chelton, "The Public Library as a Sex Education Resource for Adolescents," *Collection Building* 3.1 (1981): 41.

15. For the brave: a program on condom availability in the *library*. See Martha Cornog, "Condoms: Check 'Em Out!" *Journal of Information Ethics* 2.2 (1993): 20–26.

16. Christopher Bowen, "You Want to Display What!!!" *IFRT Report* 39 (Winter 1995): 3.

17. Mary Alice Deveny, "Teens in Transition: A Workshop on Teen Sexuality and AIDS for Youth Serving Professionals," *Voice of Youth Advocates* 16.4 (October 1993): 209–210.

18. James LaRue, "Reading with the Enemy," *Wilson Library Bulletin* (January 1994): 43–45.

19. Dallas Denny, *An Annotated Bibliography of Gender Dysphoria* (Decatur, GA: American Educational Gender Information Service, 1992): 20.

20. Chelton: 31.

21. "Cuffies," *Publishers Weekly* (January 4, 1993): 53. Believe it or not, there are some, for example, *Period* (C32, Gardner-Loulan) and *Growing and Changing* (C40, McCoy & Wibbelsman). Some other books discuss body changes and mention masturbation, but not sexual intercourse. See the Books for Pre-Adolescents section in Chapter 11.

22. An excellent brief guide to courteous and effective reference service is Catherine Sheldrick Ross & Patricia Dewdney, "Best Practice: An Analysis of the Best (and Worst) in Fifty-Two Public Library Reference Transactions," *Public Librarian* (September/October 1994): 261–266.

23. Response received in a survey of *Playboy* in public libraries, reported in Cornog, "What Happens . . ." (D115): 159. The number in parentheses indicates responder code. The two quotes following are from the same survey.

24. John Maxwell Hamilton, "Is There a Klepto in the Stacks?" *Library & Archival Security* 12.1 (1993): 47–54. Hamilton's top 10 categories: the Bible; books about preparing for various examinations; sex books; books on the occult; *Steal This Book*, by Abbie Hoffman, and other anti-establishment titles; law books; *Encyclopaedia Britannica*; classics assigned by teachers; Audubon's *Birds of America* and other rarities; and books opposed by conservative or radical factions, who steal them to lessen support for The Opposition.

25. Linda Perkins, speaking during the panel presentation "Beyond *Daddy's Roommate*: The Evolving Market in Children's Books," American Library Association Annual Conference, Miami, June 27, 1994.

8 Censorship and Other Considerations That Vary by Type of Library and Type of Collection

CENSORSHIP—IN GENERAL

> The intensity with which some people express their personal reactions, beliefs, or attitudes, however, is not relevant to whether or not an item falls within the scope of your collection or meets someone's need for information or recreation.[1]

> To switch metaphors, how can people make up their minds about things if we start palming the evidence? Surely we need more books in our libraries, not fewer.[2]

> But if censorship is always wrong, doesn't it follow that any form of social protest whose aim is objecting to or denouncing library materials is also unwarranted? . . . Even in theory, it would be a mockery of the protesting process to keep the protester from seeing his or her objection ever effecting change in society. This would be akin to having a suggestion box whose contents are never read.[3]

> The "great debate" of civil life is really about control of various "pulpits." Parenthood is a pulpit. . . . A public library is a pulpit. . . . What librarians often deplore as censorship is when someone besides the "professionals" want to have a say in establishing selection policies. It is a battle for control of the "pulpit committee."[4]

Sexuality books have always been high on the list of materials challenged in libraries.[5] First, we present some general thoughts about censorship and later confront it more thoroughly, together with related matters specific to different types of libraries and collections.

Some Theoretical Issues

It is a long held truism that librarians do not buy books about sex—even books about AIDS[6]—because they are afraid of public antagonism. Yet, evolution has occurred. The censorship fights in the 1990s have been about *The New Joy of Gay Sex* (B62, Silverstein & Picano) and Madonna's *Sex*, both with explicit pictorial and unvanilla sex, in contrast to the 1980s fights about the more "normal" albeit pictorial *The Joy of Sex* and, earlier, about the unillustrated *Tropic of Cancer*. Moreover, nearly all recent library literature urges combating censorship under all circumstances. Few librarians today will admit to being "censors"—referring to "selection," or using "good judgment" or "common sense" when they do not buy certain books.

Nonetheless, several questions require discussion. Retaining books now seems always a victory, whereas relocation, restriction, or removal seems a defeat. But if retention is to be supported regardless, is the validity of social protest thus unfairly overridden? "How can we justify an individual's right to challenge a particular book in a particular library if we would never allow the book in question to be removed?"[7]

Another theoretical issue is professional versus populist jurisdiction. In earlier days of purchasing sex books, librarians overcame professional traditions of the "guardianship of society"[8] by agreeing to "give the public what it wants"—that is, to buy books reflecting the needs and interests of an increasingly permissive community. Populist interests were granted status equal to or even greater than the professional judgment of an elite cadre of librarians. But librarians now face the possibility that populist interests do *not* want certain books, in defiance of the (now more permissive) professionals. If populist interests are to be respected in both circumstances, then perhaps challenges of materials need to be taken seriously for this reason as well.

Finally, we must address the deepest question raised by censorship: Are there works that truly must be hidden from readers? All arguments that answer *Yes* assume that certain books are so dangerous that their suppression is not only warranted but mandated by a Higher Good. For sexuality works especially, censors frequently allege that such books can damage the "moral fiber of society" and offer particular harm to women and children. Let us turn to these questions.

Is ensuring success of social protest itself a reason to remove books from the library? No. If so, then one could argue that removing books about Jews is therefore necessary to let anti-Semites have a few victories. The very best we can say about this argument is that it is treacherous—and a good deal worse can be said. The proposer of this idea likens disdaining such protests to ignoring the suggestions in a suggestion box. Indeed so—and *we* think it is a fine idea to ignore suggestions that Jews be slaughtered or that books be burned.

There are many ways to respond to protests about books without removing the books themselves: by adding other books to the collection more in line with protesters' tastes, or by holding programs about the controversy in which all sides are given ample "pulpit" time, or by encouraging protesters to contribute comments to library newsletters, bulletin boards, handouts, and so on. We urge librarians to devise these sorts of response rather than acquiescing to the storm troopers in removing or restricting challenged materials.

We are not saying that librarians should *never* restrict or remove a challenged book. We *are* saying that a book should never be restricted or removed solely *because* of a challenge. Every challenge filed in writing should invoke a full reconsideration procedure, as specified in library policy. This procedure should require review of the book by a committee that incorporates wide representation of different community segments. Information that led to the original purchasing decision should be read, plus any new information or reviews. Only then can *the committee* recommend restriction or removal by using criteria established in advance independent of the particular book challenged—*but not the protester or a librarian or administrator acting alone.*

It is one thing to remove a book without process, from fear of conflict or fear of public reaction or fear of harassment from a pressure group— or because of prejudice. It is quite another to relocate, restrict, remove, or replace a book after due process involving all appropriate groups, and after collecting data and opinions. Such machinery inhibits people from challenging books lightly but still responds to both protests and interests from *many* community viewpoints.

The philosophy of including many viewpoints in reviewing book challenges allows us to respond to the questions about listening to populist interests and about whether some books are truly dangerous to readers. Again, some history.

Ancient Rome produced the first censors—in fact, the word itself is Latin. And all censorship ever since has depended upon one and the same requirement: an elite cadre of censors who rules upon the moral value of works for a far broader and presumably less elite populace. In the past, the elite have been educated male readers only, with historical and cultural power to prevent other men and—especially!—women and (female) children from reading. Such men have included the educated clerics of the Middle Ages and, later, the educated men of the universities, many of whom felt no hesitation about telling the uneducated mob what would and would not "harm" them. Still later, at the turn of the century, educated librarians took over some of the censor's role. Originally, most were male, such as F.B. Perkins of Chapter 3, but gradually more women rose to power among this elite in library management and policy-setting.

Accordingly, the basic claim of all censorship—that it prevents "harm"— depends on literate, originally male, elites to define "harm" who have empowered themselves to judge and suppress works that they deem harmful. And when no one else can read, who can argue? Yet even the Romans had an answer: *Sed quis custodiet ipsos Custodes?* But who guards the Guards themselves? (Juvenal, *Satires*, vi. 347, C.E. 60–c. 130). How come you censors can read these books and *not* be harmed? Or, in plain English, Who died and left *you* boss?

In the late 20th century United States, the notion of an elite telling— especially adult—readers what they may and may not read is not acceptable to most people. In earlier times, the answer to *Who guards the guardians?* was *We few who can read are thereby enabled by our education and literacy to judge morality for others*. But when literacy became the universal norm, as it has in this country, then many voices indeed rose up to contest the censors' claim to "know" what causes harm.

Simultaneously, as the populace acquired the education and intellectual exercise formerly a privilege only of an elite, it has also taken upon itself some of the desire of that elite to censor. So a cacophony of censors now all claim to "know" what harms readers. Unfortunately, this cacophony disagrees with itself most noisily. Thus, Christian conservatives and many feminists appear to "agree" that pornography is harmful but do not agree about why—or about what books to censor. Canadian experience with the censorious Butler law illustrates the point, for the law was originally touted by many feminists as a blow against material harmful to women. Yet its implementation has focused more heavily on gay and lesbian material imported into Canada than on the sort of heterosexual male-oriented material that feminists see as most damaging. *Quis custodiet ipsos Custodes*, indeed. For every would-be censor of a book, there is another who would censor the books desired by the first censor.

Under this sort of "democratization of censorship," a curious dilemma emerges that drastically undercuts traditional arguments favoring censorship. Take the quote from the beginning of this section: "it would be a mockery of the protesting process to keep the protester from seeing his or her objection ever effecting change in society." The argument makes a certain naive sense—after all, don't we all *want* protest to succeed?—even though it is actually an exercise in rhetorical trickery. It evokes a "liberal" goal (successful protest) to support a "conservative" technique (censorship). But trickery aside, *to which group of protesters shall we listen?* No longer do we have Juvenal's problem of guarding a single set of Guards. Today we have so many self-appointed "Guards" that listening to one brings down all the others. In a pluralistic society, *there is no solution to this dilemma of censorship.* To heed each and every censor is to defoliate the library, and to heed only one is utterly arbitrary.

Accordingly, censorship has become self-defeating even if certain books *are* harmful—a proposition that we doubt in any case. No individual or group can speak authoritatively about "harm" because all have their own opinions and not infrequently credentials to boot—and write books to prove that the first set of censors are completely wrong-headed or that what *they* call harm is actually a positive good. We no longer have a single educated elite that can legitimately or illegitimately arrogate to itself alone the right to define what is and is not "harmful" for everyone else.

Those who argue otherwise must explain to a very dubious reading public why *their* view is the *only* right view—and then justify their self-appointment as censor of everyone else's reading. So censorship has a peculiarly American solution, at least for libraries: buy them all and let readers sort them out.

What If They Complain: Some Practical Pointers

Patron complaints and challenges against library materials are probably as old as libraries. The burning of the Alexandria library by Christians can be taken as one huge patron complaint against the religious—i.e., pagan—content of the collection.[9] If we are to avoid a repeat performance of the Alexandria incident, user complaints about sexuality materials must be anticipated, prepared for, and given fair hearing in procedures that nonetheless protect the holdings.

We stress the importance of preparedness within an overall philosophical view of how libraries should handle sexuality materials. Ad hoc responses seem simply not to work, if only because they suggest that the library did not know what it was up to when it purchased the offending titles. Indeed, patron complaints about sexuality materials can be used as a litmus test for library public relations: too many complaints—or a few that are very intense—suggest that relationships between library and community are out of register and need adjustment. We urge that complaints not be taken as indexing Evil Intentions but as opportunities for increased networking and communication between the library and those who feel that it is not doing its job.

Yet we must not be too idealistic. Some complainants are not satisfied by meeting with a library director or having their complaint heard—and possibly rejected—by a committee or library board. Other complainants may be the tip of a user iceberg and represent, organized or not, a much larger body of community opinion. These implications hold true regardless of the "politics" of the complaint—whether from conservative Christians or from representatives of a liberal-appearing gay and lesbian group. Either way, complaints provide significant feedback to the library by telling you that more work is needed.

Much writing about censorship in libraries includes practical approaches to coping with book challenges. Such approaches stress that dealing with complaints is just one more part of managing a library collection about sexuality (or anything else) and can have important benefits for library relationships with its community:

1. Consider the possibility, suggested by a number of writers,[10] that librarian self-censorship via failure to buy diverse and potentially controversial materials is probably more frequent and influential in library collections than censorship by patrons.

2. Have a selection philosophy/policy (see Chapter 5) and a reconsideration policy. The procedures for reconsideration should always require the protester to fill out a form in writing, and should include giving the protester full information as to why and how the offending material was selected.

3. Establish committees to assist in selection and reconsideration, and include representatives of all parties involved in the censorship attempt: library staff, administration (of school or other parent body), governing boards, parents, patrons, children, community organizations. Try for a wide cross-section of the community, and include minorities and even nonpatrons. A large committee can be divided into subcommittees by topic or interest area.

4. Include in the reconsideration policy what criteria will be accepted as valid for removing or relocating a book, such as out of date, new edition available, in poor condition, original cataloging not appropriate to library, no one has *ever* taken it out in 10 years, found legally obscene by a court, judged unsuitable by a majority of the reconsideration committee, and so on.

5. When people complain about library materials, treat them with tact and consideration, regardless of how much you may disagree with their protests or rhetoric. Let them know calmly and politely that you are sorry that they are upset, that they have a right to be heard, and that the library has a process for filing a complaint.

6. Whether or not protesters file written complaints, *always* ask them what titles the library could acquire to better suit their needs. Then show them that these titles are already in the library or—if they are not—buy some.

7. When a protest threatens to grow into a *cause célèbre*, turn it into a public relations opportunity by giving a press conference about the freedom to read, setting up a display of censored books or of books on different sides of the issue in question, or holding a community forum. Do not let the protesters seize the moral high ground by co-opting such buzzwords as *values*. Show that values in a democratic society are worked out by rational debate of educated citizens, not imposed through force by a few, and that rational debate requires information on all sides of the issue. Stress "We cannot remove the work you do not like, but we *can* include works you do like."

8. When dealing with administration and the press, take the stand that whereas

the library is part of and serves a particular community/school/organization, libraries have an independent responsibility as homes for intellectual innovation from all quarters and are neither slavish followers of a parent organization/community nor—conversely—hotbeds of irresponsible radicalism.

9. Know the censorship literature, particularly as it pertains to your type of library and your community.

10. Know the law in your geographic area as it pertains to sexuality materials in the library. Usually only materials for children or young adults would be affected. Those filing complaints may need to be reminded that while many acts are illegal, reading about them is not.

11. You yourself must be genuinely familiar with the particular works leading to complaints—and you must know the wider, embedding range of books that surround the controversy, even if they themselves are not under challenge. Only in this way can you discuss the issues knowledgeably and intelligently.

    Thus, if the area of controversy concerns sex education books for children, visit organizations and bookstores. Study and take notes on as many different books—and different kinds of books—as you can find. Collect reviews for these books. Consider having patrons, including young people, give independent reviews of books that the library is considering purchasing. Then when a book is challenged, you will be able to speak knowledgeably about it, why it was bought, what reviewers said (including patron reviewers), and what other books were not chosen instead. The librarian must be prepared to talk about the works available and describe books with different viewpoints.

12. Know the opposition. If protests originate in community groups, communicate openly with the groups, collect their literature for the vertical file, attend their meetings, and invite them to meet in the library (if the library has rooms for such functions). *Always* invite them to suggest books for the library to add that will serve their needs.

13. The library's strongest suit against all censors is saying this: We have in the library books you agree with and books you don't agree with. You have a right to not read (or not let your children read) books you don't agree with. But if we respond to your request and remove such books, then we would have to remove the books *you* agree with when someone else complains about them. And that we cannot do to anyone.

14. Keep in mind that you may have trouble mobilizing moderates to support your evenhanded position. Even though you probably have more moderate supporters than extremist protesters, the moderates will often remain virtually invisible simply because they are moderates.

15. Keep a file of names of outside experts with many viewpoints who can help you make a case about a particular book, including the counseling professions, educators, and clergy.

More general concerns about sexuality materials in the library can sometimes be addressed through programs—workshops about teaching children sexual values, panel discussions on erotica versus pornography—and a concerted effort to collect sexuality materials that reflect religious/conservative views as well as permissive/liberal ones. *Staff* differences of opinion about censorship and sexuality materials should be given open expression in meetings and addressed in staff training. Staff workshops could cover history and patterns of literary censorship, problems and challenges in providing library service on sensitive topics (sex, disease, adoption, and so on), and history of the literature of sexuality—using, for example, Chapter 2 of this book and *Science in the Bedroom* (D60, Bullough) as background, and even outside speakers.

But once again let us be theoretical and philosophical. What exactly *is* exercising today's censors? Many adults, especially parents, feel that the Modern World has moved too fast and that they have lost control of the trajectories of life. Their complaint about *The New Joy of Gay Sex* or about *Daddy's Roommate* is probably not so specific as it seems. Indeed, it may have taken them some time before they focused their vague feelings of helplessness on a specific title. For many such adults, library books are not the issue at all: books are merely convenient tokens of a far broader social process that they do not understand, sympathize with, or like—and that they wish to reverse when they demand that this or that book be removed. The book represents the world itself: remove the book and the evil in the world vanishes—it is healed and returned to what it should be.

The broader processes that the censor wants removed, healed, repaired—in brief, made to disappear—involve society-wide and worldwide changes in women's roles, family structure, sexuality information, and religion. So one can suggest to censoring patrons and parents that they might want to read about these embedding historical processes. Is it not the librarian's role to suggest titles of works written from *many* different viewpoints that deal with just these changes? The librarian cannot be everybody's therapist but can urge patrons to educate themselves and widen their own understanding about the social changes that so upset them. The librarian says, "You know, this book might interest you—it's about modern society and sexuality," or "Many people have such concerns—and here is a book written about just that," or "You are not alone in your worries and doubts, and you will find on the shelves many works about these very issues."

Are there such works about these worldwide transformations in sexual beliefs? Hundreds of them, and we have annotated a fairly representative sample in Part II. Yet this approach, which converts a complaint against the library into greater use of the library, requires that librarians know the modern literature on a wide range of sexuality-related issues. To an extent, that is one purpose of the present book: to give to librarians a list of titles that deal exactly with the concerns that sometimes lead to censorship attempts. But another purpose is to prepare librarians with materials that broaden the concept of "sexuality education" from teaching sexual plumbing to issues that by now are worldwide and involve everyone from cradle to grave. This approach expands the social significance of libraries from mere repositories of books all too often silent about sexuality to resource centers that can deal inventively and creatively with issues otherwise unfocused and frustrating to patrons and staff both. And in no area, perhaps, is this approach more important than in the heated arenas of sexuality information for young people, as we shall see.

CENSORSHIP AND RELATED ISSUES—BY TYPE OF LIBRARY AND COLLECTION

Throughout this book, we use the word *library* generally, as if all librarians faced similar environments when collecting sexuality materials. But public, academic, and school library environments are not the same. How do differences in type of library and collection affect sexuality materials? We will focus upon censorship and its ramifications for these three types of libraries and for their different books and clienteles.

The Backdrop of Censorship: Types of Libraries

Although all censors may be motivated by similar hopes and ideologies, the censorship climate varies greatly between public libraries and libraries affiliated with educational institutions—elementary school, junior and senior high school, or college and university. Next, within libraries affiliated with educational institutions, modalities and impacts of censorship depend on whether "children" are involved: school libraries have different relationships to censoring individuals and organizations than do college and university libraries.

One reason is the different patron base in public versus institutionally affiliated educational libraries. A second reason is that social trends in censorship affect adults' and children's materials differently, so that censorship manifests itself very differently in elementary school versus in college libraries. Significant factors in the difference include debate over the transition from childhood to adulthood; the role of state bureaucracies, political parties, and partisan groups in controlling ideologies and funding; whether libraries should function as symbolic educational entities or as reference repositories; and de facto lack of support for censoring adult reading— thereby leaving materials for young people as the only place censors can still work freely.

We first discuss public libraries and then turn to libraries with educational affiliations.

Public Libraries

Public libraries play a major and unique role in censorship debates, and we believe there are two reasons for this. One is diversity of the patron base and the other is "cross-over" reading, meaning that children can access adult materials.

Public library clienteles differ widely in ages, interests, and outspokenness, and represent different ethnic, cultural, and socioeconomic groups. With such varied backgrounds and tastes, it would be unusual if a few people did *not* sometimes react uncomfortably to books read by others. A goodly number of complaints and challenges in public libraries seem inevitable.

When adult materials are challenged, librarians have many response options, as we stress throughout. One can cite use by other groups, the "We have to be fair to everybody" argument. Reference to positive reviews is of course also valuable. But most useful may be a simple explanation of the library's purpose: where else can you find works of diversity and difference *except* in a library? Libraries accumulate books—they do not pass judgment: that is *your* prerogative as reader. For challenges to adult reading materials, these approaches ought to work—as censors know well because they have almost completely dropped challenging books for adults in favor of attacking the books they dislike as "unsuitable" for young people, of which more later.

Other issues stem from diverse patrons and reading habits. Public library patrons use the collection for different purposes, and so tension develops among library functions: information provision, research, education, recreation. To which should the library give greatest support? If you ask patrons, they may list the first three, but their actual usage may reflect the last. Thus a situation might arise where library purchase of erotic novels leads to criticism, but the sexy novels that the library *does* have circulate like crazy. Public libraries must consider such questions when drafting collection development philosophy and policy documents and decide what weight to give circulation statistics in determining collection emphasis.

Patron diversity also creates problems in buying sufficient variety in subjects and viewpoints to serve borrowers adequately. In adult collections, selection may be a greater problem than patron demands that books be removed. One reason is that many reader groups may be invisible to librarians, who therefore conclude that few titles are needed on homosexuality or that "sexual harassment is not a problem in our town"—so we don't need many books about it. A rape victim is not likely to tell a librarian that all the books on rape survival have been checked out, so can the library please buy some more? The only solution is for librarians to buy books on many sexual subjects, based upon local and national incidents reported in the news, and monitor what circulates, disappears, or is vandalized. Those patterns will show where the needs are.

Similarly, when adults do not find the library collection hospitable to their viewpoints, they will simply vote with their feet and not visit again. If all the sex books reflect permissive views, many conservative individuals will not borrow them and may not come back to the library. And then they will not support the library in a censorship battle: "Yes, the library *does* have too much on sex that shouldn't be there. All I saw were books promoting masturbation, promiscuity, and homosexuality." Librarians absolutely must buy some religious and conservative books on sex, both so that these people can receive some sex education (they may not be able to find such books in bookstores) and to enlist their support of the library as fair and evenhanded.

Public library adult collections on sexuality must also allow for a variety of reading abilities and format preferences, from grade 9 reading levels and even comic books to more sophisticated and complex works. Unfortunately, few sexuality titles seem to be available for reluctant or beginning adult readers.

Patron variety causes problems in an additional way. Sexual harassment by patrons is likely to be most bothersome in public libraries because the library is open to the entire community—and the more varied the community, the more likely there will be people who behave in sexually inappropriate ways. In addition, as U.S. citizens become richer and large bookstores more widespread, library use may decline among the "haves," leaving the "have-nots" to predominate among patrons. Public library clientele may increasingly concentrate more marginal individuals, including people with marginal sexual self-control. With this in mind, public librarians should think about different user needs and about how to deal with possibly increased deviant behavior among patrons.

Cross-Over Reading in Public Libraries

Public libraries serve all ages, creating a "cross-over" readership problem where children can access adult books—not because librarians give such books to children, but because kids find them on their own. And, once found, sex books are interesting if only for being (usually) proscribed. The presence of sexuality materials in public libraries is acceptable to many—not all!—library patrons, providing they visualize a grown-up reading the book. But when it comes to the *children* reading *The Joy of Sex*, many patrons will react with horror.

Cross-over reading leads to censorship efforts in part because few libraries today tolerate challenges to adult reading. The trend away from censoring materials for adult readers belongs to a far broader class of social changes, many external to libraries. Among many others, these include widespread public discussion of AIDS; legitimation of X-rated zoning by city councils; Supreme Court decisions based on the Rehnquist concept that a free marketplace of ideas includes sexuality works for adults; extensive publicity campaigns urging condom use; and increasing media coverage of homosexuality and other sexual minorities. One consequence is de facto access for adult readers to materials and ideas that once would have been condemned out of hand.

But another consequence has been a shift of censorship focus to the only remaining area: children's access to sexuality materials. The fear of cross-over reading accordingly leads to a wide variety of challenges in public libraries, aimed at removing books not because they are bad for adults but because they are allegedly "unsuitable reading for innocent children." Indeed, books for modern adult readers do represent a wide variety of sexual viewpoints and genres, and are often far more detailed and explicit than children's books. Therefore confrontations can readily arise between librarians and citizens' groups about young people's seemingly overeasy access to such adult materials.

This theme recurs in complaints directed against adult classics—*The Catcher in the Rye* is especially notorious—when they are included in school libraries, but the problem is certainly prominent in public libraries. Some public libraries may prevent children from entering adult reading rooms, but most do not so sharply segregate visitors by age, making the perceived problem more acute. Although school libraries have their own problems with censorship—as discussed below—their collections are more homogeneous.

Since the ALA guidelines mandate completely open collections for all patrons[11] and since physical and administrative separation of adult and young people's collections is cumbersome to implement, many public libraries resist complaints about dangers of cross-over reading. Librarians also quite rightly disclaim responsibility for monitoring children's library use, telling parents in one way or another that they must control their own children's reading—whether in the children's or adult collection.

Nonetheless, some public libraries do attempt to limit or prevent youthful use of adult materials, for example by physical barriers, separate library cards for youth and adults, "behind-the-desk"-only access to the most explicit or controversial sex books, parents' approval for children to check out adult titles, parental access to children's circulation records, and so on. Sometimes these measures are presented as compromises to censors who threaten to defoliate the adult collection so long as young people have access to it.

The only defensible compromise—if one *can* compromise with censorship—is open access by default, coupled with restriction by special request. Thus, a particular parent may sign a form authorizing the library to refuse circulation to his or her child for certain books or certain classes of books. This approach is still cumbersome to administer but less so now in the age of computerized circulation. While contrary to ALA guidelines, this system at least does not deprive other library patrons of access because of the complaint of one.

Dual Library Citizenship?

However, the cost of restricting cross-over reading is to create a sort of dual library citizenship: one class for adults, another for children. One can wonder if teaching young people that certain books are off-limits engages their interest in reading or sends them the directly opposite message. To be sure, that message may be the censor's purpose in life, but should libraries endorse it? Setting aside rhetoric about the freedom to read, we can suggest that when stratagems of library censorship are taught to children, the outcome is a guaranteed reduction in library clientele when these young people grow up. From the viewpoint of long-term growth, censorship has a stunting effect that at a minimum teaches that libraries are *not* the place to find information at all. Indeed, to the contrary.

A personal recollection from one of us (TP) illustrates the point. I had a library card when I was a boy, and used to like my local library very much. Slowly, I realized that not all the books were available to me—the nice librarians would ask me if I had my mother's permission to read that book. Since I had my mother's permission to read anything whatever, I would say yes, but the librarians didn't seem to believe me and even wanted it in writing. Many decades later, I walked past the building where that library used to be. *Used to be*: it's some kind of store now. I stood and looked, wondering sadly about where the library went. Maybe I know: it lost all its readers. They grew up and remembered the kid's lesson: *libraries don't let you read their books.*

It is not a good idea, this telling children that they cannot read books in libraries. It makes them ask if libraries are necessary in the larger social scheme of things, and it creates suspicion of libraries when, as adults, they have to vote on library budgets. But it also violates a principle: books were written not to be sequestered away from readers but to be read. So we can hope for—and assuredly we urge—librarians to make available the holdings they have to all who want them, children through adults.

Academic Libraries

University and college libraries have a history different from the public library that alters much about them and how they handle censorship challenges. Indeed, universities and libraries have historically been essentially synonymous: cohabitation between books and scholars dates back to the earliest collections of scrolls and papyri held by priests, physicians, and other literate individuals in antiquity, and was the centerpiece of all medieval and Renaissance intellectuality. Today, a university without a library—and probably a large one—could not be accredited as an institution of higher education.

Accordingly, few materials bought by academic librarians are likely to be questioned, even when purchases are not curriculum-related. The great bulk of a university library's holdings fits into the category of "reference work"—meaning thereby not the librarian's concept of encyclopedia but the scholar's concept of any book at all that says anything even remotely connected to topics even more remotely interesting (maybe) to what a faculty member does, wants to do, or is thinking about doing. The range of potential interest—and therefore value—is perhaps the widest of all in the academic library.

So censorship challenges are far less frequent in academic libraries than in either public or school libraries—except, perhaps, in smaller, mostly denominationally oriented colleges or universities. In that setting, librarians, faculty, and administrators may all agree that the collection should focus on doctrinally appropriate works and should exclude materials judged heretical or morally inappropriate. The second category may include works on sexuality, as Hippenhammer has documented for patron challenges to holdings in Christian colleges and universities.[12] In secular universities, particularly state supported ones, such challenges seem practically nonexistent. Certainly they would be easier to handle if only because the U.S. Constitution mandates separation of church and state. Nonetheless, when librarians, faculty, and administrators of a denominationally based college agree to exclude certain categories of work, the outsider must not cry *Censorship!* without first understanding that a private college has the right to collect what it wishes. An outsider might regret the narrowness of such collections, if narrowness it be, but one cannot argue that such decisions about the collection criteria are foolish or baseless.

Because denominationally based college holdings represent a special circumstance, we set them aside to return to the secular academic library. Here, our impression is that censorship problems rarely come from patrons, that is, college students. Occasionally deans or library staff will challenge sexuality materials; but even then, such challenges are likely to be confined to "leisure reading" such as *Playboy* magazine. Librarians defending the collection can expect much campus-wide sympathy for the freedom to read counter-argument.

Nonetheless, this glowing picture of academic noncensorship has its flaws. One concerns the so-called hate speech rules, and the other concerns omission of material representing society's fringes, be it conservative, particularly Christian material, or radical/anarchist, or material from alternative sources, including comix, zines, and much else.[13]

The recent movement in academia towards limiting "hate speech" tries to ban or render socially unacceptable discourse considered derogatory or dangerous to women or other groups. We gather that these policies have had relatively little or no impact—yet—on library holdings, but instead have been confined to speech per se. Occasionally, such sentiments have led to the removal of *Playboy* from college bookstores. At least some of these policies have been overturned by courts as violating the First Amendment to the Constitution. Nonetheless, in some universities, repercussions could be felt in library collections.[14]

In these situations, librarians can probably best respond by steadfastly sticking to freedom to read/First Amendment/academic inquiry arguments. A *reductio ad absurdum* approach might prove useful: if the library were to remove all materials considered derogatory to various groups, research collections on Nazism or Communism or the Civil War would be completely gutted, and the history department would firmly object.

In challenges to "leisure reading" erotic materials, students should be invited to participate in defense. Given a typical campus, several student organizations would issue angry denunciations of the material, a few would stand by it, and most students would worry about their exams. The faculty would divide along lines they have always divided along, with everyone nonetheless agreeing that It Is the Faculty's Prerogative to Oversee the Library's Holdings. Ultimately, the university president would issue a Proclamation Condemning Sexism and Other Forms of Prejudice, while simultaneously announcing that the collection would remain untouched. The students will then graduate, the faculty will go back to arguing about teaching loads and about Why Our Budget Isn't Large Enough, and the library will (again) be forgotten. Nonetheless, during these debates, the library should bring out data on actual circulation patterns of the material. Everyone will listen politely, knowing that if a *real* challenge came up, the library would be preserved even in the face of maddened monks carrying "Burn It Again, Sam" placards bedecked with pictures of Alexandria.[15]

Students can be asked to contribute to a fund to buy leisure reading materials such as *Playboy* if certain administrators raise a harangue about university resources being used for "sexist pornography." It is quite a different matter if faculty teach courses on sexually explicit communication and request that the library buy *Playboy*, *Penthouse*, titles from Masquerade Books or Blue Moon Books, or even *Hustler* or *Screw*. In that case, faculty and librarians are in it together if flak ensues. The major onus would devolve upon the faculty teaching the course, but library staff should be prepared to gather extensive background materials to support course selection and design.

In sum, serious challenges to university libraries are not likely to get very far, although occasionally patron disapproval will show itself through targeted vandalism and theft. But *a priori* censorship via selection is still an issue and especially affects collecting "alternative" materials either from the Right, Left, or Fringe. If funding is available, a "collect it all" philosophy should prevail, but no library has King Midas in the basement to convert crumbling journals into gold once they have been microfilmed. And—alas—one result is distinctly selective collection policies that tend to ignore a variety of extremely interesting and valuable materials.

Among these, we stress the need for collecting sexuality material written from conservative, religious and Christian, radical left, and anarchist/libertarian perspectives. Holdings in these genres, particularly pertaining to sexuality, are often notably weak in university library collections. In part, the lack reflects faculty indifference to these genres—and therefore lack of course support—but the problem also reflects the tendency to read and consider important mostly those materials representing one's own perspective. For most universities, these are the liberal, scientific/medical, and historical/social critical genres. Nonetheless, all university libraries should collect at least a sampling of these alternative views.

School Libraries

School libraries are strongly tied to the educational purposes, bureaucracies, and regulations of the parent school system. The young clienteles of elementary, junior, and senior high schools are more homogeneous than those of public or academic libraries; but, unlike those clienteles, have relatively little direct say in selecting or deselecting the library's holdings. Instead, state and local educational bureaucracies—the "school system"—as well as teachers and parents by and large determine for schoolchildren what the library buys, where books are shelved, and whether or not materials are retained after challenge. Nonetheless, the marriage of school and library is not fully harmonious. From this uneasy match comes a variety of problems, including those relating to censorship, that are notoriously difficult to resolve.

First, there may be general job-level tension between librarians and school personnel. Most school librarians are trained as teachers and have additional understanding of teachers and administrators because they answer constantly to their requests and demands. However, school administrators and practicing teachers are not librarians, and it is much less likely that administrators and teachers understand librarians and library functions—largely because they don't have to. So it is squarely up to the school librarian to educate teachers and administrators about libraries.

Tension also arises at functional levels. Everyone agrees that the school library supports the curriculum. But to what extent does it go beyond it? How do freedom to read considerations apply to school libraries? Should the library acquire materials on different sides of an issue if the curriculum does not cover other viewpoints? What about leisure reading? Should school librarians buy genre fiction series such as "Nancy Drew" or the Piers Anthony Xanth adventures that have no curriculum tie-in? Public libraries that buy adult romances and Louis L'Amour novels are hardly likely to debate similar fiction for youngsters, but school libraries may be far less hospitable. Perhaps this literary reluctance is proper, but the librarian must still consider why a choice is made one way or the other. Moreover, conflict may develop at the broader level of institutional philosophy versus library philosophy. May a parochial school library collect both sides of the abortion debate? How about materials on birth control?

Finally, there may be tensions about who controls acquisition and collection policies. State or city boards of education as well as local school boards may simply assume that theirs is the sole prerogative to control what a school library stocks, so that the librarian becomes little more than a book distribution clerk in a school bureaucracy. Are librarians' suggestions for purchase treated as advisory only, as urgent recommendations, or as mandates? What about the librarian's veto power? Whereas these issues plunge deeply into how school libraries are administered—which is not our topic—nonetheless such organizational relationships between librarian, school principal, school board, and higher level state and federal government agencies may impact profoundly on a librarian's own view of how to handle sexuality materials.

Are there solutions to these dilemmas? We cannot discuss administrative issues in any detail, in part because they vary from school district to school district. Instead, we address more generally how the institutional setting of a school library delimits and constrains the censorship debate, and then make observations about some of the books themselves and how they are read.

Our discussion elaborates on several points about school library censorship and selection issues. One is that debates on censorship in schools seem driven far more by adult obsessions with politics than by concern for providing youngsters with reading material. A second point develops the idea that the censoring impulse, foiled from controlling adult reading, has turned to children. In addition, children and young adults have reading interests of their own that are independent and paradoxical. Adults see messages that young people do not, and young people draw conclusions that adults do not foresee. These processes all affect how censorship occurs—or does not—in school systems. To some extent, they also affect how censorship occurs in public library children's collections, so our discussion has relevance to all children's librarians.

Adult Power Struggles Versus the Library Philosophy

At the microscopic level of a particular school library, individual decisions will determine how a censorious challenge is handled—and those decisions are often affected by the sheer chance presence in one institution of a few anti-censorship advocates among librarians and teachers, but their absence in another. However, at the macroscopic level, we sense that there

is no profession-wide consensus in education on how to handle the proliferation of sexually related works written for—or attractive to—young people. The importance of such consensus brings us once again to matters of
philosophy and purpose.

Achieving this consensus will be no easier than it is for society at large,
if only because school systems, libraries included, are a microcosm of society. In the *long* run, it will be the responsibility of university teaching
programs in education and educational librarianship to bring these matters
into undergraduate and graduate curricula, but what about in the mean-
time?

First, we can offer general advice about handling censorship challenges.
Librarians, teachers, and administrators must clarify roles, functions, rules,
and ways for resolving institutional conflicts. Librarians need to prepare
thoroughly for any potential conflict, document all decisions, and gather
as much support as possible both from inside and outside the school. It
doesn't hurt to "know everybody"—a person known is less threatening
than a person unknown. So one must get out of the library, to talk to
teachers, administrators, and parents—as well as children. And talk about
everything, as people to people: gardening, home repair, the transit strike.
Common interests make people seem less different, less alien, more credible.
If people listen to you attentively when you share information about replacing a doorknob or growing tomatoes, they will be more likely to listen
to you about sexuality materials in the library.

But being a nice person and listening and talking to lots of people will not
solve the underlying lack of philosophical vision. Indeed, the school library
environment has a peculiarly strong need for a library philosophy. We can illustrate by a hard-headed look at the realities of restriction rules, be they purchasing restrictions based on morality, a mandate to include only the most
immediately needed curriculum-related material, or a sense of burned-out "I
just work here" surrender to rules and regulations. Let us not consider a genuinely poverty-stricken school district but look instead at a system sufficiently wealthy that it actually can afford to buy recreational fiction for the
schoolkids—such as one of Piers Anthony's Xanth books.

In a genuine sense, any debate about this purchase is a tempest in a
teapot—and the smaller the teapot, the worse the tempest. But the debate
is irrelevant to what the children do and do not read. Instead, it concerns
adult issues of power and symbol. Thus, any child drawn to science fiction
and fantasy—Anthony's genre—will already have found his books in bookstores and catalogs, from friends, or through online chats on the Net. The
others don't care about Anthony. To be sure, one or two or three children
might start a life as a science fiction fan because they picked up an Anthony
novel in their school library, but most will find him through other channels.

If one chooses an example of a "more serious literary novelist"—such
as Thomas Hardy—it starts to become laughable that any large number of

children will immediately run to the school library amidst childish cries of enthusiasm: "Oh, gee, our school library has the new edition of *Tess of the D'Urbervilles!* I want to borrow it!" Dream on.

So, when adults debate what books a school library should have, exactly what are they debating? Only rarely is the issue what the youngsters will read, because most of them do not read anything at all. Instead, the debate concerns an adult issue: shall we grown-ups place our symbolic stamp of approval on this book by Putting It into the Hands of Children? For now, we disregard that these hands are mightily uninterested in most things grown-ups give them, as opposed to their own world of peers, television, sports, surviving recess, and the like.

Children's reading has become the battleground for adult power struggles: control over what children read has come to symbolize control over society. We suspect that these efforts stem from censors knowing all too well that attempts to limit adult materials are doomed by the very plurality of voices we have been emphasizing. One consequence has been the emergence of a *pseudo*-consensus that says, "We're not censors, we just don't want *our children* reading this." The censor still wants desperately to tell others what is and is not right, and to require that others grant the censors moral superiority over social problems. Now the censoring impulse—at root, this sense of beleaguered moral superiority to others—has seemingly found a way to ground itself in deeper concerns for the health and well-being of children. But, in turn, that is the problem with such efforts: censors are less concerned with children than they are with censoring books in the *name* of children. If the censor cannot speak for society as a whole, then the censor "knows" what is good for children and speaks for *them*. Indeed, in a society where adults no longer heed the censor's superior moral tone, the only ones left are children—*because they cannot talk back.*

We are tempted to respond, "Pick on someone your own size." But this raises the question, do children have the "right to read," and how should librarians handle children's requests for books and information that run counter to implicit or explicit policies and permissions? Supposing Jennifer's parents have signed a form forbidding her access to the adult collection, and librarians see the girl hunkered down with *Our Bodies, Ourselves,* which someone has left out on a table? Some librarians, remembering their own childhoods, aid and abet the children. And who can blame them?[16]

Nonetheless, individual efforts to let children read "forbidden books" do not substitute for an overarching philosophical commitment from the library and its affiliated educational institutions. The greatest obstacle to implementing a free-access-to-books-for-children policy is a deeply felt moral repugnance among many parents and religious leaders to the sexuality materials themselves, no matter who might read them; second, revulsion against the authors and promoters of such materials; and third, a deepset fear that children will be enticed into immorality. Yet, unstated by most censors, there is a fourth issue: sexuality materials in the hands of children have come to symbolize the loss of adult moral values and therefore of adult moral superiority and power over children. Such parents and others genuinely fear that their children will be lost to them completely if the children slip away into a modern world of sexuality. In this, sexuality plays a role not so much via physical intercourse but as a social symbol of battles between opposing phalanxes of adults: some write Bad Books (which end up in the kids' hands), and others view with alarm (and try to take the books away). At root, it is still a battle of adult viewpoints.

These issues are only worsened when concerned and frightened parents organize groups that attempt to exercise political influence over school boards and libraries. Yet, in the long run, we uphold the view that politics is by its very nature transitory and that a solidly held, thought-through philosophy of acquisition and access will prevail. But with sexuality, the difference is even greater between visualizing the school library as a monument to ideal morality and visualizing it as an archway opening to further knowledge. And this, it seems to us, is the great decision facing school libraries about sexuality materials: What is your purpose?

There is no easy answer to this philosophical question about school libraries, except to insist that it *is* a philosophical question and deserves careful thought. The fundamental problem raised by school library censorship efforts centers on distinguishing issues of what children actually want and need from issues of adult power struggles over symbols of What We Want Our Children to Read. Any school library book may evoke challenge when parents or other concerned citizens worry about All the Wrong Books in The Library. That is one philosophical pathway: to argue that even if the kids don't read—and perhaps especially if they don't—the purpose of a school library is to accumulate books (mostly unread) symbolizing what adults believe is right and proper. The library becomes a monument not to reading but to a social ideal presented to children. The other philosophical pathway starts with knowing that children live in a very dangerous and nasty world and that their reading is often complex in motivation and effect. One then concludes that school libraries should contain as many books as might entice further reading from those just discovering books and that will open new worlds to those who have already found them.

The Foreground of Censorship: The Books Themselves and How They Are Read

We turn next to considering children's books that can—and have—elicited censorship challenges. We offer here not the usual list of challenged titles—librarians know it by heart anyway—but try to create a broader framework that makes sense of what is challenged and why. It does not suffice to say, "Conservatives object to *The Catcher in the Rye*"; we must look more carefully at the way children and young people in fact read such books.

Children's books are more homogeneous than adult books, with less divergence in viewpoints. Until recently, many topics were virtually untouched. Books with gay and lesbian themes are beginning to take up a large part of this "formerly untouched" group—the most challenged book of both 1993 and 1994 was *Daddy's Roommate*. Certainly, challenges to children's materials have increased precisely because such books have departed from classical canons of children's stories. These, we sense, developed in the 19th century and were elaborated in the 20th into depictions of childhood as a sanitized, golden age to which adults—who wrote these books and who bought them for children—wished devoutly they themselves could retreat. In parallel, the traditional animated cartoon, like Disney's *Cinderella* and *Snow White*, dwelt in a world made attractive for its extraordinary divergence from adult realities of the Great Depression, World War II, Hiroshima, and the Cold War. *Winnie the Pooh* is as unrealistic as any adult escape fiction could ever be. And sexuality simply did not exist.

By contrast, young people themselves—pre-adolescents and up—took to the comic book and *True Romances* with open hearts. *Mad Magazine*'s idiot grinning Alfred E. Newman became the perfect anti-icon against the saccharinity of children's official literature and official culture. By the time the Hulk came grunging through the comics, an alternative youth culture was firmly in place—and long before Ninja Turtles or the Power Rangers.

So, from the outset, paradoxes loom large. Children do not read books the way adults think they do. We are reminded of a 1960s *Punch* cartoon: a mother is reading to her young son. "This is the story of Freddie Fox . . ." The boy—maybe eight years old—is visualizing a dashing fox with a walking stick and a great furry tail. ". . . Grandma Goose . . ." He visualizes a rather dowdy goose with pocketbook and flowered hat. "And," mother continues, "Barbara Bunny." He now sees a buxom young woman in a Playboy Bunny costume.[17] And yet part of the point is that his expression never changes: if we have Freddie Fox and Grandma Goose, why, then, Playboy Bunnies are part of the same world.

It is a paradox: adults know that Barbara the Playboy Bunny does not belong in the category of children's fictional characters. Adults would never confuse the world of dowdy Grandma Goose and the world of a sexy Playboy model. But for the child, each belongs to the *same* world: the one he lives in—or she, if it be a little girl. But adults react to children's reading on adult bases, seeing in children's books what adults know rather than what children see.

This paradox is illustrated elegantly by the debate over *Daddy's Roommate*. Basically a simple story of two gay men, one a father with a young son, adults have taken it as a profoundly important symbol of What We Are Teaching Our Children. Its publication was heralded as a gay-friendly event, and conservatives quickly countered with their own children's book—*Alfie's Home* (C6, Cohen; see Chapter 11). This is a semi-autobiographical tale of a boy seduced by his uncle, yet who finds an adult man to counsel him, enabling him finally to decide that he will *not* grow up homosexual. Our copy of *Alfie's Home* contains a variety of praising comments from conservative writers and critics, including Judith Riesman, and on the book's back pages describes the author's therapeutic institute for healing homosexuality in *adult* men. These are all adult political statements addressing adult morality—and they are aimed at adults.

But a boy reading *Alfie's Home* in all likelihood will pay no attention to these boring quotations and institutional purposes and might even pass over a several page illustrated ending where Alfie grows up, marries Nancy, and becomes father of Jared and Jennifer, all living happily together in "Alfie's Home." Instead, the boy reading *Alfie* might decide that it is perfectly OK for him to have sex with men when he's a boy, because when he grows up he can have sex with girls. This reading is not that of an adult who sees the political symbols—that is, the tempest in the teapot—but of a child who simply reads the words and story of *Alfie's Home* and who reaches a decision about sexuality diametrically opposed to the author's stated intentions.

We may call this phenomenon "paradoxical reading." It means that grown-up authors and critics see one message in the text, while youngsters may find exactly the opposite message. And the philosophical question that must underlie all debate about books in school libraries is whether to focus on adult symbols and meanings *or* on what the book actually, if paradoxically, may say to young readers. If the first path is taken, then by all means argue about excluding Piers Anthony or *The Catcher in the Rye* or *The Wizard of Oz*. If the second path is taken, then include as much material as you can afford to purchase because you *cannot* tell what young readers will infer, conclude, or learn. Adults may cry that *The Catcher in the Rye* is filth, is immoral, promotes rebellion—but the kids either won't read it at all or will laugh at its hopelessly outdated picture of growing up in America. And a few will find it fascinating not for its "immorality" but for its world.

But we need not rely on Salinger to illustrate the trickiness of paradoxical reading. One illustration in *Alfie's Home* shows him being called "faggot" and "queer" by other boys. It is a realistic enough image of Alfie's unpleasant situation. The intention may be clear to adults: they know they are supposed to identify with poor Alfie and sympathize with him. But at least some boy readers—paradoxically—will promptly adopt these taunts to cause hurt. For all too many boys who seek modes of antisocial expression, the effect is the same as if the book had the taunters calling another child "nigger." The intentionally sweet ending—Alfie marries Nancy and they live happily in their little home—can paradoxically be swamped by alternative readings.

Children's reactions to writing and visual material are thus startlingly idiosyncratic. It is *very* difficult to tell what will and will not upset them. Would all children find Mike Diana's cartoon cannibalism of sexual organs *that* much more disturbing than Wile E. Coyote being flattened for the nth time in pursuit of Roadrunner? (See the Humor and/or Cartoons section in Chapter 12.) No one, including us, really wants to test the question! But most of us have at least survived Nick Chopper's dismemberment en route to his rebirth as the Tin Woodman of Oz. Is it a good idea to include in a school library a tale of two children who are beheaded, and their blood poured all over a statue in order to bring it to life? It sounds like ritual Satanic abuse, or Elizabeth Bathory, or even Vlad the Impaler. But millions of kids have read this tale: it is the story of Faithful John in *Grimm's Fairy Tales*. The crucial point was made by Bruno Bettelheim in a thoughtful analysis of just such tales of horrible gore. They neutralize the infinitely worse nightmares of childhood—and the realities as well, such as being pushed down a flight of metal stairs by another kid.[18]

Actual reading tastes of children tend to get lost in censorship battles, but alert librarians will notice that children's preferences in books sometimes conflict with adult notions. Whom does the library serve? Many children love bathroom humor, food-dirtying, and far-fetched wordplay.[19] Does the library buy *Everyone Poops* (by Taro Gomi; Kane/Miller, 1993) or *The Story of the Little Mole Who Went in Search of Whodunit* (by Werner Holzwarth and Wolf Erlbruch; Stewart, Tabori & Chang, dist. by Workman, 1993), both of which apparently have great appeal for children, even though many adults find them disgusting? (The latter book carried in its cataloging-in-publication the probably quite rare subject heading DEFECATION—FICTION.) How about *The Gas We Pass: The Story of Farts* (by Shinta Cho; Kane/Miller, 1994)? (We have heard of only one other book on this subject: *It's a Gas: A Study of Flatulence*, by Eric S. Rabskin and Eugene M. Silverman, Xenos Books, 1991—but this is written for adults by a Ph.D. and a physician).

Are you shocked and startled by Alfie and Grimm and all the rest? If you are, you are among many adults, but only some children. If you are a mother, you may be firmly opposed to placing such horrible works in the hands of your children—and that is your right. But do not justify your decision by saying that little boys and little girls are too weak, too moldable to risk exposing them to such horrors. Jenny Davis coined terms such as "cockroach guts with whipped cream on top" and "crunchy barfola" for an individual whom adult ideology says ought to have been one of her nearest and dearest: her own brother. And Jenny was only eight years old when she wrote *Anchovy Breath to Zoo Food: 175 Names to Call Your Brother When You're Mad* (Avon, 1994).

Nor is modernity solely responsible for Jenny Davis. She had a counterpart in 13-year-old Mary Weller, who taught six-year-old Charles Dickens how to tell a story. Folklorist and critic Andrew Lang called her a "true genius." Her tale of Captain Murderer, who killed each of his brides on their wedding day, and his genuinely satisfying end can be found in Dickens' "Captain Murderer and the Devil's Bargain." Not even little girls are as nice as we think.[20]

Our point should be clear. Adult concerns about children's reading are arguments among adults about what is good for children, and only sometimes—rarely?—do they correspond to children's views of the matter. Accordingly, debates about school library books must be understood not in the context of children's lives but in the contexts of adult political and religious debates about adult moral viewpoints. In this, the children are unwitting pawns in a game they know little about. One must distinguish between the rhetoric of adult moral vision and the realities of children's needs as children see them.

Children's Collections—How to Cope

In coping with censorship challenges to children's books, librarians can again cite community diversity. "Yes, we believe that sexual values are important, including your values. We want you to teach your sexual values to your children. But not all parents in this town (school) agree with your values. You have the right to teach your values only to your own children, and you have a right to control only your own children's reading. You don't have the right to control other parents or other children." The parents who do not want their child to see *Daddy's Roommate* should be told, "You can prevent your child from reading the book and checking it out. But not all parents feel as you do. You do not have a right to prevent *other people's* children from reading it."

But then librarians must ask these parents what sort of books they do want for their children, and then buy some—*Alfie's Home*, for example, or some of the religious-based sex education books for young people that stress the rightness and beauty of sexuality only in the context of heterosexual marriage.

Issues in children's tastes, preferences, and right to read are another matter, and we have no ready answers. We suspect that more data should be gathered about children's spontaneous likes and dislikes, plus what they want to know. Using children as book reviewers might reveal some quite interesting information. As regards sexuality, *Show Me Yours!* (C86, Goldman & Goldman) is a start, and *every* librarian having contact with children of any age *must* read it. (Note: this is *not* the same book as *Show Me! A Picture Book of Sex for Children and Parents*, by Will McBride, St. Martins, 1975.)

As we noted, the ALA espouses open access for children, as for adults, to all materials. Ideally, that principle presupposes children having sympathetic adults to turn to whenever they find a book disturbing. On the other hand, children are victimized far more severely by poverty, street crime, violence, and abuse. If any children need the protection of sympathetic adults, it is these victims, much more than children made uneasy by sexual images in a book. As a result, we are not overly sympathetic to the hand-wringing of adults afraid that their innocent offspring will be "harmed" by *Talking with Your Child About Sex* by Mary Calderone and James Ramey or by Mark Schoen's *Bellybuttons Are Navels*. Much discourse about children's sexuality books needs to get priorities straight.

Young Adult Collections

> "Colonel Brandon is certainly younger than Mrs. Jennings, but he is old enough to be *my* father; and if he were ever animated enough to be in love, must have long outlived every sensation of the kind. It is too ridiculous! When is a man to be safe from such wit if age and infirmity will not protect him?"
>
> "Infirmity!" said Elinor. "Do you call Colonel Brandon infirm? I can easily suppose that his age may appear much greater to you than to my mother, but you can hardly deceive yourself as to his having the use of his limbs!"
>
> —Jane Austen, *Sense and Sensibility*, Chapter 8

The first speaker is the unforgettable Marianne Dashwood, all of 17 years old; Elinor, her sister, is 19—and their mother is "hardly forty." Needless to say, Marianne eventually marries Colonel Brandon, but it takes two years and several hundred pages.

And so it is that teenage sexuality forms the locus of the greatest debates of all about sex education and about library holdings. All the issues raised by children's collections also surface with young adult (middle school, junior high, high school, plus public library) collections, but are as pale shadows when compared to issues surrounding sexuality books for teenagers.

Traditional 19th and early 20th century books for teenagers about sex urged avoidance of all sexuality, even masturbation. Some modern books agree, taking deeply conservative religious views (see Chapter 11). Unfortunately, to persuade adolescent readers to eschew sex, traditional authors presented it as a terrible danger leading to physical and moral degeneration. In recent years, the physical degeneration theme is reiterated much less often, but the morally degenerative consequences of sex—especially for young women—are still strongly stressed.

But today's works on sexuality for teens are far more diverse than before because they are coming to reflect the genres of adult writing about sex.

Some present strict, religion-derived views that not only demand coital abstinence but urge avoiding all physical intimacy beyond light kissing. Others, representing the medical/scientific genre, describe male/female sexual anatomy and stress how sexual development occurs within the reader's own body. Such works often discuss contraception and abortion, as options made available by medical knowledge. These works are "liberal" in the sense that they emphasize an individual's personal choice and responsibility for his or her life. A few works for teenagers adopt feminist views, often urging young women to resist sexual forces of patriarchal males. However, very few take the historical-critical view, even though many teenagers would doubtless be interested in the history of courtship and marriage. All titles are *very* careful about legal issues of depicting underage individuals— for example, few photo or art books depict nude youngsters. Anarchist and libertarian genres of sexuality writing for teenagers are also dramatically underrepresented in titles available from mainstream publishers.

Fiction presents a somewhat broader spectrum. There are romances and love stories of varying sexual explicitness, including the famous *Forever* by Judy Blume; considerable cross-over readership by teenage female readers probably exists for gothics and Harlequin romances. Women's fiction has always been strongly erotic and romantic—except for strength of personality, Marianne Dashwood is not at all unusual. Nor is oblique but clear expressiveness of language unusual in women's writing: when Elinor Dashwood suggests that Colonel Brandon surely has use of his limbs, the context makes it clear that such limbs are all of them to be used for the bodily purposes of love. Modern women writers have kept pace with these traditions of women's fiction: Judy Blume is not as radical as she might seem to the shocked sensibilities of prudes. Women's fiction has never denied or censored the fact that one consequence of marriage is pregnancy, even if anatomical mechanisms of impregnation might not be described as directly as in the genres of medical and health oriented nonfiction.

It seems hard to write a convincing modern novel about a young woman in which her virginity is assumed and not an issue. Even *Sense and Sensibility* would lose most of its power if Willoughby had not invited Marianne to tour his future home unchaperoned. Marianne describes with some pleasure a "pretty sitting room upstairs"—the implication is clear that the couple had been examining the bedrooms also. (And given Marianne's great distress when Willoughby later abandons her, perhaps the couple had examined far more than the bedroom furniture.) Elinor contents herself by saying it was "indiscreet" on her sister's part to have accepted the invitation. Yet novels by women about women's lives in pre-contraceptive England and America center strongly on how to find a husband who genuinely loves the woman, thus surrounding virginity with a veil of being not much more than a temporary inconvenience.

These books are all among today's fiction and nonfiction sexuality titles for and about teenagers. As of 1964, the nonfiction group was subcategorized by John Farley as follows:

1. Adult marriage manuals (although today we would say "sex manuals")
2. Books dealing with birth control (and today we would add abortion)
3. Books dealing with sexually transmitted diseases
4. Books describing human reproduction with diagrams or illustrations
5. Books describing human reproduction without diagrams or illustrations
6. Sex education books written specifically for teenagers and recommended by national or local educational and library organizations
7. Sex education books written specifically for adolescents but not recommended by national or local educational and library organizations.[21]

These are still useful categories. Has anything much changed in 30 years?

The answer is yes—and Farley's work provides a sudden and startling glance backward. In 1964, there were two categories of books that *all* his librarians would censor: works about contraception and works about venereal disease. Today, in large cities entire stores specialize in condoms alone—and you cannot read a newspaper without encountering AIDS. Of course, Farley's librarians characteristically held the view that "bad effects" would assuredly result if teenagers read bad books on sex, arguing that obscene literature caused juvenile delinquency, as had been proven (they felt) by J. Edgar Hoover and by Frederic Wertham's study of comic books. Nonetheless, none of Farley's librarians denied that adolescents were interested in sex education books. Indeed, one librarian said that "students were always stealing books about sex and automobiles." So Farley concluded— we think sensibly—that "this interest seemed to be an embarrassment to many librarians, rather than the spur to acquire more and better books that a demonstrated student interest in some other subject might have been."[22] Well, failing to find "more and better" books, some of these self-same 1964 high school students grew up and wrote them. And in Farley's oddly prophetic words we see foreshadowed the immense explosion of works on sexuality over the past three decades. Yet that is not the only process at work.

Since oral contraception was introduced in 1961, a youth culture of sexuality has flourished not through mainstream institutional channels like churches or schools, or with parental support, but because teenagers *themselves* have created it. This culture includes zines, Riot Grrrls, campus slang like CFM, and much else that is irreverent—and very much the target of conservatives' angry denunciations.[23] We have found little research on the history of female youth culture in recent years, although the work of Sharon Thompson is a welcome exception. She finds that young women's narratives of sex break into two types: high melodrama, where the girl is seduced and abandoned in emotional distress and "hurt for a long time," and gleefully sexy tales of romantic comedy of how she seduced him and he "didn't know what hit him." It is thus hard to maintain the delusion that teens do not know a good deal about sex.[24]

Nonetheless, one still hears personal stories about young women becoming pregnant and not knowing how it happened. Accordingly, both informal and institutionally sanctioned sexuality education still has far to go. How can libraries, particularly school libraries, help?

Young Adult Collections—How to Cope

Sometimes sex *is* dangerous, particularly for young adults. They often do not know the limits of their own ignorance, and they may be too immature to pick up on books and experts who can help them. Nurtured on media simplifications, they may think themselves super-experts on sex and not seek additional knowledge. Or, when they do, do not know what to ask. The only remedy is to promote open discussion and information exchange in an overall educational atmosphere where there are no stupid questions even if there are also no easy answers.[25]

We maintain that libraries serving teenagers—either in schools or public libraries—must stock a balanced representation of existing genres of teenage sexuality writing, including both "official" adult-authored and "youth culture" titles. There is great need for clear, directly written material describing sexual development and the physical bases of sexual intercourse and contraception. Young adults need facts about sexual anatomy, processes, and consequences. Likewise, libraries must stock representative titles of moral and religious genres, chosen to reflect local religious and cultural history and life. Materials on gay and lesbian teenagers are much needed. It is especially important to find analyses and critiques of sexuality messages in the media—not enough books on this topic are available. Adolescents also need to know something of the history of sexuality and the debates about it through the centuries. And they need guidance in making their own decisions—which they will make, regardless of what adults say—whether for abstinence, noncoital sexual intimacy, or (hopefully protected) coitus.

Teenage sexuality information raises a unique "variety of materials" problem: because sexuality information is so crucial, young adult collections must address "reluctant readers" and those with learning or reading disabilities. This means books for lower reading levels, comic books, picture books, audiovisuals—whatever tells the story in ways these patrons will find interesting. By the same token, young adults with more advanced reading skills should have access to adult level materials. Thus, a 14-year-old girl who reads easily at the college level cannot be denied access to college level material, even if someone says she is "too young" to read it. (It seems reasonable that the person best able to make this decision is the reader herself.)

Similarly, access must be as simple and anxiety-free as possible, with as few titles as possible hidden behind desks or in offices. Protection from vandalism or theft is likewise crucial, so open access and high protection may be opposing goals. One solution may be buying many inexpensive copies of key titles, thus maximizing access at bearable risk. However, this method will not ensure protection from someone bent on wholesale destruction—not an impossibility if teenagers scrawl "faggot" all over everything. In locales with potential for teenage gang homophobia, library security can become important.

As if these issues regarding children's and young adult collections were not enough, legal restrictions intrude also. Some states have laws limiting access by minors to certain materials,[26] and there are of course the national child pornography laws.

With all of this, we find it amazing that sex education books get into young people's collections at all! For legal questions, we defer to experts. We are not sure what books among those commercially available might possibly fall under various laws or regulations. Probably very few, but librarians should check this out. Probably the most cost effective approach would be for a state library association to hire a lawyer to research the issue for all school and public libraries in that state.

Even if funding and shelf space are adequate to achieve a balanced and genuinely helpful young adult collection, there remain complaints and challenges from parents and others. These efforts are grounded in a hope of preventing exposure to undesirable and disturbing ideas that might "soil the innocence" or "corrupt" young people. In this view, certain books are intrinsically dangerous.

We do not agree. Nor do we know of evidence suggesting that when libraries remove *The Catcher in the Rye,* Judy Blume, *Changing Bodies, Changing Lives, Playboy,* or even the Fabulous Furry Freak Brothers, there then follows the disappearance of prostitutes, X-rated movie houses, drug use, AIDS, teenage date rape, or sexual abuse. Indeed, censors have argued since Plato that Some Books Are Evil—but never has the removal of books done anything except please censors.

Indeed, if censorship of youth materials is aimed at reducing phenomena like prostitution, it hardly seems likely that changing the reading habits of 16-year-olds in some high school will alter how hookers parade themselves along the Strip. It's like trimming the marigolds hoping to change how fish swim. So kids won't grow up into prostitutes if they don't read Judy Blume? You mean that women become whores because they *have* read her novels? Don't be naive. This isn't an attack on sexual immorality, it's an attack on reading and on people who read. It is *fundamentally* anti-intellectual. In the last analysis, we doubt whether censorship ever had any positive effects whatsoever. At base, censorship of youth materials is aimed at control over youthful behavior itself, as a set of prohibitions directed by grown-ups who want power and who like exercising it.

And although passionate, these impulses to censoring children's and young adult collections often have a somewhat theoretical air about them. Their claim to preserve and enhance virtue is circumlocuitous and a downright waste of time. The censor's proof of effectiveness is tautological: Judy Blume's books are immoral and when we remove them, we have therefore reduced immorality. Hardly a persuasive argument.

On the other hand, many books for children and teenagers about sex probably discomfort parents, and the possibility of children masturbating or "playing doctor" upon exposure to sex books upsets them. Yet neither is generally accepted as a grave danger to either the child or society, as compared, say, to lunatics with bomb-filled trucks. Again, it is a matter of priorities. Removing Piers Anthony's centaurs from a young adult collection achieves only the tautological: again we call it immoral, again we remove it, and then again we congratulate ourselves for ridding the world of immoral filth.

However, some adult concerns regarding exposure of young adults to erotic and sex education materials might seem more reality-based. Such people worry that teens and pre-teens will go out and *do it*—with pregnancy and disease likely sequelae, quite apart from concerns for morality and "corruption." It is an interesting theory of psychosexual development that adolescents read books and *therefore* decide sex is the thing to do. The body plays no role—just reading those books is what does it. But how come, if books make you do it, people had sex before books existed? You know, we don't believe such silliness. The "blame-the-books" argument collapses under the merest glance of common sense.

To be sure, many sexual conservatives and liberals agree that teens and pre-teens should not have coitus. Both sides thus agree on the desirability of sex education for young adults and even agree on a major goal of coital abstinence, but they do disagree about how to teach abstinence. Conservatives say that permissive teaching materials "promote promiscuity" and are "value free," while the permissive wing calls conservative materials "just say no" and "fear-based." Well, let them argue. Meanwhile, include both in the library, and let the teenagers consider both sides.

There are no easy answers about sex. And whereas young adult books have more variety of presentation and viewpoint than do children's books, they still give only a limited slice of the richness of historical and cultural responses to sex. Our young people need more than that, and anthologies may be useful particularly when young adults do not have access to, or guidance for using, adult collections of books on sexuality. But ideally all materials should be available to young readers.

Twigs and Branches

'Tis education forms the common mind;
Just as the twig is bent the tree's inclined.
—Alexander Pope, *Moral Essays*, Epistle I, line 149

The foundation of every state is the education of its youth.
—Diogenes

The future of America is not [shaped] by who sits in the Oval Office
[of the White House] but by who sits in the principal's office.
—Ralph Reed, Jr., Executive Director of the Christian Coalition[27]

Thus sayeth educators from time immemorial—and how better to bend people like vegetation than to make sure they read only Right and Proper Books in their youth? One result is that school libraries can be arenas for desperate struggles fought over the Minds and Hearts of Our Children. But once again some realism may help set into perspective the nature and likely outcome of these battles.

To reiterate, it hardly seems likely that school libraries do in fact *presently* shape much of young people's character, morality, or opinions. Far more effective than books are the realities of childhood, not peaceful and sweet—that is a politicized symbol, not a reality—but startlingly tricky to negotiate. Some children seem to be born rebels who argue with teachers, parents, other children—and books. Others are more complaisant, accepting what they are given and seeming peaceful enough. But unlike the conservative image of people as trees or foundation stones—immobile, solid, stolid, and unchanging—real people and real children tend towards flux and variation.

If giving only Good Books to children made them into decent citizens solidly accepting their role as trees and stones, do you think censorship would even exist? No one would even *write* Bad Books because children, having read Good Books, would grow up to write only more Good Books. Yet to the profound dismay of conservatives, something *does* occur between birth and adulthood that makes today's children—and children throughout history—somewhat less than real-life exemplars of the moralities presented in moralizing children's books. Grown-ups may try to bend children like twigs, but children—being animals, not plant matter—resist and growl, or accept and then later simply ignore what they were taught, or accept in part and modify in part and invent the rest for themselves.

So there are at least three visions of the ideal school library. One—which we like the most—would present children with the full panoply of children's and adult books and let them pick and choose as they like. Few children will spontaneously pick up heavy tomes of academic psychosexology (few adults do so!) but they will find other materials—some sexy, some not—and read this, that, and the other. In this vision, the school library provides a user-friendly menu of options, uncensored and unrestricted.

The second and third views put forward a far stronger link between classroom curricula and library holdings, but differ in the side they take in debates about sexuality that rage among adults outside of school systems. These polarize into "liberal" and "conservative" viewpoints.

The "liberal" ideal would provide school-age readers with primarily the sorts of literature found in SIECUS-style curricula. These teach sexual responsibility, particularly mutual contraception, and stress that sexuality is one's own to discover and, it is hoped, enjoy in sane, anxiety-free ways. In this view, a school library's holdings in sexuality would provide factual information based on the medical and social sciences, set into age-appropriate texts that emphasize both individual choice and individual responsibility.

The "conservative" ideal, typified by abstinence-only curricula, would prune the library's holdings of all works that appear to accept other paths than abstinence and replace them with books stressing a moral vision of sexuality as proper only for married adult couples. This view presents sexuality as something *they* do—meaning married parents—because they love each other and because they want babies to love. The emphasis is on moral and moralizing titles that give as little scientific/medical information as possible and instead stress moral relationship issues.

Nonetheless, liberal and conservative ideals coincide in agreeing that a children's sexuality collection should present versions of what each side holds up as its own favorite adult genre of sexuality writing. Thus, *Daddy's Roommate* presents the adult liberal, gay-friendly view of adult male homosexuality and does not mention the dangers of AIDS or describe hustling or the bar scene. The male couple is "just like" a married man and woman: they have a loving relationship, a home, friends just like the reader's Mommy and Daddy. In *Alfie's Home*, Uncle Pete—the pedophile who seduces Alfie—is a man without family, a loner, a man who is sexual but not loving and who seems to tempt Alfie into a life of unnormal adult homosexuality. In *Alfie*, we meet no gay men who have long-term lovers, who enjoy their own lives, or who are healthfully involved with gay issues, like AIDS activism. Each book skews the world it depicts to favor one or another adult vision of sexual right and wrong.

There appear to be two alternatives to surrendering to the agendas of these visions. Now we assume that the school library has some active say in what books are shelved, rather than merely automatically implementing curriculum-only book selections. One is to ban both sides as provoking bothersome controversy—to return to the traditional silence about sex. The second is to insist on balance. If *Daddy's Roommate* is a watered-down version of adult liberalism, then in it goes. If *Alfie's Home* is a watered-down version of adult conservatism, then in it goes also.

This course could bring out the worst in each side. Liberals are likely to be infuriated by *Alfie's Home*, and conservatives may continue in their detestation for *Daddy's Roommate*. Neither will praise you for suggesting the library stock their preferred book: it goes without saying that *of course* the library ought to stock it. But they very possibly will harangue you about how wrong it is to include the other book. Nonetheless, we think librarians should stick to their guns and get both.

So we believe in the second alternative: we insist that children are not twigs or decorative plant life but small, interested animal beings who explore and investigate all kinds of interesting stuff. They ignore some of it, dislike some of it, and become attached to other parts of the totality of their worlds. And their reading is paradoxical: they do *not* draw the conclusions from books that adults find so obvious. A boy reading *Alfie's Home* might quite possibly decide that he can have sex with both men and women; a girl reading *Daddy's Roommate* may decide that men like that should pay attention to females, not males. Some children, upon reading both books, will learn that homosexuality exists, that people write books about it, and that it poses problems. Children will create a unified world into which *both* books fit comfortably, even if adults are sure that the two books disagree so fundamentally that they could hardly even have been written in the same universe, let alone the same nation.

You cannot tell what children are thinking in their most un-twiglike little minds. Assuredly it is not what *you* think it is.

Handled properly, children can be the utmost delight for librarians. Many things that make them irritations to teachers—curiosity, question-asking, dislike for constraints about what to do now—are eliminated in the library, because the librarian tells them to Find Books You Like and Read Them. For children, a library can be the most permission-giving environment that exists.

This fact creates what is perhaps the most fundamental tension between school curricula and school libraries. Curricula are designed to shape twigs and foundation stones: they limit knowledge transfer to predetermined areas. Libraries are the opposite. *Alfie's Home* sits next to *Daddy's Roommate*, and together they open up worlds of immense possibility. All sorts of things exist in books. Ultimately, the library *opposes* the curriculum, not through reasons of personnel, administration, training, or conflict with bureaucratic mandate, but because the messages sent by curricula and by libraries are fundamentally different. One says Learn Only What I Say; the other says Read It All.

Throughout our discussion of libraries and education, we have insisted that stocking a library is *not* like developing a curriculum. And so we hold that school libraries must not be mere handmaidens of school curricula.

We resist the idea that libraries are tools for twig-bending or for shaping immobilized stones. Instead, we see the deepest tension between school libraries and curricula not as fights between liberals and conservatives but as an ancient conflict between expanding and narrowing life itself. In this conflict, we side with opening up possibilities, and accordingly see school libraries—and indeed libraries of all kinds—as containing the past history of such efforts. It is in the juxtaposition of *Daddy's Roommate* and *Alfie's Home* that children—and adults, if they bother to read the books themselves—will find the larger reality of life's choices, not a prettified picture of What We Want Our Children to Believe but of a world suitable for small, investigative minds—not plants or twigs, but people.

CONCLUSIONS

Ultimately, when we talk about restricting access to books, we are talking about barriers of control erected to prevent people from finding out what others have said, thought, and written. At their deepest, all censorship efforts are antisocial, no matter how prettily they are dressed up in fancy moral tones about the Higher Good. They separate, isolate, and destroy the human instinct to communicate with one another. At no level and for no topic can such vandalism of the human spirit be permitted.

In its ideal form, the library is the direct opponent of censorship because libraries accumulate books and ideas. They protect and disseminate the personhood of anyone who has ever written a single line. Thereby they protect the personhood of readers as well, and indeed the library in its ideal form serves to connect and relate people. As with all human interaction, sometimes encounters with a writer are unpleasant; but then again no one promised that everybody would always love everybody else. Disagreement is inevitable.

Do libraries have the right to restrict access to works on sexuality? No. But that answer arises not because sexuality is privileged in our philosophy for its ability to escape censorship but *because no censorship of anything at all is legitimate, and that includes sexuality materials*. Restriction of access in the service of protection against vandals is a worst-case compromise, undesirable in principle. Sexuality materials are uniquely interesting to human beings, and, if anything, sexuality materials should be offered the greatest opportunity for encountering readers, even readers critical of a book's message. At rock bottom, the ideal must be upheld that all books must be available to all people about all topics, including—and especially—sexuality.

NOTES

1. Cal Gough & Ellen Greenblatt, "Services to Gay and Lesbian Patrons: Examining the Myths," *Library Journal* (January 1992): 63.

2. James LaRue, "Reading with the Enemy," *Wilson Library Bulletin* (January 1994): 43.

3. Mark Stover, "Libraries, Censorship, and Social Protest," *American Libraries* (November 1994): 914.

4. James L. Sauer, "In Defense of Censorship," *The Christian Librarian* 36.2 (1993): 51.

5. Some especially valuable articles and books about coping with library censorship challenges: Frances M. Jones, *Defusing Censorship: The Librarian's Guide to Handling Censorship Conflicts* (Phoenix: Oryx, 1983); People for the American Way, *Protecting the Freedom to Learn: A Citizen's Guide* (Washington, DC: PFAW, 1989); Henry Reichman, *Censorship and Selection: Issues and Answers for Schools*, rev. ed. (Chicago: ALA, 1992); Office of Intellectual Freedom, American Library Association, "Before the Censor Comes: Essential Preparations," *Intellectual Freedom Manual* (Chicago: ALA, 1992): 205–240; Diane McAfee, "Put It in Writing: What You Should Know About Challenges to School Library Materials," *School Library Journal* (January 1993): 26–30; Martha Cornog, "Is Sex Safe in Your Library?" *Library Journal* (August 1993): 43–46; "Into the Lion's Den— Youth Access to Religious Materials: Building Strategies, Building Coalitions, Building Collections," *Journal of Youth Services in Libraries* (Fall 1994): 37–52.

6. See L.B. Woods & Claudia Perry-Holmes, " 'The Flak If We Had the Joy of Sex Here,' " *Library Journal* (September 9, 1982): 1711–1715; Edmund F. SantaVicca, "AIDS in the Minds of Librarians: Opinion, Perception, and Misperception," *Library Journal* (February 15, 1987): 113–115; Catherine Lemann, "AIDS and Public Libraries: A Look Back and a Look Forward," *RQ* 32.4 (Summer 1993): 505–514. Responding to the question, "If it isn't on the curriculum, do school libraries still have an obligation to collect materials on teen pregnancy and AIDS?" one school librarian stated, "I feel it is completely reasonable not to buy materials on teenage pregnancy and AIDS if these topics are not taught in the curriculum," so long as "there's a public library in the near vicinity" where requests on these topics could be forwarded. See Larry Amey, ed., "Issues," *Emergency Librarian* 21.3 (January/February 1994): 28.

7. Stover: 914.

8. Evelyn Geller, *Forbidden Books in American Public Libraries, 1876–1939: A Study in Cultural Change* (Westport, CT: Greenwood, 1984).

9. The 1994 *Encyclopedia Americana* reports that three separate incidents destroyed the great Alexandria library. The main library was damaged by Julius Caesar's legions when he besieged Alexandria in 47 B.C.E., and later ravaged by civil war under Roman emperor Aurelian in the late 200s C.E. An offshoot at the Temple of Jupiter Serapis survived until 391, when it too was destroyed, this time by Christians following an anti-pagan edict of Roman emperor Theodosius.

10. See Marjorie Fiske, *Book Selection and Censorship: A Study of School and Public Libraries in California* (Berkeley: University of California Press, 1959); John J. Farley, *Book Censorship in the Senior High School Libraries of Nassau County, New York*, Ph.D. diss., New York University, 1964 (Ann Arbor: University Microfilms, 1967): 336–337; Sanford Berman, " 'Inside' Censorship," *Wilson Library Bulletin* 77.1 (Spring 1981): 21–24; Judith Serebnick, "Self-Censorship by Librarians: An Analysis of Checklist-Based Research," *Drexel Library Quarterly* (Winter 1982): 35–56; Carol Hole, "Who Me, Censor?" *Top of the News* 40 (1984): 147–

153; Gene D. Lanier, "Censorship—The Enemy Is Us," *Media Studies Journal* (Summer 1992): 81–89; Celeste West, "The Secret Garden of Censorship: Ourselves," *Library Journal* (September 1, 1993): 1651–1653.

11. "The American Library Association opposes all attempts to restrict access to library services, materials, and facilities based on the age of library users. . . . Librarians cannot predict what resources will best fulfill the needs and interests of any individual users based on a single criterion such as chronological age, level of education, or legal emancipation." See Office of Intellectual Freedom, American Library Association, "Free Access to Libraries for Minors: An Interpretation of the Library Bill of Rights," *Intellectual Freedom Manual* (Chicago: ALA, 1992): 16–17.

12. Craighton Hippenhammer, "Patron Objections to Library Materials: A Survey of Christian College Libraries: Part I," *The Christian Librarian* 37.1 (November 1993): 12–17; Hippenhammer, "Patron Objections to Library Materials: A Survey of Christian College Libraries: Part 2," *The Christian Librarian* 37.2 (February 1994): 40–47.

13. Some libraries do acquire fringe material, usually in special collections. Lately founded and noteworthy are the *Factsheet 5* Collection at SUNY Albany and the Katzoff Collection at Brown University. The *Factsheet 5* Collection centers on the papers and zines amassed by Mike Gunderloy, who was the founding editor of *Factsheet 5*, a periodical reviewing zines of all types. The Katzoff Collection focuses upon homosexuality, especially male homosexuality; and since the recent donation of writer John Preston's papers, books, and estate, has begun to veer towards S&M and the radical/anarchist genre of sex writing.

14. See Robert Labaree, "When Policies Collide: Speech Codes and the Anti-Censorship Mission of the Library," *Library Issues Briefings for Faculty and Administrators* (January 1994): 1–3.

15. For any academic librarian attempting to understand faculty politics, the definitive analysis—nay, skewering—is F.M. Cornford's pamphlet, *Microcosmographia Academia: Being a Guide for the Young Academic Politician* (New York: Halcyon-Commonwealth Foundation, 1964), originally published in 1908.

16. See Ruth Gordon, "I Helped Children Lie," *School Library Journal* (February 1995): 42.

17. J.W. Taylor, cartoon, *The Punch Line*, ed. William Cole (New York: Simon & Schuster, 1969): 66.

18. Bruno Bettelheim, *The Uses of Enchantment: The Meaning and Importance of Fairy Tales* (New York: Vintage/Random, 1977): 116–135.

19. One of us (MC) remembers with great fondness Mrs. Pigglewiggle's giving a dirty child's mother seeds to plant secretly in her offspring's deepening outer crust. Soon the child becomes a veritable bush of green leaves and vines. How fascinating! Of course many adults love the same topics—but often feel guilty.

20. As James Thurber also observed in *Fables for Our Time*, when his Little Red Riding Hood hauls out a .45 and blows away the wolf. For Captain Murderer, see *The Complete Ghost Stories of Charles Dickens*, ed. Peter Haining (New York: Washington Square Press/Simon & Schuster, 1983): 24–35; for details about Mary Weller, who was Dickens' nursemaid, see Peter Haining's introduction.

21. John J. Farley, *Book Censorship in the Senior High School Libraries of Nas-*

sau County, New York, Ph.D. diss., New York University, 1964 (Ann Arbor, MI: University Microfilms, 1967): 199.

22. Works about contraception and venereal disease: Farley: 201; obscene literature causes juvenile delinquency: Farley: 147, plus Frederic Wertham, *Seduction of the Innocent* (New York: Rinehart, 1954); quote about books on sex and automobiles: Farley: 197; quote about embarrassment: Farley: 210.

23. CFM = Sexually suggestive: She had a CFM skirt on. From Come Fuck Me. See Pamela Munro, ed., *U.C.L.A. Slang: A Dictionary of Slang Words and Expressions Used at U.C.L.A.* (Los Angeles: Department of Linguistics, UCLA, 1989): 28.

24. Sharon Thompson, "Changing Lives, Changing Genres: Teenage Girls' Narratives About Sex and Romance, 1978–1986," in *Sexuality Across the Life Course*, ed. Alice S. Rossi (Chicago: University of Chicago Press, 1994): 209–232.

25. Parents need education as well. A colleague who teaches human sexuality in a university recently told us about a young woman who had asked her mother, in fear and alarm, what was happening to her when she had her first period. Her mother told her that she was bleeding because she had been "drinking too much Hi-C fruit juice." The young woman told our professor friend how much she appreciated learning the real facts in his course.

26. For example, Ohio prohibits furnishing to juveniles any material knowingly "obscene or harmful to juveniles" and also prohibits allowing any juvenile to be exposed to such material. "Harmful to juveniles" is defined as "representation in lurid detail" of various violent acts. However, a provision of this law exempts certain professionals, including librarians, when the material is provided for a medical, educational, or other "proper purpose." See Matthew L. Reger, "Freedom to Read: What Is a Library's Responsibility to Minors?" *Ohio Libraries* (Summer 1994): 14–15.

27. Jeffrey H. Birnbaum, "The Gospel According to Ralph," *Time* (May 15, 1995): 31.

II RESOURCES AND COMMENTARY

GUIDE TO READING PART II

This part of *For SEX EDUCATION,* See *Librarian* contains brief annotations for 597 books grouped into 48 topical sections, which in turn are grouped into five chapters for convenience. We discuss in the Introduction how we identified these books, why we selected some topics and not others, and what criteria we used for inclusion.

The Topical Sections. Each topical section begins with a brief narrative introducing the books in that section, and telling how to obtain information about additional titles; it also gives cross-references to titles in other sections. We often mention interesting works that we did not annotate, either because we lacked the space or the time or because we could not examine them personally.

The Annotations. The narrative is followed by the annotations, in alphabetical order by author for each section. Each annotation has been given an alphanumeric designation, which is used whenever that work is mentioned in Part I or Part II. Annotations give author/editor name(s), title, publication information, and notations about length, illustrations, notes, glossary, organization list, bibliography and/or reference list, and index. ISBNs usually refer to the paperback if one was available.

An Asterisk for "Best." An asterisk (*) before the title or designation number marks books we particularly liked and respected for doing very well what they were trying to do, according to criteria we discuss in the Introduction.

Suggested Age Levels. For many books in Chapter 11, and for a few books in other chapters, we have provided grade levels: birth (B), kindergarten (K), grades 1–12 (G1–12), college (C), and adult (A). Books not labeled should be assumed suitable for adults and many college students. Please note that these levels are estimates, not recommendations.

9 Sexuality and Behavior

GENERAL AND REFERENCE WORKS

We begin with basic reference books: encyclopedias, handbooks, and general research summaries. For dictionaries, see the Language and Sex section (Chapter 12).

Five encyclopedias of sex, from cozy to kinky, have been published in the last few years. *The Sex Encyclopedia* (A2, Bechtel) is short, readable, and solid, but not comprehensive. It would be good for circulating collections in high school, college, and public libraries. *Dr. Ruth's Encyclopedia of Sex* (A19, Westheimer) is much more comprehensive and is written for both younger and older readers. *Human Sexuality: An Encyclopedia* (A3, Bullough & Bullough) is more technical than Westheimer's work and suitable for college and larger public libraries. The esoteric Eastern traditions of mystical and sacred eroticism are addressed in *The Encyclopedia of Erotic Wisdom* (A5, Camphausen), probably best for university and larger public library collections. The kinky is well documented in *The Encyclopedia of Unusual Sex Practices* (A8, Love), a comprehensive, well-done work with something to appeal to or offend everyone. Outside of special interest newsletters, it is probably the only published source of information, and cautionary warnings, about many "unusual" sexual activities.

A number of general books summarize much knowledge about sexuality in lay language. Two excellent family reference books present comprehensive, complementary viewpoints and belong in every public library and college library, and probably most school libraries: *The Family Book About Sexuality* (A4, Calderone & Johnson) and *Sex Facts for the Family* (A12, Penner & Penner), the latter with a Christian perspective. *Sexuality: Health Facts* (A17, Stang & Miner) is a very concise presentation of basic information. A more informal presentation of similar material is *Sex for Beginners* (A15, Selkirk), using a lively, "sound-bite" semi–comic book style that would appeal to younger people.

Many readers like question/answer formats. *The Kinsey Institute New Report on Sex* (A14, Reinisch & Beasley) gives detailed and comprehensive information in readable Q&A narrative. From a sex therapist comes *Ask Me Anything* (A7, Klein), and from a sex columnist comes the entertaining *Let's Talk Sex* (A1, Alman).

For summaries of research, we recommend the recent *Heterosexuality* (A10, Masters et al.) and *Sexuality* (A16, Sprecher & McKinney). Older but valuable are the classic *Human Sexual Response* (A9, Masters & Johnson) and *Handbook of Human Sexuality* (A20, Wolman & Money). A recent large-scale survey of sexual attitudes and behavior has been published for popular audiences as *Sex in America* (A11, Michael et al.) and for scholars as *The Social Organization of Sexuality*, by Edward O. Laumann, John H. Gagnon, Robert T. Michael, and Stuart Michaels (University of Chicago Press, 1994, not annotated). The 1948 and 1953 "Kinsey reports" are discussed in the Female Sexuality and Male Sexuality sections.

It goes without saying that the major works of Sigmund Freud are essential to a basic sex collection, particularly *Three Essays on the Theory of Sexuality* and *A General Introduction to Psychoanalysis*. While many of Freud's observations have been supplemented and supplanted by later work, his writings have been fundamental in shaping scholarly and public attitudes about sex in this century.

An important type of general work is the anthology of opinions and views. Dushkin publishes two, highly valuable for high school, college, and public libraries: *Taking Sides: Clashing Views on Controversial Issues in Human Sexuality* (A6, Francoeur) and *Human Sexuality 94/95* (A13, Pocs). Both are updated regularly. A larger collection entitled *Sexuality* is available on subscription as part of the social/critical issues series from SIRS (Social Issues Resources Series, P.O. Box 2348, Boca Raton, FL 33427), not annotated. Another, widely varied, anthology is *The Erotic Impulse* (A18, Steinberg), which brings together scores of sex-positive intellectual heavy hitters: Anaïs Nin, Robert Bly, Camille Paglia, Gore Vidal, and so on. We feel that anthologies of people's own sexual experiences are an important component of general works. Here we suggest *Good Sex: Real Stories from Real People*, by Julia Hutton (Cleis, 1992), not annotated. (See also *Bad Sex*, noted in Chapter 6.)

Some general works about sex are included in the SIECUS bibliography,

Current Books on Sexuality, and some are covered in standard library review media. See Chapter 5.

See also the Homosexuality—General Works section in Chapter 10.

Annotations

A1   Alman, Isadora. *Let's Talk Sex: Q & A on Sex and Relationships*. Preface by Michael Castleman. Freedom, CA: Crossing, 1993. 216p. index. ISBN 0-89594-632-7. Questions and (sometimes witty) answers about all aspects of sexuality, reprinted from the *San Francisco Bay Guardian*. Viewpoint is permissive, emphasizing communication and responsibility. Covers common and uncommon sexual behaviors.

A2   Bechtel, Stefan, & the eds. of *Men's Health* and *Prevention* magazines. *The Sex Encyclopedia: An A–Z Guide to the Latest Information on Sexual Health, Safety, and Technique from the Nation's Top Sex Experts*. New York: Simon & Schuster, 1993. 365p. index. ISBN 0-671-74324-4. (Also published as *The Practical Encyclopedia of Sex and Health*.) Easy-to-read collection of entries on 115 sexual topics, *abstinence* to *yohimbine*, covering sexual behavior, sexual enhancement, contraception, STDs/AIDS and safer sex, dysfunctions, and disabilities. Short list of "Books on Better Sex."

***A3**   Bullough, Vern L., & Bonnie Bullough, eds. *Human Sexuality: An Encyclopedia*. New York: Garland, 1994. 643p. article refs. index. ISBN 0-8240-7972-8. Over 200 articles on sexual behaviors, physical and medical concepts, social issues, anthropological topics, and brief biographies of important figures in sexology. Over 100 contributors, most with advanced degrees and university affiliations. Appendix describes how to find further information.

***A4**   Calderone, Mary S., & Eric W. Johnson. *The Family Book About Sexuality*. Rev. ed. Illus. by Vivien Cohen. New York: Harper & Row, 1989. 288p. refs. (6p.). index. ISBN 0-06-091685-0. Family reference covering sexual development/ response, reproduction, family planning, marriage, family communication, sexual dysfunctions, diseases, social problems, sex and gender throughout life, and sex education. Pro and con of abortion presented. Stresses knowledge, acceptance, and responsible sexuality. Concise A–Z encyclopedia at end.

A5   Camphausen, Rufus C. *The Encyclopedia of Erotic Wisdom: A Reference Guide to the Symbolism, Techniques, Rituals, Sacred Texts, Psychology, Anatomy, and History of Sexuality*. Rochester, VT: Inner Traditions, 1991. 269p. illus. bibliog. (10p.). index. ISBN 0-89281-321-0. Over 1,000 entries on sexual traditions, myths, key individuals, and practices throughout history in various cultures, particularly from Indian, Asian, and other traditions of sacred sexuality and erotic spirituality. Cross-references and theme indexes allow readers to focus on a particular topic.

***A6**   Francoeur, Robert T., ed. *Taking Sides: Clashing Views on Controversial Issues in Human Sexuality*. 4th ed. Guilford, CT: Dushkin, 1994. 294p. chapter refs. index. ISBN 1-56134-249-1. Anthology of opposing viewpoints on 17 sexual issues, viz.: gender differences, sexual addiction, infidelity, pornography, RU486, condoms in schools, surrogate motherhood, abortion, date rape, homosexuality, prostitution, sexual harassment, and AIDS. Prior editions have different issues and contributors.

A7 Klein, Marty. *Ask Me Anything: A Sex Therapist Answers the Most Important Questions for the '90s*. New York: Simon & Schuster, 1992. 339p. bibliog. (4p.). index. ISBN 0-671-76114-5. Straightforward question/answer reference guide. Covers topics related to the body (contraception, menstruation, aging, STDs), arousal (orgasm, fantasy, masturbation, erotica), love and intimacy (monogamy, sex roles, homosexuality, spirituality), dysfunction and rape, and parenting (sex education of children, pregnancy, child abuse). Emphasizes communication, responsible decision making, and variety of sexual expression.

A8 Love, Brenda. *The Encyclopedia of Unusual Sex Practices*. Intro. by Michael Perry. Fort Lee, NJ: Barricade, 1992. 336p. illus. glossary (11p.). appendix of suppliers (2p.). bibliog. (10p.). index. ISBN 0-942637-64-X. Over 700 entries describing sex practices ranging from generally accepted, common, and safe (e.g., massage, kissing, body painting, masturbation) to bizarre, rare, and dangerous (e.g., autoerotic asphyxia, lust murder, castration, certain types of S&M) and in between (e.g., fornicatory dolls, spanking, orgies, bondage). Cautionary note included for all risky behaviors. Entries also include reference items such as sex clubs, sex conferences, and sexology.

A9 Masters, William H., & Virginia E. Johnson. *Human Sexual Response*. Boston: Little, Brown, 1966. 366p. glossary (10p.). refs. (19p.). index. ISBN U/K. A classic. Reports findings from laboratory and clinical observations of 694 men and women about anatomy and physiology of sexual response, with clinical/therapeutic considerations and psychological factors. Includes sexual response during pregnancy and in older individuals.

A10 Masters, William H., Virginia E. Johnson, & Robert C. Kolodny. *Heterosexuality*. New York: HarperCollins, 1994. 595p. illus. notes (67p.). index. ISBN 0-06-019041-8. Comprehensive sourcebook on heterosexual response, behavior, relationships, and related issues. Presents up-to-date information and summary of research in lay language; not a how-to. Covers love and intimacy, sexual response, sexual dysfunctions/compulsions, conception and contraception, abortion, STDs and HIV/AIDS, sexuality during adolescence and aging, and extramarital sexuality.

A11 Michael, Robert T., John H. Gagnon, Edward O. Laumann, & Gina Kolata. *Sex in America: A Definitive Survey*. Boston: Little, Brown, 1994. 300p. footnotes. index. ISBN 0-316-07524-8. Results of interview survey of 3,432 randomly selected U.S. people about sexual attitudes and behavior. Covers finding sex partners, number of partners, frequency of sex, practices and preferences, masturbation, erotica, homosexuality, STDs and HIV/AIDS, forced sex, and beliefs and attitudes.

*A12 Penner, Clifford, & Joyce Penner. *Sex Facts for the Family*. Dallas: Word, 1992. 336p. bibliog. (9p.). index. ISBN 0-8499-3287-4 (Rev. ed. of *A Gift for All Ages*). Comprehensive coverage of sexual topics pertaining to marriage and raising children, from Christian perspective. Includes family planning, effect of pregnancy and children upon parents' sexuality, teaching children about sex, single sexuality, sexual abuse, sexual addictions, STDs, and special situations (unconsummated marriage, in-laws, illness, aging).

A13   Pocs, Ollie, ed. *Human Sexuality 94/95.* 19th ed. Guilford, CT: Dushkin, 1994. 240p. glossary (6p.). index. ISBN 1-56134-279-3. Articles from the popular press on variety of sexuality topics: sex and society, biology, behavior and orientation, relationships, reproduction, sexuality through the life cycle, STDs/AIDS, sexual exploitation, and men vs. women.

*A14   Reinisch, June M., with Ruth Beasley. *The Kinsey Institute New Report on Sex: What You Must Know to Be Sexually Literate.* Ed. & comp. by Deborah Kent. New York: St. Martin's, 1990. 540p. illus. chapter refs. index. ISBN 0-312-05268-5. Very comprehensive collection of questions and answers about human sexuality, arranged by topic. Answers are clearly written and based upon factual information established from research, and give no "advice" other than sometimes referring questioners to a physician or counselor.

A15   Selkirk, Errol. *Sex for Beginners.* Illus. by Naomi Rosenblatt. New York: Writers & Readers, 1988. 221p. bibliog. (2p.). ISBN 0-86316-011-5. "Illustrated, often humorous documentary comic book that examines human sexuality from the standpoints of history, social relations, and sexual politics." Discusses meanings and functions of sexuality, sex and gender roles, nature vs. culture, rape, pornography, the sexual revolution, advertising and consumption, and AIDS. Quotes many viewpoints. (G10–12,C,A)

*A16   Sprecher, Susan, & Kathleen McKinney. *Sexuality.* Newbury Park, CA: Sage, 1993. 184p. refs. (26p.). index. ISBN 0-8039-4291-5. Overview of theory and research about close sexual relationships, primarily heterosexual; some coverage of gay/lesbian relationships. Topics: attraction, dating, sexual attitudes and behaviors, cohabitation and marriage, sexual satisfaction, sexual coercion, sexual standards and scripts, and safer sex.

*A17   Stang, Lucas, & Kathleen R. Miner. *Sexuality: Health Facts.* Santa Cruz, CA: ETR Associates, 1994. 116p. glossary (8p.). orgs. (2p.). refs. (2p.). index. ISBN 1-56071-187-6. Concise, ready-reference for key facts about sexual anatomy and physiology, pregnancy, birth, contraception, puberty and adolescence, romantic/erotic love, sexual response, sexual expression, and sexual orientation. Designed for health educators but suitable for many others. (G10–12,C,A)

A18   Steinberg, David, ed. *The Erotic Impulse: Honoring the Sensual Self.* New York: Tarcher/Perigee, 1992. 312p. ISBN 0-87477-697-X. Anthology of 51 mostly reprinted contributions about sexuality: essays, some fiction and poetry. Covers erotic impulse, sexual initiation, erotic imagination, differences between men and women, suppression of sexuality, and erotic spirituality. Contributors include many well-known writers.

*A19   Westheimer, Ruth K., ed. *Dr. Ruth's Encyclopedia of Sex.* New York: Continuum, 1994. 319p. illus. glossaries (11p.). bibliog. (4p.). index. ISBN 0-8264-0625-4. Over 240 entries on social and medical sexual topics, *abortion* to *zoophilia*, with 70 contributors, most physicians. Written "for the general reader and especially for high school and college students." (G10–12,C,A)

A20   Wolman, Benjamin B., ed.; John Money, consulting ed. *Handbook of Human Sexuality.* Northvale, NJ: Jason Aronson, 1991 (c1980). 365p. photos. chapter refs. index. ISBN 0-87668-775-3. Moderately technical essays summarizing much past research on human sexual development and behavior (prenatal through aging); sex and society (male/female relationships, discrimination, law, pornography); and sexual disorders and treatment (psychoanalytic, behavioral, and holistic approaches).

FEMALE SEXUALITY

In the following sections on female and male sexuality, we include general and reference works, scientific studies, and works about fantasy, sexual enhancement (making sex better and fixing what's wrong), and "sexual politics." We also include a few books on circumcision.

The revised classic *The New Our Bodies, Ourselves* (A24, Boston Women's Health Collective) and *Ourselves, Growing Older* (A26, Doress et al.) are good general references and cover much more than sexuality. Another good source is *The A-to-Z of Women's Sexuality* (A32, Kahn & Holt). An especially distinctive work that we class as reference is *Femalia* (A23, Blank), a sort of visual encyclopedia of adult women's genitals.

Although several recent studies discuss both men and women (see *Sex in America*, A11, Michael et al.), relatively few research-based books concentrate solely on women's sexuality. Three classics are *Sexual Behavior in the Human Female* (A33, Kinsey et al.), from 1953 but still the most comprehensive and never replaced; *The Hite Report* (A30, Hite), criticized as unscientific but highly worthwhile for portraying women's lives; and *The Redbook Report on Female Sexuality* (A37, Tavris & Sadd), focusing on married women. Author Nancy Friday has published a "progress report" updating her older work on women's sexual fantasies, so that we have both her 1970s classic *My Secret Garden* (A27, Friday) and her 1991 *Women on Top* (A28, Friday). A title summarizing for lay readers much scientific and feminist work on female sexuality is *Sexual Salvation*, by Naomi McCormick (Greenwood, 1994, not annotated).

We recommend five works for women on sexual enhancement. *For Yourself* (A22, Barbach) and *For Each Other* (A21, Barbach) are widely cited and highly regarded even though over a decade old. More recent and also often cited is *Becoming Orgasmic* (A29, Heiman & LoPiccolo). *Sexual Happiness for Women* (A41, Yaffé & Fenwick) takes a problem-solving approach to women's sexual dissatisfactions. *Ordinary Women, Extraordinary Sex* (A35, Scantling & Browder) is part research, part how-to, correlating heightened experience to fantasizing and selective self-absorption.

By "sexual politics," we mean various feminist perspectives on women's social and sexual behavior and roles, particularly relating to men. *Pleasure and Danger* (A39, Vance), *Sex, Power, and Pleasure* (A38, Valverde), and *Powers of Desire* (A36, Snitow et al.) examine the major issues, whereas the excellent *The Sexual Liberals and the Attack on Feminism* (A34, Leidholdt & Raymond) documents some feminists' disappointment and disagreement with goals and results of sexual liberation. A classic on women's overdependence on self-delusionary romance to "justify" sexuality is *Swept Away* (A25, Cassell).

Several recent works discuss female circumcision: the exhaustive *The Hosken Report* (A31, Hosken) and the more literary *Warrior Marks* (A40, Walker & Parmar). Another, not annotated, is *Female Genital Mutilation*, by Nahid Toubia (Toubia, 1993, from Women, Ink, 777 United Nations Plaza, New York, NY 10017).

Few theologically grounded books about sex are directed to women or men separately, although a large number of religious-based "sex-for-married-couples" books exist (some included in the Sexual Enhancement section). The reason, we suspect, is that conservative Christian teaching places sexuality into heterosexual marriage rather than seeing it as proper for individuals to explore in singlehood or solo, for example, by masturbation. Accordingly, the Christian books are written for couples and deal, sometimes gingerly, with couple-oriented issues and problems, not with the sexuality of women as women, or men as men.

The mainline media review a good many books on female sexuality. Browsing in bookstores is another route to titles. Some selections may be found in the Sexuality Library catalog, the SIECUS Current Books on Sexuality bibliography, and Focus on the Family's Women-Related Issues resource list. (See Chapter 5.) *A Research Guide to Human Sexuality* (D120, Lichtenberg) has subdivisions pertaining to women in many of its chapters.

The *Encyclopedia of Associations* lists dozens of organizations concerned with women's issues and feminism, of which the best known is the National Organization for Women (NOW). Although none focuses on women's sexuality per se, some address women's health, including contraception, abortion, STDs, menstruation, and rape. We list a few of these:

National Women's Health Network
1325 G Street NW
Washington, DC 20005
  Newsletter, advocacy, and answers to queries.

National Women's Health Resource Center
2425 L Street NW
Washington, DC 20037
  Newsletter, advocacy, information packets, answers to queries.

Melpomene Institute for Women's Health Research
1010 University Avenue
Saint Paul, MN 55104
  Journal, resource center, brochures, and information packets.

In addition, various medical organizations publish women's health news-letters, such as *Harvard Women's Health Watch*.

Many publishers have "women's issue" or "feminist" minicatalogs, including Greenwood, Haworth, and the University of Chicago Press. Other presses have an exclusive or near exclusive women focus, such as Hunter House, The Feminist Press at The City University of New York, and Women's Press.

Some catalog services specialize in books by and for women, particularly from small presses and including health and sexuality issues: Bookwoman Books (Box 67, Media, PA 19063), Old Wives Tales (1009 Valencia St., San Francisco, CA 94110), Pandora Book Peddlers (885 Belmont Ave., North Haledon, NJ 07508), and Women, Ink. (777 United Nations Plaza, New York, NY 10017). *Feminist Bookstore News* is a major guide and source of reviews for this general area.

See also the Sexual Enhancement section (Chapter 9), Disabilities and Dysfunctions section (Chapter 13), Books for Pre-Adolescents and Books for Adolescents sections (Chapter 11), plus "issue-related" sections such as Birth Control, Abortion, and Rape.

Annotations

A21   Barbach, Lonnie. *For Each Other: Sharing Sexual Intimacy*. New York: Anchor/Doubleday, 1982. 305p. notes (5p.). index. ISBN 0-385-17297-4. Manual for women about improving intimacy and sexuality with partners. Primarily heterosexual. Discusses common sex-related relationship problems and resolving them via understanding, communication, and enhancing sexual stimulation. Includes exercises.

A22   Barbach, Lonnie Garfield. *For Yourself: The Fulfillment of Female Sexuality*. New York: Anchor/Doubleday, 1975. 218p. notes (5p.). bibliog. (8p.). index. ISBN 0-385-11245-9. Manual for women about becoming orgasmic and enhancing sexual experience. Primarily heterosexual. Covers female sexual anatomy, masturbation, exercises for enhancement, communicating with a partner, sex and pregnancy, menopause and aging, and teaching children about sex. Pre-AIDS.

A23   Blank, Joani, ed. *Femalia*. Photos by Tee A. Corinne, Michael Perry, Jill Posener, & Michael A. Rosen. San Francisco: Down There, 1993. 72p. bibliog. (1p.). ISBN 0-940208-15-6. Thirty-two photographs of vulvas of adult women, diverse in age and race. Each vulva is normal, healthy, and aesthetically unique. Designed to answer girls' and women's concerns about normality of their own genitals, and to serve as reference for health professionals and laypeople.

A24   Boston Women's Health Collective. *The New Our Bodies, Ourselves: A Book by and for Women*. Updated and expanded. New York: Touchstone/Simon & Schuster, 1992. 751p. illus. chapter refs. index. ISBN 0-671-79176-1. Comprehensive feminist self-help health guide. Covers heterosexual and lesbian sexuality and relationships, pregnancy and childbearing, birth control, abortion, STDs and

HIV/AIDS, growing older, medical problems (e.g., endometriosis, breast cancer, toxic shock syndrome), and women in the medical system.

A25 Cassell, Carol. *Swept Away: Why Women Fear Their Own Sexuality*. New York: Simon & Schuster, 1984. 206p. notes (16p.). bibliog. (8p.). ISBN 0-671-45238-X. Describes how many women become sexually involved with men only by creating a self-delusion that they have been "swept away by love." Suggests that some women become involved too quickly with unsuitable men without taking responsibility for their own sexual participation. Stresses that women should take responsibility for their own lives and sexuality, and choose men realistically.

A26 Doress, Paula Brown, Diana Laskin Siegal, & the Midlife and Older Women Book Project, in cooperation with the Boston Women's Health Book Collective. *Ourselves, Growing Older: Women Aging with Knowledge and Power*. Illus. by Roselaine Perkis. New York: Simon and Schuster, 1987. 511p. resources (63p.). index. ISBN 0-671-64424-6. Feminist self-help source for women over age 40 about health, sexuality, medicine, and needs re work, retirement, housing, and economics. Covers self-care for "aging well," sexual functioning, birth control, childbearing, menopause, and common medical matters, e.g., hysterectomy, incontinence, osteoporosis, and hypertension.

A27 Friday, Nancy. *My Secret Garden: Women's Sexual Fantasies*. New York: Trident/Simon & Schuster, 1973. 361p. ISBN 671-27101-6. Nearly 250 sexual fantasies, from interviews and letters from over 400 primarily heterosexual women. Discusses function of fantasies, major themes, sources of inspiration, guilt about fantasizing, and sharing fantasies with a partner. Afterword by Martin Shepard discusses psychological factors.

A28 Friday, Nancy. *Women on Top: How Real Life Has Changed Women's Sexual Fantasies*. New York: Simon & Schuster, 1991. 559p. ISBN 0-671-64845-4. Collection of women's sexual fantasies, with three major themes: seductive and sexually controlling women, women with women, and insatiable women. Discusses evolution of women's fantasies and importance of masturbation for sexual health and self-acceptance.

A29 Heiman, Julia R., & Joseph LoPiccolo. *Becoming Orgasmic: A Sexual and Personal Growth Program for Women*. Rev. ed. New York: Fireside/Simon & Schuster, 1988. 266p. bibliog. (8p.). index. ISBN 0-671-76177-3. Workbook for women's sexual enhancement, especially for problems with orgasm. Heterosexual. Includes detailed guidance and exercises for exploring sexuality alone and with partner, plus information about sexual anatomy and response.

A30 Hite, Shere. *The Hite Report: A Nationwide Study on Female Sexuality*. New York: Macmillan, 1976. 466p. notes (3p.). ISBN U/K. Results of questionnaire study of 3,000 women, mostly middle class or in the women's movement, about female sexuality. Covers experiences, preferences, and opinions concerning masturbation, orgasm, intercourse, clitoral stimulation, the sexual revolution, growing older, and defining female sexuality. Text is mostly quotes, illustrating a rich variety of responses.

A31 Hosken, Fran P. *The Hosken Report: Genital and Sexual Mutilation of Females*. 4th ed. Lexington, MA: Women's International Network News (187 Grant St., Lexington, MA 02173), 1993. 439p. chapter notes. bibliog. (11p.). ISBN 0-

942096-09-6. Comprehensive record of female genital mutilation (FGM, also referred to as female circumcision). Covers facts and statistics, history, description of FGM in African countries and elsewhere, politics of FGM, and actions for change.

A32 Kahn, Ada P., & Linda Hughey Holt. *The A-to-Z of Women's Sexuality: A Concise Encyclopedia.* Rev. ed. Alameda, CA: Hunter House, 1992. 362p. illus. bibliog. (24p.). index. ISBN 0-89793-095-9. Over 2,000 short entries about women's sexuality, *abdominal hysterectomy* to *zygote.* Includes terms re fertility and reproduction, anatomy and physiology, sexual behavior, STDs and sexual dysfunctions, marriage, and psychology.

*****A33** Kinsey, Alfred C., Wardell B. Pomeroy, Clyde E. Martin, & Paul H. Gebhard. *Sexual Behavior in the Human Female.* Philadelphia: Saunders, 1953. 842p. bibliog. (48p.). index. ISBN 0-7216-545-09. The classic "female Kinsey report": interviews and extensive statistical data from 5,940 white U.S. women, covering types of sexual behavior and their relationships to biological and sociocultural variables. Discusses anatomy, physiology, and psychology of sexual response and orgasm in both women and men, and male data from the previous Kinsey report (A48).

*****A34** Leidholdt, Dorchen, & Janice G. Raymond. *The Sexual Liberals and the Attack on Feminism.* New York: Teachers College Press, 1990. 244p. chapter refs. index. ISBN 0-8077-6238-5. Essays mostly based on a 1987 conference at New York University. Holds that sexual liberalism is a "concerted assault on goals, principles, and achievements of the women's movement" and perpetuates women's exploitation. Contributors include Andrea Dworkin, Catherine MacKinnon, Mary Daly, and Gena Corea.

A35 Scantling, Sandra, & Sue Browder. *Ordinary Women, Extraordinary Sex: Every Woman's Guide to Pleasure and Beyond.* New York: Dutton/Penguin, 1993. 248p. bibliog. (11p.). index. ISBN 0-525-93640-8. Results of questionnaire/interview study of 86 women about ecstatic sexual pleasure and increasing one's ability to experience it. Reports that such experiences relate to "flow" and "peak experience," and correlate with ability to become fully absorbed in the moment as well as to fantasize and daydream.

A36 Snitow, Anne, Christine Stansell, & Sharon Thompson. *Powers of Desire: The Politics of Sexuality.* New York: Monthly Review Press, 1983. 489p. chapter notes. ISBN 0-85345-610-0. Feminist collection on whether sexual freedom enriches or diminishes women's lives. Addresses differences between men's and women's erotic natures, and activism about sexual issues. Historical and sociological emphasis; some fiction and poetry.

A37 Tavris, Carol, & Susan Sadd. *The Redbook Report on Female Sexuality: 100,000 Married Women Disclose the Good News About Sex.* New York: Dell, 1977. 252p. bibliog. (8p.). index. ISBN 0-440-17342-6. Results of classic questionnaire survey of 100,000 married women about sexual attitudes and behavior. Covers premarital sex, marital sex, and extramarital sex, and summarizes much other research.

A38 Valverde, Mariana. *Sex, Power, and Pleasure.* Philadelphia: New Society, 1987. 212p. notes (6p.). ISBN 0-86571-108-9. Examines sexuality from balanced, feminist perspective, rejecting both "sexual pessimism" and "sexual libertarian" extremes of feminist sex debates. Discusses the body, eroticism, heterosexuality, lesbianism, bisexuality, pornography (as produced/consumed by both men and women), desire, and sexual ethics.

A39   Vance, Carole, ed. *Pleasure and Danger: Exploring Female Sexuality*. Boston: Routledge & Kegan Paul, 1984. 462p. bibliog. (2p.). index. ISBN 8-7102-0248-2. Papers, "images," and poetry originally presented at the ninth Scholar and the Feminist Conference, "Towards a Politics of Sexuality" (Barnard College, 1982). Contributions explore tension between sexual pleasure and sexual danger in feminist theory and women's lives in Euro-America during the last century. The conference was, and still is, highly controversial in feminist circles.

A40   Walker, Alice, & Pratibha Parmar. *Warrior Marks: Female Genital Mutilation and the Sexual Blinding of Women*. New York: Harcourt Brace, 1993. 373p. photos. orgs. (2p.). bibliog. (2p.). ISBN 0-15-100061-1. Describes making a documentary film about female genital mutilation in West Africa. Includes narrative, letters, interviews, transcripts, and several poems.

A41   Yaffé, Maurice, & Elizabeth Fenwick. *Sexual Happiness for Women: A Practical Approach*. 2nd ed. Illus. by Charles Raymond. New York: Holt, 1992. 159p. orgs. (1p.). recommended reading (1p.). index. ISBN 0-8050-2214-7. Assists readers in establishing a sexual profile and in identifying specific problems and enhancements. Covers sexual techniques, overcoming inhibitions, improving response, lesbianism, (male) partner compatibility, infidelity, contraception, sex and pregnancy, single sexuality and relationships, and STDs.

MALE SEXUALITY

When we wrote the women's sexuality section, we divided the books into general and reference works; scientific studies; and works about fantasy, sexual enhancement, and sexual politics. Then we took on the "male books." We found we could use the same categories, but the books were quite different.

Nearly all the male sexuality books were either scholarly studies or fell into what for women we had called sexual enhancement. But, for women, we had meant by that phrase efforts to make sex and sexual relationships better and to overcome dysfunction. By contrast, many male sexual enhancement books read more like repair manuals: the approach seemed to be "it doesn't work—let's fix it." It is not clear that this "Mister Fix-It" approach represents how men actually think; more likely it is how authors, agents, and editors *think* men think. At the very least, this writing style— mechanistic, pseudo-chummy, and disconnected emotionally—is a marketing stratagem for selling books about men and sex. The premise seems to be that men are uninvolved emotionally in their own sexuality. Unfortunately, relatively few books therefore deal directly with male sexual emotions and happiness, as opposed to male sexual machinery and performance.

Librarians need to be aware of this gender difference in sex books. Whereas books by and for women will focus on sexual relationships, sexual feelings/response, and "understanding your body," books marketed for men describe sex more as tinkering with a car or debugging a computer. These books do not assume that readers might consult them through curiosity or a desire to enhance self-awareness. Instead, the stereotyped marketeer man is reading about sex *only* because he is dissatisfied about something and wants to *get it fixed, dammit*.

Furthermore, books about male sexuality written for men sometimes surprise women by sprinkling quips and sexual humor in with the advice. Does this mean that the author does not take sex seriously? By no means. Sexuality and male sexual function are subjects of great anxiety for many men. The humor is put in—or this is the idea, at least—to keep the man focused and to keep him reading.

But one of us (TP) has a different opinion, based partly on my experiences with a false alarm about prostate disease. Every man I spoke to was deeply emotional about such matters: sometimes sympathetic, sometimes cynical about the medical care system, sometimes saddened and frightened. Not one person ever said *Gotta get it fixed . . .* There are some deep unrealities about how men and male sexuality are so often described in books, magazines, and elsewhere.

With that in mind, let us turn to another group of very good sex books, although there are fewer than in the women's collection. We found only two that we class as basic reference—and the titles illustrate our point about the fix-it approach. *Men's Private Parts: An Owner's Manual* (A44, Gilbaugh) is concise and nicely illustrated. Its complement is *The Male Sexual Machine* (A52, Purvis), more jocular, comprehensive, full of all sorts of interesting information including anecdotes from history and research—unfortunately unreferenced.

Five varied works represent the "research" category. Two classics for women have male equivalents: *Sexual Behavior in the Human Male* (A48, Kinsey et al.) and *The Hite Report on Male Sexuality* (A46, Hite). The other three studies treat special yet significant populations. *A Sexual Profile of Men in Power* (A47, Janus et al.) and *Male Sexual Armor* (A55, Suraci) both uncover a surprisingly passive/receptive aspect to macho and powerful men. *The Sexual Man* (A45, Hart) studies conservative, married men from a Christian perspective.

The most significant women's sexual fantasy books also have a male equivalent: *Men in Love* (A43, Friday).

The most general enhancement manuals are *The New Male Sexuality* (A57, Zilbergeld), *Sexual Solutions . . .* (A42, Castleman), and *Sexual Happiness for Men* (A56, Yaffé & Fenwick). All discuss basic information and address relationships with women as well as describing sexual techniques with some fix-it elements. *Male Sexual Awareness* (A50, McCarthy) is particularly nicely done and would appeal to women readers also.

Libraries may want to buy several books about prostate disorders. The

disease has increasing prevalence in older men, and drugs for prostate disorders have recently been promoted in mass-market magazines. Moreover,
the prostate serum antigen (PSA) test now enables physicians to detect prostate problems much earlier than previously. We do not recommend reading
instead of seeing a doctor, but for background two good books are *Prostate: Questions You Have . . . Answers You Need*, by Sandra Salmans (Al-
lentown, PA: People's Medical Society, 1993), and *The Prostate Book:
Sound Advice on Symptoms and Treatment*, by Stephen N. Rous (Yonkers,
NY: Consumer Reports Books, 1992)—neither annotated.

Few books about male sexuality discuss circumcision. Nonetheless, an
active and vocal male anti-circumcision movement makes available books
recommending that parents should reconsider this so-called normal, routine
operation. Two are *Male Circumcision in America* (A49) and *Say No to
Circumcision!* (A53, Ritter). Another, not annotated, is *Circumcision: What
Every Parent Should Know*, by Ann Briggs (Birth and Parenting
Publications, 1985).

The Intimate Connection (A51, Nelson) is an interesting book that deals
with sexual politics from a Christian perspective. *Refusing to Be a Man:
Essays on Sex and Justice* (A54, Stoltenberg) provides a theoretical critique
of male sexuality that is compatible with much feminism.

Focus on the Family makes available a Materials for Men resource list,
but it contains little about male sexuality. The Sexuality Library catalog
and the Current Books on Sexuality bibliography from SIECUS have small
sections on male sexuality. (See Chapter 5.) In addition, *A Research Guide
to Human Sexuality* (D120, Lichtenberg) has subdivisions pertaining to
men in many of its chapters. Standard review media cover some items, but,
as is true of enhancement and female sexuality books, a major way to learn
of new material about men and sex is to visit a large bookstore and scan
the shelves.

The "men's movement" includes organizations often concerned more
about divorce reform, child custody, and discrimination than about male
sexuality. Books that do include material on sexuality include *Men Freeing
Men*, edited by Francis Baumli (New Atlantis Press, 1985), *The Myth of
Male Power*, by Warren Farrell (Simon & Schuster, 1993), and *Good Will
Toward Men*, edited by Jack Kammer (St. Martin's Press, 1993)—none of
these annotated. Some of the organizations:

Coalition of Free Men
P.O. Box 129
Manhasset, NY 11030
  Newsletter, *Transitions*, has book and film reviews and lists of publications.

Men's Defense Association
17854 Lyons Street

Forest Lake, MN 55025-8107
    Mostly divorce reform concerns. Several books and pamphlets.

Men's Rights, Inc.
P.O. Box 163180
Sacramento, CA 95816
    Concerned with fighting sexism against men and self-destructive aspects of the
male role. Packet of "news and views."

National Organization for Men
Eleven Park Place
New York, NY 10007
    "Preservation of men's rights and fighting social and legal gender bias," including
divorce and custody advocacy. Newsletter *Quest* mentions some publications.

Man International
3250 Orchard Drive
Palm Harbor, FL 34684
    Suggested Reading List 1994, covering fatherhood, sex roles, custody, divorce,
incest, men's movement, pedophilia, child sex abuse, battered husbands. No annotations.

    See also the Sexual Enhancement section (Chapter 9), Disabilities and
Dysfunctions section (Chapter 13), and Books for Pre-Adolescents and
Books for Adolescents sections (Chapter 11).

Annotations

A42   Castleman, Michael. *Sexual Solutions for Men and the Women Who Love
Them.* Rev. ed. New York: Touchstone/Simon & Schuster, 1989. 301p. illus. bibliog. (7p.). index. ISBN 0-671-66488-3. Guide to sexuality and enhancement for
heterosexual men: sensual/sensitive lovemaking, male sexual problems (premature
ejaculation, nonejaculation, impotence), women's sexuality, rape, birth control,
STDs, and sexual self-care.

A43   Friday, Nancy. *Men in Love: Men's Sexual Fantasies: The Triumph of Love
over Rage.* New York: Delacorte, 1980. 527p. ISBN 0-440-05-264-5. About 200
sexual fantasies, gathered via letters from 3,000 primarily heterosexual men. Commentary discusses experiences of men masturbating, sharing fantasies with a wife/
partner, and major fantasy themes.

A44   Gilbaugh, James H., Jr. *Men's Private Parts: An Owner's Manual.* New
York: Crown, 1993. 120p. illus. glossary (3p.). index. ISBN 0-517-88064-4. Concise introduction to male genitourinary system. Covers impotence, cancer, STDs,
and prostate and bladder problems. Addresses myths and misinformation, masturbation, nocturnal emissions, infertility, artificial insemination, condoms, vasectomy,
and sex vs. athletic performance. Heterosexually oriented.

*****A45**   Hart, Archibald D. *The Sexual Man: Masculinity Without Guilt.* Dallas:

Word, 1994. 223p. notes (5p.). orgs. (2p.). ISBN 0-8499-1076-5. Results of clinical interviews, 600+ essays, and 600 questionnaires from sexually conservative, religious men, aged 17–72, many clergy. Covers sexual development, feelings and thoughts, masturbation, pornography, fantasy, teenage sexuality, marital sex, workplace sex, and sex and religion. Includes advice. Gender-equal perspective. Some graphs do not match text.

A46 Hite, Shere. *The Hite Report on Male Sexuality.* New York: Knopf, 1981. 1129p. ISBN 0-394-41392-X. Results of questionnaire study of 7,000 men about male sexuality. Covers experience, preferences, and opinions re being male, relationships with women, sexual behaviors, women and sex, rape, prostitution, pornography, homosexuality, and aging. Text is mostly quotes, illustrating rich variety of responses.

A47 Janus, Sam, Barbara Bess, & Carol Saltus. *A Sexual Profile of Men in Power.* Englewood Cliffs, NJ: Prentice-Hall, 1977. 190p. chapter refs. bibliog. (5p.). index. ISBN 0-13-807487-9. Results of interview survey of 80 high-class prostitutes and madams about powerful clients: politicians, judges, diplomats, executives. Suggests that powerful men are more likely to prefer unconventional sex, especially masochistic behaviors. Relates these preferences to psychology of power.

***A48** Kinsey, Alfred C., Wardell B. Pomeroy, & Clyde Martin. *Sexual Behavior in the Human Male.* Philadelphia: Saunders, 1948. 804p. bibliog. (22p.). index. ISBN 0-7216-5445-2. Results of landmark survey of 5,300 white U.S. males about lifelong sexual behavior. Data on biological and sociocultural factors interacting with type of sexual behavior: masturbation; nocturnal emissions; "petting"; premarital, marital, and extramarital intercourse; homosexual activity; intercourse with prostitutes; and animal contacts.

A49 *Male Circumcision in America: Violating Human Rights; A Consciousness Raising Primer and Resource Guide.* 2nd ed. San Francisco, CA: NOHARMM (P.O. Box 460795, San Francisco, CA 94146), 1992. 191p. illus. orgs. (2p.). resources and order forms (20p.). ISBN U/K. Articles, papers, testimony, and reports from various sources against male circumcision (removal of penile foreskin, usually shortly after birth). Covers human rights issue, historical and cultural overview, current medical knowledge, aspects of harm, legal implications, stories from men, foreskin restoration, religious perspectives, and information for parents.

***A50** McCarthy, Barry. *Male Sexual Awareness: Increasing Sexual Satisfaction.* New York: Carroll & Graf, 1988. 294p. suggested reading (2p.). ISBN 0-88184-348-2. Comprehensive, literate guide to male sexual experience and enhancement. Covers myths, anatomy, masturbation, single sex, contraception, marriage, pregnancy and childbirth, role models and sex education re children, sensuality, fantasy, oral sex, sex and aging, sexual dysfunctions, extramarital sex, sex when divorced or as widower, homosexuality, STDs, and finding a therapist. Moderately liberal.

A51 Nelson, James B. *The Intimate Connection: Male Sexuality, Masculine Spirituality.* Philadelphia: Westminster, 1988. 140p. notes (8p.). ISBN 0-664-24065-8. Describes traditional and contemporary masculinity and male sexuality, and redefining and reexperiencing them more positively and joyfully through Christian spiritual recognition and reevaluation. Discusses sexual relationships, homophobia, male friendship, mortality, and masculinity. Heterosexual.

A52   Purvis, Kenneth. *The Male Sexual Machine: An Owner's Manual*. New York: St. Martin's, 1992. 210p. index. ISBN 0-312-07031-4. Colloquial, sometimes amusing description of male sexual anatomy, function and operation, and problems. Covers genitalia, hair patterning, testosterone, erections, orgasm, semen, aphrodisiacs, impotence, male menopause, prostate problems, sperm production, infertility, and vasectomy.

A53   Ritter, Thomas J. *Say No to Circumcision! 40 Compelling Reasons Why You Should Respect His Birthright and Keep Your Son Whole*. Fwd. by Ashley Montagu. Aptos, CA: Hourglass Book Publishing (P.O. Box 171, Aptos, CA 95001), 1992. 90p. illus. glossary (1p.). notes (1p.). ISBN 0-9630482-0-1. Discussion of reasons why male circumcision is abusive, dangerous, traumatic, and not medically, sexually, or socially necessary.

A54   Stoltenberg, John. *Refusing to Be a Man: Essays on Sex and Justice*. New York: Meridian/Penguin, 1989. 225p. notes (15p.). ISBN 0-452-01043-8. Describes socially and personally destructive aspects of sexual macho and supports vision of society based on sexual justice. Covers rape, ethics, sexual objectification, father-son relationships, disarmament, men and abortion, pornography, and feminism.

A55   Suraci, Patrick. *Male Sexual Armor: Erotic Fantasies and Sexual Realities of the Cop on the Beat and the Man in the Street*. New York: Irvington, 1992. 323p. bibliog. (5p.). index. ISBN 0-8290-2467-0. Results of questionnaire study of over 1,500 men and interviews with 800 men, contrasting police officers with civilians re sexual feelings, fantasies, desires, beliefs, and behaviors. Provides insight into sexuality of men in a macho profession vs. other men.

A56   Yaffé, Maurice, & Elizabeth Fenwick. *Sexual Happiness for Men: A Practical Approach*. 2nd ed. Illus. by Charles Raymond. New York: Holt, 1992. 159p. resource guide (2p.). index. ISBN 0-8050-2215-5. Assists in establishing a sexual profile and identifying problems. Covers attitudes and expectations, heterosexual/homosexual orientation, erection and ejaculation, increasing pleasure, partner and relationship issues (communication, sexual boredom, understanding women, contraception), and sexual health and STDs (including AIDS).

*A57   Zilbergeld, Bernie. *The New Male Sexuality*. New York: Bantam, 1992. 580p. refs. (19p.). index. ISBN 0-553-08253-1. Guide for heterosexual men about sexual stereotypes vs. realism, enhancing awareness and partner communication, and resolving problems. Focuses on emotions and sensitivity to partner. Appendix: effects of drugs on male sexual response.

SEXUAL ENHANCEMENT

The expression "sex book" most likely calls to mind the "sex manual"—in older times, the marriage manual—with its how-tos, graphic illustrations, and exercises. So as we prepared this bibliography of nearly 600 "sex books," we took care not to slight the sex manual.

One gets the distinct impression that librarians and the library press feel that sex manuals are trouble. Indeed, *The Joy of Sex* makes regular appearances in the *Newsletter on Intellectual Freedom* because of censorship attempts. But sexual enhancement works are not all cut from the same cloth. Some emphasize technique, some communication, some heterosexual coitus, some variations and toys. Some have explicit photos and art, some only pen-and-ink anatomy diagrams with lots of labels. A whole genre is illustrated with prettified, arty gouache images, sepia-tone charcoal sketches, or watercolory pictures. In their moral and ethical vision, some embrace "anything goes," others—often religious minded—look fondly at marital coitus alone. In this variety, we have tried to touch upon different viewpoints. Enhancement books written specifically for women, for men, and for gay/lesbian readers are covered in other sections.

One of the newest, most complete, and most freewheeling sexual enhancement books is *The Good Vibrations Guide to Sex* (A68, Winks & Semans), from staff at the Good Vibrations sex toy store in San Francisco. It describes a wide variety of activities and sex aids but not dysfunctions. Neither does our oldie but goodie, reincarnated as *The New Joy of Sex* (A59, Comfort), also focusing exclusively upon enhancement techniques all quaintly designated with French expressions and culinary metaphors, the title being borrowed from *Joy of Cooking*. A new closing section addresses "health and other issues." Two other quite competent books spend more time with sexual dysfunctions, sexual problems, and communication: *Sexual Awareness* (A63, McCarthy & McCarthy) and *Sexual Pleasure* (A60, Keesling). We cannot omit the indefatigable, delightful Dr. Ruth, herself a veritable sex book industry. Her *Dr. Ruth's Guide to Good Sex* (A66, Westheimer) is particularly lively reading since it includes excerpts from her radio show. All her books have the advantage of being easy and entertaining.

Two special topic books stand out. *Hot Monogamy* (A62, Love & Robinson) concerns how to enhance a long-term relationship, while *Making Love During Pregnancy* (A58, Bing & Colman) covers an important and usually neglected subject.

Christian sex manuals seem overlooked in libraries, but we hope to rectify that situation. Several are sexologically very good indeed, with authors experienced and trained in sex therapy and counseling (we cannot speak for their theology). These books tend to have fewer and less explicit pictures, which some librarians may appreciate. We especially recommend *Intended for Pleasure* (A67, Wheat & Wheat) and *The Gift of Sex* (A65, Penner & Penner). They complement each other by covering slightly different topics. The first is rather more detailed, for example, about birth control, but each is clear and well written. Both express deep appreciation of sex as a gift to be enjoyed in marriage.

Two additional Christian books include reports about sex surveys of religious couples—which makes them interesting on this basis alone. These and the preceding two all emphasize the clitoris and Kegel exercises for helping women to orgasm. *Sexual Happiness in Marriage* (A64, Miles) is more informative on birth control and recommends "interstimulation" (petting to orgasm) as a learning experience for honeymooners. Tim and Beverly LaHaye's *The Act of Marriage* (A61) has a more disapproving tone, especially of homosexuality and some fantasy. (See also *The Sexual Man*, A45, Hart.)

These four books are widely cited in the religious sex literature and remain in print despite distant publication dates. Several are in subsequent editions, indicating long-standing popularity. These are the books that your Christian patrons may have heard of.

To these secular and religious sex manuals, we add two classics from the past: the *Kama Sutra* by the Maharishi Vatsyayana (c. 1st to 6th centuries) and *The Perfumed Garden* by Shaykh Sidi Mohammed el Nefzawi (c. 15th century). Both are basic to sexology collections and exist in numerous editions (not annotated).

Historically, the *Kama Sutra* and *The Perfumed Garden* are among the most famous representatives of what once was called "erotology." The term implies a thoughtfulness about sexuality that centers it in a cultured appreciation of one of life's joys. Each contains much that is fascinating about other cultures and times (India and Islam), showing ways people elsewhere have treated sex with refinement, grace, and elegance. They are old-fashioned in our days of computer video sex games and sleazeware and, by that very token, offer much of value.

The Sexuality Library catalog, the SIECUS Current Books on Sexuality, and the Sexuality resource list from Focus on the Family are good sources for enhancement books. Some books are reviewed in *SIECUS Report* and in library review media. A visit to a large local bookstore will also yield likely titles that would be missed otherwise.

See also the Female Sexuality, Male Sexuality, Variations, and Sexual Sadomasochism sections in this chapter, and the Homosexuality—Sexual Behavior and Enhancement section in Chapter 10.

See also *The Yin-Yang Butterfly: Ancient Chinese Sexual Secrets for Western Lovers* (D62, Chu) and *Love and Sex After 60* (C83, Butler & Lewis).

Annotations

A58 Bing, Elizabeth, & Libby Colman. *Making Love During Pregnancy*. Drawings by David Passalacqua. New York: Noonday Press/Farrar, Straus and Giroux, 1977. 165p. glossary (3p.). notes (2p.). further reading (1p.). ISBN 0-374-52201-4. First person accounts of women's sexual feelings and experiences in pregnancy, with discussion of women's and men's variations in physical, sexual, and emotional responses to pregnancy. Based upon letters from several hundred couples, plus experiences of authors as childbirth educators.

A59 Comfort, Alex. *The New Joy of Sex*. Illus. by John Raynes. Photos by Clare

Park. New York: Crown, 1991. 253p. index. ISBN 0-517-58583-9 (Rev. ed. of *The Joy of Sex*.) Gracefully written sex manual for heterosexual couples. Characterized as "menu," not rule book, with "ingredients," "appetizers," "main courses," and "sauces." Encourages sexual elaboration, creativity, and play. Substantial information on health and safety.

A60   Keesling, Barbara. *Sexual Pleasure: Reaching New Heights of Sexual Arousal & Intimacy*. Alameda, CA: Hunter House, 1993. 209p. photos. suggested reading (1p.). index. ISBN 0-89793-148-3. Well-organized guide to sexual enhancement. Primarily heterosexual. Discusses sexual touching and response, sensate focus, male and female arousal, mutuality and intimacy, and help for common problems. Many exercises.

A61   LaHaye, Tim, & Beverly LaHaye. *The Act of Marriage: The Beauty of Sexual Love*. Grand Rapids, MI: Zondervan, 1976. 294p. chapter notes. bibliog. (3p.). ISBN 0-310-27061-8. Conservative Christian introduction to marital sexuality. Covers Biblical basis, meaning and practice of lovemaking, contraception, and dysfunctions. Disapproves of homosexuality and most fantasy. Reports results from sexual behavior survey of 1,700 couples who attended pre-marriage counseling. Includes section on filling humanity's spiritual void through fellowship with God and Christ.

A62   Love, Patricia, & Jo Robinson. *Hot Monogamy: Essential Steps to More Passionate, Intimate Lovemaking*. New York: Dutton, 1994. 310p. notes (8p.). recommended reading (6p.). products and sources (4p.). index. ISBN 0-525-93649-1. Manual for married or committed couples about enhancing and revitalizing their sexual relationship. Covers communication, desire differences, intimacy, techniques, variety (G-spot, oral sex, lingerie, romance novels and erotica, anal stimulation), romance, body image, sexuality, and finding a counselor.

*****A63**   McCarthy, Barry, & Emily McCarthy. *Sexual Awareness: Enhancing Sexual Pleasure*. 2nd ed. New York: Carroll & Graf, 1993. 272p. illus. further reading (1p.). ISBN 0-7867-0015-7. Heterosexual couple-based sexual enhancement manual. Covers sensuality and genital pleasuring, communication, sexual techniques, sex and aging, overcoming male and female sexual problems, and choosing a therapist. Includes exercises.

A64   Miles, Herbert J. *Sexual Happiness in Marriage: A Christian Interpretation of Sexual Adjustment in Marriage*. 3rd ed. Illus. by R. Earl Cleveland. Grand Rapids, MI: Pyranee/Zondervan, 1982. 198p. chapter notes. suggested reading (2p.). ISBN 0-310-29221-2. Rather intellectual discussion of Christian marital sexuality. Covers Biblical basis of marital sexuality, anatomy, techniques and enhancements, the honeymoon, female anorgasmia, contraception, affairs, and oral sex. Includes results from sexual behavior survey of 151 couples attending pre-marriage counseling.

*****A65**   Penner, Clifford, & Joyce Penner. *The Gift of Sex: A Guide to Sexual Fulfillment*. Dallas: Word, 1981. 352p. illus. annotated bibliog. (3p.). index. ISBN 0-8499-2893-1. Guide to sexual enhancement within marriage, from Christian perspective. Covers sex-positive messages in the Bible, anatomy/physiology, sexual response, learning about and enriching sexual activities, barriers, sexual dysfunctions, and finding help. Authors trained with Masters and Johnson.

A66 Westheimer, Ruth. *Dr. Ruth's Guide to Good Sex.* New York: Warner, 1983. 397p. recommended reading (2p.). index. ISBN 0-446-34529-6. "Guidebook to sexual fulfillment," with many excerpts from author's radio show. Broad coverage of many topics with overall theme of sexual literacy and enhancing enjoyment responsibly. Some coverage of adolescent, elderly, and gay concerns.

*A67 Wheat, Ed, & Gaye Wheat. *Intended for Pleasure.* Rev. ed. Grand Rapids, MI: Fleming H. Revell/Baker Book House, 1981. suggesting reading (2p.). index. ISBN 0-8007-1253-6. Manual for sexual education, enhancement, and enrichment in heterosexual marriage, from Christian perspective viewing husband as head of home. Covers lovemaking techniques, preorgasmia in women and impotence in men, birth control and promoting conception, sex during pregnancy, and aging. Stresses Biblical priority for marital sexual enjoyment, communication, intimate privacy, and mutual pleasuring. Authors trained with Masters and Johnson.

*A68 Winks, Cathy, & Anne Semans. *The Good Vibrations Guide to Sex.* Illus. by M.B. Condon. Pittsburgh: Cleis, 1994. 258p. resources & bibliog. (23p.). index. ISBN 0-939416-84-0. Heterosexual/homosexual sexual enhancement manual. Emphasizes variety of activities/techniques, and using sex toys and erotica. Covers safer sex but not dysfunctions. With quotes from Good Vibrations (sex toy store) customers.

VARIATIONS

Although most general sex books discuss some sexual variations, none have the monomorphic focus of those in this section. We have tried to make this a small smorgasbord of both commonplace and rare.

Nearly everyone kisses, and *The Art of Kissing* (A70, Cane) gives more information than readers may think existed. A tiny, charming collection of art and literary excerpts is *A Kiss*, compiled by Rosemarie Jarsky (Simon & Schuster, 1994, not annotated). Similarly, everyone engaging in sex must do something afterwards, and *Afterplay* (A71, Halpern & Sherman) highlights these moments.

Three most noteworthy topics come next.[1] Oral sex has become quite popular in recent years, and *Oragenitalism* (A73, Legman) is a literate guide to technique. Whereas two other books about oral sex are in print, each with strong points, neither is as complete nor as interesting.[2] *Anal Pleasure and Health* (A74, Morin) is an important classic, now updated on HIV/AIDS. And while the "G-spot" is still hotly debated in sexology, *The G Spot* (A72, Ladas et al.) presents original research that female readers can compare to their own responses.

Sex toys grow in popularity for solo and coupled eroticism, and *Good Vibrations* (A69, Blank) is an entertaining guide to selecting and using vibrators.[3] Aphrodisiacs of all types are described in *Love Potions* (A78, Watson & Hynes). An appealing and nicely illustrated work on massage is *Erotic Massage* (A77, Stubbs & Saulnier).

Pedophilia, or the sexual attraction of adults to children, has been illegal and controversial in many countries. It is hotly debated in the U.S. gay male community, of which the small but visible North American Man/Boy Love Association (NAMBLA) considers itself a part.[4] Most books, including those in the Incest and Child Sexual Abuse section in Chapter 13, discuss pedophilia as a social problem or crime. Very few study pedophiles in their own sociopsychological settings. Exceptions include *Male Intergenerational Intimacy* (A76, Sandfort et al.), an international scholarly anthology representing the unique experience of its Dutch editors, where certain forms of what Americans define as pedophilia are legal.[5] An interesting scholarly study of pedophiles in England is *The Child Lovers: A Study of Paedophilia and Society*, by Glenn D. Wilson and David N. Cox (Peter Owen, 1983, not annotated). These books speak to an adult audience, and we have much to learn from them. For readers who can deal with this issue only as crime, these books will prove illuminating: even sexual deviations deemed abhorrent can be the subject of well-presented scholarship and science.

Neither of these books is a work of pedophilic erotica nor does either contain photographs of nude or partially clad children. Neither is in any way a work of "kiddie porn." We do not encourage or advocate the production or distribution of any materials that run afoul of U.S. law. We also do not believe that these books contradict such laws. Readers should keep in mind that our comments do not necessarily constitute an endorsement of the ideas contained in these books.[6]

Relatively few serious informational books are available for the general public on sexual fetishism and the more esoteric paraphilias,[7] although a number of underground zines and newsletters are written by and for fetishists of various kinds (see Chapter 6). An exception is *The Sex Life of the Foot and Shoe* (A75, Rossi). Some others (not annotated) are published by Prometheus: *The Breathless Orgasm: A Lovemap Biography of Asphyxiophilia* by John Money, Gordon Wainwright, and David Hinsburger (1991), and *The Horseman: Obsessions of a Zoophiliac*, by Mark Matthews (1994). A comprehensive, also very readable work on bestiality is *Dearest Pet: On Bestiality*, by Midas Dekkers (Verso, 1994), not annotated.[8]

We found no bibliographies on these sexual variations except the older ones of the Kinsey Institute. However, the Sexuality Library catalog (see Chapter 5) includes many of the books annotated in this section and a few others like them.

See also the Sex for One—Or None and Sexual Sadomasochism sections below, Chapter 10 on Homosexuality and Gender Issues, and *The Encyclopedia of Unusual Sexual Practices* (A8, Love).

Annotations

A69 Blank, Joani. *Good Vibrations: The Complete Guide to Vibrators*. Burlingame, CA: Down There Press, 1989. Rev. ed. 65p. Illus. by Marcia Quackenbush. Preface by Betty Dodson. selected readings (2p.). ISBN 0-940208-12-1. Guide to vibrators for sexual stimulation: history, types, purchasing, using alone and with partner. Vibrators are recommended for intense sensation, self-exploration, and overcoming orgasmic dysfunction, particularly for the disabled.

A70 Cane, William. *The Art of Kissing*. New York: St. Martin's, 1991. 169p. ISBN 0-312-05378-9. Lighthearted manual about kissing. Uses results from interview study of 300+ people. Includes instructions for 23 kinds of kisses, descriptions of kisses from different cultures, and tips on techniques.

A71 Halpern, James, & Mark A. Sherman. *Afterplay: A Key to Intimacy*. New York: Stein and Day, 1979. notes (2p.). bibliog. (3p.). index. ISBN 0-8128-2572-1. Reports results from questionnaire study of what couples do after sex and what they would *prefer* to do. For women, satisfaction with afterplay was more highly correlated with overall relationship satisfaction than foreplay, intercourse, or orgasm; and for men, second only to foreplay.

A72 Ladas, Alice Kahn, Beverly Whipple, & John D. Perry. *The G Spot; And Other Recent Discoveries About Human Sexuality*. New York: Holt, Rinehart & Winston, 1982. 236p. illus. notes (8p.). bibliog. (11p.). index. ISBN 0-03-061831-2. Description/discussion of the Grafenberg spot, female ejaculation, importance of pelvic muscle tone for orgasm, and continuum of orgasmic response. Authors summarize own and others' research. Findings are controversial but significant in understanding female sexuality and for sex therapy.

A73 Legman, G. *Oragenitalism: Oral Techniques in Genital Excitation*. New York: Julian Press, 1969. 319p. refs. in text. ISBN U/K. Literate, detailed, and sometimes humorous guide for cunnilingus, irrumation, fellatio, and "sixty-nine." Eclectic, somewhat Freudian viewpoint re techniques and psychological factors. Primarily heterosexual.

*A74 Morin, Jack. *Anal Pleasure and Health: A Guide for Men and Women*. 2nd ed. Illus. by Jen-Ann Kirchmeier & Tom Till. Burlingame, CA: Yes Press, 1986. bibliog. (7p.). index. ISBN 0-940208-08-3. Tasteful, sympathetic guide to safe sensual/sexual pleasure from anus and rectum. Covers self-exploration; anatomy and physiology; diseases and problems, including AIDS; psychology and body image; and anally directed sexual activities, with statistics. For men and women, heterosexual or homosexual. Tasteful illustrations also.

A75 Rossi, William A. *The Sex Life of the Foot and Shoe*. New York: Ballantine, 1976. 298p. illus. bibliog. (5p.). index. ISBN 0-345-27110-6. Discussion of role of foot and shoe in eroticism throughout history, fashion, and cultures, among sexually "normal" people and fetishists.

A76 Sandfort, Theo, Edward Brongersma, & Alex van Naerssen, eds. *Male Intergenerational Intimacy: Historical, Socio-Psychological, and Legal Perspectives*. New York: Harrington Park/Haworth, 1991. (Orig. published as special issue of the *Journal of Homosexuality*.) 325p. chapter refs. ISBN 0-918393-78-7. Editor and contributors are clinical and social scientists from Britain, Europe, the Mideast, and the United States. Psychological and sociohistorical scholarly essays about man-boy sexuality (pederasty or pedophilia). Papers address diversity within pedophilic relationships, viewpoints and self-concepts of pedophiles, pedophilia themes in literature, existence of pedophilia cross-culturally, legal prohibitions plus societal and gay community reactions against pedophilia, and anti-pedophile distortions and critiques regarding current research. Considers nonproblematic more than problematic relationships.

This book is not a work of pedophilic erotica nor does it contain photographs of nude or partially clad children. It is not in any way a work of "kiddie porn." We do not encourage or advocate the production or distribution of any materials that run afoul of U.S. law. We also do not believe that this book violates such laws. Readers should keep in mind that our comments do not necessarily constitute an endorsement of the ideas contained in this book.

A77 Stubbs, Kenneth Ray, with Louise-Andrée Saulnier. *Erotic Massage: The Touch of Love; An Illustrated, Step-by-Step Manual for Couples.* Illus. by Kyle Spencer. Larkspur, CA: Secret Garden (P.O. Box 67-ECA, Larkspur, CA: 94977-0067), 1993. 112p. O-939263-02-5. Simply written, detailed guide to giving a full-body massage. Includes health guidelines and section on eroticizing safer sex.

A78 Watson, Cynthia Mervis, with Angela Hynes. *Love Potions: A Guide to Aphrodisiacs and Sexual Pleasures.* Los Angeles: Tarcher/Perigee, 1993. 272p. resource list (5p.). bibliog. (10p.). index. ISBN 0-87477-724-0. Guide to chemical and mood altering sexuality enhancers: scents, colors, foods, nutritional supplements, exercise, herbal/plant tonics, homeopathy, and flower essences. Also covers effects upon sex of tobacco, alcohol, street drugs, and legal medications, plus special needs of men, women, and people during illness.

SEXUAL SADOMASOCHISM (S&M, S/M, S-M, OR SM)

Once, no one except a few Victorian pornographers and a much hidden sexological subculture would ever even have heard of sexual sadomasochism, called S&M, S/M, S-M, or SM. Its name combines those of the Frenchman Donatien Alphonse François, Marquis de Sade and the Austrian nobleman Leopold von Sacher-Masoch, who wrote novels, treatises, tracts—call them what you will—extolling their sexual preferences. For de Sade, these admixed sexuality with power over another person; for Sacher-Masoch, *he* was that "other person," and the powerful one a woman. Today, however, most definitions of S&M stress forms of eroticism based upon *consensual* exchange of power.

For many years, de Sade's and Sacher-Masoch's books were both banned and circulated in clandestine versions: for example, de Sade's *The Philosopher in the Boudoir* and *Justine*, and Sacher-Masoch's *Venus in Furs*. But then appeared the Victorian pornographers, with their endless (and so badly written) books about Miss Whippingham's School of Discipline for Bad Boys—our parody of St. George Stock's *The Whippingham Papers*, a collection of flagellation pieces to which poet Algernon Charles Swinburne contributed anonymously.[9]

Presumably, de Sade and Sacher-Masoch would have been proud as punch that their names have thus been immortalized, for vanity, display, and theatrical exaggeration are very much part of S&M, then and now. After the turn of the century, these sexual preferences came to Sigmund Freud's attention, and his psychoanalytic essays—particularly his views of female masochism—have fertilized a rich, if arcane, field that has sprouted much later psychoanalytic writing. These include, for example, *Sadomasochism: Etiology and Treatment*, by Susanne P. Schad-Somers (Human Sciences Press, 1982), and *Pain & Passion: A Psychoanalyst Explores the World of S&M*, by Robert J. Stoller (Plenum, 1991), neither annotated. We cannot begin to summarize this literature, but a library with comprehensive holdings in clinical psychology should of course have copies of these and many other technical and scholarly works about S&M.

Today, the Freudian view has dwindled in importance and no longer represents the center of clinical thought. But certainly S&M itself has not dwindled. Indeed, by the end of the 20th century, S&M has moved from subculture and psychoanalytic couch to the mass media. Once our innocently prurient forebears would have been aroused (or disgusted) by an image of a woman in a peekaboo negligee; now one can buy mainstream publications with men and women in leather, chains, safety pins, masks, collars, all photographed in appropriately grainy black and white or in throbbing color. By the end of the 20th century, fashion has adoringly accepted much of once arcane gear of S&M in what might be called "S&M chic." And with it has grown an elaborate set of distinctions, sub-distinctions, and sub-sub-distinctions among S&M, bondage and discipline (B&D), the leather scene (gay and straight), Gothic sex, and a host of specialties that defy characterization and that need specialized dictionaries to understand—and include the SM Church of San Francisco. From a weird pose of affected nobility, through psychoanalytical perversion, to video fantasex, S&M has become multibucks—and multibooks.[10]

Its practitioners, not a single group but extraordinarily diverse, stress that S&M is characterized by its theatricality enacted scenarios and consensual exchange of power between participants. And, of course, many critics, particularly feminists, deny all such claims, root, stock, and branch. Again, out of the 19th century off to the printing presses: more books.[11]

And then followed the fiction writers, no Victorian Whippingham amateurs they: Anne Rice (a.k.a. A.N. Roquelaure) with her sexy vampires and sleeping beauties; Dominique Aury, finally identified as "Pauline Réage," author of Olympia Press's perennial best-seller *Story of O*;[12] Pat Califia, John Preston, and many more (see Chapter 6). Fairly speaking, some is erotica, some not. But it is all popular, even as book publishers subspecialize in heterosexual S&M, gay male S&M, lesbian S&M, and a category-defying collection of other sorts. S&M is perhaps now best defined not merely as a sexological variant, but also a literary, cultural, and publishing phenomenon.

And this phenomenon renders moot Freud's controversial view that women are constitutionally masochistic. S&M texts thrive on dominant men, submissive women—and also on dominant women, submissive men. In fact, the dominatrix has become if not a cultural icon, then a recognizable symbol in literature and film: Barbara Steele's daughters have grown up. In pornography, themes of male domination are common enough, but in the realities such as Stoller (see above) and "Mistress Ayesha" describe, the dominatrix is the popular money-maker.[13]

And an important point emerges about collection building. S&M is no longer a minority affectation of the elite or the perverse. In various forms, some vanilla-dilute, some not, the images, themes, and issues raised by S&M have become mainstream. So S&M is already in the library. It has percolated onto the shelves via mass-market distribution of magazines, popular novels, films, and advertisements. But even so, we perceive four reasons why library collection building may not ignore newer and less ameliorated books on this topic.

First, patron curiosity: what about that dominatrix interviewed on television? Are she and her clients just oddball sickos or more than that? Second, S&M literature is not easy to find. University collections may have the psychological titles but not the popular or semi-popular works—and moreover, such libraries are not easily accessible to the public. Here, gays have an advantage over straights, for while gay bookstores carry S&M books, straights will not find many questions answered by either Dr. Ruth or *The Joy of Sex*. Indeed, the sex shelf at one's friendly chain bookstore rarely will include any titles mentioned here. Third, some S&M practices can be *extremely dangerous* if practiced without safety precautions by over-eager amateurs but can be more or less safe if one knows what one is doing. The stress on consensual planning is particularly important for the amateur. Fourth, some S&M practices are actually safe or safer sex and involve no exchange of body fluids, and such books tell readers how to "have a scene" without getting hurt and without getting AIDS.

The two basic S&M books we most recommend for libraries are *S and M* (A82, Weinberg & Kamel) and *Learning the Ropes* (A79, Bannon). The first collects scholarly papers quite suitable for lay reading, giving a good overview of S&M culture and practice. The second is a beginners' how-to manual for "safe and fun S&M lovemaking" for either the gay or straight. A few more key works round out the collection. *The Sexually Dominant Woman* (A80, Green) teaches dominatrix skills, mostly targeted at heterosexual women. Particularly for large libraries with feminist collections, *Against Sadomasochism* (A81, Linden et al.) takes the viewpoint that female involvement in S&M is not acceptable in feminist terms.

Several more advanced books (not annotated) are Pat Califia's *Lesbian S/M Safety Manual* (Alyson, 1988) and *Sensuous Magic* (Masquerade, 1993), plus *SM 101* by J. Wiseman (Alamo Square, 1993), *The Leatherman's Handbook II* by Larry Townsend (Carlyle Communications, 1989) for gay men, and *The Bottoming Book* by Dossie Easton and Catherine A. Listz (Lady Green, 1994—see A80). The practice of "fisting" has its own book: *Trust: The Handballing Manual*, by B. Herman (Alamo Square, 1991). An introduction to the leather community is *Leatherfolk: Radical Sex, People, Politics, and Practice*, edited by Mark Thompson (Alyson, 1990). There is a fair-sized literature of S&M erotica for gay men, lesbians, and heterosexuals.

Many of these materials can be found in gay bookstores, the Lambda Rising catalogs, *Lambda Book Report*, and the Sexuality Library catalog. S&M is also the subject of several Kinsey bibliographies. (See Chapter 5 and the Homosexuality—General Works section in Chapter 10.)

An *S/M Resources Manual* (not annotated) is available from Daedalus Publishing Co. (4470-107 Sunset Blvd., Suite 375, Los Angeles, CA 90027). It lists suppliers, books and magazines, organizations, and other resources for S&M aficionados. *Sensuous Magic* (above) has a shorter but good list of books and resources. A small selection of fiction and nonfiction on "domestic discipline" and some S&M is offered in The Naughty Victorian Library catalog (TNV, P.O. Box 3292, Annapolis, MD 21403-3292).

See also the Homosexuality—Sexual Behavior and Enhancement section in Chapter 10 and *The Encyclopedia of Unusual Sex Practices* (A8, Love).

Annotations

A79　Bannon, Race. *Learning the Ropes: A Basic Guide to Safe and Fun S/M Lovemaking*. Los Angeles: Daedalus (4470-107 Sunset Blvd., Ste. 375, Los Angeles, CA 90027), 1992. 157p. bibliog. (2p.). glossary (6p.). ISBN 1-881943-07-0. Guidebook to S&M sexual interactions, for the heterosexual or homosexual beginner. Covers definitions and examples, components of a scene, physical and psychological techniques, finding partners, and safety.

A80　Green, Lady. *The Sexually Dominant Women: A Workbook for Nervous Beginners*. San Francisco: Lady Green (3739 Balboa Ave. #195, San Francisco, CA 94121), 1992. 61p. illus. ISBN U/K. Guidebook for women interested in acting the dominant role ("dominatrix") in S&M encounters. Describes types of bondage, role playing, delivering sensations, safety tips, a step-by-step basic session, and sources of further information.

A81　Linden, Robin Ruth, Darlene R. Pagano, Diana E.H. Russell, & Susan Leigh Star, eds. *Against Sadomasochism: A Radical Feminist Analysis*. East Palo Alto, CA: Frog In The Well (430 Oakland Road, East Palo Alto, CA 94303), 1982. 212p. chapter notes. ISBN 0-9603628-3-5. Essays arguing through various viewpoints that lesbian sexual sadomasochism is rooted in patriarchal ideology, and has no valid defense because of destructive outcomes of power imbalance and questionable nature of "consent" in S&M contexts.

*A82 Weinberg, Thomas, & G.W. Levi Kamel, eds. *S and M: Studies in Sadomasochism*. Buffalo, NY: Prometheus, 1983. 211p. chapter refs. index. ISBN 0-87975-218-0. Essays from scholarly and popular sources on psychological and social aspects of sexual sadomasochism. Includes excerpts from Krafft-Ebing, Freud, Havelock Ellis, and Paul Gebhard (one of Kinsey's collaborators) plus sections on S&M interactions, social organization, and narratives from two dominatrixes.

SEX FOR ONE—OR NONE: MASTURBATION AND CELIBACY

Masturbation

It surprised us that one of the most universal sexual activities seems to have produced the fewest books.[14] *Subject Guide to Books in Print* lists only nine as of 1994. Despite and because of this fact, every library should have works on masturbation—it is practiced by a large majority of people and it really *is* "safe sex," even with a partner. Yet many people have questions about it. While some consider masturbation undesirable for religious or other reasons—and such is their right—all need to know that it is not physically harmful.[15]

Since the 1970s, the doyenne of masturbation, particularly for women, has been the irrepressible Betty Dodson. Her *Sex for One* (A86, Dodson) includes the meat of her earlier works plus some material for men. Lately, a work specifically for men has appeared, entitled *Solo Sex* (A87, Litten).

We wish we could add to these two self-help style manuals a choice few scholarly or semi-scholarly works summarizing history, research, and current attitudes towards masturbation. We own two such books, but they are both much dated (neither annotated). *Human Autoerotic Practices*, by Manfred DeMartino (Human Sciences Press, 1979), collects essays from many scholars and experts, including Havelock Ellis, Albert Ellis, Masters and Johnson, Helen Singer Kaplan, and Lonnie Barbach. It focuses on recent—as of 1979—behavior and attitudes. By contrast, R.E.L. Masters' *Sexual SelfStimulation* (Sherbourne Press, 1967) ranges culturally further afield, covering history and anthropology as well as attitudes and behavior. Both these works are important, valuable, and might be available through used book sources. But each needs to be read in the context of its decade. We now need some equivalent 1990s anthologies.

There seem to be no current bibliographies on masturbation save the list in *Subject Guide to Books in Print*. The most recent Kinsey bibliography was last updated in 1992.

See also *The Destroying Angel* (D74, Money), *For Yourself* (A22, Barbach), and *For Each Other* (A21, Barbach).

Celibacy

James Sauer, member of the Association of Christian Librarians (ACL), has stated that anti-censorship "librarians who buy books furthering the advancement of sexual relativism and the toleration of homosexuality" themselves are censoring other viewpoints. He asks, "And how many books have you added lately on Biblical chastity? Or about sexual abstinence before marriage?"[16]

Sauer's point is well taken. Elsewhere in this book we include works promoting chastity before marriage, and here we include four items on celibacy, chosen from the 28 items listed in *Subject Guide to Books in Print*. Aside from this list, we know of no other bibliographies on celibacy. We urge Dr. Sauer and his colleagues to put one together—with annotations—for publication in a suitable periodical such as *The Christian Librarian*, ACL's journal.

The best popular overview that we examined seems to be out of print, but it is still relevant: *The New Celibacy* (A84, Brown). It should be updated and reprinted. *Sex & Celibacy* (A88, Wolter) provides a purely personal male view, while *Women, Passion & Celibacy* (A85, Cline) is both personal and scholarly.

With a completely different tack, *Celibate Wives* (A83, Avna & Waltz) suggests that marital celibacy may require self-help or therapy, particularly if celibacy is symptomatic of deeper unresolved issues. The authors also counsel readers not to fix what isn't broken: some marriages may adapt successfully to celibacy. Patrons in this situation will be highly interested in these case studies of women who for various reasons accepted celibate marriages—or did not.

For works promoting chastity *before* marriage, see the Books for Adolescents and Sex Education sections (Chapter 11) and the Sex and Religion section (Chapter 12). For works about celibacy and the clergy, see the Sex and Religion section. See also *Religion and Sexuality: The Shakers, the Mormons, and the Oneida Community* (D132, Foster).

Annotations

A83   Avna, Joan, & Diana Waltz. *Celibate Wives: Breaking the Silence*. Los Angeles: Lowell House, 1992. 236p. bibliog. (1p.). suggested readings (2p.). orgs. (1p.). index. ISBN 0-929923-99-5. Based upon interview study of over 100 women in celibate marriages. Covers how marriages become celibate and how to cope: reestablishing sexuality, separation or divorce, or remaining married and adjusting. Includes finding a therapist and starting a support group. Sees marital celibacy as not necessarily problematic.

*A84   Brown, Gabrielle. *The New Celibacy: Why More Men and Women Are Abstaining from Sex—And Enjoying It*. New York: McGraw-Hill, 1989. 245p.

notes (4p.). bibliog. (4p.). ISBN 007-008-4394. Introduction to celibacy as chosen temporary or permanent relief from sex to provide rest, balance, and energy for other activities. Covers history, recent views, interviews with celibate people, and celibacy and higher consciousness.

A85 Cline, Sally. *Women, Passion & Celibacy*. New York: Carol Southern/ Crown, 1993. 280p. notes (10p.). bibliog. (8p.). index. ISBN 0-517-59738-1. Discusses women's celibacy from feminist perspective. Based on interviews in the U.S., Canada, and Great Britain. Covers motives for celibacy, attitudes of women and men, celibacy as appositive to sexual consumerism, virginity, past celibate communities, and "passionate celibacy" as positive choice.

*****A86** Dodson, Betty. *Sex for One: The Joy of Selfloving*. New York: Harmony Books, 1987. 178p. illus. ISBN 0-517-56676-1. Benefits and techniques of masturbation as sexual pleasure and "safe sex" for both sexes, alone or partnered. Describes author's sexual awakening and career as artist and therapist and urges self-care for overcoming substance abuse.

A87 Litten, Harold (pseud.). *Solo Sex: Advanced Techniques*. 2nd ed. Illus. by John Tucker. Factor Press (6920 Airport Boulevard, Box 117-100, Mobile AL 36608), 1992. 207p. ISBN: 0-9626531-0-1. Comprehensive, colloquial manual for male masturbation, citing appropriate scholarly research (although without full references). Covers physical techniques, use of devices, solo sensual pleasure, fantasy, phone sex, "compusex," multiple orgasms, and using abstinence to increase arousal.

A88 Wolter, Dwight Lee. *Sex & Celibacy: Establishing Balance in Intimate Relationships Through Temporary Sexual Abstinence*. Minneapolis: Deaconess, 1992. 148p. ISBN 0-925190-53-5. Tells of author's self-destructive relationships with women and decision to explore feelings and perspectives via temporary celibacy. Covers questionable motives for celibacy, benefits, and judging if celibacy will be helpful.

NONMONOGAMY: INFIDELITY, PROMISCUITY AND SEXUAL ADDICTION, "SWINGING," GROUP MARRIAGE, OPEN MARRIAGE, GROUP SEX

As practice, preoccupation, or fantasy of millions of people over millennia, multiple partnered sex—also known as adultery, swinging, group sex, open marriage, and all their terminological cousins—deserves attention from researchers and authors in proportion to its frequency and appeal. Here, we accept the usual sexological distinction between having two or more partners on tap for separate liaisons, and having sex with them all at once. Various sex surveys show that perhaps 20–50% of married people undertake a brief or lengthy sexual connection with at least one nonspousal partner.[17] In a smaller set of marriages, the partners agree that such activities are permissible. But both married and single people sometimes find themselves in simultaneous sexual activity with two or more partners. All told, perhaps 2–5% of the adult population have been involved at one time or another in some sort of group sex.[18]

The more common approach to extramarital sex is to call it plain old adultery and treat it as a serious problem, and we have included four varied works of this sort (many more are in print). *Patterns of Infidelity and Their Treatment* (A91, Brown) takes a therapeutic view, and *Adultery: The Forgivable Sin* (A99, Weil & Winter) a self-help approach. Also with self-help impact is *Addicted to Adultery* (A92, Brzeczek et al.), by a couple who founded a 12-step program. By contrast, *Affairs of the Heart* (A96, Lee) provides 18 interviews, giving a nonprescriptive window on a variety of experiences and circumstances.

A separate set of books define certain categories of compulsive sexual behavior—sometimes extramarital and usually with many partners—as "sexual addiction." Patrick Carnes is the best known expert, and his *Don't Call It Love* (A93, Carnes) covers the topic well. (His first book on the topic, *Out of the Shadows*, 2nd ed., CompCare, 1992, is also good; not annotated). *Women, Sex, and Addiction* (A95, Kasl) concentrates specifically upon women's attractions towards and experiences with compulsive sexuality, while *False Intimacy* (A98, Schaumburg) provides a Christian perspective.

Aside from issues of prevalence, adultery is a longtime favorite of novelists and readers alike: what would literature be without *Madame Bovary* or *Anna Karenina*? But few objective scholarly or semi-popular works about adultery or about multipartnered sex exist outside frameworks treating it with moral condemnation as a social problem that devastates marriages, families, and individuals. Even if multiple partnered sex interests many people in fantasy or in reality, it has produced surprisingly little research.

Yet some books do take dispassionate, scientific views of multiple partnered relationships or are even openly positive. *Threesomes* (A94, Karlen) and *Group Sex* (A90, Bartell) are both written by sex researchers, the first in psychology, the second anthropology. *Intimate Friendships* (A97, Ramey), a classic in the field, has a theoretical and utopian view of alternative forms of intimate relationships, while *Love Without Limits* (A89, Anapol) is both a reference and a how-to for couples and singles considering "responsible nonmonogamy." Another excellent work covering group marriage-type arrangements and related issues is *Loving More: The Polyfidelity Primer*, by Ryam Nearing (PEP, P.O. Box 6306, Captain Cook, HI 96704, 1992, not annotated).

Two additional works (not annotated) are *A History of Oriental Orgies* by James Cleugh (Dell, 1968) and *A History of Orgies* by Burgo Partridge (Bonanza/Crown, 1960). Both are written in a dryly British, faintly sensationalist style and give only incomplete references to a fascinating, if irretrievable, hodgepodge of older books, reports, diaries, letters, and anthropological commentary. Partridge's work is by far the better and worth acquiring through used and out-of-print book sources.

We know of no ongoing comprehensive bibliographies on nonmonogamy. *Love Without Limits* (A89, Anapol) has a short retrospective bibliography on responsible nonmonogamy. *Loving More* has a short bibliography also.

Other resources include:

IntiNet Resource Center
P.O. Box 4322
San Rafael, CA 94913
   Short list of books for sale or loan on responsible nonmonogamy. Publishes *Love Without Limits*.

PEP (Polyfidelitous Educational Productions)
P.O. Box 6306
Captain Cook, HI 96704
   Publishes *Loving More*, plus a newsletter.

Several organizations provide help with compulsive sexuality:

NSO of SAA (Sex Addicts Anonymous)
P.O. Box 70949
Houston, TX 77270
   Books, pamphlets, and tapes available.

Sex and Love Addicts Anonymous
P.O. Box 119
New Town Branch
Boston, MA 02258
   Books, brochures, and tapes available.

Sexaholics Anonymous
P.O. Box 300
Simi Valley, CA 93062
   Literature list, with recovery stories and article compilations.

See also the Sex and Religion section in Chapter 12, especially *Religion and Sexuality: The Shakers, the Mormons, and the Oneida Community* (D132, Foster).

Annotations

*A89   Anapol, Deborah M. *Love Without Limits: The Quest for Sustainable Intimate Relationships*. San Rafael, CA: IntiNet Resource Center, 1992. 180p. glos-

sary (2p.). recommended reading (30p.). ISBN 1-880789-06-X. Introduction/
guidebook for couples and singles to responsible nonmonogamy: having more than
one sexual partner during the same period and relating in an honest, responsible,
committed manner (not casual recreational sex). Forms may include open marriage/
relationship, group marriage, triad, and intimate network. Covers how, why, problems, benefits, resources, and support groups.

A90   Bartell, Gilbert. *Group Sex: An Eyewitness Report on the American Way of
Swinging*. New York: New American Library, 1971. 224p. refs. (2p.). index. ISBN
U/K. Results of anthropological study of 350 middle class suburban people in
"swinging": consensual partner swapping for sex by (usually) married couples.
Covers how swingers meet, why they swing, sex practices, why couples drop out,
and positive/negative aspects.

A91   Brown, Emily M. *Patterns of Infidelity and Their Treatment*. New York:
Brunner/Mazel, 1991. 310p. bibliog. (5p.). index. ISBN 0-87630-631-8. Purpose:
to "provide a framework for therapists to use in evaluating and treating clients
when there is an affair." Discusses types of affairs within troubled marriages, issues
in treatment, and legacies of affairs for client and therapist. Also useful for general
readers.

A92   Brzeczek, Richard, Elizabeth Brzeczek, & Sharon De Vita. *Addicted to Adultery: How We Saved Our Marriage; How You Can Save Yours*. New York: Bantam,
1989. 231p. notes (2p.). resources (3p.). ISBN 0-553-05397-3. Account of married
couple coping with the husband's obsessive adultery, and how they preserved their
marriage and founded a 12-step self-help group for couples recovering from adultery (WESOM: We Saved Our Marriage).

*****A93**   Carnes, Patrick J. *Don't Call It Love: Recovering from Sexual Addiction*.
New York: Bantam, 1991. 439p. index. ISBN 0-553-35138-9. Guidebook/work-
book for people recovering from (self-)destructive sexual compulsions. Includes data
and advice from nearly 1,000 self-designated addicts and their families. Covers signs
of addiction and behavioral types, upbringing of addicts and partners, and stages
in recovery.

A94   Karlen, Arno. *Threesomes: Studies in Sex, Power, and Intimacy*. New York:
Morrow, 1988. 370p. notes (17p.). ISBN 0-688-06536-8. Results of sociopsychological study of men and women who have had simultaneous sexual activity with
two other people, from several episodes to 10-year ménages à trois. Data: 50 in-
depth interviews, 200 briefer interviews, and 150 questionnaires from people in
organized swinging.

A95   Kasl, Charlotte Davis. *Women, Sex, and Addiction: A Search for Love and
Power*. New York: Harper & Row, 1989. 399p. orgs. (2p.). bibliog. (6p.). index.
ISBN 0-06-097321-8. Discussion of addiction in women to (self-)destructive sexual
behaviors. Covers nature and origins of addiction and codependency, multiple addictions, masochism, sexual orientation, myths and realities about men, and recovery.

A96   Lee, Virginia. *Affairs of the Heart: Men & Women Reveal the Truth About
Extramarital Affairs*. Freedom, CA: Crossing Press, 1993. 171p. ISBN 0-89594-
621-1. Eighteen interviews with people who had extramarital affairs, differing in
personalities, circumstances, and outcomes. Comments from five outside experts.

A97 Ramey, James W. *Intimate Friendships*. Englewood Cliffs, NJ: Prentice-Hall, 1976. 176p. bibliog. (10p.). ISBN 0-13-476895-7. Somewhat scholarly, utopian discussion of intimate relationships: cohabitation, "normal" marriage, adultery, comarital sex ("swinging"), sexually open marriage, group marriage, and intimate networks. Describes problems/rewards of each.

A98 Schaumburg, Harry W. *False Intimacy: Understanding the Struggle of Sexual Addiction*. Colorado Springs, CO: NavPress, 1992. 205p. notes (3p.). resources (4p.). ISBN 0-89109-711-2. Christian perspective on sexual addiction. Covers sexual addiction behaviors, definitions and causes, healing through spiritual efforts, counseling, relationships with God, responding to a sexually addicted spouse, preventing sexual addiction in one's children, and sexual addiction in the church.

A99 Weil, Bonnie Eaker, & Ruth Winter. *Adultery: The Forgivable Sin; Healing the Inherited Patterns of Betrayal in Your Family*. New York: Birch Lane/Carol, 1993. 228p. bibliog. (6p.). ISBN 1-55972-185-5. How-to book for people and couples recovering from adultery. Discusses patterns and legacy of adultery within families from generation to generation, facing affairs, forgiving, healing, and deciding when divorce may be necessary.

REPRODUCTIVE CONTROL: ABORTION

Abortion is an immensely complex issue. In the years since safe first-trimester surgery and since *Roe v. Wade* (1973), perspectives, viewpoints, and activist groups have multiplied. And so have books, pamphlets, tracts, handouts, ephemera—thus creating challenges for building collections and vertical files within a finite number of shelves and filing cabinets. Viewpoints are often simplistically aligned as either "pro-choice" or "pro-life," but many Americans favor neither a strictly pro-choice position ("abortion on demand") nor are purely pro-life (no abortion except possibly to save the life of the mother). Moreover, whereas pro-choice is usually associated with liberal causes and pro-life with religious conservatives, there are pro-life feminists, gays, and lesbians (Feminists for Life of America, Pro-Life Alliance of Gays and Lesbians) and pro-choice religious people (Religious Coalition for Reproductive Choice, Catholics for a Free Choice). We have tried to cover some of this variety.

In no area is the Freedom to Read ethic more challenged than with abortion. It is easy for librarians with one view to slight books with other views. Regardless of whether one supports or rejects abortion, one may insist that it is a duty of morality, politics, or justice to purchase only agreeable works. Yet we insist on a higher reading of the library ethic: libraries must stock many viewpoints on abortion if they are to represent adequately its complexities and thereby serve a clientele equally diverse—or puzzled—in its opinions.

To be sure, it is difficult to create a "balanced" collection of so many polarized viewpoints. Yet we found some very good books that take quite different views. And we also found books that themselves tried to represent the debate fairly and evenhandedly. These books are especially essential.

Definitive references are *Abortion: A Reference Handbook* (A103, Costa), from the excellent ABC-CLIO Contemporary World Issues series, and *Abortion* (A107, Flanders), from the Facts On File Library in a Book series. *Abortion: Opposing Viewpoints* (A104, Cozic & Tipp) offers different voices speaking about various aspects of the issue. And whereas history can be written via any of these voices, *Abortion and American Politics* (A105, Craig & O'Brian) is a carefully balanced history of U.S. controversy. *Abortion: The Clash of Absolutes* (A119, Tribe) is also a balanced history, but in addition details legal issues and ethical/moral positions, offering hope of transcending the conflict. A key work we received too late to annotate is *The Abortion Controversy: A Documentary History*, edited by Eva R. Rubin (Greenwood, 1994), which compiles 92 primary documents pertaining to abortion, from the Hippocratic Oath through congressional hearings about banning the drug RU-486.

The Politics of Virtue (A113, Mensch & Freeman) analyzes evenhandedly both pro-life and pro-choice positions, also striving for common ground. The ideal balanced library collection must include *Abortion and the Politics of Motherhood* (A110, Luker), a classic study of pro-life and pro-choice advocates, which has been widely cited since its publication. Luker's book is vitally necessary if each side is to understand the other. Another interesting work is *Abortion, Choice & Conflict*, edited by Oliver Trager (Facts On File, 1993), which compiles editorials from U.S. papers on all sides of the issue, 1988–1992 (not annotated). *Birth or Abortion?* (A112, Maloy & Patterson) presents experiences of women facing the decision to abort, some choosing birth, some abortion. An older book, *Pregnant by Mistake*, by Katrina Maxtone-Graham (Rémi Books, 1973/1990), also gives case histories of women with unwanted pregnancies, some choosing abortion, some adoption, and some single parenthood in an era before *Roe v. Wade* (not annotated). Finally, *Men and Abortion: Lessons, Losses, and Love*, by Arthur B. Shostak and Gary McLouth, with Lynn Seng (Praeger, 1984, not annotated), is particularly valuable for its discussion of how men perceive abortion.

We move next to the pro-life position. Pro-life people are not homogeneous, and these books are quite varied. A good history from this viewpoint is *Abortion Rites: A Social History of Abortion in America* (A114, Olasky). A general book addressing religious views is *Abortion: A Rational Look at an Emotional Issue* (A116, Sproul). *Pro-Life Feminism* (A118, Sweet) presents the views of feminists against abortion, a group often overlooked. A particularly important perspective, especially considering recent events, is found in *Is Rescuing Right? Breaking the Law to Save the Unborn* (A100, Alcorn). The pastor-author presents the agonies of deciding to blockade abortion clinics, thereby breaking the law in the name of civil disobedience to serve higher religious values. It also contains some how-to sections. Less controversially, *50 Ways You Can Be Pro-Life (A102, Campolo & Aeschliman) offers activities and approaches to concerned people and groups, religious or not, for making their views effective.

Pro-choice books are also plentiful and varied. *Liberty and Sexuality: The Right to Privacy and the Making of Roe v. Wade* (A108, Garrow) is a legally oriented history, while *The Pro-Choice Movement* (A117, Staggenborg) is social and political history. *Our Right to Choose* (A109, Harrison) justifies the pro-choice position ethically, while *Abortion: A Positive Decision* (A111, Lunneborg) presents positive rationales and outcomes. Less positive but still pro-choice is *Abortion: My Choice, God's Grace* (A106, Eggebroten), capturing resignation, ambivalence, and determination in Christian women's experiences. Finally, *Religious Violence and Abortion* (A101, Blanchard & Prewitt) analyzes abortion clinic bombings in relation to pro-life activism, its radical violent wing, and religious fundamentalism.[19]

We could not locate books written for women contemplating abortion—we suspect that the space of time when the decision must be made is so short that pamphlets fill this need better than books. For women who have had abortions and are troubled about the decision and experience, *The Mourning After* (A115, Selby & Bockman) provides understanding of "post-abortion syndrome." Other books on post-abortion healing, from a right-to-life perspective, are listed on National Right-to-Life Committee and Women Exploited by Abortion (W/E/B/A) bibliographies (see below).[20]

Nearly 100 organizations in the *Encyclopedia of Associations* focus upon some version of either pro-choice or pro-life positions. Many supply bibliographies or sell materials. Some major ones:

American Life League
P.O. Box 1350
Stafford, VA 22555
   Sixteen-page annotated catalog of pro-life books, videotapes, magazines, newsletters, and brochures.

Americans United for Life
343 South Dearborn St., Ste. 1804
Chicago, IL 60604
   Three-page annotated catalog/list of pro-life books, audios, videos, articles, and pamphlets.

Feminists for Life of America
733 15th Street NW, Ste. 1100
Washington, DC 20005
   Sells pamphlets and several books.

Human Life International
7845 Airpark Road, Ste. E
Gaithersburg, MD 20879
  "Pro-life/family" catalog of books, booklets, pamphlets, postcards, and handouts. Brief annotations.

National Right-to-Life Committee
419 7th Street NW
Washington, DC 20004
  "Selected bibliography" of books on abortion, post-abortion healing, and other
pro-life topics. No annotations. Sells pamphlets and some books.

W/E/B/A (Women Exploited by Abortion)
P.O. Box 268
Venus, TX 76084
  Catalog of mostly Christian books and pamphlets.

National Abortion Federation
1436 U Street NW, Ste. 103
Washington, DC 20009
  Pro-choice. Publication order form for books, factsheets, pamphlets, bulletins,
and issue papers.

Religious Coalition for Reproductive Choice
1025 Vermont Avenue NW
Washington, DC 20005
  Brochures and pamphlets.

National Abortion and Reproductive Rights Action League (NARAL)
1156 15th Street NW
Washington, DC 20005
  Several substantial publications: *Promoting Reproductive Choice: A New Approach to Reproductive Health* (1994; 59p.) and *A State-by-State Review of Abortion and Reproductive Rights: Who Decides?* (5th ed., 1995, 181p.).

  Focus on the Family has two annotated pro-life bibliographies: Pro-Life
Materials, and Materials for Right to Life Organizations (see Chapter 5).
Many books on abortion, especially the "balanced" and pro-choice works,
are covered in the standard review media. Both *Abortion: A Reference
Handbook* (A103, Costa) and *Abortion* (A107, Flanders) include good ret-
rospective bibliographies.
  See also the Reproductive Control: Birth Control section below, and the
Books for Pre-Adolescents and Books for Adolescents sections in Chapter
11.

Annotations

A100 Alcorn, Randy C. *Is Rescuing Right? Breaking the Law to Save the Unborn.* Downers Grove, IL: InterVarsity, 1990. 249p. notes (12p.). ISBN 0-8308-1301-2. Thoughtfully argued case for blockading abortion clinics ("rescuing") as ethically and Biblically justified civil disobedience. Weighs pros and cons and describes actual rescues.

A101 Blanchard, Dallas A., & Terry J. Prewitt. *Religious Violence and Abortion: The Gideon Project.* Gainesville, FL: University Press of Florida, 1993. 347p. notes (43p.). bibliog. (11p.). index. ISBN 0-8130-1194-9. Analyzes 1984 bombing of three Florida abortion clinics, within context of radically violent anti-abortion activism, religious beliefs, and fundamentalism.

*A102 Campolo, Tony, & Gordon Aeschliman. *50 Ways You Can Be Pro-Life.* Downers Grove, IL: InterVarsity, 1993. 160p. resources & bibliog. (11p.). ISBN 0-8308-1394-2. Describes approaches and programs people can pursue to promote pro-life, both as against abortion and in larger sense, e.g., addressing needs of single parents, children, disabled, people with AIDS; supporting marriage and adoption.

*A103 Costa, Marie. *Abortion: A Reference Handbook.* Santa Barbara, CA: ABC-CLIO, 1991. 258p. glossary (7p.). index. ISBN 0-87436-602-X. Comprehensive guidebook to both sides of abortion controversy. Includes historical chronology since ancient Rome; biographies; laws/policies worldwide; statistics, techniques, complications and medical/psychological effects; discussions about harassment of abortion providers and public opinion; plus organization, print, and nonprint resources.

A104 Cozic, Charles P., & Stacey L. Tipp, eds. *Abortion: Opposing Viewpoints.* San Diego, CA: Greenhaven, 1991. 216p. chapter bibs. sources & bibliog. (7p.). ISBN 0-89908-156-8. Essays presenting different views on when life begins, should abortion be a personal choice, is abortion immoral, can abortion be justified, and should abortion remain legal.

A105 Craig, Barbara Hinkson, & David M. O'Brian. *Abortion and American Politics.* Chatham, NJ: Chatham House, 1993. 382p. chapter notes. bibliog. (7p.). index. ISBN 0-934540-89-6. Detailed history of U.S. political activity, law, and public opinion re abortion, since *Roe v. Wade* (1973). Covers state and national politics, and pro-choice and pro-life positions.

A106 Eggebroten, Anne, ed. *Abortion: My Choice, God's Grace: Christian Women Tell Their Stories.* Pasadena, CA: New Paradigm Books, 1994. 238p. orgs., resources, books (4p.). ISBN 0-932727-69-7. Anthology of Christian women's experiences with abortion as a difficult but real dilemma. Includes 13 stories of individuals' experiences, 7 essays covering other perspectives (e.g., serving as a clinic escort, church-sanctioned rape, marching for pro-choice), and discussion of doctrines and Biblical passages having implications for abortion.

*A107 Flanders, Carl N. *Abortion.* New York: Facts On File, 1991. 246p. index. ISBN 0-8160-1908-8. "One-volume source for beginning research" on abortion. Includes introduction to the issue, chronology, court cases, biographical listing, basic research resources, annotated bibliography, and organization list. Appendices cover acronyms, public funding by state, and consent/notification laws by state.

A108   Garrow, David J. *Liberty and Sexuality: The Right to Privacy and the Making of Roe v. Wade*. New York: Macmillan, 1994. notes (200p.). bibliog. (30p.). index. ISBN 0-02-542755-5. History of *Roe v. Wade* (1973) Supreme Court abortion decision, from 1920s struggles by Margaret Sanger and others to repeal 1899 Connecticut statute prohibiting use and/or prescription of any form of birth control. Also covers abortion debate 1973–1993.

A109   Harrison, Beverly Wildung. *Our Right to Choose: Toward a New Ethic of Abortion*. Boston: Beacon, 1983. 334p. notes (56p.). index. ISBN 0-8070-1509-1. Detailed defense of "women's right to the conditions for procreative choice," using ethical, historical, religious, and feminist arguments and perspectives.

A110   Luker, Kristin. *Abortion and the Politics of Motherhood*. Berkeley: University of California Press, 1984. 324p. notes (27p.). bibliog. (19p.). index. ISBN 0-520-05597-7. Examines pro-life and pro-choice history, viewpoints, and positions via survey of press clippings, action group literature, and interviews with 212 activists. Relates differences to antithetical social circumstances of the two groups.

A111   Lunneborg, Patricia. *Abortion: A Positive Decision*. New York: Bergin & Garvey, 1992. 205p. bibliog. (5p.). index. ISBN 0-89789-243-7. "Prochoice feminist counseling book, written to offset the multitude of negative and 'mixed feeling' books on abortion." Stresses positive rationales, decisions, and outcomes. Data gathered from interviews with 57 women who had abortions and 47 abortion providers. Also discusses work of abortion providers.

*****A112**   Maloy, Kate, & Maggie Jones Patterson. *Birth or Abortion? Private Struggles in a Political World*. New York: Plenum, 1992. 344p. refs. & related readings (6p.). index. ISBN 0-306-44327-9. Nearly 50 stories about women and men who had to decide whether to continue or end an unplanned or medically troubled pregnancy. Some chose birth, some abortion. Explores "in depth the truths and quandaries that surround the issue," rather than simply in terms of the woman's rights vs. the fetus' rights.

*****A113**   Mensch, Elizabeth, & Alan Freeman. *The Politics of Virtue: Is Abortion Debatable?* Durham, NC: Duke University Press, 1993. 268p. notes (93p.). index. ISBN 0-8223-1349-9. Comprehensive, complex analysis and history of pro-life/pro-choice debate, as grounded in American religious moral discourse since 1950s: Catholic, Protestant, fundamentalist, and secular. Challenges extremes of both pro-life and pro-choice positions and affirms moral integrity of compromise.

*****A114**   Olasky, Marvin. *Abortion Rites: A Social History of Abortion in America*. Wheaton, IL: Crossway/Good News, 1992. 318p. footnotes. index. ISBN 0-89107-687-5. History of abortion in U.S. since 1600s, particularly pro-choice and pro-life movements. Focuses upon combating myths promulgated by both movements and recommends how pro-lifers can have greater success by learning from the past.

*****A115**   Selby, Terry, with Marc Bockman. *The Mourning After: Help for Post-abortion Syndrome*. Grand Rapids, MI: Baker Book House, 1990. 147p. notes (3p.). ISBN 0-8010-8310-9. Guide for therapists and laypeople in dealing with psychosocial distress experienced by some women after abortion, or "post-abortion syndrome." Takes neither pro-life nor pro-choice position. Covers symptoms, diagnostic criteria, stages of grief, feelings of victimization, and importance of faith.

A116   Sproul, R.C. *Abortion: A Rational Look at an Emotional Issue.* Colorado Springs: NavPress, 1990. 207p. notes (3p.). bibliog. (2p.). index. ISBN 0-89109-345-1. Presentation of Christian pro-life perspective on abortion. Includes analyses of pro-abortion and pro-choice arguments, and discussion of sanctity of life and when life begins. Presents pro-life strategies and offers adoption as model.

A117   Staggenborg, Suzanne. *The Pro-Choice Movement: Organization and Activism in the Abortion Conflict.* New York: Oxford University Press, 1991. 229p. notes (21p.). refs. (9p.). index. ISBN 0-19-508925-1. Social history of pro-choice movement in the U.S., 1960s–1990. Focuses upon activism of six national and seven local organizations, profiled in appendix.

A118   Sweet, Gail Grenier, ed. *Pro-Life Feminism: Different Voices.* Toronto, ON: Life Cycle Books, 1985 (also P.O. Box 792, Lewiston, NY 14092-0792). 234p. footnotes. ISBN 0-919225-22-5. Essays and opinion pieces, many reprinted, on pro-life feminist topics. Addresses anti-abortion, violence against women, ways pro-life feminists differ from National Organization for Women (NOW) members, and strategies for action.

*A119   Tribe, Laurence H. *Abortion: The Clash of Absolutes.* New York: Norton, 1992. 318p. notes (17p.). index. ISBN 0-393-30956-8. Comprehensive, balanced discussion of the abortion debate, U.S. and worldwide. Covers history, constitutional and legal issues, pro-choice and pro-life positions, and areas of possible cooperation and compromise.

REPRODUCTIVE CONTROL: BIRTH CONTROL

Librarians have long since accepted birth control as a suitable topic for collecting. The only question is which of the many books available should be recommended. Two works are outstanding. *The Contraceptive Handbook* (A129, Winikoff et al.) delivers concise and up-to-date information for the general public, including older adolescents. It is suitable for high school and small public libraries. For only a few dollars more, libraries may buy *Contraceptive Technology* (A121, Hatcher et al.), the vade mecum of comprehensive reproductive information. Written for medical professionals and reproductive counselors (the preface refers to "helping our patients"), it is nonetheless quite understandable to laypeople. Every conceivable method of birth control is included with full information in nontechnical language, charts, and research findings.

Both of these works include so-called natural family planning (NFP) or fertility awareness methods (FAM). NFP relies upon detection of women's fertile periods to allow couples to choose nonfertile days for intercourse, practicing abstinence on fertile days. FAM relies upon detection of fertility to allow couples to restrict contraception (spermicide, barrier method, or noncoital sex) to fertile days. Couples tend to practice NFP for religious reasons—Roman Catholic doctrine allows only NFP. Couples who practice FAM probably do so because of aversion to or difficulty with other contraceptive techniques.

In both NFP and FAM, couples must follow complex instructions for detecting fertile and nonfertile periods. Keep in mind that for many library patrons, NFP is the only birth control technique they will use, and they depend upon printed directions to apply it effectively. Thus we recommend two excellent books on this topic alone: *The Art of Natural Family Planning* (A123, Kippley & Kippley), which takes a Christian perspective, and *The Fertility Awareness Handbook* (A122, Kass-Annese & Danzer).

Books for background reading include the excellent overview of methods, their mode of operation, and associated controversies in *Preventing Birth* (A124, Knight & Callahan). Although it does not cover religious objections to birth control, some of these are addressed in *The Bible and Birth Control* (A126, Provan), while the Catholic viewpoint is covered in *Humanae Vitae: A Generation Later* (A128, Smith). *A History of Contraception* (A125, McLaren) discusses fertility control in the Western world from antiquity to the 1980s; *Woman's Body, Woman's Right* (A120, Gordon) gives a feminist history of the U.S. birth control movement. NFP history, methods, research, teacher training, and international programming are all discussed in *Proceedings of the International Seminar on Natural Family Planning & Family Life Education* (A127, Ruiz et al.).

Two organizations provide good current awareness for books on birth control and related issues:

Planned Parenthood Federation of America
Education Department
810 Seventh Avenue
New York, NY 10019
  Publishes *Current Literature in Family Planning*, an annotated monthly list of books and journal articles. Local Planned Parenthood affiliates may subscribe and allow interlibrary loan. Librarians can probably also arrange to visit nearby affiliate resource centers and look over new books acquired.

The Couple to Couple League
P.O. Box 111184
Cincinnati, OH 45211-9985
  Ten-page annotated catalog on NFP, sexuality and theology (Catholic and conservative Protestant), chastity education, and other topics.

In addition, a bibliography on fertility awareness (for NFP, FAM, or conception) is available from Planned Parenthood of Rochester and the Genesee Valley (114 University Avenue, Rochester, NY 14605).

See also the Sex and Religion section (Chapter 12) and the Books for Pre-Adolescents and Books for Adolescents sections (Chapter 11).

Annotations

A120   Gordon, Linda. *Woman's Body, Woman's Right: Birth Control in America.* Rev. ed. New York: Penguin, 1990. 570p. notes (60p.). index. ISBN 0-14-013127-2. Social history of U.S. use and acceptance of birth control (including abortion), from feminist perspective. U.S. events are traced to British antecedents. Briefly describes contraception in ancient civilizations.

*A121   Hatcher, Robert A., et al. *Contraceptive Technology.* 16th ed. New York: Irvington, 1992. 720p. illus. chapter refs. glossary (16p.). index. ISBN 0-8290-3171-5. ISSN 0091-9721. Comprehensive reference for all contraceptive methods, including abstinence, NFP, and abortion. For clinicians, but understandable to laypeople. Also covers menstrual cycle and disorders, STDs and HIV/AIDS, pregnancy testing, infertility, adolescent pregnancy, demographic methods, and global trends in family planning.

*A122   Kass-Annese, Barbara, & Hal C. Danzer. *The Fertility Awareness Handbook: The Natural Guide to Avoiding or Achieving Pregnancy.* 6th ed. Alameda, CA: Hunter House, 1992. 148p. illus. bibliog. & refs. (3p.). index. ISBN 0-89793-096-7. Clearly written manual for using sympto-thermal method of natural family planning (NFP) and fertility awareness methods (FAM) for contraception or conception. No discussion of values or religion.

A123   Kippley, John, & Sheila Kippley. *The Art of Natural Family Planning.* 3rd ed. Cincinnati, OH: Couple to Couple League, 1994. 261p. chapter refs. glossary (4p.). additional materials (3p.). index. ISBN 0-9601036-6-X. Manual for natural family planning, requiring coital abstinence during women's fertile periods. Teaches sympto-thermo method; addresses values and morality, breast vs. bottle feeding, and fertility after childbirth. Takes Christian perspective opposing orgasm outside married, heterosexual intercourse.

*A124   Knight, James W., & Joan C. Callahan. *Preventing Birth: Contemporary Methods and Related Moral Controversies.* Salt Lake City: University of Utah Press, 1989. 358p. refs. (32p.). index. ISBN 0-87480-319-5. To "contribute to the general understanding of the scientific and social aspects of contemporary birth control methods and to the public discussion of a number of the [related] moral issues." Covers history and politics of birth control; human reproductive anatomy, physiology, and endocrinology; contraceptive technologies; abortion techniques; moral issues; and future prospects.

A125   McLaren, Angus. *A History of Contraception: From Antiquity to the Present Day.* Oxford, UK: Blackwell, 1990. 275p. chapter refs. index. ISBN 0-631-18729-4. History of fertility control in Western culture, from ancient Greece to modern Britain and the U.S. Covers contraception, abortion, and infanticide.

A126   Provan, Charles D. *The Bible and Birth Control.* Monongahela, PA: Zimmer Printing, 1989. 97p. ISBN U/K. (Available from The Couple to Couple League; see p. 216.) Literate presentation of why the Bible is against all forms of controlling birth. Includes nine reasons why the Bible prohibits birth control; two alternative viewpoints and their rebuttals; responses of Protestant theologians, 1500s–1900s, to the Biblical Onan incident in support of author's thesis; and list of additional Protestant theologians who opposed birth control.

A127   Ruiz, Ramón C., John Russell, & Irene Osmund Ruiz, eds. *Proceedings of the International Seminar on Natural Family Planning & Family Life Education, July 3-13, 1988, Hong Kong.* Hong Kong: Hong Kong University Press, 1990. (Available from International Federation for Family Life Promotion, 2009 North 14th St., Ste. 512, Arlington, VA 22201.) 307p. ISBN 962-209260-8. Essays on teaching and using natural family planning to avoid or choose conception. Covers methods, effectiveness, teacher selection and training, research program development, and family life education in several countries. Authors represent 12 different countries.

A128   Smith, Janet E. *Humanae Vitae: A Generation Later.* Washington, DC: Catholic University of America Press, 1991. 425p. notes (35p.). bibliog. (14p.). index. ISBN 0-8132-0740-1. Philosophical/ethical/theological analysis of *Humanae Vitae* plus discussion of controversies and debates since its issue. (*Humanae Vitae* is a papal encyclical, issued by Pope Paul VI in 1968, laying out Roman Catholic moral teaching on limiting family size.)

*A129   Winikoff, Beverly, Suzanne Wymelenberg, & Editors of Consumer Reports Books. *The Contraceptive Handbook: A Guide to Safe and Effective Choices.* Yonkers, NY: Consumer Reports Books, 1992. 248p. illus. references (12p.). index. ISBN 0-89043-430-1. Detailed description of female and male contraceptive methods, how to use them, side effects, and failure rates. Also covers sterilization, abortion, fertility awareness/natural family planning, and new methods under development. (G10–12, C, A.)

NATURAL HISTORY/EVOLUTION

In recent years, a number of highly technical treatises have discussed the biology and evolution of human sexuality. Many are of purely specialist interest and can be omitted here. However, some books have been written for popular audiences. And although we focus on *human* sexuality, we note an entertaining and popularly written introduction to animal mating: *How They Do It* (A137, Wallace).

An elegant summary of human sexual biology and evolution is **Mystery Dance: On the Evolution of Human Sexuality* (A135, Margulis & Sagan). *Sexual Strategies: How Females Choose Their Mates* (A130, Batten) takes a more journalistic and feminist perspective on female roles. *The Evolution of Desire* (A131, Buss) is more male directed and based upon worldwide research. *The Sex Contract* (A133, Fisher) and *Anatomy of Love* (A132, Fisher) both are readable showcases for Helen Fisher's original and provocative speculations. Heather Trexler Remoff's *Sexual Choice: A Woman's Decision* (Dutton/Lewis, 1984, not annotated) is based on extensive interviews and takes a biological-evolutionary perspective to explain how and why women choose mates. All these works draw to some extent upon *The Evolution of Human Sexuality* (A136, Symons), an earlier technical classic. Also technical, but interesting for advanced readers, is primatologist Sarah Blaffer Hrdy's *The Woman That Never Evolved* (Harvard University Press, 1981, not annotated), which relates human behavior, especially women's sexual patterns, to general primate patterns and our primate ancestry. But the granddaddy of them all is Charles Darwin's *The Descent of Man and Selection in Relation to Sex* (1872; rev. ed., 1874; many subsequent editions, not annotated). It is the *fons et origo* of Darwin's theory of human evolution and of the concept later called sexual selection. Like all Darwin's work, it is lucid and astonishingly graceful—and all libraries should own a copy.

Simon LeVay's research about brain anatomy in homosexuals has raised much controversy. In *The Sexual Brain* (A134, LeVay), he discusses these and other studies about sexual identity, behavior, and brain anatomy and chemistry.

We take the liberty of mentioning a book one of us wrote, *Sex Signals: The Biology of Love* (D41, Perper). It discusses original work on human courtship and contains several chapters on theories about the biological and natural components of human sexuality. It is critical of much sociobiology.

A unique recent work is *The Scent of Eros: Mysteries of Odor in Human Sexuality*, by James Vaughn Kohl and Robert T. Francoeur (Continuum, 1995), exploring the biochemical links among pheromones, genes, hormones, and sexual behavior (not annotated).

Most books about the natural history and evolution of sex are written by respectable academics, published by mainstream presses, and reviewed in *Library Journal* or *Choice*.

See also *Gay, Straight, and In-Between* (B54, Money).

Annotations

A130 Batten, Mary. *Sexual Strategies: How Females Choose Their Mates*. New York: Tarcher/Putnam, 1992. 248p. notes (10p.). bibliog. (17p.). index. ISBN 0-87477-757-7. Popularly written introduction to human and animal mating systems as grounded in evolutionary biology, stressing role of female initiative in choosing mates.

A131 Buss, David M. *The Evolution of Desire: Strategies of Human Mating*. New York: Basic Books, 1994. 262p. notes (12p.). bibliog. (19p.). index. ISBN 0-465-07750-1. Results of a survey of over 10,000 people from 37 countries combined with much other anthropological, evolutionary, and psychological research used to explain male-female differences and human mating strategies and problems.

A132 Fisher, Helen E. *Anatomy of Love: The Natural History of Monogamy, Adultery, and Divorce*. New York: Norton, 1992. 431p. notes (44p.). bibliog. (46p.). index. ISBN 0-393-03423-2. Informed speculations about biological and evolutionary advantages and origins of modern sociosexual behavior, supported by research from anthropology, paleontology, primatology, and field zoology. Discusses courtship, marriage, adultery, divorce, child rearing, sexual anatomy, and sex-linked behavior.

A133 Fisher, Helen E. *The Sex Contract: The Evolution of Human Behavior*. New York: Morrow, 1982. 253p. illus. bibliog. (8p.). index. ISBN 0-688-00640-X. Reconstruction of evolution of male and female sexuality, much attributed to changes related to protohominids beginning to walk upright. Discusses bonding, childbirth and child rearing, female sexual receptivity, and language.

A134 LeVay, Simon. *The Sexual Brain*. Cambridge, MA: MIT Press, 1993. 168p. sources and further reading (9p.). glossary (13p.). index. ISBN 0-262-12178-6. Readable summary of research on animals and humans showing links between genetics and brain anatomy/chemistry on one hand, and sexual development/behavior on the other. Covers nature/nurture debate and evolution, brain anatomy, sex and neural mechanisms, sex/gender differences, sexual orientation, and gender identity.

*A135 Margulis, Lynn, & Dorion Sagan. *Mystery Dance: On the Evolution of Human Sexuality*. New York: Summit Books, 1991. 224p. notes & refs. (9p.). index. ISBN U/K. Thoughtful, graceful discussion of commonalities between human and animal sexuality, with possible evolutionary advantages and paths of development. Addresses courtship, promiscuity/monogamy, orgasm, body shape and preference, the phallus, and reproduction.

A136 Symons, Donald. *The Evolution of Human Sexuality*. New York: Oxford University Press, 1979. 358p. refs. (29p.). index. ISBN 0-19-502535-0. Conjectures that differences in male and female sexuality stem from different advantages needed for reproductive success during hunter/gatherer stage of evolution. Discusses female orgasm, sexual choice, marriage, sexual variety, hormones, and homosexuality.

A137 Wallace, Robert A. *How They Do It*. New York: Morrow, 1980. 172p. photos. sources (5p.). index. ISBN 0-688-08718-3. Mating habits and techniques of 48 different creatures (mammals, birds, reptiles, fish, etc.) explained in entertaining and zoologically accurate vignettes.

NOTES

1. *Sex in America* (A11, Michael et al.) reported large percentages of both sexes finding oral sex very or somewhat appealing. From 5 to 18% of women found anal sex very or somewhat appealing, and from 11 to 26% of men (pp. 146–147).

2. These books are *The Clitoral Kiss: A Fun Guide to Oral Sex for Men and Women*, by Kenneth Stubbs with Chyrelle D. Chasen (Secret Garden, 1993), and *The Ultimate Kiss: A Sensual Guide to Oral Lovemaking*, by Jacqueline Franklin and Steve Franklin (Media Press, 1990).

3. As of this writing, dildos and vibrators are illegal in Texas. In 1994, the U.S. Supreme Court refused to hear *Regaldo v. Texas*, a case challenging the Texas anti–sex-toy law, thus letting the law stand. See Lisa Keen, "Court Rejects Dildo Case," *focusPOINT* (Minneapolis) (November 3–9, 1994): 9.

4. See, e.g., Brent Hartinger, "Separating the Men from the Boys," *10 Percent* (September/October 1994): 45–47, 66, 68.

5. See Theodorus G.M. Sandfort, "Sex in Pedophiliac Relationships: An Empirical Investigation Among a Nonrepresentative Group of Boys," *Journal of Sex Research* 20.2 (May 1984): 123–142.

6. This caveat is borrowed from *Factsheet 5*, edited by R. Seth Friedman, which reviews an immense variety of zines—small, self-published periodicals, many sexually explicit (see Chapter 6). Perhaps it is sad that we and Friedman must include such a warning. But we are aware that merely by including books on pedophilia, their scholarship and internationally credentialled editors and contributors will be no bar to alarmists, to the frightened, and to those whose politics entice them to seize any pretext for censorship. And yet we also wish to reassure such people that scholarship and science can deal with these issues in ways that do not demand obliteration or book-burning even by the best-meaning guardians of social morality. And, in consequence, such works can be read fruitfully by a wide audience, for their insights are not wrongful to ponder.

7. A paraphilia is "an erotosexual and psychological condition characterized by recurrent responsiveness to and obsessive dependence on an unusual or socially unacceptable stimulus"; *The Complete Dictionary of Sexology* (Francoeur et al., D93): 463, 735–740. In other words, a person is aroused or able to reach orgasm *only* by wearing diapers or copulating with horses or wearing latex. Legal terms are *perversion* and *deviant behavior*; popular terms include *kinky* and *weird*. The term *paraphilia* is most associated with the work of sexologist John Money. See *The Destroying Angel* (D74, Money). See also the Law and Sex section, especially for the commonly illegal paraphilias, such as exhibitionism and voyeurism.

8. Sexologically, bestiality is quite interesting. There are few books about it, nearly all out of print, and *no* self-help, advocacy, or recovery groups that we know of, or zines either. Yet human-animal sex has been documented for millennia and forms the basis for countless jokes and stories, from King Kong to Swan Lake. See Martha Cornog & Timothy Perper, "Bestiality," in *Human Sexuality: An Encyclopedia* (A3, Bullough & Bullough): 60–63. Only on the Alt.sex.bestiality newsgroup within the Internet's Usenet and similar virtual locations does it seem that zoophilists have finally felt free to seek those with similar interests. See Dan Kennedy, "Sex on the Internet," *Welcomat* (November 2, 1994): 16–17, reprinted from the *Boston Phoenix*.

On the other hand, sex with vegetables (hortiphilia?) is apparently out of the closet. A recent issue of *Chuck Magazine* (#3, 1994) includes photos of a man masturbating with an avocado, and writing for women about masturbation sometimes mentions cucumbers (e.g., *Sex for One*, A86, Dodson: 146).

9. *A History of Pornography* (D10, Hyde): 139.

10. Photographed in black and white: see, e.g., *Sex*, by Madonna, with photography by Steven Meisel (Warner, 1992); *Mapplethorpe*, by Robert Mapplethorpe (Random House, 1992). Color: see, e.g., *The X-Rated Videotape Guide* (D22, Rimmer, vol. 1): 510. Dictionaries: see Thomas E. Murray & Thomas R. Murrell, *The Language of Sadomasochism: A Glossary and Linguistic Analysis* (Greenwood, 1989). The *Atlantic Monthly* has included a small ad for The Naughty Victorian, "Unique, tasteful 50 page catalog . . . [of] Victorian Corsets & Undergarments, Traditional Discipline Implements . . ." (February 1995): 114 and in other issues. A tiny silhouette shows a woman spanking a man with what is probably a hairbrush.

The Church of SM: J. Gordon Melton, *Encyclopedia of American Religions* (4th ed., Detroit: Gale, 1993): 849.

11. Practitioners: see also SAMOIS, *Coming to Power: Writings and Graphics on Lesbian S-M* (rev. ed., Alyson, 1982). Critics: *Against Sadomasochism* (A81, Linden et al.).

12. John de St. Jorre, "The Unmasking of O," *New Yorker* (August 1, 1994): 42–50.

13. Barbara Steele: *Dark Romance* (D8, Hogan): Chapter 7. Doment men: see a Masquerade Books catalog. "Mistress Ayesha": Marc Weber, "The Trial of Mistress Ayesha," *Law and Politics* (November 1993): 22–24. For those unfamiliar with classic fantasy fiction, "Mistress Ayesha" is obviously borrowed from H. Rider Haggard's novel *She*, whose title character, Ayesha, is referred to as "she who must be obeyed." An ideal *nom de fouet* for a dominatrix.

14. In *Sexual Behavior in the Human Male* (A48) and *Sexual Behavior in the Human Female* (A33), Kinsey documented that 92% of men interviewed masturbated at some point in their lifetime, and 62% of women. The recent *Sex in America* (A11, Michael et al.) reported that 60% of men and 40% of women reported masturbating in the past year. Of the (mostly) married Christian men described in *The Sexual Man* (A45, Hart), 61% reported currently masturbating. Note that Kinsey's data referred to lifetime rather than current experience.

15. Masturbation becomes harmful physically only when damage to genital tissue or other bodily function results. Patrick Carnes reports a few such cases in *Don't Call It Love* (A93): 9 and *Out of the Shadows* (Minneapolis: CompCare, 1992): 24.

16. James L. Sauer, "Community Service" (letter), *Library Journal* (October 15, 1993): 8.

17. For example, Samuel S. Janus & Cynthia L. Janus, *The Janus Report on Sexual Behavior* (New York: Wiley, 1993): 286 and elsewhere; *Sexual Behavior in the Human Male* (A48, Kinsey et al.): 583–594; *Sexual Behavior in the Human Female* (A33, Kinsey at al.): 409–445; *The Redbook Report on Female Sexuality* (A37, Tavris & Sadd): 161–168. *Sex in America* (A11, Michael et al.) asked only about current sexual partners; 5% of married people in their sample reported two or more. *The Sexual Man* (A45, Hart) reported that 30% of the conservative Christian married men in his sample had a "strong" sexual attraction to other women.

18. Extrapolating from data in *Threesomes* (A94, Karlen): 78–79.

19. A brilliant historical discussion of issues posed by abortion and violence is Faye Ginsburg's "Saving America's Souls: Operation Rescue's Crusade Against Abortion," in *Fundamentalisms and the State: Remaking Polities, Economies, and Militance*, ed. Martin E. Marty & R. Scott Appleby (Chicago: University of Chicago Press, 1993): 557–588.

20. Some Christian books from W/E/B/A for women recovering from abortion: *Helping Women Recover from Abortion*, by Nancy Michels (Bethany House, 1988), *Help for the Post-Abortion Woman*, by Teri Reisser & Paul Reisser (Pyranee/Zondervan, 1989), and *Aborted Women: Silent No More*, by David C. Reardon (Crossway/Good News, 1987).

10   Homosexuality and Gender Issues

HOMOSEXUALITY—GENERAL WORKS

Gay publishing is one of the decade's success stories. Several books the size of this one would be needed to deal adequately with the 1980s and 1990s gay and lesbian output of writers, editors, and publishers. The ALA *Gay, Lesbian, and Bisexual Task Force Newsletter* reported that over 1,200 lesbian/gay books were published in 1992 alone.[1] In this chapter, we can mention only a small sample of these riches. We have also included books about bisexuality and transgenderism, recognizing that these are related to—not subsumed by—homosexuality.

Why should libraries buy books by, for, and about lesbians and gay men? We will summarize only briefly, because much has been written elsewhere.[2]

1. Gay and lesbian people use libraries. Over and over again, gay and lesbian writers tell how, as young people, they went to the library looking for explanations of their feelings about gender and sex. And they have not stopped reading since. So an audience exists of both adult and younger readers.

2. Gay and lesbian people are represented in all communities, professions, and ages. Recognized as "gay" or not, they use your library.

3. Gay and lesbian people have some unique information needs: about psychological, health, and medical matters, and about social and legal issues.

4. As a subject area, homosexuality has been underrepresented in library collections.

5. Both mainstream and little presses are publishing more and more good books about homosexuality and related issues.

6. Because more books on this area are being published, they are no longer difficult to buy through jobbers and large volume dealers. Moreover, many catalog services sell gay/lesbian books.

7. Nor are these works unreviewed, for the standard library review media cover many titles and so do some mass circulation periodicals. In addition, several specialized review sources deal exclusively with gay and lesbian books.

We propose that a well-rounded gay/lesbian library collection should include a variety of subtopics: general guides and introductions; coming out; couples; families; history and cultural studies; works critical of homosexuality including those designed to "reform" homosexuals; religion; scientific and scholarly research; sexuality; social issues and problems; and youth and aging. Libraries should also carry works about bisexuality and cross-gender role behaviors—transgenderism, transvestism, transsexualism, female impersonation, drag queens, and butch women (these are all different phenomena).

Gays and lesbian contributions to the art world, literature, theatre, and other media are very great. Some general coverage books on these topics would be valuable in a general collection, but more detailed coverage is more likely to be the province of academic and specialized collections. The Arts and the Media section of Chapter 11 mentions books about gay and lesbian themes in literature, art, and the media.

There are literally thousands of books available on countless subtopics—including such engaging esoterica as *Garden Variety Dykes: Lesbian Traditions in Gardening* (by Irene Reti & Valerie Chase, Her Books, 1994), for lesbians who take their Burpee catalogs seriously. Librarians wishing to spread their wings might browse in gay bookstores or catalogs (see below).

Considerable controversy, often local and very heated, can break out over the question of what sorts of books about homosexuality—pro or con—a library should carry. Throughout, we have stressed that libraries must make available as wide a variety of viewpoints as exist, particularly when controversy abounds. So no library is obligated to carry only books that display homosexuality in a negative light—nor, by the same token, only in a positive manner. Together, positive, critical, and middle-of-the-road materials provide an umbrella documentation of current ideas and are therefore all appropriate for libraries.

The definitive general work on homosexuality is the two-volume *Encyclopedia of Homosexuality* (B6, Dynes). It is unfortunately rather light on lesbian topics, but a more balanced second edition is in preparation. A shorter work for ready reference is *The Alyson Almanac* (B1). Also recommended is *Homosexuality: Opposing Viewpoints* (B5, Dudley).

For gay and lesbian readers, a basic work is *Positively Gay* (B2, Berzon) and, for lesbians, the classic *Lesbian/Woman* (B9, Martin & Lyon), now in a third edition. For nongay concerned others, two books provide sensitive, comprehensive introductions: *Loving Someone Gay* (B4, Clark), and *Is It a Choice?* (B8, Marcus).

All public libraries should have directories of gay/lesbian organizations and services. The standard is the national edition of *Gayellow Pages* (B7). If state or community directories exist, they too should be stocked—such as *The Greater Philadelphia Lavender Pages* (by Elizabeth Tillman, P.O. Box 816, Morrisville, PA 19067, not annotated).

Advice columns are nonfiction for the masses, and the gay/lesbian community has its own equivalents of Ann Landers and the *Playboy* Advisor. For gay men (mostly), the Q&A columnist Pat Califia has collected some of her columns in *The Advocate Advisor* (B3, Califia). Another terrific and wildly uninhibited gay advice column (also for the heterosexually adventurous) is Dan Savage's "Savage Love" in *The Stranger* (Seattle), but we know of no book that has collected them. Nor do we know of a lesbian Q&A advice columnist who has a published book.

Gay and lesbian books have the best alerting and distribution system of any sexuality topic. In addition to coverage in library periodicals, major book review media include *The Lesbian Review of Books*, new in 1994, and *Lambda Book Report* (from the Lambda Rising bookstore—see below). *Women's Review of Books* also has some lesbian materials.

The bibliographies in *Gay and Lesbian Library Service* (D118, Gough & Greenblatt) are useful for retrospective coverage. Some regularly updated coverage is provided by the brief bibliography on gay and lesbian sexuality and issues from SIECUS (see Chapter 5). Librarians may also use the periodic annotated bibliographies published in the library literature.[3] Another interesting annotated bibliography is distributed by the Association for Gay, Lesbian, and Bisexual Issues in Counseling (Box 215, Jenkintown, PA 19046). Librarians should not forget the ALA Gay, Lesbian, and Bisexual Task Force book award recipients; a list may be requested from the GLBTF via ALA headquarters.

A number of gay/lesbian bookstores and distribution services have catalogs, sometimes with extensive subject lists and annotations. Some major ones:

Lambda Rising
1625 Connecticut Avenue NW
Washington, DC 20009
Publishes a free bibliographic newspaper, *Lambda Rising News*, plus *Lambda Book Report*, which carries reviews and is available by subscription.

Glad Day Bookshop
673 Boylston Street

Boston, MA 02116
   At least 12 book lists by subject are available on request. No annotations.

Rising Tide Press
5 Kivy Street
Huntington Station, NY 11746
   "An Annotated Catalog of Lesbian/Gay Books for Mental Health Professionals"
(all publishers, many topics).

A Different Light
458 Hudson Street
New York, NY 10014
   A Different Light Review, annotated catalog of mostly new books.

Womankind Books
5 Kivy Street
Huntington Station, NY 11746
   Catalog of lesbian books and videos, with annotations.

True Colors
16106 University Oak, Ste. 2
San Antonio, TX 78249
   Free "newsletter recommending resources for the counseling of gay and lesbian
clients": short annotated bibliographies on various topics.

   Updated lists of catalog sources (there are many others) may be found
in *Gayellow Pages* (B7). *Gay and Lesbian Library Service* (D118, Gough
& Greenblatt) contains a list current to c. 1989.
   Another way to keep up with recent books of interest to gay and lesbian
people is to visit a gay bookstore and browse. The management will probably be delighted, and will point out best-sellers and new arrivals. (We have
had wonderful help from Giovanni's Room in Philadelphia.)
   Many public libraries compile their own flyers of recommended lesbian/
gay books, including the Minneapolis Public Library, the Hennepin County
Public Library (Minnesota), and the Milwaukee Public Library. Call to
request samples.
   Numerous publishers specialize in lesbian/gay topics, from the tiny to the
large: subsidiaries of Harper, for example. A directory is included in *Gay
and Lesbian Library Service* (D118, Gough & Greenblatt).
   There are many lengthy retrospective bibliographies on homosexuality;
A Research Guide to Human Sexuality (D120, Lichtenberg) contains a five-
page list.
   Legal guides are covered in the Law and Sex section; books of primary
value to librarians are covered under the Libraries and Sex section (both
in Chapter 12). Books *for* young people (as opposed to books *about* ho-

mosexuality in children and adolescents) are included in the Books for Children, Books for Pre-Adolescents, and Books for Adolescents sections (Chapter 11).

Many works in the General and Reference Works section (Chapter 9) have extensive material on homosexuality. See also the HIV/AIDS section (Chapter 13) and *Male Intergenerational Intimacy* (A76, Sandfort et al.).

Annotations

*B1 *The Alyson Almanac 1994–95 Edition: The Fact Book of the Lesbian and Gay Community*. 3rd ed. Boston: Alyson, 1993. 350p. bibliog. (2p.). index. ISBN 1-55583-242-3. Ready reference on homosexuality: history, research, biographies, health facts, media reviews, church policies, laws by state and country, officials and voting records, travel information, publications, organizations, and hotlines.

*B2 Berzon, Betty, ed. *Positively Gay: New Approaches to Gay and Lesbian Life*. Fwd. by Barney Frank. updated ed. Berkeley, CA: Celestial Arts, 1992. 296p. chapter notes. ISBN 0-89087-676-2. Comprehensive resource for living successfully as gay/lesbian. Covers identity and social life, partnerships, family relationships, parenting, aging, religion, work, financial planning, voting, HIV/AIDS, minorities (African Americans, Latinos, Asian-Pacific Islanders, Native Americans), and the new world of gay youth. Many referrals to organizations and print resources.

B3 Califia, Pat. *The Advocate Advisor: America's Most Popular Gay Columnist Tackles the Questions That the Others Ignore*. Boston: Alyson, 1991. 237p. resources (24p.). ISBN 1-55583-169-9. Collection of question-answer gay/lesbian advice columns originally published in *The Advocate*. Covers partners and relationships, coming out, families and children, sexuality, anatomy and physiology, aging, disabilities, STDs and HIV/AIDS, "solidarity," and death.

B4 Clark, Don. *Loving Someone Gay*. Rev. ed. Berkeley, CA: Celestial Arts, 1987. 269p. index. ISBN 0-89087-505-7. Guide to feelings and experience of being gay/lesbian, written partly for gay people and mostly for family and friends of gays/lesbians and professionals with gay/lesbian clientele. Covers self-acceptance and identity, growing up, communication, coming out, and helping someone gay.

*B5 Dudley, William, ed. *Homosexuality: Opposing Viewpoints*. San Diego, CA: Greenhaven, 1993. 216p. chapter bibliogs. resources (11p.). index. ISBN 0-89908-456-7. Essays providing varying and opposing views on homosexuality: causes, societal acceptance, changing to heterosexuality, and legal sanction of relationships. Chapter prefaces introduce each topic. Includes critical-thinking exercises.

*B6 Dynes, Wayne R., ed., assoc. eds. Warren Johansson & William A. Percy, with assistance of Stephen Donaldson. *Encyclopedia of Homosexuality*. New York: Garland, 1990. 2v. entry bibs. index. ISBN 0-8240-6544-1. Comprehensive synthesis of major research and opinion on homosexuality and lesbianism, much admittedly "controversial and contradictory." Over 770 entries, many with references. Contributors include many university faculty. (G10–12,C,A)

*B7 *Gayellow Pages: The National Edition; U.S. and Canada for Lesbians, Gay Men, Bisexuals 1994, #20*. New York: Renaissance House, 1994. 448p. index.

ISBN 1-885404-02-6. ISSN 0363-826X. Directory of organizations, businesses, and services serving or welcoming lesbian/gay/bisexual people. National U.S. and Canada entries plus regional and city listings. Includes nonprofit groups, travel and recreational services, bars and restaurants, publications and media, and health and psychological services.

*B8   Marcus, Eric. *Is It a Choice? Answers to 300 of the Most Frequently Asked Questions About Gays and Lesbians.* San Francisco: Harper San Francisco, 1993. 220p. bibliog. (4p.). index. ISBN 0-06-250664-1. Basic information about lesbians, gay men, and homosexuality in question-answer format, for straight and gay/lesbian readers. Includes definitions and origins of homosexuality/bisexuality, self-discovery and coming out, family and children, sex and relationships, work, the military, religion, discrimination and violence, the media, sports, education, gay activism, HIV/AIDS, aging, and other topics.

B9   Martin, Del, & Phyllis Lyon. *Lesbian/Woman.* 20th anniversary ed. Volcano, CA: Volcano, 1991. 428p. acronyms (2p.). ISBN 0-912078-93-6. Classic work about being lesbian, originally published 1972. For lesbians and others. Many personal accounts. Covers self-image, sexuality, motherhood, growing up, fears and dangers, the lesbian movement, and gay rights progress 1973–1991.

HOMOSEXUALITY—COMING OUT

"Coming out" is the process of revealing one's homosexuality or bisexuality to oneself or another—indeed, one must come out to oneself before coming out to anyone else. "Closeted" or "in the closet" refers to those with homosexual interests/behavior who are not out to anyone, perhaps not even to themselves.

Probably most gay men and lesbians in this country are closeted in some aspects of their lives. Many may be out to certain family members and friends, but they may "pass as straight" at work, fearing discrimination and uncertain or hostile reactions from employers or co-workers.

The gay community urges its members to come out as fully as they can: "If one day every same-sex–oriented person turned green, we would soon discover the truth of the placards carried in gay rights parades: 'We are everywhere.' "[4] But most gay people fully out accept that others are not ready or willing to risk so much by joining them now.

"Outing" is different, and occurs when a second person or group deliberately reveals to the public a person's homosexuality or bisexuality without his or her consent. It is considered unacceptable to "out" ordinary people, but opinions differ as to whether celebrities or public figures have the same right to privacy.

Coming out is discussed in nearly every general book on homosexuality and noted in some way in many, many others. A smaller selection of books treat the topic exclusively.

An excellent general work is *Coming Out: An Act of Love* (B13, Eichberg), which covers coming out to family, friends, employers—and discusses the personal and political contexts for doing so. *Coming Out to Parents* (B11, Borhek) focuses upon parents, while *The Final Closet* (B12, Corley) focuses upon coming out to one's children, young or adult. A matched pair of coming-out story collections are *Testimonies* (B10, Barber & Holmes) for lesbians, and *Revelations* (B15, Saks & Curtis) about gay men. A good work on the pros and cons of outing is *Outing: Shattering the Conspiracy of Silence* (B14, Johansson & Percy).

Among the sources provided in the Homosexuality—General Works section above, Glad Day Bookshop, Rising Tide Press, and True Colors list books under the heading of coming out.

See also books about homosexuality for young people in Chapter 11: Life Cycle Issues.

Annotations

B10   Barber, Karen, & Sarah Holmes. *Testimonies: Lesbian Coming-Out Stories.* 2nd ed. Boston: Alyson, 1994. 173p. ISBN 1-55583-245-8. Collection of stories from 21 lesbians, each describing first experiences of revealing her lesbian identity and sexual orientation to self and others.

*B11   Borhek, Mary V. *Coming Out to Parents: A Two-Way Survival Guide for Lesbians and Gay Men and Their Parents.* Rev. ed. Cleveland: Pilgrim, 1993. 308p. notes (14p.). resources (2p.). further reading (9p.). ISBN 0-8298-0957-0. Guidebook for gay men/lesbians wanting to come out to their parents, and for the parents. Addresses deciding to come out, making the announcement, working through grief, and letting go. Also discusses parents coming out, religious issues, changing to heterosexuality (including "ex-gay" ministries), and HIV/AIDS.

B12   Corley, Rip. *The Final Closet: The Gay Parents' Guide for Coming Out to Their Children.* Miami: Editech (P.O. Box 611085, Miami, FL 33261), 1990. resources (12p.). ISBN 0-945586-08-6. (Rev. ed. of *The Last Closet: A Gay Parent's Guide for Coming Out to Your Children.*) Guidance for lesbian and gay parents wanting to come out to their children. Covers children's right to know, risk and process of telling, age-appropriate language, partner's relationship with children, telling adult children, legal considerations, and HIV/AIDS concerns. Many examples/case studies.

*B13   Eichberg, Ron. *Coming Out: An Act of Love.* New York: Plume/Penguin, 1990. 279p. resources (7p.). ISBN 0-452-26685-8. Guide to revealing one's homosexuality to others. Discusses barriers and benefits of coming out and how to come out to family, friends, and others. Supports enhancing self-esteem and positive attitudes. Includes many letters to/from gays and families.

B14   Johansson, Warren, & William A. Percy. *Outing: Shattering the Conspiracy of Silence.* New York: Harrington Park, 1994. 341p. chapter refs. index. ISBN 1-56023-041-X. History and discussion of outing: revelation of one's (secret) homosexuality or bisexuality by another person without permission. Addresses history and reasons for outing, the U.S. homophile movement, outing via AIDS and activ-

ts, case for/against outing, "tactical guide to outing," and legal implications. Lists
many outed people.

B15   Saks, Adrien, & Wayne Curtis. *Revelations: Gay Men's Coming-Out Stories.*
2nd ed. Boston: Alyson, 1994. 191p. ISBN 1-55583-244-X. Collection of stories
from 22 gay men, each describing first experiences of revealing his gay identity and
sexual orientation to himself and others.

HOMOSEXUALITY—COUPLES AND MATESHIPS

Most gay men and lesbians, like straight people, are either not in a coupled relationship but want to be, about to begin a relationship, currently
in a relationship, or recovering from a relationship and hoping to make the
next one better. Books in this section provide guidance and celebration for
these couples and wannabes. Fortunately or unfortunately, books for gay
people on how to meet and mingle are not the glut on the market that we
associate with the heterosexual singles scene—and the few available books
tend to be of good quality.

Gay Relationships (B22, Tessina) is highly recommended for public libraries. It covers all points in the coupling process from finding mates to
either happily-ever-after or uncoupling, and speaks to both men and
women. Just for gay men is *The Male Couple's Guide* (B19, Marcus). *The
Male Couple: How Relationships Develop*, by David P. McWhirter and
Andrew M. Mattison (Prentice-Hall, 1984), is also very good. It is a study,
not a how-to (not annotated). For women, *Lesbian Couples* (B18, Clunis
& Green) covers the basic ground. In addition, *Boston Marriages* (B20,
Rothblum & Brehony) focuses upon romantic but asexual couples, while
And Then I Met This Woman (B17, Cassingham & O'Neil) describes het-
erosexually married women who made a transition to lesbianism. Another
work is *Staying Power: Long Term Lesbian Couples* by Susan Johnson
(Naiad, 1990, not annotated).

For such long-term couples, *Lesbian and Gay Marriage* (B21, Sherman)
provides pros and cons for private vs. public commitments, with profiles
of both "private" and "public" couples and cheery "wedding" photos. For
those choosing public ceremonies, *The Essential Guide to Lesbian and Gay
Weddings* (B16, Ayers & Brown) is a delightful confection of suggestions,
tips, and stories.

True Colors and the Association for Gay, Lesbian, and Bisexual Issues
in Counseling, noted in Homosexuality—General Works above, have "couples" sections in their lists.

See also *Same-Sex Unions in Premodern Europe* (B42, Boswell) and *A
Legal Guide for Lesbian and Gay Couples* (D104, Curry et al.).

Annotations

B16   Ayers, Tess, & Paul Brown. *The Essential Guide to Gay and Lesbian Weddings.* San Francisco: Harper San Francisco, 1994. 285p. illus. resources (5p.). index. ISBN 0-06-250271-9. Comprehensive, pleasantly tongue-in-cheek guide for planning gay and lesbian commitment ceremonies. Covers engagement through ceremony, reception, and honeymoon. Suggests rituals similar to and different from heterosexual weddings, and tips for dealing with the straight world of marriage businesses.

B17   Cassingham, Barbee J., & Sally M. O'Neil. *And Then I Met This Woman: Previously Married Women's Journeys into Lesbian Relationships.* Racine, WI: Mother Courage, 1993. 176p. refs. (2p.). ISBN 0-941300-25-0. Accounts from 36 mostly middle class women about transition from heterosexual marriages to lesbian relationships. Personalities, circumstances, and experiences are quite diverse. Many recommend support groups or counselors for women in similar situations.

B18   Clunis, D. Merilee, & G. Dorsey Green. *Lesbian Couples: Creating Healthy Relationships for the '90s.* Seattle: Seal, 1993. 274p. bibliog. (11p.). index. ISBN 1-878067-37-0. Resource for lesbian couples. Covers relationship stages, living arrangements, work, money, time, sexuality, friends and family, parenthood, differences, resolving conflict, racism, disability, recovery from problems or abuse, aging, breaking up, and starting new relationships.

B19   Marcus, Eric. *The Male Couple's Guide: Finding a Man, Making a Home, Building a Life.* New York: Harper Perennial, 1992. 328p. chapter resources. resources (3p.). index. ISBN 0-06-096936-9. (Rev. ed. of *The Male Couple's Guide to Living Together.*) Comprehensive guidebook for gay men seeking or staying in couples. Covers courtship, sex, communicating, commitment, living arrangements, rituals/religion, work, play, family, parenting, money, insurance, legal issues, health, aging, relationship breakdown, and loss.

B20   Rothblum, Esther D., & Kathleen A. Brehony, eds. *Boston Marriages: Romantic but Asexual Relationships Among Contemporary Lesbians.* Amherst: University of Massachusetts Press, 1993. 210p. chapter refs. ISBN 0-87023-876-0. Perspectives on lesbian couples who are romantically but not sexually involved. Includes personal stories, research on 19th century "Boston marriages," discussion on celibacy and sexuality, research on lesbian courtship, and implications for therapy.

B21   Sherman, Suzanne, ed. *Lesbian and Gay Marriage: Private Commitments, Public Ceremonies.* Philadelphia: Temple University Press, 1992. 288p. photos. orgs. (8p.). ISBN 0-87722-975-9. Perspectives on gay/lesbian marriage and marriage-like ceremonies. Includes pro and con arguments: practical, political, and philosophical; plus interviews with same-sex couples choosing private commitments, couples choosing public ceremonies, and clergy officiating in same-sex ceremonies.

*B22   Tessina, Tina. *Gay Relationships, for Men and Women: How to Find Them, How to Improve Them, How to Make Them Last.* New York: Tarcher/Putnam, 1989. 228p. resources (4p.). ISBN 0-87477-566-3. Guidebook about healthy love/ sex relationships for lesbians and gay men. Covers finding partners, dating, commitment, living together, commitment ceremonies, sexuality, relationship dynamics, families and coming out, breaking up, and love and aging. Appendices on safer sex and homophobia.

HOMOSEXUALITY—FAMILIES AND CHILDREN

Many gay men and lesbians led heterosexually parental lives before coming out. Others, not yet parents, actively desire to raise children, often within a gay partnership. *The Lesbian and Gay Parenting Handbook* (B27, Martin) addresses both groups but primarily those who wish to be new gay/lesbian parents. *Lesbian Mothers* (B26, Lewin) and *Gay Fathers* (B23, Barret & Robinson) consider the specific problems and life-situations of each gender. Finally, *Family Values* (B24, Burke) provides a moving and witty case study of a lesbian who legally adopted as co-mother her partner's biological son.

For parents of lesbians and gay males, a definitive work is *Now That You Know* (B25, Fairchild & Hayward).

Many other books on these topics are available. From the sources provided in the Homosexuality—General Works section, Glad Day Bookshop, True Colors, and the Association for Gay, Lesbian, and Bisexual Issues in Counseling all list books on families and/or parenting. In addition, bibliographies are available from:

PFLAG: Parents and Friends of Lesbians and Gays
1012 14th Street NW, Ste. 700
Washington, DC 20005
  "Recommended readings" list, with annotations. Books can be ordered from Lambda Rising (see Homosexuality—General Works, above).

Gay & Lesbian Parents Coalition International
P.O. Box 50360
Washington, DC 20091
  Lengthy bibliography (books and articles) on gays and lesbians and their families. Some annotations.

National Gay & Lesbian Task Force
1734 14th Street
Washington, DC 20009
  Bibliographies and fact sheets. Ask about the "Families Project."

Gay & Lesbian Advocates & Defenders
P.O. Box 218
Boston, MA 02112
  "Gay & Lesbian Parenting Bibliography & Resource List"—mostly legal, mostly periodical articles and court cases. No annotations.

See also books about homosexuality for young people in Chapter 11: Life Cycle Issues.

Annotations

B23 Barret, Robert L., & Bryan E. Robinson. *Gay Fathers*. Lexington, MA: Lexington/Heath, 1990. 196p. chapter refs. resources (22p.). index. ISBN 0-669-19514-6. To help "gay fathers, their children and families, and the practitioners who interact with them to understand the various dilemmas they face." Covers social and cultural factors, myths and realities, types of gay fatherhood, children, parents and wives, and impact of AIDS. Includes case studies.

B24 Burke, Phyllis. *Family Values: A Lesbian Mother's Fight for Her Son*. New York: Vintage/Random House, 1993. 233p. ISBN 0-679-75249-8. Autobiographical, witty account of a lesbian's successful adoption, as a second mother, of her partner's biological child. Covers partner's insemination and childbirth, author's growing gay rights activism, and the adoption process.

B25 Fairchild, Betty, & Nancy Hayward. *Now That You Know: What Every Parent Should Know About Homosexuality*. Updated ed. New York: Harcourt Brace Jovanovich, 1989. 276p. bibliog. (10p.). ISBN 0-15-667601-X. Supportive guidebook for parents with gay children or those who fear their child might be gay. Covers children's coming out from parents' and children's perspective, origins and experience of homosexuality, gay couples, religious perspectives, support groups, and HIV/AIDS. Stresses understanding and acceptance.

B26 Lewin, Ellen. *Lesbian Mothers: Accounts of Gender in American Culture*. Ithaca: Cornell University Press, 1993. 233p. notes (9p.). works cited (15p.). index. ISBN 0-8014-8099-X. Results of anthropological study of 73 lesbian mothers and 62 heterosexual single mothers. Groups showed strong similarities, especially about self-definition as mothers. Covers decision to have a child; relations with kin, friends, lovers, and the father; daily life with children; and custody problems.

*B27 Martin, April. *The Lesbian and Gay Parenting Handbook: Creating and Raising Our Families*. New York: Harper Perennial, 1993. 395p. notes (5p.). bibliog. (9p.). resources (17p.). ISBN 0-06-096929-6. Comprehensive resource for lesbians and gay men contemplating biological or adoptive parenthood. Covers deciding to become parents, biological methods vs. adoption, legal issues, raising children, family life, crises and tragedy, breaking up, and being "out" as parents.

HOMOSEXUALITY—HISTORY AND CULTURAL STUDIES

We were unable to find a good general book covering the complete history of gay and lesbian life (Vern Bullough's *Sexual Variance in Society and History* is out of print). But, an encouraging trend: historians are increasingly writing period studies of ancient Greece and Rome, Europe, Britain, and the last century or so in the United States.

Another growth trend has been writing about homosexuality cross-nationally and cross-culturally. Although we lack a sweeping anthropological overview, individual area studies are proliferating. Recent books have been published on homosexuality in China (*Passions of the Cut Sleeve* by Bret Hinsch, University of California Press, 1990), in India and South Asia (*A Lotus of Another Color*, edited by Rakesh Ratti, Alyson, 1993), among Native Americans (*The Spirit and the Flesh*, by Walter L. Williams, Beacon, 1990), and in the Moslem world (*Sexuality and Eroticism Among Males in Moslem Societies*, edited by Arno Schmitt, Greenwood, 1992), none of these annotated.

Here we recommend a small collection of rather broadly based books. *Hidden from History* (B28, Duberman et al.) provides glimpses of homosexuality throughout world history. It is suggestive and evocative rather than comprehensive. By contrast, *Gay American History* (B31, Katz)—an anthology of nearly 200 historical documents covering the United States, 1566–1976—gives glimpses so fast as to produce virtually cinematographic continuity. *Making History* (B32, Marcus) takes U.S. history up to the present, while *Odd Girls and Twilight Lovers* (B29, Faderman) focuses upon lesbian experiences. *The Third Pink Book* (B30, Hendriks et al.) carries the narrative back across the globe, summarizing the current circumstances, laws, and recent events concerning homosexuals in 178 countries. (*Coming Out: An Anthology of International Gay and Lesbian Writings*, edited by Stephen Likosky, Pantheon, 1992, covers somewhat similar ground; not annotated.) Finally, *In Search of Gay America* (B33, Miller) profiles present-day lesbian and gay men's lives in communities of all sizes around the United States.

Librarians should add to their collections any books focusing upon gay/lesbian communities in their particular geographic area, for example, *Gay New York* (by George Chauncey, Harper Collins, 1994, not annotated).

Among the catalog sources mentioned in the Homosexuality—General Works section, above, Rising Tide has a History and Sociology section, and Glad Day has History/Politics and Ethnic/Cross-Cultural Studies sections.

See also *Becoming Visible* (C71, Jennings).

Annotations

*B28   Duberman, Martin Bauml, Martha Vicinus, & George Chauncey, Jr., eds. *Hidden from History: Reclaiming the Gay and Lesbian Past*. New York: New American Library, 1989. 579p. notes (99p.). ISBN U/K. Anthology providing snapshots of homosexuality throughout world history. Covers ancient world, east and west pre-industrial societies, 19th and early 20th centuries (England and the U.S.), and World War II and postwar (U.S., South Africa, and Cuba).

B29   Faderman, Lillian. *Odd Girls and Twilight Lovers: A History of Lesbian Life in Twentieth-Century America*. New York: Penguin, 1991. 373p. photos. notes (53p.). index. ISBN 0-14-017122-3. Chronology of lesbian life and experience, from early 1900s "romantic friendships," to 1920s "deviate" masculine women and bo-hemians, through 1970s radical lesbian separatism, 1980s conservative "politically correct" movements, and 1990s solidarity through diversity and return to radical activism.

B30 Hendriks, Aart, Rob Tielman, & Evert van der Veen, eds. *The Third Pink Book: A Global View of Lesbian and Gay Liberation and Oppression.* Buffalo, NY: Prometheus, 1993. 349p. bibliog. (2p.). ISBN 0-87975-831-7. Anthology describing contemporary gay/lesbian life and issues in 15 countries, plus "world survey on the social and legal position of gays and lesbians" covering 178 countries. From the International Gay and Lesbian Association.

*****B31** Katz, Jonathan Ned. *Gay American History: Lesbians and Gay Men in the U.S.A.: A Documentary History.* Rev. ed. New York: Meridian, 1992. 702p. illus. notes (100p.). bibliog. (12p.). index. ISBN 0-452-01092-6. Wide-ranging collection of historical documents with commentary, revealing experiences and views re ho-mosexuals in the U.S., c. 1528–1976. Major topics: "trouble" (oppression), treat-ment, women passing as men, Native Americans/gay Americans, resistance, and love. Includes, e.g., letters, diaries, asylum and church records, government reports, literary works, and ephemera.

B32 Marcus, Eric. *Making History: The Struggle for Gay and Lesbian Equal Rights 1945–1990: An Oral History.* New York: Harper Perennial, 1992. 534p. photos. index. ISBN 0-06-092222-2. "Selective oral history" in interviews with 52 people, documenting progress of the lesbian/gay rights movement. Includes "high profile leaders" (Evelyn Hooker, Barbara Gittings, Randy Shilts, Larry Kramer) and little known contributors.

*****B33** Miller, Neil. *In Search of Gay America: Women and Men in a Time of Change.* New York: Harper & Row, 1990. 309p. ISBN 0-06-097308-0. Visits with lesbians and gay men in small towns, farms, suburbs, and cities throughout the U.S. in late 1980s. Designed to profile American gay and lesbian life outside already well-publicized urban gay ghettos. Includes coverage of race and religion issues.

GAY REFORM/CRITIQUE

Over the past few years, many articles in the library literature have en-couraged librarians to buy books about homosexuality. The books rec-ommended are gay-friendly and gay-positive. Librarians should also be aware of books taking other viewpoints. These tend to come in two types.

Those books arising from the "ex-gay movement" focus on the notion that homosexuality can be healed, cured, or reformed. Librarians following recent struggles of the Fairfax County Public Library to retain the *Washington Blade* will remember that Fairfax added 11 such titles to its collec-tion (see Chapter 2). We mention three. Particularly comprehensive and well-organized is *Coming Out of Homosexuality* (B35, Davies & Rentzel), aimed at troubled gay people. The sympathetic and excellent *Counseling and Homosexuality* (B40, Wilson) is written for counselors to assist those wanting to change. Nearly all gay reform and gay critique books take a

Christian perspective, as do these two.[5] *Healing Homosexuality* (B39, Ni-colosi), although derived ultimately from a Roman Catholic theological viewpoint, describes case histories of a secularly based "reparative therapy" for gay men and does not use theological doctrine or rhetoric.

The second type of book critical of modern homosexuals, gay/lesbian culture, and the gay rights movement would be considered homophobic by many people. These books generally take the viewpoint that homosexual behavior and practices are psychologically abnormal, ethically immoral, contrary to the Bible and Christianity, medically dangerous, hazardous and expensive for public health, and a general threat to U.S. society. Pro-gay laws are seen as unnecessary since homosexual people have the same rights as anyone else, while anti-sodomy laws are considered necessary and should be reinstated nationwide. Authors support their arguments by citing scholarly sources and the gay press, and express the hope that with exposure of the "real facts" about homosexuality, Americans will reverse their current pattern of gradual acceptance and see the gay rights movement as pernicious and undesirable. None of these books pushes gay bashing; some preach friendly contact and Christian-based efforts to help gays and lesbians become heterosexual or celibate, and urge ministry to AIDS patients.

Perhaps the most classic and compact but somewhat dated presentation of this view is *What Everyone Should Know About Homosexuality* (B37, LaHaye). More recent and more detailed about negative aspects of homosexual culture is *Legislating Immorality* (B36, Grant & Horne). From former Congressman William E. Dannemeyer (R-CA, 102nd Congress) comes *Shadow in the Land* (B34, Dannemeyer), with a longer section on the law than other works. *Informed Answers to Gay Rights Questions* (B38, Magnuson) offers point by point counters to pro-gay arguments.

These books exemplify the two genres, of which few are reviewed in the library literature or elsewhere. The best sources for ex-gay bibliographies and books are Regeneration Books and the ex-gay ministries:

Regeneration Books
P.O. Box 9830
Baltimore, MD 21284-9830
    Annotated catalog of "Christian books on homosexuality and related issues": sexual addiction, sexual exploitation, and AIDS. Free monthly newsletter, *Regeneration News*, which "reviews latest Christian books on homosexuality." (Note: Regeneration publications do not cover the many Christian books supportive of homosexuals. See the Homosexuality—Religion section.)

Love in Action
P.O. Box 2655
San Rafael, CA 94912
    Catalog of articles and testimonies; annotated "recommended reading" book list.

Homosexuals Anonymous Fellowship Services
P.O. Box 7881
Reading, PA 19603
   "Book ministry" catalog: books, pamphlets, tapes. Few annotations.

Courage
St. Michael's Rectory
424 West 34th Street
New York, NY 10001
   Courage is a Roman Catholic ministry sponsored by the Archdiocese of New York that promotes celibacy rather than reform for gay men and lesbians. Distributes brochures, pamphlets, tapes, and a short bibliography.

International Healing Foundation, Inc.
P.O. Box 901
Bowie, MD 20718-0901
   Publisher of *Alfie's Home* (C6, Cohen). Distributes gay reform books and audiovisuals.

   Gay critique books are more difficult to identify. A few can be found in Christian bookstores. Some older works are mentioned in an article in *The Public Eye* on the right-wing anti-homosexual movement[6] or appear in the notes to *Legislating Immorality*. Another source:

Family Research Institute
P.O. Box 2091
Washington, DC 20013-2091
   Books, articles, and tapes from anti-gay psychologist Paul Cameron.

   See also the Homosexuality—Religion section below, especially *Homosexuality: A New Christian Ethic* (B48, Moberly). Two pro-homosexuality books are somewhat critical of gay culture: *A Place at the Table* (B64, Bawer) and *After the Ball* (B68, Kirk & Madsen).

Annotations

B34   Dannemeyer, William. *Shadow in the Land: Homosexuality in America*. San Francisco: Ignatius, 1989. 243p. footnotes. index. ISBN 0-89870-241-0. Holds that homosexual rights movement and liberalization of laws and attitudes towards homosexuals are dangerous for America. Covers causes of homosexuality, legal and religious issues, homosexual movement 1960–present, homosexuality in sex education, and AIDS and public policy. Recommends compassion towards homosexuals and AIDS victims, widespread HIV testing, restoration of laws against sodomy, and rejection of anti-discrimination laws.

*B35   Davies, Bob, & Lori Rentzel. *Coming Out of Homosexuality: New Freedom* *for Men and Women.* Downers Grove, IL: InterVarsity, 1993. 202p. notes (8p.). orgs. (1p.). further reading (4p.). ISBN 0-8308-1653-4. Comprehensive and intelligent guidebook from Christian perspective for people wishing to overcome homosexuality. Covers Biblical and scientific evidence for change, spiritual and practical dynamics, understanding one's past, changing behavior, forming friendships, heterosexual romance and dating, and marriage.

B36   Grant, George, & Mark A. Horne. *Legislating Immorality: The Homosexual Movement Comes Out of the Closet.* Chicago: Moody Press/Franklin, TN: Legacy Communications, 1993. 291p. notes (25p.). index. ISBN 0-8024-4919-0. Designed to expose the worst of homosexual culture and agendas, to prevent acceptance of homosexuality in America, especially by churches. Addresses promiscuity, undesirable sexual practices, and child sex advocacy; misguided promotion and acceptance of homosexuality in U.S. culture, education, politics, medicine, the military, and the church; discusses history and theology; and encourages ministry to homosexuals, especially AIDS patients.

B37   LaHaye, Tim. *What Everyone Should Know About Homosexuality.* Wheaton, IL: Loving Books/Tyndale, 1978. notes (1p.). ISBN 0-8423-7933-9. (Originally published as *The Unhappy Gays.*) Classic presentation of conservative Christian view about homosexuality as practically and spiritually dangerous to self and America. Also addresses causes of homosexuality and overcoming it, the church and homosexuality, and coping when one's child is gay. Advocates compassion and opposes homosexuals as teachers.

B38   Magnuson, Roger. *Informed Answers to Gay Rights Questions.* Sisters, OR: Multnomah, 1994. 198p. notes (24p.). ISBN 0-88070-659-7. Point by point refutation of 53 arguments favoring gay rights. Notes that sodomy and homosexual behavior are often illegal as well as revolting, promiscuous and amoral, a drain on public health resources, and facilitating of the HIV/AIDS epidemic. Uses Christian basis for some arguments.

***B39**   Nicolosi, Joseph, with Lucy Freeman. *Healing Homosexuality: Case Stories of Reparative Therapy.* Northvale, NJ: Jason Aronson, 1993. 230p. refs. (1p.). index. ISBN: 0-87668-340-5. Case studies of reparative therapy, treatment for men who want to give up homosexual behaviors and control homosexual feelings. Based upon idea that some male homosexuality is misdirection of unfulfilled childhood need for nonsexual male friendships and stronger male identity.

***B40**   Wilson, Earl D. *Counseling and Homosexuality.* Dallas: Word, 1988. 225p. orgs. (2p.). notes (6p.). index. ISBN 0-8499-0590-7. Guidelines for Christian-based counselors of homosexual clients, about supporting clients' interest towards giving up gay/lesbian erotic contacts. Detailed suggestions for handling counseling sympathetically and coping with complexity and ambiguity. Considers that much homosexuality is learned, through lack of identification with same-sex parent and/or inhibition of opposite sex attraction, and may be unlearned.

HOMOSEXUALITY—RELIGION

We are all familiar with the turmoil that has existed in the Roman Catholic church in the last twenty-five years. Many Catholics look

upon these years as an aberrant and exceptional experience while they
yearn for the peace and quiet of the pre-Vatican II church. Such a
romantic nostalgia for the lack of controversy within the church is itself
based on an illusion. . . . Controversy and tension will always be a part
of the life of the church. Without tension the church itself is dead.[7]

Indeed, one of the most divisive issues in U.S. churches today is to what
extent gay and lesbian lives may be welcomed. Is homosexuality per se an
abomination? Is the orientation morally neutral but the practice a sin? Or
should homosexuals be required to take the same morally proper sexual
paths as heterosexuals, of either single celibacy or marrying in loving and
faithful monogamy before God? May openly gay men and lesbians serve
as clergy? May gay couples be married in church?

This issue is of great concern to millions of people—not only gay men
and lesbians wishing to participate in their chosen faith but congregations
wrestling with the possibility of welcoming them. For religious gay and
lesbian people, traditional church antipathy to homosexuality poses a serious problem. Many denominations have sprouted parainstitutional affiliates that openly accept gay worshipers. But most often these lack official
blessing or recognition from the parent church or are actively opposed by
it. These gay/lesbian religious groups include, for example, Dignity (Roman
Catholic), Affirmation (Methodist), Evangelicals Concerned, Emergence International (Christian Scientist), Honesty (Southern Baptists), Integrity
(Episcopal), and many others, including Jewish groups.[8] The Metropolitan
Community Church is a Christian fellowship established specifically for
lesbians and gay people. With a somewhat different focus, Courage is a
Roman Catholic mission that does not try to reform homosexuals but urges
them to be celibate. See the Gay Reform/Critique section, above.

Books about homosexuality and religion from various denominational
viewpoints began to appear in the 1970s. Today, in the 1990s, many such
works are in print. We have included a broad sampling of Christian-related
books. We found few books about homosexuality and Judaism or the Moslem faith.

Basic to the collection is an excellent volume of pro and con positions,
Homosexuality in the Church (B51, Siker). An essential reference, although fast becoming dated, is *The Churches Speak On: Homosexuality;
Official Statements from Religious Bodies and Ecumenical Organizations*,
by J. Gordon Melton (Gale Research, 1991, not annotated).

Three works present varied Roman Catholic perspectives. *Homosexuality* (B44, Hanigan) examines scientific data and theological tradition and
concludes that homosexual unions are "incompatible with the Christian
way of life." *Building Bridges* (B49, Nugent & Gramick), with a more
evolutionary and processual approach, summarizes recent events and pronouncements in the Roman Catholic Church about homosexuality and calls

for compassion and further dialogue. A now near-classic anthology of personal accounts is *Lesbian Nuns: Breaking Silence* (B43, Curb & Manahan). A fourth work—and almost best-seller as we write—speaks about Roman Catholic tradition but has far broader implications. This is the revolutionary *Same-Sex Unions in Premodern Europe* (B42, Boswell), describing medieval church-based texts for solemnizing same-sex marriage-like ceremonies. Some readers may therefore be interested in John Boswell's earlier scholarly book, *Christianity, Social Tolerance, and Homosexuality: Gay People in Western Europe from the Beginning of the Christian Era to the Fourteenth Century* (University of Chicago Press, 1980), not annotated.

In a more general Protestant/Christian perspective, *Sex: Should We Change the Rules?* (B47, Howe) lays out the traditional position that homosexual acts are forbidden as outside of the Biblical norm of monogamous heterosexual marriage. A more psychological approach, cited in some gay reform books, is presented in *Homosexuality: A New Christian Ethic* (B48, Moberly), which holds that homosexuality can result from disruption in nonsexual bonding with the same-sex parent, and uses this framework for counseling concerned Christians about how to respond to homosexuals. Several general Christian books take permissive viewpoints. *Is the Homosexual My Neighbor?* (B50, Scanzoni & Mollenkott) thoughtfully examines the debate, suggesting that the same religious sexual ethics that are applied to heterosexuals may also apply to homosexuals. *Can Homophobia Be Cured?* (B46, Hilton) emphasizes the Biblical mandate to love and welcome others, regardless of sexual acts. *What the Bible Really Says About Homosexuality* (B45, Helminiak) is a doctrinal attempt to refute anti-gay literalist interpretations of Biblical passages by providing their historical and cultural contexts.

Finally, a key work about being gay and Jewish is *Twice Blessed* (B41, Balka & Rose), by and about gay men and lesbians who maintain ties to Judaism.

For the gay-friendly viewpoints, the following catalogs or lists have religion sections: PFLAG, True Colors, Rising Tide Press, and the Association for Gay, Lesbian, and Bisexual Issues in Counseling (see the Homosexuality—General Works section, above). In addition, the ALA Gay, Lesbian, & Bisexual Task Force distributes Religion and Spirituality: A Checklist of Resources for Lesbians and Gay Men, a lengthy but unannotated bibliography current to 1992, updated through March 1993.

The Regeneration Books catalog and religious bookstores are good sources for Christian-related books taking the viewpoint that homosexuality is sinful and a deviation from God's plan.

See also the Gay Reform/Critique section, above, and the Sex and Religion section in Chapter 12.

Annotations

B41   Balka, Christie, & Andy Rose, eds. *Twice Blessed: On Being Lesbian, Gay, and Jewish*. Boston: Beacon, 1989. 305p. resources (2p.). notes (20p.). glossary (5p.). annotated bibliog. (9p.). ISBN 0-8070-7909-X. Essays and memoirs by and about gay/lesbian Jews maintaining ties to Judaism. Covers growing up gay and Jewish, coming out, historical Jewish traditions related to homosexuality, relationships, and creating and finding community. Appendix for Jewish educators addresses teaching about homosexuality and homophobia.

B42   Boswell, John. *Same-Sex Unions in Premodern Europe*. New York: Villard/Random House, 1994. 412p. photos. footnotes. index. ISBN 0-679-43228-0. Discusses and provides samples of medieval European liturgies for marriage-like same-sex unions. Sets texts within contexts of medieval love and marriage, and same-sex unions in ancient Greece and Rome. Appendix of selected Greek texts and English translations.

B43   Curb, Rosemary, & Nancy Manahan, eds. *Lesbian Nuns: Breaking Silence*. Tallahassee, FL: Naiad, 1985. 383p. photos. chapter notes. glossary (9p.). reading & resources (11p.). ISBN 0-930044-62-2. Personal accounts from 49 nuns/ex-nuns about self-discovery as a lesbian inside or outside the convent. Contributors vary in age and ethnicity, with lifelong involvement in social service.

B44   Hanigan, James P. *Homosexuality: The Test Case for Christian Sexual Ethics*. Mahwah, NJ: Paulist Press, 1988. 193p. chapter notes. ISBN 0-8091-2944-2. Examines scientific data about homosexuality and the theological tradition, and analyzes ethical proposals regarding morality of homosexual acts. Argues that homosexual unions cannot be compatible with the Christian way of life and should not be accorded equal normative status with heterosexual unions. Roman Catholic.

B45   Helminiak, Daniel A. *What the Bible Really Says About Homosexuality*. Fwd. by John S. Spong. San Francisco: Alamo Square, 1994. 121p. annotated source list (4p.). index. ISBN 0-9624751-9-X. Summary of Biblical scholarship showing that those perceiving the Bible as condemning homosexuality are misled by faulty translation and poor interpretation. Discusses several points of view and concludes that the Bible, taken in original historico-cultural context, does not condemn homosexuality as we know it today.

B46   Hilton, Bruce. *Can Homophobia Be Cured? Wrestling with Questions That Challenge the Church*. Nashville, TN: Abingdon, 1992. 128p. bibliog. (5p.). orgs. (2p.). ISBN 0-687-04631-9. Discusses questions Christians raise about the churches' response to homosexuality. Holds that churches have a Biblical mandate to love and welcome gay/lesbian members, sexually active or not, and fight hatred and homophobia. Describes the Reconciling Congregation program of the United Methodist Church and notes objections to the ex-gay movement.

B47   Howe, John W. *Sex: Should We Change the Rules? Let Us Argue It Out*. Lake Mary, FL: Creation House, 1991. 43p. notes (1p.). ISBN 0-88419-288-1. Summary of Biblical mandate for monogamous, heterosexual marriage as the only legitimate context for human sexual intimacy or for celibacy otherwise; plus summary of Biblical proscriptions against homosexual behavior.

*B48   Moberly, Elizabeth R. *Homosexuality: A New Christian Ethic*. Cambridge, England: James Clarke & Co., 1983. 56p. notes (2p.). bibliog. (2p.). ISBN 0-227-67850-8. Psychotheological discussion of homosexuality as resulting from disruption in relationship with same-sex parent, and representing attempted fulfillment of this legitimate psychological need. Holds that while homosexual acts are improper (and ultimately ineffective) reactions to this deficit in same-sex love, it is the deficit itself that is against the will of God. Counsels Christians to support healing of homosexuals, based upon prayer, fellowship, and nonsexual same-sex friendships.

*B49   Nugent, Robert, & Jeannine Gramick. *Building Bridges: Gay & Lesbian Reality and the Catholic Church*. Mystic, CT: Twenty-Third Publications, 1992. 218p. orgs. (2p.). bibliog. (6p.). index. ISBN 0-89622-503-8. Review of Roman Catholic Church vis-à-vis homosexuality over last few decades, re education and social concerns, counseling and pastoral issues, religious and clerical life, and evolving theological perspectives. Notes that Church's major position has been that homosexual orientation is morally neutral but homosexual acts sinful. Stresses benefits of continuing dialogue and pastoral sensitivity.

*B50   Scanzoni, Letha Dawson, & Virginia Ramey Mollenkott. *Is the Homosexual My Neighbor?* Rev. ed. San Francisco: Harper San Francisco, 1994. 242p. notes (32p.). further reading (4p.). index. ISBN 0-06-067078-9. Thoughtful, in-depth examination of Christian attitudes towards homosexuality. Covers scripture, scientific data, stereotyping and stigma, homophobia, and the homosexual as "Samaritan." Summarizes proposals that homosexual couples be held to standard similar to that for heterosexual couples. Proposes a Christian ethic of the homosexual as neighbor under God.

*B51   Siker, Jeffrey S., ed. *Homosexuality in the Church: Both Sides of the Debate*. Louisville, KY: Westminster John Knox, 1994. 211p. chapter notes. bibliog. (3p.). ISBN 0-664-25545-0. Essays from both sides of Christian debate about homosexuality: homosexual relationships are less than God's intentions and sinful, vs. homosexual relationships can be fulfilling and legitimate before God. Covers scripture, tradition, moral reasoning, science, experiences of homosexuality, and making decisions. Appendix: selected denominational statements on homosexuality.

HOMOSEXUALITY—SCIENTIFIC AND SCHOLARLY RESEARCH

Science has no definitive explanation for why some people prefer the same sex as erotic partners. But, for that matter, it cannot definitively explain why many more people prefer the opposite sex. Only three statements may be made. First, some evidence suggests a biological (inborn, possibly hormonal, possibly inherited) component to some types of homosexuality, particularly male homosexuality. Second, homosexuality and heterosexuality are not mutually exclusive categories but poles of a continuum. As Kinsey said, people "do not represent two discrete populations, heterosexual and homosexual. The world is not to be divided into sheep and goats."[9] A substantial number of people have some degree of erotic attraction to and/or experiences with both males and females. Some identify as gay, some as straight, and some as the newly emerging, doubly stigmatized category of bisexual. Third, same-sex erotic/copulatory behavior is recorded across history and culture, and in many animal species.

Because we address the needs of lay readers more than scholars, we concentrate on summaries and anthologies. Our selection is only a fraction of the available quality works.

Sexual Landscapes (B55, Weinrich) is written for a popular audience. Although it covers some general topics—such as courtship, and how men versus women react to erotica—it concentrates upon the "gender transpositions" and what we know about them. More scholarly yet still comprehensible to the public is *Homosexuality: Research Implications for Public Policy* (B53, Gonsiorek & Weinrich). It is most valuable for its comprehensive coverage and lengthy bibliography, and should be the starting point for more in-depth reading. A recent work describing possible genetic bases to homosexuality is *The Science of Desire: The Search for the Gay Gene and the Biology of Behavior*, by Dean Hamer & Peter Copeland (Simon & Schuster, 1994; not annotated).

No compilation of research on sexual orientation would be complete without a work from the Kinsey Institute and one from John Money. *Homosexualities* (B52, Bell & Weinberg) from Kinsey Institute authors presents results of a large study of homosexuals about sexuality and social and psychological adjustment. While its San Francisco sample is not typical of U.S. gays and lesbians, the study is the largest to date since the original Kinsey research.[10]

John Money is a prolific author who specializes in hormonal and developmental bases of gender behavior and the paraphilias ("perversions"). *Gay, Straight, and In-Between* (B54, Money) is devoted exclusively to sexual orientation and summarizes Money's research into psychohormonal bases of gender.

The best source for bibliographies covering biosocial and psychosocial research into homosexuality is probably the Kinsey Institute, although many bibliographies are not current (see Chapter 5). Some items are listed in *Studies in Human Sexuality* (D116, Frayser & Whitby). A number of book bibliographies about homosexuality have been published.[11] Libraries with special collections on homosexuality may undoubtedly be contacted for recommendations (for example, the Labadie Collection at the University of Michigan, the Mariposa Foundation collection at Cornell University, and the collection being founded at the San Francisco Public Library; see *Gay and Lesbian Library Service*, D118, Gough & Greenblatt, for others). Fortunately, most major works are covered in the standard review media, the Lambda Rising publications, and (we expect) *The Lesbian Review of Books* (see Homosexuality—General Works, above).

See also *The Sexual Brain* (A134, LeVay).

Annotations

B52   Bell, Alan P., & Martin S. Weinberg. *Homosexualities: A Study of Diversity Among Men and Women*. New York: Simon & Schuster, 1978. 505p. bibliog. (8p.). index. ISBN 0-671-24212-1. Results of interview study of about 1,500 homosexuals, analyzed by gender and race (black/white). Covers sexual experience and feelings, social adjustment (religion, work, friends, politics, prior marriage), and psychological adjustment. Distinguishes five major "types" of homosexuals: close-coupleds, open-coupleds, functional singles, dysfunctional singles, and asexual singles.

*B53   Gonsiorek, John C., & James D. Weinrich, eds. *Homosexuality: Research Implications for Public Policy*. Newbury Park, CA: Sage, 1991. 295p. refs. (37p.). index. ISBN 0-8039-3764-4. "Attempts to summarize what science knows about homosexuality and its relevance to public policy . . . from a variety of disciplines." Addresses nature and causes of sexual orientation, ethics of mental health approaches, effects of social and legal discrimination, biological and psychological understandings, homosexuals as couples and parents, "conversion therapy," and implications of AIDS.

B54   Money, John. *Gay, Straight, and In-Between: The Sexology of Erotic Orientation*. New York: Oxford University Press, 1988. 267p. photos. glossary (45p.). bibliog. (10p.). index. ISBN 0-19-506331-7. Complex, scholarly discussion with case studies of biological and social factors contributing to sexual orientation. Describes variations in preferences and behavior relating to gender, and development of normal and abnormal lovemaps (an individual's ideal for sexual partner and sexual activity). Includes development of paraphilias ("perversions").

B55   Weinrich, James D. *Sexual Landscapes: Why We Are What We Are; Why We Love Whom We Love*. New York: Scribner's, 1987. 433p. refs. (16p.). index. ISBN 0-684-18705-1. Repackaging of much biological sex research for popular readership. Covers need for sexual science, the gender transpositions (heterosexuals, homosexuals, bisexuals, crossdressers, and transsexuals), sexual attraction and arousal, courtship, and sex and taboo.

HOMOSEXUALITY—SEXUAL BEHAVIOR AND ENHANCEMENT

Gay and lesbian community spokespeople sometimes complain that too much fuss is made about gay sexuality, overshadowing social, behavioral, and psychological similarities with heterosexuals. However, gay sex is *not* made much of in publishing. True, many books about gay/lesbian issues include sexuality and discuss safe sex. Yet few books deal exclusively with the topic, particularly when compared to the explosion of books on gay history, area studies, and social issues—and compared to the glut on the market of heterosexual sex books. Most books below are virtual classics, and all give prominent coverage to health and safety concerns.

In 1977, *The Joy of Lesbian Sex* and *The Joy of Gay Sex* were published.

The first is now out of print and out of date, but has been replaced by a quartet of very individual books. *Lesbian Sex* (B60, Loulan) and *Lesbian Passion* (B61, Loulan & Nelson) function as a complementary pair and are together quite comprehensive, particularly about sexual dysfunctions and partner compatibility. An easier to read A-to-Z book is *The Lesbian Sex Book* (B58, Caster). In *Sapphistry* (B57, Califia), now in a third edition, Pat Califia's approach is literate—she is an excellent writer—detailed, and analytical. She covers more variations than the others.

We cannot omit the engaging Susie Bright from any discussion of lesbian sex books. Her two books from Cleis Press, *Susie Sexpert's Lesbian Sex World* and *Susie Bright's Sexual Reality* (B56, Bright) constitute a witty and eye-opening travelogue through contemporary lesbian sexuality.

For gay men, *The New Joy of Gay Sex* (B62, Silverstein & Picano) revises and updates the 1977 edition. *Men Loving Men* (B63, Walker) is also a second edition. *Gay Sex* (B59, Hart) is a new publication. Both *The New Joy* and *Gay Sex* use the A-to-Z format. *The New Joy* is slightly longer and the drawings are beautifully done. One of its authors is a psychologist and psychotherapist. On the other hand, *Gay Sex* includes an appendix on the HIV transmission risks of various activities plus an annotated bibliography. *Men Loving Men* is organized by sexual activity and gives more information about each activity than the preceding, but less on relationships and lifestyles. It includes a chapter on AIDS and STDs.

Only some of the sources listed in the Homosexuality—General Works section, above, have books about sexuality. Sources with lists are Rising Tide Press, the Association for Gay, Lesbian, and Bisexual Issues in Counseling, and Womankind Books. The Sexuality Library catalog (see Chapter 5) lists a small number of gay and lesbian sex books.

See Chapter 6 for comments about lesbian/gay erotica.

See also the Sexual Sadomasochism section in Chapter 9, *Male Intergenerational Intimacy* (A76, Sandfort et al.), and *Hustling* (E107, Preston).

Annotations

B56 Bright, Susie. *Susie Sexpert's Lesbian Sex World.* Pittsburgh: Cleis, 1990. 154p. ISBN 0-939416-35-2. Witty and irreverent essays on lesbian sexuality and culture, reprinted from the periodical *On Our Backs*. Topics include sex toys, the G-spot, anal sex, safe sex, lesbian erotica, fisting, the San Francisco Gay Pride Parade, lesbian impregnation, and gay culture. *Susie Bright's Sexual Reality: A Virtual Sex World Reader* continues with more essays (Cleis, 1992, ISBN 0-959416-59-X).

B57 Califia, Pat. *Sapphistry: The Book of Lesbian Sexuality.* 3rd ed. Tallahassee, FL: Naiad, 1988. 186p. resource list (5p.). index. ISBN 0-941483-24-X. Overview about sexuality from permissive lesbian viewpoint. Covers fantasies, masturbation, sex with a partner, and communicating about sex, techniques, frequency, orgasm, youth and age issues, disabilities, variations, and STDs/AIDS.

B58   Caster, Wendy. *The Lesbian Sex Book*. Illus. by Julie May. Boston: Alyson, 1993. 191p. resource list (7p.). ISBN 1-55583-211-3. A–Z entries on lesbian sexuality and sexual behavior, from *afterplay* to *who's on top?* Includes definitions, information, advice, and often references to other books.

B59   Hart, Jack. *Gay Sex: A Manual for Men Who Love Men*. Illus. by Bradley M. Look. Boston: Alyson, 1991. 192p. annotated bibliog. (4p.). index. ISBN 1-55583-170-2. A–Z guide to gay male sexuality, *age differences* to *zoophilia*. Covers sexual anatomy, finding a partner, sexual behaviors, sex aids and turns-ons, and health considerations. Especially stresses safer sex and condoms.

B60   Loulan, JoAnn. *Lesbian Sex*. Illus. by Barbara Johnson & Marcia Quackenbush. Minneapolis: Spinsters Ink, 1984. 309p. bibliog. (9p.). ISBN 0-933216-13-0. Manual for lesbian sexual enhancement, plus discussion of coming out, identifying as lesbian (or not), being single, love and relationships, motherhood, addiction (drugs, alcohol, sex), aging, youth, and STDs (not AIDS). Several sections on disability.

B61   Loulan, JoAnn, with Mariah Burton Nelson. *Lesbian Passion: Loving Ourselves and Each Other*. San Francisco: Spinsters Book Co., 1987. 223p. list of AIDS resources (2p.). ISBN 0-933216-29-7. Essays about lesbian sexuality and relationships. Covers self-esteem, recovery from addictions and sexual abuse, sex toys and enhancements, celibacy, dating, AIDS, and results of questionnaire survey of 1,566 lesbians about sexual experiences and sexual abuse.

B62   Silverstein, Charles, & Felice Picano. *The New Joy of Gay Sex*. Illus. by F. Ronald Fowley & Deni Ponty. New York: Harper Collins, 1992. 220p. index. ISBN 0-06-092438-1 (Rev. ed. of *The Joy of Gay Sex*.) A–Z guidebook for enjoying (safer) gay male sex, *anus* to *wrestling*. Covers sexual techniques and practices, relationships and finding partners, gay culture, HIV/AIDS and related concerns, and psychological/physical health and safety.

B63   Walker, Mitch. *Men Loving Men: A Gay Sex Guide and Consciousness Book*. 2nd ed. Drawings by Bill Warrick. San Francisco: Gay Sunshine, 1994. 159p. photos. notes (8p.). ISBN 0-917342-52-6. Elegant, intellectual sex manual for gay men. Covers masturbation, fellatio, anal intercourse, S&M, and other variant tastes; for each, gives history and techniques, plus additional points of interest. Also discusses gay male sexual health, and love and gay consciousness.

HOMOSEXUALITY—SOCIAL ISSUES AND PROBLEMS

So many recent titles have appeared about homosexuality and social issues that we can review only a few areas and mention only a few works. We concentrate on discrimination and its negative sequelae: negative stereotyping of homosexuals, homophobia and violence, problems in the workplace and in certain professions (for example, law enforcement and the military), and getting along in school and college.

Three recent and excellent works address U.S. social acceptance of homosexuality: *After the Ball* (B68, Kirk & Madsen), *A More Perfect Union* (B71, Mohr), and *A Place at the Table* (B64, Bawer). The first is addressed to the gay community, while the others are directed more towards concerned straight Americans. All suggest ways to achieve greater public acceptance of homosexuals, proposing that acceptance would increase if the general public understood that most gays and lesbians do not behave like the flamboyant "fringe" featured in the media. They also urge the gay community to adopt lifestyles and modes of self-presentation more acceptable to straights and less destructive to themselves.

Homophobia and anti-gay violence have led to many local battles over "hate crime" legislation. An anthology presenting case studies and analyses is *Hate Crimes* (B67, Herek & Berrill). *Violence Against Lesbians and Gay Men*, by Gary David Comstock (Columbia University Press, 1991, not annotated), is an excellent and comprehensive sociological work recommended for research and policy collections.

For general workplace issues, we recommend *Gay Issues in the Workplace* (B70, McNaught) and *The Corporate Closet: The Professional Lives of Gay Men in America* (B72, Woods & Lucas). An interesting related work is *100 Best Companies for Gay Men and Lesbians*, by E. Mickens (Simon & Schuster, 1994), not annotated.

A good pro-con summary of the gays-in-the-military issue is *Gays: In or Out?* (B65). Favoring the right to serve are *Exclusion: Homosexuals and the Right to Serve*, by Melissa Wells-Petry (Regnery Gateway, 1993) and *Conduct Unbecoming* by Randy Shilts (St. Martin's, 1993); against it: *Gays in the Military: The Moral and Strategic Crisis*, edited by George Grant (Franklin, TN: Legacy Communication, 1993)—none annotated.

Homosexual teachers and criminal justice workers have also engendered much debate. *Coming Out of the Classroom Closet* (B66, Harbeck) addresses the teacher issue, while *Gay Cops* (B69, Leinan) discusses homosexuals working as law enforcement agents. Especially for high school students, we suggest *The Gay, Lesbian, and Bisexual Students' Guide to Colleges, Universities, and Graduate Schools*, by Jan Mitchell Sherrill and Craig Hardesty (New York University Press, 1994, not annotated). A related work is *School's Out: The Impact of Gay and Lesbian Issues on America's Schools*, by Dan Woog (Alyson, 1995, not annotated).

A Bibliography on Violence Against Lesbians and Gays, compiled by the Anti-Violence Project, is available from the National Gay and Lesbian Task Force, Policy Institute (1734 14th St. NW, Washington DC 20009). We found no other bibliographies highlighting current social issues, but a number of works are included in Glad Day Bookshop's "Selected New Titles." New arrivals are featured prominently in the *Lambda Book Report* and the Lambda Rising newsletter/catalog (see the Homosexuality—General Works section, above). For research collections, Political Research Associates (678 Massachusetts Ave., Ste. 703, Cambridge, MA 02139) sells collections of documents, "Packets on Homophobia."

See also *Male Intergenerational Intimacy* (A76, Sandfort et al.); also the Homosexuality—Religion, and Gay Reform/Critique sections, above.

Annotations

*B64   Bawer, Bruce. *A Place at the Table: The Gay Individual in American Society*. New York: Poseidon/Simon & Schuster, 1993. 269p. ISBN 0-671-79533-3. Holds that the public misunderstands gays/lesbians, homosexuality, and the "gay lifestyle," and that a vocal and visible gay minority misrepresents most gay people and gay life. Reviews homosexuality and gay rights in historical and moral perspectives, examines homophobic/homocritical positions, and considers homosexuals and their problematic relationship to both mainstream U.S. culture and gay subculture.

B65   *Gays: In or Out? The U.S. Military & Homosexuals: A Sourcebook*. New York: Brassey's/Maxwell Macmillan, 1993. 215p. ISBN 0-02-881080-5. Incorporates *Military Necessity & Homosexuality* by Ronald Ray, and *Defense Force Management: DoD's Policy on Homosexuality* by the U.S. General Accounting Office (GAO/NSIAD-92-98). The first argues to exclude homosexuals from the U.S. military; the second summarizes research and statistics suggesting that exclusion may be costly and unnecessary.

B66   Harbeck, Karen M., ed. *Coming Out of the Classroom Closet: Gay and Lesbian Students, Teachers, and Curricula*. New York: Harrington/Haworth, 1992. 271p. chapter refs. index. ISBN 1-56023-013-4. Papers originally published in *Journal of Homosexuality*. Uneven scholarship, yet highly revealing of views and experiences of gay/lesbian educators and students. Describes discrimination, harassment, and fear of discovery. Some describe overt tolerance but covert harassment. Suggests curricula for teaching about homosexuality and AIDS/HIV.

B67   Herek, Gregory M., & Kevin T. Berrill, eds. *Hate Crimes: Confronting Violence Against Lesbians and Gay Men*. Newbury Park, CA: Sage, 1992. 310p. chapter notes. ISBN 0-8039-3764-4. Research studies and essays about U.S. violence against lesbians and gay men. Covers statistics and trends, social contexts, perpetrators, surviving and responding, and policy implications. Several "survivor's story" case histories.

B68   Kirk, Marshall, & Hunter Madsen. *After the Ball: How America Will Conquer Its Fear and Hatred of Gays in the 90s*. New York: Plume/Penguin, 1990. 398p. notes (4p.). bibliog. (10p.). ISBN 0-452-26498-7. Discusses how and why Americans disapprove of gays and lesbians, nature of homophobia, and how homophobia can be stopped or reversed. Concludes with constructive critique of gay culture and promotes code of ethics.

B69   Leinan, Stephen. *Gay Cops*. New Brunswick, NJ: Rutgers University Press, 1993. 245p. notes (8p.). index. ISBN 0-8135-2000-2. Results of interview study of 41 gay/lesbian New York City police officers, varied race and age. Covers career choice, "deviant identity," closeting and coming out, harassment from co-workers, and off-duty social/sexual life.

B70 McNaught, Brian. *Gay Issues in the Workplace.* New York: St. Martin's, 1993. 151p. notes (3p.). resources (9p.). ISBN 0-312-09808-1. For employers and others concerned with issues re gay men, lesbians, and bisexuals as productive employees. Covers being gay and coming out, homophobia and harassment, needs of gay/bisexual employees, and designing corporate workshops on sexual orientation issues.

B71 Mohr, Richard D. *A More Perfect Union: Why Straight America Must Stand Up for Gay Rights.* Boston: Beacon, 1994. 125p. ISBN 0-8070-7932-4. Appeal to heterosexuals to support gay rights as consistent with U.S. traditions of equality and personal liberty. Addresses prejudice, privacy, gay marriage, equality, civil rights, HIV/AIDS, and gays in the military. Suggests actions for support.

B72 Woods, James D., with Jay H. Lucas. *The Corporate Closet: The Professional Lives of Gay Men in America.* New York: Free Press, 1993. 331p. notes (41p.). bibliog. (12p.). index. ISBN 0-02-935603-2. Results of interview survey of 70 gay men working in bureaucratic organizations. Covers heterosexual workplace assumptions, experiences of being in the closet at work and coming out, techniques for pretending to be heterosexual or evading the issue, and transition to more gay-tolerant workplaces.

YOUTH AND AGE

These books deal with societal issues of being young or aging as a homosexual, and much less with the sexuality of younger or older gay males and lesbians. They focus on self-acceptance, coming out or being out in various contexts, social relationships, and problems of various sorts, particularly discrimination. Nearly all are written for serious readers or scholars. (Many books for gay people described elsewhere in this chapter also in part address being young or growing old.)

Gilbert Herdt's books provide a thoughtful picture of gay and lesbian youth in the United States and other countries: *Children of Horizons* (B74, Herdt & Boxer) and *Gay and Lesbian Youth* (B73, Herdt). An essential directory for working with gay and lesbian youth is *You Are Not Alone* (B77). While some of the organizations listed are in *Gayellow Pages* (B7), *You Are Not Alone* is easier to use, especially by the youth themselves and by hurried counselors.

Gay Midlife and Maturity (B76, Lee) contains scholarly essays about older gay men and lesbians. *Lesbians Over 60 Speak for Themselves* (B75, Kehoe) also has scholarly grounding but seems more accessible to the non-scholar because it quotes the women interviewed.

Books about youth and for youth are commonly found in most "youth-related" sexuality book lists. The True Colors catalog and the bibliography issued by the Association for Gay, Lesbian & Bisexual Issues in Counseling have lists of this type (see Homosexuality—General Works, above). We do not know of a bibliography of books on aging for gay men and lesbians—we suspect that the area is too new and there are too few books. However, some may be available from organizations for older gay men and lesbians; the 1994 *Gayellow Pages* (B7) lists some 21 different organizations under the index heading Senior Citizens.

See also Chapter 11: Life Cycle Issues.

Annotations

B73   Herdt, Gilbert, ed. *Gay and Lesbian Youth*. New York: Harrington Park, 1989. chapter notes & refs. ISBN 0-918393-56-6. (Originally published in the *Journal of Homosexuality*.) Scholarly and informal essays about adolescence in gay males and lesbians in the U.S., Canada, Australia, Brazil, England, Finland, France, Ireland, Mexico, and Sweden. Addresses coming out, formation of homosexual identities, parental influences, male prostitution, AIDS, and multicultural contexts.

B74   Herdt, Gilbert, & Andrew Boxer. *Children of Horizons: How Gay and Lesbian Teens Are Leading a New Way Out of the Closet*. Boston: Beacon, 1993. 290p. notes (30p.). index. ISBN 0-8070-7928-6. Results of ethnographic and historical study of Chicago's gay and lesbian community; of ethnographic study of 202 gay and lesbian youth and the Horizons agency (gay/lesbian social and educational center); and of developmental study of these youth through interviews and psychological assessments. Provides data on homosexual identity development and coming out.

B75   Kehoe, Monika. *Lesbians Over 60 Speak for Themselves*. New York: Harrington Park, 1989. 111p. chapter notes. ISBN 0-918383-55-8 (Originally published in the *Journal of Homosexuality*.) Results of questionnaire survey of 100 lesbians over age 60 re coming out, family, relationships, lesbian identity, sexuality, and growing older. Compares pre-1980 research and results with earlier studies of gay men.

B76   Lee, John Allen, ed. *Gay Midlife and Maturity*. New York: Harrington Park, 1991. 232p. chapter refs. ISBN 0-918393-80-9. (Originally published in the *Journal of Homosexuality*.) Scholarly and informal essays about aging as gay men or lesbians. Topics include adjustment to aging, a theory of successful aging, survey of aging studies, support networks, pets as therapy, communication in maturing couples, sexual attitudes and behavior, and male prostitution.

B77   *You Are Not Alone: National Lesbian, Gay and Bisexual Youth Organization Directory*. New York: Hetrick-Martin Institute (401 West Street, New York, NY 10014-2587), 1993. 59p. ISBN U/K. For lesbian, gay, and bisexual youth and those helping them. Lists over 170 organizations by state, with sections covering Canada, national organizations, scholarships, and toll-free numbers. Includes adult gay organizations, youth service agencies, religious groups, and others providing counseling, emergency shelter, medical care, support services, social events, or additional services.

BISEXUALITY

Bisexuals have been both ignored and distrusted by gay and straight people, but increasingly bisexuals are being considered part of the gay/lesbian community. For example, the Gay and Lesbian Task Force of the American Library Association recently changed its name to the Gay, Lesbian, and Bisexual Task Force. However, there are still not many books published on bisexuality, so it is especially important for libraries to have scholarly and popular materials on this topic.

Bisexuality (B78, Geller) combines personal accounts with scholarly essays and a catalog/directory of groups, periodicals, lists of films and plays, and a lengthy bibliography. It is the work of choice to begin the collection. A major recent scholarly work, *Dual Attraction* (B81, Weinberg et al.), presents results of a survey of bisexuals, heterosexuals, and homosexuals. Another key purchase, *The Bisexual Spouse* (B79, Hill), addresses a life situation relevant to many people. To round out the list is an anthology devoted solely to personal accounts, *Bi Any Other Name* (B80, Hutchins & Kaahumanu).

We found no ongoing bibliographies on bisexuality other than that from the Kinsey Institute, which is updated only to 1992 (see Chapter 5). The list from PFLAG has a Spouses category with a few titles about bisexual spouses (see the Homosexuality—Families and Children section, above). A lengthy pre-1990 bibliography is included in *Bisexuality* (B78, Geller), which also lists bisexual support organizations that may be queried for bibliographies. More titles could probably be identified by querying large gay bookstores for a list of what they stock or can order: Lambda Rising, Giovanni's Room (Philadelphia), A Different Light (New York City), or Glad Day Bookshop (see Homosexuality—General Works, above).

Annotations

*B78   Geller, Thomas, ed. *Bisexuality: A Reader and Sourcebook*. Ojai, CA: Times Change, 1990. 186p. ISBN 0-87810-037-7. (Sales from Publishers Services, Box 2510, Novato, CA 94948.) Collection of 10 contributions from bisexuals about personal experiences and views, three scholarly essays (including the "Klein grid" for assessing sexual orientation), directory of bisexual groups (36p.), list of periodicals and films/plays (4p.), and bibliography (72p.).

*B79   Hill, Ivan, ed. *The Bisexual Spouse: Different Dimensions in Human Sexuality*. McLean, VA: Barlina Books (P.O. Box 7425, McLean, VA 22106), 1987. 264p. ISBN 0-937525-01-4. Accounts from married couples and others about bisexuality in their marriages. Some couples divorced, some adapted. Also results of questionnaire survey of 207 psychiatrists and 63 sex therapists about bisexuality. Comments on the survey by Judd Marmor.

B80   Hutchins, Loraine, & Lani Kaahumanu, eds. *Bi Any Other Name: Bisexual*

People Speak Out. Boston: Alyson, 1991. 379p. orgs. (1p.). glossary (3p.). ISBN 1-55583-174-5. Essays from 75 bisexuals with varied viewpoints and lives. Most describe personal experiences and observations about sexual preference and romantic attraction. Themes: psychology and self-awareness, monogamy and promiscuity, spirituality, discrimination from both gays and straights, and sexual politics.

B81   Weinberg, Martin S., Colin J. Williams, & Douglas W. Pryor. *Dual Attraction: Understanding Bisexuality*. New York: Oxford University Press, 1994. 437p. notes (11p.). index. ISBN 0-19-508482-9. Results of interview study of about 100 bisexuals, plus questionnaire study of about 400 heterosexuals, bisexuals, and homosexuals. Covers development of sexual preference, sexual activities, relationships, and changes in perceptions and experiences 1983–1988, including changes attributed to the AIDS epidemic.

TRANSGENDERISM (TRANSVESTISM, TRANSSEXUALISM, DRAG, FEMALE IMPERSONATION, BUTCH)

> The card catalogs of most libraries have a few books about crossdressing or transsexualism. Locating these books, however, can constitute a problem. Much of the time, they are not on the shelves. . . . Library staff may be able to help (if you're not ashamed to ask), but when books have been stolen, there's little the librarian can do.[12]

The public often lumps the transgendered community in with homosexuals. However, transgenderism is a separate and only sometimes overlapping series of phenomena. *Transgendered* is an overall term for people who wish to dress, live, and/or pass as the opposite biological sex on a recurring or regular basis. (We are not talking about Halloween, costume parties, or other Carnival-like reversals of dress and behavior.) Another common term is *gender dysphoria* (GD), the state of being deeply discontented with one's own biological sex. Often the phrase is used in conjunction with *transsexuality* or *transsexualism*. A *transsexual* is someone who feels so strongly that their biological sex is incorrect that they wish to change their body through sex reassignment surgery. A common phrase is "trapped in the wrong body." A *transvestite* dresses as the other sex (crossdressing) for emotional or erotic pleasure, usually temporarily or episodically; the term is generally applied to men. (Women today have greater freedom of choice in clothing, so female crossdressers are almost unnoticeable.) A *female impersonator* is a man who performs professionally in the role of a woman. A *drag queen* is a (usually) homosexual male who enjoys dressing in public in a feminine persona, often outrageously, as part of "camp" culture.[13] A *butch* is a woman who has completely rejected female traditions and the female persona. She may be mistaken for a male—or not. There are also people who prefer to dress and live as the other sex on a permanent basis (including butches), but without changing their bodies or the "sex" block on their driver's license. These are sometimes called simply *transgendered* in a narrower sense. Any of these folk can be heterosexual (particularly transvestites), homosexual, or bisexual in choice of partner.

Confused? It is much worse if one *is* a transgendered person. Homosexual resources and networks are quite visible today, especially in large cities. The media bring regular news of gays in the military or lesbian sports champions. Many bookstores have "gay studies" sections. But where can the transgendered go to learn what *they* are, how to cope, and where to find the like-minded? Only an occasional Renée Richards or Christine Jorgensen calls public attention to the existence of such people—for many transgendered individuals want desperately to pass as their target sex, and some succeed in doing so. So no one notices. Female-to-male transgendered people are especially invisible, as women in our culture can wear male clothing without stigma and no one publicly prominent falls into this group. In addition, most publications about transgender phenomena are privately printed by transgender support organizations and not available in bookstores, although gay bookstores may carry a selection.

So, yes, the library needs to have books about transvestism, transsexualism, and other transgendered behaviors. We have included a good variety in this section because these materials are not easily visible to library acquisitions departments or to the public.

The major historical and scholarly overview and guide to further reading and research, suitable for lay and scholarly audiences, is *Cross Dressing, Sex, and Gender* (B83, Bullough & Bullough). *Mother Camp* (B86, Newton) is an interesting study of female impersonators. A sympathetic photographic view of transvestites is shown in *Transformations: Crossdressers and Those Who Love Them* (B82, Allen).

Besides these books about the transgendered, libraries need books *for* the transgendered and their families, friends, and employers. A basic resource is the *1994 Who's Who & Resource Guide to the International Transgender Community* (B87, Roberts). *The Transsexual's Survival Guide* (B89, Stringer) provides sympathetic, basic information for the male-to-female transsexual; for family, friends, and employers; and to a lesser extent for the female-to-male transsexual. *Information for the Female to Male Cross Dresser and Transsexual* (B90, Sullivan) covers the female-to-male viewpoint, while *Dagger: On Butch Women* (B84, Burana et al.) is an uneven but unique anthology. Says contributor Carol Queen, "Butch is a giant *fuck YOU!* to compulsory femininity" (p. 15). *Stone Butch Blues*, by Leslie Feinberg (Firebrand, 1993, not annotated), is a fascinating fictional introduction to butch. *Coping with Crossdressing* (B88, Roberts) speaks to wives with crossdressing partners, and *The Employer's Guide to Gender Transition* (B85, Cole) addresses employers with a transsexual on staff.

A Christian "gay reform" book, not annotated, about a homosexual female impersonator who became a "Christian husband and father" is

Michelle Danielle Is Dead, by Marie S. Rice (available from Regeneration Books; see the Gay Reform/Critique section, above).

Few librarians will have heard of these publications. Yet locating them was not difficult. While the transgendered community is not as visible as the gay/lesbian community, it does have a core group of dedicated member-run organizations that produce publications and—importantly—bibliographies. We recommend for suggestions for further purchase:

International Foundation for Gender Education (IFGE)
P.O. Box 367
Wayland, MA 01778
Four-page catalog (various publishers); also publishes *TV/TS Tapestry Journal*, a major periodical for transvestites and transsexuals.

Creative Design Services (CDS)
P.O. Box 61263
King of Prussia, PA 19406
Publishes a small but valuable line of monographs and videos.

American Educational Gender Information Service (AEGIS)
P.O. Box 33724
Decatur, GA 30033
Twenty-one page Annotated Bibliography of Gender Dysphoria compiled by Dallas Denny. A much longer version, entitled *Gender Dysphoria: A Guide to Research*, was published by Garland Press, 1994. AEGIS also publishes *Chrysalis Quarterly*.

The Society for the Second Self (Tri-Ess)
Chevalier Publications
P.O. Box 194
Tulare, CA 93275
Twelve-page "Femme Store" catalog/annotated bibliography, with plenty of fiction about male-to-female crossdressing. The name of Chevalier Publications comes from the Chevalier d'Eon, a famous crossdresser in 18th century France. Tri-Ess also publishes *The Femme Mirror*.

Human Outreach and Achievement Institute
405 Western Avenue, Ste. 345
South Portland, ME 04106
Publishes *The Journal of Gender Studies*, a professional (but not technical) journal for gender and sex role issues, including transsexualism, transvestism, transgenderism, and androgyny. Includes book reviews.

There are many other organizations for the transgendered, some local, some national, some for spouses and families, all with brochures and newsletters. One IFGE brochure notes that "this community boasts over 200 local, regional, and national support organizations." See a current *TV/TS*

Tapestry Journal or the *1994 Who's Who & Resource Guide to the International Transgender Community* (B87, Roberts).

SIECUS (see Chapter 5) has a short bibliography on Gender Dysphoria that also lists periodicals and organizations.

Annotations

B82   Allen, Mariette Pathy. *Transformations: Crossdressers and Those Who Love Them.* New York: Dutton, 1989. 163p. photos. ISBN 0-525-24820-X. Photographs with interviews of American men who dress as women part-time (transvestites). The men represent a diversity of ages and races.

*B83   Bullough, Vern L., & Bonnie Bullough. *Cross Dressing, Sex, and Gender.* Philadelphia: University of Pennsylvania Press, 1993. 382p. chapter notes. index. ISBN 0-8122-1431-5. Comprehensive description and analysis of crossdressing, suitable for laypeople and researchers. Covers history and anthropology of male-to-female and female-to-male crossdressing by heterosexuals, homosexuals, and transsexuals; medical and psychological explanations; biological and social factors; and negotiating crossdressing within marriage. Includes guide to further reading and research.

B84   Burana, Lily, Roxxie, & Linnea Due. *Dagger: On Butch Women.* Pittsburgh: Cleis, 1994. 232p. photos. ISBN 0-939416-82-4. "Stories and art, essays and interviews by butches (and the women who love them)" largely from the West Coast. Themes include growing up butch, sexuality, S&M, female-to-male transsexualism, butch women in movies and comics, finding partners, and coping with "straight" society.

B85   Cole, Dana. *The Employer's Guide to Gender Transition: Information for Those Dealing with an Employee Involved in Gender Transition.* Wayland, MA: International Foundation for Gender Education (P.O. Box 367, Wayland, MA 01778), 1992. 37p. resource list (1p.). index. ISBN U/K. Supportive guidebook for employers dealing with an employee changing gender (transsexualism). Covers major questions about gender transition and how employer can smooth the process for the employee and other staff. Addresses restroom use, work relationships, sexual harassment, and social acceptance.

B86   Newton, Esther. *Mother Camp: Female Impersonators in America.* Chicago: University of Chicago Press, 1979. 136p. footnotes. ISBN 0-226-57760-0. Results of anthropological study of professional female impersonators in Chicago. Covers occupation, lifestyle, female impersonators within gay/lesbian community, types of performance, role models, and detailed descriptions of two shows.

*B87   Roberts, JoAnn, ed. *1994 Who's Who & Resource Guide to the International Transgender Community.* King of Prussia, PA: Creative Design Services (Box 1263, King of Prussia, PA 19406), 1994. 80p. index. ISBN 1-880715-14-7. Transgender resource directory. Lists noteworthy people (living and deceased), support groups worldwide and their magazines/newsletters, physicians, therapists, and businesses (mostly beauty, fashion, and publications).

B88   Roberts, JoAnn. *Coping with Crossdressing: Tools & Strategies for Partners* *in Committed Relationships.* 2nd ed. King of Prussia, PA: Creative Design Services (Box 1263, King of Prussia, PA 19406), 1992. 72p. refs. & resources (5p.). ISBN 1-880715-10-4. Guide for wives and partners of male heterosexual crossdressers (transvestites). Covers definitions, understanding transvestism, partners' issues, negotiating mutual decisions about crossdressing, and strengthening the relationship.

B89 Stringer, JoAnn Altman. *The Transsexual's Survival Guide I, To Transition & Beyond.* King of Prussia, PA: Creative Design Services (Box 1263, King of Prussia, PA 19406), 1990. 68p. index. ISBN 1-880715-04-X; *The Transsexual's Survival Guide II, To Transition and Beyond: For Family, Friends, & Employers.* 1992. ISBN 1-880715-09-0. Volume I: Description of transition from male to female physique and identity, with some discussion of female-to-male transsexuals. Covers therapy, hormones, electrolysis, sex reassignment surgery, finances, and legal issues. Volume II for family, friends, and employers of transsexuals, covers growing up transgendered, psychology and feelings, options for surgery or not, how to give support, and relationship-related issues.

B90 Sullivan, Lou. *Information for the Female to Male Cross Dresser and Transsexual.* 3rd ed. Seattle: Ingersoll Gender Center (1812 East Madison, Seattle, WA 98122-2843), 1990. 123p. photos. orgs. (2p.). refs. (3p.). readings (26p.). films (8p.). ISBN U/K. Introduction to female-to-male crossdressing and transsexualism. Covers what transsexualism is, how to pass as male, sex reassignment surgery, family/friends, sex life, and issues re children.

NOTES

1. Susan Hoffman, "Overview of the GLTF Book Awards Situation," *GLTF Newsletter* 5.3 (Fall 1993): 4–5.
2. See, e.g., Janet A.E. Creelman & Roma M. Harris, "Coming Out: The Informational Needs of Lesbians," *Collection Building* 10.3-4 (1990): 37–41; Cal Gough & Ellen Greenblatt, "Services to Gay and Lesbian Patrons: Examining the Myths," *Library Journal* (January 1992): 59–63; Carolyn Caywood, "Reaching Out to Gay Teens," *School Library Journal* (April 1993): 50.
3. Since about 1990, we have found: "Lesbian & Gay Literature for Public Libraries," *Wisconsin Women Library Workers Newsletter* (April–June 1990): 1; Elizabeth M. Wavle, "A Gay and Lesbian Core Collection," *Choice* (July/August 1991): 1743–1751; Yvonne Raaflaub, "Problems of Access to Lesbian Literature," *RQ* (Fall 1991): 19–23; Ray Olson, "By Gays and Lesbians, for Every Library," *Booklist* (June 15, 1992): 1814; Eric Bryant, "Making Things Perfectly Queer," *Library Journal* (April 15, 1993): 106–109.
4. *Coming Out to Parents* (B11, Borhek): 72.
5. We found no gay reform/critique books from a Jewish perspective. There is considerable difference of opinion—even a pitched battle—between the "ex-gay" movement and many gay writers/spokespeople as to whether a gay person *can* become "ex-gay." The first group maintains that change is possible for all or most committed gays/lesbians, and provides encouraging case studies. The second group counters that the only "ex-gays" are bisexuals who permit their heterosexual side free rein while suppressing their homosexual side—and cites *other* cases showing widespread lapses back into gayness from so-called ex-gays. A third type of gay-

critical work also exists, more common in the past; books whose heavily degreed authors deem homosexuality a medical or psychological problem and support their points with clinical case studies and/or scientific research rather than with religious doctrine. Classic Freudianism takes this view. We have not included any of these works: they tend to be highly technical and little suitable for public or school libraries.

6. Jean Hardisty, "Constructing Homophobia: Colorado's Right-Wing Attack on Homosexuals," *The Public Eye* (March 1993): 1–10, 15. (From Political Research Associates, 678 Massachusetts Avenue, Suite 702, Cambridge, MA 02139-3355.)

7. Charles E. Curran, foreword to *Building Bridges* (B49, Nugent & Gramick): vi–vii.

8. See *Gayellow Pages* (B7) for a more complete list.

9. *Sexual Behavior in the Human Male* (A48, Kinsey et al.): 639.

10. See *Sexual Behavior in the Human Male* (A48, Kinsey et al.) and *Sexual Behavior in the Human Female* (A33, Kinsey et al.).

11. See, e.g., *Homosexuality: A Research Guide*, by Wayne R. Dynes (Garland, 1987), and *Lesbianism: An Annotated Bibliography and Guide to the Literature 1976–1986*, by Dolores Maggione (Scarecrow, 1988), neither annotated. *A Research Guide to Human Sexuality* (D120, Lichtenberg) lists some of these, most published before 1990.

12. Dallas Denny, *An Annotated Bibliography of Gender Dysphoria* (Decatur, GA: American Educational Gender Information Services, 1992): 20.

13. The term *drag* is usually applied to men in female garb. But *Deneuve* magazine recently featured photos of two winners in San Francisco's first drag *king* contest, i.e., women giving appealing renditions of butchy male personae. See "What a Drag!" *Deneuve* (October 1994): 21.

11 Life Cycle Issues

BOOKS FOR YOUNG PEOPLE

Books about sex for young people can be divided approximately into:

- Books for children: birth through grade 4, or B–G4, including kindergarten (K)
- Books for pre-teens or pre-adolescents: grades 5–6, or G5–6
- Books for teens or adolescents: grades 7–12, or G7–12

We have added estimated age ranges for each work—and our estimates are just that. Books marked B or K may be read to children not yet able to read. Works also suitable for older readers are designated as college age (C) and/or adult (A). (In the rest of Part II, books without an age range should be assumed suitable for college age through adult.)

Young people's books about sex, particularly for younger children, do not have the variety of viewpoints or the depth of coverage found in books for adults. For example, far fewer are religious-based. We include some of what we did find.

What criteria apply to selecting children's books about sexuality? Accuracy and completeness are more important for young people than adults but must be age-appropriate. Medical text accuracy is hardly needed for eight-year-olds, but simplification can be carried too far and become evasion. Terminology must be accurate and avoid slang or euphemism. If the vulva/vagina is discussed, it must be called that. To be sure, some parents and perhaps some librarians may find the medical terms offensive, cold, or unemotional. But no better defense exists against censors of children's sexuality books than the book's precision in language, so absolutely needed if a child is ill, hurt, or has been abused.

Illustrations also require comment. Because of child pornography laws affecting photographs, children's books on sexuality characteristically use mostly drawings, which can vary considerably in clarity and accuracy. Gender stereotypes are particularly important—boys may be shown as active, but girls might be shown only as passive. Women giving birth might be shown with only male rather than female obstetricians. We found only one book for children mentioning a midwife and childbirth at home as well as in hospitals. The role of the father—in delivery and childcare or absent— is also a significant element, as well as how his role in procreation is described. Another issue is whether sex is described as "intended for" reproduction, pleasure, or both. Is "married family love" presented as the sole milieu for sexuality, or are such contexts completely omitted?

These represent only some of the presentation possibilities that librarians must think about when choosing sexuality books, and such presentation factors can vary extraordinarily widely. This variation is not wrongheaded but must be recognized as underlain by moral as well as educational principles that differ among authors. Of potential relevance is whether a book *explicitly* urges premarital abstinence. Depending on the targeted age range, the issue may not be mentioned, but some patrons may argue that it should be—and demand that books omitting it forthwith be removed as unsuitable for young people's collections. As we stress in Chapter 8, making these choices on an informed basis is needed preparation for dealing with sexuality books.[1]

We have excluded fiction, except for the youngest group. Much fine fiction about sexuality-related issues has been written for older children, and at the end of each age-group section we refer librarians to bibliographies containing fiction as well as nonfiction.

As we examined books about sexuality for young people, we wondered why authors and publishers do not offer integrated *series* of books to be used stepwise with children as they grow. We found only one such series: *Learning About Sex: A Series for the Christian Family* (C1, K–A), prepared under the auspices of the Lutheran Church-Missouri Synod. The integrated approach leads us to recommend this set highly, although each title is not necessarily better than competing books. Such series obviously simplify parental and librarian choice, and we wonder why there do not seem to be others. The lack is striking.

The only books in secular publishing that seem to have this broad range are Carole Marsh's "Smart Sex Stuff" books, suggested for "ages 7–17." Over 30 are available, about AIDS, STDs, puberty, abstinence education, and pregnancy, all organized in easy-to-read-and-understand "sound bites." Their style is direct and colloquial, with humor and puns. Teachers and parents can use them for discussions with younger children; older children can read them independently. We have annotated only one: *Sex Stuff for Kids 7–17* (C2, G2–12, Marsh), which seems the most general and comprehensive.

Annotations

*C1 *Learning About Sex: A Series for the Christian Family*. St. Louis, MO: Concordia House, 1988. 6v. illus. Includes: Greene, Carol. *Why Boys & Girls Are Different: For Ages 3 to 5 and Parents*. 30p. ISBN 0-570-08481-4; Hummel, Ruth. *Where Do Babies Come From? For Ages 6 to 8 and Parents*. 32p. ISBN 0-570-08482-2; Graver, Jane. *How You Are Changing: For Ages 8–11 and Parents*. 60p. glossary (3p.). ISBN 0-570-08483-0; Bimler, Richard. *Sex and the New You: For Ages 11 to 14 and Parents*. 64p. glossary (2p.). ISBN 0-570-08484-9; Ameiss, Bill, & Jane Graver. *Love, Sex & God: For Ages 14 to Young Adult and Parents*. 120p. glossary (9p.). ISBN 0-570-08485-7; Buth, Lenore. *How to Talk Confidently with Your Child About Sex: Parents' Guide*. 153p. glossary (12p.). index. ISBN 0-570-08486-5. Age-graded Christian series. Begins with anatomical differences between boys and girls and brief mention of pregnancy and birth; culminates with guidance for marital sexuality and educating children about sex. Each book stresses sex as a good gift, uniqueness of individuals, and fulfillment of God's plan for sexuality within marriage. Depicts both sexes in various sports and occupations. (K–A)

C2 Marsh, Carole S. *Sex Stuff for Kids 7–17: A Book of Practical Information & Ideas for Kids, Parents & Teachers*. 72p. Decatur, GA: Gallopade, 1993. glossary/index (3p.). ISBN 0-55609-201-6. Colloquial, humorous, and readable introduction to sex, including sexual behavior, puberty for boys and girls, dating, STDs and AIDS, sexual exploitation, pregnancy, contraception, and reasons for postponing sexual intercourse (abstinence education). No illustrations. (G2–12)

BOOKS FOR CHILDREN

Everyone knows the "where did I come from?" books for kids about birth. But, as librarians are finding out, other categories of books about sexuality are being written for the young; they include works about (adult) homosexuality, AIDS, and child sexual abuse.

For the youngest children, *Baby Brendon's Busy Day* (C15, B–G2, Jennings) addresses positive body image, genital cleanliness, and family affection, and uses correct anatomical terms. A "Baby Brenda" version is in preparation. *Bellybuttons Are Navels* (C22, B–G2, Schoen) deals with naming all the parts of the body, including sexual parts. We feel that this approach is very useful: even if each family has its own slang or pet names like "wee wee" or "Miss Polly," children must be taught correct terms for body parts quite young so that they can report pain, injury, or abuse accurately.[2]

Two other books for very young children focus on girl/boy differences: *What Is a Girl? What Is a Boy?* (C23, B–G2, Waxman) and *Girls Are Girls and Boys Are Boys, so What's the Difference?* (C13, K–G4, Gordon). Both illustrate physical differences and stress that males and females are otherwise mostly similar. *Girls Are Girls and Boys Are Boys* also very briefly describes sexual intercourse, pregnancy, and birth.

For slightly older children, a follow-up to these titles is *A Kid's First Book About Sex* (C3, G2–4, Blank), the only book for young children about sexuality per se. Barely mentioning reproduction—it is meant to complement the "where did I come from" books—it focuses upon self-image, body parts, masturbation, a little about adult sexuality, how to ask adults for more information, and other prepubescent concerns.

The "where did I come from" books are considerably more numerous: probably more than 100 are in print. They vary widely in:

- whether and how illustrations show sexual body parts, the growing fetus, and vaginal birth

- whether and how sexual intercourse and the father's role in reproduction and/or parenting are explained

- whether birth or childrearing is explained only in the context of heterosexual marriage

- whether and how religious concepts are invoked

- whether adoption, Caesarean birth, artificial insemination, and other complex concepts about birth and birth technologies are explained

Whenever possible, librarians should preview books to gauge appropriateness and to choose books with different approaches, content, and value systems.

For younger children, *How Babies and Families Are Made* (C21, K–G4, Schaffer) is quite comprehensive. Most amusing for both children and adults are *"Where Did I Come From?"* (C16, K–G4, Mayle) and *Mommy Laid an Egg!* (C7, K–G4, Cole). *Becoming* (C10, K–G4, Faison) and *How You Were Born* (C8, K–G4, Cole) focus more upon pregnancy and birth than upon sexuality. *Dr. Ruth Talks to Kids* (C24, G3–6, Westheimer) is the only book we found for young children that covers many sexual topics: how babies are made, masturbation, sexual intercourse, contraception, homosexuality, STDs, and sexual exploitation.

Two Christian books include *Susie's Babies* (C5, K–G4, Clarkson), which uses a pet hamster to discuss God's plan for human reproduction and families, and *The Wonderful Way That Babies Are Made* (C4, K–G6, Christenson), which is two books in one: large print rhymes for younger children and small print prose for older ones.

Regarding homosexuality, all librarians are familiar with the furor about *Daddy's Roommate* (C26, K–G4, Willhoite) and *Heather Has Two Mommies* (C18, K–G4, Newman).[3] These are part of a growing collection of books about children with gay relatives, many from the Alyson Wonderland imprint of Alyson Press. We especially like *Saturday Is Pattyday* (C19, K–G4, Newman), *Asha's Mums* (C9, K–G4, Elwin & Paulse), and *How Would You Feel If Your Dad Was Gay?* (C14, G2–6, Heron & Maran). April Martin cites statistics that suggest that between 6 and 14 million U.S. children are being reared in 3 to 8 million gay or lesbian families[4]—so a good many library patrons will be interested. Curiously, no children's books from a religious perspective discuss homosexuality of a relative or acquaintance. Theresa Bigalow, speaking at the 1994 ALA Annual Meeting, commented, "[As a librarian,] I'd welcome a [children's] book that discusses homosexuality from a religious perspective."[5]

Of the many books for children about AIDS, three mostly for younger ages are *What's a Virus, Anyway?* (C11, K–G2, Fassler & McQueen), *Come Sit By Me* (C17, K–G4, Merrifield), and *Be a Friend* (C25, K–G6, Wiener et al.). *Mommy, What's AIDS?* by Joan Dodge (Tyndale House, 1989, not annotated) is written from a religious perspective. The importance of the topic warrants such books, so librarians should consider it. Unfortunately, we were unable to examine it.

An increasing number of books for children concern child sexual abuse, with the message that "bad touching" is never OK and should be reported to a trusted adult. *My Body Is Private* (C12, G1–4, Girard) and *I Can't Talk About It* (C20, G1–4, Sanford) take the girls' viewpoint. The controversial *Alfie's Home* (C6, G1–4, Cohen) is especially important as well as unique since it discusses the sexual abuse of a boy by a pedophile. Young Alfie's confusion about his sexual orientation is made quite understandable in the writing. His working through towards a heterosexual self-image need not reflect upon boys who decide later that they are gay—or upon mature, *non*-pedophilic homosexuals.

The major problem with *Alfie* is not its presentation of pedophilia but that readers may equate pedophilia with homosexuality. Sexologically, these are very different phenomena. Three issues need to be distinguished. One is the (false) idea that all homosexuals are pedophiles, which never explicitly appears in the story, although readers predisposed to that view would thus interpret the plot. The second is whether homosexuality arises from incidents of child sexual abuse, and only by the reader's generalization does the story suggest the idea—again the text makes no such assertion. The third is whether or not homosexuality can be "cured"—replaced in adolescence or adulthood by heterosexuality. Issues two and three are among *the* most controversial in sexual science. *Alfie's* author believes that homosexuality can be "healed," and the book's afternotes describe his International Healing Foundation. This foundation is designed for "helping men and women transition from homosexuality/bisexuality to heterosexuality."

Alfie illustrates very strongly our previous comment that books about sexuality have moral and ideological undertexts.[6] Adults read into children's sexuality adult issues that children themselves only rarely interpret in like ways. Indeed, one can argue that "growing up sexually" means setting aside such childlike feelings as naïveté and innocence. Many—probably all—books written for children about sexuality are adult efforts to guide such growth in ways the writer deems safe and proper—and that other writers may deem unsafe and improper. These fights among the *soustextes* come with the territory. We might say that writing these books is like a costume party, where grim adults wear clown's masks and try to sugarcoat the message while arguing with each other. There is no such thing as a value-free book for kids, especially about sex.

Many children's books about sex are reviewed in the standard library media, and bibliographies of sexuality materials for this age group periodically appear in the library literature.[7] The best source is the SIECUS Growing Up bibliography. Also useful are the other SIECUS bibliographies: HIV/AIDS plus Child Sexual Abuse Education, Prevention, and Treatment, both with sections "for young people." The Sexuality Library catalog has a "family sexuality" section with a few children's books, and Planned Parenthood of Rochester and the Genesee Valley has a short annotated bibliography, Sexuality Education for Children (114 University Ave., Rochester, NY 14605). However, the Christian and conservative books about sex for this age group are difficult to identify. The Focus on the Family bibliographies mention only a few items, mainly the *Learning About Sex* (C1) series. We found it helpful to browse in a religious bookstore.

Books for children about homosexuality show up in many gay publications catalogs. Alyson Press has a particularly large line. The following sources mentioned in the Homosexuality—General Works section in Chapter 10 also list materials: Gay and Lesbian Parents Coalition International (long list), PFLAG, Rising Tide Press, and Glad Day Bookshop. A retrospective list current to 1992 is contained in *Out of the Closet and into the Classroom* (D114, Clyde & Lobban).

See also the Sex Education section, below.

Annotations

C3   Blank, Joani. *A Kid's First Book About Sex*. Illus. by Marcia Quackenbush. Burlingame, CA: Yes Press, 1983. 48p. ISBN 0-940208-07-5. Simple description of sexual feelings, genitalia, masturbation, and sexual intercourse. Covers sexual pleasure and response rather than reproduction; complements "where do babies come from" books. Discusses briefly relationships and partner choice: heterosexual, homosexual, bisexual. (nonfiction, G2–4)

C4   Christenson, Larry. *The Wonderful Way That Babies Are Made.* Illus. by Dwight Walles. Minneapolis: Bethany House, 1982. 41p. ISBN 0-87123-627-3. Christian perspective on sexual intercourse, reproduction, birth, adoption, and family life in context of God's creation. Large print verse covers simpler aspects for younger children; small print prose provides more details for older children. Multi-ethnic. (nonfiction, K–G6)

C5   Clarkson, Margaret. *Susie's Babies: A Clear and Simple Explanation of the Everyday Miracle of Birth.* 2nd ed. Illus. by Molly Alicki-Corriveau. Grand Rapids, MI: Eerdmans, 1992. 62p. ISBN 0-8028-4053-1. Introduction to reproduction, birth, and family life via story about a pet hamster's mating, pregnancy, delivery, and nurturing of offspring. No illustrations of humans. Christian perspective. (fiction, K–G4)

C6   Cohen, Richard A. *Alfie's Home.* Illus. by Elizabeth Sherman. Washington, DC: International Healing Foundation (P.O. Box 901, Bowie, MD 20718-0901), 1993. 30p. ISBN 0-9637058-0-6. Alfie's parents fight, so Alfie turns for companionship to a pedophile uncle, who sexually abuses him. Alfie thinks he might be gay, until counselors help entire family. Alfie decides he is heterosexual, marries, and has children. Stresses need for father's affection. (fiction, G1–4)

C7   Cole, Babette. *Mommy Laid an Egg! Or Where DO Babies Come From?* San Francisco: Chronicle Books, 1993. 30p. illus. ISBN 0-8118-0350-3. Lighthearted picture book about conception and birth. In humorous reversal of the usual approach, two children listen to parents' preposterous explanations of reproduction (babies growing from seeds, etc.) and give the adults correct information about conception, pregnancy, and birth, illustrated with kid-style, explicit drawings. (fiction, K–G4)

C8   Cole, Joanna. *How You Were Born.* New York: Mulberry Books, 1984. 48p. photos. illus. further reading (1p.). ISBN 0-688-05801-9. Picture book about conception, pregnancy, and birth, including Caesarean. No description of intercourse. Intrauterine photos show growth of fetus; drawings show birth process. Shows father involvement in birth and parenting. Parents' guide. Multi-ethnic. (nonfiction, K–G4)

C9   Elwin, Rosamund, & Michele Paulse. *Asha's Mums.* Illus. by Dawn Lee. Toronto: Women's Press, 1990. 23p. ISBN 0-88961-143-2. Asha's lesbian mothers sign a permission form for a class trip, but the teacher does not believe that Asha has "two mums." Asha and the class feel confused and uncertain until the "mums" speak with the teacher. (fiction, K–G4)

C10   Faison, Eleanor. *Becoming.* Illus. by Cecelia Erçin. Brattleboro, VT: EP Press, 1976. 29p. ISBN 0-9607432-0-0. Picture book about pregnancy and birth. Tissue overlays show fetal growth inside mother. No mention of intercourse. (nonfiction, K–G4)

C11   Fassler, David, & Kelly McQueen. *What's a Virus, Anyway? The Kid's Book About AIDS.* Burlington, VT: Waterfront Books, 1990. Illus. with children's drawings. resources (2p.). refs. (2p.). ISBN 0-914525-15-8. Describes viruses, HIV, and how people can and can't get AIDS. Shows that AIDS patients are otherwise like everyone else. Mentions sexual transmission, but no details. Invites further questions. (Also in Spanish.) (nonfiction, K–G2)

C12   Girard, Linda Walvoord. *My Body Is Private.* Illus. by Rodney Pate. Morton Grove, IL: Albert Whitman, 1984. 26p. ISBN 0-8075-5319-0. Julie soliloquizes about how her mother tells her about body privacy and avoiding touching that doesn't feel good. Mentions several sexually exploitative behaviors and describes how to say no and tell trusted adults. (fiction, G1–4)

*C13   Gordon, Sol. *Girls Are Girls and Boys Are Boys, so What's the Difference?* Rev. ed. Illus. by Vivien Cohen. Buffalo, NY: Prometheus, 1985. 44p. selected refs. (1p.). ISBN 0-87975-686-1. Presents and dispels stereotypes about boy and girl behavior, then shows physical differences between different age males and females. Explains sexual intercourse and birth, and mentions changes at puberty, including masturbation and nocturnal emissions. Special note for parents and educators. (nonfiction, K–G4)

C14   Heron, Ann, & Meredith Maran. *How Would You Feel If Your Dad Was Gay?* Illus. by Kris Kovick. Boston: Alyson, 1991. 32p. ISBN 1-55583-188-5. Jasmine tells her class that she and her brother have "three dads"—father and his gay lover, and mother's second husband. Conflict follows: some kids taunt them, while Noah with a lesbian mother supports them. Jasmine's dads talk with the principal, who arranges a presentation on different kinds of families. (fiction, G2–6)

*C15   Jennings, Donna A. *Baby Brendon's Busy Day: A Sexuality Primer.* Illus. by Bruce Hall. Tallahassee, FL: Goose Pond, 1994. 29p. ISBN 0-9638079-0-0. Picture book about a baby's day. Includes breast-feeding, playing and crawling, diaper changing and genital cleanliness, bath, bedtime story, and bed. Uses correct anatomical words, shows family affection, and encourages positive body image. (fiction, B–G2)

C16   Mayle, Peter. *"Where Did I Come From?" The Facts of Life Without Any Nonsense and with Illustrations.* Illus. by Arthur Robins. Secaucus, NJ: Lyle Stuart, 1973. ISBN 0-8184-0161-3. Lighthearted picture book describing male/female sex differences, sexual intercourse, conception, pregnancy, and birth. Shows stages of fetal development. Also lists common myths (e.g., the stork). (nonfiction, K–G4)

C17   Merrifield, Margaret. *Come Sit By Me.* Illus. by Heather Collins. Toronto: Women's Press, 1990. 29p. ISBN 0-88961-141-6. Nicholas has AIDS and some classmates won't play with him until his friend Karen's parents call a meeting to educate parents and teachers about AIDS. Shows casual social contact behaviors that do *not* transmit AIDS/HIV; appendix provides background information for adults. (fiction, K–G4)

C18   Newman, Lesléa. *Heather Has Two Mommies.* Illus. by Diana Souza. Boston: Alyson, 1989. 34p. ISBN 1-55583-180-X. Picture book about a girl born to a lesbian couple by artificial insemination. When Heather asks at her playgroup if everyone but her has a daddy, the other children describe their own diverse families. (fiction, K–G4)

C19   Newman, Lesléa. *Saturday Is Pattyday.* Illus. by Annette Hegel. Toronto: Women's Press, 1993. 21p. ISBN 0-88961-181-5. Frankie's lesbian mothers separate. Frankie remains with mom Allie but is reassured by mom Patty that she will always be Frankie's mom and they will always see each other on Saturday—"Pattyday." (fiction, K–G4)

C20   Sanford, Doris. *I Can't Talk About It*. Illus. by Graci Evans. 30p. Milwaukee, OR: Gold 'n' Honey Books/Multnomah, 1986. ISBN 0-88070-149-8. Sexually abused by her father, Annie confides in a dove, who assures her she's not to blame and advises her to resist father and tell mother. Annie does, and mother supports her. Stresses that father is disturbed, unhappy, and needs help. Includes guidelines for helping sexually abused children. (fiction, G1–4)

*C21   Schaffer, Patricia. *How Babies and Families Are Made (There IS More Than One Way!)*. Illus. by Suzanne Corbett. Berkeley, CA: Tabor Sarah Books, 1988. 52p. ISBN 0-935079-17-3. Introduction to types of human reproduction: insemination through sexual intercourse, artificial insemination, and in-vitro fertilization. Describes twins and multiple births, growth of fetus, miscarriage, birth (including Caesarean section), incubators for premature infants, disabilities, and different kinds of families. Multi-ethnic. (nonfiction, K–G4)

C22   Schoen, Mark. *Bellybuttons Are Navels*. Illus. by M.J. Quay. Fwd. by Mary Calderone. New York: Prometheus, 1990. 44p. ISBN 0-87975-585-7. A small sister and brother, bathing together, name 19 body parts from head to toe, including sexual body parts. Picture book to teach correct terms, model discussions of sexual anatomy, and integrate positive and gender-appropriate awareness of genitals into acceptance of whole body. (fiction, B–G2)

C23   Waxman, Stephanie. *What Is a Girl? What Is a Boy?* New ed. New York: Crowell, 1989. 34p. photos. ISBN 0-690-04709-6. Brief photo picture book shows biological/anatomical differences between males and females of different ages and behavioral similarities. (nonfiction, B–G2)

C24   Westheimer, Ruth. *Dr. Ruth Talks to Kids: Where You Came From, How Your Body Changes, and What Sex Is All About*. Illus. by Diane deGroat. New York: Macmillan, 1993. 96p. further reading (2p.). index. ISBN 0-02-792532-3. Briefly covers physical differences between boys and girls, changes during puberty, friends, feelings, crushes, masturbation, homosexuality, sexual intercourse, contraception, STDs, sexual abuse, and how babies are made (conception, pregnancy, and birth, including Caesarean). (nonfiction, G3–6)

C25   Wiener, Lori S., Aprille Best, & Philip A. Pizzo, comps. *Be a Friend: Children Who Live with HIV Speak*. Fwd. by Robert Coles. Morton Grove, IL: Albert Whitman, 1994. 40p. ISBN 0-8075-0590-0. Art and writings about HIV/AIDS from young people, ages 5–19. Some write of their own sickness; others write of siblings or parents. (nonfiction, K–G6)

C26   Willhoite, Michael. *Daddy's Roommate*. Boston: Alyson, 1990. 30p. illus. ISBN 1-55583-118-4. Simple, upbeat picture book about a boy with divorced parents, whose gay father lives with his lover, Frank. The boy, his father, and Frank are shown in familiar family activities during the boy's weekend visits. (fiction, K–G4)

BOOKS FOR PRE-ADOLESCENTS

Most sexuality books for pre-teens discuss the changes in body, mind, and emotions accompanying puberty, when human bodies become mature enough to reproduce. As a genre, pre-puberty books tend to go light on sex and birth control and heavier on body/emotion changes, menstruation, nocturnal emissions, masturbation, and health. Many are suitable for older adolescents and even adults who are reluctant readers or have learning disabilities.

The simplest, most concise books about puberty are *Changes in You . . . for Girls* (C46, G5–10, Siegal) and *Changes in You . . . for Boys* (C47, G5–10, Siegal). They can be given to even younger children and are especially suitable for reluctant readers and learning-disabled youth. *Growing & Changing* (C40, G4–6, McCoy & Wibbelsman) has more content about physical and medical matters. Most comprehensive are *The What's Happening to My Body? Book for Girls* (C36, G4–12, Madaras & Madaras) and *The What's Happening to My Body? Book for Boys* (C37, G4–12, Madaras & Saavedra), which cover all puberty and sexual topics for pre-teens and older. Two for girls are **Period* (C32, G4–10, Gardner-Loulan et al.) and *Now You've Got Your Period* (C38, G5–8, Mahoney).

Other valuable works include *Love and Sex in Plain Language* (C34, G4–12,C,A, Johnson) and *Be Smart About Sex* (C31, G5–12, Fiedler & Fiedler). The first can be read by pre-teens through adults and is more complete about sexuality, including function of genes and differences between human and animal sexuality. The second is written in question/answer format with quotes from young people. The "4th rule of safe sex" is given as: "Learn all you can about sexuality and Safe Sex right now. . . . The library is a fine place to start." It then gives Dewey numbers for sexual topics and provides other library tips. Librarians must live up to this endorsement!

We found few religious-oriented pre-puberty books. We suspect that many denominational sex educators have not aimed quite young enough, because once beyond the "where did I come from" genre, most Christian books about sex for youth are clearly labeled "for teens." *You Are Wonderfully Made!* (C35, G4–8, Johnson) is an exception, together with *Sex and the New You* (in the Concordia series *Learning About Sex*, C1). *You Are Wonderfully Made!* uses a story-plus-commentary format, designed for discussion with an adult. This work addresses sexual development and many "problem" topics like sexual exploitation, homosexuality, and abortion. We think that more sexuality materials for young people should use this story-plus-commentary format, for it draws in the reader as well as avoiding the nonstop preachiness of much nonfiction for young people.

As a genre, pre-puberty and puberty books have been around for a while;[8] more recent to appear is nonfiction for pre-teens and teens about sexual problems. Rosen's "Everything You Need to Know" (EYNTK) series and Facts On File's "Straight Talk" series are characteristically both high quality and well-packaged, with the Facts On File books particularly good. Lerner and Millbrook have some excellent offerings also.

We recommend three EYNTK titles about HIV/AIDS: *AIDS* (C50, G5–12, Taylor), *Being HIV-Positive* (C44, G5–12, Shire), and *When a Parent Has AIDS* (C30, G5–12, Draimin). From Greenhaven's "Opposing Viewpoints Juniors" series, *AIDS: Distinguishing Between Fact and Opinion* (C43, G5–8, Opheim) is valuable. *Straight Talk About Sexually Transmitted Diseases* (C28, G5–12, Brodman et al.) and *The Facts About Sexually Transmitted Diseases* (C39, G5–10, McCauslin) both provide broader coverage beyond HIV/AIDS.

A good selection is available for pre-adolescents on sexual exploitation. We especially recommend *Feeling Safe Feeling Strong* (C51, G5–8, Terkel & Rench) for its scope and its story-with-commentary format. Other good books on sexual exploitation from the EYNTK series include *Date Rape* (C45, G5–12, Shuker-Haines), *Incest* (C48, G5–12, Spies), *Sexual Abuse* (C49, G5–12, Stark & Holly), and *Straight Talk About Date Rape* (C42, G5–12,C,A, Mufson & Kranz).

We found far fewer books on other sexuality topics, including *Birth Control* (C41, G5–12, Mucciolo) from the EYNTK series, and *Drugs and Sex* (C27, G5–12, Boyd) from Rosen's Drug Abuse Prevention Library Series. Rosen has no book on abortion, but *The Abortion Debate* (C29, G5–8, Caruana) from Millbrook's Headliners series fills the gap nicely. We found only one book on homosexuality for pre-adolescents, the very good *Know About Gays and Lesbians* (C33, G5–12, Hyde & Forsyth), also from Millbrook.

The SIECUS Growing Up bibliography is the major ongoing bibliography including this age group; some materials are listed in the SIECUS HIV/AIDS bibliography. Periodic bibliographies appear in the library literature, and many mentioned in notes 7 and 12 have works for pre-adolescents. The periodical *Y-A Hotline* publishes lengthy annotated lists, such as issue 29/30: "Super Double Issue of Sex Ed Materials," issue 33: "Romance," issue 40: "Caution: Positive Thinking Alone Won't Prevent AIDS," and issue 49: "Dating." Planned Parenthood of Rochester and the Genesee Valley has a bibliography, Sexuality Education for Preteens (114 University Ave., Rochester, NY 14605). Another interesting annotated bibliography is Issues in Sexuality for Adolescents with Chronic Illnesses and Disabilities, from the National Center for Youth with Disabilities (University of Minnesota, Box 721, 420 Delaware Street SE, Minneapolis, MN 55455). Many titles appear in standard library review media.

See also the Sex Education section, below.

Annotations

C27   Boyd, George A. *Drugs and Sex*. New York: Rosen, 1994. 64p. photos. orgs. (2p.). glossary (2p.). further reading (1p.). index. ISBN 0-8239-1538-7. Discusses unwanted sex-related consequences of drugs and alcohol, such as pregnancy and STDs. Covers effects of drugs on mind and body; social pressure to use drugs; myths about drugs and sex; and positive alternatives. (G5–12)

*C28   Brodman, Michael, John Thacker, & Rachel Kranz. *Straight Talk About Sexually Transmitted Diseases*. New York: Facts On File, 1993. 138p. glossary (6p.). orgs. (3p.). further reading (1p.). index. ISBN 0-8160-2864-8. Information about eight major sexually transmitted diseases (including HIV/AIDS), prevention, and treatment. Describes STDs in the past and their spread today. Stresses both abstinence and safer sex with condoms/spermicides. (G5–12)

C29   Caruana, Claudia. *The Abortion Debate*. Brookfield, CT: Millbrook, 1992. 64p. photos. further reading (1p.). index. ISBN 1-56294-311-1. History of recent U.S. abortion law and pro-life and pro-choice responses, beginning with *Roe v. Wade* (1973). Brief chronology of abortion in America from 18th century through 1960s. (G5–8)

C30   Draimin, Barbara Hermie. *Everything You Need to Know When a Parent Has AIDS*. New York: Rosen, 1994. 64p. photos. glossary (2p). orgs. (2p). further reading (1p). index. ISBN 0-8239-1690-1. Information for a young person whose parent has AIDS. Covers facts about HIV and AIDS, preventing HIV, how AIDS affects families, telling others, illness and death, and after the parent dies. (G5–12)

C31   Fiedler, Jean, & Hal Fiedler. *Be Smart About Sex: Facts for Young People*. Illus. by Hal Fiedler. Hillside, NJ: Enslow, 1990. 128p. orgs. (2p.). glossary (6p.). helpful books (3p.). index. ISBN 0-89490-168-0. Question-answer guidebook about puberty, sexual decisions, responsible sexuality, STDs and AIDS, drugs, contraception, and safer sex. Supports abstinence and noncoital sex. Intention: to provide factual information for decision making. (G5–12)

*C32   Gardner-Loulan, JoAnn, Bonnie Lopez, & Marcia Quackenbush. *Period*. Illus. by Marcia Quackenbush. Rev. ed. 87p. Volcano, CA: Volcano, 1991. ISBN 0-912078-88-X. Introduction to puberty and menstruation. Describes body changes, physiology, menstrual process, managing menstrual flow, mood changes, and pelvic exams. Stresses self-acceptance and individual variability. No coverage of sex or reproduction. Includes removable parents' guide. Also in Spanish. (G4–10)

*C33   Hyde, Margaret O., & Elizabeth H. Forsyth. *Know About Gays and Lesbians*. Brookfield, CT: Millbrook, 1994. 96p. notes (5p.). recommended reading (2p.). orgs. (2p.). index. ISBN 1-56294-298-0. Basic information about homosexuality. Covers history and culture, gay rights movement, possible causes of sexual orientation, acceptance in religious groups and society, growing up gay, families, and homosexuality and AIDS. (G5–12)

C34   Johnson, Eric W. *Love and Sex in Plain Language*. 4th rev. ed. New York: Harper & Row, 1985. 148p. glossary (12p.). index. ISBN 0-06-015418-7. Clear description of male/female anatomy and development, sexual intercourse, fertilization, birth, differences re men vs. women and humans vs. animals, homosexuality, masturbation, sexual exploitation, contraception, STDs, and relationships. Discusses sexual values. (G4–12,C,A)

C35   Johnson, Lois Walfrid. *You Are Wonderfully Made!* Colorado Springs: NavPress, 1988. 185p. glossary (5p.). ISBN 0-8910-9235-8. Christian perspective on sexuality and growing up, in stories followed by questions for discussion. Covers anatomy, puberty, nocturnal emissions, menstruation, sexual intercourse, masturbation, birth, self-esteem, equal gender roles, dating, homosexuality, AIDS, abortion, sexual abuse, singlehood, and postponing sex until marriage. No illustrations. (G4–8)

C36   Madaras, Lynda, & Area Madaras. *The What's Happening to My Body? Book for Girls: A Growing Up Guide for Parents and Daughters.* New ed. Illus. by Claudia Ziroli & Jackie Aher. New York: Newmarket, 1988. 269p. further reading (4p.). index. ISBN 0-937858-98-6. Detailed guide for girls about body changes during puberty: size, shape, body hair, breasts and genitals, menstruation; shorter description of male puberty. Discusses briefly masturbation, sexual intercourse, birth control, AIDS and STDs, sexual abuse, and handling sexual feelings. (G4–12)

C37   Madaras, Lynda, & Dane Saavedra. *The What's Happening to My Body? Book for Boys: A Growing Up Guide for Parents and Sons.* New ed. Illus. by Jackie Aher. New York: Newmarket, 1988. 251p. further readings (4p.). index. ISBN 0-937858-99-4. Detailed guide for boys about body changes during puberty: size, shape, body hair, voice and skin, genitals (erections, nocturnal emissions, masturbation), with shorter description of female puberty. Discusses briefly sexual intercourse, birth control, AIDS and STDs, sexual abuse, and handling sexual feelings. (G4–12)

C38   Mahoney, Ellen Voelckers. *Now You've Got Your Period.* Rev. ed. New York: Rosen, 1993. 99p. illus. further reading (1p.). index. ISBN 0-8239-1662-6. Introduction to menstruation. Covers body changes during puberty, female reproductive organs, intercourse and reproduction, process of menstruation, managing menstrual flow and discomfort, and pelvic exams. (G5–8)

C39   McCauslin, Mark. *The Facts About Sexually Transmitted Diseases.* New York: Crestwood House, 1992. 48p. illus. glossary/index (3p.). ISBN 0-89686-720-X. Simple description of sexually transmitted diseases. Covers symptoms, treatment, getting help, prevention (abstinence and safer sex), telling partners, and case study vignettes. Lists STD hotlines. (G5–10)

C40   McCoy, Kathy, & Charles Wibbelsman. *Growing & Changing: A Handbook for Preteens.* Illus. by Bob Stover. New York: Putnam, 1986. 159p. index. ISBN 0-399-51280-2. Medically oriented puberty guide. Covers genital development, height, weight, hair distribution, nocturnal emissions, menstruation, body image, diet, exercise, changing emotions, and common medical problems. Includes how to talk with parents and medical professionals. No mention of sex or masturbation. (G4–6)

C41   Mucciolo, Gary. *Everything You Need to Know About Birth Control.* New York: Rosen, 1990. 64p. photos. glossary (2p.). orgs. (1p.). further reading (1p.). index. ISBN 0-8239-1014-8. Introduction to male/female sexual anatomy, sexual development, and different birth control methods: effectiveness, safety, benefits, and myths associated with each method. Also mentions IUDs, abortion, and STDs. (G5–12)

C42   Mufson, Susan, & Rachel Kranz. *Straight Talk About Date Rape*. New York: Facts On File, 1993. 123p. orgs. (4p.). further reading (1p.). index. ISBN 0-8160-2863-X. Discusses acquaintance and date rape, causes, circumstances where it occurs, how to avoid it, and how to get help. (G5–12,C)

C43   Opheim, Teresa. *AIDS: Distinguishing Between Fact and Opinion*. San Diego: Greenhaven, 1989. 31p. illus. glossary (1p.). ISBN 0-89908-633-0. Pro and con views on whether AIDS is spread by casual contact, whether the Food and Drug Administration should make AIDS drugs more available, and whether AIDS is a moral issue. Invites readers to analyze facts and opinions in all viewpoints. (G5–8)

C44   Shire, Amy. *Everything You Need to Know About Being HIV-Positive*. New York: Rosen, 1994. 64p. photos. glossary (2p.). orgs. (2p.). further reading (1p.). index. ISBN 0-8239-1689-8. Covers what HIV-positive means, emotional reactions, legal rights, medical and self-care of body/mind, preventing transmission, and decision making. (G5–12)

C45   Shuker-Haines, Frances. *Everything You Need to Know About Date Rape*. New York: Rosen, 1992. Rev. ed. 64p. photos. glossary (1p.). orgs. (1p.). further reading (1p.). index. ISBN 0-8239-1509-3. Explains date rape, how both sexes can avoid it, and how to get help. Mentions males as victims. (G5–12)

C46   Siegal, Peggy C. *Changes in You: A Beautifully Illustrated, Simply Worded Explanation of the Changes of Puberty for Girls*. Illus. by Vivien Cohen. Richmond, VA: Family Life Education Associates (P.O. Box 7466, Richmond, VA 23221), 1991. 47p. ISBN 0-9628687-0-1. Simple description of puberty: growth, hygiene, emotions, breasts, pubic hair, menstruation, masturbation, nutrition and exercise, seeing a doctor, and saying no to sexual exploitation. Stresses difference between public and private behavior and body parts. Multi-ethnic. Removable parents' guide. (G5–10)

C47   Siegal, Peggy C. *Changes in You: A Clearly Illustrated, Simply Worded Explanation of the Changes of Puberty for Boys*. Illus. by Vivien Cohen. Richmond, VA: Family Life Education Associates (P.O. Box 7466, Richmond, VA 23221), 1991. 41p. ISBN 0-9628687-1-X. Simple description of puberty: growth, voice changes, hair and shaving, hygiene, emotions, genital changes, erections, nocturnal emissions, masturbation, nutrition and exercise, seeing a doctor, and saying no to sexual exploitation. Stresses difference between public vs. private behavior and body parts. Multi-ethnic. Removable parents' guide. (G5–10)

C48   Spies, Karen Bornemann. *Everything You Need to Know About Incest*. New York: Rosen, 1992. 64p. photos. glossary (1p.). orgs. (1p.). further reading (1p.). index. ISBN 0-8239-1325-2. Describes exploitive sexual activity between adults and young people, abusers and victims, family setting, types of touching, and getting help. (G5–12)

C49   Stark, Evan, & Marsha Holly. *Everything You Need to Know About Sexual Abuse*. Rev. ed. New York: Rosen, 1993. 64p. photos. glossary (1p.). orgs. (1p.).

further reading (1p.). index. ISBN 0-8239-1611-1. Simple description of child sexual abuse, including incest and rape. Many case stories with girl and boy victims. Identifies forms of abuse and offers advice on how to get help and avoid being victimized. (G5–12)

C50   Taylor, Barbara. *Everything You Need to Know About AIDS*. New York: Rosen, 1992. Rev. ed. 64p. illus. glossary (2p). orgs. (2p). further reading (1p.). index. ISBN 0-8239-1401-1. Basic information about AIDS and the HIV virus. Covers discovery, causes, transmission, treatment, and how to protect oneself from infection. (G5–12)

*C51   Terkel, Susan N., & Janice E. Rench. *Feeling Safe Feeling Strong: How to Avoid Sexual Abuse and What to Do If It Happens to You*. Minneapolis: Lerner, 1984. 68p. ISBN 0-8225-0021-3. Six stories relate encounters of children with sexual abuse; each narrative is followed by factual information and advice. Covers kissing/touching others, child pornography, exhibitionism, incest, obscene phone calls, and rape. (G5–8)

BOOKS FOR ADOLESCENTS

Many books for adolescents address sexual development and puberty. These books are understandably more comprehensive than those for pre-teens in covering sexuality and sexual relationships, birth control, pregnancy, masturbation, same-sex attraction, and sexual exploitation. Most transcend high schoolers and are quite suitable for college age and even adults.

Changing Bodies, Changing Lives (C53, G7–12,C,A, Bell) is the most comprehensive, with many quotes from teens. *How Sex Works* (C61, G7–12,C, Fenwick & Walker) has especially outstanding illustrations and format. *Sex & Sense* (C73, G7–12,C, Kelly) and *A Young Man's Guide to Sex* (C65, G7–12,C,A, Gale) are also good. *Doctor, Am I a Virgin Again?* (C68, G7–12,C,A, Hatcher et al.) uses short anecdotes as basis for commentary and advice.

The best general Christian sex book for this age group is *Love, Sex & God* from the *Learning About Sex* (C1) series. It supports abstinence—which Christian sex education books often call *chastity*—and urges readers to postpone sexual involvement until marriage. Most such books do not say Everything-Goes-But-Coitus; they urge that teenagers stop with hand-holding and maybe some kissing.

Several others concentrate more upon abstinence education than on sex information.[9] Libraries need some of these, and a good one is *Love, Sex & the Whole Person* (C81, G7–12,C, Stafford), giving sympathetic guidance about dating, controlling sexuality, and other issues. See also *Why Wait?* (C102, G10–12,C,A, McDowell & Day). We found a good book for Jewish teenagers: *Love in Your Life* (C66, G7–12,C, Gittelsohn). A very useful survey of views on many sexual issues is *Sexual Values: Opposing Viewpoints* (D47, Orr—see Chapter 12).

Writing about HIV/AIDS has become a growth industry, as we note in Chapter 13. Writers tackling young people's sexuality education can be serious, sincere people who nonetheless may lack background in medicine—or in psychology, social work, education, or anything else that might provide professional credentials. But as parents with word processors, they feel that They Know The Answers and Are Going to Tell Everyone. And that won't wash with most AIDS books.

To be sure, the problem of amateur writing has doubtless been around ever since Thutmose the Scribe's mother invented hieroglyphics—or whoever she and he were—but nowhere is professionality more important than in writing for young people. Most of the time, nobody can tell if the writer has background in the subject matter. Timothy Murphy and Suzanne Poirier have edited a fascinating anthology on how AIDS is written. Heavy on discourse theory and Michel Foucault, it may not appeal to most library goers, but anyone reading extensively about AIDS or responsible for selecting AIDS-related works for the public should be aware of the issues it raises (*Writing AIDS: Gay Literature, Language, and Analysis*, Columbia University Press, 1993, not annotated). In addition, the librarian may want to read *Confronting AIDS Through Literature* (D19, Pastore) with its stress on the non-neutrality of writing. These plus our own experiences lead us to a somewhat jaundiced view of many HIV/AIDS books that sprout like mushrooms for adolescent consumption.

Particularly excellent is *AIDS: Trading Fears for Facts* (C69, G7–12,C,A, Hein et al.). Also very good are *100 Questions and Answers About AIDS* (C62, G7–12,C,A, Ford), *Risky Times* (C56, G7–12,C, Blake), which includes various religious views on condoms, and *Lynda Madaras Talks to Teens About AIDS* (C76, G7–12,C, Madaras). The first two contain extensive quotations from AIDS patients. *Teens with AIDS Speak Out* (C74, G7–12,C, Kittredge) is conveyed almost entirely in the voices of young people with AIDS. All mention alternative forms of "outercourse" and mutual masturbation as safer sex alternatives. Magic Johnson's *What You Can Do to Avoid AIDS* (C72, G7–12,C,A, Johnson) does not—its major drawback. We have included this book nonetheless, as Magic's fame draws readers that other books will not. AIDS in the family is discussed in Rosen's *Coping When a Parent Has AIDS* (C60, G7–12,C,A, Draimin). The only Christian book about AIDS we found for this age group is *Let's Talk About AIDS and Sex* (C64, G7–12, Gage), which has some information about AIDS and STDs, but mainly uses the disease as a platform to concentrate upon chastity education.

Many of the books listed in the HIV/AIDS section in Chapter 13 are valuable for adolescents, especially *AIDS* (E85, Flanders & Flanders), *AIDS Crisis in America* (E89, Hombs), *AIDS: Opposing Viewpoints* (E81, Biskup & Swisher), and *The AIDS Crisis: Current Controversies* (E82, Cozic & Swisher).

Books about homosexuality for teens are still evolving. A simple, positive overview, also suitable for younger readers, is *Understanding Sexual Identity* (C80, G5–12, Rench). *Becoming Visible* (C71, G9–12,C,A, Jennings) provides a historical overview of gays and lesbians for high school and college students. A particularly excellent work, **When Someone You Know Is Gay* (C58, G7–12,C,A, Cohen & Cohen), seems aimed at friends of gay people but like *Understanding Sexual Identity* is also very much for those with questions about themselves. Three very good books providing perspectives from gay and lesbian adolescents are *Two Teenagers in Twenty* (C70, G7–12,C,A, Heron), the classic *Young, Gay & Proud!* (C52, G7–12,C, Alyson), and the gutsy *Reflections of a Rock Lobster* (C63, G7–12,C,A, Fricke). *Coping When a Parent Is Gay* (C78, G7–12,C,A, Miller) discusses having a homosexual parent—for the older children of Daddy and that roommate Frank. We also suggest *The Gay, Lesbian, and Bisexual Students' Guide to Colleges, Universities, and Graduate Schools*, by Jan Mitchell Sherrill and Craig Hardesty (New York University Press, 1994), not annotated.

The Rosen "Coping" series has several books about sexual exploitation: *Sexual Abuse* (C59, G7–12,C,A, Cooney), *Sexual Harassment* (C55, G7–12,C,A, Black), and *Date Rape & Acquaintance Rape* (C79, G7–12,C,A, Parrot).[10] Particularly good is **Rape: What Would You Do If . . . ?* (C57, G7–12,C,A, Booher). We found one Christian book: *It Can Happen to You* (C77, G7–12,C, McDowell). Three other good special topic books for adolescents are *Coping with Birth Control* (C54, G7–12,C, Benson), *Abortion: Understanding the Controversy* (C67, G7–12, Guernsey), and *On the Streets: The Lives of Adolescent Prostitutes* (C75, G7–12, Landau).

Much new material in this area is reviewed in the library media.[11] See the bibliographies and selection tools listed in the Books for Pre-Adolescents section, above, plus SIECUS's bibliography Sexuality Education Resources for Religious Denominations. Planned Parenthood of Rochester and the Genesee Valley has an annotated bibliography, Sexuality Education for Teens (114 University Ave., Rochester, NY 14605). Conservative Christian materials can be difficult to identify; some materials are included in Josh McDowell's catalog (Josh McDowell Ministry, Box 1330, Wheaton, IL 60189) and from Mailbox Club Books (404 Eager Rd., Valdosta, GA 31602).

See also *Out of the Closet and into the Classroom* (D114, Clyde & Lobban) and articles in the library literature.[12]

Annotations

C52 Alyson, Sasha, ed. *Young, Gay & Proud!* 3rd ed. Boston: Alyson, 1991. 119p. recommended reading (7p.). ISBN 1-55583-001-3. "One of the earliest publications to provide an honest look at just what it was like to be a gay or lesbian teenager," updated. Covers stereotypes and myths, coming out, friends, finding community, sexuality, health, and gay people throughout history. (G7–12,C)

*C53   Bell, Ruth. *Changing Bodies, Changing Lives: A Book for Teens on Sex and Relationships*. Rev. ed. New York: Vintage/Random House, 1987. 254p. illus. chapter refs. index. ISBN 0-394-75541-3. Comprehensive guidance on puberty, sexuality (heterosexual/homosexual), relationships with friends and parents, sexual exploitation, emotions, birth control, pregnancy, and STDs. Many quotes from teens and parents reflecting different experiences and viewpoints. Strong emphasis on relationships, feelings, and emotional health. Purpose: to provide information so teens can take care of themselves. (G7–12,C,A)

C54   Benson, Michael D. *Coping with Birth Control*. New York: Rosen, 1992. Rev. ed. 204p. bibliog. (2p.). illus. index. ISBN 0-8239-1489-5. Introduction to anatomy and the menstrual cycle, pregnancy, various birth control methods including abstinence, abortion, STDs, sexual function and dysfunction, homosexuality, and rape. (G7–12,C)

C55   Black, Beryl. *Coping with Sexual Harassment*. New York: Rosen, 1990. Rev. ed. 153p. notes (1p.). bibliog. (1p). index. ISBN 0-8239-1174-8. Discusses many incidents of sexual harassment experienced by young people and ways of coping. Uses format of fictional advice column. (G7–12,C,A)

C56   Blake, Jeanne. *Risky Times: How to Be AIDS-Smart and Stay Healthy: A Guide for Teenagers*. New York: Workman, 1990. 158p. photos. hotlines list. (2p.) ISBN 0-89480-656-4. Easy-to-understand introduction to AIDS/HIV, stressing devastating experience of being HIV-positive. Covers nature of the disease, transmission, making decisions about behavior, drugs and AIDS, dying from AIDS, treatment, testing, discrimination against AIDS patients, and fighting AIDS. Many personal stories/interviews with young people who have AIDS or are AIDS activists. Covers briefly safe sex, condoms, and abstinence. Removable parents' guide. (G7–12,C)

*C57   Booher, Dianna Daniels. *Rape: What Would You Do If . . . ?* Rev. ed. Englewood Cliffs, NJ: Julian Messner, 1991. 133p. bibliog. (3p.). index. ISBN 0-671-74546-8. Comprehensive discussion of acquaintance and stranger rape. Covers personal safety and prevention, understanding the rapist, fighting back, getting help after an attack, special problems of incest, and anti-rape activism. (G7–12,C,A)

*C58   Cohen, Susan, & Daniel Cohen. *When Someone You Know Is Gay*. New York: Dell, 1989. 183p. orgs. (2p.). bibliog. (15p.). ISBN 0-440-21298-7. Introductory and sympathetic book about homosexuality. Describes growing up gay; answers common questions about homosexuality; also discusses history, possible causes, range of family attitudes, religion, and AIDS. (G7–12,C,A)

C59   Cooney, Judith. *Coping with Sexual Abuse*. New York: Rosen, 1991. Rev. ed. 137p. orgs. (18p.). index. ISBN 0-8239-1336-8. Discusses child sexual abuse, with short case histories. Covers myths, girls and boys as victims, family context, effects of abuse, treatment for victims, reporting abuse, the adolescent abuser, and preventing abuse. (G7–12,C,A)

C60   Draimin, Barbara Hermie. *Coping When a Parent Has AIDS*. New York: Rosen, 1993. 138p. glossary (2p.). orgs. (2p.). further reading (2p.). index. ISBN

0-8239-1664-2. Addresses concerns of young people when parent or siblings have HIV/AIDS, including virus transmission, seeking help, telling others, what to do in hospitals, saying good-bye, and future custodial arrangements. (G7–12,C,A)

*C61   Fenwick, Elizabeth, & Richard Walker. *How Sex Works: A Clear, Comprehensive Guide for Teenagers to Emotional, Physical, and Sexual Maturity*. London: Dorling Kindersley, 1994. illus. photos. 94p. orgs. (2p.). index. ISBN 1-56458-505-0. Guide to growing up and sexuality. Covers changes at puberty and male/female reproductive systems, menstruation, nocturnal emissions, masturbation, emotions, relationships, sexual preference, sexual intercourse, sexual difficulties, birth control, pregnancy, childbirth, unplanned pregnancy, sex and health, STDs, and sexual exploitation. Outstandingly clear illustrations. (G7–12,C)

*C62   Ford, Michael Thomas. *100 Questions and Answers About AIDS: A Guide for Young People*. New York: New Discovery/Maxwell Macmillan, 1992. 202p. illus. photos. orgs. (20p.). glossary. index. ISBN 0-02-735424-5. Comprehensive, clearly written question-answer guide about HIV/AIDS. Includes interviews with teenagers and young adults who have AIDS. Mentions abstinence; describes safer sex in detail and saying no to risky behavior. (G7–12,C,A)

C63   Fricke, Aaron. *Reflections of a Rock Lobster: A Story About Growing Up Gay*. Boston: Alyson, 1981. 116p. photos. ISBN 0-932870-09-0. Fricke stunned his high school by bringing a male date to his 1980 senior prom. He describes pain, harassment, and prejudice while growing up gay; the prom incident; and developing courage, self-esteem, and self-acceptance. (G7–12,C,A)

C64   Gage, Rodney. *Let's Talk About AIDS and Sex*. Nashville, TN: Broadman, 1992. 102p. notes (3p.). ISBN 0-8054-6073-X. Christian-based discussion of AIDS and its risks for sexually active adolescents. Stresses abstinence before marriage, resisting messages about sex from the media and popular culture, and finding direction in life from relationship with Jesus and acknowledgment of God's love. (G7–12)

C65   Gale, Jay. *A Young Man's Guide to Sex*. Los Angeles: The Body Press/Price Stern Sloan, 1988. 234p. illus. glossary (10p.). notes (1p.). index. ISBN 0-89586-691-9. Guide for young males about sexual facts, myths, pleasures, dangers, and responsibilities. Covers communication, understanding body and feelings, masturbation, sex and relationships, contraception, pregnancy, AIDS and STDs, female anatomy, and sexual problems. Mostly heterosexual. (G7–12,C,A)

*C66   Gittelsohn, Roland B. *Love in Your Life: A Jewish View of Teenage Sexuality*. New York: UAHC (Union of American Hebrew Congregations) Press, 1991. 82p. illus. chapter refs. ISBN 0-8074-0460-8. Introduction to sexual facts and conduct from Jewish viewpoint. Covers infatuation, dating, love, premarital sex, birth control, anatomy and physiology, STDs/AIDS, abortion, homosexuality, teen pregnancy, sexual abuse, masturbation, differences between men and women, and spiritual aspects. (G7–12,C)

C67   Guernsey, JoAnn Bren. *Abortion: Understanding the Controversy*. Minneapolis: Lerner, 1993. 112p. photos. notes (4p.). orgs. (1p.). glossary (2p.). bibliog. (2p.). index. ISBN 0-8225-2605-0. Summarizes pro-life and pro-choice views. Covers statistics, when life begins, roles of womanhood and motherhood, pro-life and pro-choice activists, *Roe v. Wade* and legal decisions, abortion methods, and alternatives to abortion. (G7–12)

C68 Hatcher, Robert A., Shannon M. Dammann, & Julie Convisser. *Doctor, Am I a Virgin Again? Cases and Counsel for a Healthy Sexuality*. Atlanta: Emory University School of Medicine, 1990. 232p. Illus. by Lynda Ellis. chapter bibliogs. index. ISBN U/K. Nearly 150 short case stories used as basis for commentary and counsel about sexuality. Covers youth sexuality, menstruation, pelvic exams, sexual etiquette and its abuses, contraception, STDs/AIDS, and decision making. (G7–12,C,A)

*C69 Hein, Karen, Theresa Foy DiGeronimo, & the editors of Consumer Reports Books. *AIDS: Trading Fears for Facts: A Guide for Young People*. 3rd ed. Yonkers, NY: Consumer Reports Books, 1993. 232p. orgs. (53p.). glossary (6p.). index. ISBN 0-89043-721-1. Clear, comprehensive presentation of facts about HIV/AIDS and its transmission through sex and drug use, testing, treatment, and AIDS in the future. Covers abstinence, safe sex (outercourse), and safer sex. (G7–12,C,A)

C70 Heron, Ann, ed. *Two Teenagers in Twenty: Writings by Gay & Lesbian Youth*. Boston: Alyson, 1994. 186p. ISBN 0-55583-229-6. Forty-three young men and women (ages 14–24) talk about growing up gay and coming out, most with painful experiences such as nonacceptance by relatives and friends, and difficulties finding someone understanding to talk to. (24 stories reprinted from *One Teenager in Ten*.) (G7–12,C,A)

C71 Jennings, Kevin, ed. *Becoming Visible: A Reader in Gay & Lesbian History for High School and College Students*. Boston: Alyson, 1994. 297p. notes (8p.). bibliog. (4p.). ISBN 1-55583-254-7. Selections about gay history from various periods, countries, and cultures, from ancient Greece to contemporary U.S., with commentary and questions/activities. Introduction about heterosexism and homophobia. (G9–12,C,A)

C72 Johnson, Earvin "Magic." *What You Can Do to Avoid AIDS*. New York: Times Books, 1992. 192p. illus. orgs. (26p.). index. ISBN 0-8129-2063-5. Colloquial, clearly written manual about AIDS/HIV and how to avoid exposure to the virus. Also covers avoidance and treatment of other sexually transmitted diseases. Advises abstinence, delay of intercourse, and safer sex. (G7–12,C,A)

C73 Kelly, Gary F. *Sex & Sense: A Contemporary Guide for Teenagers*. Hauppauge, NJ: Barron's, 1993. 262p. illus. glossary (8p.). orgs. (4p.). chapter refs. index. ISBN 0-8120-1446-4 (Rev. ed. of *Learning About Sex*.) Basic guide to sexuality, covering sexual values, anatomy/physiology, discovering sexual feelings and orientation, same-sex attractions, sharing sexual feelings and behavior, love and partnerships, communicating about sex, STDs, conception and contraception, and sexual exploitation. Question/answer section. (G7–12,C)

C74 Kittredge, Mary. *Teens with AIDS Speak Out*. Englewood Cliffs, NJ: Julian Messner/Simon & Schuster, 1991. 119p. glossary (4p.). orgs. (3p.). bibliog./refs. (7p.). index. ISBN 0-671-74543-3. Stories about young people who developed AIDS as teenagers. Facts about AIDS and its prevention included together with quotes describing how they got AIDS, what happened to them and their families, and living with AIDS. (G7–12,C)

C75   Landau, Elaine. *On the Streets: The Lives of Adolescent Prostitutes.* New York: Julian Messner/Simon & Schuster, 1987. 101p. bibliog. (1p.). index. ISBN 0-671-62135-1. Profiles of young male and female prostitutes, based on interviews. Covers how they became prostitutes, experiences and lives, exploitation and violence, and difficulties leaving prostitution. Provides historical background and discusses available social services. (G7–12)

C76   Madaras, Lynda. *Lynda Madaras Talks to Teens About AIDS: An Essential Guide for Parents, Teachers, and Young People.* Illus. by Jackie Aher. New York: Newmarket, 1988. 106p. further information (9p.). index. ISBN 1-55704-009-5. Basic facts about AIDS, detailed description of transmission methods, preventing transmission (abstinence, "outercourse," safer sex, and other prevention), and activism against AIDS. Includes preface for adults. (G7–12,C)

C77   McDowell, Josh. *It Can Happen to You: What You Need to Know About Preventing and Recovering from Date Rape.* Dallas: Word, 1991. 80p. notes (2p.). resources (3p.). ISBN 0-8499-3291-2. Christian perspective on date rape. Covers definitions of date rape, how to prevent it, and how to get help and recover. Addresses responsibilities of both males and females. (G7–12,C)

C78   Miller, Deborah A. *Coping When a Parent Is Gay.* New York: Rosen, 1993. 140p. orgs. (3p.). bibliog. (3p.). annotated reading list (6p.). index. ISBN 0-8239-1404-6. Traces changing makeup of families and describes experiences of parents and children when one parent is gay. Presents parents' and children's perspective in case studies illustrating different problems and circumstances. (G7–12,C,A)

C79   Parrot, Andrea. *Coping with Date Rape & Acquaintance Rape.* New York: Rosen, 1993. Rev. ed. 173p. glossary (2p.). bibliog. (3p.). index. ISBN 0-8239-1649-9. Comprehensive discussion of acquaintance and date rape. Covers what date rape is, how it happens, who's at fault, how to find help, victims' rights, preventing date rape, and males as victims. (G7–12,C,A)

C80   Rench, Janice E. *Understanding Sexual Identity: A Book for Gay and Lesbian Teens and Their Friends.* Minneapolis: Lerner, 1990. 56p. orgs. (2p.). further reading (3p.). index. ISBN 0-8225-0044-2. Simple, clearly written answers to basic questions about homosexuality, for gay/lesbian young people and others. Covers facts about homosexuality, friends, families, religion, coming out, and healthy sexuality. (G5–12)

C81   Stafford, Tim. *Love, Sex & the Whole Person (Everything You Want to Know).* Grand Rapids, MI: Campus Life/Zondervan, 1991. 262p. ISBN 0-310-71181-9. Christian question-answer advice book covering dating, breaking up, sexual choices, postponing sexual involvement, masturbation, homosexuality, marriage, pregnancy, sexual exploitation, and STDs. (G7–12,C)

SEXUALITY IN YOUTH AND AGE

Sex in youth and sex in aging tend to be widely misunderstood as nonexistent—so librarians need to consider these areas especially important for collection building. We include here books both for and about older people, as well as books about young people's sexuality. Books *for* young readers are covered in the previous sections; they are split out so that young people's librarians can access potential acquisitions directly.

Two truly excellent books about children are *Show Me Yours!* (C86, Goldman & Goldman) and *Sexual Development of Young Children* (C88, Lively & Lively). Both build an absolutely necessary groundwork for parents and educators, and stress that full and accurate sex information should be given to children at appropriate ages. Neither promotes particular sexual behavior or values. A related work is *The Intimate Circle* (C84, Ehrenberg & Ehrenberg), which discusses how parental communication about sexuality influences childhood and adult sexual attitudes, adjustment, and problems.

Regarding young adult sexuality, most books we annotated fell into either the Sex Education or Books for Adolescents sections. One fine general work included here is *Teenage Sexuality: Opposing Viewpoints* (C89, Swisher et al.). A readable case study approach is *The First Time* (C85, Fleming & Fleming), in which well-known people describe first sexual experiences.

As the "graying of America" proceeds onward with the aging of the baby boomers, myths of the sexless crone and codger are at last fading. In 1984, these myths were firmly challenged by the Consumer Reports study, *Love, Sex, and Aging* (C82, Brecher et al.).[13] The more recent *Love and Sex After 60* (C83, Butler & Lewis) is written for older readers and takes an educational and enhancement approach. *Sexual Health in Later Life* (C90, Walz & Blum) has a somewhat similar scope. Also highly educational is *My Parents Never Had Sex* (C87, Hammond), written largely for adults interested in understanding older relatives. All four books have some coverage of homosexual relationships.

Some materials about youth and aging sexuality are listed in these SIECUS bibliographies: Sexuality in Middle and Later Life, Talking with Your Child About Sexuality, and Current Books on Sexuality. See also some of the bibliographies listed in *Free or Inexpensive Sources for Sex, Health & Family Education* (D113, Charlton) and works listed in *Comprehensive Bibliography for Sex, Health & Family Education* (D112, Charlton).

Other organizations with information on teen sexuality:

The Alan Guttmacher Institute
120 Wall Street
New York, NY 10005
  Reports, statistics, and fact sheets on abortion, teen pregnancy, and contraception.

Planned Parenthood Federation of America
810 Seventh Avenue
New York, NY 10019

Publishes Adolescent Sexuality, a yearly annotated bibliography of books and articles.

See also the other sections in this chapter, plus the Disabilities and Dysfunctions section in Chapter 13 and the Homosexuality–Youth and Age sections in Chapter 10.

Annotations

*C82   Brecher, Edward M., & the Editors of Consumer Reports Books. *Love, Sex, and Aging: A Consumers Union Report*. Mount Vernon, NY: Consumers Union, 1984. 441p. index. ISBN 0-89043-027-6. Results of questionnaire survey of 4,246 people aged 50–93, about health, friendship, love, and sexuality; and opinions about masturbation, homosexuality, pornography, and sexuality and aging. Vast majority of respondents were sexually active and presented a wide variety of behaviors and attitudes. Pre-AIDS.

*C83   Butler, Robert N., & Myrna I. Lewis. *Love and Sex After 60*. Rev. ed. New York: Ballantine, 1993. 321p. glossary (9p.). bibliog. (6p.). index. ISBN 0-345-38034-7. Reassuring guide to preserving, enhancing, and rekindling sexual experience after age 60. Mostly heterosexual; some discussion of gay relationships. Covers medicine (including STDs and AIDS), fitness, physical changes, emotional factors, relationships, and finding help. Many referrals to books and organizations.

C84   Ehrenberg, Miriam, & Otto Ehrenberg. *The Intimate Circle: The Sexual Dynamics of Family Life*. New York: Fireside/Simon & Schuster, 1988. 335p. index. ISBN 0-671-62854-2. Describes sexual feelings within families and parental styles for communicating about sex: sex repressive, sex avoidant, sex obsessive, and sex expressive. To help parents understand sexual feelings and be better sex educators for children.

C85   Fleming, Karl, & Anne Taylor Fleming. *The First Time*. New York: Simon and Schuster, 1975. 319p. ISBN 0-671-22070-5. Accounts of initial sexual experiences from 28 well-known people, e.g., Maya Angelou, Nora Ephron, Liberace, Joan Rivers, Benjamin Spock, Mae West. Virtually an endorsement for sex education, these "first times" are revealed as being as naive, embarrassing, and sometimes unpleasant as those of ordinary people.

*C86   Goldman, Ronald, & Juliette Goldman. *Show Me Yours! Understanding Children's Sexuality*. New York: Penguin, 1988. 268p. notes (9p.). index. ISBN 0-14-010714-2. Results of interview study about sexual knowledge with 1,000+ children, ages 5–15, from U.S., Canada, Australia, England, and Sweden; and questionnaire study about children's sexual behavior. Addresses what children want and need to know about sex, and why parents and schools should teach them.

*C87   Hammond, Doris B. *My Parents Never Had Sex: Myths and Facts of Sexual Aging*. Buffalo, NY: Prometheus, 1987. 180p. resources (6p.). ISBN 0-87975-413-3. Discussion of sexual myths, biology, and behavior associated with aging. Covers cultural/religious/society influences on sexuality, sexual development, menopause and midlife, sexuality in long-term marriages, singlehood, homosexuality, family attitudes, health, sexuality and institutionalization, and sexual dysfunctions.

C88 Lively, Virginia, & Edwin Lively. *Sexual Development of Young Children.* Albany, NY: Delmar, 1991. 198p. illus. glossary (4p.). chapter refs. resources & bibliog. (10p.). index. ISBN 0-8273-4198-9. Comprehensive discussion about sexual development, attitudes, and behavior of young children, for teachers, caregivers, and parents. Covers normal development and learning, gender identity, children's sexual behaviors, adult behaviors affecting children, sexual abuse, and changing sexual environments. Includes many vignettes and children's drawings.

*C89 Swisher, Karin L., Terry O'Neil, & Bruno Leone, eds. *Teenage Sexuality: Opposing Viewpoints.* San Diego, CA: Greenhaven, 1994. 236p. chapter bibliogs. resources (6p.). ISBN 1-56510-102-2. Essays providing varying and opposing viewpoints on teen pregnancy, sex education, adolescent homosexuality, and teenagers' attitudes towards sex. Chapter prefaces introduce each topic.

C90 Walz, Thomas H., & Nancy S. Blum. *Sexual Health in Later Life.* Lexington, MA: Lexington/Heath, 1987. 124p. further reading (3p.). bibliog. (3p.). index. ISBN 0-669-14599-8. Explains benefits of sexual expression and maintaining sexual health beyond age 60. Covers sexuality vis-à-vis the aging process, chronic illness, medical treatment, attitudes, and mental states; plus sexual expression in community housing and nursing homes, and sexual relationships and same-sex friendships.

SEX EDUCATION

Since the topic of this book is sex education, we have tried to provide especially good coverage in this section. We first include books for parents and caretakers about how to talk to young people about sex—how to apply sex education. Another category contains books about sex education itself, including works about curricula—what sex education is or should be. We have not included curricula themselves; many are referenced in the books annotated below and also listed in the SIECUS bibliography Comprehensive Sexuality Education. Finally, we briefly address sex education for librarians.

How to educate about sex and *how much* sex education to provide are major controversies, and we stress the importance of including works taking various approaches. These range from the permissive/liberal (some say "value-free") approach to the conservative, abstinence-based (some say "fear-based") approach. However, nearly all views—permissive, conservative, or middle-ground—*do* agree on three points.

First, sex education should begin quite young, by teaching toddlers correct names and functions for body parts and basics of pregnancy and birth. Second, information and impressions about sexuality delivered via the media are often incomplete, misleading, biased, inaccurate, and pernicious. Third, parents should be the primary sex educators of their children at all ages and have the responsibility of teaching sexual values.

Indeed, it is surprising how much "liberal" and "conservative" writers *do* agree. For example, many liberals agree with conservatives that teens should postpone sexual intercourse. On the other hand, many conservatives agree with liberals that genital self-exploration in very young children, unless obsessive, is normal and should be largely ignored. Major disagreements hinge upon:

*   whether teens *can* practice "safe sex" even when they know what it is
*   whether sexual activity outside monogamous heterosexual marriage (including masturbation) is acceptable at *any* age
*   whether homosexuality should be accepted or "reformed"
*   whether schools should provide sex education at all
*   whether abortion is acceptable
*   whether or not the United States is in a moral crisis over sexual issues.

Liberal or conservative, books about how-to-do-sex-ed-at-home can talk to parents in variously relaxed, chummy styles or in tones of urgent exhortation. Again, however, most books we have seen are surprisingly alike in what they recommend either chummily or urgently:

*   Begin when children are very young.
*   Use events such as pregnant neighbors as lead-ins to conversation.
*   Answer questions promptly and honestly (although brief postponement may sometimes be practical).
*   Do not give more information than the child seems to want.
*   Do not hesitate to say "I don't know—but we can look it up."
*   *And absolutely* incorporate parental values into the discussion.

Of course, within these agreements there is room for great diversity. So we strongly urge librarians to preview *all* sex education books to determine which ones meet the needs of the collection and the community.

We suggest a range of works for parents, covering how to educate children about sexuality, from birth through adolescence. Most permissive is *Talking with Your Child About Sex* (C92, Calderone & Ramey). More middle-of-the-road and also secular are *Raising a Child Conservatively in a Sexually Permissive World* (C96, Gordon & Gordon) and *Sex Is More Than a Plumbing Lesson* (C109, Stark); a Christian middle-ground book is *Sex Is Not a Four-Letter Word!* (C104, Miller).

We include several well-written conservative Christian books. *How & When to Tell Your Kids About Sex* (C98, Jones & Jones) is particularly comprehensive. *How to Teach Children the Wonder of Sex* (C112, Willke & Willke) discusses setting limits on dating and teaching general self-control. The most exhortative, *Against the Tide* (C99, LaHaye & LaHaye), also devotes considerable space to urging parents to control adolescent dating and to stress abstinence. All describe joys of sex as God-given within marriage and the need for parents to love their children, to spend time with them and share their interests, and to set children the example of their *own* lives as a model for a satisfying, romantic, sexually fulfilling Christian marriage. A Roman Catholic work, *Parents Talk Love* (C110, Sullivan & Kawiak), includes a particularly valuable section about using television to spark family discussions. All four books include solid information about children's sexual development in addition to communication guidelines.[14]

Three additional books address the special circumstances of educating younger children. *Straight Talk: Sexuality Education for Parents and Kids 4–7* (C108, Ratner & Chamlin) is moderately liberal. *When Sex Is the Subject* (C113, Wilson) models techniques and provides suggestions, but counsels parents to adapt responses to their own values. *Does AIDS Hurt? Educating Young Children About AIDS* (C107, Quackenbush & Villarreal) covers this special topic for both parents and teachers, and also counsels parents how to convey their own values.

Conservatives in particular consider teens a high risk group for dangerous and undesirable sexual activity. Hence, many books written from a conservative Christian perspective urge "abstinence education." *Why Wait? What You Need to Know About the Teen Sexuality Crisis* (C102, G10–12,C,A, McDowell & Day) is a particularly lengthy treatment, incorporating many comments from young people. The briefer but excellent *How to Help Your Child Say "No" to Sexual Pressure* (C100, McDowell) focuses on improving the parents' marriage and parent-child relationships. McDowell's general approach would be very valuable for parents who are not so conservative to adapt. A different strategy is proposed in *Raising Them Chaste* (C94, Durfield & Durfield), which revives and enhances the traditional "talk with Mom" (or Dad) technique. For a secular, more liberal approach, *A Parent's Guide to Teenage Sexuality* (C95, Gale) is a good comprehensive choice.

A valuable finale to these selections is the excellent *No Is Not Enough* (C91, Adams et al.), which helps parents educate adolescents about date rape and sexual harassment. These topics are also covered to some extent in many of the general sex education works mentioned above.

When providing reference help in "how-to-do-sex-ed," librarians should refer parents to books offering different viewpoints—not just so patrons can choose the ones closest to their own viewpoints, but also because other books will raise other questions to which they can respond in their own fashion.

Regarding sexuality education as a social, political, and policy phenomenon in itself, two comprehensive overviews are *The Sexuality Education Challenge* (C93, Drolet & Clark) and *The AIDS Challenge* (C106, Quackenbush et al.). The conservative, pro-abstinence view is covered in *The Myths of Sex Education* (C101, McDowell), which has little mention of religion.

Guidelines for Comprehensive Sexuality Education, Kindergarten–12th Grade (C97), published by SIECUS, sets out topics and criteria for sex education programs, while *Sexuality Education Curricula: The Consumer's Guide* (C105, Ogletree et al.) evaluates sex education curricula. Opposing these two is the complementary title *Foundations for Family Life Education* (C111, Whitehead & McGraw), which sets more conservative criteria favoring "abstinence-based, family centered, directed" sex education, and describes acceptable curricula. There are *no* overlaps among the curricula described in the second and third books.

Two additional works are highly recommended. *The Other Curriculum: European Strategies for School Sex Education* (C103, Meredith) provides a perspective beyond U.S. experience. An extremely important work for the United States is *With the Best of Intentions* (E30, Berrick & Gilbert), which we annotate in Chapter 13. It describes in scholarly and statistical fashion the California experience with a sexual abuse school education program that was bureaucratically scuttled during a billion dollar budget crisis after increasing evidence that the program had failed educationally. The moral is that "the best of intentions" do not make a program successful. It is wisdom from which many of us should learn.

Finally, librarians need *themselves* to become educated about sex education. We recommend becoming familiar with the following key works.

The basics are covered in *The Family Book About Sexuality* (A4, Calderone & Johnson), with a permissive/liberal perspective; *The Kinsey Institute New Report on Sex* (A14, Reinisch & Beasley), with a scientific/medical slant; and *Show Me Yours!* (C86, Goldman & Goldman)—an indispensable social-scientific guide to what young people need to know. Librarians should also skim *Taking Sides: Clashing Views on Controversial Issues in Human Sexuality* (A6, Francoeur) and *Human Sexuality 94/95* (A13, Pocs) for an update on sexual issues.

Given media simplifications, the wide variety of Christian views on sex is important to understand. *Sex Facts for the Family* (A12, Penner & Penner) provides a conservative Christian perspective stressing joyous eros, whereas *The Act of Marriage* (A61, LaHaye & LaHaye) is a widely read, more restrained view. A liberal Protestant analysis of New Testament sexual teaching is *Dirt Greed and Sex* (D127, Countryman). The anthology *Dialogue About Catholic Sexual Teaching* (D128, Curran & McCormick) is edited by world-recognized Catholic moral theologians and is complemented by *Sex: The Catholic Experience* (D135, Greeley), a sociological, data-based study of U.S. Catholics, including liberal views.

Librarians should also keep up to date on sexuality vis-à-vis libraries. Chapter 3 provides basic background, to be supplemented by articles in the library literature about sexuality, homosexuality, HIV/AIDS, and censorship. Moreover, librarians must become experts about who and what organizations are doing sex education in the community, have sexuality collections, or have sexuality information to distribute.

Sex education in the library must begin with the librarians!

Some sex education books are reviewed in the library media and some in *SIECUS Report*. SIECUS has three relevant ongoing bibliographies: Comprehensive Sexuality Education (curricula and textbooks), Talking with Your Children About Sexuality and Other Important Issues (books for parents), and Sexuality Education Resources for Religious Denominations (curricula and books). Planned Parenthood of Rochester and the Genesee Valley also has a bibliography, Parent-Child Communication About Sexuality (114 University Ave., Rochester, NY 14605).

Conservative sex education books are not easy to identify. Some materials in the SIECUS Religious Denominations bibliography take a conservative view. Another source is the Focus on the Family's short Sex Education bibliography, with a few curricula and books. Some "chastity education" books may be found in the Couple to Couple League catalog (P.O. Box 111184, Cincinnati, OH 45211-9985), from a conservative Christian group promoting traditional sexual values and natural family planning. Josh McDowell has his own catalog, with many books for and about adolescents (Josh McDowell Ministry, Box 1330, Wheaton, IL 60189).

See also *An Easy Guide for Caring Parents* (E8, McKee & Blacklidge) and the other sections in this chapter.

Annotations

*C91   Adams, Caren, Jennifer Fay, & Jan Loreen-Martin. *No Is Not Enough: Helping Teenagers Avoid Sexual Assault*. San Luis Obispo, CA: Impact, 1984. 177p. resources (1p.). ISBN 0-915166-35-6. Guidebook for helping adolescents avoid date rape and sexual harassment. Covers myths vs. realities, talking to teens, prevention, media messages, sex role stereotypes, mistaken interpersonal communications, and recovery after assault.

C92   Calderone, Mary S., & James W. Ramey. *Talking with Your Child About Sex: Questions and Answers for Children from Birth to Puberty*. New York: Random House, 1982. 133p. reading list (3p.). bibliog. (5p.). index. ISBN 0-394-52124-2. Provides sample age-graded questions/answers between child and adult to model good communication about sexuality. Includes guidelines for different ages. Permissive approach. Considers sexuality as a primary and enjoyable lifelong function, to be channeled appropriately rather than suppressed. Pre-AIDS.

C93   Drolet, Judy C., & Kay Clark, eds. *The Sexuality Education Challenge: Promoting Healthy Sexuality in Young People*. Santa Cruz, CA: ETR Associates, 1994. 681p. chapter refs. index. ISBN 1-56071-130-2. Comprehensive sourcebook for child and adolescent sexuality education. Covers history, background, and views about sexuality education; approaches for various age/grade levels; educator training; cultural and diversity issues; types of community programs; plus evaluation and research.

C94 Durfield, Richard C., & Renée Durfield. *Raising Them Chaste: A Practical Strategy for Helping Your Teen Wait Till Marriage.* Minneapolis: Bethany House, 1991. 176p. recommended resources. (1p.). ISBN 1-55661-171-4. Christian-based program for parents about counseling teens to resist sexual pressure until marriage. Based upon "key talk" between parent and child at puberty or before, supplemented by a ring and formal commitment to chastity. Also stresses enhancing support and communication with the child.

C95 Gale, Jay. *A Parent's Guide to Teenage Sexuality.* New York: Holt, 1989. 242p. illus. glossary (15p.). notes (6p.). bibliog. (7p.). index. ISBN 0-8050-1648-1. Manual for parents and caretakers about talking to teenagers about sex. Stresses separating fact from opinion and imparting both via discussion and books. Covers puberty, sexual intimacy, contraception and pregnancy, HIV/AIDS and STDs, homosexuality, and sexual exploitation; plus tips for single parents, helping handicapped teenagers, and finding help.

C96 Gordon, Sol, & Judith Gordon. *Raising a Child Conservatively in a Sexually Permissive World.* Rev. ed. New York: Simon & Schuster, 1989. 241p. recommended reading (8p.). orgs. (2p.). index. ISBN 0-671-68182-6. Guidelines for raising children with knowledge, self-esteem, and acceptance of own and others' sexuality; plus understanding consequences and responsibilities of sexual behavior, and desirability of restricting intercourse to marriage and committed relationships. Stresses being "askable," and supports value-based school sex education.

C97 *Guidelines for Comprehensive Sexuality Education, Kindergarten–12th Grade.* National Guidelines Task Force. New York: Sex Information and Education Council of the U.S., 1992. 52p. ISBN U/K. Guidelines for comprehensive, school-based sexuality education programs. Covers goals and values, structure and use, and key concept areas and topics. For each topic, provides developmental messages appropriate to different age levels, kindergarten through high school. Key concepts: human development, relationships, personal skills, sexual behavior, sexual health, and society and culture.

C98 Jones, Stanton L., & Brenna B. Jones. *How & When to Tell Your Kids About Sex: A Lifelong Approach to Shaping Your Child's Sexual Character.* Colorado Springs: NavPress, 1993. 272p. notes (11p.). ISBN 0-89109-751-1. Christian parents' guide for educating children about sexuality. Stresses abstinence until marriage. Notes that children are sexual starting in the womb, and urges parents to begin in infancy with clear, explicit, valuebased information. Supports responsibility and assertiveness in both boys and girls.

C99 LaHaye, Tim, & Beverly LaHaye. *Against the Tide: How to Raise Sexually Pure Kids in an "Anything Goes" World.* Colorado Springs: Multnomah, 1993. 258p. glossary (22p.). chapter notes. ISBN 0-88070-578-7. Christian guidelines for raising children to be knowledgeable about sex while postponing sexual conduct until marriage (abstinence education). Covers toddlers through adolescents. Extensive discussion of setting limits for dating. Also covers sexual abuse, "myth of safe sex," and unwed pregnancy.

*C100   McDowell, Josh. *How to Help Your Child Say "No" to Sexual Pressure.* Dallas, TX: Word, 1987. 160p. resources (2p.). ISBN 0-8499-3093-6. Christian guidebook for teaching children to resist premarital sex. Covers cultural sources of sexual pressure and promotes value-based sex education and abstinence until marriage. Stresses forming supportive and enjoyable relationships with one's children to enhance self-esteem, confidence, and responsibility. Encourages parents to model positive marital sexual affection.

C101   McDowell, Josh. *The Myths of Sex Education: Josh McDowell's Open Letter to His School Board.* Nashville, TN: Thomas Nelson, 1990. 302p. notes (18p.). ISBN 0-8407-4389-0. Comprehensive manual for parents and school boards for supporting choice of abstinence-based sex education in schools. Covers false assumptions about teen sexuality and sex education, strategies for resolving teen sexuality crisis, and resources for evaluating abstinence education.

C102   McDowell, Josh, & Dick Day. *Why Wait? What You Need to Know About the Teen Sexuality Crisis.* San Bernardino, CA: Here's Life, 1987. 444p. bibliog. (14p.). ISBN 0-89840-174-7. Christian guidebook to help parents and counselors promote premarital sexual abstinence. Incorporates comments and essays from young people. Covers reasons youth have premarital sex (five chapters), reasons to wait (four chapters), and coping with sexual pressure (five chapters). Also for teens. (G10–12,C,A)

C103   Meredith, Philip, ed. *The Other Curriculum: European Strategies for School Sex Education.* London: International Planned Parenthood Federation (Regents College, Inner Circle, Regents Park, London, NW1 4NS, England), 1989. 384p. chapter refs. ISBN 0-90483-13-7. Addresses sex education in Europe and specific programs in eight countries: Belgium, Denmark, Great Britain, Federal Republic of Germany, German Democratic Republic, Poland, Sweden, and Turkey.

C104   Miller, Patricia Martens. *Sex Is Not a Four-Letter Word.* New York: Crossroad, 1994. 206p. notes (3p.). bibliog. (8p.). ISBN 0-8245-1437-8. Guidelines to parents for talking to their children about sex. Christian perspective incorporating tolerance for different beliefs and stressing unconditional love. Covers fostering children's self-esteem, stages of psychosexual development, inviting morality, loving a gay/lesbian child, sexual abuse, date rape, STDs and HIV/AIDS, and myths vs. facts.

C105   Ogletree, Roberta J., Joyce V. Fetro, Judy C. Drolet, & Barbara A. Rienzo. *Sexuality Education Curricula: The Consumer's Guide.* Santa Cruz: ETR Associates, 1994. 169p. refs. (2p.). ISBN 1-56071-345-2. Descriptions and experienced teachers' ratings of 26 school-based sexuality education curricula G1–12; lists 31 additional curricula not rated. To assist school personnel and parents in choosing school-based sex education programs.

C106   Quackenbush, Marcia, & Mary Nelson, with Kay Clark, eds. *The AIDS Challenge: Prevention Education for Young People.* Santa Cruz, CA: Network Publications/ETR, 1988. 526p. glossary (11p.). resources (6p.). ISBN 0-941816-53-2. Resource for teaching children and adolescents about HIV/AIDS. Covers facts about HIV/AIDS, educational contexts (parents, schools, youth groups, religious groups), legal and ethical issues, plus risks and prevention for minorities and special populations. Includes guidelines from national and governmental groups.

C107 Quackenbush, Marcia, & Sylvia Villarreal. *Does AIDS Hurt? Educating Young Children About AIDS.* 2nd ed. Santa Cruz, CA: ETR Associates, 1992. 149p. readings (4p.). information sources (3p.). ISBN 1-56071-084-5. Comprehensive guide for explaining HIV/AIDS to children under age 10. Covers why and how to discuss AIDS, age-appropriate questions and answers, and coping with special circumstances: foster care, AIDS patient in the family, and schools with HIV-infected students or staff. Includes basic HIV information for adults.

C108 Ratner, Marilyn, & Susan Chamlin. *Straight Talk: Sexuality Education for Parents and Kids 4–7.* New York: Penguin, 1985. 40p. illus. bibliog. (2p.). ISBN 0-14-009413-X. Simple, concise guide for families about educating small children about sexuality. Stresses open communication, using simple language, and conveying parental values.

C109 Stark, Patty. *Sex Is More Than a Plumbing Lesson: A Parents' Guide to Sexuality Education for Infants Through the Teen Years.* Dallas: Preston Hollow Enterprises (P.O. Box 670935, Dallas, TX 75367-0935), 1991. 203p. ISBN 0-9629463-0-3. Guidance for parents for talking to their children about sex. Covers positive body image, modeling positive and romantic marriage, what young people need to know at various ages, being approachable, giving meaning and values to sexuality, counteracting the "casual sex myth," and focusing upon social skills instead of orgasm for communicating.

C110 Sullivan, Susan K., & Matthew A. Kawiak. *Parents Talk Love: The Catholic Family Handbook About Sexuality.* New York: Paulist Press, 1984. 164p. bibliog. (6p.). ISBN 0-8091-2639-7. Guidebook for parents about teaching children Roman Catholic sexual values. Covers church traditions, sexual development, myths, intimacy, and using television creatively for discussion.

C111 Whitehead, Margaret, & Onalee McGraw. *Foundations for Family Life Education: A Guidebook for Professionals & Parents.* Arlington, VA: Educational Guidance Institute (927 South Walter Reed Drive, Ste. #4, Arlington, VA 22204), 1991. glossary (4p.). resources (10p.). ISBN U/K. Guidelines for abstinence-based, family-centered, age-appropriate, directive family life and sex education. Covers rationale for directive vs. nondirective approach, age-graded curriculum objectives, parent and teacher roles, and analysis of child development. Lists abstinence-based public school curricula.

C112 Willke, Dr. & Mrs. J.C. *How to Teach Children the Wonder of Sex.* 2nd ed. Cincinnati: Hayes, 1983. 117p. ISBN 0-910728-17-8. Conservative, Christian-based parental guidelines for talking to children about sex. Covers answering questions and initiating discussion with toddlers to adolescents. Addresses mandate for parents as sex educators, pleasure and goodness of sex in marriage, demonstrating love and setting example of a happy marriage, controlling dating, stopping premature adulthood, and teaching general self-control.

C113 Wilson, Pamela M. *When Sex Is the Subject: Attitudes and Answers for Young Children.* Santa Cruz, CA: ETR Associates, 1991. 101p. refs. (1p.). orgs. & books (15p.). ISBN 1-56071-064-0. Covers children's sexual learning and development of children under age 10, answering questions, plus guidelines especially for teachers and especially for parents. Gives many examples of simple, concrete answers to typical questions.

NOTES

1. See also Martha Cornog, "Is Sex Safe in Your Library?" *Library Journal* (August 1993): 43–46.

2. Ronald and Juliette Goldman collected over 60 children's "pseudonyms" for the penis and over 40 for the vulva/vagina: see *Children's Sexual Thinking* (London: Routledge & Kegan Paul, 1982): 208–212. Compared to Australia and England, North American children took the longest to learn correct sexual terms. Paul Dickson's delightful *Family Words* (Reading, MA: Addison-Wesley, 1988) contains a few words used by entire families for genitals, bathroom functions, farting, and other sex-related topics. A number of full-grown adults, singly or in couples, delight in coining private expressions for genitals and sex acts. See Martha Cornog, "Naming Sexual Body Parts: Preliminary Patterns and Implications," *Journal of Sex Research* 22.3 (August 1986): 393–398.

Some sexuality professionals believe that nicknames and euphemisms for sexual concepts prevent direct and accurate sexual discussion. Naming the penis "Luckie Chuckie," for example, could be dangerous because the male no longer takes responsibility for what his penis does. See *Coping with Date Rape and Acquaintance Rape* (C79, Parrot): 51–52. We believe that private slang for sexual concepts can be fun and need not compromise directness or responsibility if terms are used as a secondary vocabulary for sex and not the primary one—much the way someone has a nickname, but everyone knows the "real" name and can use either as appropriate.

3. *Roommate* and *Heather* have come under attack from conservative groups and readers and have also been criticized in the gay press. One reviewer observed that they lack "the bite and grit and layers of texture that ha[ve] made some non–gay-themed picture books . . . such lasting favorites with children and adults alike. . . . Heather lives the gay version of *Fun with Dick and Jane*. . . . These books are valuable contributions to children's literature. . . . I just wish they were less saccharine and less preachy." Dian J. Pizurie, "Review Essay: The End of the Rainbow," *Lesbian Review of Books* 1.1 (Autumn 1994): 19.

4. *The Lesbian and Gay Parenting Handbook* (B27, Martin), p. 6.

5. Young Alfie, in *Alfie's Home* (C6, Cohen) is seduced by a pedophile, so we have classed the book under child sexual abuse, below. Theresa Bigalow spoke during "Beyond Daddy's Roommate: The Evolving Market in Children's Books," American Library Association 1994 Annual Meeting, June 23–30, 1994, Miami. She also noted that *Alfie's Home* and *Daddy's Roommate* have similar weaknesses because both use the child's voice as a literary/ideological device for presenting *adult* viewpoints. Neither speaks with the *authentic* voice of a child.

6. *Alfie's Home* was *not* reviewed in *Publishers Weekly*—nor could we locate a review in *School Library Journal* or other library review periodicals. The editors of *PW* commented, "We find it very difficult to spotlight works we find offensive or prejudicial. Recent submissions you will not find mentioned in our forecasts section include a picture book professing to 'provide help and healing to those . . .

seeking an alternative to homosexuality.' . . . Sometimes silence speaks best."
"Forecasts," *Publishers Weekly* (November 15, 1993): 57. Will Manley called *Alfie's Home* "misguided propaganda" that "irresponsibly exacerbates the prejudice against and oppression of gays"—see his "Does Intellectual Freedom Give Libraries the Right to Lie?" *American Libraries* (October 1994): 880.

Yet *Alfie*—the story itself and not its surrounding penumbra of notes and quotes—does not assert that all homosexuals are child molesters or that all homosexuality can be cured any more than it asserts that all parents fight and neglect their children, an important and explicit plot element. Nor, to reverse the argument, does *Daddy's Roommate* assert that all homosexuals are loving and fun parents. These are inferences that adult readers believe they detect as ideological undertext, yet we wonder if children would reason that far in a global analysis of sexual realpolitik. To kids, it's a story—and they've already seen stranger things by far.

Each librarian must consider these issues for him or herself. *Alfie* is, we feel, not about homosexuality but about child sexual abuse. Alfie's Uncle Pete is never described as "gay" or "homosexual." And as in other books for young people about child sexual abuse, Alfie's solution, recommended implicitly to the reader, is to find a trusted adult and talk about his problem. It is worth noting that the trusted adult who helps Alfie is an African American man.

7. Recent and less recent examples: Dorothy M. Broderick, "Sex Education: Books for Young Children," *Top of the News* (Winter 1978): 159–161; Linda Dunbar, "The EL Buying Guide, Human Sexuality K–12," *Emergency Librarian* 16.1 (September/October, 1988): 58–59; "Children's Books on Sex and Reproduction," *Booklist* 81.13 (March 1, 1985): 990–992; Frances Bradburn, "Sex, Lies, and Young Readers at Risk," *Wilson Library Bulletin* (October 1990): 34–38; Anne Osborn, " 'Just Say No' Isn't Sex Education," *School Library Journal* (April 1991): 39–42; "Classroom Connections: HIV and AIDS," *Book Links* (November 1992): 11–15; *Sexuality in Books for Children*, special issue of *Bookbird* 32.2 (Summer 1994): 6–39; Melissa Gross, "Sex Education Books for Kids K–6," *Journal of Youth Services in Libraries* (Winter 1995): 213–216. An annotated list produced locally is "Does AIDS Hurt? A Reading List for Children, Young Readers & Teens" from the Minnesota AIDS Project and the Minnesota Library Association.

8. See *Sex Guides* (D111, Campbell).

9. "Abstinence education" Christian sex books are written for adolescents and college age, and tend to stress that the proper, Biblically sanctioned place of sexuality is within marriage, that the joys and pleasures of marital sex are blessed by God, and that it is morally and practically advantageous to postpone sex until marriage. Many stress hazards of premarital sex and discuss related issues like date rape, sexual abuse, masturbation, petting, homosexuality, unwed pregnancy, abortion, and dating non-Christians. These books tend to contain little or nothing on the mechanics of sexuality/response, birth control, or STD prevention/safer sex other than abstinence.

While respecting this vision of purity, we—as realists, we suppose—prefer books that also offer practical advice and information about these issues in addition to any rhetoric about honoring Christian values and the Bible. We mean how to say no, alternatives to sexuality in dating situations, and how to get professional or legal help for problems such as date rape and sexual abuse. Two books that we did not annotate simply because they did not offer enough practical substance are

Sex: It's Worth Waiting For, by Greg Speck (Moody Press, 1989), and *Dating, Sex & Friendship*, by Joyce Huggett (InterVarsity Press, 1985).

Please note that we have annotated many books stressing abstinence, but they all include a good deal of other information and suggestions. *Love, Dating and Sex*, by George B. Eager (Mailbox Club Books, 1989, not annotated), does not take an explicitly Christian perspective but also concentrates on abstinence education and is longer on rhetoric than practical advice or information.

10. An excellent Rosen book received too late to be annotated is *Coping with Incest*, rev. ed., by Deborah A. Miller and Pat Kelly (Rosen, 1995).

11. See also Meg Tillapaugh, "AIDS: A Problem for Today's YA Problem Novel," *School Library Journal* (May 1993): 22–25.

12. See articles mentioned in note 7; see also Christine A. Jenkins, "Young Adult Novels with Gay/Lesbian Characters and Themes 1969–92: A Historical Reading of Content, Gender, and Narrative Distance," *Journal of Youth Services in Libraries* (Fall 1993): 43–45; Helma Hawkins, "Opening the Closet Door: Public Library Services for Gay, Lesbian, and Bisexual Teens," *Colorado Librarians* (Spring 1994): 28–31; Lynn Cockett, "Entering the Mainstream: Fiction About Gay and Lesbian Teens," *School Library Journal* (February 1995): 32–33; Virginia Jeschelnig, "Let's Talk About Sex," *School Library Journal* (March 1995): 141–142.

13. Author Ed Brecher was sufficiently immersed in his topic to star in his 60s in an explicit and charming sex education film, *A Ripple of Time* (see Chapter 6). One of us (TP) has participated in college sexuality education groups where the students were surprised at how deeply moved they were by this film.

We also want to note that *Consumer Reports* has produced three titles on sex-related topics annotated in this book (A129, C69, C82). Uniformly, they were at the top of the range for excellence.

14. See also *How to Talk Confidently with Your Child About Sex: Parent's Guide*, in C1 in Chapter 11.

12   Sex and Society

THE ARTS AND THE MEDIA

> [T]astes in erotica vary widely, and . . . what is acceptable to one per-
> son may be as the bottom of a parrot cage to another; or, to put it
> another way, one lady's deep throat may be another's big yawn.[1]

In this section, we include a selection of books about the erotica/pornog-
raphy controversy, history and study of sexual literature and sex in literature, sex and art, sex and film, sex in the media, and "compusex." Please
note that *works* of sexual literature are discussed in Chapter 6.

Of these topics, the erotica/pornography controversy has generated the
most light, heat, and printed paper.[2] Three excellent summaries are *Pornography: Private Right or Public Menace?* (D1, Baird & Rosenbaum), an
anthology representing all major views and writers, including excerpts
from the 1970 President's Commission and the 1986 Attorney General's
Commission reports; *Feminism and Pornography* (D3, Berger et al.), focusing upon factions within feminism and briefly discussing major nonfeminist views; and *Pornography* (D13, Linz & Malamuth), summarizing
scientific research tending to support or invalidate three major theoretical
approaches to pornography: feminist, conservative/moralist, and liberal. A
balanced collection should also include both *U.S. Commission on Obscenity and Pornography: The Report, 1970* (U.S. Government Printing Office,

1970) and *Attorney General's Commission on Pornography: Final Report* (U.S. Department of Justice, 1986), neither annotated. Both summarize extensive research and testimony, but they reach opposite conclusions.

Several significant books opposing pornography are annotated. *Pornography: A Human Tragedy* (D17, Minnery) takes a Christian perspective against pornography and how to combat it. A similar, unannotated work is *The Mind Polluters*, by Jerry R. Kirk (Thomas Nelson, 1985). *"Soft Porn" Plays Hardball* (D21, Reisman) focuses upon what the author believes are negative effects of *Playboy* magazine. A novel and interesting male approach is provided in *What Makes Pornography "Sexy"?* (D28, Stoltenberg), describing a consciousness-raising workshop. Another male view is presented in *Men Confront Pornography*, by Michael S. Kimmel (NAL/Dutton, 1991, not annotated).

In addition, libraries should acquire representative writings of the two major feminist anti-pornography writers, Catharine MacKinnon and Andrea Dworkin: *Pornography and Civil Rights: A New Day for Women's Equality*, by Dworkin and MacKinnon (Minneapolis: Organizing Against Pornography, 1988), *Only Words*, by MacKinnon (Harvard University Press, 1993), and *Pornography: Men Possessing Women*, by Dworkin (NAL/Dutton, 1991), none annotated.

As for views in favor of freedom of expression about sexuality, specifically against censoring what critics call "porn," a major work is the detailed and analytic **Pornography: The Other Side* (D4, Christensen). A very good feminist anthology is *Caught Looking* (D5, Ellis et al.). We also recommend several other important feminist works, not annotated. An interesting if somewhat dated U.S. and Canadian collection is *Women Against Censorship*, edited by Varda Burstyn (Douglas & McIntyre, 1985). Two recent titles are *Dirty Looks: Women, Pornography, Power*, edited by Pamela Church Gibson and Roma Gibson (Indiana University Press, 1993), and *Defending Pornography: Free Speech, Sex, and the Fight for Women's Rights*, by Nadine Strossen (Scribner's, 1995).

Fewer books deal with historical and literary studies of pornography and erotica. We have tried to balance coverage of periods, cultures, and social and legal aspects. A good reference work to authors of sexual literature is *Erotic Literature* (D15, McCormick); however, it omits all sadomasochist writing. *A History of Pornography* (D10, Hyde) is a well-written worldwide history that covers British law up to the 1960s. A complementary work focusing on continental and U.S. history and law is *The Secret Museum* (D11, Kendrick), with fascinating historical and social commentary about the erotic artifacts excavated at Pompeii. Since the "dirty wall paintings" at Pompeii are world famous and since in the past women tourists were forbidden by law to view them, this book will probably interest many readers. *The Secret Record* (D20, Perkins) covers recent Western authors, 1925–1980, from a predominantly literary perspective. A much briefer, more informal treatment is provided in *Erotica for Beginners* (D24, Selkirk), which does a once-over-lightly on both sexual writing and art.

Three additional books highlight material not covered by the works above. *The Romance Revolution* (D29, Thurston) discusses the flowering of so-called women's pornography: erotic romance novels. A more multipurpose work is *Confronting AIDS Through Literature* (D19, Pastore), covering AIDS as a literary theme and discussing how to use literature to teach about it. As for sexuality in literature generally, hundreds of books have been written on sexual themes in literature, many probably more suitable to academic than public libraries.[3] We include here only the complex and controversial *Sexual Personae* (D18, Paglia).

For readers wishing to write sexual literature themselves, two highly competent titles offer help: *How to Write Erotica*, by Valerie Kelly (Harmony Books, 1986), and *The Elements of Arousal: How to Write and Sell Gay Men's Erotica*, by Lars Eighner (Richard Kasak/Masquerade, 1994)—neither annotated.

A good visual introduction to erotic art is *The Complete Book of Erotic Art* (D12, Kronhausen & Kronhausen), while *Eroticism in Western Art* (D14, Lucie-Smith) addresses history and themes of erotic art in Europe and America. *The Art of Arousal* by Ruth Westheimer (Abbeville, 1993, not annotated) also shows a good sampling of visual erotica across history and culture. Recent art is sampled in *Erotic Art by Living Artists* (D6, Franklin-Smith) and *An Anthology of 20th Century Art: Erotic Art*, by Gilles Neret (Benedikt Taschen, 1993, not annotated).

We can include only highlights of more specialized topics. *The Sexual Perspective: Homosexuality and Art in the Last 100 Years in the West*, by Emmanuel Cooper (Routledge, 1994, not annotated), focuses largely upon British painters. **Folk Erotica* (D25, Simpson) includes both varied and amusing examples of sometimes primitive graphics and sculpture. Classic erotica from other times and places are discussed in *Erotic Spirituality* (D31, Watts), *Eros in Pompeii* (D7, Grant), and *Sex or Symbol: Erotic Images of Greece and Rome* (Catherine Johns, University of Texas Press, 1982), not annotated. A feminist historical perspective on ancient Greek erotica is taken by *The Reign of the Phallus: Sexual Politics in Ancient Athens*, by Eva C. Keuls (Harper & Row, 1985), not annotated. Other books belonging here (not annotated) include Nik Douglas and Penny Slinger's *The Erotic Sentiment in the Paintings of China and Japan* (Inner Traditions, 1990) and *The Erotic Sentiment in the Paintings of India and Nepal* (Destiny Books/Inner Traditions, 1988). One edition of the *Kama Sutra* needs mention here because it is illustrated with scholarly, yet romantic and erotic, images including photographs from Khajuraho: *Kama Sutra of Vatsyayana, Complete Translation from the Original Sanskrit by S.C. Upadhyaya* (Taraporevala's Treasure House of Books, Bombay, India, 1961), not annotated. An unusual and overlooked topic, treated with serious and impeccable scholarship, is *The Sexuality of Christ in Renaissance Art and Modern Oblivion* (D26, Steinberg). And on the opposite end of the culture spectrum, we have *Sex in the Comics* (D9, Horn) and *The Pin-Up: A Modest History* (Mark Gabor, Bell Publishing, 1972), not annotated. *Planes, Names & Dames, Vol. I 1940–1945*, by Larry Davis (Squadron/ Signal Publications, 1990), not annotated, is a collection of World War II airplane "nosecone" art, with a cover illustration of a man painting the leg of "Piccadilly Lilly" on the nose of a B-17G Flying Fortress heavy bomber.

In Western art, the 19th century saw a florescence of erotic and near-erotic images centering on exotica and Orientalia. Two books on the topic are the profusely illustrated *Idols of Perversity: Fantasies of Feminine Evil in Fin-de-Siècle Culture*, by Bram Dijkstra (Oxford University Press, 1986), and the irreplaceable *Europe's Myths of Orient*, by Rana Kabbani (Indiana University Press, 1986), the latter by a Damascus-born woman scholar who combines the unique perspectives of her gender with a native's view of how Europe saw Eastern women. Although written not as art history but as an examination of the roots of Nazism, *Male Fantasies: Volume 1: Women, Floods, Bodies, History* (Klaus Theweleit, University of Minnesota Press, 1987) contains many images of genuinely perverse eroticism, including a triptych of nude women from the Führer Room of the "Brown House" in post-1933 Munich (p. 281). (None of these books are annotated.)

We mention here several books of erotic photography: *Bilderlust* (Swan, 1991), photographs from past and present; *Early Erotic Photography* by Serge Nazarieff (Benedikt Taschen, 1993), from the 1850s; *The Homoerotic Photograph* by Allen Ellenzweig (Columbia University Press, 1992), past and present; and *Erotic by Nature*, edited by David Steinberg (Shakti Press/Red Alder Books, 1988), mostly recent photos but containing some fiction and poetry. Many books are published on photography of the nude. A particularly interesting current title is *Women en Large: Images of Fat Nudes*, by Laurie Toby Edison and Debbie Notkin (Books in Focus, 1994). (None of these are annotated.)

And here we must reiterate: We urge libraries with copies of these works to protect them carefully from vandals. Many art books are oversize and are easily slashed, disfigured, or damaged beyond repair.

Although sex on film is a relatively recent cultural phenomenon, today it is perhaps more important than printed or graphic work because it is so widely accessible through video rentals and now cable TV.

Erotic Movies (D33, Wortley) surveys sex-themed cinema worldwide, while the more recent *Censored Hollywood* (D16, Miller) concentrates on the United States, with special reference to content control and censorship. Two survey works by Gérard Lenne, not annotated, are *Sex on the Screen: Eroticism in Film* (St. Martin's, 1978) and the sequel *Sex on the Screen: The Eighties* (St. Martin's, 1990). An interesting reference is *The X-Rated Videotape Guide* (D22, Rimmer), with new volumes appearing every few years. We also suggest several special topic works: *Dark Romance* (D8, Hogan), about horror films, and *Coming Attractions* (D27, Stoller & Levine), with a behind-the-scenes look at making X-rated videos. For do-it-yourselfers, there is *The Joy of Video Sex: How to Capture Your Lovemaking with a Camcorder*, by Kevin Campbell (Amherst Media, 1993, not annotated).

Homosexuality on film is discussed in several recent books (none annotated): *The Celluloid Closet*, by Vito Russo (Harper & Row, rev. ed., 1987); *Images in the Dark: An Encyclopedia of Gay and Lesbian Film and Video*, by Raymond Murray (TLA Publications, 1995), and *Screening the Sexes: Homosexuality in the Movies*, by Parker Tyler (Da Capo, 1993).

We offer three books about sex and the traditional "media"—generally understood as newspapers, magazines, radio, and television: *Virgin or Vamp* (D2, Benedict), about coverage of sex crimes, *Gay People, Sex, and the Media* (D32, Wolf & Kielwasser), and *Policing Desire* (D30, Watney), about AIDS. The newest medium of sex depiction and information is the computer, and a lively introduction to "compusex" or "cybersex" for consumers is *The Joy of CyberSex* (D23, Robinson & Tamosaitis).

We were unable to find ongoing bibliographies on the erotica/pornography debate. Some retrospective lists are provided in *Pornography: Private Right or Public Menace?* (D1, Baird & Rosenbaum), *Feminism and Pornography* (D3, Berger et al.), as well as *Feminists, Pornography, & the Law: An Annotated Bibliography of Conflict, 1970–1986*, by Betty-Carol Sellen and Patricia A. Young (Library Professional Publications/Shoe String Press, 1987), and *Sourcebook on Pornography*, by Franklin Mark Osanka and Sara Lee Johann (Lexington Books, 1989), neither annotated. As for the history and study of sexual literature and sex in literature, ongoing lists are available only for homosexuality-related topics—see the catalog sources noted in the Homosexuality—General Works section in Chapter 10, especially Glad Day Bookshop.

Concerning sex and art, the Sexuality Library stocks a small number of erotic art and photography books, and the Light Impressions Visual Resources catalog (439 Monroe Avenue, P.O. Box 940, Rochester, NY 14603-0940) offers a few books on the nude and erotic photography. Again, homosexuality-related books are easiest to find, through the many gay review sources noted in Chapter 10.

Sex in the mass media and compusex/cybersex have not generated that many books, and we know of no bibliographies other than the catalog and review sources for homosexuality topics.

Please note that *A Research Guide to Human Sexuality* (D120, Lichtenberg) lists some retrospective bibliographies for most of the topics in this section, as well as organizations and periodicals.

We suspect that some major works are reviewed in the standard library media, with *Choice* covering literary and art criticism. A source for lists and reviews of books on photography of the nude is Frank Wallis (3 Cross Hill Road, Monroe, CT 06468). *Subject Guide to Books in Print* has section headings for PORNOGRAPHY, PHOTOGRAPHY, EROTIC, and EROTIC ART, which may prove helpful.

See also the Law and Sex section, below.

Annotations

*D1 Baird, Robert M., & Stuart E. Rosenbaum, eds. *Pornography: Private Right or Public Menace?* Buffalo, NY: Prometheus, 1991. 248p. chapter notes. bibliog. (2p.). ISBN 0-87975-690-X. Anthology of viewpoints on the pornography debate. Topics: the 1970 and 1986 commission reports, feminist issues, freedom of speech vs. censorship, religious perspectives, and pornography as causing violence and social problems.

D2 Benedict, Helen. *Virgin or Vamp: How the Press Covers Sex Crimes*. New York: Oxford University Press, 1992. 309p. notes (28p.). bibliog. (5p.). index. ISBN 0-19-508665-1. Analyzes press coverage of four well-known sex-related crimes 1979–1989, three of them rapes. Suggests how reporters should cover sex crimes without ill effects for victims, offenders, or public understanding.

*D3 Berger, Ronald J., Patricia Searles, & Charles E. Cottle. *Feminism and Pornography*. Westport, CT: Praeger/Greenwood, 1991. 178p. chapter notes. refs. (26p.). index. ISBN 0-275-93819-0. Overview of various feminist views on pornography, set in context of major nonfeminist views. Includes religious-conservative and civil libertarian positions, men's perspectives, and legal context. Goal: to maintain a balanced approach to the feminist debate.

*D4 Christensen, F.M. *Pornography: The Other Side*. New York: Praeger/Greenwood, 1990. 188p. notes (11p.). bibliog. (7p.). index. ISBN 0-275-93537-X. Analytical, detailed defense of position that pornography is not morally bad and that the current anti-pornography campaign is in many ways itself morally evil. Covers sex and values, women's issues, violence, degrading content, alleged ill effects, psychological health, and legal aspects.

D5 Ellis, Kate, and others, eds. *Caught Looking: Feminism, Pornography & Censorship*. New York: Caught Looking, Inc. (135 Rivington Street, New York, NY 10002), 1986. 96p. illus. bibliog. (3p.). ISBN U/K. Feminist essays supporting freedom of sexual expression, rejecting view that male sexuality and pornography are inherently violent, damaging, and dangerous to women. Interspersed with text are many sexually explicit pictures (mostly photos, some art) from various periods and sources. From Feminists Against Censorship Taskforce (F.A.C.T.) Book Committee.

D6 Franklin-Smith, Constance, ed. *Erotic Art by Living Artists*. 2nd ed. Renaissance, CA: ArtNetwork, 1992. 69p. illus. index. ISBN 0-940899-11-6. Mostly graphics, some sculpture, in various media, from U.S. artists, both sexes. Introduction gives brief overview of erotic art across history and cultures.

D7 Grant, Michael. *Eros in Pompeii: The Secret Rooms of the National Museum of Naples*. Photos by Antonia Mulas. New York: Bonanza, 1982. 171p. ISBN 0-517-177471. Many photos of erotic art, sculpture, and implements from Pompeii

(Italy), buried by volcanic eruption, 79 C.E., and excavated in the 19th century. Extensive historical general commentary, plus annotations on each example.

*D8 Hogan, David J. *Dark Romance: Sexuality in the Horror Film*. Jefferson, NC: McFarland, 1986. 334p. photos. filmography (19p.). bibliog. (3p.). index. ISBN 0-89950-190-7. Explores pervasiveness of sexuality in horror cinema. Themes include Frankenstein offspring, Jekyll and Hyde variations, beauty and the beast, vampires, slasher killers, and teen sex. Covers films of directors such as Alfred Hitchcock and Roger Corman, and of actress Barbara Steele.

D9 Horn, Maurice. *Sex in the Comics*. New York: Chelsea House, 1985. 215p. illus. bibliog. (1p.). index. ISBN 0-87754-850-1. Traces evolution of sexuality themes, implied and explicit, in comics worldwide, 1900 to 1980s. Themes: Americana, single girls, sex and violence, superheroes, romance, satire, science fiction, fantasy, and "far-out sex."

D10 Hyde, H. Montgomery. *A History of Pornography*. London: William Heinemann, 1964. 255p. bibliog. (2p.). index. ISBN U/K. History of pornography and erotic writing, East and West, from ancient Greece and Rome to 1960s. Emphasis more upon social contexts and content; some coverage of (British) legal aspects, including the 1964 trial over *Fanny Hill* in England.

D11 Kendrick, Walter. *The Secret Museum: Pornography in Modern Culture*. New York: Viking, 1987. 288p. notes (24p.). bibliog. (10p.). ISBN 0-670-81363-X. History of sexually explicit/arousing images and literature in the West, from 1500s to the 1986 "Meese Commission" report. Covers 19th and 20th century major censorship trials in France, Britain, and the U.S.

D12 Kronhausen, Phyllis, & Eberhard Kronhausen, comps. *The Complete Book of Erotic Art: Erotic Art, Volumes 1 and 2*. New York: Bell, 1978. 312p. & 270p. (bound in 1 vol.). illus. index. ISBN 0-517-24893X. Book 1: examples of Western, primitive, Indian, Chinese, and Japanese art, with brief text about each plus description of the First International Exhibition of Erotic Art (held in Sweden and Denmark). Book 2: additional examples from above categories, plus historical foreword.

*D13 Linz, Daniel, & Neil Malamuth. *Pornography*. Newbury Park, CA: Sage, 1993. 76p. refs. (8p.). index. ISBN 0-8039-4481-0. Characterizes three theoretical perspectives re pornography: conservative-moralist, liberal, and feminist; summarizes predictions and research for each. Notes that policy makers tend to use scientific findings that bolster their own perspective and ignore conflicting findings from other perspectives.

D14 Lucie-Smith, Edward. *Eroticism in Western Art*. New York: Oxford University Press, 1972. 287p. illus. index. ISBN 0-19-519946-4. Chronological history of erotic impulse and imagery in Western art in context of changing cultural, social, and aesthetic milieux. Classifies erotic art by type of symbolism/theme and discusses conscious and unconscious messages.

D15 McCormick, Donald. *Erotic Literature: A Connoisseur's Guide*. New York: Continuum, 1992. 263p. glossary (13p.). notes (6p.). bibliog. (1p.). index. ISBN 0-8264-0574-6. A–Z listing of major authors of sexual literature, with biographic and cultural material. Includes brief history of sexual literature, covering ancient

Greece and Rome, Asian erotica, courtly love, erotic memoirs, erotic writings in code, and modern erotica. Omits S&M themes.

D16 Miller, Frank. *Censored Hollywood: Sex, Sin, & Violence on Screen*. Atlanta: Turner Publishing, 1994. 312p. photos. chronology (8p.). notes (10p.). bibliog. (15p.). index. ISBN 1-878685-55-4. History of censorship and portrayals of sexuality in American films, early 1900s to 1990s. Covers Hollywood's institutionalized censorship and activities of pressure groups of all types.

D17 Minnery, Tom, ed. *Pornography: A Human Tragedy*. Wheaton, IL: Tyndale House, 1986. 340p. chapter notes. ISBN 0-8423-4947-2. Anthology from Christian perspective about pornography, negative effects, and how to fight it. Gives examples of successful anti-porn campaigns and excerpts from *Attorney General's Commission on Pornography: Final Report* (the "Meese report"). Contributors include James Dobson, C. Everett Koop, and Charles Colson.

D18 Paglia, Camille. *Sexual Personae: Art and Decadence from Nefertiti to Emily Dickinson*. New Haven, CT: Yale University Press, 1990. 718p. illus. notes (26p.). index. ISBN 0-300-04396-1. Provocative, complex analysis of sexuality in art and (mostly) literature, ancient Egypt and Greece to 19th century America. Traces persistence of pagan themes, sexual stereotypes, and biological bases of sex differences. "I see sex and nature as brutal pagan forces. . . . The amorality, aggression, sadism, voyeurism, and pornography in great art have been ignored or glossed over by most academic critics."

D19 Pastore, Judith Laurence, ed. *Confronting AIDS Through Literature: The Responsibilities of Representation*. Urbana, IL: University of Illinois Press, 1993. 267p. annotated bibliog. (16p.). ISBN 0-252-06294-9. Viewpoints on use of literature to confront AIDS. Chronicles significance of AIDS as literary theme, offers sampler of creative writing about AIDS, and shows how to use AIDS literature in the classroom.

D20 Perkins, Michael. *The Secret Record: Modern Erotic Literature*. New York: Rhinoceros/Masquerade, 1992. 281p. bibliog. (9p.). ISBN 1-56333-039-3. Brief background of sexual literature, ancient Greece through Victorian England. Major coverage of French, English, and American authors and publishers, 1925 1980. Emphasis upon themes and content, not law.

D21 Reisman, Judith A. *"Soft Porn" Plays Hardball: Its Tragic Effects on Women, Children and the Family*. Lafayette, LA: Huntington House, 1991. 219p. notes (9p.). index. ISBN 0-910311-92-7. Discusses negative effects of *Playboy* magazine: promotion of permissive sex based on erroneous Kinsey data, promotion of drug use, sexual violence and crime, neurochemical addiction to pornography, emasculation of men, indoctrination against marriage, sexualization of children, and victimization of women.

D22 Rimmer, Robert H. *The X-Rated Videotape Guide*. Rev. ed. Amherst, NY: Prometheus, 1986. 654p. photos. index. ISBN 0-87975-799-X (1970–1985); Volume II: 625p. ISBN 0-87975-673-X (1986–1991); Volume III: (by Robert H. Rimmer & Patrick Riley) 573p. ISBN 0-87975-818-X (1990–1992); Volume IV: (by Robert H. Rimmer & Patrick Riley) 628p. ISBN 0-87975-897-X (1992–1993). Reviews and rates adult sexually explicit videos. Volume I includes about 50p. on adult film industry and history of adult film. Rating scheme addresses overall quality of videos and type of sex portrayed. Includes plot summaries.

D23   Robinson, Phillip, & Nancy Tamosaitis, with Peter Spear & Virginia Soper. *The Joy of CyberSex: The Underground Guide to Electronic Erotica.* New York: Brady/Prentice-Hall, 1993. 331p. illus. refs. & sources (16p.). index. ISBN 1-56686-107-1. Describes erotic products and services for personal computers. Mostly for heterosexual men; some for women and gay/lesbian preferences. Reviews selection of erotic games and visuals on floppy disk or CD-ROM. Describes the adult computer bulletin board services (BBS) industry and profiles 30 BBS that "represent every area of human sexuality, from the kink to the mainstream." Discusses "virtual sex," i.e., erotic experience delivered through sophisticated electronic simulation. Enclosed floppy disk contains two erotic games for IBM PC-compatibles.

D24   Selkirk, Errol. *Erotica for Beginners.* New York: Writers and Readers, 1991. 90p. illus. refs. (2p.). further reading (1p.). ISBN 0-86316-141-3. "Documentary comic book" illustrated with black and white art clips. Covers functions of erotic art and literature, and their history in classical antiquity, Europe, Asia, India, Africa, and the Americas through the present-day West. Stresses universality of erotic imagery and imagination.

*D25   Simpson, Milton. *Folk Erotica: Celebrating Centuries of Erotica Americana.* New York: Harper Collins, 1994. 144p. photos. bibliog. (1p.). index. ISBN 0-06-017108-1. "The works presented here are linked by three unmistakable traits—the American experience, nonacademic ingenuity, and a celebration of human sexuality." Selection of erotic-themed graphics, sculpture, and objects of all types in various media, from Native American pottery of c. 500 C.E. to 1990s. Brief historical overviews.

D26   Steinberg, Leo. *The Sexuality of Christ in Renaissance Art and in Modern Oblivion.* New York: Pantheon, 1983. 222p. illus. bibliog. (3p.). index. ISBN 0-394-72267-1. Discussion of Renaissance art from 14th–16th centuries in which the genitalia of Christ are given emphasis through touching, protecting, or presentation. Analyzes several hundred such works out of nearly 1,000 identified. "The member exposed . . . stands for God's life as man and for his man's death, perhaps even for his resurrection."

D27   Stoller, Robert J., & I.S. Levine. *Coming Attractions: The Making of an X-Rated Video.* New Haven: Yale University Press, 1993. 246p. refs. (1p.). index. ISBN 0-300-05654-0. Chronicles making of an X-rated video, *Stairway to Paradise,* mostly via interviews with performers, writers, directors, producers, and technicians. Includes material on technical aspects of erotic video, motivations and backgrounds of people involved, and the porn industry's view of its audience.

D28   Stoltenberg, John. *What Makes Pornography "Sexy"?* Minneapolis: Milkweed Editions, 1994. 77p. ISBN 1-57131-201-3. Description of workshop in which men are asked to imitate a *Penthouse* magazine-style pose. Other workshop participants are invited to coach the posers and compare poses to the photos. Participants then talk about how it felt to pose or to watch. Designed to give men insights about the way they see pornography.

D29   Thurston, Carol. *The Romance Revolution: Erotic Novels for Women and* *the Quest for a New Sexual Identity*. Urbana, IL: University of Illinois Press, 1987. 259p. fiction bibliog. (6p.). refs. (11p.). index. ISBN 0-252-01247-X. Documents and analyzes 1972–1985 evolution of women's romance novels, from depicting passive innocent heroines and mysterious brutal men to featuring more assertive women, egalitarian relationships with sensitive men, and romantically described explicit sexual episodes. Concludes that these novels now include true female erotica and are sexually stimulating for readers.

D30   Watney, Simon. *Policing Desire: Pornography, AIDS and the Media*. Minneapolis: University of Minnesota Press, 1987. 159p. notes (6p.). further reading (2p.). index. ISBN 0-8166-1644-2. Analyzes coverage of HIV/AIDS in American and British mass media. Shows how the disease has been "mobilized to serve a prior agenda of societal issues."

D31   Watts, Alan. *Erotic Spirituality: The Vision of Konarak*. Photos by Eliot Elisofon. New York: Collier, 1971. footnotes. ISBN U/K. The Konarak and Khajuraho temples are Indian ruins from the 11th–13th centuries, decorated with figures in erotic poses. Text gives description of temples and surroundings, plus cultural and religious contexts for the sculptures.

D32   Wolf, Michelle A., & Alfred P. Kielwasser, eds. *Gay People, Sex, and the Media*. New York: Harrington Park, 1991. 284p. chapter notes & refs. ISBN 0-918393-77-9. (Originally published in *Journal of Homosexuality*.) Essays on sexuality and homosexuality in the mass media. Major topics: gays/lesbians and the media, AIDS and the media, TV and adolescent sexual behavior, and interpreting sexual content and meaning. Includes summary of case law on lesbian and gay rights as free speech issue, and bibliography (mostly periodical articles).

D33   Wortley, Richard. *Erotic Movies*. New York: Crescent Books, 1975. 137p. illus. index. ISBN 0-517-16826-X. Chronicles eroticism and sex in films, early 20th century to about 1975. Mostly U.S. but also notes British, European, and Japanese films.

COURTSHIP AND LOVE

Courtship is the process of mutual exploration aimed towards sexual intimacy and/or marriage.[4] Surprisingly, there are relatively few serious books on the topic. *Courtship* (D36, Cate & Lloyd) summarizes much that has been written in the scholarly literature. *Hands and Hearts* (D42, Rothman), by contrast, is a lively account for scholarly and nonscholarly audiences of the history of courtship in the United States through 1920. *From Front Porch to Back Seat* (D34, Bailey) continues the analysis of U.S. courtship from 1920 to 1965. Few research studies of the courtship process have been done; one comprehensive and recent effort is *Sex Signals* (D41, Perper), which looks at how people communicate intimacy and rejection.

Many hundreds of purely popular works on courtship have been written in the "how to pick up girls" or the "how to meet Mr. Right" genre. We have not included any here—there are too many, and they would draw us far afield. However, we must include the oldest and most famous of all,

the how-to-pick-up-girls and *Cosmo* equivalent of ancient Rome: Ovid's
The Art of Love (D40, Ovid).[5]

> Ask her to pass the bread or the fruit she has touched with her fingers;
> When she passes it on, manage to touch her hand. (P. 123)

The more things change, the more they remain the same. This little maneuver—the "accidental" touch—is also described in the modern *Sex Signals* (D41, Perper). And we might add that Ovid was one of the most
popular writers of Medieval Europe, so a library without Ovid is, well,
truly out-of-date.

There is a large and ancient scholarly and semi-scholarly literature on
love, particularly romantic love. We have included only a small selection
of comprehensive and favorite (to us) titles. One of the oldest and most
fascinating works on heterosexual and homosexual love is Plato's *Symposium*, which expresses ideas underlying a 2,000 year history of love in the
West. We particularly recommend the Tom Griffith translation (University
of California Press, 1989, not annotated). *Romantic Love* (D37, Hendrick
& Hendrick) summarizes a great deal of research on the topic. We also
recommend two broad overviews: *The Natural History of Love* (D38,
Hunt) in a popular vein, and *The Nature of Love* (D43, Singer)—comprehensive, scholarly, but still accessible.

The experience of love is analyzed in three other works, all appropriate
for scholarly and lay audiences. *The Colors of Love* (D39, Lee) is a classic
analysis of "love styles." *Love and Limerence* (D44, Tennov), also a classic, characterizes a particular and common type of romantic love, "love
sickness." *Breaking Hearts* (D35, Baumeister & Wotman) looks at the
other side: when romantic love fails and one party is rejected.

We found no reviewing or purchase sources for books about courtship
and love. Librarians wanting more in these areas may begin with the bibliographies in *Courtship* (D36, Cate & Lloyd), *Romantic Love* (D37, Hendrick & Hendrick), and *Sex Signals* (D41, Perper). *Choice* covers some of
the scholarly material; *Library Journal*, *Publishers Weekly*, and so on cover
some of the popular works.

Annotations

D34   Bailey, Beth L. *From Front Porch to Back Seat: Courtship in Twentieth-
Century America*. Baltimore: Johns Hopkins University Press, 1988. 181p. illus.
notes (32p.). index. ISBN 0-8018-3609-3. History of U.S. heterosexual courtship
from 1890s family-centered system of men calling on women, through consump-
tion-based "dating" c. 1920–1965, to less structured, more gender equal patterns
1960s onward. Extensive analysis of dating re economics, sexual behavior, and sex
roles.

D35 Baumeister, Roy F., & Sara R. Wotman. *Breaking Hearts: The Two Sides of Unrequited Love*. New York: Guilford, 1992. 241p. refs. (8p.). index. ISBN 0-89862-543-2. Analyzes essays from 71 college students about rejected lover and rejecter roles in unrequited love. Describes psychologically both points of view and types of experiences, and shows how different and sometimes contradictory these are.

D36 Cate, Rodney M., & Sally A. Lloyd. *Courtship*. Newbury Park, CA: Sage, 1992. 142p. refs. (17p.). index. ISBN 0-8039-3709-1. Overview of scholarly theory and research on U.S. heterosexual courtship: history, models, stability, breakdown, sexual aggression, and violence.

D37 Hendrick, Susan S., & Clyde Hendrick. *Romantic Love*. Newbury Park, CA: Sage, 1992. 138p. refs. (9p.). index. ISBN 0-8039-3671-0. Overview of scholarly theory and research on romantic love: history, theories, love styles, functions, meaning, and sexuality. Psychosocial perspective.

D38 Hunt, Morton M. *The Natural History of Love*. New York: Knopf, 1959. 416p. notes (18p.). index. ISBN U/K. Popularly written, entertaining history of "emotional relationships between the sexes" as related to sex, courtship, social status, and romance, from ancient Greece to 1950s.

D39 Lee, John Allen. *The Colors of Love*. Englewood Cliffs, NJ: Prentice-Hall, 1976. 282p. ISBN 0-13-152348-1. Descriptions of three primary (emotional, playful, and placid) plus secondary "love styles" that characterize behavior and attitudes within heterosexual/homosexual relationships. Designed to help people understand themselves and their relationships. Discusses depictions of love in the arts. Based upon intensive interviews with 200 people.

D40 Ovid. *The Art of Love*. Trans. by Rolfe Humphries. Bloomington: Indiana University Press, 1957. 206p. ISBN 0-253-20002-4. This edition includes *The Loves*, *The Art of Beauty*, *The Remedies of Love*, and *The Art of Love*, all Roman poetry c. 5 C.E.. The latter gives entertaining and insightful tips, instructions, and illustrative examples from mythology about winning and keeping a lover. Separate sections addressed to men and to women.

***D41** Perper, Timothy. *Sex Signals: The Biology of Love*. Philadelphia: ISI Press, 1985. 323p. refs. (19p.). index. ISBN 0-89495-049-5. Results of ethnographic observational study of how men and women meet and become attracted to each other. Documents sequence of courtship behaviors that parallel growing sense of intimacy. Also discusses rejection, marriage, and recent cultural changes affecting love and mateships.

D42 Rothman, Ellen K. *Hands and Hearts: A History of Courtship in America*. New York: Basic Books, 1984. 370p. note on sources (4p.). notes (45p.). index. ISBN 0-465-02880-2. History of U.S. heterosexual courtship 1770–1920, from reminiscences, diaries, and letters. Covers ideas, feelings, and behavior re affection, sexuality, courtship, and marriage. Epilogue briefly addresses courtship, 1920–1980.

D43 Singer, Irving. *The Nature of Love. 1. Plato to Luther*. 2nd ed. Chicago: University of Chicago Press, 1984. 381p. notes (11p.). index. ISBN 0-226-76094-4; *The Nature of Love. 2. Courtly and Romantic*. 1984. 513p. notes (20p.). index.

ISBN 0-226-76096-0; *The Nature of Love. 3. The Modern World.* 1987. 473p. notes (25p.). index. ISBN 0-226-76099-5. Sweeping trilogy tracing history of philosophy and psychology of love through Western literature and scholarly writing. Focuses mostly upon romantic love.

*D44   Tennov, Dorothy. *Love and Limerence: The Experience of Being in Love.* New York: Stein and Day, 1979. 324p. notes (27p.). bibliog. (12p.). index. ISBN 0-8128-2328-1. Characterizes "limerence"—the feeling of being obsessively in love, sometimes called "love-sickness." Describes who becomes limerent (not everyone), nature of the experience, problems and social effects, and controlling limerence when unrequited.

ETHICS AND PHILOSOPHY

Much ethical and philosophical discussion of sexuality occurs within religious frameworks. Here, we suggest a small selection of works not evoking religion. Because we are trying to present the greatest diversity in the fewest books, we have chosen mostly anthologies.

A spectrum of diverse and conflicting views on sexuality and ethics is provided in *Sexual Values: Opposing Viewpoints* (D47, Orr). *Redefining Sexual Ethics* (D45, Davies & Haney) presents liberal and radical perspectives. *The Philosophy of Sex* (D48, Soble) collects in one place philosophical approaches to present-day changing sexual attitudes and behavior. In addition, a classic work on the philosophy and ethics of sex is *Marriage and Morals*, by Bertrand Russell (various editions, not annotated).

Titles about how society at large perceives sexual ethics are also important. A benchmark of sorts was set in *Sex and Morality in the U.S.* (D46, Klassen et al.), done in the 1970s—and it did not confirm any "sexual revolution" in attitudes at that time. We look forward to a contemporary study of similar scope that measures changes in attitudes towards sexual morality since then. The recent *Sex in America* (A11, Michael et al.) reports updated ethics data in Chapter 13, "Sex and Society," which shows some liberalization in attitudes but not a great deal. However, this study did not have the detailed coverage of attitudes found in *Sex and Morality in the U.S.*, and results are not easy to compare because the questions were worded differently.

We know of no ongoing bibliography on sex and ethics or philosophy other than the list in *Subject Guide to Books in Print* under SEXUAL ETHICS—which includes religious works and many other kinds of titles that happen to have some content pertaining to ethics.

See also the Sex and Religion section, below.

Annotations

D45   Davies, Susan E., & Eleanor H. Haney, eds. *Redefining Sexual Ethics: A Sourcebook of Essays, Stories, and Poems.* Cleveland: Pilgrim, 1991. 381p. notes

(17p.). ISBN 0-8298-0912-0. "Exploration of . . . sexual ethics in the context of contemporary, multicultural movements for liberation." Liberal, feminist collection highlighting sexually oppressive social patterns and identifying alternatives as resources for change. Includes guidelines for classroom use. Some coverage of religious ethics.

D46 Klassen, Albert D., Colin J. Williams, & Eugene E. Levitt. *Sex and Morality in the U.S.: An Empirical Enquiry Under the Auspices of the Kinsey Institute*. Middletown, CT: Wesleyan University Press, 1989. 462p. chapter notes. bibliog. (14p.). index. ISBN: 0-8195-6230-0. Results of 1970s interview/questionnaire study of 3,000+ adults about their sexual behavior and opinions on morality of particular sexual activities. Detailed coverage of premarital sex and homosexuality. Does not support notion of 1960s "sexual revolution."

D47 Orr, Lisa, ed. *Sexual Values: Opposing Viewpoints*. San Diego, CA: Greenhaven, 1989. 214p. orgs. (4p.). bibliog. (3p.). index. ISBN 0-89908-420-6. Different viewpoints on the "sexual revolution" and changing sexual mores: homosexuality, sex education, pornography, virginity, celibacy, sexual variation, and monogamy. Also touches upon AIDS and teen pregnancy. (G10–12,C,A)

D48 Soble, Alan, ed. *The Philosophy of Sex: Contemporary Readings*. 2nd ed., rev. Savage, MD: Littlefield Adams, 1991. 338p. chapter notes. further reading (2p.). index. ISBN 0-8226-3013-3. Eighteen academic philosophers discuss sexual attitudes and behavior, using philosophical frameworks and arguments. Essays address "sexual perversion," masturbation, adultery, homosexuality, female masochism, rape, prostitution, and pornography, as well as broader views of sexuality.

THE FOLKLORE OF SEX

Published bibliographies, for librarians and otherwise, largely ignore the folklore of sex. By "folklore," we mean stories, songs, rhymes, jokes, and other forms of expression without known authorship and transmitted anonymously.

Folklore transmission characteristically occurs through word of mouth, manuscript, and private publication. More recently, office photocopy and facsimile machines have done yeoman service for transmitting an uncatalogable array of ephemera: drawings, doggerel, bogus officialia, perversions of "Peanuts," and much else. Much of this modern "Xeroxlore" has strong sexual content, and we recommend the anthologies of Alan Dundes and Carl R. Pagter.[6]

There are few scholarly compilations of traditional sexual folklore, but those are generally excellent. We exclude from this section nearly all the many popular small press and otherwise editions of songs, limericks, and jokes. They are properly the material of archival collections, date back to the first broadsides of England, and are repeatedly updated through printing presses, mimeograph machines, and now highspeed PC-based desktop publishing. They range from the well-known and by now virtually antique "Sex to Sexty" series to the more recent "Truly Tasteless Jokes" series by

"Blanche Knott" (get it?). There are also many recent limerick collections, some of original authorship.[7]

Erotic folklore has been an interest of ours for some time, so we include a good selection here. Unfortunately, it is light in cross-cultural materials, reflecting the dearth of published works as well as space available in this book.

Any mention of erotic folklore must begin with the scholar and writer Gershon Legman, the *grand maître*—or, as he has been sometimes called, the *enfant terrible*. Now a "septuagenarian slugger" living in France, he has long threatened to publish his autobiography, which will doubtless prove at least as interesting as his many other works—these combining humor, academic sacrilege, and daunting scholarship. His basic text on erotic folklore is *The Horn Book: Studies in Erotic Folklore and Bibliography* (D52, Legman), which belongs in all public and academic libraries.

We move from pure scholarship towards exemplars. A broad collection of popular samples, published for enjoyment and lacking scholarly apparatus, is *The Bawdy Bedside Reader*, originally appearing as *The Complete Immortalia* (D51, Hart). (This is probably a descendant, accurate or otherwise, of a collection entitled *Immortalia*, privately printed in New York in 1927.)[8] A massive scholarly compilation of songs and other works from the Ozarks and their environs is the two volume *Roll Me in Your Arms* and *Blow the Candle Out* (D57, Randolph)—the two titles being phrases from a refrain of a well-known song. Much of its content is familiar throughout the United States, and both volumes combine Legman's commentary with the intrepid collecting of the late Vance Randolph.

For bawdy songs alone, *The Erotic Muse* (D50, Cray), now in its second edition, provides words, music, and scholarly commentary for over 100 British and American favorites. "*The Whorehouse Bells Were Ringing*" (D55, Logsdon) concentrates on the American West.

"Dirty" jokes and limericks, while not exclusively English language, have reached a certain flowering in the British Isles and the United States and are treated as art forms in certain circles. The definitive collections for both genres are those of Legman: *Rationale of the Dirty Joke* (two volumes, D54, Legman), plus *The Limerick* and *The New Limerick* (D53, Legman). Libraries not quite up to the full Legman treatment of limericks might consider the shorter and more sweetly innocent *The Lure of the Limerick: An Uninhibited History*, by William S. Baring-Gould (Clarkson Potter/ Crown, 1967, not annotated).

Elsewhere in the world, the erotic tale or story seems more to be the going genre. Much of this material is not readily available either because no translations exist or because the originals were published privately or by small and evanescent presses. We give as an example *Korean Sex Jokes in Traditional Times* (not annotated), "translated and described" by Howard S. Levy, published by—we are not making this up—The Warm-Soft

Village Press (Washington DC, 1972) and reprinted in 100 copies "in the Republic of China" in 1975 (ISBN 910879-99-X, LC 72-77667, if you doubt us).

Fortunately, the situation is different for some Russian folklore. *Erotic Tales of Old Russia* (D49, Afanas'ev) is a selection in a bilingual edition of amusing and scurrilous stories collected by the great Russian folklore scholar Aleksandr Afanas'ev. Its small publisher, Scythian Books, is still very much alive in Oakland, California. The interested reader will want to compare the Russian stories with *Pissing in the Snow* (D56, Randolph), equally scurrilous Ozark stories collected by Vance Randolph, and one of the few U.S. texts available. For example, the Russian story "The Soldier and the Priest" can be compared with "It Didn't Cost Him Nothing" in Randolph.

Very few serious collections of erotic folklore seem to be published, especially of cross-cultural material. With the growing public appetite for erotic anthologies (see Chapter 6), sexual folklore may increasingly be brought to light and presented for popular and scholarly consumption.

See also erotic literature discussed in Chapter 6, notably *The Book of the Thousand Nights and One Night* (the "Arabian Nights"), and the Humor and/or Cartoons section, below.

Annotations

D49 Afanas'ev, Aleksandr, comp. *Erotic Tales of Old Russia*. Selected and trans. by Yury Perkov. Illus. by Alek Rapoport. Oakland, CA: Scythian Books, 1988. 177p. bilingual Russian-English. ISBN 0-933884-59-1. Some 59 humorous bawdy stories in Russian, 30 translated into English, selected from a larger 1879 collection. Compiled to provide authentic and previously unavailable texts for students of Russian language, literature, and folklore.

D50 Cray, Ed. *The Erotic Muse: American Bawdy Songs*. 2nd ed. Urbana, IL: University of Illinois Press, 1992. 435p. bibliog. (11p.). chapter notes. index. ISBN 0-252-01781-1. Texts and variants for 125 American and British bawdy songs: classics, parodies of "clean" songs, college songs, and armed services songs. Melodies for most, plus commentary about historical, social, and psychological contexts.

D51 Hart, Harold H., ed. *The Bawdy Bedside Reader*. Illus. by Lindi. New York: Bell/Crown, 1971. 475p. index to first lines. ISBN 0-517-145502. (Formerly published as *The Complete Immortalia*.) Collection of bawdy British and American folklore: riddles, limericks, songs (words, music, guitar chords), verse (including parodies of "clean" poetry), and miscellaneous humorous short pieces.

*D52 Legman, G. *The Horn Book: Studies in Erotic Folklore and Bibliography*. New Hyde Park, NY: University Books/Carol Publishing Group, 1963. 565p. index. ISBN 0-8216-0091-5. Introduction to major genres of erotic folklore—monographs (including Burns' *Merry Muses of Caledonia*), poetry, songs, limericks, jokes—delivered with wit, passion, and daunting scholarship. Discusses censorship and fakery in sexual folklore studies, and effects of uncensored violence vs. censored sex.

D53 Legman, G. *The Limerick: 1700 Examples with Notes, Variants, and Index.* New York: Brandywine, 1970. 517p. bibliog. (c. 9p.). notes & variants (c. 90p.). index of rhymes. ISBN U/K (reprinted by Bell, 1974, and in London by Jupiter Books, 1974, and Panther Books, 1976); *The New Limerick: 2750 Unpublished Examples, American and British.* New York: Crown, 1977. 729p. bibliog. (27p.). notes & variants (100p.). index. ISBN 0-517-53091-0. Definitive 2-volume collection of sexual and scatological limericks, with notes and commentary. Volume 1 includes 60-page history of limericks; volume 2 includes 20-page section on significance and composition of limericks. (Note: editions of the first volume before 1970—there are several, including the first French edition of 1953—do not have the historical material.)

D54 Legman, G. *Rationale of the Dirty Joke: Analysis of Sexual Humor. First Series.* New York: Grove, 1968. 811p. subjects and motifs list. refs. in text. ISBN 0-253-34775-0; *Rationale of the Dirty Joke: An Analysis of Sexual Humor. Second Series* (cover title: *No Laughing Matter*). New York: Breaking Point, 1975. 992p. subjects and motifs list. refs. in text. ISBN 0-253-3477-7. (Both reprinted as *No Laughing Matter: An Analysis of Sexual Humor*, 2v., Indiana University Press, 1982.) Two-volume collection of over 4,000 jokes and tales with sexual themes, categorized by motif. Extensive, complex, eclectic, and entertaining commentary on sociological and psychological (largely Freudian) significance/implications.

D55 Logsdon, Guy, ed. *"The Whorehouse Bells Were Ringing" and Other Songs Cowboys Sing.* Urbana, IL: University of Illinois Press, 1989. 388p. photos. glossary (8p.). bibliog. (22p.). index ISBN 0-252-01583-5. Collection of 61 songs with words and music, about cowboys or sung by cowboys, with notes about origins and variants. Most have bawdy content. Describes singers, how songs were collected, history of cowboy music, and research into bawdy songs as folklore.

D56 Randolph, Vance. *Pissing in the Snow, and Other Ozark Folktales.* Intro. by Rayna Green. Annotations by Frank A. Hoffmann. Champaign: University of Illinois Press, 1976. 192p. bibliog. (3p.). ISBN 0-252-01364-6. Some 101 humorous bawdy stories, 14 from women, told by Ozark informants 1920–1954. Annotations give Thompson motif-index numbers and discuss story themes in other sources from U.S., France, Belgium, and Russia, 15th century to the 1970s.

D57 Randolph, Vance. *Roll Me in Your Arms: "Unprintable" Ozark Folksongs and Folklore. Vol. I: Folksongs and Music.* Ed. with intro. by G. Legman. Fayetteville, NC: University of Arkansas Press, 1992. 582p. ISBN 1-55728-531-5; *Blow the Candle Out: "Unprintable" Ozark Folksongs and Folklore. Vol. II: Folk Rhymes and Other Lore.* Ed. with intro. by G. Legman. Fayetteville, NC: University of Arkansas Press, 1992. 390p. bibliog. to both vols. (60p.). index. ISBN 1-55728-237-4. Large collection of U.S. bawdy folklore originally expurgated from Randolph's earlier publications. Volume II: songs without music, rhymes, riddles, children's lore, graffiti, and beliefs. Extensive commentary discusses variants, sources, and related folk/cultural material. Introduction addresses history of the manuscript, author's life, and erotic folklore scholarship.

HISTORY AND CULTURE

We include here three interlocking topics: history of sexual attitudes, customs, and behaviors; sexual attitudes, customs, and behaviors world- and culture-wide; and the history of the *study* of sexuality. The history books focus mostly upon the United States and Western culture. A great many other books exist, particularly about sexuality in Renaissance and medieval Europe, which has its own scholarly school. Victorian England is also well studied.

Sex in History (D79, Tannahill) is the major popular panorama of the entire subject, while *Intimate Matters* (D64, D'Emilio & Freedman) treats U.S. traditions well. A particularly readable period study, *The Story the Soldiers Wouldn't Tell* (D73, Lowry), treats sex in the Civil War. Covering more recent events, *The Destroying Angel* (D74, Money) is a frank and quirky look at some American manifestations of Victorianism, from one of sexology's great scholars. Most recently, World War II's widespread but generally unrecognized influence upon sexual history is documented in *Virtue Under Fire* (D63, Costello).

We suggest a variety of works to cover the contemporary scene. *Hot and Bothered* (D65, Dennis) discusses the state of love-and-sex in the 1990s, focusing upon personal relationships, while *Sex, Art, and American Culture* (D76, Paglia) looks more broadly at issues and institutions. *Public Sex* (D61, Califia) favors "deviant and defiant" radical sex, whereas other works come out against sexual freedom: *Enemies of Eros* (D67, Gallagher) and *Sexual Suicide* (D68, Gilder).

A book with considerable intellectual and academic influence is *The History of Sexuality, Volume I: An Introduction* (Michel Foucault, Pantheon, 1978, not annotated). Not truly a "history" but a personal philosophical overview, it contains Foucault's ideas about sex, society, and power. It will probably not appeal to general readers, but larger collections should consider purchasing it.

A different slant is provided in *Too Many Women?* (D70, Guttentag & Secord), which suggests that the male/female ratio in a society has marked influences upon sexual behavior. Another historical work with a particular slant is *The Poisoned Embrace* (D75, Osborne), a history of stereotypes of deadly sexual partners.

As we noted earlier, we are excluding biographies from this book. However, we could not resist the nosy appeal of *The Intimate Sex Lives of Famous People* (D81, Wallace et al.). Like potato chips, you cannot read just one. The profiles certainly reveal that unconventional and problematic sexualities have plagued famous as well as common people.

As with the history of sex, there is a substantial technical literature of the anthropology of sex.[9] We have eschewed most of the formal literature, with the exception of several excellent overviews: *The World of Human*

Sexuality (D69, Gregersen) and *Varieties of Sexual Experience* (D66, Frayser). *Sexual Meanings: The Cultural Construction of Gender and Sexuality* (Sherry B. Ortner & Harriet Whitehead, Cambridge University Press, 1981), not annotated, was a scholarly landmark in constructionist theory building. The remaining "area studies" each include some history, some anthropology, and some sociology. We have picked two for China, *Sex in China* (D78, Ruan) and *The Yin-Yang Butterfly* (D62, Chu), as they seem to complement each other with historical versus enhancement perspectives. *Pink Samurai* (D58, Bornoff) surveys sexuality in historical and contemporary Japan, *Sex and Russian Society* (D72, Kon & Riordan) does the same for Russia, while *Intimate Relations* (D71, Kakar) is a view of sexuality in the Indian subcontinent written by an Indian psychoanalyst. Indian erotology is its own field; we mention only the bibliographic *Women of India: An Annotated Bibliography*, by Harshidah Pandit (Garland, 1985), not annotated, which contains much material on Indian sexuality, law, and history.

A book we were not able to obtain was *Sexuality in Islam*, by A. Bouhdha (Routledge, 1985, not annotated). Alev Lytle Croutier's unique *Harem: The World Behind the Veil* (Abbeville, 1989), not annotated, is a profusely illustrated historical and cultural discussion of the Turkish harem, written by a Turkish woman filmmaker and scholar. It demolishes myths to present a poignant and moving history. *Woman in the Muslim Unconscious* (Pergamon, 1984, trans. from the French), not annotated, is by a Tunisian woman sociologist writing under the pseudonym Fatna Ait Sabbah; it is scholarly but striking and powerfully written.

A large collection should possess works by R.E.L. Masters and Allen Edwardes as historically significant documents. *The Jewel in the Lotus: A Historical Survey of the Sexual Culture of the East*, by Allen Edwardes (Julian Press, 1959), and *The Cradle of Erotica: A Study of Afro-Asian Sexual Expression and an Analysis of Erotic Freedom in Social Relationships*, by Allen Edwardes and R.E.L. Masters (Matrix House, 1966), well represent their style, although both are outdated in content and conclusions; neither annotated. Yet both are also well known. A classic of "sexual anthropology" is *Sexual Relations of Mankind* by Paolo Mantegazza (Falstaff Press, 1932), not annotated. Of equal or greater importance is Margaret Mead's classic *Coming of Age in Samoa* (Morrow, 1932, many editions since), not annotated, and her later study of the United States, *Male and Female: A Study of the Sexes in a Changing World* (Morrow, 1949), not annotated. We hope that historically minded anthropologists will catalog and describe the many now outdated works in this genre; they strongly affected our views of sexuality and, with Freudianism, were pivotal in altering Western sexual beliefs.

Although we have omitted works in preparation, an exception is needed for *The International Encyclopedia of Sexuality*, edited by Robert T. Francoeur, with contributions from scholars worldwide, most native to the country they describe (3 v., Continuum, in press). It will be a major contribution to the field.

We found almost no literature about the sexuality or sociosexuality of U.S. racial/cultural groups. Standing practically alone in this area is *A Completely New Look at Interracial Sexuality* (D80, Tenzer), about sexual relationships between whites and African Americans.

Sex research, or "sexology," is usually seen as a relatively recent scholarly development, dating to 18th and 19th century attempts to cope with prostitution.[10] Yet Aristotle, who lived in 4th century B.C.E. Greece, can be regarded as one founder of Western sexology, as described in the fascinating *Science in the Bedroom* (D60, Bullough). But it is imperative also to mention Plato's *Symposium*, seemingly the first written work attempting to discuss erotic love in a comprehensive and coherent intellectual fashion. It contains presentations by different individuals—our modern word *symposium* derives from the title of this book, despite its original Greek meaning of *drinking party*—whose voices represent homosexual, heterosexual, poetic/theatrical, medical, and military views, the latter in the drunken bawdiness of the Athenian general Alcibiades. Most notable of all is Socrates' presentation of ideas he explicitly and repeatedly credits to his instructress in the art of love, Diotima of Mantinea, the woman from whom all later Western philosophy obtained its theories of Eros. The *Symposium* exists in many translations, and a library without it is like a library without Ovid: simply incomplete.

The Sex Researchers (D59, Brecher) takes a closer look at the best known and most significant scholars of sex research within the last century and a half. Focusing still more narrowly, *Dr. Kinsey and the Institute for Sex Research* (D77, Pomeroy) concentrates upon the best known (and possibly most influential) of all. A conservative vision of sexological history that to us borders on conspiracy theorizing is *Kinsey, Sex, and Fraud: The Indoctrination of a People: An Investigation into the Human Sexuality Research of Alfred C. Kinsey, Wardell B. Pomeroy, Clyde E. Martin, and Paul H. Gebhard*, by Judith A. Reisman and Edward W. Eichel (Huntington House, 1990), not annotated. It needs to be complemented by *The Modernization of Sex: Havelock Ellis, Alfred Kinsey, William Masters and Virginia Johnson* (Paul Robinson, Harper & Row, 1976), not annotated.

Reviews in the *Journal of the History of Sexuality* comprise a major source of new material on sex in history and culture. There is a fair amount of recent works in this area, some covered in library review media. University press and scholarly publishers' catalogs are another good source.

See also the Homosexuality—History and Cultural Studies section (Chapter 10) and historical approaches within other topics, such as histories of prostitution within the Prostitution and Other Sex Work section (Chapter 13).

Annotations

D58   Bornoff, Nicholas. *Pink Samurai: Love, Marriage & Sex in Contemporary Japan*. New York: Pocket Books/Simon & Schuster, 1991. 492p. illus. refs. and notes (6p.). index. ISBN 0-671-74266-3. Lively description of love, sex, and marriage in Japanese mythology, history, and contemporary society. Covers modern upbringing and family life; history and myths; the extensive prostitution and sex industries; current behavior regarding homosexuality, S&M, rape, and pornography; and future for women.

D59   Brecher, Edward M. *The Sex Researchers*. Fwd. by William H. Masters & Virginia E. Johnson. New York: New American Library, 1971. 406p. bibliog. (11p.). index. ISBN U/K. History of sex research and researchers, 1800s–1960s. Covers work of Havelock Ellis, Krafft-Ebing, Freud, van de Velde, Kinsey, John Money, Masters and Johnson, plus research on female sexuality (Elizabeth Blackwell, Leah Schaefer, Niles Newton, Helena Wright, Mary Jane Sherfey), falling in love, and "swinging."

*D60   Bullough, Vern L. *Science in the Bedroom: A History of Sex Research*. New York: Basic Books, 1994. 376p. notes (59p.). index. ISBN 0-465-03020-3. Traces observations and research about animal and human sexuality from Aristotle through early social science research on prostitution, to Kinsey, Masters and Johnson, and others. Also summarizes trends and problems in sex research.

D61   Califia, Pat. *Public Sex: The Culture of Radical Sex*. Pittsburgh: Cleis, 1994. 264p. chapter notes. index. ISBN 0-939416-89-1. Essays on deviant and defiant sexual choice and social change. Addresses sex between adults and minors, antisexual feminism, pornography, S&M, nonmonogamy, gender-bending, lesbian safe sex, latex fetishism, and prostitution.

D62   Chu, Valentin. *The Yin-Yang Butterfly: Ancient Chinese Sexual Secrets for Western Lovers*. New York: Tarcher/Putnam, 1993. 253p. illus. glossary (5p.). bibliog. (2p.). index. ISBN 0-87477-747-X. Survey of traditional Chinese sexual practice as advice for modern lovers. Includes sexual enhancement instruction from past Chinese erotic writing, covering sexual positions, exercises, aphrodisiacs, and love play techniques. Many correspond to contemporary sexological findings and recommendations.

D63   Costello, John. *Virtue Under Fire: How World War II Changed Our Social and Sexual Attitudes*. New York: Fromm, 1987. 309p. notes (19p.). bibliog. (16p.). ISBN 0-88064-070-7. "Sexual history" for World War II, focusing upon liberalization of morality and coincident liberation of women. Based upon nationwide survey and extensive historical research. Discusses female troops (U.S., British, and Russian), sexualization of male troop culture, romantic films and songs, homosexuality in battle, wartime courtship and marriage, and stateside female work force.

D64   D'Emilio, John, & Estelle B. Freedman. *Intimate Matters: A History of Sexuality in America*. New York: Perennial Library/Harper & Row, 1989. 428p. notes (40p.). bibliog. (13p.). index. ISBN 0-06-091550-1. History of sexual meanings, regulations, and politics in U.S., 1600–1980s. Describes changes from family-centered, reproductive sexuality in colonial era through emerging importance of romantic intimacy in 19th century, to today's more commercialized sexuality, expected to provide personal fulfillment.

D65   Dennis, Wendy. *Hot and Bothered: Sex and Love in the Nineties*. New York: Viking/Penguin, 1992. 276p. notes (2p.). ISBN 0-670-84502-7. Lighthearted, insightful "state of the union" about contemporary (hetero)sexual feelings and behavior, based upon interviews and letters from U.S. and Canada. Covers men's and women's views and complaints re each other, courtship patterns and problems, sexual etiquette (about, e.g., STDs, oral and anal sex, fantasies, threesomes, masturbation, and saying "I love you"), marriage, and adultery.

D66   Frayser, Suzanne G. *Varieties of Sexual Experience: An Anthropological Perspective on Human Sexuality*. New Haven, CT: HRAF Press (Human Relations Area Files), 1985. 546p. bibliog. (15p.). refs. (16p.). index. ISBN 0-87536-342-3. Complex anthropological description of human sexuality from cross-species and cross-cultural perspectives. Covers biological and social aspects of sexual and reproductive life cycles in over 60 societies worldwide. Also analyzes U.S. shift from past overlap to present separation of sexuality and reproduction.

D67   Gallagher, Maggie. *Enemies of Eros: How the Sexual Revolution Is Killing Family, Marriage, and Sex and What We Can Do About It*. Chicago: Bonus Books, 1989. 283p. chapter notes. index. ISBN 0-929387-00-7. Holds that current emphasis on sexual expression, freedom of choice in all areas of life, low value attributed to children and mothering, and emphasis on androgyny at all costs is responsible for high divorce and abortion rates, poverty and unhappiness of single motherhood, juvenile problems and crime, child abuse, and male irresponsibility.

D68   Gilder, George F. *Sexual Suicide*. New York: Bantam, 1975. 338p. notes (29p.). bibliog. (10p.). index. ISBN U/K. Holds that different, complementary, and valuable sex roles for men and women are the source of civilization and stable society. Sees androgyny and promotion to both sexes of gender-linked sexual behavior as harmful, e.g., Playboy's salesmanship to women and men of single male sexual patterns; and feminism's stress upon a unisex society and work ethic for women, downplaying motherhood.

*****D69**   Gregersen, Edgar. *The World of Human Sexuality: Behaviors, Customs and Beliefs*. New York: Irvington, 1994. 438p. illus. notes (6p.). bibliog. (27p.). index. ISBN 0-8290-2633-9. Comprehensive anthropological description of sexual behavior and related themes cross-culturally, worldwide. Covers sexual techniques, physical types, physical attractiveness, clothing and modesty, marriage, incest, and prostitution. Includes history of the study of sex and discusses current developments and trends.

D70   Guttentag, Marcia, & Paul F. Secord. *Too Many Women? The Sex Ratio Question*. Beverly Hills, CA: Sage, 1983. 277p. notes (23p.). index. ISBN 0-8039-1919-0. Traces effects of number of men vs. women throughout history. More men than women correlated with men valuing, protecting, and sometimes restricting women, plus greater commitment to monogamy, marriage, and children; more women than men correlated with promiscuity, misogyny, feminism, and lesser commitment to marriage and children. Recent technological advances are seen as likely to modify these trends in the future.

D71   Kakar, Sudhir. *Intimate Relations: Exploring Indian Sexuality*. Chicago: University of Chicago Press, 1989. 161p. notes (9p.). index. ISBN 0-226-42280-1. Psychological study of sexual relationships between men and women in India, interpreted through folktales, myths, novels and plays, narratives from women from Delhi slums, Gandhi's writings, and several psychoanalytical case studies.

D72   Kon, Igor, & James Riordan. *Sex and Russian Society*. Bloomington: Indiana University Press, 1993. 168p. chapter refs. index. ISBN 0-253-33201-X. Contributions from Russian and Western scholars about sexual issues in modern Russia: eroticism and taboos in Russian history and culture, birth control, abortion, sex in films, homosexuality, beauty contests, medical sexology, and sex and youth.

*D73   Lowry, Thomas P. *The Story the Soldiers Wouldn't Tell: Sex in the Civil War*. Mechanicsburg, PA: Stackpole Books, 1994. 209p. illus. notes (18p.). bibliog. (8p.). index. ISBN 0-8117-1515-9. Lively history of sex in the Civil War: beliefs and knowledge, prostitution, venereal disease, contraception and abortion, rape, homosexuality, women passing as men, sexual escapades of generals and clergy, cursing, sexual humor, and love.

D74   Money, John. *The Destroying Angel: Sex, Fitness & Food in the Legacy of Degeneracy Theory, Graham Crackers, Kellogg's Corn Flakes & American Health History*. Buffalo, NY: Prometheus, 1985. 213p. chapter notes. bibliog. (6p.). index. ISBN 0-87975-277-7. Popularly written history of recent and present-day antisexualism in American health care and social/legal policy. Includes antimasturbation theories and campaigns, the Inquisition and anti-witch crusades, pornography and censorship, Victorianism, distorted sexuality ("paraphilias") as result of anti-sexualism, and modern scientific reactions and views.

D75   Osborne, Lawrence. *The Poisoned Embrace: A Brief History of Sexual Pessimism*. New York: Pantheon, 1993. 242p. bibliog. (5p.). ISBN 0-679-42723-6. "Sexual pessimism . . . is the equation of sexual love outside the prerequisites of reproduction with death." Traces history of eight stereotypes of deadly sexual partners across over 2,000 years: the virgin, the witch, the leper, the Jew, the noble savage, the Don Juan, the oriental, and the androgyne.

D76   Paglia, Camille. *Sex, Art, and American Culture*. New York: Vintage/Random, 1992. 337p. chapter notes. bibliog. about author (11p.). index. ISBN 0-679-74101-1. Essays on sex and popular culture, defined as "an eruption of the never-defeated paganism of the West . . . [with] brazen aggression and pornographic sexuality." Topics include Madonna and Elizabeth Taylor as sex goddesses, homosexuality, date rape, sexual harassment, feminism, religion and sex, and the shortcomings of modern academia.

D77   Pomeroy, Wardell B. *Dr. Kinsey and the Institute for Sex Research*. New York: Harper & Row, 1972. 479p. photos. index. ISBN 06-013397-X. Sympathetic biography of Alfred E. Kinsey, with description of his sexual behavior surveys, the institute he founded at Indiana University, and reactions to his research and books on sexual behavior.

D78   Ruan, Fang Fu, with ed. collaboration of Molleen Matsumura. *Sex in China: Studies in Sexology in Chinese Culture*. New York: Plenum, 1991. 208p. refs. (13p.). index. ISBN 0-306-43860-7. Survey of Chinese sexual life over past 3,000 years: philosophy, myths, techniques, erotica and sexological writings, prostitution, homosexuality, transvestism and transsexualism, and regulation of sexuality.

Stresses contributions of past Chinese culture to sexology and ineffectiveness of current repressive governmental policies.

*D79 Tannahill, Reay. *Sex in History*. Rev. ed. Briarcliff Manor, NY: Scarborough House, 1992. 475p. illus. bibliog. (17p.). notes (23p.). index ISBN 0-8128-8540-6. Popularly written history of sexual attitudes, culture, and practices. Covers prehistory, the ancient world, Asia, the Arab world, Europe, and America.

D80 Tenzer, Lawrence R. *A Completely New Look at Interracial Sexuality: Public Opinion and Selected Commentaries*. Manahawken, NJ: Scholars' Publishing House, 1990. 196p. illus. chapter notes. ISBN 0-9628348-1-5. Includes results from telephone survey of 444 U.S. white women about interracial sexuality plus scholarly commentaries on beliefs revealed in survey, in past and present sociohistorical perspective. Issues addressed include skin color symbolism, dating and marriage, antebellum history, psychological aspects, sexual misunderstandings, and future research.

D81 Wallace, Irving, Amy Wallace, David Wallechinsky, & Sylvia Wallace. *The Intimate Sex Lives of Famous People*. New York: Delacorte, 1981. 618p. photos. index. ISBN 0-440-04152-X. Entertaining vignettes about life, loves, and sexual proclivities of 207 well-known historical figures: actors, writers, musicians, politicians, psychologists, religious figures, scientists, businessmen. Based upon extensive research from, e.g., biographies, autobiographies, memoirs, interviews, correspondence, and court records.

HUMOR AND/OR CARTOONS

Can humor be sex education? Can sex laugh at itself? We think so, and we have included a small selection of less serious works including comics, and several more serious comics as well.

Two irresistible spoofs on sex manuals are the classic *Is Sex Necessary?* (D85, Thurber & White) and *The Official Sex Manual* (D84, Sussman)—which was a howling hit with my (MC) circle of college friends in the 1960s.

Sexually explicit comics have become an industry unto themselves: notable series include *Cherry* (née Cherry Poptart; we suspect that Kellogg's protested), *Young Lust, Tits 'n' Clits* (women cartoonists, and we're not making this up), and the extremely violent and disturbing but beautifully drawn work of S. Clay Wilson.[11] Publishers/distributors of these include Kitchen Sink Press, Last Gasp Press, Rip-Off Press, and Bud Plant Comic Art. The best for libraries is the *Omaha the Cat Dancer* series (D87, Waller & Worley), where the sex is an integral part of well-developed plots involving believable characters and relationships. Omaha is engrossing and entertaining, but not funny-ha-ha.

Two gay comic series are both humor and social commentary. *Dykes to Watch Out For* (D83, Bechdel) follows a group of lesbian friends and co-workers through romances, mateships, and parenthood. *Domesticity Isn't Pretty* (D82, Barela) chronicles the affections and troubles of a gay male couple in suburbia. (Howard Cruse's *Wendel*, not annotated, is another well-known gay male comic.)

Much more serious is *Tales of the Closet* (D86, Velez), a series from the Hetrick-Martin Institute about eight gay urban teens, confronting coming out, family and personal problems, violence, and romance.

Sexual humor is widespread, but books of sexual humor are not always easy to identify, particularly works with that clichéd characteristic, "enduring value." Humor and cartoons by gay and lesbian authors do get included in some of the gay catalogs and review media such as Womankind Books (see the Homosexuality—General Works section in Chapter 10).

For other works in comics format, see *Sex for Beginners* (A15, Selkirk) and *Erotica for Beginners* (D24, Selkirk). For other sexual humor, see The Folklore of Sex section, above.

Annotations

D82   Barela, Tim. *Domesticity Isn't Pretty: A Leonard and Larry Collection.* Minneapolis: Palliard Press/Dream Haven Books (1309 Fourth Street SE, Minneapolis, MN 55414-2029), 1993. 144p. ISBN 1-884568-00-9. Humorous but also serious comic strip originally syndicated in the gay press about an affectionate gay male couple in suburbia, coping with straight neighbors, an ex-wife and two children, a Jewish mother intent on grandchildren, and assorted family, career, and other problems.

D83   Bechdel, Alison. *Dykes to Watch Out For.* Ithaca, NY: Firebrand, 1986. 78p. ISBN 0-932379-17-6; *More Dykes to Watch Out For.* 1988. 108p. ISBN 0-932379-45-1; *New, Improved! Dykes to Watch Out For.* 1990. 118p. ISBN 0-932379-79-6; *Dykes to Watch Out For: The Sequel.* 1992. 133p. ISBN 1-56341-008-7; *Spawn of Dykes to Watch Out For.* 1994. 132p. ISBN 1-56341-039-7. Warm and funny cartoon strip about contemporary lesbian life, becoming a serial soap opera with regular characters midway through second volume. Gently mocks lesbian love and sex, feminism, political correctness, lesbian motherhood, and New Ageism. Originally syndicated in the gay press.

D84   Sussman, Gerald. *The Official Sex Manual: A Modern Approach to the Art and Techniques of Coginus.* New York: G.P. Putnam's Sons, 1965. 94p. illus. ISBN U/K. Parody of "plumbing"-style sex manuals, funniest in its mangled Latinesque body parts: "The giselle for instance, which is located between the avus and the splendina, above the vestibule of the frappé, is especially receptive." Bogus illustrations of male and female "generalia" and "erroneous zones."

D85   Thurber, James, & E.B. White. *Is Sex Necessary? Or Why You Feel the Way You Do.* Illus. by James Thurber. New York: Perennial/Harper & Row, 1957. 190p. glossary (5p.). ISBN 6-080344-4. The inimitable humorist James Thurber's classic 1929 spoof on "the deep and lugubrious books on sex and marriage" inspired by the then newly popular Freudianism. A period piece, yet oddly telling for today, especially the chapters "What Should Children Tell Parents?" and "Frigidity in Men."

D86   Velez, Ivan, Jr. *Tales of the Closet*. New York: Hetrick-Martin Institute, 1987–1992. 8 issues to date. ISBN U/K. Serious comic book series about eight gay teenagers going to high school in Queens, New York, and their mutual support through coming out, homophobia, violence, family and personal problems, and love. (G7–12,C,A)

D87   Waller, Reed, & Kate Worley. *The Collected "Omaha" the Cat Dancer*. Princeton, WI: Kitchen Sink Press. Vol. 1, 1987. 128p. ISBN 0-87816-031-0; Vol. 2, 1989. 126p. ISBN 0-87816-049-3; Vol. 3, 1989. 136p. ISBN 0-87816-086-8; Vol. 4, 1990. 128p. ISBN 0-87816–122-8; Vol. 5, 1993. 126p. ISBN 0-87816-257-7. Sexually explicit soap-opera comic with anthropomorphic animals, written for both male and female readers. The strong, believable characters and both the warmth and difficulty of their relationships provide context for the sexual episodes. Heterosexual and homosexual.

LANGUAGE AND SEX

Three major discourses are used for sexual communication: standard, scientific/scholarly, and slang/obscene. Libraries need material about all three.

Standard terms are covered adequately in the major dictionaries, from Webster's Collegiate to the second edition of the *Oxford English Dictionary*. Since the 1970s, the major sexual obscenities like *fuck*, *cunt*, and *prick* have been included as well.

For scientific and scholarly terms, *The Complete Dictionary of Sexology* (D93, Francoeur et al.) is the work of choice for larger public libraries, and *The Language of Sex from A to Z* (D95, Goldenson & Anderson) the choice for smaller public and high school libraries. *The Language of Sex: An A to Z Guide* (D89, Carrera) is particularly suited for young people, with its longer entries and illustrations, although not so comprehensive.

American Sign Language poses special problems, for sex-related signs figure minimally if at all in standard sign-language dictionaries. Both *Signs of Sexual Behavior* (D103, Woodward) and *Signs for Sexuality* (D99, Minkin et al.) are good choices. (Order from the bookstore of Gallaudet University, Washington, DC, which has a catalog service of books about deafness and deaf people.)

Librarians may shy away from material about obscene slang, but that would be a mistake. Whether people use such words or not, they need access to definitions, etymologies, and commentary so that they may understand the speech of others and make informed choices about their own usage. *Dictionary of Sexual Slang* (D101, Richter) should be the standard English reference for most libraries. While containing fewer words, *Wicked Words* (D100, Rawson) covers a broader scope than just sex and is both discursive and fun to read. A specialist dictionary is *The Language of Sadomasochism*, by Thomas E. Murray & Thomas R. Murrell (Greenwood,

1989, not annotated). And the most specialized work of all is *The F-Word*, edited by Jesse Sheidlower (Random House, 1995).

All libraries need guides to sexual slang in the languages of concern to their patrons. Picture the embarrassing mistakes to which language neophytes are prone: *huevos* does not mean merely *eggs* in Spanish, nor does *baiser* mean merely *kiss* in French.[12] *International Dictionary of Obscenities* (D98, Kunitskaya-Peterson) represents the absolute minimum required. The other guides listed below—and others being published as we write— would also be useful and much appreciated in libraries serving high school and college students, other people studying foreign languages, or ethnic subculture groups (D90, D91, D92, D94, D97, D102). Most are quite inexpensive, although sometimes from small publishers and not easy to order through distributors. An interesting guide to sexual language and double entendres in English, written for non-native speakers, is *A Foreign Student's Guide to Dangerous English*, by Elizabeth Claire (Eardley Publications, P.O. Box 281, Rochelle Park, NJ 07662, 1980), not annotated.

Scholarly study of sexual language has persisted at the fringes of academia for decades, and only recently have publishing strictures relaxed enough to permit this area to go mainstream. Allen Walker Read's classic discussion of *fuck* could not mention the actual word itself when it was published in the staid journal *American Speech*.[13] Reflecting the changing times, a tongue-in-cheek classic in "porno- and scatolinguistics" has recently been reprinted by a respectable linguistics publisher. Entitled *Studies Out in Left Field*, it is a bit too technical and specialized for annotation here but a real find for academic libraries with major linguistics collections.[14] Also *de rigueur* for such libraries is the complete run of *Maledicta*, "the international journal of verbal aggression," covering obscenity and taboo expression in all languages and cultures. Yes, the ancient Egyptians had sexual cursing too. Public libraries would do well to acquire *The Best of Maledicta* (D88, Aman)[15] and *Cursing in America* (D96, Jay)—which is somewhat technical but full of interesting data.

Where are the books about lovers' language? Apparently yet to be written, although a few scholarly papers are scattered across various fields. Also still to be written are books about sexual slang and other sexual language (not dictionaries) designed specifically for children or adolescents. The closest we have found is *Elbert's Bad Word*,[16] a charming and useful but oblique tale suggesting socially acceptable alternatives to (presumably obscene) invective—for Elbert's actual word is never given. In the context of that book, the omission is appropriate, so that children can fill in words that they themselves have heard and discuss them with adults. But more could be done here, we think.

Identifying newly published material in this area is not easy. Books from mainstream publishers sometimes reach the standard review media, but the more specialized slang glossaries can be difficult to find. One catalog source is In One EAR (29481 Manzanita Drive, Campo, CA 91906), and one publisher is Scythian Books, Oakland, California. We found several by browsing the foreign language shelves in bookstores.

See also *Dictionary of AIDS Related Terminology* (E90, Huber).

Annotations

D88   Aman, Reinhold, ed. *The Best of Maledicta*. Philadelphia: Running Press, 1987. 200p. index. ISBN 0-89471-499-6. Essays, some scholarly, some informal, about taboo words and expressions in various languages: graffiti, curses, insults, jokes, sexual language, and other offensive speech. Excerpted from *Maledicta, The International Journal of Verbal Aggression*, 1977–1985.

D89   Carrera, Michael A. *The Language of Sex: An A to Z Guide*. New York: Facts On File, 1992. 180p. illus. orgs. (3p.). bibliog. (4p.). index. ISBN 0-8160-2397-2. Some 300 entries for sexuality-related terms, most medical, anatomical, or referring to sexual behavior. No slang. Definitions, some lengthy; cross-references. (G7–12,C,A)

D90   Constantine, Peter. *Japanese Street Slang*. New York: Tengu Books, 1992. 190p. refs. (2p.). index. ISBN 0-8348-0250-3. Definitions and lengthy discussion of contemporary, often taboo, Japanese slang for sexual body parts and acts. Includes social contexts, examples of usage, and some etymologies. Also includes insults and drug slang.

D91   Delicio, Roland. *Merda! The REAL Italian You Were Never Taught in School*. Illus. by Kim Wilson Eversz. New York: Plume/Penguin, 1993. 114p. ISBN 0-452-27039-1. Amusing, explicit guide to Italian slang for sexual body parts, sexual behaviors, and aspects of courtship and romance. Also includes insults, obscenities, and gestures.

D92   Drummond, D.A., & G. Perkins, comps. *Dictionary of Russian Obscenities*. 3rd ed., rev. Oakland, CA: Scythian Books, 1987. 92p. ISBN 0-933884-54-0. English definitions for Russian obscene words and expressions; Russian given in Cyrillic. Covers sexual topics plus insults, expletives, intensifiers, and general vulgar slang.

D93   Francoeur, Robert T., ed. in chief; Martha Cornog, Norman A. Scherzer, & Timothy Perper, co-editors. *The Complete Dictionary of Sexology*. New, expanded ed. New York: Continuum, 1995. 790p. refs. in text. ISBN 0-8264-0672-6. Over 5,000 entries for sexuality-related terms from biology, medicine, psychology, sociology, religion, anthropology, law, and history; no slang. Definitions, some lengthy; references and cross-references; some etymologies. Appendices list philias, paraphilias, phobias, individuals profiled, U.S. Supreme Court decisions, and summarize sexual development.

D94   Geneviève [Geneviève Edis]. *Merde! The REAL French You Were Never Taught at School*. Illus. by Michael Heath. New York: Atheneum, 1986. 102p. ISBN 0-689-11649-7; *Merde Encore!* 1986. 104p. ISBN 0-689-11938-0. Amusing, explicit guides to contemporary French slang for sexual body parts, sexual behaviors, and concepts of courtship and romance. Also insults, obscenities, and irreverent idioms for many other everyday topics.

D95 Goldenson, Robert M., & Kenneth N. Anderson. *The Language of Sex from A to Z*. New York: World Almanac, 1986. 314p. ISBN 0-345-33727-1. Over 5,000 entries for sexuality-related terms from biology, medicine, psychology, sociology, folklore, some slang; plus art, religion, anthropology, literature, and history. Concise definitions and cross-references.

D96 Jay, Timothy. *Cursing in America: A Psycholinguistic Study of Dirty Language in the Courts, in the Movies, in the Schoolyards and on the Streets*. Philadelphia: John Benjamins, 1992. 273p. bibliog. (28p.). index. ISBN 1-55619-452-8. Scholarly, readable analysis of cursing, profanity, blasphemy, and other taboo speech—much with sexual terms/imagery. Summarizes research on frequency, use by different ages and sexes, offensiveness, connection with anger, and censorship.

D97 Kiełbasa, Stanisław. *Dictionary of Polish Obscenities*. 3rd ed. Oakland, CA: Scythian Books, 1994. 93p. ISBN 0-933884-93-1. English definitions for Polish obscene words and expressions. Covers sexual topics plus insults, expletives, intensifiers, and general vulgar slang.

*D98 Kunitskaya-Peterson, Christina. *International Dictionary of Obscenities: A Guide to Dirty Words and Indecent Expressions in Spanish, Italian, French, German, Russian*. Oakland, CA: Scythian Books, 1981. 93p. ISBN 0-933884-18-4. Definitions in literal and colloquial English for core selection of sexual and scatological slang in Spanish, Italian, French, German, and Russian. Russian entries in Cyrillic; pronunciation given in Roman alphabet.

D99 Minkin, Marlyn B., & Laurie E. Rosen-Ritt, with Billy Seago & Irene Peters. *Signs for Sexuality: A Resource Manual for Deaf and Hard of Hearing Individuals, Their Families, and Professionals*. 2nd ed. Seattle, WA: Planned Parenthood of Seattle-King County, 1991. 201p. illus. photos. index. ISBN U/K. Photographs with commentary for 251 sexuality-related signs, which were collected through consulting 120 deaf persons. Covers STDs, sexual abuse, sexual acts, body parts, birth control, and relationships. Includes variants.

D100 Rawson, Hugh. *Wicked Words: A Treasury of Curses, Insults, Put-Downs, and Other Formerly Unprintable Terms from Anglo-Saxon Times to the Present*. New York: Crown, 1989. 435p. sources & methods (2p.). ISBN U/K. Dictionary of nearly 1,000 negatively valued words and expressions, many with sexual meanings. Includes definitions, with linguistic, etymological, and social commentary, plus references to literary and other print sources.

D101 Richter, Alan. *Dictionary of Sexual Slang: Words, Phrases, and Idioms from AC/DC to Zig-zig*. New York: Wiley, 1993. 250p. bibliog. (4p.). ISBN 0-471-54057-9. Definitions for over 4,000 English slang expressions with sexual meaning, from archaic to current and in both U.S. and British Commonwealth countries. Includes etymologies and usage quotations, from Chaucer to Madonna, for many terms.

D102 Robinson, Linton H. *Mexican Slang: A Guide*. Bueno Books/In One EAR Publications (29481 Manzanita Drive, Campo, CA 91906-1128), 1992. 156p. index. ISBN 0-9627080-7-0. Amusing, explicit guide to Mexican Spanish slang for sexual concepts. Also insults and obscenities, plus slang for drugs, alcohol, crime, rock and roll, and "party time."

D103 Woodward, James. *Signs of Sexual Behavior: An Introduction to Some Sex-Related Vocabulary in American Sign Language.* Silver Spring, MD: T.J. Publishers, 1979. 81p. Illus. by Frank Allen Paul. notes (1p.). bibliog. (2p.). index. ISBN 0-932666-02-7. Illustrations and commentary for 131 sexuality-related signs used by deaf people, including body parts, sexual acts, birth control, health, sexual arousal, and relationships. Includes geographic variants and usage notes. Discusses implications for linguistics, anthropology, education, medicine, and law.

LAW AND SEX

Law and religion have always regulated sexual behavior, and at various times and places, the two have coalesced into one force. However, a result of the U.S. constitutional mandate separating church and state is that modern books on the two topics occupy different niches and overlap relatively little—so that "Law and Sex" and "Sex and Religion" are different sections in this book.

Richard Green wrote that "until recently, there was little interest among law students in sexual behavior and the law."[17] He describes how the gay liberation movement of the 1970s, coupled with the emergence of sex research in the late 1940s and its explosion in the 1980s, has "provided the legal profession with material from which to fashion a new subject of jurisprudence." Indeed, all the books in this section are quite recent, with one exception all are by attorneys, and more books address homosexuals and the law than sex law in general.

The most basic reference is *Sexuality and the Law* (D108, Leonard). It is quite comprehensive, reviewing over 100 cases on nine major topics, with commentary for lay readers. *Sexual Science and the Law* (D105, Green) summarizes case law, again for major topics only, with observations about how sexological findings might better inform legal decisions.

Looking at criminal behavior, *Sex Crimes* (D106, Holmes) describes various sex offenses and discusses briefly what is known about these acts and their practitioners. A better title might be "Deviant Sex Acts," for not all behaviors described seem illegal, such as mysophilia (interest in filth, including coprolagnia and urolagnia). Holmes is professor of criminal justice administration and a deputy coroner.

Because books on homosexuals and the law can focus more narrowly, they can be more complete. Those that we reviewed have been produced by dedicated people under the aegis of the gay rights movement. The all-purpose gotta-have pocket-size book is the American Civil Liberties Union's *Rights of Lesbians and Gay Men* (D107, Hunter et al.), in easy-to-read question/answer format with statutes listed in appendices and case law referenced in footnotes. A more discursive treatment is *Lesbians, Gay Men, and the Law* (D110, Rubenstein), which includes statutes, case law, interviews, commentary, and articles reprinted from research, popular, and gay media sources. *A Legal Guide for Lesbian and Gay Couples* (D104, Curry et al.) focuses more specifically on adoption, partnerships, and joint estate planning, among other topics, with sample documents and forms. Some statutes are summarized in state-by-state charts, while case law and statutes are footnoted. A more theoretical approach is taken by *Lesbian (Out)Law* (D109, Robson), not a legal guide, which describes the law in relationship to lesbians.

Coverage of legal matters in the titles we have seen is far from comprehensive. Furthermore, there are too few such books. We look forward to the publication of more comprehensive works on the following:

• History of sex and law.
• Coverage of *all* sexually related state and federal law and case law. For example, the Leonard and Green books do not cover the so-called nuisance offenses like exhibitionism, nor do they cover bestiality, nor do they cover the law relating to sex talk telephone services and obscene phone calls. A new area that must be dealt with in future books is "compusex/cybersex" and the legal, particularly criminal and First Amendment implications of sex-oriented computer bulletin boards and virtual communication.
• Cross-cultural and international studies of sex and the law.

Fortunately for book selection, law-oriented titles by qualified authors—lawyers, legal researchers, and trained academics—are generally handled by standard presses and appear in the usual review media.

The True Colors catalog has a sublist of books addressing legal issues for gay men and lesbians (see the Homosexuality—General Works section in Chapter 10).

See also The Arts and the Media section (Chapter 12) for additional books discussing pornography and the legal concept of obscenity.

Annotations

D104 Curry, Hayden, Denis Cliffort, & Robin Leonard. *A Legal Guide for Lesbian and Gay Couples*. 7th ed. Berkeley, CA: Nolo, 1993. 283p. index. ISBN 0-87337-199-2. "Designed to help lesbian and gay couples understand the laws that affect them and to take charge of the legal aspects of their lives." Covers gay marriage/partnerships, finances, housing, travel, names, parenting, health, estate planning, living together, leaving heterosexual marriage, and finding help. Appendix of sample documents.

D105 Green, Richard. *Sexual Science and the Law*. Cambridge, MA: Harvard University Press, 1992. 323p. notes (43p.). index. ISBN 0-674-80268-3. Summary of U.S. law compared with findings of sex research re fornication, homosexuality, transsexualism, pornography, intergenerational sex, sex education, prostitution, abortion, privacy, sex-linked legal defenses, and surgical/chemical castration of offenders. Highlights questions to be investigated for better legal decision making.

D106 Holmes, Ronald M. *Sex Crimes*. Newbury Park, CA: Sage, 1991. 146p. glossary (14p.). refs. (10p.). index. ISBN 0-8039-2841-6. Examines sex-related offenses and other stigmatized behavior: "nuisance" sex behaviors, sex crimes against children, homosexuality, rape and other dangerous sex crimes, and pornography. Discusses standards for "normal" sexuality and historical perspectives, plus treatment of sex offenders and victim experience.

*D107 Hunter, Nan D., Sherryl E. Michaelson, & Thomas B. Stoddard. *The Rights of Lesbians and Gay Men: The Basic ACLU Guide to a Gay Person's Rights*. 3rd ed. Carbondale, IL: Southern Illinois University Press, 1992. 220p. chapter notes. orgs. (12p.). bibliog. (1p.). ISBN 0-8093-1634-X. Current law pertinent to lesbians/gay men, footnoted to statutes and cases. Covers speech and association, employment, security clearances, armed services, housing and public accommodations, family, criminal law (sodomy, loitering, entrapment, blackmail, anti-gay violence), and AIDS/HIV. Appendix lists state statutes re consensual adult homosexual acts.

D108 Leonard, Arthur S. *Sexuality and the Law: An Encyclopedia of Major Legal Cases*. New York: Garland, 1993. 709p. chapter bibliogs. case refs. table of cases. index. ISBN 0-8240-3421-X. Detailed summaries in lay language for 119 sexuality-related court cases up to 1992, re reproduction, sexual conduct, speech and association (including censorship), the family, discrimination (civilian and military/security), education, immigration/naturalization, and inheritance. Also provides background to U.S. legal procedures and the history of sexuality 1940–1991.

D109 Robson, Ruthann. *Lesbian (Out)law: Survival Under the Rule of Law*. Ithaca, NY: Firebrand, 1992. 185p. chapter notes. ISBN 1-56341-012-5. "How can lesbians use the law without being used by it?" Theoretical discussion of state and federal law vis-à-vis discrimination in employment, the military, and housing; sexuality; child custody; enforced separation from lovers; antilesbian violence; plus effecting legal change. Not a reference or how-to.

D110 Rubenstein, William B. *Lesbians, Gay Men, and the Law*. New York: New Press/Norton, 1993. 569p. ISBN 1-565-84-037-2. Comprehensive anthology of readings and case law pertaining to homosexuals vis-à-vis legal issues: sexual acts, speech and assembly, workplace related matters (including military), relationships, and parenting.

LIBRARIES AND SEX: BOOKS FOR AND ABOUT LIBRARIANS

Books about sex and libraries are not exactly a glut on the market. We were able to identify only five reasonably current exemplars, plus an older work that we believe is still relevant. Four provide guidance or background about issues, and two survey librarians' attitudes. Also included here are seven bibliographies and guides to sexuality sources.

We strongly urge that all public, school, and academic librarians buy and read three works on library service in relation to sex: *Libraries, Erotica, & Pornography* (D115, Cornog), *Gay and Lesbian Library Service* (D118, Gough & Greenblatt), and *AIDS and HIV Programs and Services for Libraries* (D121, Lukenbill). All provide excellent, in-depth treatment of their topics, and all complement *this* book, which deals more with selection and purchasing. A related work is *Sex Magazines in the Library Collection* (D117, Gellatly). The essays in this Gellatly collection, 15 years old but still current today, are a snapshot of librarians' reactions to sexuality materials. They vary in usefulness, quality, and tone from snide to scholarly. The collection also contains Sanford Berman's classic essay, "If There Were a *Sex Index* . . ."

Two book-length reports from surveys deal with librarians' attitudes about sex. *Sex and the Undecided Librarian: A Study of Librarians' Opinions on Sexually Oriented Literature*, by Michael Pope (Scarecrow Press, 1974), out of print and not annotated, summarizes reactions of school, college, and public librarians to the possibility of purchasing particular types of hypothetical sex books. For all categories, school librarians were the least likely to purchase and college librarians the most likely, with public librarians in between. For nearly all categories, female librarians were less likely to purchase than male. It would be an intriguing research project to replicate this study in the 1990s and compare results. By contrast, *The Young Adult Librarian's Knowledge of and Attitudes About Sex* (D122, Steinfirst) is the closest the library profession has to its very own Kinsey report.[18] Librarian readers might want to compare their sexual knowledge and attitudes with their peers'.

Some—too few—books provide help to librarians and patrons for finding sexuality materials. The most recent and most significant is *A Research Guide to Human Sexuality* (D120, Lichtenberg), a must-buy for public and academic libraries. Although apparently designed for academic researchers, it is nonetheless fully accessible and highly useful for librarians, educators, clinicians, students, and the general public. It addresses types of research sources and techniques, and also contains titles of key sources.

A bibliography of considerable importance for academic and larger public libraries is *Studies in Human Sexuality* (D116, Frayser & Whitby), which provides lengthy annotations of 1,091 titles. For public and school libraries, two must-buys are *Comprehensive Bibliography for Sex, Health & Family Education* (D112, Charlton) and *Free or Inexpensive Sources for Sex, Health & Family Education* (D113, Charlton). The first is an age-graded list of books for young people and those who teach them, organized by subject and with publishers' addresses (but no annotations). The second is an indispensable guide to acquiring vertical file materials on sexuality (see Chapter 6).

Three rather more specialized works are helpful for book selection in school and public libraries. *Sex Guides* (D111, Campbell) gives the history of the "teen sex manual" and reviews modern exemplars up through 1985. *Out of the Closet and into the Classroom: Homosexuality in Books for Young People* (D114, Clyde & Lobban) treats in a similar manner homosexuality in books written for children and young adults. Both provide background to help librarians select new titles. *AIDS Information Resources for People with Disabilities* (D119, Klauber) covers an overlooked area. It is a bibliography with source addresses, permitting librarians to use it for obtaining updated lists of materials.

Books about sex and librarianship are rare but generally reviewed in the library literature. For more information about sexuality bibliographies, see *A Research Guide to Human Sexuality* (D120, Lichtenberg), Chapter 10; the Bibliographies section in *Studies in Human Sexuality* (D116, Frayser & Whitby); and the Bibliographies section in *Free or Inexpensive Sources for Sex, Health & Family Education* (D113, Charlton). See also Chapter 5 and each individual subject section of Part II of this book.

Annotations

*D111   Campbell, Patty. *Sex Guides: Books and Films About Sexuality for Young Adults*. New York: Garland, 1986. 374p. index. ISBN 0-8240-8693-7. History and analysis of "teen sex manuals" since 1892. Reviews and compares all teen sex education books 1977–1985, including fiction and religious perspectives, plus books on STDs and teen pregnancy.

*D112   Charlton, Michele D. Martin. *Comprehensive Bibliography for Sex, Health & Family Education*. Osceola, IN: Teaching Sex Education Inc. (P.O Box 128, Osceola, IN 46561), 1993. 225p. ISBN U/K. Bibliography of about 2,500 publications, mostly books, most published after 1988. Organized by topic and audience (grades K–3, grades 4–6, grades 10–12, teachers, parents). No annotations; cross-references. Covers AIDS and STDs, birth control, child development, homosexuality/bisexuality, parenting, physiology/biology, psychological aspects, reproduction, sex education, sex roles, and sexual abuse. Some material on other topics, including religion. Publishers' addresses provided.

*D113   Charlton, Michele D. Martin. *Free or Inexpensive Sources for Sex, Health & Family Education*. Osceola, IN: Teaching Sex Education (P.O. Box 128, Osceola, IN 46561-0128), 1993. 165p. ISBN U/K. Extensive list of sex education and related pamphlets and brochures, mostly free/inexpensive. Arranged by topic, *Abortion* to *Teens—Life Planning*. Also lists charts/visual aids, bibliographies, telephone hotlines, agencies/support groups, and video sources. Conservative/religious viewpoints not covered. Source addresses provided. Highly useful for library vertical file acquisitions.

D114   Clyde, Laurel A., & Marjorie Lobban. *Out of the Closet and into the Classroom: Homosexuality in Books for Young People*. Deakin, Australia: ALIA Press/ Port Melbourne, Australia: Thorpe/Reed Ref. Pub., 1992. 150p. indexes. ISBN 1-875589-02-3. Annotated bibliography of 126 books for children and adolescents with homosexual characters or themes, mostly published 1947 (*Diary of Anne Frank*) to 1991 (*Gloria Goes to Gay Pride* and others). Introduction provides background about homosexuality book publishing in children's literature.

*D115   Cornog, Martha, ed. *Libraries, Erotica, & Pornography*. Phoenix: Oryx, 1991. 314p. chapter refs. index. ISBN 0-89774-474-8. Addresses library treatment of sexuality; meanings of "pornography" and "erotica"; feminist issues; Library of Congress *Playboy*-in-Braille case; *Playboy* in public libraries; and cataloging/access tips. Lists of erotica and homosexuality research collections; bibliographies of erotica, X-rated videotapes, and nonfiction about sexuality.

*D116   Frayser, Suzanne G., & Thomas J. Whitby. *Studies in Human Sexuality: A Selected Guide*. 2nd ed. Littleton, CO: Libraries Unlimited, 1995. 737p. index. ISBN 0-56308-131-8. Bibliography with lengthy annotations of 1,091 nonfiction, mostly adult books about sexuality, many scholarly or semi-scholarly. Purpose: "to provide a selection of highly influential and informative sex books of our times and to prepare informative abstracts of those books in an unbiased manner." Covers all topics, including cross-cultural studies.

D117   Gellatly, Peter, ed. *Sex Magazines in the Library Collection: A Scholarly Study of Sex in Serials and Periodicals*. New York: Haworth, 1981. 142p. chapter refs. index. ISBN 0-917724-16-X. Eleven essays on sexuality materials in the library, varying in approach and style: snideness, scholarly professionalism, progressivism. Topics: pornography in classical antiquity, content analysis of popular sex magazines, problems and treatment of sex magazines in libraries, legal issues, scholarly sexological serials, gay/lesbian periodicals, and indexing.

*D118   Gough, Cal, & Ellen Greenblatt, eds. *Gay and Lesbian Library Service*. Fwd. by Sanford Berman. Jefferson, NC: McFarland, 1990. 355p. index. ISBN 0-89950-535-X. Guidelines and resources for all aspects of acquisitions and services to serve gay/lesbian readers, in school, public, and academic libraries. Covers special collections, cataloging, and reference service. Many bibliographies/resource lists, e.g., nonfiction, films, music, publishers, bookstores, plus two bibliographies on AIDS.

D119   Klauber, Julie. *AIDS Information Resources for People with Disabilities: A Handbook for Information Providers in Libraries, AIDS Organizations, and Disability Organizations*. Bellport, NY: Talking Books Plus (Suffolk County Cooperative Library System, 627 North Sunrise Service Road, Bellport, NY 11713), 1993. 73p. pubs. directory (5p.). ISBN U/K. Annotates AIDS books and other resources for different disabilities. Organized by disability; each section with introduction to special needs of people with that disability, resources for consumers, and resources for professionals.

*D120   Lichtenberg, Kara Ellynn. *A Research Guide to Human Sexuality*. New York: Garland, 1994. 497p. sources (2p.). index. ISBN 0-8153-0867-1. Comprehensive manual for researching sexuality topics. Lists and provides how-tos for identifying/accessing libraries, reference works, thesauri, dictionaries, literature reviews, textbooks, library catalogs and classifications, bibliographies, databases, indexes and abstracts, periodicals, book dealers, publishers, dissertations, government documents, meetings, statistics and surveys, curricula, measurement tools and data sets, nonprint media, experts, and organizations. Subdivided by topic. Appendix: Library of Congress Subject Headings and schedules pertaining to sexuality.

*D121 Lukenbill, W. Bernard. *AIDS and HIV Programs and Services for Libraries*. Englewood, CO: Libraries Unlimited, 1994. 262p. chapter notes. index. ISBN 1-56308-175-X. Practical suggestions for programs relating to HIV/AIDS, appropriate for school, public, and academic libraries in providing services in consumer health, community education, and related areas. Includes background information, models for action, and program profiles.

D122 Steinfirst, Susan. *The Young Adult Librarian's Knowledge of and Attitudes About Sex*. Metuchen, NJ: Scarecrow, 1989. 49p. notes (2p.). ISBN 0-8108-2185-0. Results of questionnaire study of 391 young adult librarians about sexual knowledge, attitudes, and experience. Most were moderate to slightly liberal in attitudes, were somewhat comfortable with recognizing and rejecting misconceptions about sex, and felt that libraries should circulate sex education materials and information.

SEX AND RELIGION

> Overall, religious publishing is enjoying new impetus outside the narrow areas of prayer and self-help. Various currents to watch for in the near future include studies in aging and caretaking, and sexuality and the church.[19]

We believe that librarians have not collected adequately or broadly enough in sex and religion. As a remedy, we describe a goodly number of books taking a variety of viewpoints.

Will people read these books? Yes. First, most Americans identify with a denomination and attend church.[20] Second, the major issues for religion in the 1990s are sexual issues, especially for Christian denominations. Abortion, teenage sexuality, adultery, sexual abuse, homosexuality, pornography, premarital sex, and marital sex are all hotly debated in congregations, pulpits, study groups, Sunday school classes, and denominational publications, and on front porches across the United States. Third, all religions have concerned themselves with sexuality; and whether we consider ourselves "religious" or not, doctrinal traditions across centuries and cultures inform our modern sexual behavior and attitudes.

We also know that there are readers for these books because so many new ones are being published. The Christian sex book boom is real, though perhaps little noted outside the tight-knit circle of religious publishers and booksellers. About 250 books are listed in *Subject Guide to Books in Print* under SEX—RELIGIOUS ASPECTS, SEX IN THE BIBLE, CLERGY—SEXUAL BEHAVIOR, HOMOSEXUALITY—RELIGIOUS ASPECTS, and CELIBACY, and many more are doubtless hidden under such headings as

SEX INSTRUCTION. Religious publishers may be motivated by goals other than money, but few are supported by subsidies or charity. These books must be selling.

A basic collection for reference, although fast becoming dated, is the series *The Churches Speak On . . .* from Gale Research. Volumes on AIDS, abortion, homosexuality, pornography, and sex and family life have appeared. Each volume collects official statements from many religious bodies and ecumenical organizations, and we hope updates have been planned.

A good selection is available for historical and general works. *Sacred Sexuality* (D130, Feuerstein) traces the history of erotic spirituality across history and religious groups, while *Sacred Sex* (D123, Bates) provides texts from some of these erotic traditions. A fascinating, almost matched pair of books are *Innocent Ecstasy* (D133, Gardella) and *The Poisoning of Eros* (D138, Lawrence). The first holds Christianity responsible for the modern pro-sex ethic, while the second holds Christianity responsible for the worst of our sex-negative heritage. A historical account of three Christian sects with alternative approaches to sexuality is provided in *Religion and Sexuality: The Shakers, the Mormons, and the Oneida Community* (D132, Foster).

Our remaining titles deal with modern sexual issues. Usually they offer the reader information and guidance about ethical and spiritual resolution. All are written from one or another sectarian viewpoint, falling loosely into conservative-orthodox or liberal-permissive camps. A middle ground exemplar is the Jewish *Does God Belong in the Bedroom?* (D134, Gold). We found few books on sexuality from a Jewish perspective; another is *Eros and the Jews* (D124, Biale), a history of Jewish sexual attitudes and traditions.[21]

As for general Christian (largely Protestant) books, liberal authors see sexuality in modern life as representing areas of challenge and revelation for the church, whereby the "old rules" require re-understanding and re-interpretation to maintain adherence to basic Christian principles. The approach is to seek God's will afresh in the face of changing historical circumstances—*rebuilding* the church. Liberal Christian books are processual attempts to walk new paths with God. On the other hand, conservative books see recent sexual trends as evidence of people's departure from God's unchanging will, and their approach is to *defend* the church against evil and chaos. Conservative Christian books are absolutist attempts to remain on the right path, changing historical circumstances or not.[22]

Of liberal-tending approaches, a good sampling is included in the anthology *Sexuality and the Sacred* (D141, Nelson & Longfellow). The excellent *Dirt Greed and Sex* (D127, Countryman) sets New Testament references to sexuality in historical and Christian context, and advocates returning to ethical principles as propounded in the Gospels by Christ Him-

self, rather than relying on the Old Testament or the later Christian interpretations. *Between the Sexes* (D125, Cahill) attempts to synthesize
common principles of Christian sexual ethics from diverse sources. The
remaining books all try to reintegrate sexuality into Christianity, almost as
a healing of something that was once sundered: *Sex for Christians* (D143,
Smedes), *Embodiment* (D140, Nelson), *The Christian Response to the Sexual Revolution* (D139, Mace), and *Living in Sin?* (D144, Spong). Several
propose "best" or "most ethical" compromise courses of conduct for sexual
circumstances that seem different today than from the past.

Of the conservative books, we recommend most highly *Sexual Chaos*
(D145, Stafford), which enumerates failures of the modern "ethic of sexual
intimacy" and proposes instead Christian-based commitment to people,
ideas, and work. A somewhat similar message is presented in *A Generation
Betrayed* (D137, Kirk), with lesser mention of Christianity. Both books
urge readers to involve themselves in ministry and activism towards reforming sexual conduct, sex education, and media influences. A far more
theological and spiritual approach towards healing "distorted sexuality" is
found in *Eros Redeemed* (D148, White). A very personal book is *Passion
and Purity* (D129, Elliot), which intersperses accounts of the author's own
chaste courtship with advice about remaining true to Christian teachings
about sexual abstinence until marriage.

Conservative Roman Catholic writing tends to be more concerned with
individual and collective spiritual health ("sin") and less concerned with
the socially bad effects from sexual transgression. *Human Sexuality: A
Catholic Perspective for Education and Lifelong Learning* (D146, U.S.
Catholic Conference) is a basic work describing official (magisterial) Roman Catholic positions on all matters of sexuality. Two other books discuss
at more length the sanctioned Roman Catholic conception of marriage: *Sex
and the Marriage Covenant* (D136, Kippley) and—more briefly—*Intimate
Bedfellows* (D131, Finn & Finn). On the liberal end, three additional works
are less constrained by magisterial Roman Catholicism as represented by
pronouncements of the curia. *Dialogue About Catholic Sexual Teaching*
(D128, Curran & McCormick) is an anthology of both doctrine and dis-
sent. *A Secret World* (D142, Sipe) looks at priestly celibacy and sexual
behavior, the latter a reality despite doctrine. *Sex: The Catholic Experience*
(D135, Greeley) analyzes data about sexual lives of lay Roman Catholics,
revealing points of congruence and difference with the church teachings
and drawing comparisons with Jews and other Christians. Finally, two
works on be-vowed celibacy take different views. *Being Sexual . . . and
Celibate* (D126, Clark) explores dilemmas and gifts revealed during many
years of monastic celibacy, and contains much useful guidance for celibates,
both laypeople and those under religious orders. On the other side, *Celibacy: Gift or Law?* (D147, Vogels) challenges the Roman Catholic doctrine
of celibacy for priests on historical and Biblical bases. See also *Mandatory*

Celibacy in the Catholic Church: A Handbook for the Laity, by Michele Prince (New Paradigm, 1992, not annotated).

Some books deal with sex and gender issues in religious contexts, including *Her Share of the Blessings: Women's Religions Among Pagans, Jews, and Christians in the Greco-Roman World*, by Ross Shepard Kraemer (Oxford, 1992), *Mary Magdalen: Myth and Metaphor*, by Susan Haskins (Harcourt, 1994), and *God's Phallus: And Other Problems for Men and Monotheism*, by Howard Eilberg-Schwartz (Beacon, 1994), none annotated. A number of works by women writers (Mary Daly, Susan Griffith, and others) are efforts to recreate a non-patriarchal "womyn's" religion, but few deal primarily with sexuality. They deserve their own treatment in another book.

Within our time limit, we were unable to locate books about sex in Islam or Eastern traditions other than those described in the History and Culture section, above.

A few religious books about sex are reviewed in the library literature. Most are not. The only ongoing bibliographies that we know of are those of SIECUS: Current Religious Perspectives on Sexuality, and Sexuality Education Resources for Religious Denominations. However, these tend not to cover many of the conservative materials. Unfortunately, the resource lists from Focus on the Family are rather sparse. (See Chapter 5.)

The only thorough approach to acquisitions in this area is to tap booksellers' trade sources, such as *Bookstore Journal*, from the Christian Booksellers Association (CBA, P.O. Box 200, Colorado Springs, CO 80901) and the catalogs of Christian Book Distributors (P.O. Box 7000, Peabody, MA 01961-7000). But there is no substitute for perusing publishers' catalogs, particularly those of Abingdon Press, Augsburg Fortress, Baker Book House, InterVarsity Press, NavPress, Paulist Press, Pilgrim Press, Westminster/John Knox, and Word.

Two other catalog sources are the Couple to Couple League: conservative Christian/Catholic, favoring natural family planning but covering other sexual issues (P.O. Box 111184, Cincinnati, OH 45211-9985); and Regeneration Books: conservative views on homosexuality and other issues, mostly Protestant (P.O. Box 9830, Baltimore, MD 21284-9830). Libraries can also get acquainted with local religious bookstores, even setting up a store account.[23]

Generally, coverage of Protestant materials is adequate, but coverage of Catholic materials is spotty.[24] Librarians should solicit patron requests from all viewpoints, especially for religion/sex titles. A recent letter to *Focus on the Family* magazine suggested to readers:

Many public libraries allocate funds to purchase new books and videos. In the absence of individual requests, the library will choose what materials to order. So why not request more Christian and *wholesome* secular books and videos for our libraries? But don't be overzealous and try to order lots of books at one time. When you call your librarian to make a request, have the book's author and publisher's information in hand. Keep in mind that you may also purchase books and videos and donate them to your library.[25]

A personalized form letter from the library to community groups and churches can help start such requests coming.

See also books from religious perspectives in many other sections, listed in the index.

Annotations

D123   Bates, Robert. *Sacred Sex: Erotic Writings from the Religions of the World.* London: Fount/Harper Collins, 1993. 282p. bibliog. (2p.). ISBN 0-00-627686-5. Anthology of texts from various religious traditions, celebrating sexuality: Hinduism, Buddhism, Taoism, Grecian and Roman mythology, Judaism, Christianity, Islam, and tribal religions.

D124   Biale, David. *Eros and the Jews: From Biblical Israel to Contemporary America.* New York: Basic Books, 1992. 319p. notes (63p.). bibliog. (4p.). index. ISBN 0-465-02033-X. History of sexual attitudes, customs, and behavior in Judaism as reflected in texts, from the Bible to Woody Allen and *Portnoy's Complaint.* Jewish sexual culture is described as complex, subject to much religious debate, and influenced by conflict in asceticism vs. gratification, procreation vs. pleasure.

D125   Cahill, Lisa Sowle. *Between the Sexes: Foundation for a Christian Ethics of Sexuality.* Philadelphia: Fortress, 1985. 166p. bibliog. (5p.). index. ISBN 0-8006-1834-3. Rather technical analysis of some major Christian writings (the Bible, Thomas Aquinas, Martin Luther) with respect to sexuality and ethics. Postulates four reference points for Christian ethics: the Bible, "tradition," philosophical accounts of "ideal" humanity, and empirical data about humans. Proposes two criteria as basic to Christians: commitment and procreative responsibility.

*D126   Clark, Keith, Capuchin, *Being Sexual . . . and Celibate.* Notre Dame, IN: Ave Maria, 1986. 182p. ISBN 0-87793-329-4. Thoughtful, personal discussion of experiencing one's own sexuality while maintaining commitment to celibacy. Stresses meeting needs for emotional intimacy with other people and with God as necessary for remaining celibate. Roman Catholic. For both clergy/religious and laypeople choosing celibacy.

*D127   Countryman, L. William. *Dirt Greed and Sex: Sexual Ethics in the New Testament and Their Implications for Today.* Philadelphia: Fortress, 1988. 290p. bibliog. (5p.). index. ISBN 0-8006-2476-9. Analysis of Old Testament sexual ethics as based upon principles of purity and property, the setting aside of these principles by the Gospels, and their subsequent re-establishment by post-Gospel writers and the later Christian church. Interprets and applies the Gospel to sexual ethics today.

*D128   Curran, Charles E., & Richard A. McCormick, eds. *Dialogue About Catholic Sexual Teaching.* New York: Paulist Press, 1993. 601p. chapter refs. ISBN 0-8091-3414-4. Documents and readings summarizing historical and contemporary

Roman Catholic doctrine on sexual matters. Includes dissenting interpretations and divergent responses to these doctrines from within the church. Addresses general sexual ethics, parenthood, contraception, sterilization, artificial insemination, in-vitro fertilization, homosexuality, masturbation, chastity, and extramarital sexuality.

D129   Elliot, Elisabeth. *Passion and Purity: Learning to Bring Your Love Life Under Christ's Control.* Grand Rapids, MI: Fleming H. Revell/Baker Book House, 1984. 192p. notes (4p.). ISBN 0-8007-5137-X. Intersperses Christian-based advice for courting couples—especially women—about remaining sexually abstinent until marriage with account of author's own five-year chaste courtship with Jim Elliot.

D130   Feuerstein, Georg. *Sacred Sexuality: Living the Vision of the Erotic Spirit.* New York: Tarcher/Perigee, 1993. 239p. notes (13p.). recommended reading (4p.). index. ISBN 0-87477-744-5. Surveys sacred sex and erotic spirituality throughout history in various religious traditions: Christianity, Judaism, goddess worship, Taoism, and Hinduism. Addresses the challenge of sacred sex today.

D131   Finn, Thomas, & Donna Finn. *Intimate Bedfellows: Love, Sex, and the Catholic Church.* Boston: St. Paul Books & Media, 1993. 85p. further reading (2p.). notes (3p.). ISBN 0-8198-3667-2. Concise, simple description of Roman Catholic teachings on premarital sex, cohabitation, contraception, and natural family planning. For heterosexual couples. No mention of masturbation or homosexuality.

D132   Foster, Lawrence. *Religion and Sexuality: The Shakers, the Mormons, and the Oneida Community.* Urbana: University of Illinois Press, 1984. 363p. notes (83p.). sources (12p.). index. ISBN 0-252-01119-8. History of three controversial religious groups that embraced alternative models of sexuality/marriage/family: the Shakers (celibacy), the Oneida Perfectionists (group marriage), and the Mormons (polygyny).

*D133   Gardella, Peter. *Innocent Ecstasy: How Christianity Gave America an Ethic of Sexual Pleasure.* New York: Oxford University Press, 1985. 202p. illus. notes (23p.). bibliog. (8p.). index. ISBN 0-19-503612-3. History of "how Christian influences, working through popular culture, led Americans to seek ecstatic pleasure and to expect freedom from guilt in their sexual relations." Covers 18th century Catholic writings, Protestant-based medicine, evangelical movements, Bernadette of Lourdes and the Virgin Mary, and the pro-sexuality of the early proponents of birth control and modern sexology.

D134   Gold, Michael. *Does God Belong in the Bedroom?* Philadelphia: Jewish Publication Society, 1992. 215p. notes (12p.). glossary (2p.). bibliog. (2p.). index. ISBN 0-8276-0421-1. Analyzes Jewish scriptures and law relating to sexual issues and proposes modern approach to sexual ethics for Jews. Covers rape and incest, adultery, nonmarital sex, marital sex, birth control and reproductive technologies, abortion, homosexuality, prostitution, pornography, and sex education.

D135   Greeley, Andrew. *Sex: The Catholic Experience.* Allen, TX: Thomas More/ Tabor, 1994. 167p. notes (5p.). ISBN 0-88347-285-6. Results of two surveys of 1,300 and 4,400 people, plus other surveys, analyzed for data about religion and sexual behaviors, attitudes, and satisfaction. Finds married and single Roman Catholics have more frequent and more playful sex than non-Catholics, and are generally accepting of birth control and premarital sex.

D136 Kippley, John F. *Sex and the Marriage Covenant: A Basis for Morality*. Cincinnati: Couple to Couple League (P.O. Box 111184, Cincinnati, OH 45211), 1991. 356p. refs. (10p.). index. ISBN 0-9601036-9-4. Discussion of thesis that God intends sexual intercourse as a renewal of the marriage covenant, and that this provides criterion to evaluate the morality of sexual acts. Roman Catholic. Covers sex and contraception inside and outside marriage, contexts for controversy, and Biblical bases. Moderately technical.

D137 Kirk, Randy. *A Generation Betrayed: It's Time to Stop the Sexual Revolution*. Lafayette, LA: Huntington House, 1993. 203p. bibliog. (1p.). ISBN 1-56384-054-5. Describes negative social effects of "sexual freedom": promiscuity, drug use, broken families, abortion, misery, disease; and calls upon Christians to maintain sexual morality in their lives and to work for sociosexual change against "illicit, promiscuous, and dangerous" sexual behaviors and their promotion through the media and sex education.

*D138 Lawrence, Raymond J., Jr. *The Poisoning of Eros: Sexual Values in Conflict*. New York: Augustine Moore, 1989. 292p. footnotes. index. ISBN 0-9623310-0-7. Describes how sex-positive traditions of early Hebrews, continued by Jesus, as revealed by the Old Testament and the Gospels, were gradually reversed into a sex-negative position by the early Christian church, which drew upon the Greco-Roman and Platonic mind/body dualism.

D139 Mace, David R. *The Christian Response to the Sexual Revolution*. Updated ed. Nashville, TN: Abingdon, 1970. 112p. notes (2p.). ISBN 0-687-07570-X. Describes basically sex-positive nature of Hebrews and the Old Testament, and sex-negative views within the early Christian church. Calls upon Christians to repudiate anti-sex authoritarianism, take a positive approach to sex, and open discussion towards finding positive Christian values and meanings for sex, bringing religion and sex together.

D140 Nelson, James B. *Embodiment: An Approach to Sexuality and Christian Theology*. Minneapolis: Augsburg, 1978. 302p. notes (21p.). index. ISBN 0-8066-1701-2. Thoughtful, discursive discussion of theologically realized sexual ethics, to produce a Christian sexual theology based upon the spiritual integration of the body. Addresses healing of mind-body dualism through grace, love and sexual ethics, marriage and fidelity, sexual variations, homosexuality, the "sexually disenfranchised" (disabled, aged, ill, mentally retarded), and the church as a sexual community. Takes flexible, processual viewpoint.

D141 Nelson, James B., & Sandra P. Longfellow. *Sexuality and the Sacred: Sources for Theological Reflection*. Louisville, KY: Westminster/John Knox, 1994. 406p. chapter notes. ISBN 0-664-25529-9. "The authors address what our sexual experience reveals about God, the ways we understand the gospel, and the ways we read scripture and attempt to live faithfully." Liberal Protestant perspective. Topics: sources for sexual ethics, sexuality and spirituality, gender, homosexuality, singlehood, marriage, celibacy, aging, disability, HIV/AIDS, sexual violence, and pornography.

D142 Sipe, A.W. Richard. *A Secret World: Sexuality and the Search for Celibacy*.

Fwd. by Robert Coles. New York: Brunner/Mazel, 1990. 324p. refs. (12p.). additional readings (2p.). index. ISBN 0-87630-585-0. Results of study about the sexuality of Roman Catholic priests, using reports and interviews from about 1,000 priests and 500 other people, collected over 25 years. Respectful and compassionate description of sexual behavior (hetero/homosexuality, masturbation, pedophilia), origin and background of celibacy, and the functions and future of celibacy in the Roman Catholic Church.

D143 Smedes, Lewis B. *Sex for Christians: The Limits and Liberties of Sexual Living*. Rev. ed. Grand Rapids, MI: William B. Eerdmans, 1994. 244p. ISBN 0-8028-0743-7. "Guide for people who are groping their way into a liberated *and* Christian experience of sexuality," letting "compassion be the cutting edge of morality." Covers the goodness, distortions, and potential of human sexuality; and specific sexual behaviors: intercourse, masturbation, homosexuality, petting, marriage, and adultery. Generally permissive within traditional viewpoint. Supports both "moral sex" and safe sex.

D144 Spong, John Shelby. *Living in Sin? A Bishop Rethinks Human Sexuality*. San Francisco: Harper San Francisco, 1990. 156p. bibliog. (4p.). index. ISBN 0-06-067507-1. Liberal Christian proposal for "a new and rigorous [sexual] morality inside a set of parameters different from those of the past," based upon scripture, history, and modern realities. Addresses divorce, homosexuality, marriage and celibacy, singlehood and sex, and women in the (Episcopal) church.

*D145 Stafford, Tim. *Sexual Chaos: Charting a Course Through Turbulent Times*. Downers Grove, IL: InterVarsity, 1993. 173p. notes (4p.). bibliog. (3p.). ISBN 0-8308-1349-7. (Rev. ed. of *The Sexual Christian*.) Analyzes weaknesses of current marriage and sexual structure, and the accompanying ill effects of divorce, child neglect, STDs, and unhappiness. Describes the modern "ethic of intimacy" and its failure. Proposes that Christians form new "sexual counterculture" based upon strengthened monogamous marriage and celibate singlehood. Advises control of sex through greater desire for commitment to a person, an ideal, or a task/work. Urges strong program of Christian sex education.

D146 U.S. Catholic Conference. *Human Sexuality: A Catholic Perspective for Education and Lifelong Learning*. Washington, DC: U.S. Catholic Conference, 1991. 121p. bibliog. (5p.). ISBN 1-55586-405-8. Overview of Judeo-Christian perspective on human sexuality and spiritual wholeness, plus Roman Catholic principles and values in general and pertaining to particular situations and behaviors: marriage, parenthood, homosexuality, celibacy, masturbation, pornography, sexual abuse, and HIV/AIDS. Includes recommendations for sex education at various ages.

D147 Vogels, Heinz-J. *Celibacy: Gift or Law? A Critical Investigation*. Trans. from the German. Kansas City, MO: Sheed & Ward, 1993. 138p. footnotes. bibliog. (6p.). ISBN 1-55612-653-0. Somewhat technical discussion challenging the Roman Catholic doctrine of celibacy for priests, based upon detailed readings and interpretation of Biblical passages and examination of church history and documents.

D148 White, John. *Eros Redeemed: Breaking the Stranglehold of Sexual Sin*. Downers Grove, IL: InterVarsity, 1993. 285p. notes (9p.). orgs. (2p.). further reading (2p.). ISBN 0-8308-1697-6. Describes spiritual roots of sexual sin, Biblical background, and historical relationship between sex and violence and its consequences. Addresses the interaction of science and scripture about gender and sex, and redemption from distorted sexuality. Conservative Christian perspective.

NOTES

1. *Erotic Movies* (D33, Wortley): 10.

2. Recent dictionary definitions characterize pornography as intending to provoke or actually provoking sexual arousal, and erotica as representing or evoking sexuality. Popular and public usage adds the value overtones that pornography is "bad" (exploitative, ugly, unaesthetic, addictive, corrupting) and erotica is "good" (fine art, aesthetic, depictions of love, egalitarian). See Martha Cornog & Timothy Perper, "Words, Libraries, and Meaning," in *Libraries, Erotica, & Pornography* (D115, Cornog): Chapter 3.

3. Some titles in this vein: *Shakespeare's Bawdy*, by Eric Partridge (Routledge & Kegan Paul, 1968), *Chaucer's Bawdy*, by Thomas W. Ross (Dutton, 1972), *Sex and Marriage in Victorian Poetry*, by Wendell S. Johnson (Cornell University Press, 1975), and *The Garden of Priapus: Sexuality and Aggression in Roman Humor*, by Amy Richlin (Oxford University Press, 1992). Regarding homosexuality in literature, a recent reference work with biographical, bibliographical, and critical information on gay and lesbian authors is *Gay and Lesbian Literature*, edited by Sharon Malinowski and Malcolm Boyd (St. James Press/Gale, 1993), also available abridged as *The Gay and Lesbian Literary Companion* (Visible Ink Press/Gale, 1994). Others include, e.g., *Sex Variant Women in Literature*, by Jeanettte H. Foster (Diana Press, 1956/1975), *The Homosexual Tradition in American Poetry*, by Robert K. Martin (University of Texas Press, 1979), and *Acting Gay: Male Homosexuality in Modern Drama*, by John M. Clum (Columbia University Press, 1994).

4. This section covers heterosexual courtship. Gay/lesbian courtship is covered in Chapter 10. See the Homosexuality—General Works, Homosexuality—Coming Out, and Homosexuality—Couples and Mateships sections in Chapter 10.

5. Librarians buying or owning *The Art of Love* should check for expurgations. In Stravon Publishers' 1949 edition, the end of Book Three is rendered only in Latin—that section advises women how to assume flattering postures during sexual activities and how to fake orgasm if necessary to keep their lovers' affection.

6. *Work Hard and You Shall Be Rewarded: Urban Folklore from the Paperwork Empire* (Indiana University Press, 1975); *When You're Up to Your Ass in Alligators: More Urban Folklore from the Paperwork Empire* (Wayne State University Press, 1987); and *Never Try to Teach a Pig to Sing: Still More Urban Folklore from the Paperwork Empire* (Wayne State University Press, 1991). These plus similar works attest to the popularity of the genre.

7. Notable examples are two collections authored by Isaac Asimov and John Ciardi, literary giants at play: *Limericks, Too Gross* (Norton, 1978) and *A Grossery of Limericks* (Norton, 1981). We also cite the delightful *Limericks Historical and Hysterical*, "plagiarized, arranged, annotated, and some written by" historian Ray Allen Billington (Norton, 1981). Its truly incredible index should win the H.W. Wilson indexing award, but of course never will.

8. Legman describes the *Immortalia* collection in *The Horn Book* (D52): 394.

9. We know you want an example of the technical literature, so here it is: Vinson H. Sutlive, Jr., editor, *Female and Male in Borneo: Contributions and Challenges to Gender Studies*, Borneo Research Council Monograph Series, Volume I (Borneo Research Council, Department of Anthropology, College of William and Mary, 1991). It contains 16 essays with topics ranging from penis pins to cosmology about babies, and is a valuable specialist's book. But it *is* a specialist's book.

10. Serious examination of prostitution began in 1769 in France with Nicholas Edme Restif de la Bretonne's *Le Pornographe* (*The Secret Museum*, D11, Kendrick: 19–20). The pioneer work of social science sex research is reported to be the investigation by Jean Baptiste Parent-Duchâtelet, published in 1836 as *De la Prostitution dans la ville de Paris* (*Science in the Bedroom*, D60, Bullough: 31).

11. One could conjecture that cartoonist Mike Diana has followed in Wilson's tradition, although Diana's somewhat primitive drawing style is almost cute, while Wilson's is both artistically skilled and lyrically vicious. Diana was convicted on March 27, 1994, in Florida on the grounds of obscenity for his zine *Boiled Angel*, "comics, drawings and poems that frequently attack Christianity while discussing and depicting serial murder, satanic sacrifices, necrophilia, bestiality, and cannibalism." "Michael Diana Convicted," *The Comics Journal* 168 (May 1994): 16. As far as we know, Wilson's work was not prosecuted when it appeared, as most "comix" of this sort were then more or less underground. We suspect his art is mostly out of print now, as very little shows up in the large comic reprint catalogs, which *do*, however, sell all of the old (and more recent) *Fabulous Furry Freak Brothers* by Gilbert Shelton and work of R. Crumb, Wilson's contemporaries. The sex in these comics, from *Cherry* to *Omaha*, tends to be integrated into improbable plots and sometimes exploited more for humor and shock value than for the reader's sexual arousal. However, there *are* comics that would qualify as definite arousal aids, many distributed by E.C. (Eros Comics), P.O. Box 25070, Seattle WA 98125. Since the appeal of these materials is highly individual, we leave it up to librarians what to purchase beyond considering, say, *Omaha*.

12. *Huevos* also means *testicles* in Spanish—"balls," and *baiser* as a verb (not noun) is a French equivalent to *fuck* in vulgarity as well as meaning.

13. Allen Walker Read, "An Obscenity Symbol," *American Speech* 9 (1934): 264–278.

14. Arnold Zwicky, Peter H. Salus, Robert I. Binnick, & Anthony L. Vanek, *Studies Out in Left Field: Defamatory Essays Presented to James D. McCawley on His 33rd or 34th Birthday* (Philadelphia: John Benjamins, 1992).

15. Another anthology from *Maledicta* has recently appeared: Reinhold Aman, ed., *Talking Dirty: A Bawdy Compendium of Colorful Language, Humorous Insults, and Wicked Jokes* (Carroll & Graf, 1993). This collection includes some of the more lighthearted, humorous, shocking, and less scholarly articles. On a less pleasant note, the references have been stripped from those articles that did have scholarly apparatus—especially annoying to us, as one of us (MC) has an article included. We recommend the Running Press collection.

16. Audrey Wood, *Elbert's Bad Word* (San Diego: Harcourt Brace Jovanovich, 1988).

17. *Sexual Science and the Law* (D105, Green): 1.

18. On a very different dimension is Will Manley's mostly jocular "Librarians

and Sex" survey, *Wilson Library Bulletin* (June 1992): 66. Its results were reported in *American Libraries* (March 1993): 258, as well as in *The Manley Art of Librarianship* (Jefferson, NC: McFarland, 1993): 207–232.

19. Amy Boaz Nugent, "Books to Keep the Faith," *Library Journal* (May 1, 1994): 46. The most comprehensive reference list of religious denominations is the *Encyclopedia of American Religions*, 4th ed., by J. Gordon Melton (Detroit: Gale, 1993), with geographic, subject, name, and keyword indexes. Page 1117 lists 17 religions/sects under sexuality-related subject headings—that is, religious groups with some component of their creed relating to sexual matters.

20. *The Janus Report*, by Samuel S. Janus & Cynthia Janus (New York: Wiley, 1993), reports that 41% of a U.S. sample were "very religious" or "religious" and an additional 36% "slightly religious" (p. 235). *The Social Organization of Sexuality*, by Edward O. Laumann, John H. Gagnon, Robert T. Michael, & Stuart Michaels (Chicago: University of Chicago Press, 1994), cites data from its own U.S. sample and several other recent U.S. surveys. Only about 8–11% of *any* of the samples answered "none" to a question about religious affiliation. To a question about religious attendance, 46–50% reported once a month or oftener; another 28–31% reported once or twice a year to several times a year. Only 8–15% reported less than once a year or "never." (*Sex in America*, A11, Michael et al., was based upon the same data as the latter book.)

Readers may wonder what are *our* religious affiliations. One of us was raised Northern Baptist; the other has a Jewish-Lutheran background. To prepare for this book, we consulted and corresponded with several Catholic scholars.

21. The answer is, So God *doesn't* belong in the bedroom? The implication is clear that of course He does. For a scholarly treatment, see Daniel Boyarin, "Are There Any Jews in 'The History of Sexuality'?" *Journal of the History of Sexuality* 5.3 (January 1995): 333–355. He cites his own book, *Carnal Israel: Reading Sex in Talmudic Culture* (Berkeley: University of California Press, 1993). It came to our attention too late to include here.

22. Timothy Perper, Robert T. Francoeur, & Martha Cornog, *Sex and Religion in Modern Conflict* (manuscript in preparation).

23. See Eric Bryant, "Librarian-Evangelical Cross Talk," *Library Journal* (May 1, 1994): 44–45; Francine Fialkoff, "Librarian-Evangelical Cross Talk II," *Library Journal* (June 15, 1994): 56.

24. *Publishers Weekly* quoted a librarian as saying, "Catholic publishers don't seem to understand the library market. Every day I receive publishers' catalogs, but none from the Catholic publishers. And the reviews of Catholic books I see in our trade journals often are of books more theological or academic in nature and less practical for our [public library] readers" ("Librarians Face a Catholic Dilemma," *Publishers Weekly*, August 15, 1994, p. 52).

25. Lucille M. Zimmerman, "Equip Public Libraries" (letter), *Focus on the Family* (January 1995): 16.

13 Sexual Problems

DISABILITIES AND DYSFUNCTIONS

Only recently have injury, illness, and birth defects not been seen as virtually total bars to sexual intimacy and enjoyment. The disabled people's rights movement has pressed for barrier-free access to public transportation and buildings, and for wide recognition that sexual rights and desires belong to all people. Nonetheless, there are relatively few books about sexuality and disability, most from smaller publishers or nonprofit organizations. Because physicians tend not to discuss sexuality with patients and patients tend not to ask, it is especially important for libraries to have some of these materials.

An excellent and comprehensive work covering many physical disabilities is *Enabling Romance* (E6, Kroll & Klein). *Reproductive Issues for Persons with Physical Disabilities* (E2, Haseltine et al.) addresses a range of topics, including sexuality, reproduction, and parenting. More specialized is *The Illustrated Guide to Better Sex for People with Chronic Pain* (E11, Rothrock & D'Amore). Regarding learning disabilities, we suggest the concise *An Easy Guide for Caring Parents* (E8, McKee & Blacklidge) and *Sexuality and People with Intellectual Disability* (E1, Fegan et al.).

Sexual dysfunctions may arise medically or psychosomatically from organic illnesses, disabilities, birth defects and—very important—medical treatments. However, physicians and therapists consider them a separate category because they are medically secondary to the primary disability and can also occur in apparently healthy individuals. Some sexual dysfunctions occur in both men and women, such as disorders of desire. In men, the better known sexual dysfunctions include erectile dysfunction, premature ejaculation, and retarded ejaculation. For women, the major dysfunctions are anorgasmia and vaginismus.[1]

The classic, groundbreaking work on sexual dysfunctions is *Human Sexual Inadequacy* (E7, Masters & Johnson), although it does not cover desire disorders. Written very technically, it can be difficult to read. A second major reference in the field is *The New Sex Therapy*, by Helen Singer Kaplan (Brunner/Mazel, 1974), also highly technical and designed for therapists (not annotated). More readable and accessible to both laypeople and therapists is *The Illustrated Manual of Sex Therapy* (E4, Kaplan). A more popular all-around work taking a Christian viewpoint is *Restoring the Pleasure* (E10, Penner & Penner). *ISD: Inhibited Sexual Desire* (E5, Knopf et al.) and *What to Do When HE Has a Headache* (E15, Wolfe) discuss desire disorders. Specifically about male problems are *Male Sexual Health* (E12, Spark), *Overcoming Impotence* (E9, Morganstern & Abrahams), and *How to Overcome Premature Ejaculation* (E3, Kaplan). *When a Woman's Body Says No to Sex* (E14, Valins) speaks primarily to women about vaginismus.

Sex therapy has been criticized for advancing practitioners' personal agendas and various other failings. One illustrious and articulate critic is Thomas Szasz, who voices his opinions in *Sex by Prescription* (E13, Szasz).[2]

An excellent annotated bibliography on sexuality and disability is prepared and updated regularly by SIECUS (see Chapter 5). Two other organizations providing materials:

Planned Parenthood of Rochester and the Genesee Valley, Inc.
114 University Avenue
Rochester, NY 14605
  Two bibliographies: Sexuality and the Physically Disabled, and Sexuality and the Developmentally Disabled.

National Center for Youth with Disabilities
University of Minnesota
Box 721
420 Delaware Street, SE
Minnesota, MN 55455
  Bibliography: Issues in Sexuality for Adolescents with Chronic Illnesses and Disabilities.

One publisher apparently specializing in this area is Paul H. Brookes. For materials for learning disabled young people, see *Changes in You . . . for Girls* (C46, Siegal) and *Changes in You . . . for Boys* (C47, Siegal); also the "Everything You Always Wanted to Know" series described in the Books for Pre-Adolescents section in Chapter 11.

See also *Signs for Sexuality* (D99, Minker et al.) and *Signs of Sexual Behavior* (D103, Woodward), guides to American Sign Language.

We were not able to locate bibliographies on sexual dysfunctions and sex therapy. A few titles are included in the SIECUS bibliography of books on sexuality for general readers; longer lists (without annotations) may be found in *Subject Guide to Books in Print* under the headings IMPOTENCE, SEXUAL DISORDERS, and SEX THERAPY. Publishers with some focus on this area include Aronson, Brunner/Mazel, Guilford, Norton, Plenum, and Sage.

Other works discussing sexual dysfunctions within the context of enhancement are covered in the Male Sexuality, Female Sexuality, and Sexual Enhancement sections in Chapter 9. See also the Sexuality in Youth and Age section in Chapter 11.

Annotations

*E1   Fegan, Lydia, & Anne Rauch, with contributions by Wendy McCarthy. *Sexuality and People with Intellectual Disability*. 2nd ed. Baltimore: Paul H. Brookes, 1993. 131p. resources (6p.). index. ISBN 1-55766-140-5. To assist parents and teachers help mentally handicapped people understand and enjoy their own sexuality. Covers puberty, social life, marriage, single sex, fertility, parenthood, homosexuality, sexual exploitation, aging, inappropriate behavior, concerns about group homes, and sex education in various contexts; also includes case stories.

E2   Haseltine, Florence P., Sandra S. Cole, & David B. Gray. *Reproductive Issues for Persons with Physical Disabilities*. Baltimore: Paul H. Brookes, 1993. 368p. chapter refs. index. ISBN 1-55766-111-1. Moderately technical essays on sex, reproduction, birth, and parenting in context of physical disabilities, several about spinal cord trauma and brain injury.

E3   Kaplan, Helen Singer. *How to Overcome Premature Ejaculation*. New York: Brunner/Mazel, 1989. 118p. illus. readings & refs. (2p.). ISBN 0-87630-542-7. Straightforward manual to help men and their partners overcome premature ejaculation. Discusses definitions, causes, treatment, and self-therapy. Notes that premature ejaculation is not always a problem.

*E4   Kaplan, Helen Singer. *The Illustrated Manual of Sex Therapy*. 2nd ed. Illus. by David Passalacqua. New York: Brunner/Mazel, 1987. 178p. footnotes. ISBN 0-87630-518-4. Concise guide covering inhibited female excitement, female orgasmic dysfunction, vaginismus, impotence, retarded ejaculation, and premature ejaculation. For each, describes behavioral treatment techniques. For therapists and laypeople; heterosexual couple–based.

E5   Knopf, Jennifer, & Michael Seiler, with Susan Meltsner. *ISD: Inhibited Sexual Desire*. New York: Warner, 1990. 300p. suggested reading (3p.). index. ISBN 0-446-39235-9. Self-help guide for people who believe they have too low an interest in sex. Covers reasons for inhibited/low sexual desire as stemming from body, mind, and relationships; plus how to make personal and relationship changes. Includes sexual enhancement exercises and brief descriptions of sexual anatomy and function. Heterosexual/homosexual.

*E6   Kroll, Ken, & Erica Levy Klein. *Enabling Romance: A Guide to Love, Sex, and Relationships for the Disabled (and the People Who Care About Them).* Illus. by Mark Langeneckert. New York: Harmony, 1992. 209p. sources (16p.). refs. (4p.). index. ISBN 0-517-57532-9. Sympathetic guidance for disabled people about enhancing sexuality, plus information for nondisabled about disabilities and their limitations. Covers self-esteem, sexual variations, reproduction, contraception, and other general issues; discusses sexual implications of particular disabilities.

E7   Masters, William H., & Virginia E. Johnson. *Human Sexual Inadequacy.* New York: Bantam, 1980 (©1970). 463p. refs. (63p.). index. ISBN 0-553-13739-5. Details treatment of premature ejaculation, erectile and ejaculatory inhibition, female orgasmic dysfunction, pain during intercourse, and dysfunctions associated with aging. Describes therapy with about 600 people addressing physiological and psychological factors, with treatment based upon sensate-focus exercises.

E8   McKee, Lyn, & Virginia Blacklidge. *An Easy Guide for Caring Parents: Sexuality and Socialization: A Book for Parents of People with Mental Handicaps.* Shasta Diablo, CA: Planned Parenthood Shasta Diablo, 1981 (updated 1986). 56p. photos. notes (1p.). ISBN 0-9606898-1-8. Concise guide for parents to teach mentally handicapped children responsible and enjoyable sociosexual behavior. Covers puberty, cleanliness/neatness, masturbation, social life, marriage, parenthood, single sex, fertility and birth control, homosexuality, STDs, and sexual exploitation and dysfunction.

E9   Morganstern, Steven, & Allen Abrahams. *Overcoming Impotence: A Doctor's Proven Guide to Regaining Sexual Vitality.* Englewood Cliffs, NJ: Prentice-Hall, 1994. 336p. glossary (23p.). orgs. (9p.). index. ISBN 0-13-146978-9. (Rev. ed. of *Live Again, Love Again.*) Comprehensive description of erectile dysfunction and overcoming it. Covers definition and history, male sexual function, causes, self-diagnosis and physician diagnosis, treatments (hormones, drugs, implants, surgery, vacuum devices, psychotherapy, sex therapy), other male sexual dysfunctions, costs and payment, prevention, and a message to the partner. Appendix lists drugs with sexually dysfunctional side effects, and drugs used to treat dysfunctions.

E10   Penner, Clifford L., & Joyce J. Penner. *Restoring the Pleasure: Complete Step-by-Step Programs to Help Couples Overcome the Most Common Sexual Barriers.* Dallas: Word, 1993. 359p. illus. notes (3p.). bibliog. (4p.). index. ISBN 0-8499-3464-8. Manual for addressing sexual dysfunctions/dissatisfactions within marriage, from Christian perspective. Covers basic sex information, Biblical support for marital sexual enjoyment, communication, and suggestions for problems of sexual desire, arousal, release, barriers to intercourse, and sexual addictions. Includes exercises.

E11   Rothrock, Robert W., & Gabriella D'Amore. *The Illustrated Guide to Better Sex for People with Chronic Pain.* 2nd ed. Illus. by Jonathan Belt. Morrisville, PA: Rothrock & D'Amore (P.O. Box 1355, Morrisville, PA 19067-0325), 1992. 35p. glossary (3p.). reading list (2p.). ISBN 0-9632602-1-9. Concise, simply written guidebook for enjoying sexual experiences despite chronic pain. Covers sexual myths, communicating with partner, planning for sex, positions, alternatives to intercourse, considerations re arthritis, and finding a therapist.

E12 Spark, Richard F. *Male Sexual Health: A Couple's Guide*. Yonkers, NY: Consumer Reports Books, 1991. 230p. illus. refs. (17p.). index. ISBN 0-89043-319-4. Moderately technical, detailed discussion of causes and treatments of erectile dysfunction. Shorter descriptions of other male sexual dysfunctions, and of prostate and fertility problems. Good illustrations. Heterosexual.

E13 Szasz, Thomas. *Sex by Prescription: The Startling Truth About Today's Sex Therapy*. Syracuse, NY: Syracuse University Press, 1990 (©1980). 196p. notes (15p.). index. ISBN 0-8156-0250-2. Provocative critique of sex therapy and sex education as promoting unnecessary medicalization of social and moral issues, as moral/social prescriptions masquerading as science, and as legitimating evasion of individual responsibility and freedom of choice.

E14 Valins, Linda. *When a Woman's Body Says No to Sex: Understanding and Overcoming Vaginismus*. New York: Penguin, 1992. 360p. notes (7p.). bibliog. (3p.). suggested reading (4p.). index. ISBN 0-14-014908-2. Describes causes, treatments, and prevention of vaginismus: involuntary spasm of vaginal muscles, making sexual intercourse difficult or impossible. Lengthy appendix on finding treatment.

E15 Wolfe, Janet L. *What to Do When HE Has a Headache: Renewing Desire and Intimacy in Your Relationship*. New York: Penguin, 1992. 303p. further reading (3p.). bibliog. (5p.). ISBN 0-14-017899-6. Guidebook for women about coping with and changing a mate's lesser sexual interest. Stresses understanding, empathy, communication, and rational self-acceptance.

SEXUAL EXPLOITATION (GENERAL WORKS)

Sexual exploitation refers generally to sexual activity occurring when one partner does not consent or when powerlessness or vulnerability creates conditions of "coerced consent"—which is no consent at all. Subcategories are rape, sexual harassment, and child sexual abuse, including incest.

First we cover the more general area of "sexual misconduct," where people in therapeutic, advisory, or teaching roles become sexually involved with someone vulnerable because of the relationship as well as because of health, emotional problems, or age. Although the other person may consent, issues of "consent" are not ethically relevant when sexual activities involve one's current patient, advisee, parishioner, or student. Such sexual relationships are always considered wrongful, marginal, or at the very least suspect. Two works on sexual misconduct in general are *Sex in the Forbidden Zone* (E24, Rutter) and *Sexual Dilemmas for the Helping Professional* (E16, Edelwich & Brodsky), the second written from the helper's perspective. *The Forbidden Apple* (E23, Ross & Marlowe) focuses on teacher/student relationships. Two excellent books about sexual exploitation in the church are *Sex in the Parish* (E20, Lebacqz & Barton) and *Is Nothing Sacred?* (E17, Fortune).

Some books deal with sexual exploitation in general and how to prevent it. *Get Smart!* (E19, Katz & Vieland) is written primarily for college women. **Talking Back to Sexual Pressure* (E21, Powell) is an excellent source for modeling assertiveness in unwanted sexual situations. A witty but still serious title is *Seduction Lines Heard 'Round the World, and Answers You Can Give* (E18, Gordon).

With an entirely different and sometimes opposing viewpoint, *The Morning After* (E22, Roiphe) takes a provocative and critical look at the feminist emphasis on women's victimization in sexual exploitation.

Many publishers offer sexual exploitation titles, including Guilford, Impact, Norton, Safer Society Press, and Sage. A general bibliography on rape, incest, and child sexual abuse is available from the National Coalition Against Sexual Assault (912 North Second Street, Harrisburg, PA 17102-3119). A catalog service with a section on (mostly sexual) abuse is Courage to Change (318 Oak Grove Court, Wexford, PA 15090-9569).

Annotations

E16 Edelwich, Jerry, & Archie Brodsky. *Sexual Dilemmas for the Helping Professional.* Rev. ed. New York: Brunner/Mazel, 1991. 272p. refs. (10p.). index. ISBN 0-87630-627-X. Comprehensive discussion of psychosocial aspects of sexual attraction and relationships between clinicians and clients. Covers elements of seduction, power, opportunity, self-interest, morality, professional and legal liability, and relationships among staff members. Summarizes recommended guidelines.

E17 Fortune, Marie M. *Is Nothing Sacred? When Sex Invades the Pastoral Relationship.* San Francisco: Harper San Francisco, 1989. 167p. notes (7p.). index. ISBN 0-06-062684-4. Case study of pastor who sexually exploited women parishioners, and how the women and the church discharged the pastor after false starts and mistakes. Shows how churches are ill-equipped to handle this problem. Appendix: model procedure for handling clergy sexual misconduct.

E18 Gordon, Sol. *Seduction Lines Heard 'Round the World, and Answers You Can Give: A World Book of Lines.* Illus. by Rita Fecher. Buffalo, NY: Prometheus, 1987. 176p. ISBN 0-87975-405-2. Varied, amusing collection of pick-up/seduction "lines" from both sexes, reported by students from the U.S. and many countries, plus suggested snappy comebacks to indicate disinterest. Provides guidance for refusing unwanted or unsafe sex.

E19 Katz, Montana, & Veronica Vieland. *Get Smart! What You Should Know (But Won't Learn in Class) About Sexual Harassment and Sex Discrimination.* 2nd ed. New York: The Feminist Press at The City University of New York, 1993. 170p. bibliog. (3p.). ISBN 1-55861-071-5. Guidebook for women college students about preventing and handling sexual discrimination, sexual harassment, and acquaintance rape on campus. Contains case studies and suggested solutions. Stresses assertiveness and persistence.

E20 Lebacqz, Karen, & Ronald G. Barton. *Sex in the Parish.* Louisville, KY: Westminster/John Knox, 1991. 279p. notes (9p.). bibliog. (6p.). ISBN 0-664-

25087-4. Results of questionnaire/interview study about sexuality in pastoral-lay relationships. Addresses behavior and ethics. Covers positive/negative aspects, sexual temptations and setting limits, a case study of overstepping limits, power and the pastoral role, experiences of women, gay/lesbian and single pastors, and role of higher church and adjudicatory bodies. Appendix: procedures for handling allegations of pastoral sexual misconduct.

*E21   Powell, Elizabeth. *Talking Back to Sexual Pressure: What to Say . . . to Resist Persuasion . . . to Avoid Disease . . . to Stop Harassment . . . to Avoid Acquaintance Rape.* Minneapolis: CompCare, 1991. 255p. resources & orgs. (15p.). index. ISBN 0-89638-239-7. Guidelines and dialogues for asserting intention to use contraception or STD preventives, and for resisting unwanted sex. Urges and gives how-tos for activism against sexual intrusion and violence.

E22   Roiphe, Katie. *The Morning After: Sex, Fear, and Feminism on Campus.* Boston: Little, Brown, 1993. 180p. notes (6p.). ISBN 0-316-75431-5. Analysis of current feminist emphasis on women's victimization via rape, sexual harassment, and pornography. Holds that this emphasis is *over*emphasis, counter to common sense, misrepresentative of the real world, and crippling to women's development and identity.

E23   Ross, Victor J., & John Marlowe. *The Forbidden Apple: Sex in the Schools.* Palm Springs, CA: ETC Publications, 1985. 99p. ISBN 0-88280-107-4. Description of sexual exploitation, assault, and harassment involving junior high and high school teachers and students. Based upon several hundred incidents collected informally. Designed to help teachers, students, parents, and administrators prevent these situations. Also addresses faculty relationships, homosexual cases, and teachers and mature students.

E24   Rutter, Peter. *Sex in the Forbidden Zone: When Men in Power—Therapists, Doctors, Clergy, Teachers, and Others—Betray Women's Trust.* New York: Fawcett Crest, 1991. 288p. resources (22p.). ISBN 0-449-14727-4. Results of study of 1,000+ case reports of male professionals having sexual contact with female patients, clients, parishioners, or students. Extensive discussion of psychological causes and outcomes of these relationships, and how to prevent them.

INCEST AND CHILD SEXUAL ABUSE

Libraries should have books on both incest and child sexual abuse. A range of titles should be acquired, especially books written for or by victims/survivors and books stressing that both boys and girls can be victims.[3]

The Broken Taboo: Sex in the Family (E36, Justice & Justice) is a good overall classic introduction to incest. By contrast, *Forbidden Partners* (E42, Twitchell) concentrates on how incest has been represented in literature and popular culture. *Incest and Sexuality* (E39, Maltz & Holman) is written for adult survivors of either sex. Finally, *Kiss Daddy Goodnight* (E28, Armstrong) provides vivid and traumatic personal accounts. Louise Armstrong's newer *Rocking the Cradle of Sexual Politics: What Happened When*

Women Said Incest (Addison-Wesley, 1994), not annotated, describes public response to the "outing" of incest over the past 15 years.

Indeed, the past decade has also seen an impressive variety of titles concerning child sexual abuse. *Childhood Sexual Abuse: A Reference Handbook*, by Karen L. Kinnear (ABC-Clio, 1995), is a new and invaluable reference source (not annotated). Many books about healing and recovery have been written for adult victims/survivors. *The Courage to Heal* (E29, Bass & Davis) and the shorter *Beginning to Heal* (Harper Collins, 1991, not annotated) are popular classics, while *The Wounded Heart* (E26, Allender) takes a Christian view. *Victims No Longer* (E37, Lew) speaks to adult male victims of child sexual abuse. *Shifting the Burden of Truth* (E33, Crnich & Crnich) advises survivors how to sue their abusers.

When the Bough Breaks (E40, Matsakis) and *No More Secrets* (E25, Adams & Fay) are helping guides for parents of sexually abused children. A work for counselors and evaluators is *Sexual Abuse of Young Children* (E38, MacFarlane et al.).

A unique perspective on preventing child sexual abuse is *Man/Child* (E34, Hunter), written by a convicted offender. *Abused Boys* (E35, Hunter) is a basic introduction to the lesser known circumstances of sexual abuse of boys. Two more general works on child sexual abuse for clergy and religious laity are *Child Sexual Abuse* (E32, Carlson) and *A Moral Emergency* (E27, Angelica), while *A Gospel of Shame* (E31, Burkett & Bruni) chronicles recent scandals of Roman Catholic priests accused of abuse. An earlier classic work is *Child Pornography and Sex Rings*, by Ann Wolbert Burgess (Lexington/D.C. Heath, 1984, not annotated).

Not all specialists believe that the child sexual abuse prevention and treatment movements take the best approach. We recommend three critical works. *Confronting the Victim Role* (E41, McCarthy & McCarthy) disapproves of "victim-centered" treatment, and proposes healing based upon strength and self-esteem. *Suggestions of Abuse* (E43, Yapko) criticizes therapists attempting to uncover "repressed" memories of abuse; this arena is a war zone in psychology and psychiatry. *With the Best of Intentions* (E30, Berrick & Gilbert) contends that current prevention programs based upon child empowerment are flawed, and recommends modifications.

Librarians will surely have no difficulty finding new books on incest and especially child sexual abuse: each is well covered in the library literature. Many major publishers have titles, including religious, self-help, and psychology presses. (See the list in the Sexual Exploitation section, above.) *Subject Guide to Books in Print* has copious lists under the headings CHILD MOLESTING, INCEST, and INCEST VICTIMS, plus a much shorter list under PEDOPHILIA.

SIECUS has a recurring bibliography, Child Sexual Abuse Education, Prevention, and Treatment, including books for children, for parents, and for professionals, and curricula. *Comprehensive Bibliography for Sex,*

Health & Family Education (D112, Charlton) has a section on sexual abuse. Occasional bibliographies appear in the library literature.[4]

Other sources of bibliographies:

Voices in Action
P.O. Box 148309
Chicago, IL 60614
  Bibliography on both incest and child sexual abuse.

Clearinghouse on Child Abuse and Neglect Information
P.O. Box 1182
Washington, DC 20013-1182
  Bibliographies are available on all aspects of child sexual abuse: prevention, treatment, offenders, and victims. Request Catalog of Services and Publications.

See *A Research Guide to Human Sexuality* (D120, Lichtenberg) for other organizations providing literature suitable for the vertical file, plus the *Encyclopedia of Associations*.

Several published bibliographies cover older works: *Incest: An Annotated Bibliography*, by Mary De Young (McFarland, 1985), *Child Molestation: An Annotated Bibliography*, by the same author (McFarland, 1987), and *Incest: The Last Taboo: An Annotated Bibliography*, by Rick Rubin and Greg Byerly (Garland, 1983).

See also books for young people, in the Books for Children, Books for Pre-Adolescents, and Books for Adolescents sections in Chapter 11.

See also *Male Intergenerational Intimacy* (A76, Sandfort et al.).

Annotations

E25 Adams, Caren, & Jennifer Fay. *No More Secrets: Protecting Your Child from Sexual Assault*. San Luis Obispo, CA: Impact, 1981. 90p. orgs. (1p.). resources (2p.). ISBN 0-915166-24-0. Detailed suggestions for parents about preventing child sexual abuse. Covers definitions, protection techniques, teaching children to avoid and report problems, sample dialogues, instructional games, symptoms of abuse, how to cope after abuse, and taking collective action.

E26 Allender, Dan B. *The Wounded Heart: Hope for Adult Victims of Child Sexual Abuse*. Colorado Springs: NavPress, 1990. 255p. notes (2p.). annotated bibliog. (5p.). ISBN 0-89109-289-7. Christian perspective on recognizing and healing child sexual abuse. Primarily for adult victims. Detailed discussion of identifying abuse and its damages, and seeking healing, growth, and justice through Christian love for self and others.

*E27 Angelica, Jade C. *A Moral Emergency: Breaking the Cycle of Child Sexual Abuse*. Kansas City, MO: Sheed & Ward, 1993. 169p. glossary (2p.). orgs. (5p.). notes (14p.). bibliog. (5p.). ISBN 1-55612-617-4. Call to congregations and religious groups of all faiths to confront child sexual abuse. Includes statistics of abuse, myths and realities, case studies, denominational responses, recommended ministry programs, and sample sermons.

E28   Armstrong, Louise. *Kiss Daddy Goodnight: A Speak-Out on Incest*. New York: Pocket Books, 1978. 296p. bibliog. (4p.). index. ISBN 0-671-82668-9. Vivid accounts of exploitative incest experiences, contributed by adult women victimized by fathers or older brothers. Commentary by the author/editor.

*E29   Bass, Ellen, & Laura Davis. *The Courage to Heal: A Guide for Women Survivors of Child Sexual Abuse*. 3rd ed. New York: Harper Perennial, 1994. 604p. resource guide (54p.). index. ISBN 0-06-095066-8. Comprehensive, detailed guidebook for women healing from childhood sexual abuse. Includes data, quotes, and stories from over 200 survivors. Covers taking stock, the healing process, patterns of change, case studies, advice for supporters of survivors, and response to backlash against survivor credibility.

E30   Berrick, Jill Duerr, & Neil Gilbert. *With the Best of Intentions: The Child Sexual Abuse Prevention Movement*. New York: Guilford, 1991. 210p. notes (29p.). index. ISBN 0-89862-530-0. History and analysis of child sexual abuse prevention programs. Holds current approaches as flawed; recommends alternative model based more upon protection than empowerment, and emphasizing body awareness, communication, "secret touching" as bad, and adult responsibility.

E31   Burkett, Elinor, & Frank Bruni. *A Gospel of Shame: Children, Sexual Abuse, and the Catholic Church*. New York: Viking, 1993. 292p. notes (24p.). index. ISBN 0-670-84828-X. Chronicle of U.S. child sex abuse cases over last few decades involving Roman Catholic clergy. Details case histories, victim reactions, lawsuits and aftermath, reactions of priests and church hierarchy (initially, evasion and cover-up), and reforms implemented.

E32   Carlson, Lee W. *Child Sexual Abuse: A Handbook for Clergy and Church Members*. Valley Forge, PA: Judson, 1988. 79p. notes (1p.). annotated bibliog. (10p.). ISBN 0-8170-1133-1. Guide for clergy and laypeople (any denomination) for dealing with child sexual abuse in the congregation/synagogue. Covers causes and signs of sexual abuse, understanding offenders and victims, ethical and theological response, confidentiality, treatment and healing, and educating the congregation.

E33   Crnich, Joseph E., & Kimberly A. Crnich. *Shifting the Burden of Truth: Suing Child Sexual Abusers—A Legal Guide for Survivors and Their Supporters*. Lake Oswego, OR: Recollex, 1992. 251p. glossary (6p.). index. ISBN 0-9631608-3-4. Handbook for childhood sexual abuse victims about suing abusers. Provides detailed guidance about whether to sue, possibilities of winning, finding an attorney, and the lawsuit process. Includes case histories, questions and answers, list of attorneys, and list of statutes and decisions.

E34   Hunter, Howard. *Man/Child: An Insight into Child Sexual Abuse by a Convicted Molester, with a Comprehensive Resource Guide*. Jefferson, NC: McFarland, 1991. 237p. orgs. (19p.). annotated bibliog. (70p.). index. ISBN 0-89950-528-7. Description for parents of child sexual abuse patterns, drawn from experiences of the author and fellow inmates incarcerated for molesting. Summarizes much other research. Covers typical seduction scenarios and how to prevent them, indicators of abusers and abuse, and legal aspects.

E35   Hunter, Mic. *Abused Boys: The Neglected Victims of Sexual Abuse.* New York: Fawcett Columbine, 1990. 339p. notes (26p.). resources (6p.). bibliog. (16p.). index. ISBN 0-449-90629-9. Introductory work about sexual abuse of boys. Covers definitions and frequency of abuse, impacts and factors affecting impacts, recovery, and healing. Includes first person stories from survivors.

E36   Justice, Blair, & Rita Justice. *The Broken Taboo: Sex in the Family.* New York: Human Sciences Press, 1979. 304p. notes (20p.). bibliog. (6p.). index. ISBN 0-87705-482-7. General introduction to incest. Covers incest in history and religion, who commits incest, why incest occurs, cues and consequences, and what can be done via individual treatment and public policy.

E37   Lew, Mike. *Victims No Longer: Men Recovering from Incest and Other Sexual Child Abuse.* New York: Harper Collins, 1990. 325p. orgs. & bibliog. (10p.). index. ISBN 0-06-097300-5. Guide to self-understanding and healing for adult male victims/survivors of child sexual abuse. Covers myths vs. realities, feelings, sexuality, survival adaptations and aftereffects, recovery, telling others, relationships and social support, individual and group counseling, confronting the abuser, and letting go. Describes other forms of therapy and gives suggestions for partners, family, and friends. Includes case studies.

E38   MacFarlane, Kee, & Jill Waterman, with others. *Sexual Abuse of Young Children: Evaluation and Treatment.* New York: Guilford, 1986. 355p. refs. (14p.). index. ISBN 0-89862-675-1. Detailed discussion of evaluation and treatment of young victims of child sexual abuse, written for professionals, caretakers, and parents. Covers child development, medical evaluation, interviewing, effects of abuse, legal considerations, individual and group treatment, and helping parents.

E39   Maltz, Wendy, & Beverly Holman. *Incest and Sexuality: A Guide for Understanding and Healing.* Lexington, MA: Lexington/Heath, 1987. 166p. notes (1p.). bibliog. (2p.). suggested reading (2p.). index. ISBN 0-669-1408-X. Guidebook for adult survivors of childhood incest about reclaiming positive, healthy sexual attitudes. Summarizes research and interviews concerning patterns of incest, effect on sexuality, and how survivors and partners can find help. Appendix on male incest survivors.

E40   Matsakis, Aphrodite. *When the Bough Breaks: A Helping Guide for Parents of Sexually Abused Children.* Oakland, CA: New Harbinger, 1991. 258p. chapter bibliogs. notes (6p.). orgs. (3p.). ISBN 1-879237-00-8. Guidebook for parents of sexually abused children. Describes sexual abuse, with two case histories. Covers helping the child grieve and heal, treatments (therapy, hospitalization), and helping oneself as parent.

E41   McCarthy, Barry, & Emily McCarthy. *Confronting the Victim Role: Healing from an Abusive Childhood.* New York: Carroll & Graf, 1993. 222p. further reading (2p.). ISBN 0-7867-0011-4. Critique of victim-centered "adult child," codependence, and 12-step therapy programs for child abuse and child sexual abuse, with guidance for emphasizing survivorship, strength, self-esteem, responsibility, and dealing with reality. Includes guidelines for choosing therapists and self-help groups.

E42   Twitchell, James B. *Forbidden Partners: The Incest Taboo in Modern Culture.* New York: Columbia University Press, 1987. 311p. illus. notes (19p.). bibliog.

(21p.). index. ISBN 0-231-06413-6. Scholarly, readable description of attraction/ anxiety associated with incest taboo in Europe and U.S., revealed by literature and popular culture 1800s–present. Appendix summarizes biological, psychological, and sociological views.

E43   Yapko, Michael D. *Suggestions of Abuse: True and False Memories of Child-hood Sexual Trauma.* New York: Simon & Schuster, 1994. 271p. notes (12p.). bibliog. (14p.). index. ISBN 0-671-87431-4. Carefully researched discussion and critique of therapies designed to uncover repressed memories of childhood sexual abuse. Reports data from questionnaire survey of over 800 therapists about nature of memory and hypnosis, and compares them with scientific findings, revealing therapists' misconceptions.

RAPE

The category "rape" is less simple than it appears. Complexities arise because the word is defined not only by law, but also by common experience and everyday use of language. For example, a man is not legally a rapist unless he has been convicted by a court, but in common speech the term is used more freely. Issues of marital rape have posed even wider definitional problems.

These issues are not limited to dictionary writers. Instead, they represent changing visions of what is and is not acceptable sexual behavior—and those opposing one or another form of sexual activity tend to use the most pejorative terms available. The result widens our consciousness of sexual misconduct, but simultaneously dilutes the meaning of once restricted but very powerful terms. The sense of evil and malice implicit in older or legal uses of the word *rape* may become weakened when, in an effort to spread an umbrella of evil over both, it is used to describe an over-ardent and none-too-bright teenager wooing a reluctant young woman.

The issue is central in understanding and evaluating books that attempt to broaden the definitions of rape: many are powerfully felt efforts to see malice where previous generations saw only bad behavior. These newer voices in writing about rape have widened the discourse about sexual exploitation and are reflected in the many and varied new books in the field. One consequence is that books on "rape" deal with matters ranging from knife-point stranger rape to the fumblings of inexperienced young men.

Indeed, writing about rape has proliferated and diversified. All libraries should have books on rape by men of women (general), rape in marriage, acquaintance or "date" rape, gang rape (which may also be acquaintance rape), rape *of* men (by women or by other men), and advice for rape victims/survivors. We have emphasized books describing the behavior/offense, its offenders, its victims, and general prevention strategies. Books about sex between adults and individuals younger than puberty are covered in the Child Sexual Abuse section.

Many books about rape have been published in the last twenty years, reflecting a maturing of public (and publisher) consciousness. The books below are certainly not the only worthy books available.

A good comprehensive up-to-date introduction to the research and literature on all aspects of rape is *Rape: The Misunderstood Crime* (E45, Allison & Wrightsman). *Men Who Rape* (E52, Groth & Birnbaum) is a classic seminal study of rapists, published in 1979 and widely cited since. Two excellent books focus on prevention: *Stopping Rape: A Challenge for Men* (E51, Funk) and—for women—*Stopping Rape: Successful Survival Strategies* (E46, Bart & O'Brian).

A variety of voices, largely feminist, comprise the anthology *Transforming a Rape Culture* (E50, Buchwald et al.), including contributions from many well-known writers. We also recommend the classic feminist work that alerted so many people to the prevalence of rape and sexual violence: *Against Our Will* (E49, Brownmiller). Male viewpoints appear in *Men on Rape* (E47, Beneke).

Three books about date or acquaintance rape also address prevention and recovery: *I Never Called It Rape* (E60, Warshaw), *Dating Violence* (E54, Levy), and *Sexual Assault on Campus* (E48, Bohmer & Parrot).

Other types of rape are covered by several additional important titles: *Rape in Marriage* (E57, Russell), *Fraternity Gang Rape* (E58, Sanday), and *Male Rape: Breaking the Silence on the Last Taboo* (E56, McMullen).

Regarding recovery from rape, we include *Free of the Shadows* (E44, Adams & Fay) and—from a Christian perspective—*Sexual Assault: Will I Ever Feel Okay Again?* (E59, Scott). A matched set of concise books is written for women rape victims and male significant others: *If You Are Raped* (E53, Johnson) and *If She Is Raped* (E55, McEvoy & Brookings).

There seem to be few bibliographies on rape or acquaintance rape alone. However, lengthy lists are included under both topics in *Subject Guide to Books in Print*. Some older published bibliographies are listed in *A Research Guide to Human Sexuality* (D120, Lichtenberg), together with organizations providing information other than bibliographies. See the general bibliographies and sources listed in the Sexual Exploitation section, above.

For books for young people about rape/acquaintance rape, see the Books for Pre-Adolescents and Books for Adolescents sections in Chapter 11.

Annotations

E44 Adams, Caren, & Jennifer Fay. *Free of the Shadows: Recovering from Sexual Violence.* Oakland, CA: New Harbinger, 1989. 208p. resources (6p.). ISBN 0-934986-70-3. Daily readings for rape victims: practical suggestions for dealing with emotions, sexuality, self-protection, the legal system, and other sequelae to victimization. Also suggestions for family, friends, and therapists. Mostly for women, but mentions male victims.

*E45 Allison, Julie A., & Lawrence S. Wrightsman. *Rape: The Misunderstood Crime*. Newbury Park, CA: Sage, 1993. 306p. refs. (27p.). index. ISBN 0-8039-3707-5. "Comprehensive up-to-date review of the crime of rape from a psychological perspective." Summarizes much theory and research, and addresses characteristics of rapists and rape, reactions of and towards rape victims, legal aspects, treatment of victims and rapists, and prevention.

E46 Bart, Pauline B., & Patricia H. O'Brian. *Stopping Rape: Successful Survival Strategies*. New York: Pergamon, 1985. 199p. chapter refs. bibliog. (6p.). index. ISBN 0-08-032813-X. Results of interview study of nearly 100 women, half of whom were raped, half who avoided rape. Analyzes how avoiders had prevented rape, what strategies worked, and other factors influencing outcomes.

E47 Beneke, Timothy. *Men on Rape*. New York: St. Martin's, 1982. 174p. orgs. (3p.). ISBN 0-312-52951-1. Overview of common male attitudes about rape of women. Excerpts from interviews with husbands, lovers, friends, lawyers, doctors, policemen, and a rapist. Includes brief introduction about rape and modern sexual culture, and a response from an advocate for rape victims/survivors. Appendix of male anti-rape groups.

E48 Bohmer, Carol, & Andrea Parrot. *Sexual Assault on Campus: The Problem and the Solution*. New York: Lexington/Macmillan, 1993. 280p. notes (14p.). refs. (7p.). index. ISBN 0-02-903715-8. Describes patterns of rape and acquaintance rape at colleges and offers advice to prevent and respond to incidents. Combines social science research; legal analyses; and interviews with victims, parents, and campus officials.

E49 Brownmiller, Susan. *Against Our Will: Men, Women and Rape*. New York: Bantam/Simon & Schuster, 1975. 541p. notes (51p.). index. ISBN 0-553-02974-6. Classic feminist work on rape by men. Discusses psychology, history and law, police treatment, rape as power, myths of rapist and victim, case studies of women raped and prison rape of men, and combating rape.

E50 Buchwald, Emilie, Pamela R. Fletcher, & Martha Roth, eds. *Transforming a Rape Culture*. Minneapolis: Milkweed Editions, 1993. 467p. orgs. (2p.). additional reading (3p.). index. ISBN 0-915943-06-9. Essays about sexual violence. Addresses how U.S. culture perpetuates rape, strategies for change, activism, and "visions and possibilities." Authors include Naomi Wolf, Susan Griffin, Gloria Steinem, and Andrea Dworkin.

*E51 Funk, Rus Ervin. *Stopping Rape: A Challenge for Men*. Philadelphia: New Society, 1993. 178p. contact list (2p.). bibliog. (6p.). ISBN 0-86571-268-9. Feminist-oriented guide primarily for men about understanding and ameliorating male sexual violence. Covers personal and societal effects of rape, rape culture and causes, ways men can stop sexual violence, and how to respond to rape survivors. Includes exercises and workshop outline.

E52 Groth, A. Nicholas, with H. Jean Birnbaum. *Men Who Rape: The Psychology of the Offender*. New York: Plenum, 1979. 227p. footnotes. index. ISBN 0-306-40268-8. Results of classic psychological and clinical study of over 500 sexual offenders (some convicted, some not). Covers rape myths vs. realities, types of rape, assessment, treatment, and other aspects of rape such as intoxication and sexual dysfunction.

E53 Johnson, Kathryn M. *If You Are Raped: What Every Woman Needs to Know.* Holmes Beach, CA: Learning Publications, 1985. 166p. glossary (6p.). refs. (7p.). index. ISBN 0-918452-72-4. Briefly describes rape and self-protection strategies. Lengthy discussion of coping with being raped: stages of psychological recovery; finding support from family, friends, and others; relationships with husbands, lovers, and children; acquaintance rape; getting medical attention; legal help and action; and anti-rape activism.

E54 Levy, Barrie, ed. *Dating Violence: Young Women in Danger.* Seattle: Seal Press, 1991. 315p. refs. (19p.). index. ISBN 1-878067-03-6. Collected essays about dating violence, including date rape. Includes case studies and covers contexts of dating violence, intervention strategies, education, and prevention.

*E55 McEvoy, Alan W., & Jeff B. Brookings. *If She Is Raped: A Guidebook for Husbands, Fathers and Male Friends.* 2nd ed. Holmes Beach, CA: Learning Publications, 1991. 132p. orgs. (4p.). suggested readings (9p.). ISBN 1-55691-062-2. For male family/friends of female rape survivors. Addresses understanding the assault, understanding her reactions, helping her recover, dealing with the legal system, and coping with his own feelings.

E56 McMullen, Richie J. *Male Rape: Breaking the Silence on the Last Taboo.* London: Gay Mens Press [*sic*], 1990 (dist. by Alyson). 247p. bibliog. (21p.). ISBN 0-85449–126-0. Discusses rape of males, mostly by other men but some mention of women attackers. Covers male rape and (English) law, causes, types of victims, consequences, statistics, and prevention. Appendices include guidance for counseling victims and summarize 13 research studies.

*E57 Russell, Diana E.H. *Rape in Marriage.* Rev. ed. Bloomington: Indiana University Press, 1990. 421p. notes (19p.). bibliog. (10p.). index. ISBN 0-253-20563-8. Results of interview study of 930 women about sexual abuse in marriage. Covers theory and statistics of wife rape, characteristics of the husbands and wives, women viewed as property, cases of torture and murder, wives' strategies, and international perspectives. Includes summary of state statutes.

E58 Sanday, Peggy Reeves. *Fraternity Gang Rape: Sex, Brotherhood, and Privilege on Campus.* New York: New York University Press, 1990. 201p. bibliog. (5p.). ISBN 0-8147-7961-1. Discussion of heterosexual gang rape on U.S. college campuses. Includes detailed case study, briefer descriptions of several other incidents, and anthropological description of male-oriented "campus party culture," including fraternity culture and sexual behavior.

E59 Scott, Kay. *Sexual Assault: Will I Ever Feel Okay Again?* Minneapolis: Bethany House, 1993. 207p. chapter refs. ISBN 1-55661-325-3. (Rev. ed. of *Raped.*) Story of author's rape and struggle towards recovery, from Christian perspective. Also includes questions and answers about rape, plus statistics and stages of recovery.

*E60 Warshaw, Robin. *I Never Called It Rape: The Ms. Report on Recognizing, Fighting and Surviving Date and Acquaintance Rape.* New York: Harper & Row,

1988. 229p. bibliog. (5p.). resources (8p.). index. ISBN 0-06-096276-3. Results of questionnaire survey of about 6,000 college men and women about sexual assault. Describes acquaintance rape, why women are victimized, responses of authorities, prevention, recovery, and responsibility of men and of parents, schools, and lawmakers.

SEXUAL HARASSMENT

Sexual harassment is another area with a recent publishing boom. The books below are only a few of approximately 100 currently available titles and deal with definitions and descriptions, personal experiences, prevention, treatment of victims, and the law. Our choices were made with an eye to variety.[5]

Sexual Harassment (E62, Eisaguirre) is a basic reference, recommended for all public libraries and clear enough for high school libraries also. *Primer on Sexual Harassment* (E65, Lindemann & Kadue) addresses legal aspects in much greater detail and is designed for nonlawyers, whether employers or employees. Another basic work is *Sexual Harassment No More* (E61, Conway & Conway), which covers the subject broadly, from a Christian perspective.

Like all sexual issues, sexual harassment calls forth many opinions, attributed causes, and remedies. A diverse sample may be found in *Sexual Harassment: Current Controversies* (E69, Wekesser et al.) and *Sexual Harassment: Confrontations and Decisions* (E67, Wall), anthologies of different perspectives.

Four other books contain quite valuable material. *Back Off* (E64, Langelan), a how-to, presents success stories of women succeeding in fighting harassment. *Harassed* (E66, McCann & McGinn) shows the range of women's perceptions about sexual harassment. *Shockwaves* (E68, Webb) documents sexual harassment worldwide, and *When NO Means NO* (E63, Gomez-Preston & Reisfeld) is a case study of a woman police officer who won a million dollar sexual harassment settlement.

Nearly uniformly, these books assume that men are the harassers and women the victims. Only *Primer on Sexual Harassment* (E65, Lindemann & Kadue) is worded in a completely gender-neutral manner. Perhaps harassment by women of men and homosexual harassment are both truly rare, or perhaps social factors lead to their underreporting. However, some general works in the Sexual Exploitation section above cover women as aggressors.

New books on sexual harassment are relatively easy to track, as mainstream publishers and review media cover this topic well. An older bibliography is *Sexual Harassment*, by Dawn M. McCaghy (G.K. Hall, 1985, not annotated).

We found two organizations active in this area:

Association for the Sexually Harassed
P.O. Box 27235
Philadelphia, PA 19118
   Run by Cheryl Gomez-Preston, author of *When NO Means NO* (E63). Write for information.

Women Refusing to Accept Tenant Harassment
607 Elmira Road, Ste. 299
Vacaville, CA 95687
   Source of advice and clippings about women tenants sexually harassed by landlords.

   See also *Coping with Sexual Harassment* (C55, Black) and *No Is Not Enough* (C91, Adams et al.).

Annotations

E61   Conway, Jim, & Sally Conway. *Sexual Harassment No More.* Downers Grove, IL: InterVarsity, 1993. 207p. notes. (7p.). ISBN 0-8308-1631-3. Guide for men and women about recognizing, preventing, and dealing with sexual harassment, from Christian perspective. Covers harassment settings (workplace, dates, marriage, education, religion), insights about men and male harassment, insights for women to reduce harassment, and personal values to counter harassment.

*E62   Eisaguirre, Lynne. *Sexual Harassment: A Reference Handbook.* Santa Barbara, CA: ABC-CLIO, 1993. 217p. glossary (3p.). index. ISBN 0-87436-723-9. General reference on sexual harassment and guide to further research. Covers major feminist, legal, management, and male perspectives; chronology of events; biographical sketches; overview of laws; statistics; surveys; characteristics of harassers and victims; costs and effects; organizations; and bibliography.

E63   Gomez-Preston, Cheryl, with Randi Reisfeld. *When NO Means NO: A Guide to Sexual Harassment.* New York: Birch Lane/Carol, 1993. 183p. ISBN 1-55972-143-X. Describes author's harassment experiences (she won a $1.2 million settlement against the Detroit Police Department), what sexual harassment is and its effects, how and where it happens, what those harassed should do, and how to take a case to court. Also covers educating companies, employees, and children about combating sexual harassment. Mentions harassment of men.

*E64   Langelan, Martha J. *Back Off! How to Confront and Stop Sexual Harassment and Harassers.* New York: Fireside/Simon & Schuster, 1993. 380p. resources (9p.). notes (12p.). ISBN 0-671-78856-6. Guide for women about confronting and challenging sexual harassers. Covers why men harass women, how-to's for nonviolent confrontation, and case studies of women and girls successfully confronting harassers taken from letters solicited through the District of Columbia Rape Crisis Center.

E65   Lindemann, Barbara, & David D. Kadue. *Primer on Sexual Harassment.* Washington, DC: Bureau of National Affairs, 1992. 302p. table of cases. index.

ISBN 0-87179-764-X. Comprehensive, somewhat technical manual about sexual harassment, primarily for employers. Covers employer liability, sources of legal protection, action required, and litigation issues. Appendices: Equal Employment Opportunity Commission documents, sample anti-harassment policy, auditing a policy, and summary of the 1991 Civil Rights Act.

*E66   McCann, Nancy Dodd, & Thomas A. McGinn. *Harassed: 100 Women Define Inappropriate Behavior in the Workplace*. Homewood, IL: Business One Irwin (Homewood, IL 60430), 1992. 128p. ISBN 1-55623-796-0. Results of questionnaire survey of 100 "reasonable women" providing reactions to 50 actual workplace events, re offensiveness of event, emotional response, and actions recommended. Covers background, impacts, and prevention of sexual harassment. Reveals areas of consensus and nonconsensus among women.

E67   Wall, Edmund, ed. *Sexual Harassment: Confrontations and Decisions*. Buffalo, NY: Prometheus, 1992. 262p. chapter refs. ISBN 0-87975-787-6. Collection of different views on sexual harassment from lawyers, scholars, and researchers. Covers harassment at university and workplace, explanations/causes, and legal responses.

E68   Webb, Susan L. *Shockwaves: The Global Impact of Sexual Harassment*. New York: MasterMedia, 1994. 434p. resources (61p.). refs. (8p.). ISBN 0-942361-90-3. Resource manual about sexual harassment worldwide. Covers recent U.S. definitions and legal decisions; sexual harassment and responses in U.S. and other countries; actions from the European Communities, United Nations, and the International Labour Organization; and what can be done.

*E69   Wekesser, Carol, Karin L. Swisher, & Christina Pierce, eds. *Sexual Harassment: Current Controversies*. San Diego, CA: Greenhaven, 1992. 208p. orgs. (1p.). bibliog. (2p.). index. ISBN 1-56510-020-4. Essays providing varying and opposing points of view on whether sexual harassment is a serious problem, its causes, how to reduce it, and whether broad legal definitions can be effectively used in the courts.

SEXUALLY TRANSMITTED DISEASES (STDs) AND SAFER SEX

We think an "ideal" STD book should include straightforward information on symptoms, transmission, diagnosis, and treatment of the dozen or so major STDs, plus information on prevention via abstinence, mutual long-term—not serial—monogamy, safe sex, and safer sex.[6] In the 1990s, more books are available about AIDS than on other STDs singly or collectively, and a number of books about safer sex have appeared. The next section covers books on AIDS alone; here we deal with STDs in general, AIDS included, plus "safer sex" books.

201 Things You Should Know About AIDS and Other Sexually Transmitted Diseases (E75, Nevid) comprehensively describes STDs and how to prevent them, including safe and safer sex and condoms. *S.T.D.: Sexually Transmitted Diseases, Including HIV/AIDS* (E72, G10–12,C,A, Daugirdas) is also comprehensive. It has many drawings and some photographs of symptoms, and is geared graphically and in language to college age and younger adults. A particularly concise presentation is *STD Prevention* (E76, G10–12,C,A, Stang & Miner), also suitable for adolescents. The most complete book on STD diagnosis and treatment we reviewed was *Safe Sex* (E73, McIlhaney); it takes a conservative viewpoint, recommending abstinence and marriage as the safest preventives. Not a how-to or diagnostic aid, *No Magic Bullet* (E70, Brandt) provides a social history of the major STDs other than AIDS over the last century.

The Complete Guide to Safer Sex (E74, McIlvenna) includes much material usually found in enhancement-type sex manuals to make safer sex appeal to everyone, including people with non-mainstream erotic tastes. *How to Persuade Your Lover to Use a Condom* (E71, Breitman et al.) supplies valuable model dialogue for talking to a partner about safer sex and condoms.

We found few nonspecialist bibliographies on STDs other than AIDS (we exclude medical, epidemiological, and world public health bibliographies). *Subject Guide to Books in Print* includes material under the entries SEXUALLY TRANSMITTED DISEASES, HERPES SIMPLEX VIRUS, GONORRHEA, and SYPHILIS. Both STDs and safer sex are sometimes covered to some degree in general bibliographies, and safer sex especially in bibliographies on HIV/AIDS (see the HIV/AIDS section). We located most of the books in this section by perusing publisher catalogs and browsing local bookstores. Some books are listed in *Comprehensive Bibliography for Sex, Health & Family Education* (D112, Charlton).

Two organizations providing information:

American Social Health Association
P.O. Box 13827
Research Triangle Park, NC 27709
  Distributes *Managing Herpes*, Herpes Bibliography, and HPV (Herpes Papilloma Virus) Bibliography. Many flyers and pamphlets are available about herpes and all STDs and treatment.

Centers for Disease Control/Center for Prevention Services/Division of Sexually Transmitted Diseases
Building 1, Room 4037
Atlanta, GA 30333
  Publishes a Resource List for Informational Materials on STDs.

For somewhat older material, there is *Sexually Transmitted Diseases: An Annotated Selective Bibliography*, by Stephen Margolis (Garland, 1985, not annotated).

See also books for young adults about STDs, in the Books for Pre-

Adolescents and Books for Adolescents sections in Chapter 11. For books about AIDS, see the next section.

See also *Talking Back to Sexual Pressure* (E21, Powell) and *Seduction Lines Heard 'Round the World* (E18, Gordon).

Annotations

E70 Brandt, Allan M. *No Magic Bullet: A Social History of Venereal Disease in the United States Since 1880*. Expanded ed. New York: Oxford University Press, 1987. 266p. notes (49p.). index. ISBN 0-19-504237-9. History of social uses, impacts, and meanings of STDs from late 19th century to 1980s. Covers syphilis, gonorrhea, herpes, and AIDS. Focuses on tension in prevention and treatment campaigns between medical and moral approaches, and between civil liberties and public health considerations.

*E71 Breitman, Patti, Kim Knutson & Paul Reed. *How to Persuade Your Lover to Use a Condom . . . and Why You Should*. 2nd ed. Rocklin, CA: Prima Publishing (P.O. Box 1260BK, Rocklin, CA 95677), 1987/1993. 85p. orgs. (2p.). ISBN 1-55958-437-8. Techniques of persuading partner to accept condom use during sex. Discusses using condoms to prevent pregnancy and disease, facts about STDs and birth control methods (including the female condom), and how to buy and use condoms.

E72 Daugirdas, John T. *S.T.D.: Sexually Transmitted Diseases, Including HIV/ AIDS*. 3rd ed. Hinsdale, IL: Medtext, 1992. 149p. illus. orgs. (2p.). glossary (3p.). ISBN 0-9629279-1-0. Simply written, lively, and complete coverage of STDs, plus prevention, diagnosis, and treatment. Also addresses STDs during pregnancy and other non-STD causes of genital irritation. Prevention chapter covers abstinence, monogamy, condoms, and assertiveness. (G10–12,C,A)

E73 McIlhaney, Joe S., Jr. *Safe Sex: A Doctor Explains the Realities of AIDS and Other STDs*. Grand Rapids, MI: Baker Book House, 1991. 173p. ISBN 0-8010-6294-2. Description of STDs, plus course of infection, diagnosis, treatment, dangers, and implications for each. Notes that infected person can transmit STDs without either partner knowing disease is present, and cites dangers of "serial monogamy." Stresses abstinence and monogamous marriage as best preventives; also mentions condoms plus contraceptive foam. (C,A)

*E74 McIlvenna, Ted, ed.; authored by the senior faculty of the Institute for Advanced Study of Human Sexuality. *The Complete Guide to Safer Sex*. Fort Lee, NJ: Barricade, 1992. 252p. notes (6p.). glossary (22p.). ISBN 0-942637-58-5. Comprehensive, detailed, sex-positive manual for understanding and avoiding AIDS transmission. Gives many safe and safer alternatives to risky sex, including self and mutual masturbation, sextalk, erotica, sex toys, use of condoms and dental dams, and inducing partner to practice safer sex. Includes tips for safer group sex, S&M, and other special situations.

*E75 Nevid, Jeffrey S. *201 Things You Should Know About AIDS and Other Sexually Transmitted Diseases*. Boston: Allyn & Bacon, 1993. 182p. glossary (3p.). orgs. (4p.). notes (15p.). ISBN 0-205-14873-5. Complete, detailed coverage of

STDs, plus prevention, diagnosis, and treatment. Five chapters cover AIDS/HIV, seven chapters other STDs. Also discusses safer sex, abstinence, masturbation, communicating sexual limits, and using condoms.

*E76   Stang, Lucas, & Kathleen R. Miner. *STD Prevention: Health Facts*. Santa Cruz, CA: ETR Associates, 1994. 62p. glossary (4p.). orgs. (2p.). refs. (2p.). index. ISBN 1-56071-183-3. Concise, clear description of STDs, symptoms, and treatment. Also covers prevention (abstinence and safer sex), control, risk factors, and effects specific to women. (G10–12,C,A)

HIV/AIDS

There is bad news and there is good news about AIDS books. The bad news is that there are so many of them: how to keep up? The good news is also that there are so many of them: librarians can choose among many titles.

The 20+ books we annotate are not the only good works on HIV/AIDS. They were chosen to illustrate the type and quality of books that libraries should own: general and reference works, histories, guides for people with HIV, guides for families and caregivers, religious perspectives, and special topics.

Not all who write about AIDS need be physicians, but medical credentials or other experience/degrees in health care do indicate value. Of course, memoirs, histories, and religious works, for example, need not have this grounding.

Research guides are indispensable: *How to Find Information About AIDS* (E91, Huber), *AIDS Crisis in America* (E89, Hombs), from ABC-CLIO's excellent Contemporary World Issues Series, and *AIDS: Library in a Book* (E85, Flanders & Flanders), from the Facts On File Library in a Book series. *Dictionary of AIDS Related Terminology* (E90, Huber) constitutes a necessary, complete glossary. A good general foundation is provided by *AIDS: Opposing Viewpoints* (E81, Biskup & Swisher) and *The AIDS Crisis: Current Controversies* (E82, Cozic & Swisher),[7] together with *AIDS in the World* (E94, Mann et al.). We also recommend *HIV Prevention* (E98, Stang & Miner), plus *About AIDS* (E77), which is written for adults with low literacy skills and is also useful for younger people. A large collection of articles, entitled *AIDS Crisis*, is available on subscription as part of the Social/Critical Issues Series from SIRS (Social Issues Resources Series, P.O. Box 2348, Boca Raton, FL 33427-2348), not annotated.

Three histories of HIV/AIDS each take a somewhat different perspective: the classic *And the Band Played On* (E97, Shilts), the more recent *Against the Odds* (E79, Arno & Feiden), which focuses more on AIDS drugs, and Robert Gallo's autobiographical *Virus Hunting* (E88, Gallo). An award-winning historical book that we did not get to see is *History of AIDS: Emergence and Origin of a Modern Pandemic*, by Mirko D. Grmek (Princeton University Press, 1993, not annotated). Libraries should also collect some personal history/memoir-type books about AIDS, such as *Borrowed Time: An AIDS Memoir*, by Paul Monette (Harcourt Brace, 1988), and *Days of Grace: A Memoir*, by Arthur Ashe & Arnold Rampersad (Knopf, 1993). A superb work from a physician and highly recommended is *My Own Country*, by Abraham Verghese (Vintage, 1995). (None of these are annotated.)

Guides for people with AIDS include *The Guide to Living with HIV Infection* (E80, Bartlett & Finkbeiner) from Johns Hopkins, now in its second edition, and *Immune Power* (E92, Kaiser). Bartlett and Kaiser are physicians. The first concentrates on medical treatments, doctor visits, hospitals, and so on. The second describes a therapy system based on self-help through diet, diet supplements, and mind-body work coupled with standard medical therapies.

For families and caregivers, *After You Say Goodbye* (E86, Froman) is a classic manual for handling grief and practical matters. Kübler-Ross' *AIDS: The Ultimate Challenge* (E93, Kübler-Ross) talks generally about AIDS counseling and help. Much more concise, and practical in thrust, *The Caregivers Guide* (E83, Denniston) concentrates upon the logistical details of medical, business, and legal arrangements a caregiver must understand and possibly handle. A new work we did not inspect is *AIDS Care at Home: A Guide for Caregivers, Loved Ones, and People with AIDS*, by Judith Greif and Beth Ann Golden (Wiley, 1994, not annotated).

A number of books about HIV/AIDS have been published by religious presses—an understandable trend since AIDS ministry fits into long-standing traditions of church work with the sick. Yet AIDS ministry also poses special problems for the church, arising from the sexual transmission of the disease and its association in the United States with stigmatized and "sinful" lifestyles: homosexuality, drug use, prostitution, and promiscuity.

A problem for *librarians* is that religiously motivated books on AIDS, while concentrating on the authors' theological opinions, to which they are entitled, may present inaccurate medical information. *The AIDS Epidemic* (E99, Wood & Dietrich), written by two physicians, is an excellent work from the conservative Christian perspective. Its authors spend an entire chapter refuting claims in earlier conservative/religious books (written by nonphysicians) that HIV/AIDS is spread by casual contact.[8]

Several religious books written by non-physicians deal with church responses to AIDS rather than with its medical aspects. *AIDS and the Church* (E96, Shelp & Sunderland) contains theological discussion as well as a survey of how different denominations have responded to the AIDS crisis. An AIDS ministry case history is provided in *When AIDS Comes to Church* (E78, Amos), which concentrates much more on preparation and techniques for AIDS ministry; readers are conscientiously advised to get their AIDS education directly from the medical community. A particularly good pamphlet on AIDS and the Christian church is *The AIDS Crisis: The Facts and Myths About a Modern Epidemic*, by Andrés Tapia (InterVarsity Press, 1988, not annotated).

Ethical aspects of the AIDS crisis are addressed very well in **AIDS & Ethics* (E95, Reamer). These issues have salience for millions of people independent of religion.

Several additional works warrant serious consideration. The highly controversial *The Myth of Heterosexual AIDS* (E87, Fumento) is exhaustively researched and deserves a place in the library collection. In addition, *Blacks and AIDS* (E84, Duh) summarizes penetration of HIV/AIDS into the African-American community. A more current and also interesting work, *Risky Sexual Behaviors Among African-Americans*, by Ernest H. Johnson, (Praeger/Greenwood, 1993), is not so broadly based and not annotated here.

There are also many excellent books about women and AIDS: *Women, AIDS, and Activism*, by ACT UP/New York Women and AIDS Book Group (South End, 1992), *The Invisible Epidemic: The Story of Women and AIDS*, by Gena Corea (Harper Collins, 1992), and *Until the Cure: Caring for Women with HIV*, edited by Ann Kurth (Yale University Press, 1993), none annotated.

The library press reviews a goodly number of books about HIV/AIDS, and many publishers have titles in the area. The gay press and the catalog and review sources for homosexuality books are also good sources (see the Homosexuality—General Works section in Chapter 10). As for bibliographies, SIECUS makes available a fine recurring bibliography on HIV/AIDS books for the public (see Chapter 5). Two sources for religious materials:

Christian General Store
2130 Fourth Street
San Rafael, CA 94901
   Catalog: Quality Christian Materials on Issues Related to HIV/AIDS.

Love in Action
P.O. Box 2655
San Rafael, CA 94912
   Love in Action is a gay-reform-type organization. It has a Love in Action AIDS Catalog, including mostly articles and short pieces, distributed by Love in Action for the Christian AIDS Services Alliance (P.O. Box 3612, San Rafael, CA 94912-3612). Includes a Select Bibliography on HIV/AIDS, of mostly Christian books.

   Other organizations providing interesting information:

AIDS Information Network
1211 Chestnut Street

Philadelphia, PA 19107
  Referrals to print and other sources of information via telephone, fax, and online.

Centers for Disease Control National AIDS Clearinghouse
P.O. Box 6003
Rockville, MD 20849-6003
  Several catalogs of materials of all types, including pathfinders and bibliographies/resource guides on religious resources and AIDS in the workplace.

National Leadership Coalition on AIDS
1730 M Street NW, Ste. 905
Washington, DC 20036
  Distributes brochures, pamphlets, sample policies, and fact sheets about AIDS in the workplace.

Center for Women Policy Studies
2000 P Street, Ste. 508
Washington, DC 20036
  Sells *The Guide to Resources on Women and AIDS*, a recurring directory, and other materials about women and AIDS.

  Many additional organizations provide AIDS information. Consult *How to Find Information About AIDS* (E91, Huber), *AIDS Crisis in America* (E89, Hombs), and *AIDS: Library in a Book* (E85, Flanders & Flanders). The *Encyclopedia of Associations* lists a large number of AIDS organizations.
  Sporadic articles about providing HIV/AIDS information appear in the library literature, and some bibliographies are produced by individual libraries.[9] An interesting-sounding bibliography that we did not annotate is *The AIDS Dissidents: An Annotated Bibliography*, by Ian Young (Scarecrow, 1993), covering alternative treatments, "alarmist and hateful views," unofficial research, and other voices.
  Books about HIV/AIDS for young people are included in the Books for Children, Books for Pre-Adolescents, and Books for Adolescents sections in Chapter 11. Books about how to tell young people about HIV/AIDS are covered in the Sex Education section in Chapter 11. Guides to safer sex practices are covered in the Sexually Transmitted Diseases (STDs) and Safer Sex section, above.
  See also *Confronting AIDS Through Literature* (D19, Pastore) and *AIDS and HIV Programs and Services for Libraries* (D121, Lukenbill).

Annotations

E77 *About AIDS*. Produced in collaboration with the National Association of People with AIDS. Syracuse, NY: New Readers Press, 1994. 127p. illus. glossary

(3p.). ISBN 1-56420-019-1. Simply written introduction to AIDS. Covers what HIV/AIDS is, risky and nonrisky sexual and nonsexual behaviors, talking with children and others about AIDS and safer sex, drugs and needles, getting tested for HIV, symptoms and treatment, helping people with HIV/AIDS, workplace and legal issues, benefits and money, and sources of help. (G4–12,C,A)

E78 Amos, William E., Jr. *When AIDS Comes to Church*. Philadelphia: West-minster, 1988. 129p. orgs. (7p.). notes (1p.). ISBN 0-664-25009-2. Story of how a Baptist church in Florida responded to AIDS-infected congregation members and their families. Discusses pastor's preparation for responding, basis for AIDS min-istry, and how churches can respond and minister.

E79 Arno, Peter S., & Karyn L. Feiden. *Against the Odds: The Story of AIDS Drug Development, Politics and Profits*. New York: Harper Perennial, 1992. 314p. sources (30p.). chronology (14p.). index. ISBN 0-06-092359-8. History of discovery of AIDS; development, approval, and marketing of AIDS-effective drugs; and strug-gle among Food and Drug Administration, federal government, pharmaceutical companies, physicians, and AIDS activists to influence the process.

E80 Bartlett, John G., & Ann K. Finkbeiner. *The Guide to Living with HIV Infection, Developed at the Johns Hopkins AIDS Clinic*. Rev. ed. Baltimore: Johns Hopkins University Press, 1993. 356p. resources. (6p.). glossary (34p.). index. ISBN 0-8018-4664-1. Comprehensive guidebook and reference for HIV-positive people, families, caregivers, and friends. Covers understanding HIV, preventing transmis-sion, effects of HIV infection on body/emotions/relationships, medical care and treatments, legal and financial considerations, preserving mental health, and pre-paring for death.

*E81 Biskup, Michael D., & Karin L. Swisher, eds. *AIDS: Opposing Viewpoints*. San Diego, CA: Greenhaven, 1992. 215p. chapter bibliogs. glossary (2p.). orgs. (6p.). bibliog. (3p.). index. ISBN 0-89908-165-7. Essays offering different view-points on seriousness of AIDS, moral issue or not, effectiveness of testing, prevent-ing transmission, and treatment. (G10–12,C,A)

E82 Cozic, Charles P., & Karin L. Swisher, eds. *The AIDS Crisis: Current Con-troversies*. San Diego, CA: Greenhaven, 1991. 240p. orgs. (2p.). bibliog. (2p.). in-dex. ISBN 0-89908-584-9. Essays providing varying and opposing viewpoints mirroring "the mosaic of opinions encountered in society." Topics: seriousness of AIDS epidemic, funding of research and treatment, AIDS testing, treatments, and prevention. (G10–12,C,A)

E83 Denniston, Elizabeth R. *The Caregivers Guide: A Labor of Love*. Bangor, ME: Eastern Maine AIDS Network (P.O. Box 2038, Bangor, ME 04401), 1993. 51p. ISBN U/K. Guide to caring for someone with HIV/AIDS. Covers preparation (e.g., settling business and medical relationships, supplies and equipment to buy), caring for self-as-caregiver, intensive caregiving (e.g., community health services, giving shots and medications, dealing with visitors), and handling final death and loss.

E84 Duh, Samuel V., *Blacks and AIDS: Causes and Origins*. Newbury Park, CA: Sage, 1991. 153p. chapter refs. ISBN 0-8039-4347-4. Explores prevalence and transmission of AIDS in U.S. and African black populations. Covers health status of black Americans, history and epidemiology of AIDS, AIDS in Africa, genetic vs.

environmental transmission, control of AIDS in the U.S. and Africa, and financing AIDS control.

*E85   Flanders, Stephen A., & Carl N. Flanders. *AIDS: Library in a Book*. New York: Facts On File, 1991. 248p. glossary (3p.). index. ISBN 0-8160-1910-X. One-volume source for research on AIDS. Includes overview, introduction to AIDS epidemic, chronology, court cases, biographies, research guide, annotated bibliography, and organization list. Appendices cover acronyms and structure of U.S. public health system.

E86   Froman, Paul Kent. *After You Say Goodbye: When Someone You Love Dies of AIDS*. San Francisco: Chronicle Books, 1992. 270p. resources (2p.). suggested reading (2p.). ISBN 0-8118-0088-1. Guidance for coping with loved one's death from AIDS. Covers grieving and taking action; plus coping with depression, anger, fear, and guilt. Sections cover different practical matters arising from death of partner vs. relative vs. friend; plus "caregiver burnout" and helping another person grieve.

E87   Fumento, Michael. *The Myth of Heterosexual AIDS*. Washington, DC: Regnery Gateway, 1993. 463p. notes (55p.). index. ISBN 0-89526-729-2. Provocative, well-researched presentation on how HIV/AIDS risk to most heterosexuals has been misrepresented and exaggerated. Contends that while AIDS poses some risk to heterosexuals, transmission through heterosexual intercourse is and will be considerably rarer than current "authoritative" estimates. Maintains that needs of at-risk populations are shortchanged by overemphasis on heterosexuals.

E88   Gallo, Robert. *Virus Hunting: AIDS, Cancer, and the Human Retrovirus: A Story of Scientific Discovery*. New York: Basic Books, 1991. 352p. index. ISBN 0-465-09815-0. AIDS researcher and HIV co-discoverer Gallo narrates in technical detail the discovery of cancer-causing retroviruses in humans and subsequent discovery of HIV virus. Also includes brief description of his upbringing and training, and includes answers to common questions about AIDS and what can be done.

*E89   Hombs, Mary Ellen. *AIDS Crisis in America: A Reference Handbook*. Santa Barbara, CA: ABC-CLIO, 1992. 268p. glossary (16p.). index. ISBN 0-87436-648-8. Basic reference for HIV/AIDS information. Covers definition and transmission, demographics, public policy issues, chronology, biographical sketches, facts and statistics, excerpts from key reports, legal issues, directory of organizations (34p.), and lengthy annotated print and nonprint reference bibliography.

*E90   Huber, Jeffrey T. *Dictionary of AIDS Related Terminology*. New York: Neal-Schuman, 1993. 165p. ISBN 1-55570-117-5. Approximately 1,100 definitions related to HIV/AIDS: medical terms, pharmaceutical drugs, names of doctors and other key people, sexual behaviors, organizations, and intravenous drug culture terms. Abbreviations, acronyms, slang terms, and product names are cross-referenced to main entries.

*E91   Huber, Jeffrey T. ed. *How to Find Information About AIDS*. 2nd ed. Binghamton, NY: Haworth, 1992. 290p. index. ISBN 1-56024-140-3. Directory of "key access points" into the massive amount of AIDS information. Lists major organizations (national, state, and local), state health departments, research/grant/training institutions, hotlines, electronic sources (databases, bulletin boards, etc.), major print sources (indexes, abstracting services, bibliographies, periodicals, books), and audiovisual producers/distributors. Some brief annotations.

*E92   Kaiser, Jon D. *Immune Power: A Comprehensive Healing Program for HIV.* New York: St. Martin's, 1993. 240p. notes (2p.). refs. (8p.). index. ISBN 0-312-09312-8. Treatment regimen for HIV-positive patients combining diet, nutritional supplements, herbs, exercise, stress reduction, emotional healing, and standard medical therapies. Reports dramatic results among 134 HIV-positive patients over 4 years (89% stable or improved, 98% survival).

E93   Kübler-Ross, Elisabeth. *AIDS: The Ultimate Challenge.* New York: Collier/Macmillan, 1987. 329p. ISBN 0-02-089143-1. Essays addressing counseling and ministering to AIDS patients and families. Describes efforts to start AIDS hospice for children in Virginia and includes transcript of emotional and confrontational public meeting, plus letters to the editor. Chapter on AIDS in prison.

E94   Mann, Jonathan M., Daniel J.M. Tarantola, & Thomas W. Netter, eds. *AIDS in the World.* Cambridge, MA: Harvard University Press, 1992. 1037p. notes (77p.). index. ISBN 0-674-01266-6. Project of the Global AIDS Policy Coalition. Provides detailed analysis 1980–1992 of the AIDS epidemic worldwide and global response. Many statistics and tables, some by country. Covers status, impact, interactions with other diseases, research, programs and coalitions, prevention and care, funding, human rights, global vulnerability, and past and future of viral epidemics.

*E95   Reamer, Frederic G., ed. *AIDS & Ethics.* New York: Columbia University Press, 1991. 317p. chapter refs. index. ISBN 0-231-07359-3. Essays summarizing ethical issues re HIV/AIDS and how public, organizational, and legal reactions have reflected particular viewpoints. Covers public health vs. civil liberties, mandatory testing, human subjects research, health insurance, AIDS education, activism, obligation to treat, privacy, and AIDS and the law.

E96   Shelp, Earl E., & Ronald H. Sunderland. *AIDS and the Church: The Second Decade.* Louisville: Westminster/John Knox, 1992. 238p. notes (25p.). refs. (6p.). ISBN 0-664-25202-8. General middle-ground Christian discussion of AIDS, stressing compassion and ministry. Covers history and effects of AIDS, religious groups' responses, Biblical basis for ministry, plus nature and types of ministry suggested. Takes the viewpoint "Judge not."

E97   Shilts, Randy. *And the Band Played On: Politics, People, and the AIDS Epidemic.* New York: Penguin, 1987. 646p. notes on sources (7p.). index. ISBN 0-14-011369-X. Powerful, detailed account of discovery of AIDS/HIV and growth of the AIDS crisis, told in episodic accounts about patients, physicians, researchers, politicians, activists, and others. Documents "too-little-too-late" responses to the epidemic from politicians, scientists, health professionals, and the gay community.

*E98   Stang, Lucas, & Kathleen R. Miner. *HIV Prevention: Health Facts.* Santa Cruz, CA: ETR Associates, 1994. 90p. glossary (8p.). orgs. (4p.). refs. (3p.). index. ISBN 1-56071-184-1. Concise, ready-reference presentation of key facts about HIV/AIDS: origins and scope of epidemic, immune system effects, transmission and testing, treatments, and public policy challenges. Designed for health educators but suitable for many others.

*E99   Wood, Glenn G., & John E. Dietrich. *The AIDS Epidemic: Balancing Compassion and Justice*. Portland, OR: Multnomah, 1990. 435p. chapter notes. glossary (8p.). bibliog. (7p.). ISBN 0-88070-309-1. Medically accurate general work about AIDS from conservative Christian viewpoint. Covers history, medical aspects, the church and AIDS, and society and AIDS. Stresses compassion and ministry. Considers both homosexuality and homophobia sinful.

PROSTITUTION AND OTHER SEX WORK

Even a small library collection about prostitution should reflect four subtopics: history, policy/law, behavior of prostitutes and clients, and voices of the sex workers themselves (as they sometimes self-designate). Usually these topics overlap within a particular work.

All adult collections should have *Prostitution: An International Handbook* . . . (E102, Davis) and *Women and Prostitution* (E101, Bullough & Bullough); both have excellent coverage of history and policy, and some description of behavior. *Uneasy Virtue* (E104, Hobson) adds in-depth perspective on American social and legal policies. Many books—too many to include here—describe the lives of prostitutes, singly as biography or autobiography, or as a group by journalists or social scientists. They may be identified from bibliographies in the works above and from Kinsey Institute bibliographies (see Chapter 5). Libraries may want to emphasize regional studies—for example, Western libraries acquiring *Gold Diggers and Silver Miners: Prostitution and Social Life on the Comstock Lode*, by Marion Goldman (University of Michigan Press, 1981), or New York libraries buying *Working Women: The Subterranean World of Street Prostitution*, by Arlene Carmen and Howard Moody (Harper & Row, 1985), neither annotated.

Three excellent anthologies give voice to prostitutes and other sex professionals themselves: *Sex Work* (E103, Delacoste & Alexander), covering a variety of sex work, *Good Girls/Bad Girls* (E100, Bell), addressing the uneasy dialogue between feminists and sex workers, and *A Vindication of the Rights of Whores* (E106, Pheterson), touching upon international aspects of the prostitutes' rights movement.

Adjunct to the voices of working prostitutes are the self-help organizations run by ex-prostitutes that publish pamphlets, monographs, and shorter works. PA (Prostitutes Anonymous) and WHISPER are two major groups; both provide vertical file material, but only PA has monographs. *Sold Out* (E109, Williams) comes in full-length, condensed, or pamphlet versions and is another *must* for all public libraries. The condensed and pamphlet versions are a desirable acquisition for high school libraries in large cities.

The male side of prostitution seems largely overlooked in publishing.[10] We did find a few fascinating and unconventional works. *Hustling* (E107,

Preston) is a male-male prostitution how-to with a good deal of general information, while a pseudo-fictional treatment is *Understanding the Male Hustler*, by Samuel M. Steward (Harrington Park Press, 1991, not annotated). From the 1970s comes *Gigolos* (E108, Ramsey), an entertaining pop sociology study, now updated by the more journalistic but also well-written *Gigolos: The Secret Lives of Men Who Service Women*, by Dane Taylor and Antonia Newton-West (Mt. Ivy Press, 1994, not annotated). *Black Players* (E105, Milner & Milner) is an interesting work of urban anthropology.

Most works on prostitution are published by mainstream and feminist (sometimes lesbian-feminist) presses. *Choice* and *Women's Review of Books* doubtless cover some of the new items. The ex-prostitutes' organizations are good sources of vertical file and other materials:[11]

PRIDE (from PRostitution to Independence, Dignity and Equality)
c/o Family & Children's Service
Lake Street Branch
3125 East Lake Street
Minneapolis, MN 55406
Flyers; short bibliography c. 1991; notebook of clippings, case stories, and information about PRIDE.

PA (Prostitutes Anonymous; address mail to "PA" only)
11225 Magnolia Avenue #181
North Hollywood, CA 91601
Newsletter with organizational information. Publishes *Sold Out* (E109, Williams), listed in latest catalog as *Complete Recovery Guide* and *Condensed Recovery Guide*.

WHISPER (Women Hurt in Systems of Prostitution Engaged in Revolt)
P.O. Box 65796
St. Paul, MN 55165-0796
Flyers, reprints, newsletters, other educational materials.

See also *On the Streets: The Lives of Adolescent Prostitutes* (C75, Landau).

Annotations

E100   Bell, Laurie, ed. *Good Girls/Bad Girls: Feminists and Sex Trade Workers Face to Face*. Seattle: Seal Press, 1987. 231p. glossary (4p.). ISBN 0-931188-57-1. Essays and debate from 1985 Toronto conference of feminists and sex workers: prostitutes, strippers, porn performers. Addresses conflicting views about sexuality, feminism, censorship, prostitution, pornography, and sex workers' experiences and rights.

*E101   Bullough, Vern, & Bonnie Bullough. *Women and Prostitution: A Social History*. Buffalo, NY: Prometheus, 1987. 374p. bibliog. (7p.). notes (36p.). index. ISBN 0-87975-372-2. (Rev. ed. of *Prostitution: An Illustrated Social History*.) Comprehensive history of female prostitution worldwide, from animal precedents and early prehistory to the 1980s. Addresses social, legal, and medical factors.

*E102   Davis, Nanette J., ed. *Prostitution: An International Handbook on Trends, Problems, and Policies*. Westport, CT: Greenwood, 1993. 403p. chapter refs. bibliog. (6p.). index. ISBN 0-313-25754-X. Prostitution patterns in 16 countries, including U.S. Addresses social and legal definitions, history and trends, social organizations, theories, status and lifestyle, law enforcement, politics, intervention, and social policy.

E103   Delacoste, Frédérique, & Priscilla Alexander. *Sex Work: Writings by Women in the Sex Industry*. Pittsburgh: Cleis, 1987. 349p. bibliog. (19p.). ISBN 0-939416-11-5. Contributors include prostitutes, pornography actresses, strippers, massage parlor workers, and exotic dancers. Diverse contributions cover day-to-day work experiences; connections with feminism, lesbianism, and other external social collectivities; and activist organizing. Mostly nonfiction; some fiction, some poetry.

E104   Hobson, Barbara Meil. *Uneasy Virtue: The Politics of Prostitution and the American Reform Tradition*. Chicago: University of Chicago Press, 1990 (orig. pub. 1987). 275p. illus. notes (25p.). index. ISBN 0-266-34557-2. History of politics of prostitution in U.S., encompassing attempts at control and reform by political and social groups, 1800 to 1980s. Covers prostitute groups, including COYOTE and WHISPER, and modern European policies.

E105   Milner, Christina, & Richard Milner. *Black Players: The Secret World of Black Pimps*. Boston: Little, Brown, 1972. 329p. glossary (16p.). notes (10p.). bibliog. (5p.). ISBN 0-316-57411-2. Anthropological study of black pimps and their prostitutes in San Francisco. Covers social organization, male-female expectations and roles, mechanics of pimping, and pimps' philosophy and world view.

E106   Pheterson, Gail, ed. *A Vindication of the Rights of Whores*. Preface by Margo St. James. Seattle: Seal Press, 1989. 293p. ISBN 0-931188-73-3. Anthology reflecting international prostitutes' rights movement and perspectives from prostitutes worldwide. Contributions include presentations from the First Whores' Congress (Amsterdam, 1985) and the Second Whores' Congress (Brussels, 1986).

E107   Preston, John. *Hustling: A Gentleman's Guide to the Fine Art of Homosexual Prostitution*. New York: Masquerade, 1994. 175p. ISBN 1-56333-137-7. How-to book also containing much information about patterns in male-male prostitution. Covers hustler and customer characteristics, places/types of work, starting a business, handling customers and money, erotic specialties, and why *not* to hustle.

E108   Ramsey, Lynn. *Gigolos: The World's Best Kept Men*. Englewood Cliffs, NJ: Prentice-Hall, 1978. 161p. illus. bibliog. (3p.). ISBN 0-13-356360-X. Results of informal worldwide interview study of gigolos: men paid for sexual activities and/or social companionship with women. Describes types of gigolos and clients, and profiles individual men.

*E109   Williams, J.L., ed. *Sold Out: Recovery Text for Prostitutes Anonymous*.

North Hollywood, CA: PA World Services Office (11225 Magnolia Blvd. #181, North Hollywood, CA 91601), 1992. 140p. ISBN U/K. Introduction to Prostitutes Anonymous, 12-step recovery programs for sex workers, and guidance for men and women about getting out of the sex industry. Includes personal histories and letters. Comes in smaller, condensed version (113p.) containing fewer case histories (1991). Key information is also available in 18p. booklet form, titled *Sold Out: The Booklet; A Recovery Guide from Prostitutes Anonymous for Those Who Wish to Leave the Sex Industry (or for Those That Love Them)* (1990).

NOTES

1. Other terms for desire disorders are *inhibited sexual desire* and *desire phase dysfunction*. Helen Singer Kaplan (*The Illustrated Manual of Sex Therapy*, E4: xiii) describes two subcategories: hypoactive sexual desire (simple lack of sexual interest) and sexual aversion disorder. A third subcategory not noted by Kaplan is sexual desire conflict, or discrepancy in desire between partners. For men, the classic rather vague term usually referring to erectile dysfunction is *impotence*; retarded ejaculation may also be called *inhibited male orgasm* or *ejaculatory incompetence*. For women, anorgasmia may be termed *inhibited female orgasm* or—optimistically!—*preorgasmia*. *Frigidity* is an older, imprecise, and pejorative word applied to women and used variably for inhibited sexual desire, anorgasmia, or even inability to experience pleasure in sexual activities.

2. An articulate and recent critique of sex therapy re sexual abuse accusations is Spencer Harris Morfit's "Challenge to Psychotherapy: An Open Letter to Psychotherapists Concerning Clinical Practice as Seen Through the Lens of the 'Recovered' or 'False Memory' Debate," *Journal of Sex Education and Therapy* 20.4 (Winter, 1994): 234–245. See also the Incest and Child Sexual Abuse section in this chapter.

3. In most categories of sexual exploitation, both the terms *victim* and *survivor* are used to refer to exploited individuals.

4. Two within the last 10 years: Margo Hittleman, "Sexual Abuse: Teaching About Touching," *School Library Journal* (January 1985): 34–35; Michael S. Carifio, "Child Sexual Abuse: Selected and Recent Resources," *Choice* (October 1990): 268–273.

5. We have not included books about the "Tailhook" harassment of women naval personnel nor about Anita Hill's challenge of Clarence Thomas' Supreme Court nomination. Each has resulted in some interesting titles, many reviewed in the library literature.

6. Liberal and conservative voices disagree about "safe sex." Condoms not being 100% foolproof in preventing STD transmission, some voices proclaim that "safe sex isn't," and therefore only abstinence and sex within long-term, monogamous marriage should be promoted as STD preventives. Such clamor has led liberal sex educators and writers to use *safer sex*. Now some educators and writers make a distinction between *safer sex*, meaning sexual activities involving some risk of transmission, such as intercourse and oral sex with condoms and dental dams, and *safe sex* where virtually *no* risk exists, such as mutual masturbation, massage, sharing fantasies, telephone sex, etc.

7. We asked Greenhaven about the difference between the Opposing Viewpoints and Current Controversies series. Greenhaven told us that the Current Controversies series has the "same concept as Opposing Viewpoints books, with these differences: articles are longer, and they are not placed in a precise pro/con format. Instead, each side of the issue is covered with anywhere from 3–10 viewpoints. . . . They are not revised as frequently as the Opposing Viewpoints books." Both series are "suitable for classrooms"—presumably, high school and college age, but also seem appropriate for adult collections.

8. Librarians should accordingly examine cautiously, e.g., *Power in the Blood*, by David Chilton (Brenthood, TN: Wolgemuth & Hyatt, 1987), *The AIDS Cover-Up?* by Gene Antonio (San Francisco: Ignatius, 1987), *The AIDS Plague*, by James McKeever (Medford, OR: Omega, 1987), *What the Bible Says About AIDS*, by David R. Reagen and Thomas Baker (McKinney, TX: Lamb and Lion Ministries, 1988), and *The Truth About AIDS*, by Patrick Dixon (East Sussex, UK: Kingsway, 1987). All are criticized in *The AIDS Epidemic* (E99, Wood & Dietrich) for giving inaccurate medical information about transmission. Yet "truth" is a sticky and inexact criterion for building the library collection: as Jefferson Selth points out, you cannot defer to the judgment of experts for what constitutes truth, "if only because (a) they do not always agree among themselves, and (b) if they do all agree upon something today, they may not agree on it tomorrow." Jefferson Selth, *Ambition, Discrimination, and Censorship in Libraries* (Jefferson, NC: McFarland, 1993): 122 and the entire chapter "Waiting in the Wings." We are not suggesting that librarians exclude matters of accuracy in evaluating books, but that "accuracy" is not so firm a foundation for selection as it would seem.

9. Several articles: Edmund F. SantaVicca, "Integrating AIDS into the Academic Curriculum: Realistic Roles for Libraries," *Urban Academic Librarian* 8.2 (Winter 1991/1992): 41–45; Jean Hofacket, "Intensive Care: Materials on AIDS and HIV," *Library Journal* (January 1993): 65–68; C. Lehman, "AIDS and Public Libraries," *RQ* (Summer 1993): 505–514. A library-produced HIV/AIDS bibliography and pathfinder is AIDS: Research and Resource Guide, from the Free Library of Philadelphia.

10. Certainly male prostitution—with male or female clients—has existed for centuries but seems to have attracted nowhere near the attention accorded female prostitution. We cannot think of explanations beyond the doubtful cliché that "all men are interested in sex anyway," and therefore males seem perfectly natural as vendors in the sex trade. Thus for moral reasons, it is the *women* in the sex trade who garner the fascination and the reform efforts. Presumably, the opinion is that most male prostitutes, at least over the legal age of consent, are past moral rehabilitation.

11. We tried to track down the well-known prostitutes' rights group COYOTE (Call Off Your Old Tired Ethics), founded by the equally well-known Margo St. James, to see if it provides any interesting materials. However, every address we tried resulted in inquiries returned as "addressee unknown." According to *A Research Guide to Human Sexuality* (D120, Lichtenberg), COYOTE's address is 2269 Chestnut Street, #452, San Francisco, CA 94123, plus COYOTE-Los Angeles, 1626 North Wilcox Ave. #580, Hollywood, CA 90028. They do not appear to supply either publications or bibliographies, but they do have an archive, located at Radcliffe University.

Index

This index does not attempt to replace the indexes of the nearly 600 books annotated in the main text. Instead, it directs readers to broad topics, such as abortion, under which are listed references to annotations and to text pages. It also provides pointers to "viewpoints," such as feminist, where we group books sharing common viewpoints across different topics. Because many books cover a wide spectrum of sexological phenomena, we have highlighted only the major topics covered in each book. The reader is directed to the annotations themselves for further details. We have also indexed books under reader groups (e.g., children, preadolescents, adolescents, young people).

Many topics cold be indexed specifically under Sex, Sexuality, Libraries, or Erotic. A topic or book is rarely indexed under these four words to eliminate pages of repeat entries. For example, "Sexuality materials, access to" is indexed under "Access to sexuality materials."

All name entries include pages where books authored by that person are mentioned, whether or not the author's name appears in the text.

Boldface alphanumerics refer to annotations: for example, **A11** is eleventh book annotated in Chapter 9. **B** refers to book annotated in Chapter 10, **C** to Chapter 11, **D** to Chapter 12, and **E** to Chapter 13. In Chapters 9 through 13, all annotations are given in sequential, numerical order.

About the Authors

MARTHA CORNOG, M.A., M.L.S., edited *Libraries, Erotica, & Pornography* (1991), which won the American Library Association's Eli M. Obeler Award for Intellectual Freedom in 1992. With her husband, Timothy Perper, she has written articles on sexuality materials in the library for *Library Journal, Collection Building, Journal of Information Ethics*, and *SIECUS Report*. She has also published on sexual language and communication and contributed to *The Complete Dictionary of Sexology* (1995) and *Human Sexuality: An Encyclopedia* (1994). She and Timothy Perper are currently preparing a work on *Sex and Religion in Modern America*. She has been active in the Society for the Scientific Study of Sex and served on the editorial board of *The Journal of Sex Research*. She is manager of membership services for the American College of Physicians.

TIMOTHY PERPER, Ph.D., is the author of *Sex Signals: The Biology of Love* (1985) and co-editor of *A Descriptive Dictionary and Atlas of Sexology* (Greenwood, 1991). He has published on human as well as animal sexuality, contributing to *Human Sexuality: An Encyclopedia* (1994) and authored or co-authored three chapters in *Libraries, Erotica, & Pornography* (1991), edited by his wife, Martha Cornog. An independent writer, researcher, and lecturer, he is active in the Society for the Scientific Study of Sex and a former book review editor of *The Journal of Sex Research*.